SPECIAL CHILDREN:
AN INTEGRATIVE APPROACH

Bernard G. Suran
Northwestern University Medical School

Joseph V. Rizzo
Barat College

Alfred Hirshoren
University of Georgia
Contributing Author

SCOTT, FORESMAN AND COMPANY Glenview, Illinois
Dallas, Tex.   Oakland, N.J.   Palo Alto, Cal.   Tucker, GA.   London, England

Library of Congress Cataloging in Publication Data

Suran, Bernard G
  Special children.

  Bibliography: p. 496
  Includes indexes.
  1. Exceptional children—Education.   I. Rizzo,
Joseph V., 1942–   joint author.   II. Title.
LC3965.S9   371.9   78-15497
ISBN 0-673-15068-2

Acknowledgments

(p. 11) "The Privy Council Grants the Virginia Company Authority to Coerce Children, 1620" from ACTS OF THE PRIVY COUNCIL OF ENGLAND, 1619–1621. Published 1930. Cited in Robert H. Bremner, CHILDREN AND YOUTH IN AMERICA: A DOCUMENTARY HISTORY, Cambridge: Harvard University Press, 1970, p. 8. Reprinted by permission of Her Majesty's Stationery Office. **(p. 13)** From "Tythingmens Duty," Council/Court Records, Volume 5: 233, Archives of the Commonwealth, Boston, Massachusetts, October 15, 1679. Cited in Edmund S. Morgan, THE PURITAN FAMILY, Harper and Row, Publishers, Inc., 1966, pgs. 148–149. Reprinted by permission of Edmund S. Morgan and The Commonwealth of Massachusetts, Office of the Secretary, Archives of the Commonwealth. **(p. 18)** "A Bill of Rights", by Irving N. Berlin from ADVOCACY FOR CHILD MENTAL HEALTH, edited by I. N. Berlin. Copyright © 1975 by Irving N. Berlin. Reprinted by permission of Brunner/Mazel, Publishers, New York, New York. **(pp. 27, 29)** From DEVELOPMENTAL DIAGNOSIS: NORMAL AND ABNORMAL CHILD DEVELOPMENT, CLINICAL METHODS AND PEDIATRIC APPLICATIONS by Arnold Gesell and Catherine S. Amatruda, Second Edition. Copyright 1947 by Arnold Gesell. Reprinted by permission of Harper and Row, Publishers, Inc., Hagerstown, Maryland. **(p. 44)** Adapted from "Imitation of Film-Mediated Aggressive Models", by Albert Bandura, Dorothea Ross and Sheila A. Ross, *Journal of Abnormal and Social Psychology,* Volume 66, Number 1; 1965. Copyright © 1965 by the American Psychological Association. Reprinted by permission of the American Psychological Association and Albert Bandura. **(p. 55)** "Conclusions of the Project on the Classification of Exceptional Children" from THE FUTURES OF CHILDREN: CATEGORIES, LABELS, AND THEIR CONSEQUENCES by Nicholas Hobbs. Copyright © 1975 by Jossey-Bass Publishers. Reprinted by permission of Jossey-Bass Publishers. **(p. 79)** With permission. From *Webster's New World Dictionary,* Second College Edition. Copyright © 1974 by William Collins + World Publishing Co., Inc. **(p. 89)** Adapted from "The Eight Basic Principles," by Virginia M. Axline, in CHILD PSYCHOTHERAPY: Practice and Theory, edited by Mary R. Haworth, © 1964 by Mary R. Haworth, Basic Books, Inc., Publishers, New York. **(p. 116)** Adapted from "Hearing Problems of School Age Children" by John K. Duffy, Report 5 in Volume 1 of the Maico Audiological Library Series as cited in Irving S. Fusfeld, ed., A HANDBOOK OF READINGS IN EDUCATION OF THE DEAF AND POSTSCHOOL IMPLICATIONS, 1967. Courtesy of Charles C Thomas, Publisher, Springfield, Illinois, Maico Electronics and Dr. John K. Duffy. **(p. 155)** Excerpt from CARE AND MANAGEMENT OF EXCEPTIONAL CHILDREN by Juanita Fleming. Copyright © 1973 by Meredith Corporation. Reprinted by permission of Appleton-Century-Crofts, a publishing division of Prentice-Hall, Inc. **(p. 166)** Adapted from "Separation Crisis in Two Blind Children" by Selma Fraiberg in THE PSYCHOANALYTIC STUDY OF THE CHILD, Volume

Preface

To become involved in the world of special children is an exciting, challenging venture. The heartache one feels from sensing a child's distress, the exhilaration that comes from helping a child achieve even a small objective, the fatigue and sometimes the disappointments that follow a hard day in the clinic or classroom or playroom, the sense of worth one knows from doing something that is quite worthwhile —these are but a few of the experiences in store for those who choose to work with special children.

Most of us become involved with special children for personal reasons. Perhaps it simply feels good to be engaged in the helping process. Perhaps our lives have added meaning from the sense of giving to the lives of others. Perhaps we are following in the footsteps of someone we respect and admire. Beyond these personal reasons for becoming involved with special children, however, are the children themselves. Knowing them. Attempting to help them. This is the attraction in the study of special childhood.

Many of the students who read this book may be unsure of the reasons for their interest and uncertain of their future goals. Such uncertainty is often necessary at the beginning of a quest. It is the source of wonder and concern. It prompts us to study and to want to know more. Such is the purpose of this book: to organize and to clarify the desire to know more about special children.

This textbook is intended to provide a comprehensive introduction to the study of special children. We define children as special because of the presence of some physical, cognitive, emotional/behavioral, or social factor that makes difficult the realization of the child's fullest potential. These factors tend to require skilled intervention in order for normal or reasonably normal development to occur. Our approach is frankly humanistic. We are guided by the belief that the individual child is valuable simply because he or she is a human being. In addition, our approach is eclectic but integrative. We entertain a variety of viewpoints and theoretical rationales, but we try to bring together the most relevant perspectives in psychology, education, medicine, social work, and so forth. We feel that this introductory textbook can be equally helpful to students of psychology, education and special education, nursing and pre-medicine, and many other of the professional disciplines concerned with special children. We have sought not to exercise a particular theoretical view or to instruct in the subtleties of a particular professional discipline. In each chapter, our rule-of-thumb has been to determine what is most relevant to the particular area of special childhood being studied. Our emphasis is directed at the whole child as a member of a society that is increasingly valuing and supporting the rights of special children.

We are indebted to many individuals for their help in bringing this book to completion. Limitations of space will not permit us to thank them all. We thank our colleagues for their comments and suggestions early in the manuscript development: John W. De Mand, Kansas State University; Solomon E. Feldman, Northern Illinois University; Bernardine Chuck Fong, Foothill College; Benjamin B. Lahey, University of Georgia; and C. Lamar Mayer, California State University. Further, we thank those who read and commented on the manuscript: Sharon S. Brehm, University of Kansas; Raymond Hawkins, University of Texas at Austin; Marjorie L. Lewis, Illinois State University; Joel D. West, Northern Michigan University; and Rosalind C. Oppenheim, Director of the Rimland School for Autistic Children, for her comments on Chapter 14, *Special Parents*. Al Hirshoren, University of Georgia, contributed his expertise to Chapter 15—*Special Education and the Schools*—and also commented on the chapter drafts, for which we are grateful. James L. Romig must be acknowledged for his initial enthusiasm that was responsible for getting the project off the drawing board. The assistance of Joanne M. Tinsley in editing the manuscript and managing the technical aspects of production has been so invaluable that the book would not have been completed without her help. A special thank you is in order to Ellen Barnett, Paula Cummings, Virginia Gilman, and Lynda Wilson for their untiring assistance in the preparation of the manuscript. Perhaps most importantly, thank you to Mary Elizabeth Suran and Joyce Rizzo for their constant review of the manuscript through its several versions and especially for their emotional support of the authors who, like the manuscript itself, would not be complete without them.

B.G.S.
J.V.R.

Contents

PART THREE

Children with Learning and Cognitive Differences

PART FOUR

Children with Emotional and Behavioral Differences

PART FIVE
Applications to Special Children

PART ONE

Special Children and the Problems of Child Development

CHAPTER ONE

An Introduction to the Study of Special Children

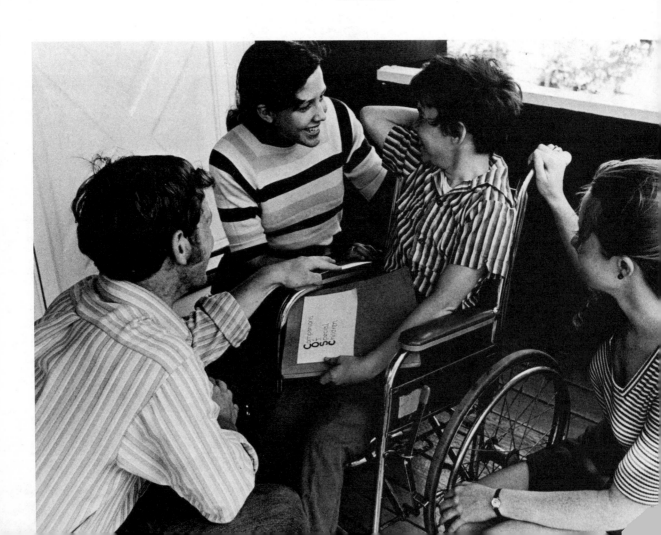

I lay it down as a prime condition of sane society, obvious as such to anyone but an idiot, that in any decent community, children should find in every part of their native country, food, clothing, lodging, instruction, and parental kindness for the asking.... the children must have them as if by magic, with nothing to do but rub the lamp, like Aladdin, and have their needs satisfied.

George Bernard Shaw, *Parents and Children* (1914)

A DEFINITION OF SPECIAL CHILDREN

What is it like to be a "special child"? There are probably as many answers to this question as there are special children. Being a child is a very personal affair; this is no less true for the special child. The unique experiences of one's own childhood lie at the very roots of each person's individual being. For most of us, childhood seems a wondrous and mysterious phenomenon of human experience: a time of growth, a time of learning and unlimited potential, a time of fantasy and play, a time of living in one's mind the many things that one will yet become. For some, childhood can also seem a time of frustration, a time of confinement, a time of disappointment. For special children, the latter can often be the case.

In a philosophical and humanitarian sense, all children are special. However, in this text, we are concerned with special kinds of children who are significantly different from other children in some important dimension of human functioning. These **special children** are those for whom the presence of a physical, psychological, cognitive, or social factor makes difficult the realization of their needs and full potential. For these children skilled intervention and special care are needed in order to help them reach their potential. This definition of special children encompasses the deaf, the blind, the speech disabled, the crippled, the mentally retarded, the emotionally disturbed, to mention but a few. Even gifted children with high IQ's must be recognized as special because skilled intervention by trained professionals might well be required in order for them to develop to their fullest potential. In the case of an intellectually gifted youngster, of course, the child is capable of achieving at a level in advance of what is typically expected of other children; but the realization of this potential is a critical part of such a child's development.

Over the years a number of general terms have been used to refer to special children—among them, "exceptional," "disabled," "handicapped," "dysfunctioning." Though we recognize these terms and will use them at times throughout the text, we have chosen to highlight the term "special" because

6
An introduction to
the study of special
children

we feel it points up not only the fact of difference in special children but also implies the need they have for a particular kind of care and understanding.

The Kinds of Special Children

Although every child is unique and must be considered in highly personal terms, it is often useful in a discussion of special children to group them in terms of common characteristics. This approach reflects the **scientific method,** which relies on systematic observation to provide data that can describe common characteristics and general trends and can aid in predicting patterns of behavior. In our study of special children, this approach will be seen in discussions of the various kinds of special children in terms of those aspects or patterns generally characteristic of each group. To maintain the objective distance of the scientific method throughout, however, runs the risk of losing the highly personal excitement and richness true only of the individual. To avoid this, we will look at a variety of case studies of special children, reflecting the **clinical method,** which applies the data of the scientific method to the actual assessment, treatment, and care of the individual. As such, this textbook will subscribe to both the scientific and the clinical methods; although there will be frequent emphasis on the individual child, the format of the text will be structured by the consideration of the various kinds of special children.

There is no single consistent and universally accepted method of describing the different kinds of special children. Educators, social workers, physicians, psychologists, biomedical scientists, and others are all involved in helping the special child; and professionals in each of these areas tend to use a slightly different framework for classifying special children. For the purposes of this textbook, three major categories of special children will be studied: (a) children with sensory, motor, and physical differences (including hearing and speech disabilities, visual impairments, and physical health disorders); (b) children with learning and cognitive differences (including mental retardation, learning disabilities, and giftedness and creativity); and (c) children with behavioral and emotional differences (including personality problems, conduct disorders and delinquency, and severe emotional problems).

Many special children are difficult to classify and will not fall easily into one specific category. Some special children may have two or more disabilities but be identified only by a single classification; for example, a child may be both emotionally disturbed and mentally retarded, but if the emotional disturbance predominates, the child may tend to be classified only as emotionally disturbed. In other cases, a child with two or more different disabilities may actually be classified as *multiply handicapped;* for example, a child who is both crippled and blind clearly needs very different kinds of services for each disability, and the classification as multiply handicapped tends to underline that child's more complex needs. We have not reserved a specific chapter for the discussion of multiple handicaps, since this would largely involve a duplication of material presented in the other chapters. In a similar vein, we have chosen to cover disadvantaged children in a later chapter devoted to the education of special children. Though this decision may seem arbitrary to some, we feel that the problems of disadvantaged children are primarily educational, and our intent is not to overemphasize the problems they face. We shall discuss in more depth the difficulties inherent in labeling and categorizing in Chapter 3 on assessment and diagnosis.

Many of the special conditions of childhood are experienced by large numbers of children and require the services of various skilled professionals. Estimates of the numbers of children who experience various types of special conditions vary widely, and the difficulties involved in estimating rates of prevalence for individual categories of special childhood will be discussed in relevant chapters. Although no single government agency is charged with the responsibility of keeping accurate statistics for all categories of special childhood, it is possible to gain a general estimate of the numbers of children who experience special conditions. Exhibit 1.1 draws together estimates from several sources regarding the prevalence rates of various categories of school-age special children. An examination of this data indicates that almost every fifth child (20 percent) in the United States will be born with or will develop some identifiable special condition that can potentially inhibit the child's normal development.

Toward Understanding Special Children

Since special children are first of all children, it is important to our understanding of them that we understand normal childhood. It is a curious notion, however, that even though we have all had a firsthand experience of childhood, we can scarcely speak of it with anything but guarded caution and the dawn-

EXHIBIT 1.1

ESTIMATED PREVALENCE RATES OF SCHOOL-AGE SPECIAL CHILDREN

	Percent of Population	Number of Affected Children
Hearing disabilities	.57*	313,500**
Speech disabilities	3.50*	1,925,000**
Visual disabilities	.22*	121,000**
Orthopedic disabilities	.50*	275,000**
Other physical health disorders	5.00***	2,750,000**
Mental retardation	3.00*	1,650,000**
Learning disabilities	2.50*	1,375,000**
Behavioral and/or emotional disorders	2.00*	1,100,000**
Juvenile delinquency (ages 10 thru 18)	2.90****	1,112,500****
Multiple handicaps	.06*	33,000**
	20.25	10,655,000

  * Based on Craig (1976)
 ** Based on 1978 population estimate of 55,000,000 school-age children
*** Based on Mattsson (1972)
**** Based on U.S. Dept. of HEW (1972)

8

An introduction to
the study of special
children

ing awareness that adults have always had difficulty understanding children. The meaning of "childhood" changes not only from generation to generation and from culture to culture but also from individual to individual. For the most part, childhood today is recognized as a time of physical and emotional development and preparation, a time during which—somehow—the child "grows up" into an adult. This is not to say that childhood is merely a period of preparation for adulthood. Childhood is a time of life that has a meaning and rhythm all its own; but much of the meaning and rhythm has to do with development, change, and the acquisition of new skills and ways of being. Life itself is a process of change and adaptation, and people are constantly changing throughout the various periods of life. In the child, however, change is more rapid, more regular, more important. In this respect, the special child is no exception.

It seems ironic that, knowing the importance of growth and change to children, so much of it should be beyond their control—that is, in terms of their physical, psychological, cognitive, and social development. Human childhood is relatively unique among the species of the animal kingdom in that the human infant comes into the world very dependent and considerably undeveloped. In this respect, striking changes continue to occur long after birth, and the human infant requires an extensive period of development prior to the acquisition of biological and emotional maturity.

For example, in humans 25 to 30 percent of the actual life-span is a time of biological immaturity in which the developing person continues to undergo dramatic physiological and psychological changes. During this time, the child is dependent upon adult care and protection. For the special child, the dependence often seems even greater and the time longer.

As we shall see, different societies have responded to the obvious period of childhood immaturity in different ways, and a variety of adults have assumed varying degrees of responsibility for a child's development. We can say, however, that two major factors distinguish childhood as a unique period, whatever the society: (a) rapid developmental changes at both the physiological and psychological levels and (b) dependence upon responsible adult "caretakers" in order to ensure the integrity of the child's development. For the special child, many of the developmental changes will not follow the norm; and much of the dependence upon the care of others is greater. We might add a third factor that is a growing part of childhood: (c) the right to as normal a development as possible and the opportunity to grow to one's fullest human potential. Effective caretaking during this period of growth and development is essential to this goal. This is equally true for special children, and it is here that the added hurdles in special childhood make effective caretaking even more crucial.

From our discussion thus far, several key points have been made that will be helpful to our understanding of special children. First, special children are both similar to and different from other children. The similarities exist, and it is important to understand and remember them. But special children are also different from other children in some important dimension of human functioning (such as the lack of sight or the inability to learn by conventional means). Second, special children, as do all children, have the right to as normal and complete a development as possible. Third, special children need skilled intervention or special services (such as psychotherapy or special education placement).

THE HELPING ORIENTATION

In recent years there have been major gains in society's ability to provide sophisticated care in order to help special children develop to their full potential. One of the purposes of this book is to describe various populations of special children and to examine the kinds of intervention and help possible in order to increase their possibilities for a more meaningful life.

The presence of a helping orientation toward special children, however, cannot be taken for granted in any society. There is ample room for major improvement in current programs; but the prospects of a special child in contemporary society are vastly superior to those that were available in most previous societies. Current efforts toward helping the special child have been made possible by two major circumstances: (a) a changing social philosophy that emphasizes the value of the individual and the rights of children and (b) the increasing sophistication of various treatment approaches that has created the hope that help is always possible. In order to understand the care and management of the special child in contemporary society, a brief consideration of the past may provide a useful perspective.

The Emergence of a Social Conscience Toward Children

It is only in the eighteenth and nineteenth centuries that clear attempts to help the special child came to light. Considering the management of children in general, however, it can safely be assumed that special children fared poorly in most previous societies. Genuine care for special children requires a social sensitivity toward them, and the study of history provides sorry testimony to the fact that we are only slowly acquiring a social conscience toward the needs and the rights of all children.

The ability of a society to provide services to help special children requires not only the technical skills to do so (such as medical intervention, special education, psychotherapy) but also a social philosophy that recognizes the child as an active, feeling person who has a value independent of any other purpose. This valuing of the child as a person in his/her own right has not been easily achieved by most societies. In ancient biblical societies, for example, children were frequently viewed in terms of their value for preserving the intellectual and religious traditions of Judaism (Despert, 1970); the issue of the child's individual needs tended to be less relevant than the critical social function provided by children in maintaining stable religious traditions. In the city-states of ancient Greece, children were clearly viewed as servants of the state; in the militaristic city-state of Sparta, for example, male children who seemed physically capable of developing into warriors were formally adopted by the state at an early age, though left in the custody of the mother until age seven (Good & Teller, 1969). At age seven these youngsters

Unlike attitudes in past centuries, today's outlook holds a growing sensitivity for the needs of children, as reflected in the growth of day-care programs.

began rigorous training and "hardening"; that is, they were deliberately exposed to the worst hardships so that they would be more likely to be successful in the military endeavors of the state.

In ancient Roman society, a shift began to take place away from viewing the child primarily as a useful object of the state. The family became the basic unit of socialization and was regarded as sacred (Despert, 1970). Childrearing was the responsibility of the family rather than of the state, but the father retained absolute power in the family and had the right to reject the child at birth. The child of ancient Roman society continued to be viewed as a passive recipient of adult values and knowledge, and education and training were frequently accomplished by harsh and brutal treatment (deMause, 1974).

During the Middle Ages, and with the decline of the Roman Empire, the powerful influence of the Church stressed the importance of spiritual rather than worldly values. Children were frequently valued in terms of potential service to God and religion. At times, children themselves identified with the religious fervor of the times, as in the Children's Crusades of the twelfth and thirteenth centuries; others were rejected by their parents, exploited, sold into slavery, or killed. With the emergence of the commercial and industrial revolutions of the sixteenth and seventeenth centuries, children were seen to be an economic advantage because of their considerable work potential; children became valuable commodities and were frequently purchased and sold as apprentices, slaves, or servants (see Exhibit 1.2).

The lessons of history in this regard are that children are the most de-

EXHIBIT 1.2

11
The helping
orientation

THE PRIVY COUNCIL GRANTS THE VIRGINIA COMPANY AUTHORITY TO COERCE CHILDREN, 1620
January 31, 1620

Whereas we are informed that the City of London hath, by an act of the Common Council, appointed one hundred children, out of the multitudes that swarm in that place, to be sent to Virginia, there to be bound apprentices for certain years with very beneficial conditions for them afterwards, and have moreover yielded to a levy of five hundred pounds for the appareling of those children and towards the charge of their transportation; wherein, as the City deserveth thanks and commendations for redeeming so many poor souls from misery and ruin and putting them in a condition of use and service to the State; so forasmuch as information is likewise made that among that number there are divers unwilling to be carried thither and that it is conceived that both the City wanteth authority to deliver and the Virginia Company to receive and carry out these persons against their wills, we have thought meet, for the better furtherance of so good a work, hereby to authorize and require as well such of the City as take charge of that service as the Virginia Company, or any of them, to deliver, receive, and transport to Virginia all and every the foresaid children as shall be most expedient. And if any of them shall be found obstinate to resist or otherwise to disobey such directions as shall be given in this behalf, we do likewise hereby authorize such as shall have the charge of this service to imprison, punish, and dispose of any of those children, upon any disorder by them or any of them committed, as cause shall require, and so to ship them out for Virginia with as much expedition as may stand with conveniency. For which this shall be unto all persons whom the same may any way concern a sufficient warrant.

From Bremner, Barnard, Hareven, & Mennel (1970, p. 8)

---

fenseless members of society, and the inherent weaknesses of any given society are frequently first directed at children. Before services for special children can be provided, a society requires both a philosophy of humane understanding as well as a means of protection for children in general. A thorough discussion of this phenomenon would take us far afield, but it is worth noting that by the seventeenth century both a philosophy of humane care as well as institutions of social protection began to take root in Western society.

A philosophy of humane care
At the core of many of the major social changes that took place in the seventeenth and eighteenth centuries was the growing awareness of the rights of individuals. The influence of John Locke (1632–1704), the noted English philosopher, on the founders of the American and French revolutions is well known. Locke was also a physician, however, and he exerted considerable influence on attitudes and practices of both childbirth and childrearing. In keeping with his philosophy regarding the rights of individuals, Locke was concerned that children be raised with thought and care, recognizing the child

12

An introduction to
the study of special
children

as emotionally responsive and emphasizing the importance of an empathic understanding of the child (Illick, 1974).

In the same manner, the romanticism of Jean Rousseau (1712–1778), the noted French social philosopher, also influenced attitudes toward children. In his classic work, *Emile,* he invited an empathic understanding of childhood, suggesting that it is the teacher who learns from the reactions and responses of the child (Cruchon, 1969). Rousseau praised and prized the innocence of childhood, and many members of the middle and upper classes were exposed to his ideas. It became fashionable to idealize the freedom of youth and the spontaneity of childhood, and to view with nostalgic tenderness those lost aspects of one's own life.

The wide dissemination of such ideas among the middle and upper classes began to affect even the less educated strata of society. Concepts of child-rearing became firmly imbedded in the cultural traditions of Western society. It was the presence of such humane attitudes toward children in general that served as the eventual source of an attitude of caring for the needs of the special child.

Early institutions of social protection

With the colonization of America came both the best and the worst of European traditions. In early New England, for example, children were frequently treated harshly and repressively. At the same time, however, consciousness of the child as an individual and a member of the community was also emerging. Many colonists had themselves been victims of religious persecution and had become sensitized to the need for laws to protect the defenseless.

The New Englanders were unique in enacting legislation to care for illegitimate and orphaned children as public charges, and they attempted to ensure that parents fulfilled their responsibilities in caring for their children. In the 1670s, for example, the office of "tithingman" was established in Massachusetts; these men were to be selected from "the most prudent and discreet" members of the community and were charged with monitoring family government and the behavior of children and parents with respect to each other (see Exhibit 1.3). In many respects, the tithingman was quite similar to the contemporary "child advocate" who is coming to be a recognized protector of children's rights. The evolution of these humane approaches to the care of children, symbolized by the presence of such innovations as the tithingman, prepared the way for some of the first attempts to provide professional help aimed at accommodating the conditions of special childhood.

The Emergence of a Helping Orientation Toward Special Children

The possibility of a helping approach toward children with particular problems was prepared for by the gradual changes in social perspective described in the previous section. In the past two centuries many individuals and movements, too numerous to recount here, have made significant contributions to understanding and helping special children with various problems. Many of their contributions will be discussed in appropriate chapters throughout this book. The work of Jean-Marc Itard with a boy called Victor and the work of

EXHIBIT 1.3

13

The helping
orientation

RESPONSIBILITIES OF TITHINGMEN, 1679
Mass. Records, VI, 240–241.

It is ordered . . . that henceforth the selectment of each town take care that tithingmen be annually chosen in their several precincts of the most prudent and discreet inhabitants, and sworn to be the faithful discharge of their trust . . . .

The tithingmen are required diligently to inspect the manner of all disorderly persons, and where by more private admonitions they will not be reclaimed, they are from time to time to present their names to the next Magistrate, or Commissioner invested with magistratical power, who shall proceed against them as the law directs. As also they are in like manner to present the names of all single persons that live from under family government, stubborn and disorderly children and servants, night-walkers, tip-plers, Sabbath breakers by night or by day, and such as absent themselves from the public worship of God on the Lord's days, or whatever else course or practice of any person or persons whatsoever tending to debauchery, irreligion, profaneness, and atheism amongst us, whether by omission of family government, nurture, and religious duties, [or] instruction of children and servants, or idle, profligate, uncivil or rude practices of any sort, the names of all which persons with the fact whereof they are accused, and witnesses thereof, they shall present to the next Magistrate or Commissioner, where any are in the said town invested with magistratical power, who shall proceed against and punish all such misdemeanours by fine, imprisonment, or binding over the county court as the law directs.

From Bremner et al. (1970, p. 42), cited from Morgan (1966)

Samuel Gridley Howe with a girl named Laura Bridgman are worthy of note here, however, because they are genuine milestones in the history of child psychiatry and special education.

Jean-Marc Itard and the case of Victor
One of the first documented efforts to work with a special child was undertaken by Jean-Marc Itard (1775–1838). In 1799, a child of about twelve years of age was discovered living in the forests near Aveyron, France. Brought to Paris by civil authorities, the boy soon became the object of popular attention as rumors spread that he had been reared by animals. Instead of the "noble savage" of Rousseau's romantic philosophy, however, the boy was dirty, nonverbal, incapable of attention, and insensitive even to basic sensations of heat and cold. He spent his time eating, sleeping, and rocking back and forth. Despite the child's appearance, Itard believed that appropriate environmental conditions could humanize him, and he undertook the responsibility for making this effort, rather than allow the child to be sent to an asylum. Itard's (1962) account of his work with this boy, whom he called Victor, is a very poignant detailing of the optimism, frustration, anger, hope, and despair that he experienced in working with a special child. His experiences are familiar to anyone who has undertaken a similar responsibility.

Using crude diagnostic methods, Itard had determined that Victor's sensory organs, though intact, were often "dull," or insensitive. He did not

14

An introduction to
the study of special
children

seem to react to extremes of hot and cold, and of all his senses, his hearing appeared the least sensitive: Victor would not respond to loud noises—even to the sound of a pistol being fired as an experimental test of his hearing abilities. And yet, Itard observed, Victor would respond to such subtle sounds as the cracking of walnuts. It seemed as though Victor had an unusually developed ability to "screen out" sounds that he was not interested in hearing.

Following John Locke's contention that all human learning takes place through experience, Itard determined that his work with Victor must begin with the sensory stimulation and discipline which are the basis of learning. Itard used a variety of means to bring Victor to an awareness of his sensory experiences: hot baths, massages, tickling, emotional excitement, even electric shocks. Many of these techniques have now become commonplace in the treatment of autistic and schizophrenic children (see Chapter 13). Itard also attempted to increase Victor's ability to engage in social contacts: he taught him a few basic signs with which to communicate his wants; he taught him to solve simple problems and even to recognize a few simple words; he taught him to relate, though in a primitive manner, to other human beings.

After five years of work, Victor had become moderately socialized but not, as Itard had naively hoped, "normal." Victor died in 1828 at about forty years of age. Though Victor's ability to learn and Itard's ability to teach are important historically, they are overshadowed by the caring relationship that developed between them. Itard's is perhaps the first account in history in which we experience an adult's attempt to understand—really to feel with and know—the mind and emotions of a special child. This deep investment on the part of an individual in the needs and feelings of another person's child remains a key component of the helping orientation.

Samuel Gridley Howe and the case of Laura Bridgman

Perhaps the first special children to attract the organized efforts of helping persons were the deaf and the blind. In the eighteenth century, particularly in France and England, a number of individuals sought to develop specialized approaches for the training of deaf and blind persons. In 1784, for example,

Laura Bridgman (left) was the first to benefit from Samuel Gridley Howe's (right) efforts to provide formal training for the deaf and blind.

Valentin Haüy (1745–1822) founded the first school for the blind in Paris. These efforts spurred considerable activity in the United States, not the least of which was the work of Samuel Gridley Howe (1801–1876). Educated at Brown University and Harvard Medical School, Howe was hired in 1831 by the New England Asylum for the Blind to devise methods for educating sightless persons. Howe founded his school with only two students initially, but the school soon served increasing numbers of blind children. Howe's work is particularly interesting because, like Itard, he was keenly sensitive to the subjective experience of the special child. It was this unique ability to understand the inner world of the child that enabled Howe to make a significant breakthrough in working with special children.

Perhaps Howe's best known and most successful work with a special child took place in his efforts to educate a deaf and blind child, Laura Bridgman, who entered his school in 1837. Howe became the first professional to undertake work with a deaf and blind child, and his extensive reports on her education and development are an outstanding legacy to the entire field of work with special children in general and the deaf and blind in particular. Case Study 1.1 on page 16 provides some relevant selections from Howe's reports of his work with Laura Bridgman.

In the combined work of Itard and Howe, one can see the emergence of a helping orientation toward the special child take firm root as a means of enhancing the developmental potentials of children with a variety of problems.

The Children's Rights Movement

As social attitudes toward children in general began to change, the legal system, as an expression of changing social attitudes, was also beginning to enter a phase of defining and treating children as persons with rights of their own. The rights of children became an increasingly important issue at three distinct levels: (a) the decisions of the courts, (b) social legislation enacted by Congress, and (c) policy statements of national and international organizations.

The courts and children's rights

As long ago as 1869, in *Fletcher et al.* v. *Illinois,* parental rights began to be defined in terms of restrictions imposed by the rights of children. In the Fletcher Case, the court ruled: "Counsel urge, that the law gives parents a large discretion in the exercise of authority over their children. This is true, but this authority over their children must be exercised within the bounds of reason and humanity. If the parent commits wanton and needless cruelty upon his child, either by imprisonment of his character or by inhuman beating, the law will punish him. . . . It would be monstrous to hold that under the pretense of sustaining parental authority, children must be left, without the protection of the law, at the mercy of depraved men or women, with liberty to inflict any species of barbarity short of the actual taking of life" (cited in Bremner et al., 1971, p. 119).

In recent years, the actions of the courts have required recognition of children's rights in a number of areas: equal access to educational opportunities (e.g., in *Brown* v. *The Board of Education,* 1954); fair procedures for classi-

16

An introduction to
the study of special
children

CASE STUDY 1.1

THE EDUCATION OF LAURA BRIDGMAN, 1837

The first knowledge I had of Laura's existence was from reading an account of her case written by Dr. Mussey, then resident at Hanover. It struck me at once that here was an opportunity of assisting an unfortunate child, and, moreover of deciding the question so often asked, whether a blind-mute could be taught to use an arbitrary language. I had concluded, after closely watching Julia Brace, the well-known blind-mute in the American Asylum at Hartford, that the trial should not be abandoned, though it had failed in her case, as well as in all that had been recorded before.

It was rather a discouragement . . . to find that Laura had no sense of smell; or to be more precise, only the latent capacity for using it; the organ of that sense not having been destroyed by the disease, as had those of sight and hearing . . . I determined, however, to make an attempt to reach her mind through the one remaining sense, especially as there was something about her which seemed to give promise of her aiding the attempt as much as she could . . . .

I found that she had become familiar with much in the world about her. She knew the form, weight, density, and temperature of things in the house. She used to follow her mother about, cling-

ing to her dress, and feeling her arms and hands when she was doing any work. The faculty of imitation of course led her to strive to do whatever she perceived others doing, whether she could understand it or not . . . .

Slowly and patiently, day after day, and week after week, exercises . . . went on, as much time being spent at them as the child could give without fatigue. Hitherto there had been nothing very encouraging; not much more success than in teaching a very intelligent dog a variety of tricks. But we were approaching the moment when the thought would flash upon her that all these were efforts to establish a means of communication between her thoughts and ours . . . .

The poor child had sat in mute amazement, and patiently imitated everything her teacher did; but now the truth began to flash upon her, her intellect began to work, she perceived that here was a way by which she could herself make up a sign of anything that was in her own mind, and show it to another mind, and at once her countenance lighted up with a human expression; it was no longer a dog or parrot—it was an immortal spirit, eagerly seizing upon a new link of union with other spirits!

From Howe (cited in Dennis, 1972, pp. 63, 66)

fication of the mentally retarded (e.g., *Mills* v. *State Board of Education,* 1972); humane treatment of the institutionalized retarded (e.g., *Wyatt* v. *Stickney,* 1972); and adversarial protection in juvenile court proceedings (e.g., *In re Gault,* 1967). Such legal decisions obviously do not result in immediate changes in the treatment of children; both the courts and society are still trying to deal with the problems treated in *Fletcher* v. *Illinois.* Nonetheless, the actions of the courts toward children's rights represent the prospect of orchestrated legal change that is typically more effective than the independent actions of a few isolated individuals.

Social legislation and the needs of children

The recognition of the child as a person has also prompted Congress to enact legislation to safeguard the welfare of children. In 1912, for example, Congress created the United States Children's Bureau and gave this agency broad powers to investigate the interrelated problems of child health, child dependency, child labor, and child delinquency. As the Children's Bureau grew in influence, it brought about the first White House Conference on Children in 1930. This first conference addressed itself particularly to problems relevant to the care of children, such as nutritional problems, inadequate medical care, infant mortality, and the conditions of poverty resulting from worldwide depression. Subsequent White House Conferences have continued to focus attention on the current needs of children and special children.

In recent years, Congress has continued to enact legislation establishing various agencies and commissions that are involved in protecting the rights of children. In 1961 the President's Panel on Mental Retardation was founded to address the needs of the retarded child; in 1963 the National Institute of Child Health and Development was charged with the responsibility of reviewing and stimulating research in the area of child health and development; in 1965 the Joint Commission on Mental Health of Children was given the responsibility of advocating children's needs; in 1967 the Office of Child Development was established in the Office of the Secretary of Health, Education, and Welfare; in 1970 the Developmental Disabilities Program was made responsible for promoting the development of life-long assistance programs for mentally retarded, cerebral palsied, and epileptic children.

Perhaps the most important single piece of legislation currently affecting special children is Public Law 94-142—The Education for All Handicapped Children Act—enacted in 1975 by Congress. This law (which is discussed at greater length in Chapter 15) was designed to ensure a free and appropriate public education for all special children between the ages of 3 and 21. Public Law 94-142 provides a formula by which the federal government makes a commitment to pay an increasing percentage of the costs associated with special educational services necessary for handicapped children. Through this legislation, the federal government has attempted to assure that the rights of special children are protected by helping subsidize the cost of services involved in special educational programs of various types.

Policy statements regarding the rights of children

The role of the White House Conferences as an advocate for children's rights has already been noted. These Conferences led, indirectly but unquestionably, to the adoption by the United Nations General Assembly (1959) of the *Declaration of the Rights of the Child*. This declaration demanded a recognition of the rights of children to develop to their full capacity—"physically, mentally, morally, spiritually, and socially in a healthy and normal manner and in conditions of freedom and dignity" (Principle 2); "to grow and develop in health; to this end special care and protection shall be provided . . . , including prenatal and postnatal care" (Principle 4). Of particular interest to us is Principle 5: "The child who is physically, mentally, or socially handicapped shall be given the special treatment, education, and care required by his/her particular condition." More recently, in 1976, the General Assembly of the United Nations declared 1979 the International Year of the Child (IYC). Key objectives during this year are the promotion of child advocacy and the call to action on

18

An introduction to
the study of special
children

the part of nations, organizations, and individuals to meet the physical, intellectual, psychological, and social needs of all children.

Another significant statement of the rights of children was set forth by the Joint Commission on the Mental Health of Children. In 1970 this commission published its first report, entitled *Crisis in Child Mental Health,* to advise the government of the health needs of children and to make recommendations for the programs to meet those needs. An important part of this report included a statement regarding the rights of children. This statement has subsequently been revised by Berlin (1975) as a "Bill of Rights" and is reproduced in Exhibit 1.4. Such statements of children's rights, of course, can only serve to spur society's recognition of its responsibilities. There continues to be a dramatic disparity between the needs of special children and society's ability to respond to those needs in an adequate manner. In most cases, the fate of a special child lies directly in the hands of understanding and concerned parents and a few competent professionals who are able to lend their expertise to the resolution of that child's problems.

The Helping Professions

It has been noted that a helping orientation to the needs of special children has been made possible by a number of historical changes in social attitudes as well as by legal decisions and social legislation that protect the rights of

EXHIBIT 1.4

A BILL OF RIGHTS

We hold these truths inalienable for all children:

ONE: The Right to Be Born Wanted.
TWO: The Right to Be Born Healthy.
THREE: The Right to Live in a Healthful Environment.
FOUR: The Right to Live in a Family Whose Basic Economic Needs Are Met.
FIVE: The Right to Continuous and Loving Care both at Home and in School.
SIX: The Right to Acquire Intellectual and Emotional Skills for Effective Citizenship.
                a. The Right to Dignity in School.
                b. The Right to Humane and Concerned Treatment Under the Law and by Courts.
                c. The Right to Child-Centered Divorce and Custody Laws.
SEVEN: The Right to Meaningful Employment.
EIGHT: The Right to Diagnostic, Treatment, and Rehabilitative Care through Facilities which are Appropriate to Children's Special Needs and Which Keep Them as Closely as Possible within Their Normal Social Setting.
NINE: The Right to Racial and Ethnic Identity, Self-Determination, and a Real and Functional Equality of Opportunity to the Above Rights.
TEN: The Right to Political Participation through Education for Informed Citizenship.

From Berlin (1975, p. 5)

children. In the case of each special child, however, help is made possible by the persistence of parents and/or advocates in securing relevant professional and paraprofessional assistance. For each special child, the prospects for a normal development have been greatly enhanced by many changes within and between the professions that provide services for special children. Though the many types of professional help will be discussed in more detail in later chapters, it is important here to have a general picture of the professionals involved. Exhibit 1.5 summarizes the various professional services in terms of five major areas associated with special children: (a) medical/paramedical, (b) social/legal, (c) educational, (d) psychological, and (e) special modalities.

It is obvious from Exhibit 1.5 that there are many different kinds of professionals who can provide a particular type of expertise in helping a special child. Few, if any, special children require all, or even most, of these professional services. It is not unusual, however, that a special child may require the services of several different professionals, each of whom views the child's needs in terms of the perspective of his/her particular discipline. It would be

EXHIBIT 1.5

A SAMPLING OF THE HELPING PROFESSIONS

MEDICAL/PARAMEDICAL	SOCIAL/LEGAL	EDUCATIONAL	PSYCHOLOGICAL	SPECIAL MODALITIES
Pediatrician	Caseworker	Teacher	Counselor	Speech pathologist
Neurologist	School social worker	Regular	School psychologist	Audiologist
Orthopedist	Psychiatric social worker	Special	Clinical child psychologist	Optometrist
Otolaryngologist	Probation officer	Remedial specialist	Behavior therapist	Music therapist
Optometrist	Child advocate	Itinerant		Art therapist
Ophthalmologist	Attorney	Clinical/ diagnostic		Recreation therapist
Psychiatrist		Principal		Child-care worker
Nurse		School Nurse		
Physical therapist		Guidance counselor		
Occupational therapist				

20

An introduction to
the study of special
children

rare, indeed, that a single person would possess all the skills necessary to help a special child.

Because of the complex nature of the diagnostic and treatment services possible in contemporary society, professionals have learned the overriding importance of teamwork and coordination of services—in essence, a **team approach** to helping. Within any given hospital, school, or clinic, professionals regularly form teams that pool the expertise of different skills in order to provide the child with effective and coordinated management. Within the school, for example, a given child may be enrolled in a special education class, be seen regularly by the school psychologist, and be followed by the school nurse; some of that child's classes may also be taught by the regular classroom teacher. All of the persons involved would form the child's team in the educational setting. That same team may also have contact with the child's pediatrician or neurologist, or with a caseworker provided by a state's department of children and family services. This is a very "usual" situation for a special child, and during the course of the child's development, several other professionals may also be involved. With different kinds of special children, of course, different professions have a greater or lesser involvement. Since several disciplines are typically involved in a child's care, however, the team approach is usually a must if the child is to benefit most.

PLAN OF THE BOOK

This book is intended to serve as a comprehensive introduction to special children. Although a multidisciplinary emphasis is maintained, particular attention is paid to the psychological and educational aspects of special childhood. The remaining chapters in the first section of the text discuss issues central to the consideration of all special children: normal and special development (Chapter 2), diagnosis and assessment (Chapter 3), and the helping process itself (Chapter 4).

The second, third, and fourth sections of this book provide nine chapters dealing with particular populations of special children: included are children with sensory and motor differences, learning and cognitive differences, and emotional and behavioral differences. Within each of these chapters, the following material is discussed for each special condition under consideration: (a) definition and classification, (b) incidence and etiology, (c) diagnosis and identification, (d) developmental consequences, and (e) intervention.

The fifth and final section of the book considers in detail three aspects of special childhood that merit in-depth discussion: parents of special children (Chapter 14), educational services for special children (Chapter 15), and provision of services and child advocacy for special children (Chapter 16).

SUMMARY

1. Special children are defined as those for whom the presence of a physical, psychological, cognitive, or social factor makes difficult the realization of their needs and full potential.

2. It is estimated that 20 percent of the general population of children can be classified as special.

3. Two major factors distinguish childhood as a unique period in the human life cycle: rapid developmental changes and dependence upon adult caretakers.

4. Two important circumstances have influenced current efforts toward helping special children: a social philosophy that emphasizes the value of the individual, and the increasing sophistication of treatment approaches.

5. The rights of children in contemporary society have been refined by three major factors: decisions of the courts, enactment of social legislation by Congress, and policy statements by powerful national and international organizations.

6. The needs of special children typically require the help of a team of professionals, each having a unique expertise.

Models of Child Development

There was a child went forth every day,
And the first object he looked upon, that object he became,
And that object became part of him for the day or a certain part of
  the day,
Or for many years or stretching cycles of years.

Walt Whitman

THE NATURE OF CHILD DEVELOPMENT

There are few experiences in this world as packed with pleasure and awe as the sight of a child delighting in the discovery of some new-found skill or previously unknown dimension of existence. A four-month-old learning to grasp and shake a rattle; a one-year-old calling out "Mama" and "Dada" to proud parents; a three-year-old mastering the pedals of a new tricycle; a preschooler making a first "real" friend outside of the family; a second grader reveling in the rudiments of writing and reading and arithmetic; a pre-teenager dealing with issues of "right" and "wrong"; a teenager experimenting with a newly emerging sense of independence and social identity—such accomplishments in the process of human development serve as signposts by which we can measure a child's growth and development. Indeed, the very fact of change and becoming is a natural, central feature in the life of the developing child.

Each of us, at every age and every stage, is constantly changing. Sometimes the changes are obvious, while at other times they are quite subtle. When one meets an old friend after a long absence, it may be readily apparent that he/she has gained a girthful twenty pounds on a frame that can ill support the additional baggage; it may be less apparent, however, that the same person may have divorced a spouse, been converted to a new religion, grown more serious than humorous, or even have found some sense of inner peace that makes the whole world seem different.

Physical change is more easily noticed than psychological change. Together, they form the simple data of experience. By looking at how we change—both physically and psychologically—over the years, we can gain a better sense of where we have come from and what we have become. In essence, we can see how we have developed.

In living organisms, and especially in humans, some changes are more regular and more specific than others. Some changes seem almost predictable. When an infant starts standing, aided or unaided, we assume that the time is near when he/she will start walking. Standing represents a change in the child's scope of abilities, but it also represents a significant indicator that many

23

other changes will soon follow. Parents know this fact well as, almost without thinking, they begin to place valued or dangerous objects out of the inquisitive reach of their soon-to-be walking and higher-seeking infant.

Changes can genuinely be identified as "development" when they represent an increasing capacity for a wider range of behavior. Such changes are particularly noticeable in childhood because it is then that the most rapid physical growth and obvious learning usually occur. For the most part, these changes take place in a developing child in an orderly and predictable way, and they tend to enhance the child's ability to master the environment. **Child development,** therefore, might be seen as a series of changes, usually patterned and predictable, that foster the child's ability to cope with and master the external environment. For the special child, the changes may be more difficult, and they are not always patterned or predictable.

MODELS OF CHILD DEVELOPMENT

Over the years a number of viewpoints, or models, have evolved that attempt to explain the usual pattern of child development. Though to date no one model is universally accepted, some have become more prominent than others. We use the term *model* because each viewpoint is based on different premises that provide us with a different guide, or model, for understanding child development. It is important that those of us concerned with special children understand these models of "normal" child development so that we may understand better the similarities and differences in the development of the special child. With a sound knowledge of these models, we can see more clearly the significance of the deviations that often occur in the development of a special child. This is especially important if we seek to help these special children develop to their fullest.

As such, it is our intent in this chapter to look briefly at four basic models of child development: *maturational, psychodynamic, cognitive,* and *learning.* Each of these models emphasizes a slightly different aspect of development. We shall review these models of child development with the express purpose of selecting the central constructs and characteristics especially applicable to understanding the problems of special childhood. Then, beginning on page 45, Case Study 2.1 will look at one special child from the perspectives of each of the four models.

A MATURATIONAL MODEL: ARNOLD GESELL

A basic issue facing the student of special children is the question of *how children grow.* Physical growth in childhood is a matter of common experience, but for the special child physical growth is particularly significant. It is not uncommon, for example, for the cute and cuddly three-year-old thought to be somewhat slow in social development to become a physically awesome, and perhaps frightening, brain-damaged adolescent. Children with a variety of problems continue to mature physically, and the dimension of physical development is a central consideration in each and every child.

Arnold Gesell (1880–1960) is the investigator most closely identified with the study of the physical growth of children, commonly known as **maturation.** As an undergraduate at Clark University, Gesell was drawn to the blossoming new study of child development. Early in his training, he became convinced that the key to understanding child development was to be found on a physical basis. He went on to pursue this line of thought in medical school and later as Director of the Yale Clinic of Child Development, where he had occasion to assess thousands of normal and special children. Because Gesell was a physician who wrote popular books on child guidance, many of his more scientific writings have been overlooked. Gesell's view of child development, however, has much to offer the student of special childhood. It is presented here as a maturational model that can be of considerable use in understanding any individual special child. Our discussion of Gesell will focus on three of his major contributions, namely the view of the child as an organism, the concept of norms of development, and the practice of developmental diagnosis.

The Child as an Organism

As a physician, Gesell sought a physical explanation to the question of how children grow and develop. First and foremost, Gesell saw the infant and developing child as an *organism* governed by natural laws of biological functioning:

> *What is an organism? It is living, growing protoplasm. The mind, so far as we can fathom it by direct observation, is an expression of the organization of this protoplasm, manifested in visible patterns of behavior.* (Gesell & Ilg, 1943, p. 20)

Gesell's view of the child as an organism led him to propose two important principles regarding growth and development: *growth is unitary* and *growth is organized by the nervous system.* The concept of unity of growth

Arnold Gesell, seen here examining an infant, believed that physical development, or maturation, is the key to understanding a child's development.

implies that all growth—physical, psychological, cognitive, social—is part of the same fabric of development. In this sense, all growth is likewise governed, or organized, by the nervous system:

> *The growth of the mind is profoundly and inseparably bound up with the growth of the nervous system. . . . How does the mind grow? It grows like the nervous system; it grows with the nervous system. Growth is a patterning process. It produces patterned changes in the nerve cells; it produces corresponding changes in patterns of behavior. (Gesell & Ilg, 1943, pp. 17–18)*

In brief, Gesell's model of child development is termed *maturational* because it views the development of the nervous system itself as the organizer of growth processes. A maturational view of child behavior maintains that growth in the child is governed by naturally occurring and regulating processes innate to the maturing nervous system, of which *increasingly complex behavior* is the observable expression. In essence, development is a function of a "built-in timetable" fixed by the maturation of the central nervous system. Gesell assumed that such developmental changes in the child are lawful and meaningful because they represent the highest attainments of millions of years of evolution of the human nervous system. This view enabled Gesell to proceed with what might be considered his greatest achievement— the establishment of norms of development.

Norms of Development

Gesell felt that one of the major purposes of a science of child development should be to observe and record with great precision the actual behavior changes that take place as a presumed function of the maturation of the nervous system. As a scientist, he felt that his job was simply "to see what happens," and in this respect he and his colleagues were tremendously successful. In his many writings and filmed interviews, Gesell has rightfully achieved distinction as one of the great describers and catalogers of infant and child behavior.

Gesell believed that the most sensible way to understand problems in child development is first to gain a clear and accurate understanding of the processes that take place in the normally developing child. To this end, his lifelong work involved accumulating developmental data on thousands of infants and children. In the early 1930s, Gesell was a pioneer in using film techniques to record and study the developing child as a total complex action system—that is, an organism—that changes with age (Gesell, 1935).

Gesell's extensive research on infant and child behavior almost single-handedly gave credence to the concept of **norms of development.** These norms, sometimes described as **developmental milestones,** are based on careful research and rigorous data showing that there are specific age levels at which infants and children are typically able to perform various critical behaviors (such as crawling, standing, or using first words). A lengthy presentation of this normative data would be beyond the scope of this discussion, but Exhibit 2.1 gives some examples of Gesell's norms of development.

EXHIBIT 2.1

27
A maturational
model

EXAMPLES OF GESELL'S DEVELOPMENTAL NORMS

16 weeks: gets excited, laughs aloud
spontaneous smile in response to people
anticipates eating at sight of food
sits propped for ten to fifteen minutes

28 weeks: smiles and vocalizes to a mirror and pats at mirror image
many vowel sounds
sits unsupported for brief period and then leans on hands
takes solids well
when lying on back, places feet to mouth
grasps objects and transfers objects from hand to hand
when held standing, supports most of weight

12 months: walks with only one hand held
says "mama" and "dada" and perhaps two other "words"
gives a toy in response to a request or gesture
when being dressed, will cooperate
plays "peek-a-boo" games

18 months: has a vocabulary of some ten words
walks well, seldom falls, can run stiffly
looks at pictures in a book
feeds self, although spills
can pull a toy or hug a doll
can seat self in a small or adult chair
scribbles spontaneously with a crayon or pencil

24 months: walks up and down stairs alone
runs well, no falling
can build a tower of six or seven blocks
uses personal pronouns ("I" and "you") and speaks a three-word
    sentence
identifies simple pictures by name and calls self by name
verbalizes needs fairly consistently
may be dry at night
can pull on simple garment

36 months: alternates feet when climbing stairs and jumps from bottom stair
rides a tricycle
can copy a circle and imitate a cross with a crayon or pencil
comprehends and answers questions
feeds self with little spilling
may know and repeat a few simple rhymes

48 months: can dry and wash hands, brushes teeth
laces shoes, dresses and undresses with supervision
can play cooperatively with other children
can draw figure of a person with at least two clear body parts

60 months: knows and names colors, counts to 10
skips on both feet
can print a few letters, can draw identifiable pictures

From Gesell & Amatruda (1947)

Developmental Diagnosis

By carefully specifying the ages at which developmental milestones typically take place, Gesell laid the basis for considering the normal potential or possible problems of a given child. Gesell's key to assessing the capacities and potentials of any given child is the "developmental diagnosis," which has been helpful to pediatricians who seek to identify as early as possible children who may have developmental and health problems. **Developmental diagnosis** includes a physical examination of the child as well as a detailed health history and parent interview. The main focus of the examination, however, is an assessment of the child's behavior patterns. The behavior patterns most central to this assessment include the following:

a) **adaptive behavior:** the child's capacity to organize stimuli, to perceive relationships, to dissect wholes into meaningful component parts, to coordinate eyes and hands in reaching and manipulation, to initiate new adjustments to problem situations;

b) **gross motor behavior:** the child's capacity to maintain head balance, to sit, to stand, to crawl or creep, to walk;

c) **fine motor behavior:** the child's ability to use hands and fingers to grasp and manipulate objects in an increasingly refined fashion;

d) **language behavior:** the child's ability to use visible and audible forms of communication, such as facial expressions, posturing, vocalizations, words, phrases, sentences;

e) **personal-social behavior:** the child's personal reactions to his/her immediate environment and changes in it, such as adaptability to independent play and cooperation and responsiveness to toilet training or to learning to eat solid foods.

These basic *fields of behavior* are presumed to be the major indicators of the integrity of a child's development, which proceeds stage by stage, in an orderly sequence and increasing degree of maturity. (Exhibit 2.2 illustrates how a pediatrician might record the developmental diagnosis of a small child.) The evaluation of any single item of behavior, or indeed of an entire behavior repertory, is made by comparing a given child's behavior pattern to the expected ages at which particular behaviors are known to develop. Various behaviors (such as crawling, standing, first words) are known to occur at particular age levels, and the normal behavior pattern—established and defined by controlled investigation of the course of development typical of healthy children—is presumed to be a general criterion of maturity. The very term "normal" is understood to be synonymous with "healthy" (Knobloch & Pasamanick, 1974, p. 6).

According to Gesell's perspective, then, the normal (or healthy) child is one who demonstrates behavioral development in a manner consistent with the expected norms of development. Children who fail to develop according to normal patterns might be considered to be experiencing **developmental delays.** Such delays might well be an indication that the child might have some disabling condition that requires special attention to help the child back into the "norm." In this respect, Gesell made a significant contribution to

EXHIBIT 2.2

29

A maturational
model

GESELL'S ILLUSTRATIVE BEHAVIOR INTERVIEW

Name: Jane Doe   Age: 40 wks.   Date: 6–10–40   CCD No.

Informant: Mrs. Doe
  Relationship to child: Mother

Motor behavior (include handedness and manner of manipulation of objects)
  Sits alone well
  Creeps all over the house
  Pulls to her feet and stands—no cruising—lowers self
  Steps when hands held, no walking

Language behavior (include gestures)
  dada and mama   Comprehends name
  baba (bottle)   no
  imitates sounds   patacake, bye
                                   where's daddy

Play behavior (include toys)
  Plays with toys, bangs together
  Picks up crumbs
  Pokes into holes
  No in and out play

Domestic behavior (feeding, dressing, toilet, cooperation)
  Takes part each feeding from cup, chokes, refuses
  Holds bottle, feeds self cracker
  bm. regularized

Emotional behavior (dependency, management, playmates, specific behavior
    deviations)
  Good baby, plays alone happily
  Friendly with strangers if not approached too fast
  Sleeps all night, sucks thumb at sleep time
  Some resistance to cup—takes new foods well

Health history
  2 teeth
  has been well since last visit

From Gesell & Amatruda (1947, p. 100)

---

the study of special children by providing clear-cut and unambiguous norms by which to measure the developmental progress of any child.

It is worth noting, however, that Gesell's model focuses primarily on behavior that is closely related to neurological maturation. Though Gesell was a vigorous campaigner for the social and psychological needs of children, his model of child development relies heavily on the assumption that development is controlled by innate tendencies and appears to underestimate the degree to which environmental factors may influence the inner determination of behavior. The notion of a built-in timetable becomes somewhat suspect in instances where children demonstrate developmental delays in the absence of neurological deficits. Nonetheless, the work of Gesell and his associates has provided a pragmatic approach to the understanding of normal infancy and early childhood as well as to the early assessment and identification of potential problems in a child's development.

PSYCHODYNAMIC MODELS: SIGMUND FREUD AND ERIK ERIKSON

A second approach to understanding the development of special children comes from theorists and clinicians who are particularly interested in the unseen aspects of the child's inner life. Such approaches are typically described as **psychodynamic** because they assume that human behavior is a function of inner, unconscious mechanisms of motivation. Although many persons have made significant contributions to psychodynamic theories, the most important contributions, for our purposes, are those of Sigmund Freud and Erik Erikson.

Freud's Psychosexual Theory of Child Development

In a sense, all psychodynamic approaches are indebted to the work of Sigmund Freud, the founder of psychoanalysis. Freud maintained that childhood experiences are so critical that they can unconsciously influence the behavior of individuals throughout their adult lives. Freud attempted to explain human behavior by postulating the presence of an unseen psychosexual energy—the **libido**—as the motive power behind human behavior. He maintained that this motive power manifested itself in five distinct and significant childhood stages: (a) the **oral stage,** in which the infant's needs are almost totally directed toward oral gratification; (b) the **anal stage,** in which the infant's focus of libidinal energy is on the anal area and the mastery of processes of elimination and toilet training; (c) the **phallic stage** (beginning late in the preschool years), in which the child is thought to discover the genital area as a major source of pleasure; (d) the **latency period** (from early school years to adolesence), in which the child's libido is thought to be somewhat diffused or even curiously inactive; and (e) the **genital stage** (beginning in adolescence and representing the culmination of psychosexual development), in which the adolescent's libidinal satisfaction focuses on genital stimulation with others.

Freud, of course, has been both roundly criticized and widely praised for his theory of psychosexual development, but the Freudian approach to the understanding of human behavior continues to hold a place of eminence and influence among major theories of personality. It should be remembered, however, that in his original formulation, Freud's central purpose was to explain adult behavior through an understanding of childhood experiences. Freud's own clinical work was almost exclusively with adult patients, and he attempted to develop a theory of personality that would make sense of the unconscious determinants affecting adult behavior. Although many practicing psychoanalysts continue to use Freud's classical model in therapy with children, there have been considerable developments in the psychoanalytic approach to children that constitute more genuine models of child development. Of these, the work of Freud's daughter, Anna Freud, is especially praiseworthy as an extension of his now-classic theory. And yet, the psychodynamic model of child development that perhaps has the most relevance in our understanding of the special child is that of Erik Erikson (1902–   ).

Erikson's Psychosocial Model of Child Development

The work of Sigmund Freud served both as a frame of reference and a point of departure for Erik Erikson's view of child development. Erikson's unique contribution to the understanding of special childhood lies in his construction of a model that is equally comfortable in describing both normal and special development. Freud needed a theory of child development in order to explain the origins of abnormal behavior in adults; Erikson was interested in childhood in its own right, and his model seeks to comprehend what it is in the nature of child development that is central to the psychological health of every child. Erikson's response to this issue is to view childhood as beset with conflicts and composed of a typical sequence of nuclear crises that are experienced by all individuals in the course of their development. The essentials of Erikson's theory will be presented here under two major headings: the psychological "ground plan" and the psychosocial stages of development. But first, some information about the man himself should help put his model in perspective.

Erikson's father died shortly after his birth. When he was three, his mother remarried. His stepfather wanted him to become a physician; instead he be-

Erik Erikson has interpreted psychological development as a series of psychosocial stages, each offering the child an opportunity to work out a conflict between inner needs and social requirements.

came an artist. Even as an artist, however, Erikson specialized in baby pictures and portraits of children. Although he lacked formal university training, the young artist soon became interested in psychoanalysis and was trained in child analysis by Anna Freud and August Aichorn at the Vienna Institute of Psychoanalysis. At the time, Erikson was teaching at a small American school in Vienna, and in the early 1930s he published his first papers on the application of psychoanalytic concepts to the education of children. In 1933 he accepted an invitation to lecture and practice analysis in the United States, and in the mid-1930s Erikson conducted research at both Harvard and Yale on children's play behavior. In 1950 he published *Childhood and Society,* a work that introduced a major new theory of child development. Erikson's approach is sometimes described as a **psychosocial model** because it seeks to explain the complex of interactions and relationships that exist between the developing child's inner life and the personal-social environment.

The psychological ground plan

Erikson assumes that psychological growth parallels physical growth. Just as Gesell set forth a schedule of physical development based on observable behaviors, Erikson sought to understand and explain the unobservable psychological schedules within the child. Erikson described this inner schedule in terms of the *epigenetic principle:* "Somewhat generalized, this principle states that anything that grows has a *ground plan,* and that out of this ground plan the *parts* arise, each part having its *time* of special ascendancy, until all parts have arisen to form a *functioning whole*" (Erikson, 1959, p. 52). The ground plan of development consists of a particular type of crisis faced by a child at each stage of development so that the resolution or weathering of these crises produces specific personality strengths that form the basis of the child's maturing personality. Erikson, therefore, has interpreted the ground plan of psychological development as a series of psychosocial stages, each of which offers the developing child a unique opportunity to work out a conflict between inner needs and social requirements.

The psychosocial stages of development

Erikson proposed eight stages of personal growth; the last three stages encompass the adult years and are therefore beyond the scope of this discussion. The five childhood stages, however, have proven to be very useful to the understanding of both normal and special development and provide considerable insight into the underlying meanings of the behavior of both normal and special children. The five stages of the developing child are as follows:

a) *Infancy and the crisis of* **trust vs. mistrust:** Erikson locates the cornerstone of all personality development in the infant's ability to develop a sense of basic trust. The infant stage (from birth through 18 months) requires a clear degree of physical comfort, regularity of caretaking, minimal experiences of fear and uncertainty, and formation of a psychological bond with the caretaking person, usually the mother. The infant needs to be able to learn "to get what is given and to experience particular givers and forms of giving" (Erikson, cited in Tanner & Inhelder, 1971, p. 170). The acquisition of a sense of basic trust helps infants grow psychosocially by developing an inner sense of well-being that prepares them for willing acceptance of new experiences. Children who experience unpredictable and highly frustrating infancies may be inhibited in development because of the establishment of a basic sense of mistrust that interferes with their ability to experience a sense of consistent satisfaction of basic needs.

b) *Early childhood and the crisis of* **autonomy vs. shame and doubt:** As the growing infant gains trust in parent figures and a consistent, predictable environment, he/she enters early childhood (18 months through 3 years). Here the main focus is on the integration of a sense of self as an autonomous unit able to exist in an independent fashion. The child's muscular development ushers in the era of toddlerhood as well as the typical age in which toilet training becomes a social necessity. The central psychological issue for the child involves his/her capacity to learn self-control in accordance with certain expectations demanded by the culture. A child who is unable to exert self-control—possibly due to excessively harsh or excessively lax parenting—may well develop a sense of shame or doubt associated with being weak and uncontrolled. Autonomy, therefore, forms the basis for self-regulation in the child's continuing development.

c) *The play age and the crisis of* **initiative vs. guilt:** Healthy development during the child's preschool years (ages 3 through 6) involves the successful dealing with issues of increasing sexuality (the Freudian phallic stage) as well as a sense of direction and purpose. The developmental emphasis is on movement toward goals, many of which are experienced through fantasy and play. "The emphasis is on initiative in the sense that the child is passionately preoccupied in reality and in fantasy with what he wants to get at, where he wants to go, what he wants to see and touch, what question he wants to understand" (Erikson, cited in Tanner & Inhelder, 1971, p. 177). The child's persistence in approaching various goals is far more extensive than his/her actual ability to master goals, and the inner issue becomes one of whether or not the child will integrate a sense of initiative or will become fearful of others and restricted in imagination and creativity. The danger during this period is that the child's initiative might produce real or imagined fears or guilt regarding the consequences of his/her actions.

d) *The school age and the crisis of* **industry vs. inferiority:** Erikson is fond of William Blake's quote, "The child's toys and the old man's reasons are the fruit of the two seasons." In a similar way, the fruit of the school age can be a sufficient sense of initiative so that the child's initial experience of formal schooling (ages 6 through 11) will be marked by a sense of scholarship and industry. Children in most cultures are expected to "move away" from their families and enter more directly into the larger society of school and neighborhood; healthy development requires the acquisition of both beginning technical skills (reading and writing, etc.) as well as social competence. Children who are unable to perform satisfactorily in this regard risk developing a sense of inferiority and inadequacy that can be associated with failure in school tasks or ineptitude in social relations with peers.

e) *Adolescence and the crisis of* **identity vs. role confusion:** Erikson's model is especially well-suited to understanding the turmoil and chaos of adolescence, the stage he has termed the "identity crisis." With the beginning of physiological puberty, childhood itself comes to an end, and the age of youth begins:

> *The growing and developing youths, faced with this physiological revolution within them, and with tangible adult tasks ahead of them are now primarily concerned with what they appear to be in the eyes of others as compared with what they feel they are, and with the question of how to connect the roles and skills cultivated earlier with the occupational prototypes of the day. (Erikson, 1963, p. 261)*

The emphasis in psychosocial development now involves the issue of positively affirming and becoming comfortable with oneself. The danger in development involves the potential for confusion about who one is or the inability to discover an appropriate social and personal role for oneself. Normal independence issues and movements toward emancipation from parental authority may become so exaggerated that various antisocial or delinquent activities may result. The inner harm, however, may be even more damaging if the adolescent fails to discover an inner continuity of self as well as the self's meaning for others.

These five childhood stages in Erikson's conception of the life cycle repre-

EXHIBIT 2.3

FREUD'S PSYCHOSEXUAL STAGES AND ERIKSON'S PSYCHOSOCIAL STAGES

Freud's Psychosexual Stages	Corresponding Libidinal Development	Erikson's Psychosocial Stages	Corresponding Ego Tasks
Oral stage (birth to 2 years)	Mouth is focus of libidinal satisfaction, and feeding is crucial experience.	Trust vs. mistrust (birth to 18 months)	I am what I am given.
Anal stage (2 to 3 years)	Anal area is focus of libidinal pleasure, and toilet training is crucial experience.	Autonomy vs. shame & doubt (18 months to 3 years)	I am what I "will."
Phallic stage (3 to 6 years)	Genital area becomes source of libidinal pleasure, and curiosity about sexuality begins.	Initiative vs. guilt (3 to 6 years)	I am what I imagine I can be.
Latency period (6 to 11 years)	Libidinal energy is diffusely directed.	Industry vs. inferiority (6 to 11 years)	I am what I learn.
Genital stage (12 to adulthood)	Libidinal energy focuses on genital area, and sexual interests are oriented toward others.	Identity vs. role confusion (12 to early adulthood)	I know who I am.

sent important areas of concern for anyone who works with special children. His theory of normal development easily extends to considerations of the development of special children, and his model has had considerable influence in the applied areas of child psychology and education.

A COGNITIVE MODEL: JEAN PIAGET

A third approach to the study of child development is based primarily on the importance of knowledge as a critical factor in child development. Cognitive models of child development emphasize such issues as the way that knowledge is acquired, the way that information is processed, and the role of such knowledge acquisition and information processing in the child's overall development. Although there are many viewpoints that stress cognitive factors in development, the most thorough, and perhaps most intriguing, is that of the eminent Swiss psychologist and educator, Jean Piaget (1896–   ). Piaget's approach to understanding child development is relevant in the diagnosis and treatment of the special child because it provides cues to the ways in which a child might be experiencing the world. In addition, Piaget's work is particularly meaningful to the educator, who bears the responsibility of developing the most appropriate paths to learning for special children.

Jean Piaget came to the study of child development by a rather circuitous route. Originally trained as a zoologist, his doctoral dissertation dealt with mollusks rather than children. Even as a youngster, however, he was actively interested in logic and philosophy, and the problems of human knowledge. Following the completion of his doctoral work, this interest was rekindled, and he went to Paris to work with Alfred Binet, the pioneer of children's intelligence tests. The young Swiss psychologist soon came to be known for the construction of highly ingenious research techniques to study child development, techniques that also included detailed recording of the child's spontaneous questions and comments. Almost from the start, Piaget was interested in *what the child was experiencing*. The birth of his own three children aroused a scientific as well as a fatherly interest in their development, and many of his conclusions are based on his detailed observations of them.

Like Erikson, Piaget's method has been to probe for the causes that underlie behavior. He has also been interested in trying to define what goes on behind a child's behavior, within the child's inner activities; unlike Erikson, however, Piaget's focus has been on the evolving mind of the child and the specific ways in which children understand themselves and the world about them. The wealth of detail he has provided regarding the cognitive processes that occur in the course of development, combined with his child-centered approach to learning, have brought Piaget to the forefront of contemporary theorists of childhood education. Those who work with special children have found two particular contributions of Piaget to be most relevant: his concept of development and his stages of cognitive development.

Development as Organization of Experience

Piaget's interest in logic and intelligence led him to focus his studies of child development on the organizational activities of thought and understanding

*Jean Piaget (far left) has based much of
his model of cognitive development on
his observations of children at work and
play.*

that occur within the child. The impact of experience is the very stuff by which
the child grows, and each new experience demands some form of cognitive
organization or reorganization in the child's evolving mental structures. In
Piaget's thinking, therefore, *development is the continued reorganization of
mental structures*. In this sense, all the attributes and dimensions of a child's
personality are a function of the child's cognitive capacity to organize experience. Piaget's concept of the function of stimulating experiences as the condition of continued development lies at the very heart of many efforts to work
with special children in the classroom.

The Stages of Cognitive Development

Piaget began with the question of how a child learns; this led to a model of
phases that characterize the cognitive development of children. He considers
development to be an inhering, evolutionary process that affects the whole
child, and yet he places primary emphasis on the child's increasing capacity to
organize experience. As a model of cognitive development, Piaget described

five distinct stages in which the child experiences increased capacities to comprehend the world of experience.

a) **The sensorimotor period:** Piaget believes that newborn infants are "locked in egocentrism," a state including not only the self-centeredness of infants but also their lack of awareness of anything beyond themselves. Newborns are conscious only of themselves, and Piaget agrees with Freud that for them, "the world is essentially a thing to be sucked" (Piaget, 1967, p. 9). Gradually, infants gain experience through their senses and absorb such experiences into evolving patterns of motor behavior. This sensorimotor period begins at birth and continues throughout the second year. It consists primarily of the processes of receiving information and stimulation from the environment **(assimilation)** and modifying existing patterns of motor behavior to cope with different conditions **(accommodation).** Through assimilation and accommodation, infants learn that certain actions have specific effects in the external world. Language also begins to develop during this period and enables infants to begin representing their experiences through the medium of a thought or a word. A primitive internal representation of the world begins. Cognitive development in the sensorimotor period, therefore, is characterized primarily by information acquired through infants' physical explorations of the environment and various forms of sensory stimulation.

b) **The preconceptual period:** During the third and fourth years of life, intellectual growth involves the construction of beginning ideas or notions— what Piaget terms **preconcepts**—about the properties of things. Children during this period are constantly investigating their environment and discovering new symbols to use in communicating about the environment. Their ideas, nonetheless, continue to hold a highly personal reference for them; through self-discovery, the world is being born to them, and they continue to locate themselves at the center of this world. Children at this stage are not yet able to form true concepts, and their attempts to generalize to classes of things are fuzzy and confused. For example, Piaget's daughter Jacqueline (at age 3 years and 2 months) defined a "daddy" as "a man who has lots of Jacquelines" (Piaget, 1951). Children are not yet able to generalize beyond their own understanding of themselves. During this period, children are also quite *animistic,* attributing to objects the characteristics of life. When, for example, Piaget's son Laurent was informed (at age 3 years and 7 months) that they had missed their train, he inquired, "Doesn't the train know we aren't on it?" (Piaget, 1951). Such "confusion" in the child's understanding of the world prompted Piaget to describe this period as the preconceptual phase. Clearly, *egocentrism* remains a major characteristic of the child's mode of understanding during this phase.

c) **The intuitive period:** During the years from 4 to 7, children begin to form a widening interest in their social world and demonstrate an initial capacity to give reasons for their beliefs and actions. Their broadening social interactions and ever-increasing capacity to use words effectively are important factors in contributing to their growth away from an egocentric view of the world. For example, Piaget's daughter Jacqueline, at age 5 years and 11 months, made the following observation about the night sky: "You'd think the stars are moving because we're walking." Here she showed a beginning awareness that the world functions independently of her own actions. By 6 years and 3 months, after a dizzy bout of whirling herself around, she observed, "You can feel it going round but things aren't really turning" (Piaget, 1951, pp. 260, 265). One can see here a sense of intuition about the way the world works; the child's reasoning moves from a single premise to a conclusion in one simple jump. Similarly, a child in this period may well know how to count without understanding the meaning of numbers. The intuitive period, nonetheless, enables children to attain new and more advanced levels of organizational thinking, despite the fact that they have not yet mastered a formal logic.

d) **The period of concrete operations:** From the ages of 7 to 11, children become capable of engaging in *operational thought,* by which Piaget means the mental capacity to relate an object or event to a total system of inter-related parts. *Operations,* the genuine inner activities of the mind, refer to a child's capacity to relate experience to an organized and meaningful whole. During the early primary school years, Piaget believes that such mental operations are predominantly concrete, in the sense that they are concerned only with real-life, existing objects; in the words of Piaget, "concrete operations consist of nothing more than a direct organization of immediately given data" (Piaget, 1958, p. 249). In terms of problem-solving abilities, children at this stage may not be able to perform mental operations if problems are presented verbally and without physical counterparts; for example, "2 + 2" may be a meaningless exercise, whereas the presence of "2 red apples + 2 red apples" may be quickly seen to add up to "4 red apples." Children in this period require physical materials as a means of facilitating cognitive development. Such considerations are especially important for a child whose development may be otherwise impeded by some special condition.

e) **The period of formal operations:** By the time normal children are age 12, their cognitive development is characterized by mental operations very similar to those of adult thought. The term "formal" means that children at this stage have developed the structure, or form, of thinking. They are able to begin reasoning abstractly and to use concepts in the absence of physical counterparts. Between the ages of 11 and 15, youngsters become theory-builders, "an individual who thinks beyond the present and forms theories about everything, delighting especially in considerations of that which is not" (Piaget, 1950, p. 148). It is not until the stage of formal operations that older children or adolescents are truly capable of thinking beyond their own world or sets of conventions. Entering into the world of ideas proper, adolescents may well take genuine pleasure in examining relationships, both physical and human, and reevaluating the world from a variety of viewpoints. The acquisition of formal operations liberates youth from the restrictions of an enclosed reality and provides the possibility of experimenting with a new order of things. The "identity crisis" described by Erikson from the standpoint of psychosocial development is made possible by this newly acquired capacity to think beyond the limitations of the given situation. It is no wonder, then, that many adolescents resent being treated like children, since the power of their mental processes has moved them into the complexities of the adult world.

The five stages described by Piaget are not intended to represent chronologically fixed milestones but rather descriptions of the major rhythms of cognitive advance in the child. Piaget provides a frame of reference for analyzing the continuum of mental growth and a means by which to predict the ways in which children are able to perceive certain issues and events in the course of their development. This broad theory of mental development sets forth the magnificent process of inward growth over the entire area of mental life and identifies the ways in which the minds of children develop to full organizational capacity. This model also points to the ways in which the thinking processes of children are radically different from those of adults; in this respect, a serious reading of Piaget will readily dispel the notion that children are merely "miniature adults." (Exhibit 2.4 on page 40 presents a summary of Piaget's stages of cognitive development.)

In Piaget's panoramic view of intellectual "unfolding," the stages of cognitive development are believed to be experienced regularly in the course of every child's growth. Although there has been relatively little direct application of his model to special childhood, Piaget's model affects every professional involved in the education of children and raises questions regarding the education of special as well as normal children. His child-centered approach rings a warning alarm for any teacher who does not listen for cues from children themselves as meaningful, evolving entities. In this respect, the cognitive model of Jean Piaget has profound implications regarding the ways in which we attempt to educate, constantly holding out to the educator the need for an awareness of the inner mental capacities of children "in process." Education, both normal and special, is less a means of imparting and acquiring knowledge than a means of stimulating the expansion of the mind itself. Piaget reminds us that every child's capacity to learn is founded in a unique experiential history and innate curiosity about the world rather than in a prefabricated format about what he/she is supposed to know. How much more so is this the case with children whose development has in some way been threatened or impaired.

LEARNING-BASED MODELS: ROBERT SEARS AND ALBERT BANDURA

A fourth approach to understanding the development of special children comes from the learning theory tradition of studying human behavior. The basic thrust of *learning theory* applied to issues of child development is that the increasing elaboration of observable behavior in the course of development is best understood as a continuing formation of relationships between stimuli and responses. In the traditional formulations, *stimulus events* are understood to be the many chemical, physical, biological, and social events that act upon the individual; *response events* are simply the overt and covert activities of the individual. It should be mentioned here that learning theory is not limited to strict stimulus-response psychologies, but the considerable scientific achievements of learning approaches have been made possible primarily because of a commitment to studying behavior in terms of observable stimuli and responses.

EXHIBIT 2.4

PIAGET'S STAGES OF COGNITIVE DEVELOPMENT

Descriptive Name	Age Level	Nature of Cognitive Activities
Sensorimotor period	Birth through 2 years	Mode of experience and learning relies on sense and motor activities—first internal representations of the world Information acquisition—learns that certain actions have specific effects Recognition of the constancy of external objects
Preconceptual period	2nd through 4th year	Initial use of symbols, but inaccurately and egocentrically Language makes possible use of beginning ideas
Intuitive period	4th through 7th year	Advances reasons for ideas without displaying adequate logic Conclusions are based on feelings or on what one would like to believe
Period of concrete operations	7th through 11th year	Uses mental operations to reason about things, yet cannot generalize Able to reason only about objects immediately present or in direct experience Coherent organization of ideas—child appears genuinely "rational"
Period of formal operations	11th year through adulthood	Able to deal with abstractions and use deductive reasoning Able to form ideals and develop hypotheses The world of reality is able to include the possibility of it being different

Reinforcement of behavior is an important concept that explains continuing development. A **reinforcer** is considered to be any specific environmental event that strengthens the tendency of a response to occur again. A hungry child who says, "Mommy, I'm hungry" and is immediately given cookies and milk demonstrates that he/she has learned a way to satisfy needs; but the child has also been reinforced for social behavior, and the tendency to behave in a communicative manner has been strengthened. Such reinforcement is termed **primary reinforcement** because it results in the reduction of a primary drive, hunger. Praising a child for putting away toys is also a reinforcement; in this case, it is called **secondary reinforcement,** or *social reinforcement,* involving the reduction of social drives for approval and affection. There are many different approaches in learning theory, and each of them views the mechanics of learning somewhat differently. Nonetheless, reinforcement in its many forms is typically considered to be a key mechanism by which learning takes place and through which development occurs. Learning-based approaches to understanding and treatment are being increasingly applied to the problems of special children, and knowledge of developmental learning theories is now essential for anyone who works with special children.

A Learning-Based Definition of Child Development

Although much of the research in learning theory has focused on laboratory situations that seem remote from the human condition, learning theorists are becoming increasingly involved in the application of a strict scientific method to the analysis of human development. This experimental approach has brought increased vigor as well as a highly novel understanding to the issues of child development. Bijou and Baer (1965), for example, attempted to define developmental psychology from the viewpoint of experimental learning theory:

> *Developmental psychology specializes in studying the progressions in interactions between behavior and environmental events. In other words, it is concerned with the historical variables influencing behavior, that is, with the effect of past interactions on present interactions. . . . Developmental psychology concentrates on* the history of an organism's previous interactions. *(p. 14)*

Learning theory places great emphasis on the events that take place in the individual's environment and regards the environment as a potentially powerful factor in the development of various behaviors and/or personality traits. In this sense, learning theory is sometimes considered an environmental approach because it assigns such importance to environmental factors in the development of a child's behavior patterns. For Bijou and Baer, for example, the most important task of developmental psychology is to specify the nature of the relationships that exist between a child's evolving behavior and the environmental factors that facilitate or inhibit the behavior. The history of the child's interaction with the environment is, of course, considered to be a highly important aspect of a child's current behavioral capacities and/or limitations.

Among the learning theorists, several investigators have taken a special interest in the social environment as a critical variable in child development. The human infant's prolonged period of dependency on parents or parent substitutes places the developing child in close interaction with a number of people who constitute the child's social environment and who have the capacity to shape the child's behavior and personality. **Socialization** is understood to be the general process by which a child acquires the beliefs, skills, values, behavior patterns, and other characteristics considered appropriate for a particular society; from the standpoint of learning theory, socialization is a general rubric for an extensive array of learning situations critical in the formation of a child's personality. Our current discussion will focus on two of the more prominent social learning theorists, namely Robert Sears and Albert Bandura.

Robert Sears: Interpersonal Influence and Personality Formation

A pioneer in the study of socialization has been Robert R. Sears (1908–   ). Sears' interests tend to typify the social learning approach to child development. As an undergraduate at Stanford University he was active in drama and literary affairs, but as a doctoral candidate at Yale he was toughened on "hard science." Throughout his scientific and professional career, Sears has combined a humanistic awareness of the complexity of life with the conviction that only the experimental method could yield useful information about the nature of behavior. His writings and research, therefore, combine an appreciation of the clinical richness of Freudian psychodynamics with the need for precise definition and measurement of behavior in objective terms.

Although the majority of Sears' work has been with normal children, many of his findings have relevance to the understanding of special children. Early in his career, Sears began developmental research on the effects of childrearing methods on children's personalities. He spent a great deal of time observing the interactions of mothers and children in contrived laboratory situations. He also insisted, however, that behavior must be studied in a natural setting, so he evolved techniques—such as the study of a child's doll-play activity—to measure freely occurring behavior. One of his most important contributions to the study of childrearing has been the construction of standardized interviewing techniques to review various aspects of the childrearing process with mothers.

Sears' major research interests have been in the area of aggression and dependence in children, and yet these studies have always been part of a broader interest in the effects of social interaction between the child and

Research by Robert Sears (left) on interactions and interpersonal influence, and by Albert Bandura (right) on observational learning, has contributed greatly to our understanding of the nature of learning in child development.

the parents on the child's developing personality. Sears described these interactions as "the mechanics of interpersonal influence" (Sears, Maccoby, & Levin, 1957, p. 466). For Sears, the study of child development is essentially the study of the most fruitful conditions under which learning takes place, namely the consistent interactions or interpersonal influences between the child and significant others. It is these interactions, Sears concludes, that are most central in the formation and maintenance of the child's personality.

According to Sears, the child is born with basic drives (such as hunger) that become "socialized" through interaction with parents, slowly evolving into motivational systems within the child's personality. Although he does not postulate stages of child development, Sears clearly notes two distinct stages of socialization: the learning in which the family is the initial agent of socialization; and the learning that occurs through interaction with social agents beyond the family, such as peers and teachers. Development is thus understood to be an orderly process in which the child's evolving behavior meets with certain types of social responses, or reinforcements, so that consistent patterns of reinforcement produce consistent patterns of behavior. In terms of the special child, the emphasis is on the importance of all consistent patterns of interaction between the child and other people, including therapists, special education teachers, and parents.

The Observational Learning Model of Albert Bandura

Through the work of his students and colleagues, Sears' original applications of learning theory to the study of personality have been considerably extended and expanded. Perhaps the most important strides have been made by Albert Bandura (1928–   ), a long-time colleague of Sears. In 1953 Bandura joined the faculty of Stanford at the same time that Sears was assuming chairmanship of the psychology department. Bandura, however, has taken social learning theory in a new direction. Accepting the many empirical studies demonstrating that social learning takes place through experience and reinforcement, Bandura has gone beyond the theoretical position that social learning is a phenomenon to be accounted for solely on the basis of reinforced behavior. He has also taken his fellow behaviorists to task for taking to extremes their belief that environment exerts total control over human behavior (Bandura, 1974).

As a social learning theorist, Bandura has taken the position that both children and adults are able to observe the effects of their own actions and are able to exert conscious control and choice over a wide range of behavior. Bandura has arrived at this humanized brand of behaviorism by his own extensive research in the area of observational learning. Through a series of investigations, Bandura has demonstrated that learning by example, through *imitation* or *modeling,* is a basic mechanism by which children acquire many social behaviors. (See Exhibit 2.5 for an example of Bandura's research on imitation.) Bandura has steadfastly advanced the position that the most significant learning does not take place through reinforcement, shaping, or trial-and-error but rather through the observation of social models. **Observational learning,** or **modeling,** refers simply to the process whereby an ob-

BANDURA'S RESEARCH ON IMITATION OF AGGRESSIVE BEHAVIOR

Bandura has done a number of studies investigating whether aggressive behavior is learned by observing others behaving in an aggressive manner. In one study, Bandura and Huston (1961) found that children readily imitated aggressive behavior they saw exhibited by a model. In another study, Bandura, Ross, and Ross (1961) showed that children who observed aggressive models in one setting also behaved aggressively in a new setting when the model was absent. The hypothesis then arose that children might tend to imitate aggressive behavior when it is presented through films or on television.

In order to test this hypothesis, Bandura, Ross, and Ross (1965) chose as subjects 48 boys and 48 girls between the ages of 35 to 69 months who were enrolled in the Stanford University Nursery School. Subjects were divided into four groups: one group viewed real-life aggressive models; a second group viewed the same models behaving aggressively on film; a third group viewed a film of a cartoon character behaving aggressively; and a control group had no exposure to aggressive models. For the three experimental groups, the aggressive act portrayed was that of a large plastic "Bobo doll" being punched, hit with a mallet, and tossed and kicked, in addition to being verbally "assaulted" by the model.

After exposure to their respective situations, each group was observed during a 20-minute play period in a playroom that included a variety of toys (both aggressive and nonaggressive) and, of course, the Bobo doll. Imitative behavior by each child in the play period was measured by the responses the child exhibited that were similar to those of the model.

Data from this study indicated no significant differences between the three experimental groups—all responded with much higher aggressiveness than the control group. In fact, the data suggested that, of the three conditions, "exposure to humans on film portraying aggression was the most influential in eliciting and shaping aggressive behavior." The children actually modeled their play behavior after the film models. The implications are obvious: film media—especially television—may be a key source for the learning of social behavior.

---

server (e.g., a child) acquires a new behavior or alters an existing behavior by reproducing some distinct response or series of responses that have been exhibited by some model (e.g., parents, sibling, peer, or television character).

In essence, Bandura has departed from the early stimulus-response model of learning to a model of behavior that recognizes that *mediational processes* such as thinking must be considered even though they are difficult to measure and demonstrate:

> In social learning theory, it is assumed that behavior is learned and organized chiefly through central integrative mechanisms prior to motor execution. By observing a model of the desired behavior, an individual forms an idea of how response components must be combined and temporarily sequenced to produce new behavioral configurations. In other words, patterned behavior is largely guided by symbolic representation rather than formed through reinforced performance. (Bandura, 1971a, p. 14)

By recognizing the functioning of the whole person in the scientific study of behavior, Bandura has brought to the mainstream a more humanistic approach to learning and development.

The fact of learning cannot be underemphasized as a critical factor in child development, and the various learning-based models of development act as a set of reminders that one cannot discount the influence of environmental factors as powerful variables in both normal and special development. In the applied areas of child development, social learning theories, as well as the more explicit conditioning approaches, are proving highly effective in working with special children. Bandura (1971b), for example, has described the psychotherapeutic use of modeling, and O'Leary and O'Leary (1972) have demonstrated the extensive applications of learning approaches to the classroom management of special children.

CASE STUDY 2.1

LINDA: THE APPLICATION OF DEVELOPMENTAL MODELS TO A SPECIAL CHILD

Identifying Data

Linda, a pretty, young girl with long black hair and large brown eyes, was admitted to a metropolitan children's hospital at the age of 2 years 8 months because she had stopped walking and eating solid foods. The parents, a helpless and highly dependent-appearing couple, had brought her to the hospital's outpatient clinic because they were concerned that she was "retarded" and was "getting worse." At the time of admission, the parents showed very little ability to interact with their daughter, and Linda seemed very withdrawn and depressed. She was unable to hold eye contact with nurses and staff, made bizarre gestures and stared into lights, and did not speak. The parents were unable to offer any reason for her failure to walk or inability to take solid foods.

Extensive physical and medical examinations revealed no clear organic or physiological causes for her condition. Investigation of her home situation revealed that each of her parents had medical problems—her father was epileptic and her mother was hypertensive. A nurse who visited Linda's home reported that Linda slept on a bare mattress on the living-room floor. The three-room apartment was only barely furnished, shades were drawn during midday, and the home atmosphere was extremely drab and impoverished; the parents had

received an eviction notice from the landlord. There were two younger children, ages 20 months and 6 months, and the mother was again pregnant. Both parents seemed well-intentioned but were confronted by so many personal and social problems that they had little energy to attend to the needs of their children. Psychiatric examination of the parents revealed that both were childlike and highly dependent; they were themselves an extremely deprived couple —emotionally, intellectually, and socioeconomically.

Consideration of the Case from a Maturational Model

From a maturational perspective, the primary consideration regarding Linda's behavior would be the *delay in the accomplishment of developmental milestones.* Linda had learned to say "mama" and "dada" at 15 months but had not acquired any other active language; in normal language development, children have 6 to 10 words by 15 to 18 months and by 2 years of age use simple phrases as well as the personal pronouns "I" and "me." In terms of motor behavior, Linda had been achieving gross motor milestones at approximately a normal rate until her refusal to walk. With regard to personal, social, and adaptive behavior, Linda gave evidence of severe delays. She had acquired almost no skills relating to self-feeding and self-care; she showed no capacity to imitate others in any way; she could not use toys in a functional manner. Although she had begun eating solid foods at 18 months, at the time of admission she could be bottle-fed only, and she handled the bottle awkwardly and ineptly. Normal children of 18 months typically can do such things as use a spoon successfully with little spilling, take off their own shoes and socks, and carry and hug a doll.

Although there was no gross evidence of organic damage, a maturational perspective might attribute Linda's developmental delays to inadequate nutrition and/or insufficient caloric intake. Such children are frequently described as "failure-to-thrive" children. Such delays might also be attributed to emotional neglect or maternal deprivation.

Linda's actual diagnosis by her pediatrician was "severe developmental delay due to prolonged emotional neglect." Linda was assigned to a foster mother while in the hospital. A nutritional program was designed to meet her needs and an emotional stimulation program was initiated by a staff psychologist. She began making immediate progress.

Consideration of the Case from a Psychodynamic Model

From a psychodynamic perspective, Linda's refusal to walk or to eat solid foods could be understood as a form of *regression,* a return to an earlier form of behavior no longer appropriate. The regressive behavior might be considered a symptom of an underlying conflict producing so much internal stress that Linda was regressing to a more infantile stage. It would almost be as if she were saying that it was safer to be a baby than a 2-year-old.

According to Erikson's psychosocial model, inner stress is understood to be a function of the nuclear crises that attend each psychosocial stage. In the first year of life, the child faces the issue of trust versus mistrust in terms of the degree to which the child is able to experience the mothering figure as nurturant, caring, and predictable. From Linda's standpoint, it might well be that her mother was quite adequate during Linda's first months of life, but within

a short time her mother was again pregnant. The foundation for basic trust was provided but never had an opportunity to become consolidated. As she entered the stage of autonomy versus shame during her second year, she was not fully equipped to manage this crisis because she had not internalized a sense of well-being associated with the safety of an adequate mothering figure. Linda could not manage the autonomy required by development of motor skills (walking, climbing, running) that allow for more extensive exploration of her environment. The barrenness of human resources in Linda's life led to a severe solution: total withdrawal and regression to a more infantile stage.

From this perspective, the attempt to treat Linda's special condition of regression in development would necessarily require the provision of a more adequate, nurturing mothering figure to help resolve the inner crisis.

Consideration of the Case from a Cognitive Model

In the cognitive model of Piaget, Linda exists in a constantly changing interplay between herself and her environment. Linda's symptoms would be seen as a breakdown in her ability to adapt to the environment, a failure to grow and an inability to make use of experience for the purpose of continued organization and growth. Piaget uses the term *equilibration* to describe the inner processes of self-regulation by which a child comes to achieve a sense of coherence and stability in the developing conceptions of the world. Such equilibrium—the hallmark of normal development—allows for the prospect of continuing adaptation and the ongoing reorganization of mental structures. From a cognitive standpoint, Linda's special condition would involve an incapacity during the sensorimotor period to transform her experience into useful, adaptive knowledge and the resultant inability to achieve a sense of coherence between herself and the world.

In terms of helping Linda, the cognitive model would maintain that the major goal of intervention would be to help her organize and respond meaningfully to her ongoing experiences of the world.

Such intervention would necessarily require a child-oriented educational environment to help her discover that her motor behavior and exploration of the world can be cognitively useful. In helping Linda learn to organize her experience for the purpose of understanding herself and the world, a therapeutic preschool program would be the treatment of choice. It should be pointed out that this form of intervention would not preclude other forms of treatment (such as a nutritional program or foster-mothering) but would simply take into account the fact that cognitive development is essential to her overall growth as a person.

Consideration of the Case from a Learning Model

From the standpoint of a learning-based model, Linda's refusal to walk and to eat solid foods, her inability to maintain eye contact and to use language in a functional fashion, and her unresponsiveness to people would best be understood not as symptoms of underlying conflicts but rather as simple *behavior deficits*. The source of these behavior deficits would be assumed to be found in the history of Linda's interaction with her environment and with the system of stimulus-response associations established between herself and significant

social agents (parents, siblings, etc.). Linda's *behavior disorder*, therefore, would be seen as a function of the failure of the social environment to reinforce prosocial behavior.

In this analysis, an environment that fails to reinforce smiling, eye contact, approach to people, and so forth will produce a very low frequency of such behaviors in the child. Even behaviors previously established (such as walking and eating solid foods) may stop occurring if reinforcement is withdrawn. In the experimental literature, this phenomenon is known as *extinction* and tends to occur when a previously established response is no longer followed by a reinforcement.

The treatment approach for Linda would require the systematic restructuring of her environment so that more socially appropriate learning could take place. This treatment might include the availability of more adequate social models to provide new experiences for observational learning. Or treatment might require the provision of more effective childrearing patterns directed at reinforcing socially meaningful behavior. In addition, target behaviors would likely be established (eating, eye contact, walking) and carefully reinforced and shaped in the direction of competent development.

THE APPLICATION OF DEVELOPMENTAL MODELS TO SPECIAL CHILDREN

We have seen in Chapter 1 that the special child is a child who experiences some form of impediment in the realization of developmental potentials. In Chapter 2 we have reviewed some of the more significant models of development to illustrate various ways of understanding growth and change in childhood. It is clear that the current state of knowledge of child development does not provide an integrated understanding of all its relevant aspects. Those who work with special children, however, must have some guides in their efforts to help these children achieve the realization of their developmental potentials. These efforts will likely involve one of the models discussed in this chapter, or perhaps, less fortunately, dependence on less explicit expectations of the child's course of growth.

In applying any model of child development to the needs of the special child, the first question that must be asked is, Where is the child in his/her *own* course of development? Each of the approaches described above will formulate a unique framework for addressing the developmental aspects of special childhood. Using Gesell's maturational model, the question might be asked, At what pace is the child acquiring the normal milestones of motor behavior, language, adaptive behavior, and personal-social behavior? From a psychodynamic standpoint, the question might be, How is the child being influenced by inner stages of psychosocial or psychosexual development? From Piaget's cognitive viewpoint, the question is simply, How is the child able to organize and understand the experience of reality? A learning-based approach would be more likely to ask, How can the child's environment be better organized to promote learning and development?

Every model of child development emphasizes slightly differing dimensions of change and growth. No model is "more correct" or "more true" than any other model. As long as a model makes its assumptions explicit, its utility can be tested empirically in the experimental laboratory and in clinical work with children who need help. Each of the models discussed in this chapter has shown the capacity to be useful in organizing information about change and growth. In the same manner, each of these models can be applied clinically to the case of a particular special child, as can be seen in Case Study 2.1 above.

In the next two chapters, the questions of diagnosis and treatment of special children will be addressed. For the simple reason that children are constantly changing and growing, developmental considerations are central in all questions of diagnosis and treatment. Many approaches to diagnosis and treatment, unfortunately, have failed to integrate a developmental perspective, and we must all be ready to act as critics when developmental aspects are being forgotten. One of the more blatant examples of failing to understand the significance of developmental aspects in treatment and diagnosis can be found in the now-decreasing custom of enforced separation of physically ill infants from their mothers while being hospitalized. This practice produced a near-epidemic of *hospitalism,* a condition involving severe depression and apathy in the child as a result of the maternal deprivation. Throughout this book, therefore, a developmental perspective will be maintained wherever possible, and the student should be ready to formulate developmental questions in each and every consideration of special children.

SUMMARY

1. *Child development* is defined as a series of changes, usually patterned and predictable, that foster the child's ability to cope with and master the external environment.
2. Gesell's model of child development is called *maturational* because it views the development of the nervous system itself as the organizer of growth processes.
3. Gesell described child development in terms of the achievement of developmental milestones, or norms of development.
4. The models of Freud and Erikson are called psychodynamic because they assume that human behavior is a function of inner, unconscious motivational forces.
5. Erikson's five stages of child development include: infancy (trust vs. mistrust),

early childhood (autonomy vs. shame and doubt), the play age (initiative vs. guilt), the school age (industry vs. inferiority), and adolescence (identity vs. role confusion).

6. Piaget's model of child development is called a cognitive model because it stresses the manner in which knowledge is organized as the critical factor in child development.

7. Piaget's five distinct periods of cognitive development include: the sensorimotor period, the preconceptual period, the intuitive period, the period of concrete operations, and the period of formal operations.

8. Learning-based models of child development stress the significance of past and present interactions between the child's behavior and environmental events.

9. Sears is best known for his study of the effect of childrearing patterns on the development of children's behavior.

10. Bandura has demonstrated that observational learning is a basic mechanism through which children acquire many social behaviors.

11. Each model of child development provides a different but equally important way of viewing children's behavior.

Diagnosis and Assessment of Special Children

In the waiting room of a child guidance and development clinic, a ten-year-old patient sat pensively observing a four-year-old patient who was vigorously rocking back and forth on a toy rocking horse. The younger child gleefully made high-pitched squeals and showed little awareness of anything or anybody except the rocking horse. The older child did not know the four-year-old, but he seemed studious and quizzical of his younger peer's behavior. When the ten-year-old's therapist approached him at the appointment time, the youngster asked, "Is that there kid a 'mental' or an 'emotional'?" Taken by surprise, the therapist asked his patient to clarify his terms. "You know what I mean," the youngster replied. "Is that kid a 're-tard' or a 'crazy'?"

THE MEANING AND FUNCTIONS OF DIAGNOSIS

Children obviously develop their own systems of classification and diagnosis, and at times their diagnoses of their peers can be used cruelly and harshly. And yet, the use of labels by children is no more than a reflection of practices of the adult world. The issue of diagnostic labels as a means of categorizing a person's condition or behavior is a complex and controversial problem that affects the daily life of anyone who works or lives with special children. More importantly, it is an issue that can have profound consequences in the life of a special child. The misuse of a diagnostic label "can blight the life of a child, reducing opportunity, diminishing his competence and self-esteem, alienating him from others, nurturing a meanness of spirit, and making him less a person than he could become" (Hobbs, 1975, p. 1). On the other hand, the appropriate use of a diagnostic label can enable a child to enter into a social system of medical, educational, and psychological services that he/she needs to become a more fully functioning human being. Adequate diagnosis is the key to understanding, treatment, and prevention of the problems of children.

Diagnosis as Process and Product

The term "diagnosis" is derived from the Greek roots *dia* ("apart") and *gigno-skein* ("to know"). Because the process of diagnosis has long been associated with medical practice, it has come to suggest "the knowing apart of a disease entity." Traditionally, in medicine, the presence of certain symptoms occurring together consistently has been viewed as indicative of a particular illness or disease with identifiable characteristics. Medical research and clinical practice have jointly proceeded from this initial recognition of a **symptom syndrome** (the specific characteristics of an illness) and have sought to discover the **etiology** (cause) of the illness, its **incidence** (frequency and distribution in the population), and its **prognosis** (likely course or outcome). In many instances, diagnosis has also guided the course of treatment and research into modes of prevention.

This *medical model* of the diagnostic process has been very influential in the development of various nonmedical professions, including clinical psychology, special education, speech therapy, and occupational and physical therapy. These professions all function through interrelated processes of diagnosis and intervention that stem from the logic and practice of physicians dealing with disease and dysfunction.

In many cases, the medical model of the diagnostic process is directly applicable to the problems of special children. A "disease entity" is recognized on the basis of a set of common symptoms; it is named and classified; research and clinical experience produce conceptions of causation and treatment; and modes of prevention are developed.

In many more cases, however, the problems of special children are not related to identifiable "disease entities," and the medical model does not provide an adequate basis for conceptualizing developmental disorders. In these cases it is particularly important to maintain a clear conceptual distinction between *diagnosis as a process* and *diagnosis as a product*. As a process, diagnosis is the comprehensive study of the individual child based on findings derived from *assessment procedures* that measure physiological functions, physical development, intellectual development, and behavior. This study of the whole child functioning within the context of family, school, and neighborhood leads to a "product," the development of a **diagnostic label,** or **classification,** that permits us to compare our knowledge of the individual child with a classification system which includes all the major developmental problems children may develop. The diagnostic process and the diagnostic classification help us organize our knowledge of the individual child and relate it to accumulated knowledge about particular kinds of problems. At times, however, diagnostic labeling and classification can create serious problems.

Classification and Labeling

For a variety of reasons, diagnosis as classification has been considered by many to be one of the major obstacles to progress in psychiatry, clinical psychology, special education, and related professions (Braginsky & Braginsky, 1969, 1971; Stuart, 1970). Foremost among these reasons is the lack of a valid and reliable classification system that can order and relate developmental problems in any usable fashion. The two most prominent classification systems relevant to special children have been that of the American Psychiatric Association in the 1968 Second Edition of its *Diagnostic and Statistical Manual (DSM II)* and that of the Group for the Advancement of Psychiatry (1966). While both these systems are comprehensive, both are based on a nineteenth-century conception of psychological disorders as falling into clear-cut categories with specific patterns of causation. These systems are based heavily on the medical model, and they make little room for consideration of a variety of developmental disabilities and behavioral problems that do not fit easily into broad categories without distortion of our understanding of an individual child.

Put in most basic terms, currently available classification systems have often forced a correspondence between an abstract category and the behavior of a real child. In addition, a classification system should yield consistent agreement among different diagnosticians in classifying disorders, and there is ample research indicating that recent classification systems do *not* produce such consistency (O'Leary, 1972; Stuart, 1970). Whether an upcoming Third Edition of the American Psychiatric Association's *Diagnostic and Statistical Manual (DSM III)* overcomes these hurdles remains to be demonstrated. However, other problems would remain even if an adequately realistic and consistent classification scheme were available.

One such problem is the fact that different languages and modes of understanding characterize different professional disciplines. For example, a pediatrician might view symptoms of a speech disorder as a function of subtle central nervous system damage. A psychologist might see the same behaviors as the outcome of faulty parental management. An educator might view the same symptoms as a result of a poor educational environment. And a speech pathologist might suspect that hearing defects are producing communication difficulties that eventuate in a speech disorder. As a function of differing diagnostic perspectives and labels, parents may receive a wide array of treatment recommendations, and the child may be burdened with a variety of conflicting diagnoses.

Another factor that contributes to the problem of labeling a child's condition is the social and semantic issue of "What do the words mean?" Ideally a diagnosis ought to identify a real condition and lead to appropriate interventions. However, the literal meaning of a diagnosis is often compounded by real or imagined stigma that society associates with certain terms. The linguistic and social awkwardness of diagnostic labels is nowhere more apparent than in the proliferation of terms regarding special children. A youngster whose intellectual development is well below appropriate age level might be viewed as retarded, disabled, handicapped, damaged, pathological, impaired, defective, and so forth. The social response to different words varies from time to time within the same society and at the same time among different lay and professional groups. The language of labeling is regularly confounded by trends affecting the social acceptability of certain terms and by changes in the professional understanding of their meanings.

Another problem in the use of labels requires particular caution. While the appropriate use of diagnostic labels is descriptive, labels are often used in an explanatory fashion. It often happens that a word or phrase describing a condition is reified (made real) in practice so that it comes to imply an explanation of the condition. The use of the term "developmental delay," for example, literally explains nothing, but it is often used as though it explains something about the nature of a condition. Thus it is not uncommon to encounter phrases in a diagnostic report to the effect that: "Johnny is apparently experiencing a significant developmental delay," or "Susie's reading difficulties are a consequence of generalized developmental delay." Understanding is implied where none exists.

A final problem that might be mentioned has to do with the iatrogenic effects of diagnostic labels on oneself and others (Stuart, 1970). Literally, *iatrogenic* means "doctor produced," and an **iatrogenic effect** in a general way is an unforeseen consequence of treatment efforts by a professional agent. A suggestible patient seeking assistance with stomach distress might be asked by a physician whether he/she also has frequent headaches. If the patient subsequently begins having headaches without any other changes in physical condition, the headaches might well be an iatrogenic effect of the diagnostic examination.

A diagnostic label may also have negative effects in the way an individual is perceived by others. In the case of a special child, a diagnostic label may lead parents and teachers to form negative perceptions of the youngster. The label may lead to inappropriate classroom placement and restrict learning opportunities. Eventually, a label may lead the child to develop negative perceptions of the self as worthless or as helpless and needing the continuous support and assistance of others. In any of these cases the iatrogenic effects of a diagnostic label may create more problems than are solved.

Briefly, diagnosis as classification is subject to numerous problems leading to parental and professional confusion, stigmatization, and negative developmental consequences. Research may be discouraged because an illusion of understanding is fostered where none exists, and inappropriate treatment may be encouraged because of misplaced confidence in the state of our understanding of the problems of special children (see Exhibit 3.1).

Where diagnostic classification is properly understood as primarily a descriptive, shorthand means of communication with a potential for disclosing commonalities among problems, then it can be used constructively. With this in mind, there are a number of important positive functions of diagnosis that we shall now examine.

DIAGNOSIS AND THE SPECIAL CHILD

From the standpoint of the helping professions involved with special children, diagnosis is best viewed as the *process* of attempting to discover (a) whether a given child in fact exhibits a developmental problem; (b) what the problem is; (c) the causes of the problem in the child's constitution, history, or current environment; (d) the potential course and developmental consequences; and (e) the best approaches to intervention and remediation.

Determining If a Problem Exists

The first step in the diagnostic process should involve a determination of whether a problem warranting intervention really exists. Making such a determination is not nearly as easy in practice as it might seem. Wide variability in the attainment of developmental tasks often makes it difficult to decide whether a child is developing slowly but normally, or whether a child is showing the first indications of a developmental problem that calls for immediate intervention. Even the use of such respected guidelines as those provided in the developmental research of Arnold Gesell (see discussion in Chapter 2) may not provide clear-cut evidence, because one can speak of

EXHIBIT 3.1

55

Diagnosis and the
special child

CONCLUSIONS OF THE PROJECT ON THE CLASSIFICATION OF EXCEPTIONAL CHILDREN

1. Classification of exceptional children is essential to get services for them, to plan and organize helping programs, and to determine the outcomes of intervention efforts.

2. Public and private policies and practices must manifest respect for the individuality of children and appreciation of the positive values of their individual talents and diverse cultural backgrounds. Classification procedures must not be used to violate this fundamental social value.

3. There is growing public concern over the uses and abuses of categories and labels as applied to children, and there is widespread dissatisfaction with inadequate, uncoordinated, and even hurtful services for children; we assume that all citizens share responsibility for these unsatisfactory circumstances, as well as for their repair.

4. Special programs for handicapped children should be designed to encourage fullest possible participation in the usual experiences of childhood, in regular schooling and recreational activities, and in family and community life. When a child must be removed from normal activities, he should be removed the least possible distance, in time, in geo-graphical space, and in the psychological texture of the experience provided.

5. Categories and labels are powerful instruments for social regulation and control, and they are often employed for obscure, covert, or hurtful purposes: to degrade people, to deny them access to opportunity, to exclude "undesirables" whose presence in some way offends, disturbs familiar custom, or demands extraordinary effort.

6. Categories and labels may open up opportunities for exceptional children, facilitate the passage of legislation in their interest, supply rallying points for volunteer organizations, and provide a rational structure for the administration of governmental programs.

7. Our nation provides inadequately for exceptional children for reasons linked to their being different; it also provides inadequately for exceptional children because it provides inadequately for all children. There is urgent need for a quickened national conscience and a new national policy with this as a goal: to nurture well all of our children, in body, mind, and spirit, that we as a people may grow in wisdom, strength, and humane concerns.

From Hobbs (1975, pp. 5–14)

normal development only in terms of composites and averages. An individual child is never average in the sense that internal developmental rhythms and rates can never be matched exactly with idealized norms.

Variability in the attainment of developmental milestones is further complicated by the fact that the very young child is incapable of reporting anything about subjective experience. Even older children are poor "informants" because of language limitations and because they have not developed standards for comparing their own experiences with those of others. Furthermore, the temptation to minimize or ignore indications of potential problems is often irresistible, and professionals as well as parents may for too long adopt a "wait and see" attitude. Finally, even the best diagnostic procedures often fail to produce consistent, dependable results because of technical problems; and those that are technically adequate typically require extensive interpretation, opening the door to disagreement among diagnosticians.

With all these potential problems in mind, the child-care professional—teacher, psychologist, pediatrician—must approach the initial step of the diagnostic process with thoroughness, caution, and as much precision as permitted by the current state of knowledge. The diagnostician must be thoroughly conversant with normal patterns of development and acceptable margins for individual variation. Using these guidelines, meticulous observation of a child's behavior and abilities must be undertaken, and such observations must be placed within an overall developmental framework. The diagnostician must further be skilled in gathering information from a variety of sources—including parents, teachers, and the child—and then be able to collate and integrate this information in coherent fashion. Finally, the diagnostician must be a technical expert in the administration and interpretation of assessment procedures characteristic of his/her specific professional orientation. Under such circumstances, a decision that a problem does or does not exist can lead in the direction of obtaining appropriate services for the child.

Determining the Nature of the Problem

If it is determined that a problem does exist on the basis of marked deviations from developmental norms or on the basis of clinical examination, it then

The exercises these children are working on not only help them increase their cognitive skills but also aid their teacher in determining the nature of any possible visual-motor problems they might have.

becomes necessary to determine the nature of the problem, that is, an idea of what the problem might be. In some cases, the very existence of the problem also discloses its nature. For example, research data have definitely linked several specific physical characteristics with Down's Syndrome; if such characteristics are apparent at birth, the diagnosis of Down's Syndrome inevitably follows.

In many more cases, however, the nature of the problem is not immediately evident. For example, a five-year-old child's failure to begin talking is a symptomatic indication that a problem exists. But extensive investigation may be necessary before it can be determined what it is that is impeding the child's development or use of speech. Decisions regarding the nature of the problem are critical, since they often affect predictions regarding the child's future developmental potential or appropriate intervention approaches.

A given set of symptoms may be associated with a variety of possible disorders. **Differential diagnosis,** the precise specification that a given set of symptoms is indicative of one disorder rather than another, requires extensive diagnostic skill, experience, and the availability of sound technical procedures. In some instances, the diagnostician may still be baffled despite the skilled use of assessment procedures. It is critically important in establishing a differential diagnosis that the diagnostician recognize realistic limitations and share these openly with collaborating colleagues and with the parents. Adequate differential diagnosis of the special child almost always requires a multidisciplinary team approach in which professionals share the data obtained in their independent investigations and integrate this information into a total picture of the individual child.

Once a differential diagnosis has been developed, it will further guide investigation into the causes of the child's problem.

Determining the Etiology of the Problem

Understanding the etiology, or causation, of a problem is not an end in itself, though, unfortunately, it is sometimes viewed in this way. Rather, knowing the cause of a developmental problem is a step in the diagnostic process leading in the direction of rationally based treatment. Understanding etiology can often help lead to intervention based on appropriate psychological, educational, or medical strategies.

For example, it may be discovered that a disorder is a function of a biochemical or metabolic disturbance, in which case medical treatment would be indicated. Or it may be that the cause of a disorder in organic malfunction is irreversible, in which case treatment must be focused on educational and psychological intervention that is based on awareness of the organic disability. The fact that a problem may be medically irreversible only means that child-care professionals must devise educational and psychological measures that circumvent or compensate for the problem. In certain cases it may be discovered that the causes of a problem lie in past or present environmental conditions. Naturally, such knowledge will support intervention approaches that have little to do with medical techniques, but which require a thorough understanding of the child's developmental history and present life circumstances. Countless other etiological possibilities may confront the diagnostician.

The important point here is not to catalog these possibilities, but rather to emphasize that an adequate understanding of the causes of a disorder is critically important in the overall goal of facilitating the child's further development.

Determining the Prognosis of the Disorder

Knowledge accumulated thus far in the diagnostic process can enable the diagnostician to make tentative predictions regarding the child's ongoing development and the potential developmental consequences of a disorder. Such a prognosis is important in planning for future care and treatment of the special child.

Decisions regarding home-based treatment or institutional care, special educational placement or placement in a regular classroom, and many others should be based on the best possible predictions regarding the child's future development. Adequate professional care must be provided for, and parents have the right to the best information possible regarding the child's potential course of development in order to make provisions for treatment and, where necessary, ongoing care. In some cases, predictions about the development of the special child will affect all family members as decisions are made about how and where the family will live in order to facilitate the optimal development of the special child.

While information regarding prognosis can be important in arranging the best possible care for the special child, it should *never* be used to make finalistic predictions that will limit services or the child's ability to develop. Again, the diagnostic process can be misused by barring a child from opportunities and services if it is seen as a seal on the child's developmental potential. Diagnostic predictions should, therefore, always be framed in terms that will point to available services and that will permit and encourage parental planning.

Determining the Best Intervention Strategies

Most importantly, diagnosis should eventuate in detailed, rationally based plans for intervention. We will discuss intervention strategies in detail in Chapter 4, but it is important to note here that intervention may take a variety of forms, ranging from medical procedures to advice to parents on managing the child's behavior in the home. In order to determine which interventions are appropriate and will maximize the child's developmental potential, it is imperative that the diagnosis include a series of detailed, descriptive statements about the child's condition and behavior. Further, diagnostic statements must be sufficiently concrete so that each can be related to specific intervention techniques. To say, for example, that a youngster is "mildly retarded" says very little of practical utility. To say, instead, that a youngster cannot distinguish among a penny, a nickel, a dime, and a quarter, and does not recognize their relative values, is diagnostically more useful, since such a statement can lead directly to intervention strategies designed to remedy this deficiency. Used in this way, no diagnostic statement is ever hopeless, nor an impediment to services. On the contrary, *adequate diagnosis serves as a vital, ongoing guide to intervention* on the part of the special educator, the psychologist, the pediatrician, the parents, and any individual who is concerned with the child's welfare.

Good diagnosis is always more than classification. It is the first step taken to provide services and opportunities that will maximize the developmental potential of the special child.

ASSESSMENT PROCEDURES

Each of the helping professions working with special children has attempted to evolve formal assessment procedures that facilitate the diagnostic process. Though such procedures vary widely, any formal assessment procedure should include a standardized observation method with demonstrable validity and reliability. By means of such a procedure, a diagnostician can examine and evaluate a child in order to obtain a comprehensive and individualized conception of the child's condition.

Though this procedure may appear somewhat formidable at first glance, most of its elements are already familiar. First, it should be emphasized that **assessment procedures** are nothing more than observation methods used under controlled conditions, often with refinements designed to permit greater precision and accuracy. Thus the term **standardization** simply refers to the fact that the conditions of observation are held constant across children so that variations in observations may be attributed to the child's developmental level rather than to chance variations among observers or observation conditions.

In order for these standardized observations to be useful, they have to be replicable or consistent. This consistency in observations is technically called **reliability.** A final key element in producing usable information about a child's development is **validity.** That is, standardized, reliable observational methods must assess the target behavior that the diagnostician is aiming at. In barest terms, validity simply means that the assessment procedure measures what it is intended to measure.

It is important to strive for these conditions of observation regardless of the perspective of the diagnostician. Whether a medical geneticist is conducting an analysis of amniotic fluid to assess potential chromosomal abnormalities or an educator is using an achievement test to assess academic progress, the criteria of standardization, validity, and reliability must be evaluated in order to determine the worth of the assessment procedure. Naturally, these criteria vary according to the specific assessment tools being used. Reliability, for example, may be quite high in the measurement of blood serum components, or notoriously low in the assessment of type and severity of psychological disturbance (Kanfer & Saslow, 1965; O'Leary, 1972). Similarly, standardization may vary from the extensive and rigidly controlled procedures in the development of an intelligence test to the idiosyncrasies of an individual interview between a clinician and a child. The important point is that the criteria of standardization, reliability, and validity be evaluated in the use of any assessment procedure, since the information gathered is rarely better than the procedure used to gather it.

It is beyond the scope of this chapter to review and evaluate the staggering variety of procedures available to assess the physical, cognitive, social, and emotional development of children. In medicine alone, the number of procedures used to detect subtle organic abnormalities is bewildering; in psychology and education, ability and personality tests number literally in the thousands. Despite this array of specific assessment procedures, however, each of the professions dealing with special children has developed an identifiable orientation toward diagnosis and assessment that is a result of practical necessities of the profession as well as dominant theoretical frameworks.

Since the professional who works with special children has frequent need to review the assessments of other professionals, it is important that he/she be familiar with the most commonly used assessment procedures within and among different child-care specialties. In the remainder of this chapter, we will survey a few of the most commonly used assessment procedures employed in the diagnosis of the special child. These include the pediatric evaluation, the psychiatric mental status examination, psychological and educational assessment procedures, target behavior assessment, and speech and hearing evaluations.

The Pediatric Evaluation

Ideally, the medical care of a child should begin with the identification of the mother's pregnancy. In this way it is possible both to take preventive health measures and to bring needed attention to possible "high-risk" pregnancies in which there is medical concern for the health of either the child or the mother. In most situations, however, direct health care of the child begins shortly after birth, with the customary pediatric examination of the new baby prior to discharge from the hospital. The **pediatrician,** trained as a physician and a specialist in the prevention and care of childhood medical problems, typically continues to be the major source of health care for a child throughout infancy and childhood. The pediatric evaluation frequently constitutes the first in a series of specialized assessment procedures intended to determine the nature of a special child's problems. As such, it is often the pediatrician who first suspects the existence of a problem and begins working with the parents as a coordinator for the various services that may be necessary for a special child.

Health history

A diagnostic assessment by a pediatrician consists initially of taking the health history of the patient. A thorough pediatric history is basic not only in the diagnosis of special children, but also in the ongoing care of normal children who often exhibit developmental deviations that, nevertheless, do not constitute or suggest the presence of a disorder (Hughes, 1975). It is through the health history that the physical, emotional, psychological, and social aspects of the child's situation first come to light. Viewed collectively, these factors can provide clues to the nature of an existing disorder; they can also con-

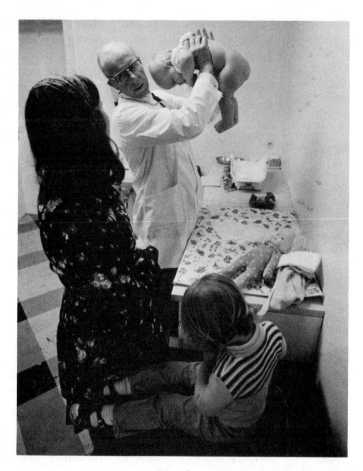

It is often the pediatrician who first suspects the existence of a problem and begins working with the parents as a coordinator for the many services necessary for a special child.

tribute significantly to further determinations of etiology, prognosis, and treatment strategy.

In the case of a child patient, the pediatrician usually receives most of the health history from an interview with the parent or parents. As such, the pediatrician must be skilled in interviewing techniques so that spontaneous descriptions by the parents can be elicited with ease and also so that specific questions can be asked which clarify the parents' accounts.

A thorough health history should include a statement or description of the following aspects as they relate to the child (Seidel & Ziai, 1975; Silver, 1974):

a) the parents' "presenting concern," that is, the reason they are seeking assistance;

b) the symptoms involved in any presenting illness;

c) previous illnesses and general health quality;

d) developmental milestones;

e) personality characteristics and patterns of interpersonal relations;

f) school progress and educational development;

g) the family history, including ages of parents, number and ages of children in the family, marital relationship, and related factors on the general tone of family relationships;

h) the family's socioeconomic characteristics, such as educational and occupational level, type of neighborhood and school;

i) the child's habit patterns (eating, sleeping, toileting) and temperament;

j) a review of specific physiological systems (sensory, respiratory, digestive, neuromuscular, genitourinary).

The skilled pediatrician will also use the health history as an opportunity to evaluate the parents' attitudes toward the child, the basic emotional stability of the parents, and the likelihood that the parents will respond to suggestions regarding management of the child's illnesses or developmental problems (Hughes, 1975).

Physical examination

The physical examination of the child constitutes the second major focus of the pediatric evaluation. The nature of the examination varies considerably depending on the age of the child, but the general orientation remains much the same. The physical examination begins with observations of the child's general appearance and behavior and includes specific physical measurements (height, weight, head circumference) as well as temperature, blood pressure, and the examination of individual physiological systems. These include the abdomen, chest, heart, extremities and neuromusculature, rectum and genitalia, and sensory systems. Routine laboratory analyses complement the examination.

Though the pediatric evaluation depends heavily on the skill and judgment of the diagnostician, it is by no means either totally subjective or impressionistic. On the contrary, though absolute precision is never possible, adequate pediatric evaluation is based on established developmental norms, such as those originally developed by Gesell and others. Physical and behavioral observations of the individual child are translated into age equivalents and compared with carefully derived standards that have demonstrated reliability and validity. It is important to recognize that such an approach focuses on normal developmental processes. *Assessment proceeds from an initial assumption of normality,* and only deviations from healthy patterns of development lead to conclusions that development may be amiss. By remembering this, the pediatrician guards against iatrogenic problems that can be a by-product of a clinical orientation.

As indicated by the pediatric evaluation, further medical investigation may be undertaken by a variety of medical specialists. Indications of neurological dysfunction may prompt a referral to a **pediatric neurologist,** a physician specializing in the diagnosis and treatment of children's nervous system disorders. Similarly, other indications of problematic functioning or development may lead to further investigation by a variety of medical and nonmedical specialists.

Whereas the pediatrician is primarily concerned with the overall health and development of the child, the child psychiatrist is primarily involved in the diagnosis and treatment of childhood psychiatric disorders. It should be made quite clear at the outset that these professional demarcations are rarely clear-cut or absolute in practice. The concerns and functions of various child-care professionals characteristically overlap and complement each other, and in a multidisciplinary child-care team, distinctions are more a matter of emphasis than of mutually exclusive functions. Consequently, the mental status examination may alternatively be conducted by a psychologist or a social worker.

Within the context of a multidisciplinary approach to the care of the special child, the child psychiatrist traditionally assesses the psychological functioning of the child—including degree and severity of disturbed behavior—through observation, interview, and scrutiny of the child's play behavior. The **child psychiatrist**—trained as a physician and specialist in childhood psychological disorders—brings extensive background to the diagnostic approach that has come to be termed the **mental status examination,** an examination of intellectual, emotional, behavioral, social, and general personality dimensions (Cramer, 1975).

The mental status examination is not a well-standardized procedure in the sense that we have been using the term, and reliability and validity are difficult to assess. Individual psychiatrists and psychologists vary considerably in how they conduct the mental status examination, and each clinician-child interaction is characterized by its own idiosyncratic patterns. Despite this variability in procedure, however, the consistency of the results of the mental status exam is surprisingly good (Goodman & Sours, 1967).

The attempt to understand a child's inner psychological life by asking questions is considerably more difficult than with adults. Even a verbal and articulate youngster may conceal or minimize difficulties because of a fear of consequences or the need to appear as normal as possible. Few children seek psychiatric help of their own accord, and children are frequently coerced into psychiatric evaluations by concerned adults. Direct questioning, therefore, is often useless, and considerable skill is required to assist a child in describing his/her psychological experiences.

With preschool children the mental status examination relies less on organized conversation between child and clinician and more on observations of the child's behavior. Frequently the child is seen in a playroom or in an office equipped with selected age-appropriate toys. In the play situation the appropriateness, quality, organization, constructiveness, and content of the child's play form the bases upon which assessment of the child's functioning is appraised.

To a great extent the methods and concepts that guide the psychiatric evaluation are derived from the psychodynamic concepts of theorists (such as Freud and Erikson) who view expressive behavior as a manifestation of the child's level of psychological development. The child's play, for example, may point to emotional conflicts or unresolved psychosocial crises involving trust, self-acceptance, independence, and sexual development. Inferences regarding unconscious sources of conflict and anxiety are checked against one another to develop an integrated picture of the child's psychological and interpersonal functioning.

Although differences exist in the specific examination procedures of individual clinicians, there is general agreement regarding the essentials of an adequate mental status examination (Brophy, 1974; Chess, 1969; Cramer, 1975; Goodman & Sours, 1967). These include evaluation of the following areas: (a) general appearance and physique; (b) activity level; (c) coordination and motor skills; (d) speech and language development and patterns; (e) intellectual functioning, general information, and organization of thinking; (f) specific modes of thought, orientation to time, place, and person, and unusual perceptions; (g) style of interpersonal functioning, such as dependency and aggression; and (h) dreams and fantasies.

The information gleaned from observation and examination of these areas is then integrated into a coherent diagnostic picture with suggestions regarding etiology and treatment.

Psychological and Educational Assessment

Upon initial suspicion of the presence of a developmental problem, one of the most frequent specialized referrals made is to a clinical child psychologist or a school psychologist. A **clinical child psychologist** usually holds a Ph.D. in psychology and has specialized in the diagnosis and treatment of children's

Though child psychiatrists use a variety of assessment techniques, observation plays a key role in working with young children.

psychological and developmental disabilities. A **school psychologist,** at a minimum, has an M.A. in psychology and state certification.

In some instances, preliminary assessment using diagnostic tests may be conducted by a **special education teacher,** an individual who has been trained and certified to use specific educational methods with special children. Diagnostic assessment procedures appropriately used by psychologists or special educators are indicated in the following sections.

In many respects, the psychological evaluation is similar to the pediatric evaluation and the mental status examination, since each explores patterns of development and current behavior. However, one of the aspects of evaluation that has come to be associated with the psychologist is the use of psychological tests. Though such tests number literally in the thousands, a smaller number have come to be considered classics in assessing the intellectual abilities and personality characteristics of special children. Even within this smaller group of instruments it is practically impossible to become skilled in the use of more than a few tests appropriate to a given clinical situation. An excellent series of resources that describe current tests are the *Mental Measurement Yearbooks,* published periodically depending on the number of new tests available. The *Seventh Mental Measurements Yearbook* (Buros, 1972) and its predecessors are invaluable tools in evaluating the appropriateness and technical adequacy of a wide variety of psychological and educational tests.

What makes a test technically adequate? Here we can revert to familiar criteria. An effective test is one that is based on sound norms derived from uniform standardization procedures and that has adequate reliability and validity. Ideally, these technical problems should be solved by the creator of a test, but this is not always the case. As such, it is the responsibility of the examiner to make a judicious choice of assessment instruments on the basis of available research data, since the individual psychological examiner can be no more accurate in his/her assessment than is permitted by the technical precision of the assessment instruments used.

The formal evaluation of a child is founded on the careful selection and administration of appropriate tests, but it also includes interview and history information and observations of the child's behavior before, during, and after formal testing. The trained examiner integrates test findings with observations and information from other sources to develop a diagnostic picture.

Varieties of Psychological and Educational Tests

Tests and other assessment procedures may be categorized in a variety of ways. One useful approach distinguishes among tests on the basis of the kind of stimulus situation presented and the kind of response required. Using this approach we can distinguish among three broad groups of assessment devices: objective tests, subjective tests, and projective techniques. Within each of these groups respectively, the stimulus situation (that is, the test item or question) becomes increasingly ambiguous, and the subject response becomes more variable and less consistently predictable. Expectably, reliability and validity decrease as the stimulus situation and subject response become less structured.

Objective tests

Probably the most familiar psychological and educational assessment devices
are *objective tests,* in which a clearly structured series of questions is presented, calling for subject responses that can be unequivocally categorized
as right or wrong. Most ability and achievement tests are of this type regardless of whether they are teacher-made devices for assessing classroom progress
or expensive, nationally standardized devices.

A major class of objective tests of interest to those who work with special
children are those designed to measure **general ability,** or **intelligence.** Intelligence tests were originally constructed to study school success in retarded
children. In 1904 Alfred Binet first attempted to assess the intellectual ability
of Paris schoolchildren, and this original instrument has been a prototype
for most later intelligence tests. Because of its origin in an educational context, the original Binet-Simon Scale was heavily weighted with questions designed to measure academic potential. Consequently, this early scale and
most successors are really more accurately viewed as tests of academic aptitude rather than overall intellectual potential (Anastasi, 1975). One might go
even further in refining the meaning of an intelligence test. Since any test can
only measure behavior that is exhibited in a given situation, what is really
being assessed is current achievement. Viewed in this way, some of the
mystery is removed from the intelligence test, which is often viewed popularly as capable of tapping some undefined reservoir of intellectual potential.
However, removing the mystery does not diminish the utility of such tests,
and they are appropriately used to assess the presence of abilities considered
important in a child's educational development. Intelligence tests are by no
means infallible predictors of academic success, but they are an important
means of assessing a child's intellectual development and hypothesizing about
future academic performance.

In addition to tests of general ability, such as familiar intelligence and
scholastic aptitude tests, other objective tests are designed to measure
specific abilities. Various perceptual-motor tests, for example, have been
developed to assess the child's accuracy of perception in controlled situations
and his/her ability to perform specific motor responses. Such tests often require a child to copy a printed figure (such as a square or diamond), to trace
a figure, or to arrange colored blocks in a specified design.

In other cases, specific ability tests are designed to assess numerical
ability, verbal ability, and ability to comprehend spatial relations. Tests such
as these are useful indicators of a child's readiness for certain school tasks,
or, in some cases, they can be used to investigate the possibility of neurological problems (Lourie & Rieger, 1974). Whereas general ability tests are
often used to assess overall level of intellectual development and can aid
in the identification of giftedness or retardation, special ability tests may be
used to identify skills or deficits in specific areas of functioning.

Another type of objective test measures **achievement** and is designed to
assess the extent to which a child has acquired certain skills or knowledge
directly from the educational process. "Achievement tests may be said to
measure the effects of learning under partially known and controlled conditions, whereas intelligence tests measure the effects of learning under
relatively uncontrolled and unknown conditions" (Anastasi, 1975, p. 2082).

Objective tests are administered both by psychologists and educators. Because such tests have objectively determinable right and wrong answers, they are usually easily scored and interpreted, provided appropriate norms are available. However, the use of certain objective tests is restricted to psychologists or others trained in their administration and interpretation. This is usually the case with individually administered intelligence tests, which require extensive training in administration, scoring, and interpretation.

Subjective tests

The group of assessment procedures included in this category are not really tests in the familiar sense of the term. Rather, these instruments are designed to gather information about a given individual's attitudes, feelings, perceptions of self and others, and behavior. Such *subjective tests* do not produce answers that can be evaluated as right or wrong; instead they yield a picture of an individual's functioning in specific areas. The term "test" is used here descriptively because these instruments are characteristically developed with attention to standardization and development of norms, and because statistical information regarding reliability and validity is usually available. Two examples of subjective assessment instruments are self-report inventories and rating scales.

Self-report inventories typically take the form of a series of statements that are evaluated as true or false as applied to the individual. The statements used may tap a relatively specific set of attitudes or behaviors, or they may be broadly inclusive and sample many domains of behavior and feelings. Self-report inventories are a useful way to gather a relatively large amount of information about a person in a short time, and the standardized format permits comparison of an individual subject's responses with previously developed norms.

Rating scales are similar to self-report inventories in that they, too, are a series of descriptive statements; they differ, however, in that the evaluation is made by someone other than the subject of the statements. Thus, rather than asking a child whether he/she often feels frightened (as in a self-report inventory), for a rating scale the diagnostician might ask a parent or teacher to evaluate the extent to which the child appears to be fearful. An additional difference between the two approaches is more technical than substantive: the self-report inventory typically asks whether a behavior is true or false as applied to the subject, whereas a rating scale asks instead for an estimate of the frequency or intensity of a characteristic.

Unlike objective tests, self-report inventories are often restricted to use by psychologists, and test publishers will sell these instruments only to those with appropriate training and credentials. Rating scales are used by psychologists, educators, and others. Though care is required in their use, rating scales are really nothing more than formats for systematizing observations of a child's behavior.

Projective tests

The third broad category of tests is used by psychologists rather than educators, and consists of a variety of approaches and techniques that are collectively called *projective tests*. All of these tests share common characteristics of presenting the subject with a relatively ambiguous and unstructured stimulus situation and requesting a highly subjective response. The projective test provides an opportunity to understand otherwise inaccessible personal constructions of the self and the world. Because the subject lacks guidelines as to what constitutes a socially appropriate response, it is assumed that a highly personalized interpretation of the stimulus situation will occur in which the subject "projects" meaning onto an ambiguous stimulus. This projection will reveal unconscious and/or suppressed emotions, perceptions, and attitudes as well as the degree of psychological integration or disorganization of the individual's personality.

One of the simplest forms of projective techniques is the **projective drawing,** in which the child is asked to draw a picture of a person or a house or a family, or a series of such figures. Tests of this kind have come to be seen as a means of assessing a child's concept of self, awareness of body functioning, perception of others in relation to the self, and a general projection of important personality characteristics. Koppitz (1968) has published a scoring system for children's figure drawings that has helped in producing some standardization in interpretation of responses, but projective drawings remain very much a clinical art rather than an objective science. Projective drawings are particularly helpful in the assessment of young children who are not sufficiently verbal to respond to other forms of personality assessment and who are easily interested in self-expression through drawing.

Probably the most familiar projective test is the **Rorschach Inkblot Technique,** named after its creator, Hermann Rorschach. The Rorschach consists of ten inkblots that are successively presented to the child with the question, "What might this be or what does it remind you of?" As a child shares personal perceptions of the inkblots, the examiner records the child's responses, and on subsequent analysis scores and codes the responses on the basis of comparison with the responses of others who have taken the test. Responses are interpreted to construct notions of the child's inner thoughts and response tendencies.

Other widely used projective techniques include a variety of **picture-story tests**—in which the child is presented with a series of standard pictures and asked to relate a story about each picture—and various **completion techniques**—in which a child is given a fragment of a sentence or a story and asked to complete it.

Projective testing constitutes a widely used and significant approach to assessment of the special child's strengths and problems and is seen as a key to tapping struggles, fears, and conflicts that the child cannot or will not verbalize. Evaluation of the utility of projective techniques is difficult and highly controversial. Despite the availability of more than 2000 theoretical and research articles evaluating such techniques, it is unclear whether they contribute information that is sufficiently valid and reliable to serve as a guide in the diagnostic appraisal of the special child (O'Leary, 1972). Exhibit 3.2 gives a number of examples of currently used assessment procedures.

Target Behavior Assessment

A promising approach to assessment that has come into increasing use in recent years—and one that may be used by the special educator as well as

EXHIBIT 3.2

EXAMPLES OF PSYCHOLOGICAL AND EDUCATIONAL ASSESSMENT PROCEDURES

Type of Test	Name	Description
Objective test (general ability)	Stanford-Binet Intelligence Scale	A large number of verbal problems and a few motor tasks at younger ages. Age range from 2–superior adult. Yields an IQ score along with a large amount of information regarding specific areas of functioning. Good standardization, reliability, validity.
Objective test (general ability)	Wechsler Intelligence Scale for Children, Revised (WISC-R)	Wide range of verbal and motor tasks for ages 6–16. Yields an IQ score along with observational information about intellectual and personality style. Good standardization, reliability, validity. Has advantage of yielding separate subtest scores in various areas of intellectual and motor functions.
Objective test (specific ability)	Illinois Test of Psycholinguistic Abilities	A large number of verbal items with some requiring motor responses. Assesses child's ability to understand and use language appropriately based on a theoretical model of specific language functions. Subtest scores permit isolation of deficits in understanding language, internal use of language, and responses based on language. Good reliability; further study of validity required.
Objective test (achievement)	Peabody Individual Achievement Test	Individually administered test measuring achievement in arithmetic, reading recognition, reading comprehension, and general information. Yields age and grade equivalents and percentile ranks. Acceptable standardization; good validity and reliability.
Subjective test (rating scale)	Vineland Social Maturity Scale	Observer—usually a parent—reports on child's ability to carry out a variety of self-care, language, and social activities. Adequate standardization and norms. Moderate reliability; validity questionable under some circumstances.
Subjective test (self-report inventory)	16 P.F. Test	Forms available for children requesting self-report on a wide variety of items ranging from general interests through self-report of specific behaviors. Yields scores on 16 personality factors such as assertiveness, practicality, apprehensiveness. Excellent reliability; needs more extensive validation research.
Projective test (inkblot technique)	Rorschach Inkblot Technique	Child describes perceptions of a standard series of inkblots. Responses are scored on basis of content, use of color, shape, movement, shading. Highly controversial clinical technique with inadequate evidence of reliability and validity.
Projective test (picture-story technique)	Children's Apperception Test	Series of pictures depicting groups of animals in different situations. Child makes up a story about each picture. Based on psychodynamic theory of development, pictures are designed to tap areas of psychosexual development. Questionable validity and reliability.

the psychologist—is **target behavior assessment** (O'Leary, 1972). Sometimes referred to as *functional analysis of behavior* or *applied behavior analysis,* this approach is intended to supplant psychiatric and psychological assessment procedures that have questionable validity and reliability (Bijou & Grimm, 1975). Target behavior assessment includes a variety of possible approaches that rely on the direct observation and measurement of precisely defined behaviors. Derived from the work of social learning theorists and psychologists concerned with applied behavior analysis, these assessment techniques avoid inferences as to the meaning of behavior. Instead, any defined target behavior is taken at face value, and an attempt is made to specify the conditions under which the behavior occurs (or fails to occur). Subsequently, environmental conditions or social contingencies are systematically manipulated to determine their effects on the behavior in question. One can conceive of this approach very much as experimental research designed to study the behavior of an individual child, since the steps consist of pretreatment observation, systematic manipulation of variables, and assessment of treatment outcomes.

Target behavior assessment has a number of advantages in diagnostic assessment. First, because behaviors are specified in explicit terms, a high degree of reliability in the description of behaviors is possible. With fewer inferences made, there is less room for disagreement among observers and less room for discrepancies in the observations of a single observer at different times. Second, because target behavior assessment is focused directly on the behavior at issue, the question of validity does not even arise. There is no question about what is being measured, though care must be taken to select target behaviors that are important to the child's ongoing development. A third advantage of target behavior assessment is that diagnosis of a specified behavior or set of behaviors is directly linked to intervention possibilities. Where a problem behavior is identified as functionally related to given environmental or social conditions, intervention procedures can be developed directly in relation to conditions that need to be changed.

Naturally, target behavior assessment may not be directly useful in instances where constitutional factors or physical impairments are directly responsible for the developmental problem. However, even under these circumstances, target assessment may be helpful in pointing toward alternative diagnostic and treatment procedures or in suggesting ways of compensating for the physical impairment. Finally, this approach to assessment is inherently self-correcting and leads to a continuous interaction between diagnostic and treatment processes.

This last factor can be spelled out more fully in an explicit description of the steps involved in target assessment. (a) *The initial step involves the selection and specification of target behaviors.* Such selection is often a function of identifying the behaviors that constitute the child's problem as perceived by parents, teachers, or pediatrician. On occasion, target selection is a more subtle process as the "problem" perceived by others may be a byproduct of their own behavioral excesses or deficiencies. For example, a normally active youngster might be perceived as "hyperactive" by a mother who is herself extremely tense and high-strung. (b) *Once specified and defined, target behaviors are observed carefully during a "baseline" period prior to any intervention.* The target behavior is counted or its intensity measured under specific, naturally occurring conditions. During this period additional information may also be gathered using more traditional techniques of testing, parental description, inventories, and rating scales. (c) Armed with information regarding the frequency and conditions of occurrence (or nonoccurrence) of a target behavior, *a treatment strategy is developed on the basis of empirically derived principles of learning and behavior change.* The program is instituted along with continued monitoring of the target behavior to determine empirically whether the behavior is changing in the desired direction. Appropriate changes indicate the accuracy of the diagnosis and effectiveness of the treatment procedure. Undesirable changes or no changes at all in the target behavior clearly indicate the need for revisions in the diagnostic picture and modification of the intervention strategy. Thus the burden of producing change lies in the assessment and treatment plans. The child is not viewed as intractable or incurable. Rather, diagnosis and intervention strategies are viewed as needing modification and revision until some form of intervention proves successful in implementing change.

As in the case of other assessment procedures, target behavior assessment should form a part of a comprehensive diagnostic effort—including pediatric evaluation, the mental status examination, and psychological and educational assessment—in order to develop a precise and functional diagnostic picture of the special child.

Speech and Hearing Evaluations

The presence of a speech impairment or hearing loss can severely impair a child's intellectual, social, and personal development. In some situations, such as a child born with cleft lip or palate, both current and potential problems can be immediately identified and an intervention program can be initiated. Language, however, is a complex function that is slow to develop, and difficulties in both speech and hearing may not be immediately apparent, even to the practiced eye. For these reasons, speech and hearing evaluations are often included as components of the diagnostic process with special children. It is extremely difficult for the layperson to recognize or assess the presence and extent of a hearing loss. As many as 50 percent of parents of hard-of-hearing children whose behavior is socially inadequate do not even suspect a hearing difficulty in their child, sometimes for several years (Newman, 1975). Both speech and hearing disorders require sophisticated diagnosis in order to specify the nature and severity of a problem as well as to initiate appropriate intervention.

Diagnosis and assessment of problems in speech and language is one of the primary functions of the **speech pathologist,** a specialist in the assessment and treatment of language disorders. The speech pathologist approaches the assessment of the child with certain basic questions in mind: (a) Is the child's language level appropriate to age and apparent intellectual potential? (b) If not, how far does the child's language behavior deviate from established norms? (c) What are possible reasons for the child's deficiencies? An awareness of the diagnostic possibilities and potential disorders of childhood is important in this respect because language difficulties may be symptomatic of a wide variety of disorders.

Speech and language evaluation is a clinical art that has not yet reached a high degree of technical precision. In general, the diagnostician assesses a child on the basis of language development norms, behavioral observation, examination of speech musculature, and several standardized tests. But specifying quality and quantity of language is only one aspect of speech evaluation. A thorough assessment will analyze the entire expressive behavior pattern of the child as well as receptive language abilities and modes of concept formation.

Although a speech pathologist can determine the presence of hearing difficulties in a special child, hearing is best evaluated by an **audiologist,** a specialist in the assessment of hearing functions and hearing impairments. Audiology, as a discipline, is evolving increasingly precise measurement procedures. Ideally, a valid and reliable assessment procedure would be one that did not rely on the child's active participation to determine hearing ability (Northern & Downs, 1974). Objective tests of hearing typically rely on methods of recording autonomic physiological responses that result from the presentation of auditory stimuli. Naturally the audiologist is aware that hearing is a complex process requiring more than sensory awareness. Hearing also requires the meaningful interpretation of sounds, and the audiologist also views the diagnostic process from the perspective of the child's overall functioning. As such, speech and hearing assessments are characteristically conducted within the context of the other diagnostic procedures we have surveyed. Speech and hearing evaluations add critical perspectives to the

Regular hearing evaluations are important as children develop. Here a sixth-grader hesitates in her response as to which ear is hearing the signal.

diagnostic picture and, together with other assessment procedures, contribute to a more complete diagnostic understanding of the developmental problems of the special child.

The Multidisciplinary Approach

It is evident by now that diagnosis is an extremely complex process requiring technical skill and experienced clinical judgment. Each of the child-care professions has developed distinctive assessment techniques that can contribute importantly to the diagnostic process, and adequate study of the developing child usually requires information in each of these major areas of the child's development. Yet despite the distinctions among the diagnostic and assessment techniques of these different professional specialties, we must remember that these distinctions often become blurred in practice. Regardless of professional identification, no child-care specialist can afford to overlook any bit of information, and it is often the case that a specialist in one area will discover problems in another aspect of the child's functioning while conducting his/her own specialized assessment. For this reason, diagnosis must be viewed in relation to the child's total development and requires the collaborative efforts of many specialists, each of whose findings contributes to understanding the child as a developing individual. Developmental problems do not occur as isolated defects in the child. Rather, an impairment in one area of functioning inevitably has pervasive effects on the child's overall development. The multidisciplinary team approach to diagnosis is an acknowledgment of the unitary nature of the special child's development. The importance of this multidisciplinary approach is perhaps best illustrated through detailed review of the diagnosis and assessment of an individual child. This is done in Case Study 3.1, the diagnosis of Noam.

CASE STUDY 3.1

NOAM: A MULTIDISCIPLINARY DIAGNOSIS

Noam was a handsome 6-year-old boy with dark eyes, brown hair, and slender but angular build. When Noam was age 3, his 4-year-old sister Elaine had begun kindergarten, and his mother had enrolled Noam in a Montessori school so that she could work as a part-time secretary and be "more than just a housewife." Noam began having problems at the school almost immediately. He acted restless and agitated, constantly moving about and frequently displaying emotional outbursts or tantrums; he would refuse to listen to the directives of his teacher and would sometimes even strike out at the other children. His teacher informed his parents that Noam did not seem "normal," and she recommended that he be evaluated medically. The fam-

ily had only recently moved to the city and were referred to a pediatric neurologist. A physical examination, behavioral observation of hyperactivity, and positive findings on an EEG suggested mild neurological dysfunction. The neurologist concluded that Noam had minimal brain dysfunction, and he recommended a trial of medication that included both Ritalin and Dilantin.

Noam continued to show problems both in school and at home. At home, he would refuse to get up in the morning, to get dressed for school, or to eat his breakfast. His mother felt increasingly unable to cope with him, and began regularly using verbal threats of physical violence. To friends, she confided that she had impulses to hurt Noam, that she despised him, and that she wished he were not her child. Fortunately, Noam's suburban school district had a special education class at the preschool level, and he was placed in a small class of eight children with a very sensitive teacher. His behavior at school, however, grew increasingly unmanageable, and he frequently needed to be physically restrained by the teacher aide. An appealing and likeable boy despite his behavior, Noam often did quite well in his special education class. He was clearly a bright youngster; he was very verbal and articulate and showed more talent than most of the children in his class. Noam would often seek affection from his teacher and teacher aides; and yet, within the span of a few minutes, he would suddenly become provocative and antagonizing. The project coordinator called in his parents and told them that Noam would need more extensive evaluation and planning than the school could possibly provide. At the school's suggestion, the parents brought Noam to a multidisciplinary children's center, where Noam was evaluated over a six-week period by a team of child health professionals. Noam was now 6 years 3 months and had had the benefit of 2 years of preschool special education in a highly regarded program, as well as a year at a Montessori school. Noam's diagnostic evaluation was coordinated at the clinic by a clinical psychologist, but he was also evaluated by a clinical educator, a psychiatrist, a pediatric neurologist, and a speech pathologist, and his parents' history was taken by a social worker.

Excerpts from the Social History

Noam's parents, Mr. & Mrs. M., were extremely uncomfortable during the interview. The history was taken over two sessions and was marked by frequent disagreements between the parents and much casting of blame. Mrs. M., a 31-year-old overweight woman who had completed two years of college, appeared to be extremely needy, dependent, and ineffectual. She readily admitted to feelings of hostility toward Noam, and in this context her personality became much more animated and aggressive. Her history indicated that she was the oldest in a family of three children,

with a younger brother and younger sister. Mrs. M. related an extremely unhappy childhood in which she was constantly pressured by her father to achieve academically and was frequently beaten for her failures. Although her father was a successful professional, he often beat both Mrs. M. and her younger sister. Her mother was a passive, submissive woman who was unable to intervene for her and prevent such physical abuse.

Mr. M., a 34-year-old electrical engineer, was the only child of first-generation immigrant parents who did not attend school in the United States. Mr. M. stated, "I despised school," pointing out that his parents' unfamiliarity with American schooling often placed him in difficult circumstances. It appeared that his own childhood had been extremely unhappy, and he was often ashamed that his parents were different from American-born parents. He described himself as a "loner."

Mr. and Mrs. M. first met when their families arranged a blind date for them. After a one-year courtship, they married. Their ten-year marriage was fraught with conflict and unhappiness. Early on, they began to have explosive arguments. Each blamed the other for their problems. Mr. M. would often scream and throw things, and then he would withdraw into silence. Mrs. M. would feel helpless and defeated, and then she would tend to overeat. Arguments were seldom, if ever, resolved with a sense of understanding. Their first child, Elaine, was born after two years of marriage and seemed to introduce more stability into their relationship. When Noam was born, Mr. M. admitted, "I wasn't really ready for the second kid." About Noam's birth, Mrs. M. said, "Throughout my pregnancy, I wondered how I could really love another child like I loved Elaine. But when I came home from the hospital, I resented Elaine and wanted to be alone with Noam. I felt he was special. He was just what I wanted—a handsome son of my own."

Noam's developmental milestones were all within the normal range: he sat up at 6 months, stood at 9 months, took his first steps at 12 months, had several first words before 1 year, spoke in sentences before 2 years and was easily toilet trained at 2-½. He was initially a cuddly child who was relaxed and quiet. By the age of 2, however, he became much more active and exploratory. The normal negativism of the 2-year-old was too much for Mrs. M. to manage. In time, Noam was no longer special to his mother, and she became increasingly resentful of him. Mr. M. continued to play the role of the "loner" and refused or was unable to intervene in the frequent conflicts between mother and Noam. In sum, the history revealed a normal birth and early development impeded by severe conflicts in the family, through which Noam gradually became an object of hatred.

Excerpts from the Psychological Evaluation

During psychological testing, Noam proved to be an enthusiastic but demanding youngster who was highly distractible and in need of much support and control. His speech seemed very infantile, raising concerns about an articulation problem. He appeared nervous and under pressure to achieve. At several points he began screaming and crying because of his inability to solve a problem. His verbalizations were frequently indicative of thought confusion; for example, when he was unable to solve a puzzle problem successfully, he began crying, "I can't do it. I can't do it. I hope it's bad 'cause I can't do it." Despite these difficulties in test-taking, Noam was able to complete all the tests. As the testing proceeded, however, he showed increasing panic and needed much assistance from the examiner in order to continue the testing.

On the Wechsler Intelligence Scale for Children (WISC), Noam achieved a Verbal Scale IQ of 125 (superior range), a Performance Scale IQ of 115 (above average range), and a Full Scale IQ of 123 (superior range).

On projective tests (Rorschach, Thematic Apperception Test, and Projective Drawings), Noam displayed an extremely active fantasy life, and under stress he seemed unable to distinguish fantasy from reality. On Card 4 of the Thematic Apperception Test (a picture of an adult man and woman), for example, Noam incorrectly perceived the stimulus figures as a little boy and his mommy, relating the following brief story: "The little boy

is mad and the mommy wants him to go some place and he won't go there. Is that a true story?" Noam's inner sense of combativeness with the maternal figure dominated his responses to projective tests, and he introduced this theme inappropriately to stimuli that normally elicit other themes. At the same time, Noam's projective drawings of human figures indicated that he had bizarre perceptions of himself and others.

In sum, psychological testing indicated that Noam was an intellectually gifted child who also demonstrated a moderate to severe degree of emotional disturbance. Diagnostically, he would be best understood as a borderline psychotic youngster.

Excerpts from the Speech and Language Evaluation

The speech diagnostician conducted the examination in the presence of Noam's mother, who was openly hostile toward Noam during the examination. Noam remained seated for almost a full hour of evaluation, but his behavior was immature, impulsive, and very manipulative. Administration of The Arizona Articulation Proficiency Scale revealed the presence of a mild articulation disorder. Speech was intelligible—although noticeably defective (approximately 16 percent); this was in contrast to a usual 3 percent error score at the 6-year level. Speech pattern was characterized by immature consonant substitutions and omissions, such as w for l initially (e.g., "wight" instead of "light"). Noam, however, could generally correct a mispronounced word when the examiner repeated it to him in a correct fashion. It was the examiner's impression that Noam's articulation problems did not have any organic basis. Rather, his immature speech was presumed to be a function of an emotional disorder. The prognosis for the acquisition of normal speech was thought to be excellent.

Excerpts from the Psychiatric Examination

Noam appeared overly anxious throughout the interview. He was in constant motion and changed rapidly from one distraction to another with little ability to focus on one topic for more than half a minute. He would be euphoric one moment and anxious the next. His speech was tangential, with evidence of loose associations, occasional flights of ideas and blocking. He spoke of a concern about danger of physical harm and fantasies of being omnipotent. There was no overt evidence of hallucinations or systematized delusions, but Noam's ability to test reality was grossly impaired for his age (e.g., he professed anxiety and vulnerability to sharks in the examiner's office, which was located on the fourth floor of an eight-story building in the heart of a midwestern city). His impulse control was very poor, and he displayed an extremely low tolerance for frustration. Perceptions of self were also quite distorted, and his knowledge of body parts was very primitive. Noam had many questions about sexual differences, volunteering that he did not understand how women urinate and that he thought babies came from the mother's anus. The examiner concluded that Noam was a severely anxious child who was experiencing a borderline psychosis of childhood.

Excerpts from the Neurological Evaluation

Noam was a tall, well-developed and well-nourished child (height 48¼" and weight 47½ lbs.). Head and chest circumferences were within normal limits (19½" and 23"); ears, nose, throat, heart, lungs, abdomen, and genital-urinary systems were within normal limits. It was noted that Noam's mother was diagnosed as diabetic in the past year and because of Noam's high birth weight (10 lbs. 5½ oz.), his mother may well have already been a diabetic at Noam's birth. It was also noted that Noam was currently receiving the medication Cylert from the family pediatrician for his hyperactivity; the Cylert was producing insomnia, and, as a consequence, Noam was receiving Benadryl to get a night's rest. Previously, he had been medicated on Ritalin, Dilantin, and Mellaril, all of which were discontinued because they lost their effectiveness. The evaluation indicated the presence of a mild neurological problem based on the following: previously abnormal findings on the EEG, hyperactive behavior, bilateral positive Babinski's (extension of the toes of both feet instead of flexion when stimulating the soles of the feet), mild generalized hypotonia (flaccidity or subnormal tension of the muscles). The neurologist noted, however, that Noam's emotional disturbance did not seem to be related to or caused by the mild neurological problems.

Excerpts from the Educational Evaluation

The clinical educator noted that Noam was active and provocative during the testing, displaying fantasies of grandiosity and aggression. He was responsive to the examiner's directions, however, and was able to complete all the tests. On the Wide Range Achievement Test, Noam scored above grade level on all three subtests: grade level 1.8 on arithmetic, 1.6 on spelling, and 1.3 on reading. On the McCarthy Scales of Children's Abilities, he scored in the average range on all subtests, and his best abilities were on subtests involving fine motor and gross motor skills. It was the opinion of the clinical educator that Noam's behavioral, emotional, and neurological problems had not impeded his ability to achieve academically.

Communication of Findings

When all examiners had completed their evaluations of Noam, a staffing conference was held. This conference included the various diagnosticians who had examined Noam and several representatives from Noam's school. The following findings and recommendations were discussed:

a) It was agreed that the previous diagnosis of minimal brain dysfunction was inaccurate and that Noam would be best diagnosed as a child with borderline childhood psychosis. Although the conferees recognized the possible stigma that might be involved in categorizing a child as emotionally disturbed, it was recognized that this diagnosis was necessary in order to provide appropriate treatment and management.

b) It was recommended that Noam be hospitalized for psychiatric treatment for a period of 3 to 4 months in order to help him deal with his emotional problems in an intensive fashion.

c) It was recommended that a trial of Thorazine be instituted following hospitalization to reduce anxiety and to help Noam be more receptive to the milieu therapy of an inpatient psychiatric unit.

d) It was recommended that Noam's parents begin marital therapy to help them develop more effective ways to manage their conflicts. Noam could join the parents for family therapy sessions when the parents had made more progress in their relationship with each other.

The psychologist then met with the parents and presented the findings and recommendations. Mr. M.'s response seemed somewhat detached, but he did ask appropriate questions about the nature of Noam's and the parents' therapy and the nature and causes of Noam's emotional problems. Mrs. M. initially responded very hysterically, blaming herself for Noam's problems and threatening that it would be better if she committed suicide. The examiner emphasized that an entire family system was involved in Noam's problems and that Noam himself contributed to the workings of this system. By the end of the session, both parents appeared able to understand and accept the findings and recommendations, and arrangements were made for Noam's hospitalization. It was agreed that Mr. and Mrs. M. would enter marital therapy with the psychologist who had coordinated the diagnostic evaluation and that the psychologist would also be involved in Noam's therapy during hospitalization. In Chapter 4, "Helping Special Children," we shall see how Noam has fared in therapy.

SUMMARY

1. The medical model of diagnosis includes recognition of a symptom syndrome, its etiology, incidence, and prognosis, and approaches to intervention and prevention.
2. Diagnosis may be viewed both as a process and as a product.
3. Diagnostic classification is an important step in organizing knowledge about special children, but it can potentially create problems in the form of iatrogenic effects, stigmatization, and misunderstanding.
4. The diagnostic process consists of determining whether a problem exists, what the problem is, how it is caused, what effects it has on development, and how to remedy it.
5. Differential diagnosis is the process of deciding which of several problems is impeding a child's development.
6. The diagnostic process makes use of assessment procedures—controlled observation techniques—that have been standardized and have adequate reliability and validity.
7. Typical components of the diagnostic process with special children include pediatric evaluation, mental status examination, psychological and educational assessment, target behavior assessment, and speech and hearing evaluation.
8. Psychological and educational assessment procedures may be categorized as objective, subjective, and projective instruments.
9. Target behavior assessment is a diagnostic procedure that relies on the precise definition and direct observation and measurement of behavior within the context of environmental events.
10. Target behavior assessment consists of specification of the target behavior, baseline measurement, and intervention procedures.
11. Speech and hearing are key functions in normal development, but problems in these areas are often difficult to detect. For this reason, speech and hearing evaluations are often included in the diagnostic study of the special child.

Helping Special Children

help, *vt. 1. to make things easier or better for (a person); aid; assist; specifically, a) to give (one in need) something necessary, as relief . . . . 2. to make it easier . . . to exist, happen, develop, improve, etc.; specifically a) to make more effective, larger . . . ; aid the growth of; . . . b) to cause improvement in; remedy; alleviate; relieve . . .*

From *Webster's New World Dictionary of the American Language, Second Edition* (1974)

THE NATURE OF THE HELPING PROCESS

"Helping" is a general term, nontechnical in meaning. We have chosen to use it in this discussion because it can encompass the many different approaches currently in use to correct or alleviate the problems of special children. Intervention procedures are not the exclusive province of any one profession; rather, aiding the growth of the special child is a multidisciplinary effort that demands the cooperative work of many individuals with widely varying skills and training.

Because the specific tools and techniques of various helping professionals differ so greatly, the helping process is often conceived in terms that are idiosyncratic to specific professional groups. Even the languages employed become peculiar to specific helping orientations. As a result, it often happens that the language of one orientation is not understood clearly by individuals of another orientation. Even more confusing is the fact that certain terms and concepts are used by several helping professions, but have different meanings for each. To minimize potential confusion we shall propose a few broad distinctions.

Intervention is a general term that refers to the application of professional skills to maintain or improve a child's potential for ongoing healthy development. The physician prescribing medication, the teacher using touch and hearing to augment visual channels in teaching reading, or the social worker seeking foster-home placement for a child are all engaged in intervention procedures designed to facilitate a child's development. Naturally, each of these interventions requires particular skills and training, but all of them constitute intervention procedures designed to help special children.

Therapy is the treatment of an illness or disabling condition, and the terms *therapy* and *treatment* are often used interchangeably. Traditionally, therapy and treatment have been identified with medical practice and refer to procedures employed in the control or cure of identified disease processes. With the advent of nonmedical health professions, however, the term "therapy" is now often used to describe a variety of helping approaches independent of medical practice. For example, behavior therapies developed in the laboratories of psychologists are obviously different from the drug therapies used in medical practice, and yet both constitute genuine therapy. These and many other intervention procedures can be used in a systematic way to enhance a child's development. As the concept of therapy is increasingly employed by a variety of helping professions, it may be appropriately viewed as an organized process of causing or aiding physical, psychological, cognitive, or social changes to enhance development.

Management and **care** are additional forms of helping. These terms typically refer to processes of coordinating and monitoring various aspects of intervention. For example, when a child is said to be "under a doctor's care," it is understood that a physician is coordinating treatment procedures. "Management" is a particularly important concept in residential and hospital settings, where all phases of the environment and the treatment process are closely supervised. In this sense, management includes planning, directing, implementing, coordinating, and evaluating the activities of various helping agents involved with a patient. Within this general framework, management has also acquired particular meanings. In behavior therapy, for example, *contingency management* refers to a set of procedures by which the behavior modifier associates certain reinforcers with a child's specific behaviors. For example, praising or rewarding a child each time he/she completes a homework assignment will likely encourage such behavior. Recently, *parental management* of the behavior of special children is also being recognized as an important part of the helping process. There is now a growing recognition that management procedures implemented by both parents and professionals are key components of the helping process.

Rehabilitation refers to intervention procedures that seek to restore a child to normal or optimal functioning following illness or injury. Efforts at rehabilitation focus initially on those skills lost or impaired during the course of development. In this respect, rehabilitation includes various physical, occupational, and behavioral therapies that seek to restore lost functions. At the same time, rehabilitation often includes efforts to assist in personal, educational, or vocational adjustment and development. With children, primary rehabilitation concerns in cases of accident, acute illness, or injury focus on the child's response to education and the degree to which the child is able to recover previously acquired skills.

Another important component of the helping process is **remediation,** a concept that is used largely by educators and is the educational counterpart of therapy as used by physicians and psychologists. The goal of remediation is to correct deficits in skills and abilities, and the focus is typically on the correction of a specific deficit, such as a reading or speech deficit. Remediation has often been considered as an alternative to special educational placement for youngsters who exhibit specific deficits in skills or learning levels.

Probably the most widely known form of educational intervention is **special education,** in which appropriate facilities, specialized methods and materials, and specially trained teachers are provided. Many forms of remedial programs attempt to keep the child in the conventional classroom while providing some form of focused intervention within this context.

Intervention, therapy, management, rehabilitation, remediation, and special education are thus major components of the helping process with special children. There are many avenues of intervention, and many of these are sufficiently complementary that the same child may be simultaneously and most effectively helped through a variety of interventions. It is not unusual, for example, for a learning-disabled youngster who also shows emotional and behavioral problems to be placed in a special education classroom; teacher and psychologist might consult in the development of behavior modification procedures designed to help the child develop behavioral controls; the child might be placed on medication and managed by a pediatrician or psychiatrist; in addition, the child and parents might be in family psychotherapy to work out mutual conflicts; and the parents might be assisted by a social worker in finding appropriate resources for additional assistance.

The helping process is comprised of the multidisciplinary skills of medicine, allied health sciences, education, and the behavioral and social sciences. Each of these disciplines has developed forms of intervention with individual children that reflect their own expertise and traditions.

In the remainder of this chapter we will survey the major forms of intervention available for special children. Our discussion will follow traditional divisions and modes of organization, but it is important to remember that these distinctions are often artificial and may break down in actual practice. It is convenient to think of the psychologist as expert in applying principles of behavior modification; but every teacher working with an individual child is also modifying behavior. It is comforting to view the physician as expert in the evaluation and administration of medication; but evaluation of the effects of medication must depend on the careful observations and thorough reports of parents and teachers, and the wise physician is guided by their assistance.

With these general considerations regarding the helping process in mind, this chapter will examine five major forms of intervention with special children: (a) medical, (b) psychotherapeutic, (c) behavioral, (d) educational, and (e) social. Although this division is somewhat arbitrary and by no means exhaustive, these five approaches to intervention represent the basic approaches to caring for and helping the individual child. An understanding of them will be useful in working effectively with special children. Case Study 4.1 demonstrates the general process of intervention.

CASE STUDY 4.1

NOAM: INTERVENTION WITH AN EMOTIONALLY DISTURBED CHILD

Noam M. (see diagnostic Case Study 3.1, p. 73), age 6 years 3 months, was admitted to a children's inpatient psychiatric unit with a diagnosis of borderline psychosis of childhood. His emotional disturbance was manifested by the following behaviors: a tendency to engage in infantile speech; inability to maintain attention and interest in ongoing activities; poor self-image; high anxiety level; need to constantly test the ability of caretakers to set limits and controls on his behavior; inability to deal with feelings; excessive preoccupation with fantasies; disorganized thinking; constant attempts to manipulate others to have his own way; inability to interact appropriately with his peers. Intervention with Noam included the following types of treatment: drug therapy (Noam was given a 25 milligram dosage of Thorazine four times a day); group psychotherapy (two one-hour sessions per week with five other children in his age range; group psychotherapists were a male psychologist and female social worker); daily milieu therapy (management of disturbed behaviors by nursing staff, child-care workers, and other professional staff); marital therapy for Noam's parents (weekly one-hour session with a clinical psychologist); and coordinated planning with Noam's school district for his eventual return to special education.

The effects of Thorazine were almost immediately evident in Noam's behavior, greatly reducing his level of agitation and rendering him more receptive to psychological interventions. Noam's anxiety level was lessened by medication, and he showed an increasing capacity to stay interested in ongoing activities.

Group therapy afforded Noam considerable feedback about his behavior from both the therapists and his peers. Infantile, manipulative behavior by Noam was ignored, rather than rewarded with attention. When he behaved appropriately, he was encouraged and supported for his behavior. Group therapy was most effective in helping Noam deal more effectively with his peer relationships and helping him gain a more effective image of himself.

The major changes in Noam's behavior, however, were a function of milieu therapy. Separated from his family through hospitalization, the milieu established a new network of experiences for Noam by coordinating the responses of staff to his behavior on a 24-hour-a-day basis. For example, infantile speech patterns were corrected each time Noam engaged in them; if he said, "Come on, pway with me," the staff worker would reply, "If you want me to play with you, Noam, say 'play' and not 'pway'." When Noam would cry instead of expressing anger, he would be encouraged to express the anger. When he would become preoccupied with fantasy instead of inter-acting with others, he would be required to stop fantasizing and become involved with the persons who were actually present. Within three months, Noam's behavior had greatly improved, and he seemed ready to be returned to his home.

During his hospitalization, Noam's parents were seen in weekly, and sometimes biweekly, marital therapy sessions. Noam's parents engaged in frequent arguments, blaming each other for a variety of problems. The initial goal in their treatment was to help them examine their need to blame each other as a defense against examining themselves. The conflictual aspects of their interaction were greatly reduced, and during the last month of his hospitalization, Noam began joining the sessions with his parents for family therapy. The goal here was to help the parents learn to respond to Noam in the same ways that the staff had found to be effective.

When Noam was discharged from the hospital, he was placed in a special education class for emotionally disturbed children. Halfway through the first semester of this class, he began taking his afternoon classes with the regular first grade. At the end of the first semester, Noam was placed in the regular first-grade class on a full-time basis. Noam's parents continue in weekly marital therapy sessions, and Noam joins these sessions on an occasional basis. Frequent consultations between the therapist and Noam's teachers continue to be necessary, but with teacher support and understanding Noam has been able to function in a regular classroom. Noam and his parents will likely require some form of psychotherapy throughout his development, but Noam's prospects of living a normal life have been greatly enhanced through the multiple interventions of medication, hospitalization and milieu therapy, group and family psychotherapy, and marital therapy for his parents.

MEDICAL TREATMENT

Although medical intervention can be extremely varied and complex, the most common forms of medical treatment fall into a few major categories. These include the controlled use of medication, surgical procedures, and procedures for management and supportive therapy. Sound medical practice—though oriented toward treatment of organic disease and physical disability—always focuses on caring for the whole person. This is particularly the case in pediatric medicine, the medical specialty involved with the diagnosis, treatment, and prevention of childhood problems. Within the context of this holistic concern for the welfare of the growing child, however, drug therapy and surgical procedures are exclusive to medical practice and are the unique contributions of the physician.

Chemotherapy and Psychopharmacology

Historically, **chemotherapy** has referred to the *use* of drugs to combat an infecting agent or to inhibit the growth of aberrant cells. A more inclusive definition views chemotherapy as the treatment of organic dysfunction by the use of biochemical agents. Chemotherapy includes such diverse drug treatments as the use of antibiotics for acute infectious illness, the use of steroids in the treatment of leukemia, or the use of hormones in the treatment of endocrine disorders. In the latter case, for example, thyroid hormones are used in cases of hypothyroidism to prevent the development of *cretinism,* a syndrome involving mental retardation and aberrations in physical development.

Although there is a continual search for more widely applicable or more effective drugs, medicine has already made dramatic achievements in the biochemical treatment of organic illness.

By contrast, **psychopharmacology**—the study of the use of drugs to induce psychological effects on mental functioning, behavior, and emotional responsiveness—is a relatively new field. This form of treatment involves administration of drugs known to affect the central nervous system in such a way that changes in behavior result from biochemical action in the central nervous system. Although treatment relies on biochemical action, the intention is one of behavioral change. For this reason, this form of treatment is also referred to as **behavioral pharmacology** (Thompson, Pickens, & Meisch, 1970).

The specific application of psychopharmacological treatment techniques to the problems of special children began with research by Charles Bradley (1937). Bradley was the first to treat "specific educational disabilities" and hyperactive behavior in schoolchildren with a stimulant drug (Benzedrine). As a result of drug administration, Bradley noted overall improvement in the children's mood, activity level, and educational achievement. In a few instances, negative effects were noted in the form of increased irritability or fearfulness.

Psychopharmacological approaches to treatment have increased dramatically in the decades since Bradley's pioneering research. In addition to continued investigation of stimulant drugs to alter behavior levels and mood, investigators have also studied the use of (a) amphetamines for hyperactivity (Connors, 1972b); (b) the major tranquilizers for aggression in autistic and schizophrenic children (Eisenberg, 1968); (c) antidepressants for bed-wetting (Halverstadt, 1976; Henderson, 1976); and (d) antidepressants for symptoms of depression (Frommer, 1967). Various medications have been administered to learning-disabled children, emotionally disturbed youngsters, the mentally retarded, and those with behavior disorders; and the effects of medication on activity level, attention, mood, and motor performance have been studied extensively (Sprague & Werry, 1974). Exhibit 4.1 summarizes several of the major psychopharmacological agents commonly used with children.

The implications of this body of research and clinical experience are not yet clear. For example, though some researchers claim that drug therapy is effective with 70 percent of hyperactive children (White, 1975), others raise serious questions regarding the efficacy or ethics of using medication to control children's behavior (Connors, 1972a; Offir, 1974; Sprague & Werry, 1974; Walker, 1974).

EXHIBIT 4.1

SOME DRUGS USED IN THE TREATMENT OF SPECIAL CHILDREN

Classification	Generic Name	Trade Name	Used to Treat	Effects
Stimulant	dextroamphetamine amphetamine methylphenidate	Dexedrine Benzedrine Ritalin	Hyperkinetic disorders, specific learning disabilities, and behavior disorders.	Effective in reducing hyperactivity, impulsiveness, destructiveness; increases frustration tolerance; stabilizes mood; occasionally reduces fear and depression in neurotic children. Clearest results in treating extreme hyperactivity and hypoactivity.
Antianxiety (tranquilizer)	chlordiazepoxide diazepam	Librium Valium	Personality problems in which anxiety and fearfulness are prominent features.	Effectiveness variable in reducing anxiety or stabilizing mood. Research results mixed; may produce hyperexcitement.
Antipsychotic	chlorpromazine haloperidol trifluoperazine	Thorazine Haldol Stelazine	Schizophrenia and psychoses in which agitation and aggression are prominent; autism.	Effects variable, though research suggests some usefulness in reducing agitation and aggression. May stimulate alertness in severely disturbed children; however, alertness and learning may be impaired in less disturbed children.
Anticonvulsant	phenobarbitol	Phenobarbitol	Convulsive seizure disorders.	Effective in reducing seizure frequency.
Antidepressant	imipramine	Tofranil	Nocturnal enuresis in young children; depressive symptoms in adolescents.	Reduces frequency of bedwetting in some children.

It is difficult to estimate the frequency or effectiveness of drug therapy for behavior problems in children, but the hope that a given medication can cure or control a child's symptoms is widespread among anxious parents and busy physicians. Thus, despite lack of clear research results, drugs continue to be used extensively with periodic cautions appearing in the popular and professional literature.

Common misconceptions regarding the potential benefits and dangers of drugs have prompted a number of investigators to offer guidelines and suggestions for effective drug usage (Connors, 1969; Eisenberg, 1968). These typically include regular monitoring of dosage levels, primary effects on target behaviors, and side effects; frequent consultation with parents and teachers regarding their observations; reduction or elimination of medication as early as possible; and simultaneous educational/psychological programming to amplify or maintain behavior change subsequent to cessation of drug therapy.

As increasing research and sophistication produce more specific and effective chemical agents, it is likely that drug therapy will be seen as one of several treatment alternatives for the problems of special children in conjunction with educational and psychological intervention procedures, and with increasing specificity and precision.

Surgery

In the past few decades, remarkable advances have taken place in the use of surgical procedures with children. In the early 1900s, there was no formal pediatric surgical training available anywhere in the United States, and prior to this time surgical treatment of the special child did not really exist in this country (Hertzler & Mirza, 1974). By the late 1930s, however, pediatricians and surgeons began to recognize the need and possibility of surgery for a number of childhood disabilities and diseases. The surgical treatment of children is now so complex and extensive that nearly half of the admissions to children's hospitals are for surgical treatment (Owings, 1973), and subspecialties within the field of pediatric surgery have emerged (Wilkinson, 1975).

Extraordinary developments in the surgical treatment of children have made it possible to prevent many deaths. Improved procedures have also made it possible to correct or improve many birth defects that are not life-threatening but are seriously handicapping. For example, in *pyloric stenosis,* a narrowing of the sphincter muscles in the stomach that prevents digestion, surgical intervention has reduced mortality rates from 75 percent early in the century to less than 1 percent today (Dennison, 1974).

Since surgical treatment has effectively prolonged the lives of many children subject to birth defects, a large number of these children eventually enter into continuous health and special education services, increasing the need for other forms of specialized intervention. Again using pyloric stenosis as an example, recent research has shown that children treated for this disorder in infancy may later develop problems in learning and general adjustment (Klein, Forbes, & Nader, 1975). The effects of infantile health problems may have widespread effects on development that only become noticeable later as the child fails to accomplish developmental tasks.

While we cannot undertake a general survey of surgical treatment of special children, several areas of surgical intervention are particularly important for us to recognize, since they often occur in the medical histories of special children. These include *reconstructive surgery,* for the surgical repair of physical abnormalities such as cleft lip and/or cleft palate; *neurosurgery* for disabling conditions of the brain and spinal cord; and *orthopedic surgery* for problems of the skeletal system that often occur in youngsters with multiple congenital anomalies. Although many other surgical subspecialties have emerged, these are the most common forms of surgical treatment for special children.

Reconstructive surgery, neurosurgery, and orthopedic surgery typically require lengthy hospitalizations, and they often require other forms of intervention such as long-term care and management, physical therapy, occupational therapy, and speech therapy. Upon return to home and school, the child may also require psychotherapy and remedial education to assist in readjusting to normal activities.

Medical treatment constitutes a highly sophisticated form of intervention that involves a variety of specialists with unique skills. Medical intervention offers assistance in conditions where identifiable organic or physical disorders exist, and in the current state of the art and science of medicine, drug therapy and surgery are the most distinctive forms of assistance.

PSYCHOTHERAPY

Psychotherapy is the most common form of intervention for children who display emotional or behavioral problems, interpersonal conflicts, or somatic symptoms for which there is no organic cause. The intent of psychotherapy is to provide treatment for problems that are psychological in nature. **Psychotherapy** is typically defined, therefore, as the planned management of an interpersonal process intended to relieve the child's initial distress and to enhance developmental processes (Stuart, 1970). Though there are often radical differences in theoretical orientation or tactical approaches among the several dozen different approaches to psychotherapy, all focus on the use of the patient-therapist relationship as a vehicle for improving patient functioning (Patterson, 1974; Swanson, 1970).

Rather than attempting to enumerate the sometimes subtle distinctions among the various therapeutic strategies, we will look at some generally accepted notions regarding child psychotherapy and examine the major modalities commonly employed. These include individual psychotherapy, family therapy, and group psychotherapy.

Individual Psychotherapy

One of the first published reports of psychotherapeutic interaction with a child was Jean Itard's work with Victor, the Wild Boy of Aveyron (discussed in Chapter 1). Itard's work, while educational in intent, can also be viewed as psychotherapy because it involved planned interactions with Victor to promote a strong relationship between child and "therapist" that might bring Victor closer to normal functioning.

Subsequent to Itard's work with Victor early in the nineteenth century, little further development took place in the individual psychotherapy of children for the next hundred years. Then, in 1909, Sigmund Freud published his famous study of "Little Hans," a 5-year-old boy who had developed a phobia for horses. Though Freud's report of the case of Hans is an excellent example of psychoanalytic reasoning in the study of childhood psychological disorder, it is hardly an example of psychotherapy as currently understood, since Hans was actually treated by his own father who consulted with Freud by letter.

The most significant advances in the psychodynamic treatment of the individual child were provided by Melanie Klein (1932) and Anna Freud (1946), both of whom recognized the importance and meaning of a child's play as a context for psychotherapeutic interaction. Traditional forms of psychotherapy had relied heavily on verbal transactions between therapist and patient, but in working with children, therapists soon discovered that verbal treatment was often ineffective. The recognition that children communicate through play in much the same way that adults communicate through words made it possible to develop play therapy as a treatment technique unique to work with special children.

Play therapy, therefore, is a form of psychotherapy in which the child's play is considered to be the medium by which the therapist helps the child resolve inner conflicts and tensions. Most therapists agree that the key to effective play therapy is the capacity of the therapist to respond sensitively to the child's unspoken needs and feelings (e.g., Harrison, 1975; Swanson, 1970). In play therapy the physical setting enhances the child's capacity to communicate through fantasy and to express subjectively experienced conflicts and anxieties. Typically, a playroom is the setting for treatment; it is furnished with a variety of toys including puppets, human and animal dolls, paints and paper, modeling clay, and games. At times a water table and sandbox may be included. These play materials are used in such a way that the therapist encourages self-expression and self-exploration while attempting to help the child better understand feelings, fears, and problems in relating to others.

Psychodynamic therapists (e.g., Bornstein, 1945; Klein, 1932; Maenchen, 1970) believe that the source of a child's problems lies in internal, unconscious conflicts that must be brought to consciousness. Therapists using *psychodynamic play therapy* rely heavily on frequent and direct interpretations of the unconscious meaning of the child's play. For example, a child engaging in angry, aggressive doll play is assumed to be expressing underlying hostility. The play behavior is interpreted to the child, and the therapist makes tentative suggestions regarding the underlying nature and object of the child's anger. In a way, the therapist says for the child those things that are too terrifying to experience or express directly and helps the child recognize that feelings are not in themselves dangerous.

A less interpretive, less directive approach to play therapy has been described by Virginia Axline (1947). In *nondirective play therapy,* the child's play is the very essence of treatment. Axline assumes that the child possesses inherent drives toward health and self-realization. For some children, external

In play therapy, this 4-year-old, provided with a "family" of dolls, is able to structure the family situation in ways that reflect his feelings about his parents and siblings and his place in the family.

pressures block this inner drive and inhibit healthy development. In nondirective play therapy, the goal of the therapist is to create conditions of warmth, empathy, and unconditional acceptance so that the child eventually feels free to engage in genuine self-exploration and self-acceptance. In the absence of environmental pressures that make acceptance by others conditional on the child being a certain kind of person, the child can tentatively explore real feelings and begin to understand that such feelings are legitimate and the self worthwhile for no other reason than that the child is a person.

In addition to psychodynamic play therapy and nondirective play therapy, there are also situations where a child may benefit from talking about problems. Whereas play therapy is often appropriate for children between the ages of 3 and 10, it is sometimes the case that a bright and articulate child may be able to discuss feelings and problems without the use of play as an expressive medium. With older children, psychotherapy resembles more closely the verbal interaction that characterizes psychotherapy with adults.

Individual psychotherapy with children is often a lengthy process in which child and therapist may meet once to several times a week for a few months to several years. The range of potential events that occur in treatment is as broad as in any interaction between two people and impossible to specify with any precision. The therapist must approach the treatment situation with a basic respect for and acceptance of the child patient and an ability to be comfortable with the youngster's style and level of communication. Beyond these prerequisites, the therapist must also be flexible, creative, and knowledgeable about child development and child treatment so that adult understandings may be translated into an effective therapeutic relationship with the child. A good summary of eight basic principles important to the child psychotherapist is presented in Exhibit 4.2.

Family Therapy

Child psychotherapists generally believe that the treatment of a child requires some degree of therapeutic contact with parents. When a child is being seen in individual psychotherapy, it is common practice for therapist and parents to communicate necessary information regarding the child's treatment. In these situations the therapist might well facilitate the child's progress by sharing with the parents relevant understandings of their child's behavior or by giving the parents advice about managing their child's behavior. In other circumstances, the therapist might not work with the child at all, deciding instead to work with the parents to increase their capacity to provide effective parenting for their special child. In still other situations, the parents might be seen by one therapist to work individually or jointly on personal or marital problems while the child is seen separately in psychotherapy. All of these formats for intervention can provide some degree of help for the family of a child identified as the patient.

EXHIBIT 4.2

AXLINE'S EIGHT BASIC PRINCIPLES OF PSYCHOTHERAPY WITH CHILDREN

1. The therapist must develop a warm, friendly relationship with the child, in which good rapport is established as soon as possible.

2. The therapist accepts the child exactly as he/she is.

3. The therapist establishes a feeling of permissiveness in the relationship so that the child feels free to express his/her feelings completely.

4. The therapist is alert to recognize the *feelings* the child is expressing and reflects those feelings back to the child in such a manner that he/she gains insight into his/her behavior.

5. The therapist maintains a deep respect for the child's ability to solve his/her own problems if given an opportunity to do so. The responsibility to make choices and to institute change is the child's.

6. The therapist does not attempt to direct the child's actions or conversation in any manner. The child leads the way; the therapist follows.

7. The therapist does not attempt to hurry the therapy along. It is a gradual process and is recognized as such by the therapist.

8. The therapist establishes only those limitations that are necessary to anchor the therapy to the world of reality and to make the child aware of his/her responsibility in the relationship.

From Axline (1964, pp. 93–94)

During the 1960s an additional approach began to gain wide acceptance among psychotherapists. Instead of viewing contact with the family of the special child as an important adjunct to the child's treatment, many therapists began to feel that the focus of treatment should be on the family as an on-going system of relationships and events. This approach—based on the rationale that the system of disturbed or troubled relationships needs inter-vention rather than only the individual child who is the referred patient—has become known as **family therapy.** Typically, the family therapist works with child, parents, and siblings in joint sessions. In this family context, there is no need for secondhand reports regarding interactions, since the family interacts in the presence of the therapist who can make direct observations and interventions in the patterns of relationships. Furthermore, interactions or insights prompted in the therapist's office can more readily be carried over into family interactions in real-life situations.

The prospect of developing an effective treatment program for a given family depends on many factors. For example, the availability and motivation of other family members are important elements; the extent of disturbance of the family system must be determined; and the skills of the therapist in becoming a participant-observer in the family unit must be assessed. It is important to note that family therapy is most appropriately used in situations where the child's emotional problems appear to be a function of disturbances within the family system (Graham, 1976). Under such circumstances, family therapy offers promise of enhancing total family functioning as well as the growth of individual family members.

Group Psychotherapy with Children

Still another widely used form of psychotherapy with children is the treat-ment of children in groups. The distinguishing factor in **group therapy** is the simultaneous treatment of several children, usually in the same age range, treated together in order to make use of group processes and face-to-face peer interactions as primary vehicles for change.

Group psychotherapy with children originated in the 1930s when S. R. Slavson began working with children in a format he called *activity group therapy.* Slavson's procedure was to bring together emotionally disturbed youngsters between the ages of seven and twelve and to provide them with various activities including art, crafts, and games. Slavson (1950) viewed the group as a substitute family and the therapist as a substitute parent, whose interaction with the children helped them express and resolve developmental conflicts and fears.

In recent years, group therapy with children has evolved to the extent that there are several distinguishable orientations and ways of conducting group interaction. Ginott (1961), for example, introduced a form of group play therapy in which the focus remained on the individual child as the child interacted with group and therapist. Ginott maintained that the group facili-tates the opportunity for any individual child to achieve personal gains by identifying with the therapist or other group members. Speers and Lansing (1965) organized group therapy experiences for severely disturbed preschool children who lacked adequate language, were not toilet trained, and were extremely withdrawn. Despite the severity of disturbance in these youngsters, Speers and Lansing maintained that the group experience was instrumental in helping these children develop a sense of self. Although most group therapy rationales are based on peer influence or group experiences as the essential elements of treatment, Rose (1972) has instead seen the group as an ideal setting for the implementation of behavior therapy, which we will discuss shortly. Rose has attempted to translate group processes into behavior modification concepts and to construct a group treatment experience that is based on behavior modification procedures.

Group therapy has evolved into an important mode of psychological intervention with special children. Not identified with any single theoretical orientation, it has been a flexible treatment modality that can combine various activities and potential treatment influences including play, verbal interaction, peer influence, socialization experience, modeling by the group or by the leader, mutual support, and behavior modification techniques.

Individual, family, and group psychotherapy represent major approaches to psychological treatment of children. Within these formats are a wide range of theoretical rationales and specific intervention techniques. Many of these specific approaches to treatment will be discussed in later chapters. Suffice it to say here that the effectiveness of psychotherapy with children is a hotly disputed issue (Donofrio, 1970, 1976), and it has been difficult to develop clear-cut research conclusions on its effectiveness. Nevertheless, the direct clinical experiences of helping professionals in psychology, psychiatry, social work, and education have produced a strong conviction in many that psychotherapy is an important mode of intervention for special children.

BEHAVIOR THERAPY

A discussion of behavior therapy as distinct from psychotherapy is debatable. We have chosen to do so for two reasons. First, the years since 1960 have produced a virtual explosion of clinical and research literature. Most of this literature is presented apart from traditional psychotherapy, and much of it is highly critical of the kinds of approaches discussed above. Second, behavior therapy is sufficiently distinct in origin and practice from traditional psychotherapy to warrant separate consideration. Whereas psychotherapy originated in clinics, hospitals, and consulting rooms, behavior therapy originated in psychological laboratories and makes use of behavior change technology as the basis for therapeutic intervention. Psychotherapy relies on the interpersonal skills of the therapist, while behavior therapy relies on empirically validated principles of behavior change.

Behavioral approaches to the treatment of the special child take their inspiration from carefully designed laboratory studies exploring the ways in which behavior is learned, maintained, and changed in human and animal subjects. In essence, behavior therapy is the application of research findings to the alleviation of developmental problems within the context of ongoing empirical evaluation of the effects of treatment.

The terms "behavior therapy" and "behavior modification" are sometimes distinguished, but there is ample justification for using them interchangeably (Wilson & Franks, 1975), and we will not make any distinctions in this discussion. Furthermore, we feel it is important to emphasize the fact that behavioral approaches to treatment hardly fit popular conceptions of them as rigid, narrow, and mechanistic. Contemporary behavior therapy is more aptly represented by rigorous adherence to the facts and principles revealed by empirical research than by doctrinaire adherence to any particular set of concepts (Bandura, 1975). Recognition of this fact could dispel much pointless controversy and confusion.

To repeat then, **behavior therapy** is no more nor less than the application of scientifically derived principles of experimental and social psychology to the alleviation of human problems within the context of generally accepted ethical principles. As we examine specific applications, we will see that a number of techniques have been developed for treating special children within a behavioral framework.

In behavior therapy with children, behavior is understood to be an observable and measurable response of the child. Examples of symptomatic behavior include hyperactivity, distractibility, inappropriate aggression, bedwetting, infantile speech, excessive fearfulness, and the child's reports of anxiety. Such symptomatic behaviors are assumed to result from interaction among the child's hereditary-constitutional endowment, current environmental conditions, and previous learning history. In order to eliminate inappropriate behaviors or to develop new behaviors, stimulus conditions in the environment are altered, or attempts are made to modify the child's understanding and perception of the environment. Two important approaches for producing these changes are respondent conditioning and operant conditioning.

Respondent Conditioning

The classic example of *respondent conditioning,* also known as *classical conditioning,* is Pavlov's research on the salivation response of dogs. In 1899 the Russian physiologist Ivan Pavlov began conducting a series of studies in which he demonstrated that the occurrence of a chance event in the environment could acquire the power to elicit certain behaviors. Pavlov observed that a dog would naturally salivate (*unconditioned response*) to the presentation of powdered meat (*unconditioned stimulus*). He further observed that by pairing the presentation of powdered meat with the sound of a tuning fork (*conditioned stimulus*), the dog would, after several trials, salivate (*conditioned response*) to the sound of the tuning fork alone. Pavlov's work represented a key development in modern psychology and has had profound influence on subsequent understanding of human behavior.

Watson and Rayner (1920) demonstrated that the concepts of conditioning developed by Pavlov offered a powerful explanation of human as well as animal behavior, and they showed that these concepts were useful in understanding abnormal behavior. Watson and Rayner found that an 11-month-old boy named Albert showed no initial fear when presented with a white rat. However, when the presentation of the rat was accompanied by a sudden, loud noise, Albert showed a dramatic fear response, trembling and crying. After several trials in which the loud sound (unconditioned stimulus) was paired with the presentation of the rat (conditioned stimulus), Albert acquired an intense fear of the rat alone. In essence, a neutral stimulus, the white rat, had become a conditioned stimulus eliciting a conditioned fear response. Watson and Rayner reasoned that the principles of respondent conditioning could effectively explain the development of phobic behavior. Since we are all constantly experiencing a wide variety of internal and external stimuli, it seems plausible that any of these, potentially, can assume the role of a conditioned stimulus if associated with the experience of fear.

Shortly after Watson and Rayner's work with Albert, Mary Cover Jones (1924) used the principles of respondent conditioning in treating a 3-year-old boy named Peter who was very afraid of white rabbits and also showed a generalized fear response to other white, fluffy objects (such as cotton or fur). In a well-designed and carefully controlled treatment study, Jones successfully eliminated Peter's fear of rabbits by a series of presentations of a rabbit under pleasant circumstances. Jones began by placing Peter in a room with children who liked to pet and play with a rabbit. Later, she presented the rabbit at gradually closer distances while Peter was eating and enjoying his food. After a total of 45 sessions, Peter showed a real fondness for the rabbit, and he displayed no fears of cotton, fur, or other materials that had been associated with his fear of white rabbits.

These experiments by Watson and Rayner and Jones laid a foundation for the use of respondent conditioning in the treatment of children's phobias. In contemporary behavior therapy, derivatives of this early work are important in the treatment of a wide range of emotional problems (e.g., Rudestam & Bedrosian, 1977; Wolpe, 1973).

In addition to treating intense fears, respondent conditioning procedures have proven effective with other problem behaviors. Mowrer and Mowrer (1938) developed a simple conditioning procedure for the treatment of night-time bed-wetting (*nocturnal enuresis*). The Mowrers used a pad placed on a child's bed and wired to ring a bell when the sleeping child began to urinate. The bell would awaken the child, inhibit urination, and also condition the response of sphincter contraction to inhibit further urination. The Mowrers' original study demonstrated 100 percent effectiveness on 30 children using the "bell and pad" treatment procedure, and this apparatus is still widely used in the treatment of nocturnal enuresis (Jehu, Morgan, Turner, & Jones, 1977).

Operant Conditioning

Operant conditioning, also known as *instrumental conditioning*, refers to a second set of behavioral mechanisms by which learning takes place. The pioneering research in operant conditioning was conducted by B. F. Skinner and his colleagues. Skinner (1938) reformulated Pavlov's conditioning theory, pointing out that conditioning involves more than just stimulus-response associations. In addition, Skinner noted that much human behavior occurs naturally and is spontaneously emitted to operate on the environment with specific consequences. Skinner distinguished between *respondent behavior,* which is elicited by an environmental stimulus, and *operant behavior,* which is spontaneously emitted by the organism. In a series of carefully controlled studies, Skinner demonstrated that operant behavior in rats, pigeons, and monkeys is controlled by its immediate consequences. A key concept in operant conditioning is the experimental definition of a *positive reinforcement* as any stimulus event that, when following an organism's response, increases the strength or frequency of that response. *Punishment* is any stimulus event presented consequent to a response that decreases the strength or frequency of that response. Hundreds of subsequent studies of the principles governing operant behavior have demonstrated the importance of frequency of reinforcement, timing of reinforcement, and other variables in affecting the nature of operant learning.

Research in operant conditioning has had tremendous impact on the development of educational and psychological treatment procedures, and applications have been developed for helping a number of children who are mentally retarded, physically impaired, learning disabled, or emotionally disturbed. In fact, operant conditioning techniques (summarized in Exhibit 4.3) have been ingeniously applied to so many situations that we can only provide a flavor for the kinds of treatment approaches that have been attempted.

EXHIBIT 4.3

SUMMARY CHART OF OPERANT TECHNIQUES

Positive Reinforcement
Presentation of a positive reinforcer contingent upon the occurrence of a specified response. A positive reinforcer is defined empirically as anything that increases probability, strength, or frequency of the response. E.g., praising a child for mowing the lawn.

Negative Reinforcement
Cessation of an aversive stimulus contingent upon a specified response to increase the probability, strength, or frequency of the response. E.g., allowing a child who has been "grounded" to begin seeing friends again contingent upon a polite apology for the offense being punished.

Punishment
Presentation of an aversive stimulus contingent upon a specified response to reduce the frequency of the response. As in the case of a positive reinforcer, a punisher is defined empirically by its effects on the response. E.g., scolding a child who has taken a toy from a younger brother or sister.

Extinction
Nonreinforcement of a response to reduce its frequency. E.g., completely ignoring a child whenever the youngster speaks in a "whining voice." Should normally be combined with positive reinforcement for some alternative desired behavior (such as speaking in a normal voice).

Token Reinforcement
Presentation of a symbolic positive reinforcer contingent upon a desired response. The token is later exchanged for a backup reinforcer such as money, food, or privileges. E.g., allowing a youngster to paste a star on a daily chart each day the youngster remembers to empty the trash; at the end of a week or month, etc., the youngster exchanges the filled chart for a trip to the zoo.

Response Cost
A fine imposed contingent upon a specified response. Used in conjunction with a token economy. E.g., in addition to earning stars for a specified behavior, the youngster may lose a star on his/her chart every time he/she fights with a sibling.

Time-out from Positive Reinforcement
The child is removed from *all* positive reinforcers contingent upon a specified response. E.g., a child is told to sit on a chair away from the rest of the family whenever he/she uses foul language.

Differential Reinforcement of Other Behavior (DRO)

A specified response is reduced in frequency by consistent, positive reinforcement of alternative responses incompatible with the undesired response. E.g., shouting and speaking quietly are incompatible, and a parent reinforces the child whenever a quiet voice is used in speaking.

Behavior Shaping

A novel response is developed by careful, immediate reinforcement of successive approximations to the novel response beginning with some behavior already in the child's repertoire. E.g., a youngster may be taught to make a bed by first reinforcing straightening of sheets, then straightening of sheets and blankets, then correct placement of pillows, etc.

Modeling

Imitation of a desired behavior first emitted by a model is reinforced. E.g., Mary, age 5, observes Johnny, age 10, washing dishes. Mary asks if she may help wash dishes and is praised by her parents for helping.

Contingency Contracting

An explicit, mutual contract is developed in which each party agrees to perform (or refrain from performing) specified behaviors in order to obtain desired positive reinforcement from the other party. E.g., mother and Johnny agree that regular bathing is important, and if Johnny bathes regularly for one week, mother will help him complete a club project.

In an early study, Hingtgen, Sanders, and DeMyer (1965) sought to increase the capacity of six children diagnosed as severely schizophrenic to engage in cooperative behavior. They taught these youngsters to press a lever to obtain a candy reinforcer. When the children had learned this response, the candy reward was then made contingent on each child's cooperation with another child in alternating lever pressing. This simple operant procedure increased the frequency of physical contact between the children and enabled them to develop more appropriate social responses to each other. The use of positive reinforcement techniques to develop or increase behaviors is currently an extremely important technique in the treatment of severe emotional disturbance (Rimland, 1974; Stevens-Long & Lovaas, 1974), mental retardation (Trace, Cuvo, & Criswell, 1977), delinquent behavior (Hobbs & Holt, 1976), and many other problems of special children.

Operant methodology can also be used to decrease undesirable behaviors. An operant principle often used in such situations is called *extinction* (nonreinforcement of the maladaptive target behavior). Williams (1959), for example, taught parents to extinguish severe tantrum behavior in a 20-month-old child by helping them stop reinforcing tantrums through excessive attention. A rule of thumb often presented to parents and teachers in eliminating undesirable behavior is to "ignore or praise." That is, when undesirable behavior occurs, ignoring it is often an effective approach to eliminating it.

An alternative approach to eliminating a behavior is to reward incompatible behavior. Patterson (1965) eliminated hyperactive and destructive classroom behavior in a 9-year-old boy by reinforcing the child for remaining in his seat and being quiet and nondisruptive. Patterson did so by mounting a small light and counter on the child's desk. The light was flashed after predetermined intervals of quiet sitting, and the light signal was subsequently backed up with a candy reward presented by the teacher. Intervals between reinforcements were gradually increased to lengthen intervals of quiet, in-seat behavior.

In addition to their use with individuals, operant procedures have been used effectively in the management of groups of children in settings ranging from special classrooms to residential institutions and hospitals. One approach to the management of group behavior is the *token economy,* a system in which symbolic rewards (*tokens*) given for predetermined appropriate behavior can be exchanged for tangible reinforcers such as food, money, toys, privileges, or play time.

One of the first systematic accounts of a token economy was presented by Ayllon and Azrin (1968) who developed a system for increasing appropriate patient behavior in a mental hospital. Patients earned tokens for a variety of behaviors including good personal hygiene, appropriate table manners, and cooperation. Tokens were exchanged for commodities or privileges important to each patient.

These boys, participants in Project Re-Ed—a program designed to reeducate and foster more adaptive behavior on the part of "emotionally disturbed" or "socially discordant" children—are seen here in a group therapy session with their counselors. The program relies on a number of behavioral techniques in pursuing its goals.

The use of a token economy in working with special children has been effectively demonstrated by work at Achievement Place, a cottage-style treatment facility for predelinquent and delinquent youngsters referred by a juvenile court (Bailey, Wolf, & Phillips, 1970; Phillips, 1968). The token economy at Achievement Place was designed to reward relevant social and academic behaviors and to eliminate antisocial and undesirable behaviors. The system is based on a reinforcement strategy of earning points that can be used to purchase privileges such as watching television. At the same time, inappropriate behaviors are punished through a "response-cost" procedure involving a system of fines. The effectiveness of the Achievement Place model has prompted replications in other places (e.g., Liberman, Ferris, Salgado, & Salgado, 1975).

Another significant application of operant conditioning principles is in the area of parent training. In Chapter 14 we will review many of the challenges faced by parents of special children and specific approaches parents can employ in helping their children, but it is worth noting in this context that behavior modification techniques can be very important tools in helping parents effectively manage problem behaviors in children. In an early study, Wahler, Winkel, Peterson, and Morrison (1965) studied the behavior of parents whose children displayed a variety of problems. The experimenters observed mothers interacting with their children and scored the frequency of deviant behavior displayed by the children. It became apparent that much of the children's undesirable behavior was being reinforced inadvertently by the mothers who attended to such behavior. At the same time, those mothers seemed to pay little attention to constructive behavior. The experimenters developed a treatment program to reverse these contingencies. Green and red lights were placed in the treatment room where mother and child interacted. Mothers were instructed to pay attention to their children when the green light was on, thereby reinforcing the children with attention. When the red light was on, the children were to be ignored. Using these signals, the experimenters trained mothers to reinforce appropriate behavior and to extinguish inappropriate behavior. In less than half an hour, deviant behavior dropped almost to zero frequency while appropriate behavior increased in frequency. A simple training program proved to be a powerful tool in helping parents cope effectively with behavior problems in their children.

Behavior therapy offers a very promising approach to the treatment of those children who can benefit from environmental modification. The behavior therapies are frequently contrasted with other approaches—favorably or unfavorably—but such comparisons are becoming increasingly unnecessary. In many respects, the behavior therapies now offer a supplement or alternate to both drug therapy and psychotherapy. The practicality of this approach will likely ensure an ever widening application to the problems of special childhood.

EDUCATIONAL INTERVENTION

In a recent survey of directors of state special education programs, 28 of the 50 respondents agreed that "the major controversy in special education today involves labeling handicapped children and the related problem of where to place them" (State-Federal Information Clearinghouse, 1973, p. 4). The mandate of P.L. 94-142 to provide appropriate education for all children has prompted educators to describe various categories of special children and to organize educational programs that are responsive to their special needs.

Special education is a form of intervention that focuses on the appropriate placement of the child within the educational system and constructs placements that are helpful to the special child. However, the special skill of the educator is the ability to coordinate and facilitate learning through sensitive utilization of curricula and materials suited to the needs of the individual child. Special education is designed to provide (a) specific appropriate facilities, (b) specialized methods and materials, and (c) specially trained teachers for children with a wide range of developmental problems (Reger, Schroeder, & Uschold, 1968).

For the most part special education has been a means of providing a useful educational experience for youngsters who have been medically or psychologically defined as different. These include mentally retarded, emotionally disturbed, physically or orthopedically impaired, blind or partially sighted, deaf or hard-of-hearing, speech deficient, and gifted children. However, the best method of providing appropriate educational experiences for special children has been the subject of ongoing controversy, and educators are still debating the relative merits of placing special children in special environments or educating them in regular classroom settings. Because this is a critical issue, here we will discuss educational intervention in terms of the options of special placement and mainstreaming. Then, in Chapter 15, we will present in more detail both the issues involved in and the educational techniques for providing special children with the most beneficial but least restrictive educational environment.

Special Placement

School systems have traditionally educated children by organizing more or less homogeneous classes based on some defined characteristic such as age or ability. The concept of **tracking** emerged in education as a means of grouping children with similar educational needs into homogeneous classes. The most familiar example of this procedure is the conventional division of "fast track" and "slow track" students based on reading or arithmetic ability. In a real sense, special placement of the impaired child is simply another method of tracking students into homogeneous groups. It is this principle of homogeneous grouping that has produced special schools for the physically disabled, special classes for the educable or trainable retarded, and special classes for the behaviorally or emotionally disturbed.

The special school
Special schools for handicapped children include both residential institutions and day schools. In the **residential school,** a child is separated from family—and frequently from community—and is placed institutionally with other children who have similar problems requiring specific services from trained

staff. A residential school for the deaf was established in Connecticut in 1817, and over the years residential schools have been founded for children with various types of handicap or exceptionality. The well-known Project Re-ED, for example, consists of a series of residential schools for emotionally disturbed children in which innovative concepts of education are implemented by trained teacher/therapists (Hobbs, 1966). The goal of Project Re-ED is to restructure the disturbed child's attitude toward education by providing an intensive treatment experience of some six-months' duration. Other types of residential schools involve long-term placement for the child who needs ongoing care.

An alternative to the residential school was provided by day schools, which began as early as 1871 with the establishment of a day school for deaf children in Boston. The **day school** has the merit of keeping the child in the family and community while still providing a core of specially trained teachers and professionals to guide the child's education and development. In most urban communities, day schools provide therapeutic educational services for a variety of children, ranging from those who have specific impairments such as cerebral palsy to those who exhibit severe emotional disturbance.

A relatively recent innovation in day schools is the "noncategorial" therapeutic preschool (Cook, 1966). This type of day school is operated by a child clinic or hospital; it does not categorize or label children but rather provides programs for children based on their level of social development. Such schools clearly have the advantage of drawing on the institution's entire staff, including clinical teachers, psychologists, psychiatrists, pediatricians, and physical and occupational therapists. However, such day programs are usually quite limited in the number of youngsters they can serve; most clinic or hospital schools provide educational treatment services for no more than 25 or 30 children at a time. Private day schools are also limited in this respect and are very expensive as well, so that there is an obvious and pressing need for larger, publicly-funded day school programs administered by regular school systems.

The special class

An alternative to both the residential school and the day school is the special class in the normal public school, sometimes described as the **self-contained classroom.** Any classroom that brings together children with similar disabilities under the direction of specially trained teachers so that the child's total educational needs are provided in the class by the teacher is both a self-contained classroom and a special class. The special class constitutes placement for the child outside the normal school structure with the intention of providing therapeutic education that is responsive to the child's needs and level of functioning.

Shortages of funding and personnel frequently make it impossible for every school to have special, self-contained classrooms, so special children are often transported to schools distant from their home neighborhoods. However, within a given urban school district, provisions have now often been made for special classrooms for mentally retarded, learning disabled, emotionally disturbed, blind, deaf, physically handicapped, and gifted children.

The residential school, day school, and special class are the major types of educational placement for the special child. It is important to remember that special placement, despite its extensive history and good intentions, frequently comes under attack by educators and by the general public as well. Critics maintain that special placement dramatizes the nature of a child's problems, prevents normal developmental experiences, isolates the child from interactions with normal children, and impairs the development of a healthy self-concept. Unfortunately, clear research evidence either to support or refute such criticisms is not yet available.

Mainstream Education

The concept of **mainstreaming** refers to provision of educational programs for the special child while keeping him/her in a regular classroom setting. Advocates of mainstreaming seek to normalize the educational treatment of the special child by bringing treatment perspectives and services to the child in the regular classroom situation—without removing the child from important social contacts and experiences.

Mainstreaming has been a controversial issue for some years, but recently it has received increased support. Meeting the needs of special children in the regular classroom, of course, creates a variety of demands on the child, the teacher, and other children in the class, and on the resources for professional care within the school system. Despite these issues, several alternatives to full-time placement of a child in a special school or special class have become matters of conventional practice. Foremost among these options are (a) the resource room, (b) the itinerant teacher, and (c) the classroom consultant.

The resource room

The resource room provides an opportunity to provide special services while mainstreaming the majority of the child's educational program. The resource room permits maintenance of the child in the regular classroom for most of the school day while also enabling the child to spend some part of the educational process in a special "resource" class structured to meet his/her special needs. This approach has become especially prevalent for youngsters who display specific learning disability or mild emotional/behavioral problems.

The itinerant teacher

The itinerant teacher is a specially trained educator who provides individual assistance to a child for specific periods during the normal school schedule. Itinerant teaching is, in effect, a form of tutoring by a highly trained specialist who is familiar with the individual child and the specific techniques that can help the child develop most effectively. For example, a gifted youngster might be given special tutoring to enrich the curriculum and challenge the youngster's abilities by an itinerant teacher who has been trained in educating unusually talented children. In addition to the special educator who serves as an itinerant teacher, school systems may employ a number of itinerant professionals, including speech and language therapists, reading specialists, counseling psychologists, and social workers.

The classroom consultant

A third approach that can help maintain the special child in the regular classroom is the use of clinical professionals as consultants to teachers and schools regarding the educational management of the special child. The psychiatric consultant, for example, may provide sufficient assistance to a teacher regarding understanding and management that an emotionally disturbed child will be able to remain in a regular classroom setting. Or teacher and psychologist might consult in the development of behavior modification procedures to reduce disruptiveness in a predelinquent youngster. Stennis (1973) saw the functions of the classroom consultant as: (a) the service role of diagnostician, (b) the administrative role of program development, (c) the preventive role of teacher-educator, and (d) the research role of developing individualized instruction techniques. Organized professional consultation can supplement the skills of educational personnel so that the particular needs of the special child can be met more adequately.

These approaches to mainstream education are not mutually exclusive and can often be used most effectively in conjunction with each other. Regardless of format, however, mainstream education demands the individualized education of the child. In this sense, advocates of mainstreaming are also philosophical supporters of individualized instruction as central to educational technology. However, the question of whether individualized instruction for the special child can best be accomplished by mainstreaming or special placement remains unresolved.

Reading specialists can provide individualized tutoring for specific periods during the normal school schedule.

Studies comparing special placement and mainstreaming have produced mixed findings that do not permit easy conclusions (Barker-Lunn, 1970; Blackman & Heintz, 1966; Dahllöf, 1971; Findley & Bryan, 1971). Mainstream advocates argue that assignment of a child to a special class is simply an administrative action rather than a responsive form of educational intervention. Advocates of special placement maintain that placing a special child in a regular classroom will not in itself normalize development nor lead to academic success even with supportive services.

The controversy is further confused by the fact that some special children have no need of special educational programs, and by the unfortunate reality that special education is often not very special. Special education is clearly in a period of transition, and concepts of educational intervention are changing rapidly. The practice of mass education in the United States has brought the schools to the forefront of intervention with exceptional children, and the various approaches to educational services discussed here likely account for more hours of treatment than all other forms of therapy combined. With the heavy demands for specialized educational services always on the increase, educational programs will continue to evolve innovative strategies of intervention and treatment.

SOCIAL INTERVENTION

The network of social service and social welfare programs that currently help special children is far removed from colonial practices of selling orphaned or indigent children at public auction to families willing to support them. Social work has become one of the key components of the helping process, and caseworkers are often the special child's major source of assistance.

The social services provided by caseworkers range from helping needy families obtain necessary financial assistance from public agencies to counseling regarding the management of life circumstances surrounding medical disabilities. The historical role of the **social worker** has been one of helping identified clients receive assistance from relevant social institutions; today, many social workers are also trained in counseling and psychotherapy. However, our discussion will focus on an aspect unique to social work: intervention in the social placement of special children.

Although the prevailing philosophy in social work and related professions emphasizes the maintenance of children in their families, situations sometimes arise where it is necessary for the well-being of the child or community to place a youngster in a special environment. Those forms of intervention that involve the placement of the child in a special environment will here be called *social intervention*. This form of intervention stems from the recognition that certain circumstances arise that require alteration of the child's social environment. The movement of a child from family of origin to an alternative social placement may be necessary for several reasons and may take place in several ways. A delinquent youngster may require placement in a correctional institution; a child who has lost natural parents through death, abandonment, or their inability to parent may need placement in a foster home or orphanage;

a rejected or disturbed child may need the support of a residential milieu. Our discussion will focus on two of these alternatives: *foster placement* (placement with a family other than the natural family) and *residential placement* (placement in an institution).

Foster Placement

In terms of our considerations, the most common situations that might require foster placement are such cases as children with birth defects who are not wanted by natural parents, emotionally disturbed children who must be separated from inadequate or emotionally disturbed parents, and children who have been battered or neglected by their natural parents. The need for child placement arises when a family has been unsuccessful in providing an adequate environment to care for a child's physical or psychological needs. As a form of intervention, foster placement manipulates the external social environment to protect the child's physical growth and emotional development.

Although placement with a foster family historically provided a means of caring for a child's material and physical needs, the child development professions have become increasingly aware of the subtle influences of the caretaker-child relationship in promoting the child's physical, social, and emotional well-being. Goldstein, Freud, and Solnit (1973) have argued forcefully that all child placements must be based both in principle and in the law on the child's right to consistent and adequate parenting as well as physical care. In developing a theoretical basis for legal considerations in child placement, Goldstein et al. prepared a series of definitions that could serve as a basis for legal decision-making regarding child placements. Among the most important of these definitions are the concepts of the *wanted child* and the *psychological parent.*

Goldstein et al. defined the wanted child as "one who receives affection and nourishment on a continuing basis from at least one adult and who feels that he or she is and continues to be valued by those who take care of him or her" (1973, p. 98). In a similar vein, they defined the psychological parent as "one who, on a continuing, day-to-day basis, through interaction, companionship, interplay, and mutuality, fulfills the child's psychological needs for a parent, as well as the child's physical needs" (1973, p. 98).

As a form of intervention with the special child, then, foster placement is intended to provide for the child's best developmental interests by establishing and encouraging a parent-child affinity. Except in temporary emergencies, provident care of the special child recognizes the need for permanency in the parenting of a youngster. The wanted child-psychological parent relationship could well form the basis of optimal use of foster placement interventions.

Residential Placement

In recent years there has been a movement away from large, state-supported custodial institutions where children are placed because of delinquency, intellectual retardation, physical disability, or emotional disturbance. Critics of institutionalization have argued that institutions provide little genuine treatment and are merely a means of removing special children from society (Braginsky & Braginsky, 1969, 1971). Newer approaches to residential treatment have sought to establish a substitute for the family experience in smaller, more personal settings, an approach termed "milieu therapy."

Milieu therapy is a form of residential treatment that involves careful planning of the physical and social environment. The term "milieu" is actually synonymous with "environment" but is reserved almost exclusively for the environment of the residential setting. In one of the first thorough reviews of milieu therapy with emotionally disturbed patients, Cumming and Cumming (1962) defined milieu therapy as "the scientific manipulation of the environment aimed at producing changes in the personality of the patient" (p. 5). Ideally, the therapeutic milieu should be so designed that every aspect of the environment contributes toward the development of the patient: physical setting, daily routines, personnel should all contribute to improvement in the child's functioning. Depending on the nature of the child's problems, the milieu approach is an important alternative to foster placement.

Residential placement, of course, involves many different kinds of facilities, including residential schools for the deaf or the blind and residential treatment agencies for the emotionally disturbed. The placement of the delinquent adolescent in a correctional institution is a form of residential placement, as is the psychiatric hospitalization of the psychotic child. Placement of profoundly retarded children in institutions that provide custodial care is still another form of residential placement. In each of these cases, the reasons for placement are quite different, and the nature of the intervention offered within the institution will differ considerably from case to case. Residential placement, in its many forms, is a necessary type of intervention for many different types of special children.

The Lambs—a residential setting in Libertyville, Illinois, for the mentally retarded—provides work/training programs through which the mentally retarded can find meaning in their lives through productive jobs and learning experiences. In one such program, money management skills are taught to enable individuals, such as Marc shown here, the opportunity to directly serve customers at the register.

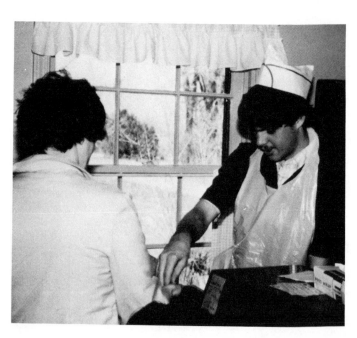

Helping the special child is a complex and demanding process. As we have seen, intervention in the life of the special child may require the skills of a number of helping agents in an ongoing, extensive attempt to maximize the child's developmental potential. Nevertheless, the time, the effort, the expense involved in these interventions are not privileges of special children, nor are they charitable options on the part of our society. On the contrary, adequate intervention and help is the right of every special child, and it is our obligation to provide this help. In the following chapters, specific groups of special children will be considered, and the treatment aspects for each of these populations will be considered in greater detail.

SUMMARY

1. The helping process is described in terms of intervention, therapy, management and care, rehabilitation, remediation, and special education.
2. The major forms of medical intervention are medication and surgical procedures.
3. Psychotherapy is the planned management of an interpersonal process intended to relieve the child's initial distress and to enhance developmental processes.
4. Psychotherapy with children includes individual psychotherapy (both verbal and play therapy), family psychotherapy, and group psychotherapy.
5. Behavior therapy is the application of scientifically derived principles of experimental and social psychology to the alleviation of human problems.
6. Behavior therapies make use of a wide variety of reinforcement or conditioning procedures.
7. Special education is designed to provide specific appropriate facilities, specialized methods and materials, and specially trained teachers for children with a wide range of developmental problems.
8. Special education includes both special placement and mainstream education.
9. Those forms of intervention that involve the manipulation of the child's home environment are called social intervention.
10. The concept of the wanted child is a critical aspect in foster placement, whereas milieu therapy is a key factor in residential placement.
11. The major forms of intervention available to the special child include medical intervention, psychotherapy, behavior therapy, educational intervention or special education, and social intervention or placement.

PART TWO

Children with Sensory, Motor, and Physical Differences

CHAPTER FIVE

Children with Hearing and Speech Disabilities

Be of good cheer. Do not think of today's failures, but of the success that may come tomorrow. You have set yourselves a difficult task, but you will succeed if you persevere; and you will find a joy in overcoming obstacles—a delight in climbing rugged paths, which you would perhaps never know if you did not sometime slip backward—if the road was always smooth and pleasant. Remember, no effort that we make to attain something beautiful is ever lost. Sometime, somewhere, somehow we shall find that which we seek. We shall speak, yes, and sing, too, as God intended we should speak and sing.

Helen Keller (1896)

AN INTRODUCTION TO DISABILITIES AND HANDICAPS

Children who are born with a disability in hearing or speech—or who acquire such a disability during the course of development—are invariably required to cope with much more than the direct effects of the disability itself. Impaired hearing creates tremendous complications in a child's ability to comprehend many physical and interpersonal aspects of the world; yet perhaps even more problematic are potential indirect effects: being viewed by parents or teachers as slow, being unable to grasp schoolwork that is presented without recognition of an impairment, being viewed by peers as aloof, unfriendly, different. Similarly, impaired speech limits a child's ability to communicate needs and feelings in a clear and easy manner; yet more difficult to manage are the indirect effects in the form of difficult interactions with others who do not understand what the child is saying or who poke fun at readily detected speech problems.

Every child with a disability in speech or hearing must cope not only with the disability itself, but also with the potentially handicapping circumstances created by the disability. This distinction between disability and handicap is an important key to understanding all special children. A **disability,** or **impairment,** is a defect in physical makeup or functioning that can be specified and described objectively. A **handicap,** by contrast, is a potential limitation in functioning that may arise when obstacles imposed by physical impairment interfere with optimal development. A disability inevitably produces complications in the development of the special child, but it is only when these complications limit the child's development that we can view the individual as handicapped. In some respects the distinction is a subtle one, and yet we can perhaps understand it more clearly when we think of the deaf person who has successfully coped with a disability only to have others behave in a patronizing manner or assume the presence of limitations, other than deafness, that do not exist.

Throughout this and the next several chapters we will maintain the distinction between *disability* or *impairment* as an objective condition and *handicap* as an obstacle to personal development. Many individuals with physical disabilities dislike the term *handicap* because they feel it is discriminatory or because they do not experience themselves as being any more handicapped than individuals without significant disabilities. For many the term *impairment* is preferred since it seems less value-laden.

Our objective in this chapter is to review basic knowledge regarding hearing and speech disabilities. In so doing, we will also develop a format for studying the problems of special children that will be used in subsequent chapters of the book. Beginning with a technical definition of a specific disability, we will proceed to look at *incidence of the disorder, causal factors, clinical approaches to diagnosis and identification, developmental consequences, and approaches to intervention.* Not all of the problems of special children fit neatly into this organizational format, and at times we will depart from it as necessary. However, it will be helpful to you in your study of special children to keep in mind these basic questions: (a) What is the nature of the disability? (b) How often does it occur? (c) What factors cause the problem? (d) How is it manifested? (e) How does it affect development? (f) What are the best available approaches to intervention?

CHILDREN WITH HEARING DISABILITIES

The type and intensity of problems experienced by hearing-impaired children are very much a function of the severity of the hearing loss and the time of its occurrence. Children with less severe hearing loss who are identified and treated early may be subject to minimal disability and little or no sense of handicap. On the other hand, children who are born deaf typically require special help both educationally and psychologically, since serious hearing impairment poses unique problems in a child's interactions with others.

In normal development the acquisition of language occurs spontaneously and almost effortlessly, but the child with a serious hearing impairment must overcome severe obstacles in order to master even the rudiments of communication. Indeed, the extent to which human communication is a function of sound and spoken words really becomes clear only as we observe the struggles of a hearing-impaired child learning to speak. Without early identification and intervention, children with severe hearing impairments may be subject to many handicaps, including inability to realize intellectual potential, problems in personal and social adjustment, and inability to participate in normal developmental experiences. Such youngsters are often incorrectly diagnosed as mentally retarded, emotionally disturbed, psychotic, or autistic.

Different but equally important issues arise for children with less severe hearing impairments. These youngsters frequently remain unidentified and may well experience educational and social problems precisely because the hearing impairment is not identified or understood. It is not unusual, for example, for a child with a relatively mild hearing loss to remain undiagnosed throughout the early school years. As problems in development come to the attention of teachers and school personnel, such a child may be informally labeled as a "slow learner," a "behavior problem," a "learning-disabled" child, or even less benignly, as "stubborn" or "lazy." These labels are applied because the unidentified hearing disability creates difficulties in the child's abilities to adjust to educational and social demands that are less problematic for normally developing children.

Children with hearing disabilities typically show no physical signs of impairment even though the consequences of the impairment may be quite extensive. Educationally, hearing-impaired children may require special accommodations so that they are not handicapped in a learning environment designed for normal-hearing children. Accommodations might include special seating arrangements close to the teacher or extra planning on the part of the teacher to ensure that the child has an opportunity to augment hearing with information from other sensory channels. On a social level, the hearing-impaired child will encounter more difficulty than others in communicating or may even be stigmatized because of the need for a hearing aid. Such experiences, in turn, can affect the child's developing self-concept and induce a sense of social handicap.

Any degree of hearing loss can pose problems in the child's development. However, recent advances in the technology of hearing aids, along with ongoing developments in the education of hearing-impaired children, have minimized many potential developmental difficulties. Such is not the case with children who are born deaf. For deaf children the developmental consequences of hearing disability are significant and pervasive, and the major focus of our discussion will be on children who are born with profound and irreversible hearing impairment.

DEFINITION AND CLASSIFICATION OF HEARING DISABILITIES

There are two major approaches to the definition and classification of hearing loss: (a) degree or severity of loss and (b) physiological site of the loss. The first of these approaches recognizes the importance of the degree of impairment and its interference with normal hearing. The **decibel (dB),** a unit for measuring the loudness of perceived intensity of a sound, is used as a means of classifying the degree of functional hearing. The range of human hearing extends from 1 to 130 decibels. Sounds louder than 130 dB are experienced by the normal ear as painful, and persistent exposure to such loud sounds may damage the hearing mechanism. Exhibit 5.1 presents examples of the decibel levels of familiar sounds.

Classification According to Severity

Using the decibel as a measure of loudness, classification according to degree of hearing loss is based on the amount of hearing in the better ear and includes five categories: mild, moderate, severe, profound, and total.

EXHIBIT 5.1

**LOUDNESS OF COMMON SOUNDS
AND LEVELS OF HEARING LOSS**

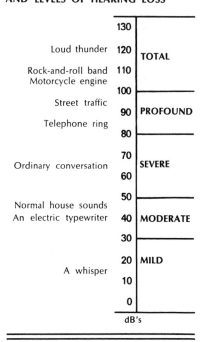

130	
Loud thunder 120	**TOTAL**
Rock-and-roll band 110	
Motorcycle engine	
100	
Street traffic	
90	**PROFOUND**
Telephone ring	
80	
70	
Ordinary conversation	**SEVERE**
60	
50	
Normal house sounds	
An electric typewriter 40	**MODERATE**
30	
20	**MILD**
A whisper	
10	
0	
dB's	

Mild hearing loss

Children with mild impairments cannot hear sounds below about 30 dB. This is in the borderline range between normal hearing and genuine impairment. A hearing aid is often advisable for children with losses in this range, and professional intervention may be important in maintaining good speech patterns since mildly hearing-impaired youngsters may not hear some consonant sounds that are typically spoken at slightly diminished volume.

Moderate hearing loss

Children with moderate hearing loss cannot hear souds below 50 dB, and amplification with a hearing aid is needed if such youngsters are to learn adequate receptive and expressive language. These frequently used terms refer simply to ability to understand **(receptive language)** and to speak **(expressive language).** The expressive language, or speech, of children with moderate hearing loss shows characteristic omission of unheard consonant sounds, giving an impression of infantile articulation patterns.

Severe hearing loss

Children with severe hearing loss cannot hear sounds less than 80 dB and are unable to develop adequate receptive or expressive language without professional intervention because they simply cannot hear ordinary spoken language. Even with intervention that includes amplification, auditory training, and speech therapy, speech patterns are likely to be quite unusual because amplification cannot replicate ordinary conversational sounds.

Profound hearing loss

Children with profound hearing loss cannot hear sounds below 100 dB, and even with amplification they cannot hear ordinary language sounds accurately. Intervention by a special educator for the deaf is essential to minimize the handicapping consequences of profound impairment.

Total hearing loss

Children with total hearing loss, a condition known technically as **anacusis,** cannot hear anything more than noise-type sensations. Intervention is critical if totally deaf children are to develop any receptive or expressive language in the form of manual signs, finger spelling, speechreading, or writing.

Classification According to Site of Loss

The second major method of classifying hearing impairments is based on identification of the anatomical site responsible for interference in normal auditory functioning. Classification according to site of loss is, of course, compatible with classification based on severity. The two systems together provide a comprehensive description of the nature of the impairment. Classification according to site of hearing loss includes four categories: conductive, sensorineural, mixed, and central auditory.

Conductive hearing loss

Children with conductive hearing loss experience interference in the transmission of sounds from the auditory canal to the inner ear. A purely conductive hearing impairment usually involves malfunction of the tiny bones of the middle ear but does not involve any damage to the inner ear or the cerebral cortex. In many cases conductive hearing loss can be medically treated or surgically corrected.

Sensorineural hearing loss

Children with sensorineural hearing loss have some degree of physical damage to the auditory nerve or to the nerve endings of the inner ear. Hearing loss due to sensorineural damage usually cannot be corrected medically.

Mixed hearing loss

In some children, hearing loss may be a consequence of impairment in the conduction of sounds and of sensorineural damage. Only the conductive elements of such a hearing loss can be corrected medically.

Central auditory hearing loss

Hearing loss of this type is perhaps more appropriately referred to as dysfunction because it involves subtle neurological damage in the cerebral cortex that interferes with the perception, organization, and comprehension of sounds rather than a loss in the ability to hear sounds.

Other Factors in the Classification of Hearing Loss

In addition to identification of the severity and the site of hearing impairment, adequate diagnosis must also include a consideration of the age of onset of the impairment. A hearing disability present at birth either as a result of hereditary factors or problems during intrauterine development is referred to as a **congenital** hearing impairment. A hearing disability developed any time after birth is referred to as an **acquired** hearing impairment. Age of onset is a critical factor, since it affects the potential success of intervention efforts in minimizing developmental handicaps. Congenital hearing impairment, for example, appears inevitably to affect every aspect of communicative development from birth onward (Sanders, 1971). Acquired hearing loss occurring during the prelingual period—the early months of development prior to the appearance of language—also has devastating effects on later communication ability. The importance of impairments during the prelingual period stems from the fact that language acquisition appears to be biologically programmed as a critical period during the latter part of the first and the second years of life (Lenneberg, 1967). An impairment of hearing during this critical period may preclude adequate language development later—even with intervention. A hearing impairment acquired after the development of speech is usually less devastating to the child's overall development.

An additional factor that must be considered in the diagnosis of hearing impairment is whether the loss is **unilateral,** affecting only one ear, or **bilateral,** affecting both ears. Other factors being equal, a unilateral loss is less likely to impede normal development than a bilateral loss. Intervention approaches will vary depending on whether an impairment is classified as unilateral or bilateral.

To sum up, a complete description of a child's hearing disability includes a specification of (a) the severity of loss, (b) the site and physiological cause, (c) the age of onset, and (d) whether the impairment is unilateral or bilateral.

For both educational and social purposes, the major classifications of hearing disabilities are characteristically reduced to the **deaf** and the **hard of hearing.** The Advisory Committee on the Education of the Deaf (1971) suggested that the dividing line between the deaf and hard of hearing should be a hearing loss of 75 to 80 dB in the better ear. Although it is difficult to determine whether actual practices correspond to these recommendations, there is some evidence that the majority of public residential schools for the deaf use a hearing loss of 60 dB or greater as the criterion for definition of deafness (Hall & Talkington, 1972).

INCIDENCE AND ETIOLOGY OF HEARING DISABILITIES

Since many children with mild hearing loss remain undetected, it is difficult to determine accurately the incidence of hearing disabilities, and estimates vary widely. The National Advisory Council on Neurological Disease and Strokes (1969) estimated that there are 8.5 million persons in the United States who have hearing losses less severe than total deafness, and approximately 3 million of these are estimated to be children (Diller, 1972). Figures drawn from the Bureau of Education for the Handicapped indicate that there are 52,000 deaf children and 350,000 hard-of-hearing children under 19 years of age who are currently being served in special education programs (Hobbs, 1975), while about 500,000 hard-of-hearing children are being educated in regular classes (Northern & Downs, 1974). Incidence estimates by Proctor and Proctor (1967) indicate that one child in every 2,000 births has profound and irreversible deafness. The discrepancies in these various estimates are due largely to differences in the definitions of hearing disabilities that underlie different studies.

In addition to creating difficulties in developing accurate incidence estimates, the problem of diverse definitions also creates difficulties in sorting out the various causal factors that lead to hearing impairment. An extensive discussion of the etiology of deafness is beyond the scope of this text, but it is important to recognize that the causes of hearing disabilities are quite varied and include (a) hereditary chromosomal defects, (b) congenital malformations (birth defects), (c) perforation of the tympanic membrane as a result of injury, (d) chronic infections of the middle ear, (e) skull fractures, (f) exposure to extremely loud noises, (g) viral diseases such as rubella (German measles) during the mother's pregnancy, and (h) congenital syphilis.

In an important study of the causes of hearing impairment Vernon (1969a) examined the records of 1,468 children who entered or applied for admission to the California School for the Deaf in Riverside, California. Vernon found that the major causes of deafness in this population were hereditary factors (5.4 percent); Rh factors, that is, blood incompatibilities between mother and fetus (3.1 percent); prematurity (11.9 percent); meningitis (8.1 percent); and rubella (8.8 percent). In 32.3 percent of these cases the cause of deafness was some factor other than the five major etiologies noted above, and in 30.4 percent the examining physician was unable to identify a cause for the child's hearing disability. The fact that no specific cause of hearing impairment was identifiable in nearly a third of the cases in this study is ample evidence of the work that remains to be done in understanding hearing impairments.

DIAGNOSIS AND IDENTIFICATION OF HEARING DISABILITIES

The early identification of hearing loss is of paramount importance in helping an impaired child achieve as normal a development as possible. As the infant reaches toddlerhood and more complex behaviors develop, the handicapping effects of an impairment can become cumulative so that the child experiences increasing difficulty in attaining developmental milestones. At the same time, failure to establish certain behaviors, especially the use of functional speech, may be early clues that the child is not developing normally.

During the first year of life, deaf children vocalize and babble in a manner similar to infants with intact hearing. Developmental research by Gesell and others demonstrates that between 12 and 18 months the child who is developing normally begins to use first words. At this point, however, the vocalizations of deaf childen fail to evolve in the direction of functional speech. If there is no functional speech by the end of the second year, there is a strong possibility of hearing impairment. But diagnosis is not simple, because difficulty in language acquisition can be due to many factors, including lack of a stimulating home environment, emotional conflict, childhood autism, mental retardation, or even temporary developmental slowness. Exhibit 5.2 presents several possible signs of hearing impairment.

Assessment of Hearing Loss in Infants

Despite the importance of early identification, it is extremely difficult to develop valid and reliable tests of hearing during infancy and later preschool years. This is because adequate diagnostic procedures require, on the part of a youngster, consistency of response that can be related to the capacity being measured. In order to assess hearing capacity, we must first be sure that the child will respond to a given auditory stimulus consistently, and then we must be able to vary that stimulus in such a way that the child will make observably different responses to differences in stimuli. In practice, this means that the

EXHIBIT 5.2

POSSIBLE SIGNS OF UNDETECTED HEARING IMPAIRMENT IN SCHOOL-AGED CHILDREN

The child fails to pay attention when casually spoken to.

The child gives the wrong answers to simple questions.

The child "hears" better when watching the speaker's face.

The child is functioning below his potential ability in school.

The child often asks the speaker to repeat words or sentences.

The child has frequent earaches and running ears.

The child has frequent colds.

The child has upper respiratory infections like sinusitis and tonsilitis.

The child has allergies similar to hay fever.

The child has become a behavior problem at school and at home.

The child fails to articulate correctly certain speech sounds or omits certain consonant sounds.

The child often fails to discriminate between words with similar vowels but different consonants (e.g., mistakes "wood" for "hoot").

The child is withdrawn and does not mingle readily with classmates and neighbours.

From Duffy (1967, pp. 33–34)

child must be able to discriminate among sounds of differing intensity or tone and then be able to communicate these discriminations. With older children this presents no problems, since we can simply ask for a verbal response regarding the presence or absence or variations among sounds. The problem is much more complex with infants: they cannot follow instructions or respond verbally.

In order to assess the hearing of an infant, we must rely on the youngster's basic environmental awareness and capacity to make behavioral responses to the stimuli presented. By the age of about 5 months, infants typically have sufficient muscular control and awareness to turn their heads toward the source of a sound. These emerging capacities are a source of delight to parents, and they are also critical in the diagnostic process. In 1944 Ewing and Ewing first described the systematic use of "noisemakers" to elicit orienting responses (such as head turning) in infants; the observation of head and eye movements continues to be an effective approach to testing hearing in infants (Feinmesser & Bauberger-Tell, 1971).

The *Crib-O-Gram* (Northern & Downs, 1974) is a relatively new diagnostic instrument that refines assessment of these basic response capacities of infants. The Crib-O-Gram consists of a multiple-response recorder that monitors motor and respiratory activity. At twenty predetermined intervals during the day, a test sound is delivered to the infant, and the multiple-response recorder monitors variations in respiration and motor responses that indicate whether or not the infant heard the sound. By varying the tone and intensity of auditory stimuli while monitoring basic physiological responses, it is possible to determine what sounds an infant can hear. The Crib-O-Gram is clearly

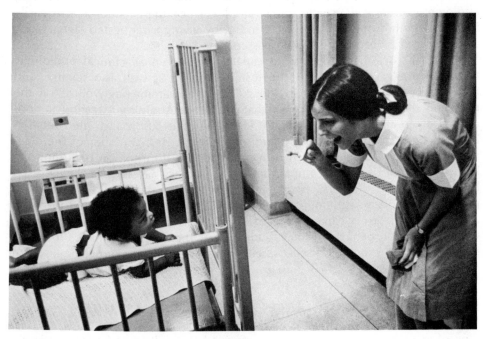

Testing to see if an infant will turn toward the source of a sound is a first step in diagnosing possible hearing loss.

an objective measure of auditory capacity and offers promise as an assessment procedure, but considerable research remains to be done to determine its accuracy and precision.

Another currently used test of hearing capacity in infants involves arousal of a sleeping infant by the administration of a loud sound. This arousal test typically involves presentation of a 90 dB sound via a loudspeaker. Tests of this type clearly are intended to screen infants with potential hearing loss in the severe to profound range.

Assessment of Hearing Loss in Young Children

In assessing 2- and 3-year-olds, the diagnostician can make use of their capacity for more complex responses than can be made by infants. Assessment of hearing in the preschooler may involve *behavioral play audiometry*. In this technique, the child is fitted with earphones and then allowed to engage in a structured play session that sustains interest and cooperation while a variety of auditory stimuli are presented through the earphones. At the same time, the diagnostician employs various conditioning procedures to establish consistent response patterns. For example, the child may be rewarded initially for placing a block in a box when he/she sees a drum being beaten; the drum is then gradually faded out of sight, and to be rewarded the child must place a block in the box when sounds presented through the earphones are heard. Since many children in this age range have limited language and communication skills, the conditioning of a behavioral response such as placing a block in a box is a means of establishing a communication system during testing.

With older preschoolers (4- and 5-year-olds) and school-age children, audiometric testing is usually much simpler, since these children can easily indicate whether or not they hear a sound by giving a requested signal, such as a nod of the head or a simple "yes" or "no."

Formal assessment of hearing capacity is known as **clinical audiologic testing.** In the case of children, this testing is an art as well as a science, and its accuracy depends heavily on the skill of the examiner as well as on the precision of technical instruments that are used. Audiologic testing is conducted by an **audiologist,** a specialist in the administration and interpretation of audiometric techniques and in auditory training. As a member of the diagnostic team, the audiologist can provide important information regarding the kind and extent of hearing impairment. The primary assessment device used by audiologists is the *audiometer,* an instrument that permits the controlled presentation and measurement of sounds. Audiometry can be used in direct assessment of hearing capacity or adapted for use in procedures such as the Crib-O-Gram or behavioral play audiometry. Increased sophistication currently permits the audiologist to screen more children at younger ages than ever before possible.

DEVELOPMENTAL CONSEQUENCES OF HEARING DISABILITIES

One of the most critical aspects of profound hearing loss and deafness is the type and degree of interference that is caused in the fulfillment of normal developmental potentials. Do the hearing impaired think differently than the hearing? Does profound hearing loss produce mental retardation? Does the deprivation of hearing produce particular types of personal or social problems? Questions of this nature raise the issue of handicap, the cumulative result of obstacles that physical impairment poses between the individual and his/her maximal functional level. The notion of handicap, therefore, involves consideration of the developmental consequences of hearing disability on such basic human abilities as language, thinking, educational achievement, and personal-social skills. There is now an extensive body of research dealing with the consequences of profound hearing loss and deafness. A brief review of this research will help clarify the relationships between hearing disability and potential developmental consequences.

Language Factors

Although we will examine speech disabilities in a later section, the interdependence of hearing and language development make it important that we consider the linguistic consequences of hearing impairment here. Diminished language skills are the outstanding problem for children with severe and profound hearing impairments (Suppes, 1975). Historically, deaf children experienced so much difficulty in the acquisition of language that the deaf came to be known as the "deaf and dumb," meaning that they could neither hear nor speak. It is only in recent years that research is beginning to reveal the complexity of the relationship between hearing and speaking.

For example, Lenneberg, Rebelsky, and Nichols (1965) found that deaf infants differ very little from hearing infants in patterns of vocalization during the first few months of life. Differences in vocalization between hearing and deaf children become more apparent during the last six months of the infant's first year, and it is clear that the inability to hear spoken language exerts a dramatic effect on language acquisition during the second year. Lenneberg (1967, 1970) has produced persuasive arguments and considerable evidence for a "critical stage hypothesis" of language learning. This hypothesis suggests that speech is a function of maturational changes in the central nervous system which occur at critical stages of infant development. If language is not acquired during these critical periods of biological programming, severe difficulties will be encountered in later attempts to acquire language. Whatever the eventual merits of the critical stage theory prove to be, such thinking has been influential in directing intervention efforts toward earlier and earlier stages of preschool development.

The poor intelligibility of the speech of those with severe and profound hearing impairments is clearly the result of a variety of factors. Even under conditions of optimally effective intervention, the spoken language of deaf children suffers from low intelligibility because of problems in sound production, articulation, voice quality, and tone discrimination, as well as problems in the actual content and structure of language (Oyers & Frankmann, 1975).

Several studies have shown that there are considerable differences between deaf and hearing persons in both the structure and content of language. For example, Brannon (1966, 1968) analyzed the verbal responses of normal-

In learning to speak, the deaf or hard-of-hearing child can use earphones to enhance any residual hearing but must rely in large part on the sight and "feel" of speech.

hearing, hard-of-hearing, and deaf children to a series of stimulus pictures. Hard-of-hearing children were found to use fewer adverbs, pronouns, and auxiliaries than hearing children. Deaf children used even fewer modifiers, prepositions, adverbs, and pronouns than the hard-of-hearing children. An analogous study of the written language of the deaf showed it to be less complex, more rigid, and more prone to grammatical errors than the language of hearing children (Power & Quigley, 1973). Quigley, Wilbur, and Montanelli (1976) studied the written language of 427 deaf students (aged 10 to 19) and 60 hearing children (aged 8 to 10). They asked the students to judge the grammatical correctness of sample sentences and found that even the youngest hearing students obtained consistently higher scores than the deaf students on indices of grammatical correctness. Throughout the literature on the language of the deaf, such findings are consistent with clinical observations regarding language difficulties in deaf children.

Conceptual Abilities and Educational Achievement

Though many congenitally deaf individuals attain considerable levels of achievement, such is more often the exception than the rule. In fact, before the advent of more sophisticated forms of communication training for the deaf, it was widely believed that deaf persons were also mentally defective. This unfortunate view was based primarily on observations of language disabilities in the deaf. As we have seen, however, language deficiencies are more likely due to lack of auditory experience than to mental deficiency or psychopathology.

A number of studies are now available that demonstrate rather conclusively that deaf children are similar to hearing children in the distribution of intelligence. This is not to say that patterns of intellectual development in deaf children are identical to those in hearing youngsters. The very fact of language disability precludes this possibility and makes it necessary to develop special educational programs that can facilitate intellectual development. Nevertheless, the intellectual potentials of deaf children are normal and should not be underestimated because of language deficits. Case Study 5.1 clearly illustrates the results of this kind of error.

In addition to research demonstrating similarity in intellectual potential between deaf and hearing children, investigators have also studied the process of thinking itself. Comparisons of concept formation and abstract thinking between the deaf and hearing consistently demonstrate similarity in thinking processes when the tasks involved are not dependent on language (Furth, 1964, 1966, 1971; Vernon, 1967). Although a few studies have shown differences between deaf and hearing children on nonverbal cognitive tasks, Furth

CASE STUDY 5.1

DEAFNESS IS NOT RETARDATION: A CASE OF MISDIAGNOSIS

Robert was 7 years old. His mother had died when he was 2, and the identity of his father was unknown. Since his mother's death, Robert had been cared for by an aunt. At age 5, he was placed in a day-care center for severely retarded children. Robert was a friendly child who seemed eager to please others, and he responded enthusiastically to gestures of affection. However, Robert had no expressive language at all, and it was difficult for day-care staff to determine whether he understood any language. Nevertheless, he appeared to understand gestures and was able to follow a few simple directions. Most staff members never questioned the fact that Robert was retarded and appropriately placed in the facility.

The speech pathologist at the day-care center had insisted, shortly after Robert's arrival, that he should be evaluated by a psychologist and an audiologist. Having observed Robert closely, she was convinced that he was not retarded, but rather suffered from a severe hearing impairment. However, it took her nearly two years to overcome others' objections and secure referrals to appropriate professionals. Since Robert had no language, psychological evaluation was based on behavioral observations, ratings on objective behavior scales, and a nonverbal intelligence test. Results indicated that Robert was functioning in the normal range of ability. Audiological evaluation demonstrated that Robert did indeed have a severe hearing impairment. These studies eventuated in Robert's placement in a state school for the deaf where he was fitted with a hearing aid and given auditory training and training in manual communication. Robert made a good adjustment to this residential setting and flourished on the attention he received. He responded well to training in manual communication, and his development reflected normal intellectual ability. However, despite amplification with a hearing aid, Robert was unable to learn to communicate verbally.

(1961) suggested that such differences are a function of deficiency in cognitive stimulation and social-emotional acceptance of deaf children rather than a direct function of language deficiency. Taken together, these various conclusions strongly suggest that language disabilities resulting from deafness directly interfere with intellectual performance, and that language disabilities indirectly affect thinking by inhibiting normal patterns of cognitive stimulation and interpersonal interaction. The handicapping effects of these factors are apparently cumulative, since there is evidence that early similarities between deaf and hearing children later develop into a situation in which deaf children increasingly fall behind in concept attainment abilities (Meadow, 1975).

Despite similarities in intellectual potential and thinking processes, studies of the educational achievement of deaf children clearly demonstrate their deficiencies as compared with hearing children (Vernon, 1969b). McClure (1966) reported that only 5 percent of graduates from educational programs for the deaf attain a tenth-grade level of educational achievement, only 41 percent achieve a seventh- or eighth-grade level, and 30 percent are functionally illiterate.

Vernon (1969a) found that deaf children with deaf parents achieved in school at about two-thirds the rate of hearing students. Children who became deaf because of blood incompatibilities with the mother (Rh factors) achieved at a rate of about one-half that of hearing students, and children deafened by reason of prematurity, rubella, or meningitis achieved at a rate slightly lower than one-half that of those with normal hearing. Vernon concluded that the better educational progress of deaf children with deaf parents may be due to early exposure to sign language by the deaf parents who can thus provide a mode of early cognitive stimulation as well as communication.

Personal and Social Factors

It is an unfortunate but nonetheless real fact that deaf children lead more isolated lives than children with normal hearing. Living in a world devoid of sound and hampered in communication with others, deaf children often turn inward and have difficulty establishing a sense of self-worth and confidence in relating to others.

While the incidence of severe emotional disturbance in the deaf is no greater than in hearing persons (Altshuler, 1971; Grinker, 1971), there are inevitable problems in psychosocial development. In infants and young children problems may occur because of inability to comprehend aspects of emotionality that are communicated verbally and are an important part of the mother-infant bond (Altshuler, 1974). As the child develops, parental expectations may not be understood as readily and may lead to experiences of mutual frustration. In some cases, parental concern over the child's failure to develop normally can lead to rejection or overprotection; in either case, the child must adapt to the attitudes and behavior of caregivers. Often the necessity for such adaptations in the absence of adequate receptive or expressive language leads to overdependency in the deaf child (Mindel & Vernon, 1971). Restricted in interactions to those with whom communication is possible, the child may develop a self-concept that is dependent largely on parental responses and acceptance. Occasionally, however, inability to hear may lead the child in the direction of greater independence and self-reliance, as needs that cannot be expressed are met by direct and independent coping strategies.

In an interesting study of personal and social characteristics of deaf children, Schlesinger and Meadow (1971) observed mothers interacting with their deaf children and found the mothers to be less permissive, more intrusive, more didactic, less flexible, and less approving than mothers of hearing children. In interviews, parents of the deaf said their children needed more constant supervision, and they relied more heavily on spanking for discipline. These parents generally experienced more frustration in child-rearing.

Deaf children themselves consistently have more adjustment problems than hearing children. They tend to be rigid, egocentric, lacking in creativity, impulsive, and lacking in empathy (Meadow, 1975). Often, the lack of language facility in young deaf children increases the need to express frustration physically, by temper tantrums, rather than verbally (Mindel & Vernon, 1971).

As the deaf child develops and begins to move from the family to the larger world of neighborhood and school, problems are often intensified. If

Interpersonal relationships are important to personal growth. Too often, the deaf child's inability to communicate clearly results in frustration, ridicule, and isolation. Though sign language does limit one to communicating with those who understand signing, it has clearly helped the deaf teenagers pictured here to interact with their peers.

the child is fortunate enough to have access to well-designed educational programs, educational achievement may be minimally impaired. However, the child must also cope with adults and peers who have little empathy and even less understanding of the nature of severe hearing disability. Rather than being a source of self-esteem, the peer group may instead become a source of humiliation if the child is subjected to misunderstanding, rejection, even ridicule. These problems are further intensified during adolescence, when peer esteem and heterosexual relations become critically important as sources of self-value.

Dozens of specific problems could be enumerated, but most reduce to this basic issue: severe hearing impairment and its impact on language can potentially interfere with most interpersonal relationships and lead to a diminished sense of self-worth and personal competence. These are not necessary consequences, but the probability of their occurrence demands that caregivers be acutely aware of the psychological and social factors in the development of the hearing-impaired child.

INTERVENTION WITH THE HEARING-IMPAIRED CHILD

As children with physical impairments, the deaf and hard of hearing require considerable intervention services in terms of health care, education, rehabilitation, and various therapeutic interventions. Ideally, intervention would begin at birth with routine examination by a pediatrician and early identification of high-risk infants. Coordinated care between medical specialists and clinical audiologists would provide early medical correction where possible, fitting with a hearing aid, auditory training, and manual communication training even during early preschool years. Selection of a preschool should ideally be a function of the child's abilities and could include a mainstreaming preschool for both disabled and nondisabled children. Parents should be assisted by a social worker in the identification of services available to them and their child and given assistance in child management or treatment of childhood psychological problems by psychologist, psychiatrist, or social worker.

The range of services in an ideal system would be both extensive and expensive, but many of the components of an ideal service system are available even today. The problem is that such services are not always easily identifiable, and they suffer from lack of coordination and interprofessional competition. The family that seeks help for a hearing-impaired child could benefit greatly from the availability of a *child advocate* whose primary function would be to help families identify and obtain services within the community and to speak honestly on the issues regarding competing programs and methods. The futures of deaf children are very much dependent on the ability of society to ensure that they receive the services they need, and the child advocate could provide such guarantees.

Currently, intervention with deaf children involves two major objectives. The first is the possible correction of the hearing loss itself. In this respect medical intervention and amplification are the most significant approaches to correction. Many forms of hearing loss are not correctable, however, and in these cases intervention is focused on minimizing educational and psycho-social consequences of hearing impairment through provision of services specifically designed for the hearing-impaired child.

Medical Intervention

Medical intervention can occur at two levels: through prevention and through treatment. An important new concept that can have far-reaching implications in the prevention of many of the adverse consequences of any disability— including deafness—is the "high-risk register" (Black, Bergstrom, Downs, & Hemenway, 1971). As applied to infants and young children, the notion of **high risk** refers to increased probability that a given youngster will develop some specific disability because of complications during the mother's pregnancy or delivery, certain postnatal conditions, or the socioeconomic background or medical history of the parents. For hearing disabilities, the high-risk register is a listing of various medical factors associated with increased risk of hearing loss. The register can be used in newborn nurseries as a means of early identification of those infants who have a higher probability of hearing loss, that is, infants who are "at risk." Specific factors listed in a high-risk register for hearing impairments include the following:

a) **prenatal conditions** (present before birth by reason of genetics or complications during pregnancy)—such as family history of deafness, maternal rubella during pregnancy, maternal infection;
b) **perinatal conditions** (occurring during delivery)—such as prolonged labor, prematurity, complications during delivery;
c) **postnatal (neonatal) conditions** (occurring after birth)—convulsions, low birth weight (less than 4 pounds), high birth weight (more than 11 pounds).

The high-risk checklist provides an extensive and exhaustive listing of such conditions to alert medical and nursing staffs in newborn nurseries of the possibility of hearing loss in an identified infant. The use of the register in conjunction with ongoing screening during preschool years can be a significant step toward early detection and intervention.

The actual remediation of hearing impairments by medical intervention is limited. There are no surgical or drug treatments known to be effective in the treatment of sensorineural or central hearing losses. Parents of deaf children frequently hope for miracle cures, but there are no known cures for deafness. In the last decade research has begun on the use of electronic implants that are intended to stimulate the auditory nerve directly, but this technique is experimental and is not used with children (Merzenich, Schindler, & Sooy, 1974).

Conductive-type hearing losses are sometimes amenable to correction either by surgical or pharmacological treatment. The treatment of choice depends on whether the conductive impairment is a function of infection, structural defect, or both. Generally this type of medical intervention has a good prognosis for partial or complete recovery of hearing loss.

Hearing Amplification

A hearing aid is simply a device used to intensify sounds reaching the ear. This intensification of sound is commonly referred to as **amplification** and can be achieved either by mechanical or electrical means. Cupping one's hand around the ear is a simple way of amplifying sound mechanically, and the earliest hearing aids were mechanical devices such as ear trumpets. This kind of amplification is minimally useful and characteristically amounts to no more than 5 or 10 dB.

In the past three decades significant technical advances have been made in the electrical amplification of sounds, and modern technology now provides an extensive number of hearing aids that can amplify whatever residual hearing a child has.

Although a large number of effective hearing aids are now available, the problem of selecting and fitting an aid to a young child may be quite difficult. The infant or young preschooler may not understand the purpose of the aid and may resent and reject it. Even the child who is trained to accept the aid may break it accidentally or smear it with food or dirt. Children simply do not stay as clean as adults. Zink (1972) found that over half of 92 children who had hearing aids had broken them but had not told anyone. Consequently, children who wear hearing aids must have them tested regularly to determine if they still work.

The value and benefits of amplification have increased proportionately to technological advances within the field. Children with hearing losses as small as 15 dB, as well as children with profound nonremedial deafness, are currently considered equally good candidates for hearing aids precisely because of the increased sophistication in electronic amplification devices (Northern & Downs, 1974). The child with very mild hearing loss who is experiencing learning problems may well get sufficient help from an aid to reduce the intensity of the learning problem. In addition, the profoundly deaf child may show some small increase in hearing as a result of amplification that can still lead to considerable alteration of capacities. Despite these advances, many deaf children cannot benefit from amplification, and even where amplification is effective, there are inherent problems in that all sounds are intensified and, to some extent, distorted. For some youngsters the fact that amplification is indiscriminate may produce problems in flooding the child with auditory stimulation that can be quite disconcerting. Yet even with these problems amplification is an important aid and should be available to every child who can potentially benefit from it.

Educational Intervention

The best method of educating the deaf child has long been a matter of controversy. The heart of this conflict is the long-standing conflict regarding teaching oral language as opposed to manual language, and the issue has been debated for well over a hundred years.

The direct teaching of oral language or **speech (lip) reading** is considered by its proponents to be an important step in integrating the deaf child into a

Sign language can open up the world of communication to many deaf children. The deaf child shown here is using sign language to chat with her companion—perhaps about the third party.

hearing world in which others rely on speech for communication. On the other hand, those who favor manual training methods, such as the use of **sign language** or **finger spelling,** point out that deaf children cannot acquire language at normal developmental levels and are thus unable to achieve at the same level as hearing children. Although sign language enables the deaf child to speak only with those who speak the same language (typically special teachers, parents, and deaf peers), the acquisition of signing skills is considered to be an important step in both communication and socialization skills.

Research in this area has been somewhat limited, but the data tend to favor the conclusion that manual training is probably more advantageous than oral training (that is, speech reading). Stevenson (1964) found that children taught by manual means demonstrated better educational achievement than those taught speech reading. Montgomery (1966) found that the acquisition of sign language in a group of deaf children had no adverse consequences on the simultaneous acquisition of speech- or lip-reading ability. Moore (1976) described the Rochester Method of deaf education first used in the United States at the Rochester School for the Deaf in New York in 1878. This approach combines training in finger spelling with simultaneous training in speech reading. Like Montgomery, Moore concluded that finger spelling does not interfere with good oral techniques. Further, finger spelling in combination with speech reading leads to improved educational achievement in deaf students, especially in areas where meaningful language is involved. Studies by

OPEN ISSUE

Speech reading or manual communication? Each has its proponents, and research can be cited pointing to the advantages and disadvantages of each. On the one hand, speech reading promises easier assimilation of the hearing-impaired child into normal life patterns. The only accommodations others need to make are to speak clearly and directly to the hearing-impaired child. The potential advantages of mainstream education and normalization are obvious.

At the same time, however, research suggests that manual communication or signing enables the child to utilize intellectual potential more fully and to develop more adequate skills in expressive communication. The primary disadvantage is that the youngster is largely restricted in communication to those who are familiar with the manual communication system he/she has learned. Normalization and mainstream education necessarily suffer.

Which is the better approach? There is at present no answer to this question, and the special educator must reach his/her own decisions after careful examination of the issues and research. However, some possible relevant issues that have not been adequately investigated include the impact of speech reading or manual communication upon the child's developing self-concept, effects on patterns of family interaction, reactions of others to the hearing-impaired child, and restrictions on participation in games and sports. Research in these areas might provide important ancillary information in resolving this open issue.

Vernon and Koh (1970, 1971) further support the notion that deaf children trained in manual communication demonstrate better educational achievement than children taught by oral methods. The weight of the evidence appears fairly clearly in favor of manual training, but an optimal approach would probably combine finger spelling with oral training.

CHILDREN WITH SPEECH DISABILITIES

Study of severe hearing impairment readily convinces us of the critical importance of communicative processes in all phases of development. The child who cannot hear inevitably suffers impairment in ability to communicate. But many children who can hear quite adequately nevertheless suffer from an inability to communicate clearly and efficiently. Like the hearing-impaired child, the speech-disabled youngster experiences a variety of potentially handicapping consequences in virtually all areas of development, including—most importantly—cognitive and educational achievement and personal-social development.

Because speech impairments are usually obvious and readily detectable, the speech-impaired child is often so labeled early by parents, teachers, and peers. Unfortunately, the labels applied rarely reflect the nature of the impairment itself. Instead, the labels often reflect notions about the intellectual ability or personality of the speaker. The child who exhibits articulation problems in the form of immaturities of speech is often viewed as intellectually and socially immature as well. The child with a language disorder that interferes with the correct naming of objects might be viewed as "dumb" or "crazy." In neither case does the common-sense inference have much to do with the realities of the child's developing personality; however, the glib application of such labels can have serious effects on the educational and interpersonal development of the speech-impaired child. In the remaining sections of this chapter, we will examine some of these consequences and look at approaches to intervention. First, however, we will examine the current thinking regarding definition and classification, incidence and causation, and diagnosis and identification of speech disabilities.

DEFINITION AND CLASSIFICATION OF SPEECH DISABILITIES

Speech disabilities may be manifested in a staggering array of distinct forms, including delayed onset of speech, speech usage below age expectations, oddities of articulation, peculiar usage of language, stuttering, unusual intonation or voice quality, paucity of speech, inability to recall or use appropriate words, poor self-expression, or total absence of speech (Chess & Rosenberg, 1974). However, all speech disabilities have in common an *impairment of effective verbal communication to the extent that the intelligibility of spoken language is reduced.* While this inclusive definition is applicable in a general way to speech problems stemming from mental retardation or childhood psychosis, we will restrict our discussion to speech disorders in children of normal intellectual potential.

In the interest of simplicity, it is useful to think of speech disabilities as falling within four major categories: (a) articulation disorders, (b) timing disorders, (c) voice disorders, and (d) language disorders.

Articulation Disorders

Articulation disorders include errors in which the child omits or distorts word sounds, substitutes one word sound for another, or adds irrelevant sounds to words. **Lisping** is a familiar articulation disorder in which one sound is substituted for another. For example, a *th* sound may be substituted for an *s* sound so that "simple" becomes "thimple." Or an *sh* sound may be substituted for an *s* sound and "simple" becomes "shimple." Another familiar articulation problem is **lalling,** in which *r* and *l* sounds are distorted. Problems in articulation are common characteristics of developing speech, and all children produce them in learning to talk (Milisen, 1971). The persistence of such distortions beyond appropriate ages, however, can be quite problematic, since it inhibits clear communication and produces frustration in both speaker and listener. Further, the youngster who cannot overcome articulation problems is often seen as using "baby talk" and the immaturity present in speech patterns is generalized to the child's personality. As development proceeds, articulation disorders can be a source of social ridicule and damaged self-esteem.

Timing Disorders

The most familiar example of speech disability is actually a problem in the sequential timing of speech and is caused by a disability in breath control while speaking. We are referring, of course, to **stuttering.** Analysis of stuttering reveals that this speech disability consists of repetitions of words or word elements, hesitations in speech, and prolongations of speech sounds (Robinson, 1964). As with articulation disorders, the disruptions in the flow and rhythm of speech characteristic of stuttering are common in early speech development. In observing the emerging speech patterns of toddlers, it is easy to observe repetitions of words or speech sounds (referred to as **clonic blocks**) or prolongations of sounds and hesitations between sounds (referred to as **tonic blocks**). Such interruptions of normal speech rhythm are often accompanied in the young child by excitement and a drive to spill out a burst of words. A similar intensity of emotional arousal is also apparent in the stutterer, but as a more or less permanent aspect of verbal communication rather than as a passing stage of development.

A related problem in the timing and fluency of speech is **cluttering,** in which speech is excessively rapid, erratic in rhythm, and occasionally slurred, garbled, and unintelligible (Perkins, 1971). Weiss (1964) suggested that, unlike the stutterer, the clutterer is unaware of problems in the intelligibility of speech patterns, and it is only in recent years that speech pathologists are beginning to recognize cluttering as a specific speech disability. Perhaps cluttering has for so long been overlooked as a distinct problem because of lack of subjective awareness of difficulty in communicating and because the erratic timing and direction of cluttered speech make it seem to be more a problem in organization of thinking than a problem of verbal expression.

Voice Disorders

One aspect of verbal expression is the quality of voice that the speaker employs. Characteristically, normal speech is varied in tone and inflection, and voice volume is modulated in relation to circumstances. In some individuals, however, these patterns of control and variation are disrupted so that voice quality is too loud or too soft, too high- or low-pitched, or stereotyped in inflection. As in the case of other speech disabilities we have discussed, there are normal developmental occurrences that exemplify the kind of problem that can develop. A familiar example of a transient voice problem is the adolescent boy whose voice will occasionally jump an octave into a falsetto (Van Riper, 1972). However, just as the teenage boy is embarrassed by his uncontrolled variation in pitch, so is the individual who displays a chronic voice disorder and must engage in constant self-monitoring in an attempt to control voice quality. Such acute self-awareness can easily become a hindrance to free, comfortable communication and lead to hesitation in speaking.

Language Disorders

Often referred to as "expressive aphasia" or "severe language delay," a language disorder involves a central nervous system dysfunction that impedes the comprehension or use of words (Myklebust, 1971b). Actually, an aphasic disorder may be receptive or expressive and may occur in modalities other than speech. **Aphasia** is a general term referring to a disability in use of words. If the disability impedes comprehension of spoken language, it is a **receptive aphasia.** If the disability involves inability to find the correct word to express an idea or to communicate verbally, it is an **expressive aphasia.** Both types of disorder may occur within the same individual, and they may occur with or without subjective awareness that a problem exists. In some instances the aphasic disorder may be circumscribed and limited in its impact on overall communication. Thus, for example, an adult stroke victim may experience only minimal interference in expressive language; however, cortical damage may sometimes be extensive enough to lead to total inability to communicate. In children brain trauma may have the same consequences, though expressive aphasia is more often observed in a failure to develop language, that is, severe language delay.

While the foregoing classification system is in common usage (e.g., Perkins, 1971; Van Riper, 1972), it is by no means exhaustive. Speech disabilities may arise as well from conditions of severe social deprivation or from a physical disability such as cerebral palsy. As noted earlier in this section, mental retardation and severe emotional disturbance can also result in some form of speech disability. Furthermore, the various classifications are not mutually exclusive, and several types of speech disability may coexist in the same individual. Finally, there is the important matter of speech disability consequent to severe hearing impairment or deafness that is not included in this fourfold classification system. Having noted these exceptions, however, we will continue to use the distinctions outlined above as the most useful basis for an introduction to speech disabilities.

INCIDENCE AND ETIOLOGY OF SPEECH DISABILITIES

Estimates of the incidence of different disabilities and problems of childhood must always be viewed with some reservations. As in the case of hearing impairment, for example, incidence estimates are partly a function of populations sampled and partly a function of the definitions employed. Studies by Myklebust (1964) and Wood (1969) suggest that approximately 5 percent of school-age children in the United States have speech impairments severe enough to impede education. More recent estimates suggest that between 1,925,000 (Craig, 1976) and 2,440,000 (Hobbs, 1975) children exhibit speech disabilities of one kind or another.

A recent study by Calnan and Richardson (1976) is impressive in scope and design. These investigators used data from a longitudinal study of all children in England, Scotland, and Wales born during one week in 1958. A follow-up conducted when these children were 11 years old included an assessment of speech development. Parents, teachers, and physicians were asked to evaluate the speech of the children in terms of whether or not the children were easy to understand in verbal communication. While this procedure hardly constitutes adequate diagnostic evaluation, it is useful as an initial screening device. Analyses of their data led Calnan and Richardson to suggest that approximately 16 percent of the children in their study showed some degree of speech defect. The probability that a boy would exhibit a speech problem was more than twice as high as for girls, and children from lower socioeconomic classes had more speech problems than those from higher socioeconomic groups. These sex and social class differentials are similar to those reported by other investigators (e.g., Milisen, 1971). If comparable incidence estimates were applied to children in this country, between 4 and 6 million youngsters would be viewed as having some kind of speech disorder. However, Calnan and Richardson include speech problems arising from social disadvantage in their estimates, and this would account for the discrepancy between their incidence estimates and those of Hobbs (1975) and Craig (1976). Specifying the incidence of major categories of speech disabilities is even more problematic than overall incidence estimates. However, a study published by the American Speech and Hearing Association (ASHA) in 1961 suggested the following rough estimates: articulation disorders—80 percent; stuttering—7 percent; voice disorders—2 percent; language disorders—3 to 5 percent; and other disorders—5 to 6 percent. With these general incidence figures in mind, we can briefly examine causative factors in speech impairments.

Causes of articulation disorders

Articulation defects can stem from several possible sources. They may simply be errors in sound production that have become habitual. Initially, such errors may be produced because of inadequate coordination of oral and facial muscles. In some cases, specific physical disabilities such as cerebral palsy or cleft palate contribute directly to difficulties in the formation of sounds. In the large majority of cases, however, such defects are not present, and articulation disorders appear to result from deficiencies in learning (Winitz, 1977). Interestingly, the most obvious inference made in connection with articula-

In young children, alleviating an articulation disorder is often a matter of helping them recognize different sounds and then reinforcing them for correct reproduction of those sounds.

tion problems—that the child is "lazy" or using "baby talk"—has not been confirmed by empirical research. In fact, children with articulation disorders do not differ from other children in anatomical variables, auditory variables, intelligence, or personality (Powers, 1971). However, some evidence that articulation problems may be learned errors comes from findings that firstborn children and children of higher socioeconomic status have lower rates of articulation errors (Winitz, 1969). Winitz suggested that these differences reflect differences in amount of language stimulation and reinforcement for correct sound production. Another factor that fits the hypothesis that articulation disorders result from faulty learning is evidence suggesting that mothers of these children tend to be demanding, critical, excessively high in their standards for their children's behavior, and negative toward their children's speech (Powers, 1971). However, it is possible that maternal attitudes *resulted from* rather than contributed to the causation of speech errors.

Causes of stuttering

The single speech disability that has been the subject of more research and theorizing than any other is stuttering. Prescientific notions held that stuttering was a result of possession by evil spirits, and subsequent thinking has run the gamut from causation by faulty parenting to beliefs that stuttering is a mild form of epilepsy or is caused by attempts to make a left-handed child use the right hand during early home and school training. While we cannot examine all these theories, a few are worth mentioning as representative of different viewpoints.

The belief that stuttering is an outcome of undetected organic dysfunction is represented by the *dysphemia theory* (West, Kennedy, & Carr, 1937) and the concept of *cerebral dominance* (Orton, 1937). Roughly, this theory suggested that effective speech requires that impulses from the brain reach paired oral and facial muscles simultaneously in order that these paired structures can operate in unison. However, if one cerebral hemisphere is not dominant and able to coordinate the messages to the muscles, a disruption of speech occurs in the form of speech hesitations, prolongations, and repetitions. Vulnerability to "mixed dominance" in which neither cerebral hemisphere coordinates muscular activity was thought to occur because of hereditary factors or because of attempts to change handedness during early home and school training.

At this point in time, there is no clear evidence that stutterers are any different biologically from nonstutterers. However, observation of familial tendencies among stutterers and a clear preponderance of male over female stutterers continue to spur searches for subtle constitutional factors.

From a psychodynamic view, stuttering is thought to be a symptom of neurosis stemming from a conflict between an unconscious wish to express a socially unacceptable impulse and the need of the ego to repress the impulse to maintain social acceptance. Stuttering is seen as the result of conflict between id and superego. The hesitancies and prolongations can be seen as symbolic expression of the internal, unconscious conflict (Travis, 1971).

While stutterers are, in fact, more tense, withdrawn, and socially sensitive as a group than nonstutterers, there is no evidence that these characteristics support the notion of internal conflict and neurosis. A more likely explanation is that such characteristics develop as a consequence of stuttering and the apprehensiveness it causes in social situations.

Probably the most useful approach to understanding stuttering is to view it as the result of multiple causative factors including potential constitutional vulnerability, cumulative results of faulty learning, and resultant apprehension and anxiety related to speech (Perkins, 1971). As the child learns to speak, natural dysfluencies may become sources of anxiety so that the vulnerable child learns to fear speech. If this apprehensiveness is reinforced by parents or teachers who set unrealistically high speech standards or who are generally critical and demanding, the child may come to view any occasion to speak with intense fear and self-consciousness that then disrupts fluent speech. Eventually, the child begins to develop a concept of self that includes speech dysfluency. It is further possible that stuttering also has paradoxically reinforcing effects in that it may bring attention or it may give the child a built-in excuse for avoiding social demands.

The variety of approaches to understanding stuttering need not be confusing since, in effect, many of the ideas reviewed here are compatible with each other. However, none of them has received sufficient research support to suggest that we yet understand the development of stuttering. On the contrary, the question of causation is open, and intervention approaches need to be based on outcomes rather than theories.

Causes of voice disorders

Voice disorders are less adequately investigated than other speech disabilities, and notions regarding causal factors vary depending on the specific kind of voice disorder in question. For example, some problems affecting voice quality stem from disease processes that directly affect the voice musculature. A familiar example is *laryngitis,* in which the larynx is inflamed as a result of respiratory infection. The result is hoarseness in voice quality. More serious problems affecting laryngeal tissue include the growth of tumors on the vocal cords or tissue ulcerations. While surgically correctible in many cases, some growths may require the removal of the larynx, a procedure called *laryngectomy.* In cases such as these the individual must undergo a process of relearning to speak by means of exhalation of breath through the esophagus. This kind of speech is called *esophogeal speech* and is readily recognized by its characteristic low, hoarse quality.

Disorders of pitch, in which voice quality is too high-pitched or too low-pitched or monotonous in pitch, may result from emotional conflicts, habitual misuse of voice, general physical weakness, or hearing loss. The last of these causes is frequently encountered as the hearing-impaired child develops distortions in voice quality because of inability to hear pitch variations in the voices of self and others and is thereby unable to reproduce normal variations in voice tone or volume.

Causes of language disorders

Language disorders truly constitute an interdisciplinary problem. Stemming as they do from some form of central nervous system dysfunction or damage, most of these disorders are medically untreatable. As a result, they become problems in educational programming, psychological treatment, and language training.

The child with language delay, the cerebral-palsied child, the aphasic child, and the learning-disabled child may all have difficulty in developing the conceptual ability to use language without any implications of mental retardation. Rather, damage to areas of the cerebral cortex involved in language comprehension and/or production may be more or less specific in producing speech disability (Myklebust, 1971a). Subsequently, of course, inability to use language may in turn lead to educational difficulties and eventuate in retarded intellectual development as well.

Language disorders may be congenital in nature and stem from prenatal causes in heredity or intrauterine development. In a smaller proportion of children, language disorders may result from disease or injury occurring perinatally or postnatally leading to damage of cortical tissue. In these cases language disorders may be viewed as a form of *learning disability*. In still other cases, language disorder may be related to mental retardation or severe emotional disturbance. A lack of clear understanding of the nature of language disorders naturally inhibits effective treatment, but this is an area of active research. Efforts to develop compensatory language training procedures—despite a lack of understanding of the nature of some of these disorders—are promising.

DIAGNOSIS AND IDENTIFICATION OF SPEECH DISABILITIES

The diagnosis of speech disabilities is a process of varying complexity depending on the kinds of problems a child exhibits. For example, articulatory problems are usually first recognized by parents or teachers. Diagnostic evaluation by a speech diagnostician is more a matter of confirming that articulation patterns are discrepant from age expectations and then trying to isolate the specific nature of the articulation errors. Characteristically, assessment procedures used in the diagnostic study of articulation problems are straightforward and require the child to produce vowel, consonant, and diphthong sounds both as independent elements and as components of words. The child is asked to repeat words that have specific sounds placed at the beginning, middle, or end. For example, a child might have no problem pronouncing the initial s in "simple," but might have more difficulty with the middle s in "basket" or the terminal s in "trees." Responses can be evaluated immediately, or the child's sound reproductions can be taped for later study. Analysis of the child's sound reproductions is used to determine patterns of error and possible causal factors as well as to plan for intervention.

Similarly, assessment of timing disorders such as stuttering involve straightforward analysis of the child's verbal behavior. In this case the diagnostician is concerned with rate of speaking, frequency and intensity of hesitations, prolongations, and repetitions, as well as visual indications of stress, such as facial grimaces (Darley, 1964). Checklists derived from studies of children who stutter have been devised as a means of increasing the reliability of assessment in the case of an individual child. In some cases, a complex assessment battery is used, consisting not only of analyses of stuttering behavior but also personality assessment devices, self-rating scales, and measures of attitudes toward communication (Guitar, 1976).

Because articulation and timing disorders are manifest in observable behavior, assessment procedures can attain a high degree of reliability and validity, and agreement in the judgments of independent observers regarding stuttering symptoms is usually quite good.

While techniques for assessment of voice problems have not attained the wide degree of usage that characterizes techniques for assessment of articulation and timing problems, clinical techniques are available for evaluating voice quality. Beginning with a determination of "natural voice level," attempts are made to determine the extent to which habitual speech varies from this level. Natural voice level is a function of physical voice musculature and simply refers to the middle of the tonal range readily producible by a given individual. For example, natural voice level in adult males is characteristically lower in tone than females'. Natural voice level may be assessed clinically by asking the individual to hum a series of notes in ascending and descending order and evaluating the point at which a peak of voice intensity occurs. Alternatively, a speech diagnostician may use tactile cues from vibrations felt in the bones of

A necessary step in diagnosing a speech disability is first getting the child to speak. For years, speech pathologists visiting classrooms have found that a puppet can be a big help in relaxing children enough so that they will speak freely.

the nose or jaws. Highest intensity of vibration occurs at natural voice level. Obviously, this kind of procedure relies heavily on clinical experience and judgment, and its accuracy is a function of the skill of the speech diagnostician.

Having determined natural voice level, the diagnostician can evaluate habitual speech to determine the extent to which usual voice quality varies from it in pitch. Instruments are available that allow precise measurement of variations from natural voice level. Procedures for evaluation of voice quality can be useful in tracing the causes of voice disorders, since specific kinds of variations are typically related to certain causal factors. For example, unusually high pitch is often associated with problems in the vocal folds of the larynx; unusually low pitch may suggest the presence of metabolic or neurological disturbances. While assessment techniques for voice evaluation do not have the technical reliability and objectivity of articulation and timing assessment techniques, they are nevertheless important approaches that permit surprising precision in assessment in the hands of a skilled diagnostician.

By contrast, evaluation of language disorders does not approach the clarity or straightforwardness of other speech assessment procedures. Assessment of language disorders depends on the degree of understanding of language development that is available. Because language development is a highly complex process dependent on central nervous system functioning, intellectual potential, personality development, and sociocultural factors, it is evident that assessment can be problematic. This is because the disorder may stem from any one or a combination of these factors. Case Study 5.2 illustrates the problems in diagnosis of language disorders.

A large number of assessment procedures have been developed for evaluating language disorders, and these vary widely in reliability. The question of validity is difficult to evaluate and often requires complex experimental analyses. One widely used language assessment technique is the Illinois Test of Psycholinguistic Abilities (ITPA) (Kirk, McCarthy, & Kirk, 1968). This complex technique attempts to assess the interaction of cognitive and linguistic functions at *representational* and *automatic sequential* levels. Subtests that assess representational capacities attempt to evaluate the child's use of language in mediating the meaning of linguistic symbols. Automatic sequential subtests evaluate capacity to retain and automatically execute acceptable grammatical habits. Analysis of a child's responses permits the development of hypotheses about the nature of the language problems.

Such problems may occur in *encoding,* or understanding language; *decoding,* or using language to express meaning; and *association,* or the central nervous system mediating processes that relate encoding and decoding and permit the use of linguistic symbols in communication. While the ITPA is probably as good as any test of this type and is therefore widely used, it cannot approach the technical precision of articulation tests. Because they are simpler and directly measure observable behavior, articulation assessment devices are not subject to problems inherent in making inferences about complex internal linguistic and cognitive functions that simply cannot be measured directly. Tests such as the ITPA are limited in reliability and validity by the very complexity of the processes they attempt to assess. Furthermore,

PROBLEMS IN THE DIAGNOSIS OF LANGUAGE DISORDER

Charlie G., age 5, was brought to a child-guidance clinic by his parents because they could no longer tolerate his extremely aggressive behavior. Charlie, they complained, would frequently attack other children without provocation and would hit his parents when they attempted to control him. They had tried spankings and other forms of punishment, but Charlie persisted in violent temper outbursts. Apart from his aggressive behavior, however, Mr. and Mrs. G. felt Charlie was developing well, and they were particularly proud of his physical agility which, upon probing, appeared to be more accurately described as hyperactivity.

Charlie was a handsome, well-built youngster who accompanied the psychologist willingly at their first meeting. However, the examiner was immediately taken aback by the fact that Charlie's speech was barely understandable, a fact that the parents had not even remotely implied. Charlie's articulation was quite infantile, and it took some time for the examiner to be able to penetrate his halting, lisping speech and cluttered language. After several sessions during which the psychologist became more accustomed to Charlie's speech and able to understand some of it, it was still difficult to comprehend Charlie's idiosyncratic use of words.

Consultation with a speech pathologist and intensive review with the parents of Charlie's developmental history confirmed diagnostic suspicions. A speech pathologist conducted an independent diagnostic study and was able to determine that Charlie had little comprehension of language and was merely parroting words. The speech pathologist was unable to specify the causal factors involved in Charlie's infantile articulation patterns, but there was no doubt that Charlie exhibited an aphasic disorder of moderate severity. The parents had, apparently, assumed that infantile speech was Charlie's only communication problem and that he would outgrow it.

Review of Charlie's developmental history with the parents revealed that he had had a serious accident at about age 3. He had fallen off a second-story porch while riding a tricycle and suffered a concussion, though no bones were broken and the parents had not noticed significant changes in his behavior afterward. They had not mentioned the incident during initial interviews because they felt the incident reflected badly on them as parents and were embarrassed by their "neglect."

Psychological testing confirmed the diagnostic suspicions of the speech pathologist and indicated that Charlie experienced problems in concept formation as well as understanding and using language. The parents' description of Charlie's accident further supported diagnostic conclusions: Charlie was suffering from central nervous system damage sustained during his fall from the porch. The language disorder was a result of this injury, as was the explosive violence that caused the parents to seek help in the first place. Charlie's hyperactivity was another manifestation of the injury.

The diagnostic study eventuated in special educational placement for Charlie along with ongoing speech therapy and psychotherapy. Mr. and Mrs. G. were seen in regular meetings with a psychologist to assist them in understanding and managing Charlie's behavior and to try to relieve some of the guilt they felt as a result of Charlie's accident and resultant developmental problems.

While Charlie's initial school adjustment seemed to be good, the parents terminated their meetings after a few months. Attempted follow-up after 18 months revealed that the parents had divorced, and Mrs. G. had moved to a different city with Charlie. No further information was available on Charlie's development.

the ITPA and similar tests require some competence in the use of language to begin with and are therefore not applicable to cases in which there is severe language delay or severe receptive or expressive language problems.

The diagnosis of speech disabilities is a complex process that requires extensive training and clinical skill. The child-care professional who typically conducts the diagnostic study of speech problems is the speech pathologist. As a profession, speech pathology is fairly new among those that deal with special children, and the American Speech and Hearing Association (ASHA) is only about 40 years old. Nevertheless, in a relatively short span of time, speech pathology has established itself as a key part of the multidisciplinary team that is concerned with helping special children.

The **speech pathologist,** or speech therapist, must be certified by the ASHA. Specific requirements for certification include a master's degree or equivalent in clinical experience, supervised professional experience, and recommendation by a mentor attesting to professional abilities (Perkins, 1971). On a personal level, West and Ansberry (1968) suggested that speech pathologists should be interested in people, accepting, responsible, independent, highly ethical, and, above all else, have good speech patterns themselves.

Since the speech pathologist is basically a clinician who applies the findings of medical and behavioral science to the correction of speech disabilities, thorough professional preparation in addition to academic background is crucial. Throughout this chapter we have referred to a variety of specific clinical techniques used to assess hearing, articulation, voice quality, and speech rhythm and timing. The speech pathologist employs these techniques in practice and must necessarily be well aware of levels of personal competence in their use. No one can be an expert in all techniques, and awareness of one's limitations is an important professional quality.

In addition to assessment and diagnosis, the speech pathologist also employs a variety of intervention techniques. These range from basic speech training in the case of articulation disorders to highly technical therapeutic approaches in the treatment of certain voice disorders, such as those arising from corrective surgery for cleft palate or surgical laryngectomy. In applying these techniques the speech pathologist also employs educational methods and may, at times, function psychotherapeutically in providing support and understanding to the speech-impaired child. Behavior modification techniques are often employed to bring about desired changes in speech behavior and should be familiar to the speech pathologist (Drudge & Philips, 1976).

DEVELOPMENTAL CONSEQUENCES OF SPEECH DISABILITIES

The developmental consequences of speech disabilities are a function of both the nature and severity of the disability as well as the social and educational demands placed on the child. A mild articulation problem may present minimal problems and persist through adulthood without negative consequences. By contrast, severe language delay will probably affect every aspect of development and can have potentially devastating effects on educational, emotional, and interpersonal development.

In examining the developmental consequences of speech disabilities, it becomes readily apparent that certain types of speech disabilities—apart from severity—are likely to affect some areas of development more than others. For example, even mild language disorders are likely to have more serious consequences for educational development than articulation or timing problems that may be relatively severe. In the following sections it is important to remember that the kind of disorder—as well as its severity—must be considered in understanding the impact of a speech disability on a child's development.

Conceptual Abilities and Educational Achievement

Language delay and expressive aphasia inherently interfere with educational and cognitive development because this development depends heavily on the understanding and use of language. Cognitive development and education are interactive in nature and rely on a mutuality between understanding and expressing ideas. The absence of linguistic competence obviously hampers such interaction and likely interferes with optimal cognitive development. Unfortunately, there is little research bearing on the eventual developmental level attained by children exhibiting early language impairment, but what little evidence there is indicates that expressive language delay is associated with delay in nonverbal mental abilities as well as verbal abilities (Stevenson & Richman, 1976).

By contrast, timing, articulation, and voice disorders do not *necessarily* have adverse consequences on educational and cognitive achievement. Indirectly, these speech disabilities may affect educational and cognitive development if the child begins to develop a concept of self as inadequate or incompetent, or if others begin to attribute to the child traits of intellectual deficit that have no basis in fact. A further indirect consequence of these disorders is the fact that learning environments may become aversive if associated with embarrassment or anxiety arising from self-awareness of speech problems.

Personal and Social Factors

Of much greater significance in articulation, timing, and voice disorders are the potential negative consequences in interpersonal relations and development of an adequate self-concept. Extensive research has been directed toward an investigation of the psychosocial consequences of stuttering, for example. Unlike the normally speaking child, the child who stutters and, to a lesser extent, the child with poor articulation are typically subject to extensive criticism and demands for better speech production. Either directly or indirectly, the speech-disabled child receives feedback from others that implies immaturity, intellectual incompetence, and inadequacy. The messages communicated by others may be blunt: "Stop that baby talk!" Or the child may receive indirect messages: "Slow down and think what you want to say." In many instances, a scowl or a look of impatience may be all the response the child needs to begin questioning personal adequacy because of dysfluency in communication.

A common characteristic of stutterers is an acute self-awareness that almost inevitably inhibits ease and comfort in social situations. Sheehan (1971) suggested that stutterers inherently have a self-concept which includes speech dysfluency as a central component. Stutterers view themselves as different, and this view colors virtually all relationships and performance in social situations. This view of the self as different is further reinforced by the fact that others see stutterers as different in ways that are not directly related to the speech dysfluency itself. Woods and Williams (1976) have shown that stutterers are perceived as more self-conscious, tense, nervous, emotional, guarded, withdrawn, reticent, insecure, and passive than nonstutterers. Such negative perceptions exist independently of amount of contact one has with a stuttering child, suggesting that a cultural stereotype of the stutterer is a factor leading to interpersonal problems.

While stutterers do not, in fact, exhibit any greater incidence of severe emotional disturbance than normal-speaking children, they do appear more anxious, less self-confident, and more socially withdrawn (Bloch & Goodstein, 1971). However, in view of a stutterer's experiences involving negative social stereotypes, difficulties in communication, and resultant embarrassment in situations requiring verbal interaction, such outcomes are hardly surprising. Though less research data are available regarding the psychosocial consequences of articulation and voice disorders, it seems to be a safe inference that similar, if less intense, consequences apply to youngsters who exhibit these disorders as well.

INTERVENTION WITH THE SPEECH-IMPAIRED CHILD

As we have seen in this brief survey, speech disabilities differ widely in nature and causation. It is not surprising therefore, that approaches to intervention also show marked differences.

Medical Intervention

Apart from the professional specialization in the treatment of speech disabilities that characterizes the speech pathologist, the medical specialty of otolaryngology is also concerned with the treatment of speech disabilities. Characteristically, **otolaryngology** is concerned with the potential physical relationships between speech and hearing disability and with the linguistic consequences of deafness. Another area of concern is in the treatment of voice disorders through application of medication or surgical correction. The otolaryngologist is concerned specifically with the diagnosis and treatment of infectious diseases of ears, nose, and throat that may affect speech or hearing or both. The development of *neoplasms* (tumors on the larynx or esophogeal canal) may also lead to speech disability and require surgical correction. Certain oral-facial muscular problems are of concern since they may directly interfere with ability to produce correct sounds. These include abnormalities of the tongue, lips, mouth, palate, and nose. Problems in any of these areas typically can only be corrected surgically. Thus medical intervention is important in the treatment of speech disabilities that result directly from defects in the complex respiratory, oral, and facial musculature involved in speech production.

Psychological Intervention

As we have noted, the presence of any speech impairment may eventuate in adjustment problems. However, psychological intervention is most likely to occur in helping children who stutter and children who exhibit language disorders.

In the case of stutterers, both psychotherapy and behavior modification techniques have been effective in reducing the intensity of stuttering or eliminating it (Perkins, 1971; Van Riper, 1973). In a large proportion of cases, however, stuttering appears to disappear without any form of intervention (Cooper, 1972; Sheehan & Martyn, 1970), but Young (1975) suggested that such spontaneous recoveries are not likely to be either permanent or complete. Research that proposes high rates of remission without treatment is based largely on retrospective reports by adults who once stuttered, and Young reported that such reports are suspect. Though stuttering may no longer constitute a serious disability, it is, according to Young, likely to recur under specific circumstances.

Van Riper (1973) employed an eclectic approach in the treatment of beginning and young, confirmed stutterers. His programs included desensitization, emotional support, modeling, parental counseling, and, when necessary, environmental change.

Psychological intervention in language disorders has been less effective than in the treatment of stuttering. Certain assessment procedures used by psychologists can be useful in pinpointing the nature of language delay or an expressive aphasia, but treatment approaches are limited largely to behavioral techniques to increase language production and usage. To date these efforts have not been particularly effective.

Educational Intervention

The most important strategy for helping the child with a severe language delay involves the provision of a special educational setting designed to facilitate language development and usage through a comprehensive and total communication system. Thus, *simultaneous language acquisition* is currently widely used, as children are simultaneously given verbal stimulation while being taught to use a form of manual communication.

In some cases intensive efforts may be made to teach the child specific sounds and then, through repetition and drill, to form these into words that, in turn, are associated with stimulus objects (Blake, 1971). Additional approaches include emphasis on body awareness, intensive environmental stimulation, and shaping of linguistic responses. Myklebust (1971b) emphasized the importance of the dictum, "input precedes output." This means that attempts should be made to build a base of receptive language through general stimulation prior to looking for expressive language development. Despite intensive efforts, however, the child with severe language disorder may progress little.

The prognosis is better with moderate or mild language disorders, where educational intervention becomes a key factor in bringing the child as close to normal as possible in language and cognitive ability. Because many moderate and mild language disorders fall within the scope of learning disabilities, educational techniques employed with these children are specific applications of general techniques in remediation of learning disabilities. Some of these general approaches will be discussed further in Chapter 9.

Communication is the basis for human interaction, and disabilities in hearing and speech can have devastating consequences on the quality of the child's interactions and the quality of the child's life. Audiology, speech pathology, special education, medicine, and psychology have made important advances in helping the child with communication disabilities, but our ignorance of the development of these children is nonetheless profound. Still more dramatic is the fact that these disabilities affect as many as 5 million children and adolescents in this country. Much remains to be done in understanding and helping these special children.

SUMMARY

1.   A disability or impairment is a defect in physical makeup or functioning, while a handicap is a potential limitation in functioning that may arise from obstacles imposed by an impairment.
2.   Hearing disabilities may be classified according to severity of hearing loss or physiological site of the loss.
3.   Early identification of hearing loss is critical in minimizing the handicapping effects of impairment.
4.   Diagnostic assessment of hearing loss in infants and young children relies heavily on objective procedures or procedures involving conditioned responses.
5.   While hearing loss inevitably affects language development, it does not necessarily imply intellectual deficits.
6.   Primary intervention approaches with the hearing disabled include medical/surgical procedures, amplification, and educational intervention in the form of training in speech reading and/or manual communication.
7.   Speech disabilities may be categorized as articulation disorders, timing disorders, voice disorders, and language disorders.
8.   The developmental consequences of speech impairments vary according to the nature of the disability and its severity.
9.   With the exception of language disorders, diagnostic assessment of speech disabilities is relatively objective and reliable.
10.   Speech therapy, educational remediation, and psychotherapy are key intervention processes with speech-impaired youngsters.

CHAPTER SIX

Children with Visual Disabilities

Between the time I was two and five, sight imperceptibly slipped away, leaving me able to see light, shadows, and for a few years and at close range, color. I learned to perceive the objective world through sound, touch, smells, relationships. It was an instinctive process.

Rose Resnick (1967, p. 17)

AN INTRODUCTION TO VISUAL DISABILITIES

Since the days of Homer, the blind poet and storyteller of ancient Greece, attitudes toward the blind have been marked by ambivalence and uncertainty. Although the loss of vision is recognized as a physical disability of critical consequence, the social achievements and independence of spirit often encountered in the blind can easily give the impression that a severe sensory impairment such as blindness is not really handicapping. Well-known individuals—such as Helen Keller who became both blind and deaf at the age of 19 months—are held up as courageous examples of the fact that blind persons are capable of outstanding achievement.

More and more, persons who reconcile their blindness to achieve a fulfilling human existence tend to reject the notion that they are handicapped and in need of special consideration. Many blind persons in contemporary society speak of themselves as having a "characteristic" rather than a "handicap." Sighted persons who interact with the blind sometimes fail to grasp the fact that such statements do not represent a disclaimer of disability so much as a rejection of condescension. A blind person, for example, can surely benefit from the assistance of a sighted person while trying to cross a busy intersection; all that is necessary in such circumstances, however, is the offer of an arm to touch while crossing the street. The sighted person who attempts to carry a blind person physically across the street may well elicit the rebuff, "Stop! I may be blind but I'm not lame."

It is worth noting that "the blind" is no more than a shortcut expression for persons who have the disability and/or characteristic of blindness. The expression itself should not gloss over the fact that both children and adults with visual disabilities should not be categorized solely on the basis of an impairment. Blind individuals are complex human beings with varieties of qualities and talents that should not be forgotten in consideration of the disability aspect of their lives.

DEFINITION AND CLASSIFICATION

As the American Foundation for the Blind (1954) has pointed out, the legal definition of blindness is a medical one that has little relevance to the educational needs of blind children. Since medical and educational approaches have yet to arrive at a mutual system of definition and classification, it will be necessary to review each separately.

Medical-Legal Definition of Blindness

The medical-legal definition of blindness, taken from a document first provided in 1934 by the House of Delegates of the American Medical Association (see Connor, Hoover, Horton, Sands, Sternfeld, & Wolinsky, 1975), is as follows:

> A person shall be considered blind whose central visual acuity does not exceed 20/200 in the better eye with correcting lenses or whose visual acuity, if better than 20/200, has a limit in the central field of vision to such a degree that its widest diameter subtends an angle of no greater than twenty degrees. (p. 240)

Although this definition may seem somewhat technical, it can be easily understood by looking at two basic criteria used in determining legal blindness: *visual acuity* and *field of vision*.

In essence, a person's **visual acuity** is a measure of how accurate his/her distance vision is compared to normal-seeing persons. Anyone who has taken an eye examination has probably had their visual acuity measured by means of an eye chart called the **Snellen chart,** a standardized series of letters, numbers, or symbols that must be read from a distance of 20 feet. Each line of letters is of a different size that corresponds to the standard distance at which they can be distinguished by a person of normal vision. For example, a person of normal vision can read a designated size of letters on the Snellen chart at a distance of 20 feet and is said to have 20/20 vision. When a person can only distinguish at 20 feet a size of letter that a person of normal vision could distinguish at 200 feet, the person is said to have a visual acuity of 20/200 and is considered legally blind.

At the same time, the **field of vision** is also important in determining legal blindness. If a person's angle of vision is 20 degrees or less, his/her actual field of vision is reduced to the point equivalent to blindness. Such a reduced field of vision is sometimes called "tunnel vision" because the person can perceive only a narrow band within the field of vision.

"Legal blindness" does not mean "total blindness," and many individuals who are legally blind retain some degree of residual vision. This legal definition, therefore, is useful for the purpose of identifying persons whose vision is so poor that they cannot function as normally sighted and are eligible for special assistance programs provided by local, state, and federal governments.

Educational Definitions and Classifications of Blindness

The medical-legal definition of blindness is relatively useless for educational purposes because it includes persons who are completely blind in the same category with those who have some residual vision. Such distinctions are important in education: totally blind children need educational programs that

OPEN ISSUE

The most important factor in deciding whether to teach a child the use of braille involves determining the degree of functional visual efficiency that the child possesses. In order to protect the child's capacity to learn, however, many states in previous years adopted the requirement that all legally blind children be taught by means of braille. These laws were based on medical-legal definitions of blindness that are relatively useless in helping determine the appropriate mode of reading for a child. In some situations, this problem manifests itself in the absurdity in which a state law can require that a legally blind child learn braille as the mode of reading when, in fact, the child has sufficient residual vision to be educated by printed matter. At first glance, it may seem ridiculous to think that a "blind" child can actually read by vision, and yet the use of visual aids have enabled many legally blind children to read printed matter.

Studies by Jones (1961) and Nolan (1965) seriously questioned the practice of teaching braille to every legally blind student. Jones (1961), for example, studied 14,125 legally blind children and found that 58 percent used braille, 38 percent used print, and 4 percent used both braille and print. In other words, the use of low-vision aids had enabled 42 percent of the children in this study to learn to read printed material. Since printed material is much more efficient than braille as a mode of reading, special educators must be very careful in determining the appropriate mode of reading even for children who are "legally blind." Braille instruction is more and more being reserved for the totally blind or for those children whose functional visual efficiency is so poor that printed material cannot be distinguished even with the use of low-vision aids.

teach them to rely on other sense modalities for learning, whereas partially sighted children can benefit from educational programs that maximize use of residual vision. As such, accurate classification of a child's visual capabilities is central to the establishment of programs that will be responsive to the child's educational and developmental needs.

Fonda (1960) suggested some distinct classifications of visual disabilities for purposes of educational programming; Fonda's system attempted to use the visual-acuity index based on the Snellen chart as a means of classifying mode of reading instruction (for example, use of braille, use of large-print materials, etc.), but subsequent studies have shown that visual acuity is a poor predictor of mode of reading for children (Jones, 1961; Nolan, 1965, 1967). As Lowenfeld (1973) pointed out, educators have found that **functional visual efficiency**—the way in which a child uses the vision he/she has—is more important than visual acuity in determining an educational program for the child. Despite the recognized importance of functional visual efficiency as a critical basis of classification for purposes of education, however, a thorough system of classification on this basis has proven to be quite difficult to develop; for the most part, this is because testing for visual efficiency in young children is in itself a difficult task.

In the absence of a more sophisticated yet workable system of classification, educators must rely on more general guidelines to assist the child with visual disabilities. The term **visual disability** (or visual impairment) "is used to describe those children who, after correction by all possible means, have such severe limitations in vision and their use of it that they are handicapped in their school programs" (Taylor, 1973, p. 156). Within this general category of visual disability, the major classifications include the educationally blind and the partially sighted.

The educationally blind child

The educationally blind child is most easily understood as the child who cannot make use of vision for the purpose of learning. A given child who is classified as educationally blind may well retain some small degree of residual vision, but this remaining vision cannot be employed in the learning situation. In the practical sense, *the educationally blind child must rely chiefly upon touch and hearing as the major avenues of learning.* Programs for the educationally blind, therefore, must attempt to maximize the child's use of nonvisual senses. The most obvious application of this principle, of course, involves the use of braille for reading.

Headphones are a good aid for helping educationally blind children concentrate on using the senses they do have.

The partially sighted child

Visually disabled children who are able to use vision as an avenue of learning are classified as partially sighted. Though many of these children may be legally blind, *the partially sighted child has sufficient functional visual efficiency that vision, rather than touch or hearing, can be utilized as the chief avenue of learning.* Educational goals for the partially sighted child include maximal use of the child's functional residual vision by means of magnification, illumination, specialized teaching aids (such as large print books and posters), as well as exercises designed to increase visual efficiency. Several studies have shown that the visual abilities of the partially sighted can be improved by intensive visual stimulation training (Ashcroft, 1966; Ashcroft, Halliday, & Barraga, 1965; Barraga, 1964). These studies have helped resolve the question of whether extended reliance on residual vision is useful or harmful.

For example, Barraga (1964) selected ten matched pairs of partially sighted children (ages 6 to 12) from a residential school for the blind. For one child in each pair, she provided daily 45-minute visual stimulation sessions for approximately 9 weeks. The results indicated that the children who participated in the experimental program showed significantly greater functional use of vision on a posttest visual discrimination task. This study was the first documentation supporting the hypothesis that functional visual efficiency can be improved by means of visual stimulation training. Barraga's work was an important step toward recognizing that visual acuity or distance is a poor predictor of a child's potential response to training.

The use of prescription devices and low-vision aids, combined with visual stimulation training, can considerably increase a child's ability to maximize near-vision potential. Near vision, of course, is much more central to the problems of learning than is the case with distance vision. Special education for the partially sighted now recognizes that definitions and classifications for the partially sighted must be based on the realization that functional visual efficiency can be improved with training. This finding has considerable import for children with some residual vision because "partially sighted" becomes far more than a category of classification distinct from total blindness; intervention with the partially sighted seeks both to maximize the use of a child's near-vision potential as well as to improve the child's functional visual efficiency.

Often the assumption is made that the term partially sighted refers to any child who wears corrective glasses. The great majority of visual impairments do not represent serious loss of vision and can often be corrected to normal or near-normal vision through the use of corrective glasses. The partially sighted, however—even with corrective lenses—continue to experience serious loss of vision; on the visual acuity index, the partially sighted are usually classified between 20/70 and 20/200, although many partially sighted, in the sense discussed above, are legally blind. Our discussion will focus mainly on children with serious visual disabilities and will not be concerned with mild visual impairments that are correctable by prescription lenses or with perceptual-motor disabilities, which will be discussed in the chapter on learning disabilities.

INCIDENCE AND ETIOLOGY

Because of the differences described above regarding the definition and classification of blindness, accurate figures regarding the number of blind children in the general population are somewhat difficult to obtain. Apgar and Stickle (1968) estimated that among the total population of the United States, 500,000 persons were blind or had serious visual impairment. Among preschool and school-aged children, the Bureau of Education for the Handicapped estimated that 1 in 3,000 must be classified as totally blind and 1 in 500 as partially sighted and in need of special education (Craig, 1976). The Bureau further estimated that there are 70,000 children in the United States with serious visual disabilities but that only 30,000 of these youngsters are receiving special education in public and private residential and day schools.

The causes of severe visual impairments are varied—so much so that it has been difficult to conduct large-scale studies. Current confusion regarding medical-legal and educational definitions of blindness creates difficulties in adequately classifying subjects as blind, so that studies of causation tend to be specific and limited to particular causative groups. One of the first extensive studies of the causes of blindness was that by Fraser and Friedman (1968), whose subjects were 776 English children attending special educational institutions for the blind. Fraser and Friedman described four major classifications of the causes of blindness: (a) hereditary/genetic causes, (b) prenatal causes (during pregnancy), (c) perinatal causes (during or directly related to delivery), and (d) postnatal causes (occurring after the child has been born). A fifth category included combinations of the above and was described as (e) complex hereditary and environmental causes. In their study, Fraser and Friedman found 59 children (7.7 percent) to be blind due to a combination of causes.

Hereditary/genetic causes

Extensive discussion of the complex genetic mechanisms involved in the transmission of blindness would be far beyond the scope of this discussion. It is important to note, however, that 327 children (42.1 percent) in the Fraser and Friedman study were blind due to genetic causes. There are a number of hereditary diseases that can produce serious loss of vision. For example, *retinoblastoma,* a malignant tumor of the retina that usually arises in infancy or early childhood can cause blindness. This disease can be inherited as a Mendelian *dominant trait* with *incomplete penetrance,* which means that the person carrying the disease may not manifest the lesion but can still pass on the disease to offspring. In the Fraser and Friedman investigation, 43 children (over 5 percent of the total studied) were blind because of retinoblastoma. This disease is particularly severe in that, until recently, it has required the surgical removal of the eyes; although recent medical advances have made it possible to arrest the growth of the malignancy without removal of the eyes, the disease inevitably causes blindness, and even a cured patient can transmit the disease to offspring.

Congenital and infantile cataracts are another hereditary cause of serious visual disability. A cataract is an opacity or cloudiness in the lens of the eye that prevents the normal passage of light through the pupil to the retina. Cataracts can be caused by other factors, such as diabetes, but can also be inherited. Cataracts seem to occur equally in males and females, and in the Fraser and Friedman study, 55 youngsters (over 7 percent) were impaired because of cataracts. Although there are many different hereditary causes of blindness, retinoblastoma and cataracts are the most significant genetic causes in terms of the number of children affected.

Prenatal causes
A number of factors affecting the fetus in the uterus can produce birth defects, including blindness. Drugs and radiation are believed to be possible causes of blindness in the fetus, but prenatal infections such as rubella (German measles) and syphilis are the most significant and best documented causes of blindness. Fraser and Friedman found that 44 of the children studied (less than 6 percent) were blinded by prenatal causes. In this respect, the influence of antibiotic drugs in the treatment of expectant mothers has been a critical factor in reducing the effects of prenatal infections such as syphilis and rubella.

Perinatal causes
The infant who is born prematurely is typically at risk for many diseases, including blindness. In generations past, low birth weight infants frequently died soon after birth so that the possible consequences of prematurity and low birth weight were not easily evident. Medical advances, such as incubation, have made it possible to save the lives of "preemies" but not without considerable risk of vulnerability to many diseases. Fraser and Friedman found that 258 children (33.2 percent) in their study were blinded by perinatal causes. These authors noted, however, that the percentage of children blinded by perinatal causes is decreasing because of the virtual elimination of one of the major perinatal causes of blindness, namely *retrolental fibroplasia* or RLF. This catastrophic chapter in the history of medical treatment of prematurity and low birth weight merits special discussion and consideration in Exhibit 6.1.

Postnatal causes
In the Fraser and Friedman investigation, 88 of the blind children studied (11.3 percent) had become blind due to causes that occurred in infancy and childhood. Such causes included accidents, infections, inflammations of the eye, tumors, and vascular disease. Although a wide variety of factors can cause blindness in the developing infant or child, it is clear from the above that the vast majority of blind children become disabled on the basis of genetic and/or birth-related factors. The age of onset at which blindness occurs is, of course, a critical factor in a child's overall development, and it is important to note that the vast majority of blind children in the Fraser and Friedman study lost their sight either before birth or early in infancy.

Although this discussion of the causes of blindness has been somewhat cursory, we know that many cases of blindness in children could have been prevented by genetic counseling, adequate medical care during pregnancy, and rapid medical intervention in childhood illnesses and accidents. We also

OXYGEN ADMINISTRATION AS A CAUSE OF BLINDNESS

Retrolental fibroplasia, or RLF, is an eye disease first described by Terry in 1942; RLF is an abnormal growth of fibrous tissue behind the crystalline lens of the eye. During the 1940s it became common medical practice to administer oxygen to premature infants of low birth weight; since "preemies" frequently have difficulty breathing, the administration of oxygen was considered to be a harmless but potentially life-saving procedure. In 1954, however, several investigators discovered independently that the major cause of RLF was precisely the administration of high concentrations of oxygen to premature infants. The practice was immediately curtailed.

RLF is now virtually controlled as a cause of blindness, but the last generation of infants suffered considerable risk and damage because of the lack of knowledge regarding this disease. To this day, very little is known about the factors that might predispose the eyes of the infant to the potentially harmful effects of oxygen treatment. In current medical practice, sophisticated techniques are available to monitor premature and low birth weight infants, and the risk of harmful consequences has been greatly reduced. The unsuspected and unfortunate consequences of oxygen administration to "preemies" have, nonetheless, taught an important lesson—namely that great care must be taken in the introduction of unsubstantiated forms of treatment. In current medical practice, new types of treatment must be preceded by a period of careful experimental research.

know that intervention itself (as in the case of oxygen treatment and RLF) poses certain dangers that must be tested for and eliminated. In the case of prenatal infections, such as rubella and syphilis, medical advances in antibiotic therapy have greatly increased the possibility of preventing injury to the child. Preventive medical care, however, is very much dependent on an informed and concerned public making use of existing programs and facilities. Despite improved methods of prevention, many children continue to suffer from severe visual disabilities that require sophisticated medical, educational, and psychological intervention.

DIAGNOSIS AND IDENTIFICATION

We know from our discussion of the causes of visual disabilities that the great majority of children with serious visual impairments are either born with the disability or develop it early in infancy. Early identification of visually disabled children is particularly important because they can benefit considerably from specialized intervention during the preschool period. The diagnosis of visual impairment should ideally set forth specific plans of intervention designed to reduce adverse consequences of the disability on the child's development. In the case of the blind child, such planning would include increasing the child's use of the senses of touch and hearing both to reduce the consequences of loss of vision and to stimulate alternate methods of learning. In the case of the partially sighted child, early intervention would seek to make use of the child's remaining vision by means of specialized exercises or low-vision aids (e.g., magnification or large print materials). Early identification is critical, therefore, precisely because it offers the prospect of meeting the child's needs during the course of critical periods in the child's development.

The High-Risk Register for Visual Disabilities

The concept of the "high-risk register" was discussed in Chapter 5 in reference to children with hearing disabilities. The application is quite similar and equally important in the identification of children with visual impairments. The high-risk register is, in effect, a call for alertness to possible visual disability in children who have other medical conditions known to correspond with or involve risk to the child's vision. As Gardiner (1969) pointed out, however, the high-risk register for loss of vision frequently tends to be neglected "because of a prevalent attitude of mind which regards the eyes as relatively unimportant organs" (p. 59). In support of his observation, Gardiner continued:

> One might quote the example of a child with maple sugar urine disease, who had been reported in detail many times in many papers, and who at the age of five was found, virtually by chance, to have cataracts. She had been studied intensively, had a grave metabolic disorder treated by refined and artificial nutritional methods, but nobody could say whether these cataracts were new or old, or due to the disease or to its treatment. Nobody knew because nobody had made the necessary observations on her eyes before the age of five. Her miraculous survival obviously dazzled the minds of those treating her, so that they forgot about her eyes. This happens frequently. (p. 59)

Extensive consideration of the medical aspects of the high-risk register is beyond the scope of this discussion, but it is critical for every parent of a child with birth defects to inquire of the attending physician regarding the high-risk register for loss of vision. If the child is considered to be at risk for loss of vision, examination of the eyes becomes a major priority in the child's care.

Diagnostic Examinations for Visual Loss

The examination of the eyes and determination of visual ability in the infant is an extremely difficult procedure. Subjective tests of vision (such as the standard examination with the Snellen chart) require that the subject be able not only to respond to the social demands of the examination but also to report accurately his/her visual experience to the examiner. Infants and very young children are clearly unable to engage in such examination, and, as such, a number of objective assessment procedures have been developed for the diagnosis of visual disabilities in the infant and toddler.

The visual examination of the infant must rely heavily on clinical observations of the child's response to visual stimuli. Such responses include reactions of the pupil to the presentation of light, blinking in response to light presentation, eye movements in response to the movement of objects in the visual

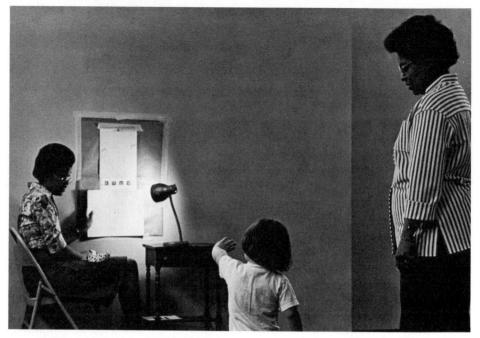

For preschool children, relatively simple eye-screening examinations can be used to detect possible visual problems.

field, fixation on stationary objects, and motor responses to visual stimuli (MacKeith, 1969). Clinical examinations of this type cannot determine the infant's actual visual ability but can yield important gross information about the child's potential for sight.

More sophisticated objective procedures for the diagnosis of visual disabilities in infancy are being developed but are not yet perfected for standard use. The *electroretinogram (ERG),* for example, is a relatively new method of objectively recording the eye's response to light. When the eye is stimulated by a bright flash of light, a momentary change takes place in the standing electrical potential of the nerves of the retina. The ERG can record this electrical activity either photographically or with an oscilloscope and make possible the determination of abnormalities within the eye. Such technical advances offer promise of the kinds of diagnostic procedures that may one day be routine in the examination of the infant or young child.

Patz and Hoover (1969) reported a very useful screening procedure that has been jointly established by the Maryland Society for the Prevention of Blindness and the Baltimore City Health Department. In essence, a portable camera is used to make photographic recordings of the eyes of infants. The photographs are then reviewed by an eye specialist in a manner similar to that of a radiologist reviewing an X ray. This procedure can reveal a large number of abnormalities of the eye without direct examination by an eye specialist; children who are identified on the screening basis can then be referred for more direct and extensive evaluation and care.

A wide variety of assessment procedures are now in use for children of preschool and primary-school age. Visual acuity testing, either by means of the standard Snellen chart or an adaptation using pictures or toys more appropriate for younger children, remains the dominant form of diagnostic vision screening in schools and preschools. In addition to testing for visual acuity, an **ophthalmologist** (a licensed medical doctor who specializes in the diagnosis and treatment of the eyes) or an **optometrist** (a licensed specialist in vision who is trained in the art and science of vision care, including examination of the eyes and enhancement of vision by nonsurgical means) can conduct a more thorough examination of the eye itself. Such examinations usually employ an *opthalmoscope,* an instrument used in examining the interior structures of the eye, or a *slit lamp,* an instrument that emits a narrow beam of strong light useful in the examination of frontal portions of the eye. A thorough diagnostic examination of the eyes, therefore, would include the typical eye-chart examination and a physical examination of the structures of the eye. Although the institution of eye-screening procedures in many states has brought trained specialists into direct contact with large numbers of children, the key people who must be sensitive to the potential visual problems of young children are parents, teachers, doctors, and nurses. In this respect, various behavioral signs (such as those given in Exhibit 6.2) might be cause for concern about a child's vision, thus prompting the need for a referral to an optometrist or ophthalmologist.

EXHIBIT 6.2

SIGNS OF POSSIBLE VISUAL DISABILITIES IN CHILDREN

Infants
Pupils do not react to light
Appears comfortable when bright light is directed toward eyes
Does not stare at surroundings
Is unable to follow a moving object with eyes
Has red-rimmed, encrusted, or swollen eyelids

Toddlers and Preschoolers
Rubs eyes frequently
Tries to brush away blur
Has pain in and about the eyes
Squints
Frowns
Is oversensitive to light
Stumbles or trips over small objects
Eyes are out of alignment (crossed eyes)
Blinks

Has repeated sties or watery, red eyes
Holds playthings close to eyes

Schoolchildren
Holds book close to eyes while reading
Tilts head forward when looking at objects
Holds head to one side while reading
Frowns when reading from a distance
Closes one eye when looking at an object
Skips words when reading aloud
Confuses the letters o and a when reading
Reads above or below the line
Eyes do not work together
Has double or blurred vision
Experiences dizziness and/or headaches following close eye work

From Fleming (1973, pp. 86–87)

DEVELOPMENTAL CONSEQUENCES

Despite the fact that many individuals who are blind from birth or become blind early in infancy are able to achieve and function as well as sighted persons of equal ability, loss of vision represents a potential handicap of considerable magnitude in the life of a developing child. The role of vision in a child's development was explored quite thoroughly by Gesell, Ilg, and Bullis (1949) in a work that still serves as an excellent reference. Vision is eminent among the sensory modalities because it assumes and retains a highly directive role in normal development; according to Gesell and his associates, vision acts as an integrator of a child's developing action systems and experiences of the world. Sighted persons become so accustomed to visual experience that they can easily overlook the fact that vision provides not only a specific sense modality but also an added dimension and qualification to the experience of other sense modalities. The loss of vision in a child's total experience is poignantly illustrated in the questions raised by a young blind girl in psychotherapy:

> Why can't I write with my eyes? Why did I always want to touch my mother? Where does the loving go when the scolding comes in the voice? Can you see the echo come back? What color is it when it is blue? (Omwake & Solnit, 1961, p. 352)

The effects of blindness and severe visual disability on a child's development must be understood in terms of both the specific effects of the lack of visual input as well as the more global effects of the lack of vision as an integrating function in overall development. In the past few decades, an increasing body of theoretical and research literature has concerned itself with various aspects touching on the development of the blind child. This material will be reviewed here in terms of (a) motor development, (b) language factors, (c) conceptual abilities and educational achievement, and (d) personal and social factors.

Motor Development

A number of studies have demonstrated that blind children who are otherwise neurologically and physiologically normal give evidence of early retardation in motor development when compared to norms for sighted children. Norris, Spaulding, and Brodie (1957) found that only 50 percent of a sample of 66 neurologically intact blind children were walking independently by age 2. Adelson and Fraiberg (1974) confirmed these findings with greater specification in a more intensive study of 10 blind infants: the blind infants closely approximated norms for sighted infants in such motor milestones as "sitting alone momentarily," "rolls back from stomach," "sits alone steadily," "takes stepping movements when hands are held," and "stands alone"; they were delayed, however, on such motor milestones as "elevates self by arms, prone," "raises self to sitting position," "stands up by furniture," and "walks alone, three steps." All of the milestones on which the blind infants were delayed involved self-initiated mobility, suggesting to the researchers that loss of vision does not affect the achievement of stable postures but that vision does play a central role in the establishment of milestones involving locomotion and mobility. Vision acts as a lure to move a sighted child toward objects at a distance. In this respect, Adelson and Fraiberg noted, "Only after [the blind child] has become practiced in reaching on sound will he begin to creep and walk, slowly mapping the concrete world about him" (1974, p. 125). Although this delay in self-initiated mobility need not exert a lasting effect on the blind child's overall motor development, such delays may well produce a spiraling effect on other personality factors. The lack of vision interferes with self-initiated mobility, and the lack of such mobility interferes with the child's capacity to explore and investigate the environment.

In this regard, Sandler (1963) maintained that the prolonged period of immobility in the blind child creates abnormal tendencies to be left alone, possibly resulting in passive self-centeredness and lack of striving toward mastery at later ages. Such observations are difficult to examine experimentally, and research evidence on the potential long-term effects of delayed mobility is lacking. Experiential observation of blind children at older ages, however, suggests that blind youngsters tend to be less outwardly mobile and frequently engage instead in self-stimulating movements, such as waving their arms, swaying from one foot to the other, and turning and twisting their bodies. These apparently directionless but rhythmic movements are known as **blindisms.** Although such unusual postural mannerisms are not distinctive to the blind (they are known to occur in children who are mentally retarded and/or emotionally disturbed), their presence in the blind child may well represent a substitute for more outwardly oriented exploration of the environment.

Language Factors

Language, both in its written and spoken form, has been created primarily by and for the use of the sighted. A large number of the words and phrases of any language are based on the experience of vision and visual imagery. An obvious example is that the word "seeing" is itself equated with "understanding," as in the case of a person who exclaims "Now I see it!" when he/she has discovered the solution to a problem. For the sighted child, the acquisition of language occurs within the context of the child's visual experience of the object world so that word and object blend together in vision and understanding. Because the blind child lacks the experience of visual association, the acquisition of a useful vocabulary takes place more slowly. In addition, spoken language requires oral movements, and the blind must learn to imitate movements of speech that they have never seen. Burlingham (1961, 1964, 1965) noted that speech development is initially somewhat delayed in the blind child, but once speech is acquired, blind children speak fluently and have excellent vocabularies. By late preschool age, blind children frequently tend to use speech excessively. This tendency of blind children to verbalize excessively or to use speech confidently about objects that they have not really experienced and do not really understand is known as **verbalism.**

Burlingham (1961) provided an interesting insight into the language of the blind:

> The blind child verbalizes in a manner similar to a sighted one in many ways, but there are differences. In one way lack of sight stimulates verbalization in the blind child, who tries to make up with words for what he does not see. He finds uses for speech that the seeing do not require, that is, for orientation, to collect characteristics for differentiating between persons, to discover some mark by which an object can be recognized. He asks questions, the main object of which is to provide clues.
>
> On the other hand, lack of sight makes many words meaningless or gives them a different meaning. Therefore, concepts may be completely misunderstood or only partially understood; or words may be used merely to imitate or to parrot the sighted. (p. 135)

The role of nonverbal communication in the blind child is very poorly understood. Since nonverbal communication is primarily visual in nature, the blind are obviously much less effective in responding to nonverbal cues. Despite this fact, it is a commonplace belief that the blind are specially gifted in terms of hearing and tactile sensitivity. This belief in "sensory compensation," namely that the blind have superior tactile and auditory senses to make up for loss of vision, has not been supported by research evidence. Bateman (1965) and Hare, Hammill, and Crandell (1970), for example, conducted studies to determine whether partially sighted children differed from sighted children on such factors as auditory decoding and sound discrimination ability; no significant differences were found in these controlled studies, and Hare et al. concluded that "the myth of sensory compensation" should be rejected.

Closely related to the belief in sensory compensation is the widespread notion that blind persons are "better listeners" than are sighted persons. Again, the popular assumption is that if a person cannot see, greater investment and

By touching miniatures of the animals she is learning about, this blind child will more readily connect the words with their concepts.

energy will be directed to listening skills. Although this issue has not been well researched, Hartlage (1963) found no significant differences in listening skills between the sighted and the blind.

For educational purposes, it cannot be assumed that impaired vision necessarily entails compensation and improved utilization of other sensory modalities. This does not mean that other sensory modalities should not be explored and used as much as possible for communication, learning, and skill acquisition. Whatever may take place instinctively in compensating for loss of vision, blind children bring no unusually developed or innately superior skills to the task of learning, and the education of the blind child must be based on the nature of the child's abilities.

Conceptual Abilities and Educational Achievement

One of the first professionals to conduct standardized assessments of blind children was Samuel P. Hayes, a psychologist who had long been involved with the Perkins School for the Blind in Watertown, Massachusetts. Recognizing that the blind child would be severely handicapped by using tests that require vision, Hayes (1941) developed a modification of the Stanford-Binet Intelligence Test suitable for work with blind children. Hayes eliminated from the Stanford-Binet (1937 revision) those test items that required the use of sight so that the test became essentially an assessment of verbal abilities. This modification—known as the Interim Hayes Stanford-Binet—paved the way for the intellectual assessment of blind children and provided one of the most extensive studies of intellectual abilities among blind children. Hayes administered his test to 2,372 blind children in residential schools; whereas the mean IQ of the sighted children on the 1937 Stanford-Binet standardization sample was 100, the blind youngsters in the Hayes' study had a mean IQ of 98.8—only slightly lower and not significantly different than the sighted group would be expected to produce in a comparable testing.

Using an adaptation of both the Wechsler Intelligence Scale for Children and the Stanford-Binet, Bateman (1963) studied 131 children enrolled in special classes for the partially sighted and the blind; the IQ scores of these youngsters were found to be normally distributed with an average IQ of 100. One finding of the Bateman study that has had far-reaching implications for the categorization of children for special education classes was the discovery that 40 percent of the sample should have been more properly classified as *learning disabled* rather than visually impaired.

Both the Hayes and the Bateman studies also found that among populations of the visually disabled, the students with the better vision tended to score lower on IQ tests than the students with less adequate vision. The reasons for this finding remain obscure but it may well be that students with the more severe visual disabilities tend to receive preferential treatment over students with less severe visual impairments.

More recently developed intelligence assessment procedures for the visually impaired have included the use of "haptic" as well as verbal assessments. **Haptic tests** rely on touch perception and use items such as specially developed formboards or shapes with raised dots. These tests are usually informal, nonstandardized procedures without adequate norms for use with children. Despite the fact that haptic tests and verbal tests are being developed, most existing tests are adaptations of tests originally developed for the sighted, a factor that could contribute negatively to the performance of blind children on such instruments. Because of these difficulties in assessment procedures, intellectual abilities of the blind have been less thoroughly studied than is the case with other populations of special children. *In general, however, when the effects of visual disability are directly controlled, intellectual abilities among the blind can be compared quite favorably with the distribution of such abilities among the sighted.*

Tisdall, Blackhurst, and Marks (1967) investigated the effects of visual deprivation on the cognitive processes of blind children. These investigators used verbal tests to assess originality of ideas, fluency of ideas, flexibility of thought, and the ability to elaborate on a stated theme. The population studied involved a group of 76 residential school blind children, a group of 76 day school blind children, and a control group of 76 day school sighted children. It was found that both sighted and blind performed equally over a range of such tests, thus lending support to the finding that the inherent nature of cognitive abilities does not differ among the sighted and the blind. Although the intellectual and cognitive abilities of the blind have not been widely investigated, research in this area gives little reason to believe that visual deprivation leads to significant differences between the cognitive abilities of the sighted and the blind.

Studies of the educational achievement of the partially sighted, however, are far less encouraging. Perhaps the most extensive investigation in this area (Birch, Tisdall, Peabody, & Sterrett, 1966) also attempted to determine criteria for the most effective type size to be used in printed instructional materials. The researchers compiled standardized reading achievement scores, as well as other descriptive data, on 903 partially sighted fifth- and sixth-grade students in special education classes in the District of Columbia and fifteen other states. They discovered that these students were far behind norms for reading achievement, irrespective of type size used in the tests. They also discovered that the students had average intelligence but were markedly overage for grade placement. The most obvious cognitive effects of visual disability, therefore, entail problems of achievement in special education programs when such programs are compared to the achievement level of sighted peers. Despite the fact that the partially sighted students in the Birch et al. study were older than sighted peers in the same grade, educational achievement was 2-1/2 years behind norms for the sighted in this grade range. No comparable studies of the partially sighted in regular classroom placements have yet been conducted, so it is difficult to determine whether such retardation in educational achievement is a function of the visual disability itself or of special education placement.

Personal and Social Factors

The assessment of personal and social development in the visually impaired child has not had a high priority among educators and psychologists, very possibly because of the difficulties involved in developing tests that are independent of visual components. Commonly used personality instruments for children, such as projective drawings and verbal responses to pictorial stimuli, are, obviously, inappropriate for assessing the blind child. Baumann (1973) noted that more suitable instruments have recently been developed using verbal questionnaires as measures, but the adequacy of such measures remains to be demonstrated. For these reasons, much of the research with blind children has been done through intensive studies of individual cases, relying heavily on intuitive and descriptive reporting.

Many such studies approach the blind child from the standpoint of psychodynamic theory, maintaining that the fact of blindness has inevitable and serious consequences on the child's development. Klein (1962), for example, noted that blindness tends to isolate the child from the environment, drastically reducing the child's opportunities for stimulation, manipulation, and interaction. In the same vein, Sandler (1963) argued that the absence of vision tends to produce a distinct line of development in the blind child toward passive self-centeredness and a lack of striving toward mastery. In spite of the fact that many blind adults are lauded for their spirit of independence, psychodynamic theory tends to look at the difficulties inherent in the development of the blind child with a view toward understanding the nature of the child's inner experience.

Fraiberg (1972), for example, presented considerable insight into the young blind child's experience of separation from the mother:

> In the case of the blind infant under one year it is difficult to isolate those conditions which mean mother is "absent" in everyday experience. In the case of the sighted child, mother is absent when she is not seen.

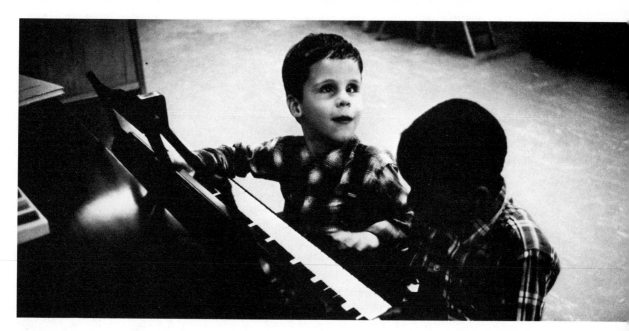

Sharing music and friendship—an important part of growth.

Vision permits the sighted child to give meaning to the "comings and goings" of his mother since he can track her with his eyes to the point at which she leaves his visual field (goes to another room, closes a door, etc.).

For the blind child, mother can be present in the room, and if she refrains from talking or moving, she has left the child's perceptual field. (pp. 356–57)

Fraiberg pointed out that the inability to track mother visually creates special problems for the young blind child because the presence and absence of the child's human partners frequently seems capricious and mysterious and unpredictable.

In addition to studies focusing on psychodynamic development in the blind child, a number of investigators have studied various other personal and social factors. Sommers (1944) studied 143 blind adolescents and their parents and found a variety of parental reactions to their children's disability. No consistent personality deviations were discovered in these adolescents, and the data suggested that personal adjustment in the blind adolescent was related to favorable parental attitudes regarding the youngster and the disability.

Cowen, Underberg, Verillo, and Benham (1961) also studied the relationship between visual disability and personal adjustment among three groups of adolescents: a group of partially sighted enrolled in a day school, a group of partially sighted enrolled in a residential school, and a control group of normally sighted children. Subjects in each group were tested on seven distinct measures of personal adjustment. No significant differences in adjustment were found among the three groups. The authors concluded that there is no inevitable relationship between visual disability and personal adjustment.

Cratty and Sams (1968) studied the concept of body imagery in 91 blind and partially sighted children, using a variety of body-image tests such as body planes, body parts, body movements, laterality, and directionality. An interesting finding in this study was that these youngsters were incapable of projecting themselves into the tester's reference system; for example, the subjects had unusual difficulty identifying the examiner's right side from the examiner's left side. This investigation raised the question of whether blind children experience others as "bodies" or as "voices which occasionally touch." Although the use of spatial orientation procedures to assess body imagery is an interesting approach to the assessment of imagery in the blind, the findings are not easily interpreted, and further research is needed.

Witkin, Oltman, Chase, and Friedman (1971) studied the relationship between absence of vision in the blind and cognitive style. Witkin and his associates defined cognitive style as "self-consistent modes of functioning which a person shows throughout his perceptual and intellectual activities, and which are, in turn, cognitive manifestations of still broader psychological dimensions" (p. 16). In general, these investigators found that the blind were less cognitively articulate and less psychologically differentiated than sighted peers. Despite the general findings, however, some blind subjects were found to be highly developed in both cognitive articulation and body image. The authors hypothesized that in some blind children, the lack of vision might actually serve as an impetus to the development of differentiation. The hypothesis advanced suggests that the blind child might well need to make a special effort to achieve an articulated concept of the world precisely because of the lack of vision and that this increased effort encourages the development of differentiation. The reasons why some blind children might make this effort while others do not remain obscure, even in theory. These findings again suggest, however, that *there is no straightforward relationship between visual disability and psychological adjustment variables.*

The above studies represent selections from the research and theoretical literature regarding blindness and personal-social adjustment. It should be clear from this brief review that psychodynamic studies of the blind tend to expect, theoretically, that blindness from birth or infancy is likely to impose extreme difficulties in ego development. Other research studies, however, do not find any clear relationship between blindness and psychological maladjustment. It must be concluded that blindness does not inevitably involve psychological or social maladjustment; nonetheless, there is a need for parents, teachers, and other professionals to be aware of the possible problems that the blind child may encounter as crisis periods in psychological and social development. An integrated theory of development in the blind child has not as yet been articulated, and psychodynamic theory currently offers considerable insight in this regard. Research on the psychological and social development of the blind child has been varied, and there is need for an integrated theory or theories to inspire more comprehensive research in this area.

INTERVENTION

Intervention with the visually disabled has a variety of purposes depending on the nature and degree of visual loss as well as the unique skills of differing professional disciplines. In general, however, the major goals of intervention in the area of visual impairments include the following: (a) preventing the occurrence of visual loss in newborns and infants; (b) protecting vision in the sighted; (c) recovering vision after a loss occurs; (d) increasing residual vision in children with visual loss; (e) helping an affected child adapt to visual disability by cultivating other sense modalities such as touch and hearing; (f) assisting the visually impaired child during crisis periods in development; (g) providing specialized facilities and aids suited to the child's intact abilities; and (h) enhancing mobility and other skills of daily living. Within the context of these general goals, several specific types of intervention are provided by certain professional disciplines. These specific forms of intervention occur most regularly through medicine, psychology, social work, and education.

Medical Intervention

Medical intervention is perhaps most widely effective at the preventive level. For example, since several major causes of blindness are hereditary, genetic counseling of parents can be an important preventive measure. Beyond that, prenatal care for mothers can be the most effective form of intervention. Treatment of maternal syphilis with antibiotics, for example, reduces risk of infection to the fetus, thus preventing possible impairment of the child's visual system. In this regard, 49 states have laws requiring prophylaxis of the eyes in the delivery room (Patz & Hoover, 1969); this common procedure of washing the eyes with a 1 percent silver nitrate solution is considered to be the most effective protection of the newborn from possible consequences of gonorrheal infection. In the same vein, mass inoculation for known childhood diseases is also a critical preventive measure.

When an infant or child is identified as having a visual disability, medical treatment varies depending on the nature of the condition. Some visual disabilities can be treated effectively by surgery or drugs, whereas others cannot be treated by any medical means. In a child with bilateral cataracts, for example, a number of different types of medical intervention are possible. Soft cataracts have traditionally been treated by a procedure known as *needling*, which involves breaking up the substance of the crystalline lens of the eye with a knife needle; a more recent innovation with the same principle is called *phacoemulsification*, a method of breaking up the cataract with the use of a low frequency ultrasonic needle. Another possible procedure for the treatment of cataracts is *atropinization*, or aspiration of the eye with an alkaloid drug known as *atropine;* this washing of the eye with an alkaloid drug is intended to produce a permanent dilation of the pupil so that the child actually "sees around" the opacity.

The possible medical treatments for various visual disabilities are too extensive to be discussed here. Despite the plethora of various treatments, medical advances in the treatment of blindness have been slow in developing, and there is no "cure-all" available in the treatment of blindness. The partially sighted child is particularly in need of regular medical evaluation to prevent deterioration and further loss of residual vision.

The use of optical aids is a highly significant form of medical intervention for the partially sighted child. There are several ways in which optical aids can improve the visual capability of the partially sighted, but the most common use is based on the principle of magnification or enlargement of the retinal image; the telescopic lens increases the visual angle and makes an object appear larger than it really is because the image that falls on the retina is enlarged. In this way, the nonseeing areas of the retina are made smaller in proportion to the total image received, thus providing reduced interference with the perception of the object. Such aids obviously can be crucial in maximizing the residual vision of the partially sighted child.

Psychological Intervention

Although a comprehensive approach to psychological intervention with the blind child is still lacking, in the past few decades mental health personnel have become increasingly aware of various treatment possibilities. In a general sense, psychological intervention with the blind child has paralleled overall developments within the mental health field; treatment perspectives, therefore, include the possibility of individual psychotherapy oriented around the disability, parent counseling, group psychotherapy with older blind children, and crisis intervention.

Innovations in recent years have attempted to focus specific programs of psychological intervention toward the developing needs of the blind child during late infancy and preschool years. Foremost among these innovations are sensory stimulation programs that attempt to provide the child with as much nonvisual stimulation as possible; these programs recognize that there is no automatic compensation for lack of vision by the other senses. Fraiberg (1971) and Fraiberg, Smith, and Adelson (1969) provide excellent discussions of a developmental guidance program for both blind children and their parents. The Fraiberg program attempts to structure the parent-child relationship in such a way that the physical closeness of the parent promotes sound and touch as the major sources of meaning and reward in the child's sensory experience. These forms of intervention seek to build in the blind child an early experience of sound-touch identity for persons and things, thus capitalizing on the child's intact sensory modalities.

Psychological intervention by mental health professionals skilled in the understanding of developmental problems in blind children can be extremely important in facilitating appropriate responses to crisis situations in the child's growth. Short-term psychotherapy, or crisis intervention, can be directed toward helping the blind child resolve specific difficulties in psychological development that are complicated by lack of vision. Case Study 6.1 gives an example of short-term psychotherapy with a mother and her blind child.

Social Intervention

For many years, one of the primary modes of intervention for the blind child involved residential placement in a school for the blind. A brief decade ago, 80 percent of the blind children in this country were enrolled in residential schools for the blind. Recent emphases on mainstream education as well as decisions by the court emphasizing equality of educational opportunities for the disabled have drastically reduced the numbers of children now placed in residential schools for the blind to an estimated 35 percent. The remainder now attend special or regular classes within their home school districts (Lowenfeld, 1973).

Residential placement for the blind child remains a desirable treatment choice in many instances. If the parents cannot cope with the child or if the child is very severely disabled, a school for the blind may be the only resource that can be effective in helping normalize the child's growth. Such decisions, however, can now be made on balance with other alternatives that include keeping the child at home and providing other forms of medical, psychological, or educational intervention.

Educational Intervention

A number of noted individuals have been associated with the development of educational approaches for blind children. In 1784, Valentin Haüy (1745–1822) founded the first school for the blind in Europe, L'Institution Nationale des Jeunes Aveugles, with 14 students. Haüy is credited with being the first to use embossed (raised) printing with his students, making it possible for them to

CRISIS INTERVENTION WITH A BLIND CHILD

Jackie was a 14-month-old boy blind from birth due to retrolental fibroplasia (RLF). He had been developing well within the average range for blind children when suddenly his mother was called away from home for three days because of the death of her father. Shortly after his mother returned home, Jackie began having screaming fits that lasted for hours: his face would become immobile and expressionless, he would engage in repetitive screams, and he would crawl in a frenzied, desperate fashion over his mother's body. He abandoned any interest in his toys, became fitful and sleepless for long periods at night, lost interest in eating and, after a few mouthfuls, would vomit. Jackie's mother became increasingly concerned at her inability to restore her son to a more normal behavior pattern; after his behavior had persisted without noticeable change for a two-week period, she contacted a child development center for assistance.

The staff at the Center was skilled in working with blind children and quickly recognized that Jackie's three-day separation from his mother had very likely precipitated a "separation crisis" which occasioned extremely regressive behavior. The staff felt that Jackie was experiencing terror and rage. In a sighted child, such separation anxiety would likely be expressed more directly, either actively (by fighting, kicking, and hitting) or passively (by ignoring the mother upon her return and instead seeking the solace of the adult who had been the caretaker

during the mother's absence). In either case, the mother of a sighted child would more easily recognize such behaviors as a sign of the child's anger at being left. The mother of a sighted child could help the child deal with the anger by identifying it, accepting it, and reestablishing a bond of effective caretaking: "You are angry with me because I had to leave you. I understand why you are angry and it's all right. Mommy is back now and will help you feel better."

As a one-year-old blind child, however, Jackie lacked the motor patterns necessary to demonstrate clearly the anger he experienced. Because Jackie lacked these motor patterns for fighting, the targets of his aggression were not immediately available to him. The staff at the Center encouraged Jackie's mother to provide him with pots and pans and banging toys whenever he engaged in his screaming fits. The banging games, in the words of the mother, "worked like magic." Jackie learned very quickly to express his anger through banging pots and pans. Within a few days, Jackie's shouting became very rare, his desperate clinging to his mother disappeared, and his general behavior returned to its previous patterns. Instead of being a helpless partner in Jackie's experience of crisis, his mother had shown she was an effective caretaker sensitive to his needs and able to provide him with help for his problems.

Drawn from Fraiberg (1972)

recognize letters by touch; in the main, however, Haüy's school sought to bring the method and content of regular education to the needs of the blind.

The most important educational innovation to be introduced for the blind was accomplished by one of Haüy's students, Louis Braille (1809–1852), the inventor of a touch system of reading that still bears his name. Braille was blinded at age 5 by an accident with one of his father's saddlery tools. At age 10, Braille entered Haüy's school and distinguished himself in both science and music. Using Haüy's earlier work with embossed printing, as well as that of Charles Barbier who had developed a system of writing with points, Braille produced a touch system that has become the basis of the braille system of writing and reading as it is used today.

In the United States, Samuel Gridley Howe (1801–1876) was the forerunner of efforts to educate the blind. A sensitive and effective educator, he was the first person in America to devote himself to the education and training of a deaf and blind child, and his work with Laura Bridgman (see Chapter 1) continues to stand as a milestone in the achievement of an empathic understanding of special children. As the first director of the New England Asylum for the Blind (founded in 1829 in Massachusetts and now known as the Perkins School for the Blind), Howe was an articulate advocate for a number of the following issues that remain paramount in special education today: (a) residential schools should be small and few in number, (b) the majority of blind children should be educated in common schools with their seeing peers, (c) every blind child must be considered as an individual who should be educated in accordance with his/her unique abilities, (d) the curriculum for the blind child should be as much like the curriculum for the sighted as possible, (e) the main purpose of education for the blind should be to train them to be socially and economically self-sustaining (Farrell, 1956).

Principles of educating the visually impaired

The history of special education for the visually impaired has shown that educators successful in teaching the blind make use of certain principles to guide the process of education. Lowenfeld (1973) has summarized these principles in three needs of the visually impaired: (a) the need for concrete experiences, (b) the need for unifying experiences, and (c) the need for learning by doing. If the education of the blind child is to be personally meaningful and self-involving, it must offer the child the opportunity to go beyond words in the construction of a sensible reality.

Concreteness of experience, unification of experience, and learning by doing require that educators of the blind orient learning experiences toward real-life events and the use of objects and special materials. Arts and crafts that involve the use of the hands are obviously very useful approaches for bringing the blind child into closer proximity with sensory experience. Fulker and Fulker (1968) present a variety of such programmed educational experiences, ranging from the use of cut-outs and models to the utilization of field trips for the blind. Exhibit 6.3 gives an example of this approach, which the authors describe as "techniques with tangibles." This exhibit demonstrates the interaction of the three principles discussed above as a means of enriching the content of the child's mental life even when language alone is the medium of learning.

Braille instruction

For the totally blind child, braille offers the most plausible entry to the world of letters, and special educators need to be familiar with it as a second written language. In the United States, the Standard English Braille system was adopted in 1932 and is the accepted approach. The system makes use of a *six-dot cell*

TECHNIQUES WITH TANGIBLES

"Let's try an experiment," the teacher of fifteen high-school age, visually handicapped students challenged his class. "Each of you must give me a detailed description of what the term 'dog' means to you, gained from a firsthand knowledge of dogs you have examined yourselves."

Notes were taken as the students described various dogs they had "seen." Then the teacher read four paragraphs which he had previously chosen describing four widely different breeds of dog. A Siberian husky was described hauling a sled, and at the opposite pole of comparison, a toy Pekingese was pictured dawdling on his mistress's lap. Then the students were asked if, in all four read-

ings, they saw a single dog image, or if it changed shape and size as they imagined the next story excerpt. Two of the students made no changes, five made only slight and very vague changes. Eight were well informed enough to distinguish clearly the different kinds of objects classified under one word, "dog."

In the process of conducting this informal experiment, both the teacher and the students learned about the types of concepts the pupils had. It illustrated in a dramatic way the impoverishment of mental images characteristic in some of our high-school-age students, even concerning such an everyday object as a dog.

From Fulker & Fulker (1968, p. 3)

devised by Louis Braille and includes 63 different characters that are alphabetical, numerical, and grammatical. Exhibit 6.4 shows the braille alphabet. Braille can be written with both a *braille writer* (a machine similar to a typewriter) or a *slate and stylus* (similar to a pencil and paper for a sighted writer). Each works by embossing points of a six-dot cell on paper. These points can then be read by touching the finger (usually the forefinger) to the page.

Blind children who become proficient in braille can read only about as quickly as a sighted reader is able to read aloud. Both reading and writing braille, therefore, are paced more slowly than is the case with sighted reading and writing, so the braille reader is at an obvious disadvantage. Another disadvantage of braille reading material is its sheer bulk. Each single braille character requires a quarter of an inch of line space, and each braille line requires two-fifths of an inch of page space. When a typical issue of *Reader's Digest* is transformed into braille, it requires four volumes that are each one inch in thickness and 11 by 13½ inches in size. The use of a shorthand symbol system can make braille material less bulky, but it still remains a cumbersome system.

Recent technological advances may well revolutionize the entire approach to reading for the visually impaired. The *optacon*, a new type of reading machine, is already being used in larger public school systems. This technological aid is a small electric camera that—when held in one hand and focused on printed material—translates the material into a sharp pulsation felt in the index finger of the other hand. Although this equipment is expensive (a single machine costs approximately $3,000), it offers the blind child an opportunity to read almost as quickly as the average sighted student in a normal classroom.

EXHIBIT 6.4

169

Intervention

THE ALPHABET IN BRAILLE SYMBOLS

An alternative to the touch reading that is the essence of any braille system is, of course, "reading with the ears." Recordings, both by tape and phonograph, provide an important source of literary material for the blind. The Library of Congress currently maintains an extensive collection of literary and reference works that have been transformed into recorded materials as well as braille.

Aids for the partially sighted

A central goal in the education of the partially sighted is to maintain or increase the child's capacity to make use of vision for the purpose of learning. Since there are many differing types of visual conditions included in the category "partially sighted," potential aids must be programmed to the individual needs of each child. The commonly used aids that can facilitate use of printed materials among the visually disabled include control of lighting conditions in the classroom, the use of optical devices for magnification and projection, and variations in the type or size of printed materials.

Although such aids can be extremely helpful in the objective sense, educators of the partially sighted must be sensitive to the fact that there are many subjective variables that influence a child's ability to make effective use of these aids for learning. As Barraga (1973) has pointed out, many partially sighted children have been taught to believe that they are blind and cannot see with their eyes; on the other hand, attempting to see with the eyes may expose the child to a feeling of potential failure. Such subjective factors frequently present subtle barriers for the teacher who is trying to facilitate use of vision in a partially sighted child. It cannot be overemphasized, therefore, that the use of aids with the partially sighted also requires sensitivity to the child's motivational and emotional states. Aids that can increase visual capability for learning through printed materials do not automatically guarantee that the child will be receptive to such assistance.

Daily living skills

An additional educational objective for all blind and partially sighted children is helping the child acquire daily living skills. If education is a preparation for a meaningful life, then the education of the blind must help equip the child for life in a sighted world. Chief among the daily living skills for which the blind child requires special training are *orientation* and *mobility*. The blind, for example, have no built-in visual feedback for appropriate head and facial orientation while engaged in conversation. Such orientation must be sensitively taught. Furthermore, the ability to move safely from place to place does not come easily when one cannot see; for the blind, it is a complex skill requiring training and encouragement. Simple grooming skills involving one's social presentation can be difficult to acquire without natural visual feedback; for the blind, such skills, taken for granted by sighted persons, must be learned slowly and by touch rather than a quick glance in the mirror. Such skills are

For years, braille (shown left) has provided the major access to reading materials for the blind. The optacon (shown right) may well change that, however. This small electric camera translates printed material into sharp pulsations that can be "read." The marvel of the optacon is that it can provide the visually impaired with immediate access to reading materials that are not in braille.

absolutely essential for social interaction with the sighted, and the education of the blind child would be sadly neglectful if it did not take them into account.

In conclusion, current medical research offers little promise for "cures" of blindness. The roles of the special educator and clinical professional, therefore, remain of primary importance in the planning and implementation of services for children with visual loss. Programs of early identification and early intervention in the educational, medical, and psychological needs of these children and their families offer the best hopes for more integrated service and consequent reduction of the handicapping aspects of visual loss. Within special education, most educators are convinced that special provisions such as resource rooms, itinerant teachers, and residential schools will continue to be necessary educational approaches to the blind and visually disabled (Lowenfeld, 1973). Social attitudes toward the blind are still much in need of modernization, and yet there has probably never been a period in history that has offered greater prospects for integration of the blind into the general fabric of society.

SUMMARY

1. The medical-legal definition of blindness stresses visual acuity and the field of vision but does not take account of the child's functional visual efficiency.
2. The educationally blind child must rely on touch and hearing as the major avenues of learning.
3. The partially sighted child is able to use vision as an avenue of learning.
4. It is estimated that 1 in 3,000 schoolchildren is educationally blind and that 1 in 500 is partially sighted.
5. The causes of blindness are varied and include hereditary-genetic, prenatal, perinatal, and postnatal factors.
6. Research studies indicate that children who are born blind are slower in acquiring developmental milestones that involve self-initiated mobility.
7. Blind children frequently give evidence of *verbalism*, a tendency to talk excessively or to use speech confidently about objects they have not really experienced or do not understand.
8. When the effects of visual disability are directly controlled, intellectual abilities among the blind compare quite favorably with the distribution of such abilities among the sighted.
9. Most research studies tend to indicate that the presence of serious psychological or social maladjustment is not significantly greater among the blind when compared to equivalent groups of sighted persons.
10. The single most important type of intervention for the blind child is special education.
11. Many children who are legally blind can still learn to read with their eyes.

Children with Physical Health Disorders

There is, perhaps, no place where the interaction between body and mind can be studied more advantageously than in a hospital for chronically ill children. What we saw demonstrated to the full was how in some instances personality development can be distorted and devastated by the affliction of the body; how in others a strong ego may triumph over the body, influence progress and recuperation, and mold the final outcome; and, finally, how helplessly exposed to their illnesses were those children whose earlier circumstances of life had deprived them of the chance of building up healthy and effective personalities.

Thesi Bergmann and Anna Freud (1965, p. 100)

AN INTRODUCTION TO PHYSICAL HEALTH DISORDERS

The presence of serious illness or physical disability in an infant or young child can be a terrifying experience for both the child and the family. The sudden experience of pain from illness or medical treatment, hospitalization and separation from loved ones, the disruption in the functioning of the family unit—events such as these are difficult enough for the adult patient, let alone for the young child who may be suddenly wrenched from the protective warmth and security of the family. Coping with serious illness or physical disability can be a traumatic challenge to a child's developing personality as well as a threat to the harmony of relationships within the family.

The care and management of children with physical health disorders is likewise an extremely demanding profession. Our hearts naturally go out to the suffering child, but competent professional care frequently requires distance and sternness of attitude. Professional caregivers must be both emotionally sensitive and emotionally tough, and sometimes they must be both at the same time. Nurses, physicians, and staff involved in the care of the hospitalized child constantly work in situations of conflicting emotion. As skilled professionals, they have commitments to quality care; as concerned persons, they seek to be understanding and empathic; at times, as helpless observers, they see lives that have barely begun suddenly end.

The study and understanding of children with severe physical health problems has advanced rapidly within the past few years, and basic knowledge of this field is essential for anyone who is involved professionally with children. Many children with physical health disorders are not placed in special educational programs; they may instead remain integrated in the local community and school. These children frequently are absent from school for long periods, require special medications, and raise many concerns for their peers and schoolmates. The child who is diagnosed as leukemic at age 8 has already had several years of close contacts with teachers and peers; a sudden hospitalization, several painful medical procedures, the loss of hair associated with medication, the return to school, the absence from school for further hospitalizations, the shadow of possible death—such events create consternation and anxiety for everyone who is involved with the child. This chapter will seek to present a frame of reference for understanding the many psychological and social issues involved in helping children with physical health disorders.

DEFINITION AND CLASSIFICATION

The definition and classification of children with physical health impairments is far from an orderly process. So many different kinds of children are included under the general rubric of "physical disability and/or physical health impairment" that it is virtually impossible to include all such children under a single set of descriptive terms and expect a homogeneous population to be thus described. The general classification of physical disability and physical health impairment includes children who are born with multiple physical defects, children who lose limbs because of accidents, children who are severely burned, children with visual or auditory disabilities, children with asthma, children with a specific chronic illness such as leukemia or cystic fibrosis, children with differing kinds of crippling conditions such as muscular dystrophy or limb deficiency, and children with cleft lip or cleft palate. All of these children have medical problems of a physical nature, require extensive medical services such as hospitalization and possible surgery, and raise concerns about the possibility of psychological problems that might arise from the physical disorder.

Definition of Terms

"Physical health disorders" is clearly a general term that includes many different kinds of physical disabilities and illnesses. These conditions, or at least certain classes of these conditions, may also be described by such terms as physical handicaps, orthopedic disabilities and handicaps, neurological impairments, chronic illness, disabling illness, and chronic physical disorders. Public Law 91-230 (the Elementary and Secondary Education Act), for example, uses the nomenclature "Crippled and Other Health Impaired." Because of the possible confusion that can arise from this multitude of descriptive labels, it would be well to elaborate on the concept of physical health disorders.

This chapter will not concern itself with childhood illnesses that are brief and self-limited; measles, mumps, and chicken pox, for example, typically run their course in a matter of a few days to a few weeks with little or no adverse consequences to the child. Many other childhood conditions, however, are not self-limited and *cannot be easily or completely cured.* An illness of this type is usually termed **chronic,** because it is long-standing, and **disabling,** because it places severe demands on the growing child's ability to lead a normal life. For our purposes, then, a **physical health disorder** is any identified physical health problem that (a) requires intensive medical attention or hospitalization, (b) cannot be easily and completely cured and is therefore long-standing, and (c) places severe demands on the child's ability to lead a normal life.

Classification of Physical Health Disorders

A satisfactory system of classification that would be equally useful to medical, educational, and mental health personnel has not yet been developed. Between 1958 and 1966, the American Medical Association suggested a series of guides to help the practicing physician classify the nature of various ailments commonly treated. These guides are based on the notion that the most useful medical guide to classification involves the specification of the physical location of the problem or the system of the body that is impaired. Thus one general classification is "extremities and back," including orthopedic disabilities, and another general classification is "cardiovascular system," including heart diseases and blood diseases. This system is helpful in organizing medical specialities but provides little useful information for the nonmedical professional.

Pless and Douglas (1971) suggested that other factors should be included in the classification of physical health disorders. They proposed a system based on three major categories: type, duration, and severity:

Type of Disability
a) *Motor*—a condition that interferes predominantly with motor function either directly or indirectly (e.g., cardiac condition or orthopedic impairment);
b) *Sensory*—a condition that interferes with vision, hearing, or speech (e.g., blindness, deafness, or cleft lip);
c) *Cosmetic*—a condition that predominantly affects social interaction (e.g., eczema or craniofacial anomaly);
Duration of Disability
a) *Permanent*—a condition that is present at age 15 and whose natural history suggests that it will continue indefinitely (e.g., heart disease);
b) *Indefinite*—a condition that is present at age 15 but whose natural history suggests that it *may* terminate at a later date (e.g., asthma);
c) *Temporary*—a condition that terminated prior to age 15 (e.g., eczema);
Severity of Disability
a) *Mild*—a condition that only prevents the child from engaging in strenuous activities (such as competitive athletics);
b) *Moderate*—a condition that interferes with normal daily activities appropriate for age and sex (such as quiet play or school attendance);
c) *Severe*—a condition that requires prolonged periods of immobilization, 18 weeks or more continuous absence from school or attendance at special schools (pp. 407–8).

This schema helps clarify those aspects of a physical health disorder that are most relevant in planning for a child's educational, psychological, and social needs. The distinct advantage of such a classification system involves its ability to assist nonmedical professionals in planning to minimize the consequences of a physical health disorder.

INCIDENCE AND ETIOLOGY

Accurate data regarding the full range of physical disorders and chronic illness in childhood are extremely difficult to obtain, primarily because of inconsistencies in defining various physical disorders. Perhaps the most extensive study of incidence rates of chronic illness was that conducted by the U.S. Department of Health, Education, and Welfare in the late 1950s and early 1960s. Although somewhat dated, this study, known as the U.S. National Health Survey, used household interviews as the means of data collection and is probably the most comprehensive study of its kind ever undertaken. The data from this study were organized by Schiffer and Hunt (1963) and published under the title *Illness Among Children*. These authors reported:

> *In the period July 1959 through June 1961, an annual average of 13,996,000 chronic conditions were reported among children under the age of 17. This means a rate of 226.1 per 1,000 population, or almost 1 condition for each 4 children. The 13,996,000 conditions were distributed among 11,116,000 children, so that almost 1 child in every 5 under the age of 17, 18.0 percent of the population in that age group, had at least 1 chronic condition. Since it is believed that the National Health Survey data err on the side of underreporting, it can safely be said that the prevalence of chronic conditions among children represents a public health problem of staggering proportions. (pp. 12–13)*

The most frequently occurring chronic conditions reported in this study were two major groups of illnesses: (a) hay fever, asthma, and other allergies, and (b) sinusitis, bronchitis, and other respiratory diseases. These two classes of illness accounted for almost half of the chronic conditions reported for children under 17, with allergic diseases accounting for 32.8 percent and resipratory diseases accounting for 15.1 percent. Paralysis and orthopedic impairments accounted for 11.6 percent, while all other chronic conditions accounted for 40.5 percent. It is interesting to note that nearly one-fourth of all days reported lost from school due to physical health disorders were lost because of asthma.

Incidence rates with regard to the full range of physical health disorders vary considerably from locale to locale and from decade to decade. There are fewer respiratory diseases in the dry climate of Arizona than in the cold, wet winters of upper New York. At the same time, medical advances reduce the prevalence of certain types of disease. The polio vaccine, for example, has drastically reduced the numbers of children who are paralyzed by virtually eliminating one of the major causes of paralysis. In the same vein, however, medical advances also tend to increase prevalence rates for certain illnesses; a decade ago, leukemic children typically died shortly after the onset of the illness; today, improved treatment approaches make it possible for many leukemic children to live through childhood and into adulthood. As leukemic children are kept alive for longer periods of time, the prevalence rate for leukemia among living children increases proportionally.

Many factors, therefore, are at work producing differences in estimates of incidence rates for various types of physical health disorders. Pless and Douglas (1971) stated that, despite this variation, "even the most conservative estimates affirm that at least one child in 20 will experience a chronic illness" (p. 405). Mattsson (1972) maintained that "even if only serious chronic illnesses of primary physical origin are included, American and British surveys still report that 7 percent to 10 percent of all children are afflicted" (p. 801).

Since physical health disorders are a general category that includes many different types of specific illnesses, causation must be seen as extremely varied. Mattsson (1972) organized the possible causes of physical health disorders in terms of the following schema:

a) **Prenatal chromosomal aberrations**—such as Down's syndrome or Turner's syndrome (a chromosomal anomaly in which the major symptoms involve dwarfism, infantile sexual development, and webbed neck);

b) **Prenatal abnormal hereditary traits**—such as clubfoot, cleft lip or palate, cystic fibrosis (a progressive disease of the pancreas), hemophilia and sickle cell anemia (blood disorders), and certain types of blindness and deafness;

c) **Prenatal harmful intrauterine factors**—such as birth defects caused by blood incompatibility between mother and fetus, radiation, and infections such as rubella or syphilis;

d) **Perinatal trauma or infections**—such as loss of oxygen or hemorrhage during childbirth that produces brain damage and subsequent impairment of neurological development;

e) **Serious postnatal trauma, injuries, or infections**—such as chronic kidney disease, rheumatic fever, tumors, leukemia, and loss of limb due to physical injury.

In a specific sense, the causes of particular illnesses may, of course, still be unknown. Leukemia, for example, is actually a group of diseases with unknown specific causes, and yet it can still be recognized as caused by postnatal events rather than hereditary causes. The etiology of leukemia obviously involves a unique set of causal factors vastly different from the loss of limb caused by an automobile accident. Because the nature of physical health disorders is quite varied, further discussion of the causes of these disorders would only take us away from the more germane considerations.

DIAGNOSIS AND IDENTIFICATION

The diagnosis and identification of children with physical health disorders is primarily a medical problem of considerable complexity. Extensive discussion of such considerations is beyond our purpose. For most educators and non-medical health professionals, however, a general knowledge of diagnostic categories combined with relevant medical information about a particular child is sufficient to deal constructively with the psychological, social, or edu-

One of the most tragic examples of a prenatal harmful intrauterine factor in the early 1960s was the case of the "thalidomide babies," children born to women who had taken the now-banned tranquilizing drug thalidomide during pregnancy. The defect was most commonly manifested in malformed arms and legs. The children in the picture above are being taught to use artificial limbs and their own limbs as much as possible; they wear head protection because their sense of balance may be faulty, and they cannot protect themselves if they fall.

cational aspects of an affected child's life. In the interest of such knowledge, Exhibit 7.1 presents relevant information regarding the major diagnostic categories of the physical health disorders of childhood.

DEVELOPMENTAL ASPECTS

The presence of a chronic illness during the formative years of a child's development clearly creates many unusual issues that must be faced by the child and the family. Both medical and psychoeducational health specialists have become increasingly concerned about the whole child rather than just about aspects of the child's illness. Adequate medical care for children involves more than the diagnosis and treatment of the physical or organic aspects of a child's illness. The child with chronic physical disorders is a unique patient because he/she is a rapidly changing, developing individual who is also a dependent member of a family unit. Illness and hospitalization may

EXHIBIT 7.1

179

Developmental
aspects

COMMON PHYSICAL HEALTH DISORDERS OF CHILDHOOD

Name	Diagnostic Description	Important Characteristics
Cerebral palsy	A crippling condition of the neuromuscular system; disorder of movement and posture; central characteristic is neurological motor dysfunction caused by brain damage (birth injury, congenital defect, infection); not a clear-cut syndrome but includes children with a variety of symptoms, such as muscle weakness or involuntary muscle movements.	Brain damage involved in CP may also affect IQ but not inevitably; however, a greater proportion of CP children are mentally retarded than is case with general population; since condition involves brain damage, it cannot be cured, but physical therapy and surgery can improve function.
Epilepsy	A condition of the neuromuscular system involving recurring attacks of loss of consciousness, convulsive movements, or disturbances of feeling and behavior; also known as *seizure* or *convulsive disorder;* caused by as yet undetermined brain damage.	Focus of treatment is the control of seizures; many effective anticonvulsant medications are now available; although many mentally retarded individuals suffer from seizures, the seizures themselves do not seem to cause mental retardation.
Spina bifida	A congenital defect of the spinal column; in its more severe forms, paralysis of lower limbs is virtually inevitable without surgical intervention; condition is evident at birth; most severe form is termed *myelomeningocele.*	Typically involves mental retardation; although the lives of these children can usually be saved by surgery, many such youngsters will have considerable physical and intellectual disabilities.
Muscular dystrophy	A degeneration of the muscles; disease is progressive and grows worse with age.	These children typically require a wheelchair in the normal course of the disease; cognitive abilities are not affected.
Limb deficiencies	Caused by genetic birth defects, amputations due to disease, or accidents.	Mechanical limbs (prosthetic devices) can frequently be fitted, but considerable training in use of limb as well as supportive attitudes are necessary.
Cystic fibrosis	Symptoms include generalized dysfunction of the exocrine glands, very high salt concentrations in sweat, and chronic pulmonary dysfunction with repeated episodes of pneumonia (with severe bouts of coughing); most lethal hereditary disorder of children in U.S.; specific cause unknown; no	These youngsters are encouraged to lead active lives and no physical restrictions are placed on behavior; cognitive development is normal and they typically remain in regular school placement; extensive therapeutic regimen is required in the home; patients frequently feel emotionally in-

Name	Diagnostic Description	Important Characteristics
	known cure, and illness is inevitably fatal; many patients, however, survive into adolescence and young adulthood.	hibited due to mucous excretions, chronic coughing, and breathing difficulty.
Leukemia	A group of diseases characterized by sudden increases of white blood cells in the bone marrow and peripheral blood; most common form of childhood cancer; a decade ago, the disease was considered fatal; recent advances in chemotherapy have made it possible to expect cure or at least long-term leukemia-free survival.	Many children can be treated with drugs on an outpatient basis; others require surgery, radiation therapy, or bone marrow transplantation; fear of death is frequent concern of child and family, even in remission, and an atmosphere of normalcy should be stressed with emphasis on positive aspects of living.
Asthma	Causes unclear; involves both psychological and somatic factors; often described as *psychophysiologic* illness; characterized by difficulty in breathing due to narrowing of airways; involves severe and life-threatening attacks of wheezing; may cause death due to inability to breathe.	Sometimes described as the "vulnerable child syndrome"; breathing attacks are frightening and parents may tend to overprotect the child; drug therapy can be very effective in preventing attacks and aerosol (fine mist spray) can be helpful in controlling attack.
Diabetes	Characterized by an inability to store sugar in the blood due to dysfunction of the pancreas; symptoms include loss of weight, frequent urination, and excessive thirstiness; treatment involves diet management and insulin therapy as needed.	With proper management, diabetes can be brought under control; risks involve diabetic coma (excess of sugar in blood causing nausea, abdominal pain, labored breathing) and insulin reaction (lack of sugar causing hunger, sweating, tremors, drowsiness).

represent a threat to life and physical health, but they may also represent a threat to psychosocial development and effective family functioning. The care of the chronically ill child, therefore, requires a sensitivity and awareness of the child as a developing person who experiences his/her physical disability as part of an evolving sense of reality and personal identity in membership with a particular family.

A Child's Concept of Illness and Disability

In a now-classic article, Anna Freud (1952) made the following observation:

> Before we can arrive at a correct assessment of this potentially traumatic experience of illness we have to work our way through the action of a large number of factors which, though they are mere by-products of the

situation, are for the child's mind inextricably intermixed with it. The child is unable to distinguish between feelings of suffering caused by the disease inside the body and suffering imposed on him from outside for the sake of curing the disease. He has to submit uncomprehendingly, helplessly and passively to both sets of experiences. (p. 70)

In a study of 264 children aged 6 through 12 years who had had short-term hospitalizations, Campbell (1975) investigated the possibility that a child's definition of illness is learned cognitively from the mother. Although Campbell discovered that the illness concept of a specific child was unlikely to resemble that of the mother, he did find that as children grew older their definitions of illness became more like those typically given by adults. In an extensive review of the literature, Vernon, Foley, Sipowicz, and Schulman (1965) concluded that the child's conception of illness is rather dominated by thoughts of punishment, mutilation, death, and abandonment.

Children, in other words, do not experience an illness or disability as an objective, comprehensible event that occurs to the body. Instead, they experience the illness subjectively and bring their own experience to bear in making sense of the illness. Young children in particular lack the ability to understand the causal relationships involved in an illness and tend to provide psychological reasons as causes for the experience of physical health disorder. Thus pain, symptoms, hospitalization, intrusive treatments, separation from parents during hospitalization, and the like can easily be seen by a child as a punishment for some actual or imagined misdeed. For example, a child with a heart defect said that he was ill because "he had run too much"; a young colitis patient blamed his illness on the fact that he had "eaten something dirty"; and a child with diabetes stated that she had acquired her disease because she "had eaten too much candy" (Mattsson, 1972). Such mistaken notions are commonly encountered in hospital settings, despite the fact that, on many occasions, very accurate information about the illness has been given to the child. Since many children avoid talking about their illness or disability, it is important that professional personnel and parents help them discuss their private feelings and ideas about the illness in order to correct possible misconceptions. Many hospitals for children have play programs to help them communicate in play what cannot be said in words.

The Hospital Experience

Hospitalization itself can be a frightening and traumatic experience, especially for the younger child, and the recognition of this fact has produced major changes in methods of hospitalization. For many years, the overriding concern in the hospitalization of the child was the illness itself, with little attention paid to the emotional or developmental needs of the child. Well into the middle of the current century, children were managed very much like adults in hospitals, with restrictions on bed confinement, visiting hours, feeding schedules, and so forth. René Spitz (1945) provided significant impetus to alter the nature of childhood hospitalization in order to be more responsive to the needs of the child; he noted that hospitalization separated the child from the mother, producing a situation of maternal and emotional deprivation. Spitz introduced the term **hospitalism** to describe the observed effects of such deprivation in infants and young children: depression, loss of weight, emotional withdrawal, and general physical wasting. Thus Spitz observed that a strange and horrible paradox was occurring: children who were hospitalized for various illnesses were acquiring a new illness, albeit a psychological one, because of the maternal deprivation that occurred during hospitalization. This increasing awareness of the potentially harmful effects of long-term hospitalization on the child's development has produced dramatic changes in the management of children who are hospitalized. As Kenny (1975) noted, this realization of the child's need for affectionate, human contact has led to a relaxation of hospital visiting policies to the extent that many hospitals provide a *rooming in* service by which parents can remain with their ill child during the hospitalization.

Since the major concerns regarding a child who is ill center about the illness itself, it can easily be overlooked that the child may be more concerned about the hospitalization than about the illness. Hospitalization represents a decisive change in a child's life; the child is removed from home, is suddenly cared for by strangers, and may well be exposed to pain or intrusive procedures as part of the diagnostic or treatment process. Hospitalization itself represents a potentially stressful experience for the child, and children frequently show this stress quite directly by crying, whining, screaming, resisting medications, struggling against treatment, or becoming tense, fearful, or with-

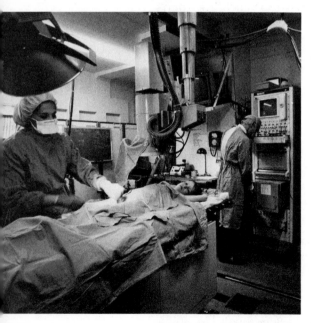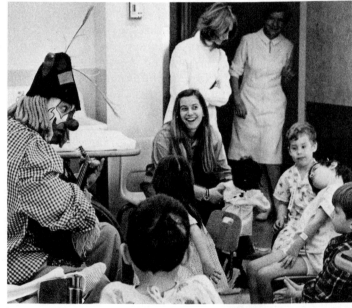

The hospital experience can be a frightening sequence of machines and unknowns. Play programs, such as the one pictured above right, can go a long way in helping children relax and communicate their concerns.

drawn (Gellert, 1958). It would be overstating the case, of course, to maintain that every hospitalized child experiences severe psychological stress or shows signs of such emotional behavior. It is important, however, for both the hospital staff and the family to recognize that even psychologically healthy children may become emotionally upset in response to the experience of hospitalization and that hospitalization may be very stressful even to the child who appears to be coping well.

Vernon et al. (1965) identified a number of factors that may contribute to psychological distress for the hospitalized child: (a) unfamiliarity with the hospital setting; (b) separation from home and family; (c) need to form and experience new interpersonal relationships with nurses, technicians, physicians, and other hospital personnel; (d) restrictions on sensory and motor movement and the fact of confinement; (e) the child's conception of the meaning of the hospitalization; (f) the age and the sex of the child; (g) the child's prehospital personality and the nature of the child's relationships with the parents; (h) the emotional responses of the parents and family to the child's illness; and (i) the specific medical procedures involved in the care of the child. Although extensive discussion of these factors would be beyond the scope of this review, it should be clear that the experience of stress during hospitalization is determined by many factors. It is important that medical and nursing staffs remain aware of the potential stress involved in hospitalization and seek to provide ways to reduce such stress during the child's stay.

Developmental Consequences

Robert Louis Stevenson, himself a victim of pulmonary tuberculosis, once observed that "Life is not a matter of holding good cards, but of playing a poor hand well." Chronic illnesses and physical disabilities in childhood represent potential problems in coping with life or even with the threat of death itself. The chronically ill or physically disabled child, of course, is first a child, and as a child is subject to the processes of growth and development that characterize the state of childhood. In addition to the obvious physical incapacities that affect the chronically ill child, physical disorders also pose problems in the child's psychological, social, and educational development. The child's ability "to play a poor hand well" is known as *coping,* and the understanding of coping behavior is a necessary prelude to working successfully with the chronically ill child.

Coping behavior

The child's ability to cope effectively with chronic illness is obviously a function of many factors, including the age of onset of the illness, the nature of the child's personality before the illness, the family interaction patterns, and the specific nature of the illness. The term "coping behavior" has recently been generally adopted to describe the many responses of children and families to the stress represented by chronic health problems, as well as other continuing disabilities. Stubblefield (1974) noted that chronic illness in children poses two major risks in terms of the child's psychological adaptation: (a) depressive reactions such as shock, apathy, and detachment, and (b) negative effects on self-esteem and self-image. Unhappiness and doubts about one's skills and abilities seem to be central concerns involved in a child's response to chronic health problems.

There is a growing interest among health professionals in attempting to identify the mechanisms or factors that enable children and their families to cope well in the face of chronic illness and/or physical disability. With regard to the child, Mattsson (1972) set forth some of the differences between youngsters who cope effectively and those who cope less effectively. Children who cope well are characterized by age-appropriate dependence on their families; ability to accept their limitations and assume responsibility for their care; ability to gain satisfaction through compensatory physical activities or intellectual pursuits and appropriate release and control of emotions; ability to maintain hope for recovery during time of crisis; and adaptive use of denial regarding the fact of an uncertain future. Children who do not cope well fall into three categories: (a) those who become passive and dependent (demonstrating fearfulness, inactivity, lack of outside interests, and marked dependency on overprotective mothers); (b) those who become overly independent, or pseudoindependent (denying realistic dangers and rebelling against guilt-ridden families); and (c) those who identify with the family's view of them as defective outsiders (displaying shyness, isolation, and loneliness, and harboring resentful, hostile attitudes toward physically healthy persons).

With regard to the family of the chronically ill child, the initial reactions to the diagnosis of serious illness typically include depression, denial, anxiety, resentment, and anger. Steinhauer, Mushin, and Rae-Grant (1974) noted that the initial crisis is usually followed by a stage of disorganization while parents attempt to work out their feelings toward their child's illness. Parents who cope well resolve the crisis by accepting the child's illness and the limitations imposed by it. Other families may simply disintegrate in the face of the illness, and the parents may "cope" by separating or divorcing. On the other hand, the parents and family may well remain in a state of crisis, responding to the child with oversolicitude and exaggerated concern or by actually rejecting the

Reading to a young child confined to a hospital bed promotes better coping behavior by averting inactivity and boredom.

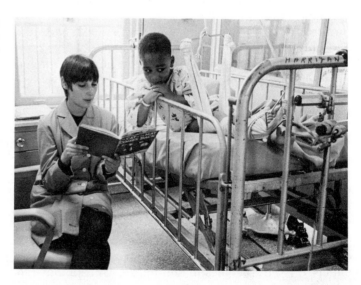

EXHIBIT 7.2

FAMILY REACTIONS TO SEVERE CHRONIC ILLNESS

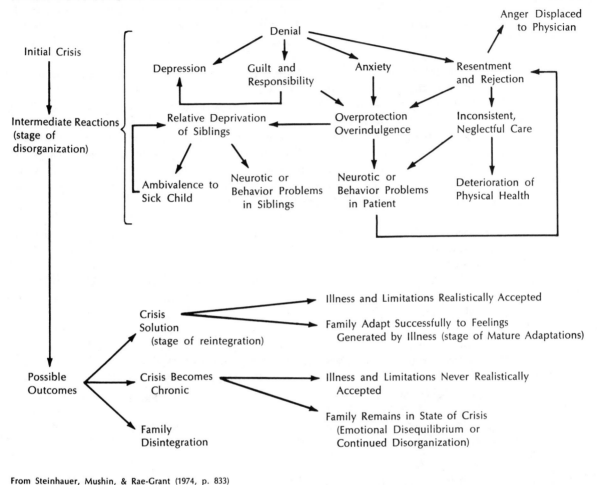

From Steinhauer, Mushin, & Rae-Grant (1974, p. 833)

child. Exhibit 7.2 presents a graphic illustration of the variety of coping patterns of parents of chronically ill children.

Personal and social adjustment
In general, both theory and research support the notion that chronic health disorders, hospitalization, and surgery have an adverse effect on the child's development. Vernon et al. (1965) noted that studies which assess changes in behavior or psychological functioning from prehospital to posthospital periods typically find that "more children change in the direction of upset than change in the direction of benefit" (p. 160). Moore (1975) maintained that surgical procedures inevitably disrupt the child's development. It should be pointed out, however, that these authors focused primarily on the immediate and short-term effects of hospitalization and surgery.

Barker, Wright, Meyerson, and Gonick (1953) theorized that children with chronic physical disorders are subject to psychological and social problems in development, and various studies—usually short-term and with specific populations of a particular illness—have tended to find confirming evidence of psychological maladjustment in children with specific illnesses. Khan, Herndon, and Ahmadian (1971), for example, studied the psychological and social adjustment of 14 children with chronic kidney problems; the findings indicated that these youngsters demonstrated evidence of depression, isolation, and feelings of inadequacy. Like most studies of chronically ill children, however, this research did not employ a control group of normal and/or healthy children, so it is difficult to know to what degree, if any, children with kidney problems may feel more depressed, more isolated, and more inadequate than is the case with so-called healthy children. This failure to provide a comparison group is a fairly common problem: many studies of chronically ill children are conducted in clinical settings and frequently fail to collect data on a comparable group of children who are not chronically ill. Langford (1961), Prugh (1963), and Apley and MacKeith (1968) reported rather favorable adjustment of small groups of chronically ill children who were followed into young adulthood, but these authors relied on clinical observation rather than objective data.

Pless and Roghmann (1971) studied the psychological adjustment of chronically ill children as a general category and compared them to children who were not chronically ill. Their study involved a 1 percent probability sample of all children under 18 years of age living in Monroe County, New York. In addition, they reviewed two other surveys of a similar nature: (a) the National Survey of Health and Development conducted in England, Wales, and Scotland (Douglas, 1964; Douglas & Blomfield, 1958), and (b) a study of 9- and 11-year-old children conducted on the Isle of Wight in England (Rutter, Tizard, & Whitmore, 1970). Although psychological and social adjustment was assessed differently in each of the studies, Pless and Roghmann arrived at a number of significant observations:

a) "With the exception of delinquency among boys, chronically ill children are, compared with healthy children, more frequently truant, more often troublesome in school, and more often socially isolated" (p. 355);

b) The incidence of psychiatric disorders among chronically ill children is much higher than the incidence of psychiatric disorders in the general population;

c) The risk of psychological maladjustment is directly related to the duration of the physical disorder, that is, the risk increases with the length of time that the physical disorder is present;

d) The risk of psychological and social maladjustment is greater if the physical disorder itself is more severe;

e) Psychological and social maladjustment is more frequent among children with permanent physical disorders than among children with temporary physical disorders.

In summary, of course, it is obvious that children with chronic physical disorders are at risk for psychological and social maladjustment. Chronic illness poses a threat to the integrity of a child's psychological and social development. It should not be presumed, however, that every child who is affected by chronic physical illness is emotionally disturbed; many children cope very effectively and valiantly with illness, and their response to physical illness can actually equip them to cope more effectively with other stresses in their lives. In general, however, chronic physical illness takes its toll on a child's capacity to achieve a normal and healthy psychosocial development.

Cognitive ability and educational achievement

The cognitive abilities and educational achievements of children with visual and hearing disabilities have been discussed in previous chapters. These children must be considered separately within the general population of children with health impairments and physical disabilities because sight and vision play such significant roles in cognitive and educational development. Another group of children who must be considered separately within the general category of physical health disorders are children with brain damage or central nervous system dysfunction that may directly affect intellectual functioning. The classic example of this class is children with *cerebral palsy (CP)*, who are frequently assessed as mentally retarded. It was once thought that the reason for the presence of mental retardation in many CP youngsters involved lack of adequate opportunity and inadequate education. Despite increasing efforts toward appropriate educational opportunities, large numbers of CP children continue to test as mentally retarded. Estimates of retardation with cerebral palsied youngsters, however, must be viewed with caution because of the extreme difficulties in testing youngsters with severe muscular impairments. The range of intellectual functioning in CP children is quite wide, and some CP children are deceptively superior in intellectual capacity despite considerable physical handicap.

Studies of the possible effects of physical health disorders on measured intelligence have been sadly lacking. Wrightstone, Justman, and Moskovitz (1953) studied a group of children with heart conditions and found them to be in the lower end of the average range (mean IQ of 94.4 compared to normal mean IQ of 100); these authors hypothesized that restriction of physical activity in this group of children may have limited opportunities for intellectual

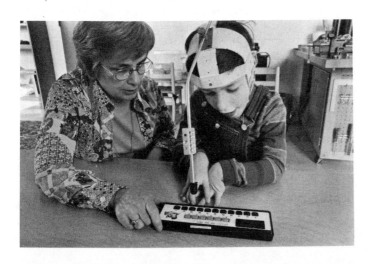

As an aid in his schoolwork, this child, who has little hand control, uses a head pointer to operate a calculator for math instruction.

stimulation, thus producing a mild deflation in measured intelligence. Our knowledge in this area is quite limited with respect to the general population of children with physical health disorders. Although it might be hypothesized that chronic illness and repeated hospitalizations might well produce an adverse effect on intellectual capacity, the possible effects of chronic illness on measured intelligence have not been well researched.

The effects of chronic illness on educational achievement are nonetheless well known. Chronically ill youngsters suffer from repeated absences from school during periods when the illness is active. A number of older studies, such as Wrightstone et al. (1953) and a study by the Ohio Commission on Children and Youth (1951) found academic underachievement widespread among children with chronic health problems. More recent studies have produced similar findings. In the Isle of Wight survey (Rutter et al., 1970), with 28 months or more of retardation in reading achievement as the criterion of academic achievement, a significantly greater number of chronically ill children were behind in educational achievement when compared to a control group of healthy children. Douglas (1964) also reported that chronically ill children score significantly below nondisabled children on tests of academic achievement. Although current large-scale studies in the United States are lacking, there is ample reason to hypothesize that the difficulties involved in the education of children with physical disorders, including frequent absence and lack of motivation, are likely to produce significant retardation in academic achievement.

INTERVENTION

The increasing attention to the needs of children with physical health disorders has brought about dramatic changes in medical care and in the very constitution of professions that provide service for these youngsters. Within the field of pediatrics, a vast number of medical and surgical subspecialities have developed in response to the specific needs of the child patient. Within clinical psychology, a new speciality known as *pediatric psychology* has developed to meet the needs of children whose problems are primarily physical but also involve many psychosocial aspects. The development of new or expanded children's hospitals has also paralleled the growth of allied health professions, such as pediatric nursing, recreational and physical therapy with children, and educational programs for hospitalized or homebound youngsters. Despite this increasing interest in and service for children with physical health disorders, however, such children frequently remain poorly understood and badly managed.

We will not attempt to undertake consideration of the many specific medical interventions involved in the treatment of children with physical health disorders. It should be obvious, of course, that the primary goal of medical intervention is the cure or control of the illness itself. With the child patient, however, medical intervention must also take into consideration the fact that the patient's medical needs must be balanced with developmental needs. In this regard, Yancy (1972) defined the three major goals of treating a chronically ill child as follows:

a) treatment of the disease itself, including correcting the specific defect as much as possible, controlling the symptoms, and arresting the disease process;

b) preventing the disease process, the treatment regimen, and the various people involved in the program from interfering with the development of the child;

c) preventing the illness, the treatment regimen, and the people involved from disrupting the family unit.

With these notions in mind, the psychological and emotional care of the hospitalized child and the education of children with physical health disorders will be considered.

The Psychological and Emotional Care of the Hospitalized Child

In a very real sense, the psychological and emotional care of the hospitalized child must begin with the recognition that hospitalization constitutes a potential threat to the integrity of a child's normal functioning and development. Such awareness can only be consistently realized when *staff education* of medical and nursing personnel includes specific course work in child development and the functioning of the whole child. As Petrillo and Sanger (1972) have noted, "Scrutiny of medical and nursing rounds will reveal in most instances that they are oriented to sickness in children rather than to children who are sick" (p. 86). The education of physicians and nurses is understandably oriented to the physical aspects of illness, but unfortunately the psychological aspects of illness are all too frequently underestimated or denied. Many of a child's significant responses to hospitalization are predictable, and such knowledge can be invaluable in caring for the child's emotional needs.

One of the most important ways of caring for a child's psychological needs is by providing continuity in the child's relationships with nursing and medical staff. Prugh, Staub, Sands, Kirschbaum, and Lenihan (1953) were among the first to advocate the concept of *case assignment nursing,* in which a single nurse provides for the complete care of a given patient. The practice has since become widespread. Petrillo and Sanger (1972) advocated a more comprehensive "systems approach" in which everyone involved in the clinical management of the child becomes a component of a system that seeks to promote health at both the physical and psychological levels. Case Study 7.1 gives an example of the way in which coordinated care by hospital personnel can provide a systematic approach to both physical and psychological needs.

Within the general context of a health-promoting milieu in the hospital, a number of specific approaches to psychological management are worthy of note. Kliman (1968) pointed out that *brief psychotherapy* by a mental health worker can be very helpful in enabling the child to work through fears regarding hospitalization. For example, Kliman noted two helpful sessions with an 8-year-old boy hospitalized to have his tonsils and adenoids removed. These two sessions focused on discussing with the child his general interests and feelings to get an idea of his personality; asking him about his ideas on the anatomy of the tonsils and adenoids and the techniques involved in anesthesia and surgery; briefly "correcting" several misconceptions he had (e.g.,

ORCHESTRATING THE PSYCHOLOGICAL CARE OF THE HOSPITALIZED CHILD

Valerie—Age Five
Was a Champion Manipulator

Although Val came to us with a variety of behavior problems, in addition to chronic kidney disease, nothing about her provoked so much response from hospital personnel as did her refusal to eat at mealtime. In short order, she managed to win the attention of people from many different departments—physicians, nurses, dietitians, cleaning and laundry personnel, and ever changing visitors. She was so appealing—cute, little, sick and abandoned by her mother. Everyone wanted to make it up to her by feeding her whatever she wanted. It appeared that there were as many ideas on how to solve her problem as there were people involved. She was bribed, coaxed, petted, and punished to no avail. Val had never had so much attention and she was not willing to give it up.

After a few weeks of struggling, it became apparent that Val was eating no better and was obviously emaciated. The head nurse decided to call a halt to all personal remedies and asked for the intervention of the mental health team.

Although some staff members disagreed, the mental health consultant decided to remove altogether the gratification Val received and to substitute other pleasures. The plan adopted was to:

1. Serve her minute portions of food without comment; to refrain from praising her for eating as well as to refrain from scolding for not eating; to remove the tray at the usual time.

2. Offer her the usual between meal snacks given to all the children, and nothing more.

3. Assign one person as a consistent mother figure.

4. Arrange for pleasurable activities within and outside of the hospital environment.

Our purpose was to get Val to eat because of hunger, and not for the purpose of pleasing anyone. We also wanted her to stop using mealtime as a way of retaliating and expressing her anger. We needed to show her that her eating habits did not matter to us one way or another.

It was not easy going. Some of the staff thought that the plan was a sadistic one: a form of starvation. A number of people were slipping her goodies just before meals. It took a few days before everyone, including visitors, understood what was required of them.

Gallantly, Val held out for 10 days. It was difficult for her to believe what was happening. She was stunned by the small quantities of food and the seeming lack of interest in her antics. On several occasions she demanded different kinds of food and was ignored; she tipped over her tray and was sent out of the dining room; she announced that she would eat if she were fed, but no one agreed to feed her.

When all of Val's maneuvers were thwarted and every illicit source of food cut off, she surrendered. She ate voraciously. It was difficult to keep the staff from praising her.

Soon after, Val was deriving much pleasure from her outings and from the concentrated attention of one nurse. The eating problem dissolved except when new personnel were assigned to the floor. On these occasions she did attempt to manipulate them by refusing to eat, but it did not work. The staff was finally united on this issue.

From Petrillo & Sanger (1972, pp. 224–25)

the belief that a dentist's drill would be used in the operation); encouraging him to fantasize the role of the surgeon and the anesthetist and to draw pictures of them. Kliman found this last technique—the use of drawings done either by the child or by the therapist at the child's direction—to be an especially useful technique for helping a young child work through fears and anxieties regarding hospitalization or surgery.

Since children frequently have difficulty in verbalizing problems associated with hospitalization and illness, *play therapy programs* are increasingly viewed as a necessary component in the effective psychological management of children in hospitals. Azarnoff (1974) noted that play itself is a necessary part of childhood, and children need to play whether they are hospitalized or not; in this respect, she pointed out that stricken children vary in the ways that they cope. Some hospitalized children will use play as a healthy escape from their overwhelming feelings about illness, whereas others will use their play to work through feelings about the illness. Adams (1976) described a structured therapeutic play program designed specifically to deal with the anxiety associated with hospitalization. The approach described by Adams actually used a "play hospital," equipped with small dolls representing patients, nurses, and doctors as well as various hospital supplies (needles, tubing, tongue depressors, stethoscopes, surgical masks and gloves, suture sets, etc.), for the child to use in fantasy play. Although wide variations are possible in conceptualization and actual formats of play, play therapy is an important procedure in the psychological management of the hospitalized child.

Still another important component in the care of the hospitalized child involves intervention with parents and families. It has already been noted that the parents' response to a child's illness and hospitalization can have a significant effect on the child's ability to manage his/her illness. At the same time, parents stricken with grief or anxiety about their child's care may require psychological intervention for their own needs. Heffron, Bommelaere, and Masters (1973) presented an excellent discussion of the use of *group therapy with parents* as a critical component in the management of leukemic children. Bringing together groups of parents whose children had similar medical problems was found to be a valuable adjunct to the management of the child, as well as a means of helping families cope in crisis periods and defining problems commonly shared by such families.

Staff education, case assignment nursing, brief psychotherapy, play programs, and group therapy with parents are only several of the ways in which children's hospitals attempt to assist in the psychological management of illness and hospitalization. The psychological care of children in hospitals, however, is still a developing area that will surely benefit from the increasing attention brought to bear by both mental health professionals and parent associations. Despite the pressure of rising costs associated with hospitalization, additional approaches to the psychological management of children are needed in order to limit the traumatic threat that can be posed by hospitalization.

The Education of Children with Chronic Physical Disorders

There is a paradoxical kind of injustice involving the education of children with chronic physical disorders. When an adult becomes ill or is hospitalized, it is commonly accepted that he/she will be relieved of both social and occupational duties. A physical illness in adulthood is typically managed by relaxing the obligations associated with work and social life. Illness in a child, however, is a far different matter. For children, work is education, and their social lives are characterized by a variety of experiences with classmates and peers. Both education and social contact are considered essential to a child's healthy development, so that the presence of a chronic illness cannot be managed by excusing the child from educational and social experiences. Without such experiences, the child's psychosocial development would be seriously jeopardized, and the management of educational experiences for the chronically ill child represents a critical aspect of the child's overall health planning.

Although there are slightly different educational considerations for children with physical disabilities (e.g., crippling conditions) as compared to children with chronic illnesses (e.g., asthma or heart conditions), there are also many similarities between these groups of children. Both crippled and health-impaired youngsters require coordination between educational and medical care, whether it involves hospitalization or convalescence when attendance at school is not possible. Because of the possibility of frequent absences, regular review of educational progress and individualized instruction are even more critical than is the case with other special conditions of childhood. Although there are many issues relevant to the education of children with chronic physical disorders, those of particular import are hospital programs, homebound programs, and the issue of mainstreaming and special education.

It is fundamental to the emotional and social growth of children with physical disorders that they participate as much as possible in everyday family responsibilities.

Hospital programs

One of the first clearly defined educational programs for children in hospitals was developed at the National Jewish Hospital in Denver, Colorado (Zipin, 1947). This program was literally a school within the hospital, serving long-term stay, tubercular children from the ages of 4 to 16. It included formal classroom work, elective projects such as leatherwork and sewing, and instruction intended to develop healthy and uncomplicated attitudes toward illness and disability. Hospital schools of this type are found mainly in hospitals that specialize in providing long-term hospitalization for children. They rely on special education teachers to provide regular, organized instruction in a classroom setting within the hospital, and students include both hospitalized children and some outpatients.

In many hospitals, such programs are not feasible, due to lack of space or widely divergent types of conditions among patients. In children's hospitals, many patients (such as a child in traction or a child with severe burns) are bedridden and immobilized for extensive periods of time. In this case, educational programs within the hospital must be flexible, and in these situations the *itinerant teacher,* who can provide highly individualized instruction, is necessary to meet the needs of youngsters who cannot easily leave their beds.

Over the past decade, there has been increasing recognition that the most desirable type of educational program in the hospital is that which most closely approximates normal school experience (Seidel, 1967). The classroom—with its blackboard, erasers, and other school-related paraphernalia—and the teacher—with workbooks and lesson plans—can provide a feeling of familiarity and reassurance amid the often sterile surroundings of a hospital environment. In the same manner, continued interaction with classmate-patients also tends to provide a more normal experience for the hospitalized child. Perhaps, most importantly, academic involvement itself helps the child both to keep pace with the educational growth of peers outside the hospital as well as to continue with the important work of his/her own self-development and enrichment.

The educational program in children's hospitals is variously named. Dombro (1967) surveyed 151 large children's hospitals or general hospitals with large children's units and found that their educational programs were called by a variety of names—among them, Play Program, Educational-Recreational Program, Recreation Program, Children's Activity Program, Hospital Teaching Program, Play Therapy-Teaching Program, Pediatric Education Program, and Child Life Program. Of the 151 hospitals surveyed, 92 (or 61 percent) reported the presence of some such organized program within the hospital; only 20 of these programs, however, were formal education programs staffed by trained educators.

Many hospital programs come under a broader designation, such as *child life programs,* in which the goals include academic instruction as well as play therapy, occupational therapy, recreational therapy, and activity therapy. The costs of these services are frequently without direct remuneration so that salaries of educators and other child therapists are managed by averaging these costs into the patients' daily bed fees. Although the need for such services seems obvious, amid an era of rapidly rising hospital expenses, many hospital administrators do not feel justified in developing or extending pro-

Recreational programs provide needed practice in body coordination skills. Here, with his therapist close at hand, this boy looks into a mirror to check for correct body position.

grams that are not directly related to the child's medical care. In the absence of state or federal funds to support such programs, there may well be a decline in the availability of these services to hospitalized children.

Homebound instruction

Homebound instruction is a method of providing short-term education for the child who is no longer hospitalized but is not yet ready to attend a formal school. This form of instruction is conducted by an itinerant teacher and is highly individualized to the child's specific needs. Obviously, it is quite costly. The teacher of homebound children must be highly competent and experienced in instructional techniques, skills in managing the child's behavior, and ability to relate well to parents in terms of advice, support, and counseling. Most school districts set minimum limits on the time that a child will likely be absent from school before he/she can qualify for homebound instruction; for example, if a child will not be homebound for at least three months, a homebound program may not be initiated. Because of the travel time and individualized nature of the instruction, the itinerant teacher in the homebound program can usually manage a load of not more than 5 or 6 children. Connor (1964) pointed out that the teacher of the homebound child experiences considerable demands on travel time and seldom is able to visit the same student more than two or three times a week.

Mainstreaming and special education

Traditionally, many children with chronic physical disorders and health impairments have been unable to attend regular schools. Public Law 94-142 (the Education for All Handicapped Children Act of 1975), however, will very likely increase the mainstreaming of such children in regular classes. In the past, crippled children in wheelchairs, for example, might not have been able to function in a regular school for the simple reason that the school was not physically equipped to manage children with such problems. Most school districts have evolved special schools or special classes for crippled and health-impaired children, but the majority of these children with normal intelligence could remain in regular classes; in the future, the percentage will surely increase to the point that almost all health-impaired children might be enrolled in regular classes.

Many youngsters with physical health disorders are in regular but reduced programs, perhaps attending school for half-days only. These situations must be carefully reviewed by administrators and teachers. Khan, Herndon, and Ahmadian (1971), for example, studied 14 children with chronic kidney problems who were in half-day and/or home tutoring programs. The children themselves expressed sadness at the arrangement because of the imposed isolation from friends. These researchers concluded that regular school attendance would have been more beneficial for these youngsters in terms of their social and emotional adjustment.

The mere placement of children with health disorders in a regular school situation, however, will not in itself ensure academic or personal-social success. Force (1956) analyzed the social interactions of 63 disabled children who were placed in regular classes and found that their status as peers, friends, and workmates was significantly lower than that of a comparable group of nondisabled children. If mainstreaming involves no more than the passive placement of health-impaired children in regular classes, it will likely prove unsuccessful.

Guralnick (1976) identified three distinct reasons to support regular education for children with physical disorders: (a) increased understanding and sensitivity to individual differences that nondisabled children, their parents, and their teachers can develop from such integration; (b) benefits to teachers that can arise from observing and working with a mixed group of children; and (c) potential benefits available to the disabled child who can observe and interact with more advanced peers. Guralnick pointed out, and rightfully so, that such potential benefits do not occur magically but rather through *planned interactions*. Speaking directly to the several studies of mainstreaming preschool children, Guralnick concluded that the data "suggest that the critical component is not the simple presence of nonhandicapped children in the class [with handicapped children], but the way in which interactions among these children are *systematically* guided or encouraged" (p. 237). Benefits for the disabled child are likely to occur when the environment is organized so that nondisabled peers can act as agents of change regarding the social and academic behaviors of disabled youngsters. As such, Guralnick concluded that mainstreaming can very likely be effective when disabled youngsters have opportunity to model the behavior of more advanced peers.

Whatever the rationale for mainstreaming, the placement of a health-impaired youngster in a group of nonimpaired peers requires planning and direction in both the academic and social aspects of classroom activity. Both mainstream and special classes, however, will likely see increasing experimentation in the use of innovative methods for educating children with health disabilities. Jones and Sisk (1967) set the mode for innovation in this regard by developing a new approach to help children with cerebral palsy increase their sensitivity to body image as well as intimate contact with others. Because of difficulties in muscle control, CP children frequently lack physical contact with peers. Jones and Sisk placed a group of CP children together in a confined space so that they could not avoid brushing against each other. In an empirical study of this *confined space* procedure, Jones, Barrett, Olonoss, and Andersen (1969) reported that participating CP youngsters improved in body awareness, peer interaction, and social, verbal, and motor activity. Such planned interactions may be several steps removed from the issues of reading, writing, and arithmetic, but programs of this type display the wide variety of educational procedures that are possible for children with different types of health disabilities. At this stage of our knowledge, there is no reason to believe that any particular method or format of education has demonstrated superiority over others (Diller, 1972).

THE DYING CHILD

Although accidents (such as those caused by motor vehicle accidents, falls, fires, drownings, poisonings, firearms) are the chief cause of death in childhood, terminal illnesses (such as leukemia and cystic fibrosis) are the most studied causes of death in childhood. A terminal illness in which the child's death is not imminent requires considerably more planning and treatment of both family and child than is the case with sudden and unexpected death. Our discussion will focus mainly on terminal illness and the difficulties experienced by the patient, the family, and the professional caregivers who are involved with the dying child.

The Child's Awareness of Death and Dying

Heartless as it may seem, studying the reactions of a dying child is necessary in order to understand the nature of the child's experience and to plan for the most appropriate care for the child and the family. In an early study of 48 dying children, Richmond and Waisman (1955) concluded that terminally ill children typically reacted to their illnesses with acceptance and passive resignation, manifesting little overt feeling or awareness of their impending deaths. Knudson and Natterson (1960), in a similar study, confirmed the findings of Richmond and Waisman but also observed that older children begin to show anxiety about death. The Knudson and Natterson study, followed by two studies by Morissey (1963a, 1963b), have generally confirmed the belief that *children under age 6 are not conceptually able to understand death*. When younger children are hospitalized with a fatal illness, their anxiety tends to be related to separation from parents and hospitalization rather than awareness of death. These studies also tend to indicate that children older than age 10 are able to understand death as an imminent event and that this awareness can be the source of anxiety and fear.

There still exists some disagreement in the literature regarding the awareness of death in children from ages 6 to 10. Children in this age range do not easily verbalize their feelings, and caregivers are frequently confused about the best way to deal with dying children in this age range. Should the diagnosis be discussed directly with the child? Will the child be able to understand what is being said? Is the child aware that he/she is dying? Will it be comforting or upsetting to talk about these issues?

Waechter (1971) asked 64 hospitalized children ages 6 to 10 to tell stories about a set of eight stimulus pictures presented to them; the children with fatal illnesses expressed more death themes than the children with nonfatal illnesses. This finding suggests that children between ages 6 and 10 do have some awareness and anxiety about death even if they do not engage in verbal discussion or overt expression.

Spinetta, Rigler, and Karon (1973) studied 25 fatally ill leukemic children and 25 children with chronic but nonfatal diseases (such as diabetes). All of these children were between ages 6 and 10, and the parents of the leukemic children maintained that the child had not been told and did not know that the illness was fatal. This study indicated that the leukemic children were much more anxious about their illnesses than were the children who had nonfatal illnesses. Spinetta et al. concluded that despite parental attempts to protect the children from the awareness that they were dying, the children had in some way understood that their illness was quite serious and threatening.

Spinetta (1974) reviewed the research in this area and came to the following conclusion:

> ...the fatally ill 6- to 10-year-old child is concerned about his illness and ... even though this concern may not always take the form of overt expressions about his impending death, the more subtle fears and anxieties are nonetheless real, painful, and very much related to the seriousness of the illness that the child is experiencing. (pp. 259–60)

Spinetta maintained that the issue of whether such anxiety should be labeled "death anxiety" is mainly a problem of semantics. He suggested that caregivers have underestimated the degree to which children with terminal illnesses experience awareness of their illness and their impending death and that this entire area is in need of investigation. Schowalter (1970) noted that by age 6 children begin to understand the permanency of death and that fatally ill children this age may well experience the thought of death as a punishment for bad behavior. In the preadolescent and early adolescent child who is dying, Schowalter maintained that the awareness of death is accompanied more by despair and resentment of unfulfillment. Continuing research regarding the inner lives and reactions of dying children may help resolve some of these questions, but in the meantime the care of the dying child is very much dependent on the intuition of the caregivers.

The Care of the Dying Child

The reaction of a dying child to his/her illness is based both on the degree of awareness of death and the reactions of family and caregivers. Both the child and the family have a right to the natural grief that such an event occasions, and professionals who attempt to talk the child and family into denying their grief do an injustice. Physicians, nurses, social workers, counselors, and clergy, however, rightly seek to reduce the pain and confusion that is touched off by a child's dying. Caregiving for the dying child and the family must begin with the issue of discussing the diagnosis. Sensitive management of this issue is critical in helping the child and family respond to the issue of dying.

Discussion of the diagnosis

When a diagnosis of terminal illness has been made, it is typically the responsibility of the attending physician to discuss it with the parents. Recognizing that this is an extremely difficult situation to manage, some physicians prefer to meet the parents in the company of a psychologist or social worker who can become more involved in helping the parents deal with their grief. Even parents who suspect the worst typically respond to the diagnosis of a terminal illness with shock and denial. Before parents can deal effectively with information about their child's illness or ways in which to help their child, they must first experience their own pain and confusion and learn to deal with it. Frequent consultations with staff who are skilled in dealing with parental reactions may be very helpful during this initial period.

One of the most critical questions that arises is whether the child should be told that the illness is terminal. Sigler (1970) maintained that children should not be told until the final stages of the illness. Sigler reasoned that efforts at intervention should be directed at making the environment as normal as possible in order to avoid despondency in the child. Kliman (1968) pointed out that children will pick up subtle cues anyway and that failing to deal with the child honestly may well produce a situation of distrust. Kalnins (1977) noted that terminally ill children easily see through parental attempts to disguise their own worries about the child. Kirkpatrick, Hoffman, and Futterman (1974) concluded that the issue of trust between child and family, on the one hand, and physicians and caregivers, on the other, is a critical aspect in the management of the dying child and the family. Honesty with the parents is always at a premium, but the discussion of the diagnosis with the child seems to be more an individual matter that must take into account such issues as the child's age, the likely progress of the illness, the strength of the family, and the child's ability to deal with stress. The decision to tell a child of his/her illness seems best guided not so much by hard and fast rules as by sensitivity to the individual case.

Life enhancement

The concept of an individual approach to the child is important in enabling his/her remaining years—or even days—to be as satisfying as possible. There is no general prescription regarding effective psychological care of children with fatal disorders. As Howarth (1974) pointed out:

> The day-to-day practical implications of this individual approach are that one is taking an interest in things of importance to the child, . . . pets, hobbies, school activities and friends. . . . But more importantly, one is constantly trying to see events and experiences from the child's point of

OPEN ISSUE

Edouard de Moura Castro, aged 7, his little frame shriveled by leukemia, demanded that doctors let his failing life take its course. He had already taped an articulate message of hope to others facing death.

Edouard asked his mother to remove the oxygen machine that was keeping him alive.

"He said, 'Mother, turn off the oxygen, I don't need it anymore,'" Barbara de Moura Castro said Tuesday. "I turned it off, then he held my hand and a big smile came to his face and he said, 'It is time.'

"Then he left."

Edouard died Jan. 10 after deciding details of his funeral and where he was to be buried.

The son of a Brazilian diplomat, Dr. Claudio de Moura Castro, Edouard lived with his mother and step-sister in Santa Barbara and spent his few years amazing those who knew him by the things he said and did.

When he was 3½, Edouard became associated with a local group that followed the precepts of the ancient Eastern religion, Vedanta. By the time Edouard died, the Vedanta swami believed his tiny friend was the reincarnation of a holy man.

"He was not a normal little boy . . . He was so full of understanding of his suffering, full of understanding of God," said Pravrajika Prabhaprana, the group's head nun.

"I don't know how he got involved with them," said Mrs. de Moura Castro, who added that her son's faith in reincarnation inspired her to believe. "He introduced me into it."

It was Edouard's fascination with the Vedanta philosophy that gave him the belief that death "was like a passageway, a walk into another galaxy," as he said on his tape.

His message was recorded by Kim Downey, a volunteer worker for a group called Hospice, which works with the dying and their families.

When Mrs. Downey asked the boy why he wanted to die, he said: "Because I am so sick. When you are dead and a spirit in heaven, you don't have all the aches and pains. And sometimes, if you want to, you can visit this life but you can't come back into your own life.

"If you don't hang onto your body and let yourself ease away," Edouard said on the tape, "it is not so painful."

About two years ago, Edouard's mother took him to a children's hospital, where doctors worked furiously to save his life with drugs. "They wanted so badly to keep him alive, they just bombarded him. They overtreated him," she said.

"Sometimes doctors want to save people very badly," Edouard told Mrs. Downey. "They try everything to cure them . . . I don't feel good, and I am too sick to live on."

There is solace for the boy's mother: "It was a privilege and an honor to go through this with my son. I hope it helps parents talk things over with their children and doctors. If he has done this in his short life, then it will have been worth it."

The rights of the child who is dying constitute an area of grave concern in current medical care. Some authorities maintain that a child has a right to share in all information and decisions about the illness. Others maintain that the child, especially the younger child, should be protected from the additional stress that may be involved in full participation. Most children cannot be as decisive as Edouard de Moura Castro. The right to live and the right to die remain perplexing issues in the care of the terminally ill child.

From Associated Press (January 25, 1978)

view and keeping alert to the child's ways of expressing feelings of unhappiness, discomfort, or anxiety. (p. 135)

It is always difficult, of course, to understand the private inner experience of another person. In this respect, Goggins, Lansky, and Hassanein (1976) suggested that projective personality tests, especially the Rorschach, can be useful in understanding underlying coping processes in children with malignancies.

Trying to experience the child's point of view is a useful way of anticipating the child's needs and of making sense of the child's communications. Morse (1970) pointed out two goals that are extremely important in the care of the dying child and family: (a) enhancement of their lives for the remaining time they have together and (b) mobilization of their strength to cope with the inevitability of death. Morse proposed four principles necessary in coping and life enhancement: (a) the provision of one strong, guiding physician to be directly responsible to the child and parents, no matter how many individuals are involved in the child's care; (b) the provision of a skilled nursing staff sensitive to the meaning of a child's emotional reactions; (c) the provision of social services to the child's parents to strengthen their resources to deal with the impending crisis; and (d) the development of understanding among the entire relevant hospital staff regarding the child's psychological defenses and the effects of the child's illness on the parents. Such principles of care are vitally important on hospital wards for dying children.

Many children who are dying do not require hospitalization until the final stages of their illness. For example, leukemic children who cannot be cured are still able to lead very normal lives until their illness has progressed to its final stages. As the mother of a child who died of leukemia reported, however, even during periods of remission when the child is at home, hospital staff are relied upon as "lifelines of support" (Craig, 1974, p. 93). If the remaining days, months, or years of a child with a terminal illness are to be as normal and enhanced as possible, the efforts of hospital staff and family must be orchestrated in this direction.

For many families, religion can often provide comfort and a means of coping with the reality of death and dying. When a child's life is coming to a close, families may well seek solace in the concept of an after-life or life-beyond-death. Easson (1970) noted that the real meaning of death—the possibility of not being—is immensely disturbing. "Every human individual responds to death by denying these more disturbing aspects of dying" (p. 93). This realization can be even more traumatic with a child whose life may seem to be just beginning.

Perhaps the most fitting conclusion to this discussion is a poem written by a 17-year-old girl suffering from Hodgkins disease (Currier, 1977, p. 81):

UNTITLED
I wander through
the pathways
of my life
looking for the beginning
of the circle
which has been

enclosing me.
Some days I am alive,
but not living.
I can look
but what do I see?
My feelings are like
the swaying leaves
falling from the trees.
Where am I today?
What will tomorrow bring?
You may see me smile
or hear me speak,
but my true feelings
remain engulfed
in my soul.
I hope soon to emerge.
I want to find
some sense of time
and to bloom
with the flowers.
I hope to come alive
once again
and live in peaceful
solitude—forever.

SUMMARY

1. A physical health disorder is defined as any identified physical health problem that requires extensive medical attention or hospitalization, cannot be easily and completely cured and is therefore long-standing, and places severe demands on the child's ability to lead a normal life.
2. Estimates of prevalence rates for physical health disorders range from 5 to 10 percent of the general population.
3. Children with physical health disorders have been found to have significantly greater psychological and social maladjustment than physically healthy children.
4. The effects of physical health disorders on measured intelligence are not sufficiently documented to allow for general conclusions.
5. Children with chronic health disorders typically achieve significantly lower scores than physically healthy children on measures of academic achievement.
6. Psychological intervention with hospitalized children includes a range of approaches, such as staff education, case assignment nursing, brief psychotherapy, play therapy programs, and group therapy with parents.
7. Educational intervention with hospitalized children includes hospital schools, itinerant teachers, and a large variety of programs that stress the needs of the total child.
8. From the age of 6 onward, children who are dying become increasingly able to conceptualize the meaning of death.
9. There is considerable disagreement regarding the discussion of the diagnosis with a terminally ill child, but the concept of life enhancement is generally viewed as the most meaningful approach to a child who is dying.

PART THREE

Children with Learning and Cognitive Differences

Children with Mental Retardation

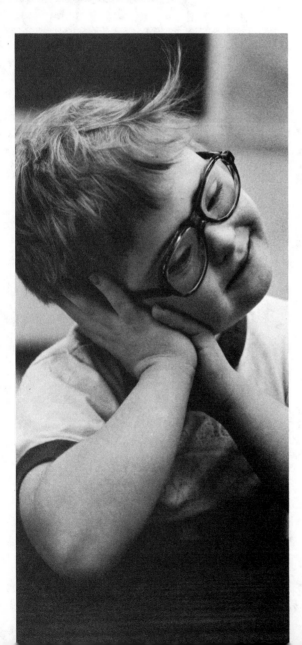

There are few sights more pitiful than the children who live in institutions for the mentally retarded. The feeling is inescapable when one sees the profoundly retarded inmates, incapacitated, needing almost total care. Yet it is, perhaps, more acute at the sight of the mildly retarded child. One's pity for the profoundly retarded is tempered somehow by the obvious nature of their defects, and one is relieved that institutions exist which assume this human burden. When one, however, encounters thousands and thousands of mildly retarded children living in the same institutions, children who in many ways so much resemble children on the outside, the pity is compounded with confusion.

Braginsky and Braginsky (1971, p. 11)

AN INTRODUCTION TO MENTAL RETARDATION

Despite the fact that there has been an active professional and scientific interest in the mentally retarded child for a full century and more, we are still unable to answer some of the more fundamental questions about this unfortunate condition of childhood. Our knowledge regarding the possible causes of mental retardation has advanced a hundredfold, and yet we are frequently powerless to provide a meaningful explanation for the maldevelopment of a single retarded child. It is true, of course, that modern society has made many advances in its understanding of mental retardation and in attempts to provide adequate medical, psychological, educational, and social services to the retarded child and his/her family. Within medicine, active research in genetics and metabolism promises the possibility of breakthroughs in the understanding and prevention of several organic retardation syndromes; past successes in the prevention of mental retardation caused by certain organic abnormalities spur valid hopes in this regard. Within clinical and experimental psychology, problems in the misapplication of psychological tests sometimes blur the genuine contributions that IQ tests have made to the needs of the retarded child; at the same time, the development of refined methods of behavior therapy and a burgeoning interest in psychotherapy with the retarded child have provided an area of rapprochement between clinical and experimental psychologists. Within education, controversy rages over the issue of mainstreaming and special education at the same time that new experiments in preventive education are demonstrating the remarkable possibilities that exist in the prevention of sociocultural retardation. Within the context of social approaches, institutionalization of retarded youngsters has been roundly criticized, and recent changes herald prospects for more community-based approaches that keep the retarded child in or near his/her home.

Perhaps more than any other condition of special childhood, retardation fans the interest of multiple professional and academic disciplines. The field is so broad and retarded children are so varied that summary generalizations are obviously difficult and perhaps superficial. At the very heart of all the wordiness and social philosophizing that has marked the field of mental retardation for so many years, however, is a very simple phenomenon: the retarded child seems to tug on something fine and clean within the human soul. Despite the frequent abuses in the treatment of retarded children, the retarded child compels the compassion and understanding of the hardened as well as the gentle heart. The accidents of birth and environment that plague the retarded can happen to anyone, and the retarded child seems to serve as a reminder of our very human struggle to overcome.

DEFINITION AND CLASSIFICATION

Historically, an extensive number of labels have been used to describe children and adults who display retarded development of critical human abilities. In retrospect, terms such as "feeble-minded," "idiot," "moron," and "imbecile" seem harsh and vindictive. Ill-intentioned and insensitive use of these terms, rather than the terms themselves, is the key factor in producing undesirable connotations. The current designations of *mental retardation* and *mental deficiency* are considered standard use and will likely remain so for some time; but these terms, too, can be misused by some as forms of insult rather than sensitive statements of a person's condition. In short, it has proven virtually impossible to develop a set of terms and diagnoses that protect children from callous or vicious exploitation.

Current Definitions of Mental Retardation

From a scientific and professional standpoint, mental retardation as a category is an unsatisfactory but necessary construct. It does not represent a homogeneous group of children, nor can it be considered a specific kind of disorder or disease. Individuals who are described as mentally retarded vary widely in almost every aspect of human behavior and human personality, and, as we shall see, the more apt category might be called "the mental retardations."

Despite its limitations, the current category of mental retardation is still important for understanding, diagnosis, and treatment of retarded individuals. As both a scientific and a social construct, its meaning changes with time and with changing scientific and social realities. In the current state of science, mental retardation is defined on the basis of behavioral criteria rather than on the basis of presumed psychological processes or inferred disease. Current definitions of mental retardation, therefore, stress explicit behavioral criteria as necessary guidelines for labeling individuals as mentally retarded.

The American Association on Mental Deficiency (AAMD) reflects the current scientific and professional views regarding the definition of mental retardation in its Sixth Edition of the *Manual on Terminology and Classification in Mental Retardation,* edited by Herbert Grossman:

> *Mental retardation refers to significantly subaverage general intellectual functioning existing concurrently with deficits in adaptive behavior, and manifested during the developmental period. (AAMD, 1973b, p. 11)*

And the American Psychiatric Association in its *Diagnostic and Statistical Manual of Mental Disorders* (DSM-II), defined mental retardation as follows:

> *Mental retardation refers to subnormal general intellectual functioning which originates during the developmental period and is associated with impairment of either learning and social adjustment, or maturation, or both. (APA, 1968)*

In the 1978 draft of a new DSM-III, the APA is moving closer to the terminology of the AAMD's definition by citing "significantly subaverage general intellectual functioning" and "concurrent deficits in adaptive behavior" occurring before age 18 as essential features of mental retardation.

In a general sense, then, mental retardation is understood to be a retardation in development. In order for a child to be considered retarded, two distinct sets of behavior criteria must be applicable: (a) subnormal or significantly subaverage intellectual functioning and (b) deficits in adaptive behavior or impairment of learning and/or social adjustment. *Both these criteria must be considered before diagnosing a child as mentally retarded.* This definition represents an advance in scientific and professional thinking, and these dual behavior criteria are intended to serve as a check on each other. The second criterion, adaptive behavior deficits, was first proposed by the AAMD in 1959 because of increasing concerns regarding the adequacy of IQ test scores as a sole criterion for diagnosing a child as mentally retarded. Soon after this, Heber (1961) proposed an adaptive behavior scale, but the measurement of adaptive behavior has not yet achieved the technical sophistication that has been the case with the measurement of intelligence.

Current definitions of mental retardation, therefore, seek more and more to protect children from misdiagnosis or false labeling as retarded. These definitions reflect changing social attitudes and scientific conceptualizations of retardation by emphasizing adherence to stricter diagnostic criteria regarding both the measurement of intelligence and social adaptiveness. Psychometric assessment of intellectual functioning as well as clinical observation of social adaptive behavior, of course, are areas that can benefit from increasing sophistication and precision in scientific measurement. At the same time, much of the more sophisticated thinking about mental retardation has not yet penetrated to the grass roots level of clinical practice; it is unfortunate but nonetheless true that many youngsters continue to be labeled retarded on the basis of a single intellectual assessment that produces a low IQ score. Clinical practice in schools, hospitals, and child guidance centers relies heavily on intellectual assessment procedures, often to the exclusion of other considerations. For many years, the labeling of children as retarded has been a function of intellectual testing or the application of presumed medical diagnostic categories. It is not unusual, therefore, to discover the presence of considerable discrepancies between current definitions of retardation and conventional practices in diagnosis and classification. Before proceeding more directly to a discussion of diagnosis and classification, it will be necessary to consider in more detail the nature of intelligence and intellectual assessment.

Mental Retardation and the Concept of Intelligence

Historically, the phenomenon of mental retardation has been best understood by aligning it with the concept of intelligence; at the same time, intelligence, both popularly and scientifically, has come to mean "that which is measured by an IQ test." Since standardized tests of intelligence were devised specifically for the practical purpose of identifying intellectual ability and aptitude for education, it was inevitable that the IQ test would become the single most important tool in the definition and measurement of mental retardation. The "IQ" has been institutionalized through extensive use by both educators and psychologists, and it is likely that both the concept of intelligence and its measurement through standardized tests will continue to function as critical factors in the understanding of mental retardation.

Standardized intellectual assessment, however, has been subjected to considerable and valid criticism. As Mercer (1975) asserted:

> Because psychologists, educators, and clinicians have neither examined the assumptions underlying traditional practices nor adequately monitored the social implications of institutionalizing procedures based on these assumptions, the standardized testing movement is now being challenged. Those who have been labeled as deviant because of their low test scores are rejecting the labels and attacking the labelers. They are protesting the taken-for-granted value frame within which psychologists, educators, and test-makers have been operating. (p. 131)

Mercer's comments underline much of the controversy that has surrounded the use of IQ tests and the identification and labeling of children as mentally retarded. The concept of intelligence and the use of IQ tests are so central to the discussion of mental retardation that it will be necessary to consider these issues in some detail.

Definitions of intelligence

Psychologists and educators have long been fascinated by the study of behavior that is presumed to reflect "intelligence." Probably more ink has been spilled and more basic research has been conducted in the study of intelligence than any other broad area of human behavior. Despite this active and dedicated interest in the study of intelligence, however, no definition of intelligence has ever proved satisfactory to a majority of theoreticians or researchers. Intelligence is an elusive concept so fundamental to the understanding of human behavior that it seems to defy consensual definition. Robinson and Robinson (1976) noted, nonetheless, that three basic considerations are common to most definitions of intelligence: (a) *the capacity to learn*, (b) *the sum total of knowledge that has been acquired by an individual*, and (c) *the ability to adjust or to adapt to the total environment, especially to new situations*.

OPEN ISSUE

The most compelling controversy regarding the nature of intelligence involves the issue of whether intelligence is *innate* (due to heredity or genetic endowment) or *acquired* (due to environment or experience). This *"nature versus nurture"* controversy has not been resolved scientifically, and there are many popular misconceptions about the concept of intelligence. One of the most unfortunate of these misconceptions is that IQ is fixed and immutable, and that measured intelligence is genetically determined. This notion can easily lead to inaccurate and unfounded racial and ethnic stereotypes.

Disadvantaged minority groups frequently test out well below the national average on standardized tests of intelligence. For example, in the 1920s, mental tests of recent immigrants from southern and eastern Europe (such as Greeks, Italians, and Poles) revealed an average IQ in the high 70s and low 80s. This was far below the measured IQs of northern and western Europeans who had immigrated to the United States generations earlier and had measured IQs around the American national average. This finding led many to the conclusion that immigrants from southern and eastern Europe were genetically inferior. Sowell (1977), however, found that the IQs of these immigrant groups of the 1920s "rose over the decades until today they are virtually equal to or exceed the national average" (p. 56). It appears likely that as the immigrants of the 1920s became familiar with and an integral part of the American society in which they lived, they acquired the skills necessary to do well on IQ tests.

Whether intelligence is innate or acquired, the simple fact of the matter is that there are no tests of innate abilities. Although the nature versus nurture problem has not been resolved, it is nonetheless true that there are no demonstrated testing procedures that can measure innate capacity. At the request of the Black Psychological Association in 1969, the American Psychological Association's Board of Scientific Affairs appointed a panel of experts to study the use of psychological and educational tests on students from disadvantaged backgrounds. The report of this panel defined intelligence as "the entire repertoire of acquired skills, knowledge, learning sets, and generalization tendencies considered intellectual in nature that are available at any one period of time. An intelligence test contains items that sample such acquisitions" (Cleary, Humphreys, Kendrick, & Wesman, 1975, p. 19). The panel further noted that this definition might be considered circular were it not for the fact that there has been a consistent consensus among psychologists regarding the kinds of behaviors that might be described as intellectual.

The point is that intelligence, in its measurable aspects, seems not to be an innate ability but an acquired set of skills. As such, it is not fixed, immutable, and unchanging; rather, it changes with time, with growth, with experience, and with specific interventions. When children are formally tested and achieve a particular IQ score, it should not be assumed that this score measures their genetic potential. Nor should it be assumed that this IQ score will be fixed and unchanging. An IQ score is only a measure of a child's current repertoire of acquired skills and knowledge.

These general components have marked various historical attempts to define intelligence and remain very popular in current usage. Wechsler (1958), for example, in his classic work on the construction of tests of intelligence, stated: "Intelligence, operationally defined, is the aggregate or global capacity of the individual to act purposefully, to think rationally, and to deal effectively with his environment" (p. 7). Wechsler's definition reflects his position that intelligence is a general characteristic of the person that cannot be separated from the personality of the entire individual.

In fact, however, there are as many coherent definitions of intelligence as there are consistent points of view about human behavior, and recent reviews in this area (Rabin & McKinney, 1972; Robinson & Robinson, 1976) have stressed the widely diverging possibilities that are available in the definition of intelligence. Some approaches to general mental capacity have stressed the *ability structure* of intelligence, seeking to define experimentally (through the sophisticated statistical technique of factor analysis) the independent abilities that comprise intelligent behavior. Still another view of intelligence has come from many *developmental psychologists* who emphasize various processes of mental development from infancy to adulthood. And yet another position is taken by those who insist that "intelligence" does not exist in nature as a complex of traits but is merely invented by theoreticians as a *hypothetical construct* to aid the understanding of behavior.

Despite the many differences that exist among scientists regarding the definition of intelligence, on the practical level considerable strides have been made in the assessment of intellectual ability for purposes of education, preparation for complex demands of social existence, assigning individuals to appropriate jobs in the military, and so forth. In this respect, the scientific study of intelligence has produced many useful dividends for modern society. Programs of planning and assistance for the mentally retarded are only one of many such dividends that flow from the accurate assessment of intellectual potential.

The measurement of intelligence

Intelligence testing, as it is known today, had its beginning in 1904 when Alfred Binet and Theodore Simon were commissioned by the French Minister of Public Instruction to devise a procedure to select out slow-learners for special instruction. The aim of this project was to discriminate normal from mentally retarded children by developing a graded scale of tests varying in difficulty to which norms could be assigned for the ages at which children should be expected to pass the items. Binet and Simon (1905) thus produced an intelligence scale consisting of 30 separate tests that included such tasks as recognizing objects in a picture, discriminating two lines as to length, defining simple words, repeating a sentence of 15 words, drawing an object from memory, and answering a list of questions (e.g., "What should you do when sleepy?"). Continued revisions of this scale in 1908 and 1911 produced a highly workable instrument that not only distinguished normal children from mentally retarded children but also was able to assign a mental age to a child's performance on the test. This was accomplished by assigning a similar number of tests to each year level; a child was credited with a specific number of months of mental age (MA) for every test passed. It was a simple procedure to compute the total number of tests passed in order to arrive at the child's **mental age,** a measure of determined mental ability based on the child's success in passing a series of tests ordered in difficulty at various age levels. If a 7-year-old who was chronologically ready for first grade achieved a mental age of only 5 years, it could be presumed that he/she would have difficulty learning as well as other 7-year-olds who had achieved mental ages of 7 years or above.

The next major step in the measurement of intelligence was taken by Lewis Terman of Stanford University. Terman produced a slightly altered but well-standardized form of the Binet tests in 1916 that became known as the Stanford-Binet Scale. (This scale has since been restandardized in 1937 and again in 1972, and has been the most widely used test of intellectual ability.) In addition to the mental-age concept, Terman introduced the **intelligence quotient,** or **IQ,** as a means of assigning a score to a child's performance on the test. Simply put, IQ is a ratio of chronological age (CA) to mental age (MA), and is determined by the following formula: $IQ = (MA \div CA) \times 100$. Thus, a 10-year-old with a mental age of 10 would have an IQ of 100; a 10-year-old with a mental age of 8 would have an IQ of 80; a 10-year-old with a mental age of 12 would have an IQ of 120.

Both the concepts of mental age and intelligence quotient were and are convenient shorthand forms of expressing the child's level of performance on a series of standardized tests. Although technically appropriate, these short-hand symbols can very easily give the mistaken impression that intelligence is a specific "thing" of which a child has a particular amount. In fact, both mental age and IQ are merely ways of quantifying an individual's behavior in a standardized testing situation.

The next significant advance in the mental testing movement was provided by David Wechsler, for many years the Chief Psychologist at Bellevue Hospital in New York City. Beginning in the 1930s, Wechsler produced a series of tests for adults, school-age children, and preschool children. One of these, the Wechsler Intelligence Scale for Children–Revised (WISC–R, 1974) is the second most commonly used IQ test for children. The Wechsler tests attempt to define intelligence as a number of measurable abilities that can be measured across all age ranges. Wechsler introduced the concept of the *deviation* IQ so that each subject's performance is compared only with that of other individuals in the same age range of the standardization sample. Since 1960, the Stanford-Binet test has also incorporated this deviation-IQ procedure, which is more empirically valid than the ratio IQ and mental-age concept.

The Stanford-Binet and the Wechsler tests are administered individually to each subject and typically require at least an hour of testing time. During the testing, the examiner also takes notes about the subject's test behavior, and these clinical observations are frequently as important in the assessment of the subject's abilities as are the quantified test scores. Although a large number of group-administered tests of intelligence are also available, individual tests like the Stanford-Binet and the Wechsler scales are much more appropriate instruments in the assessment of mentally retarded individuals. These tests are typically administered only by skilled professional psychologists, well-versed in measurement theory and behavior observation, and also sensitive to the nuances of child behavior. Thus, the skilled examiner recognizes that the child's actual test scores are only one index of intellectual ability. As Robinson and Robinson (1976) pointed out, "the tester who has engaged in face-to-face interaction with the subject is more likely to make recommendations and decisions with the subject's best interests in mind" (p. 22). When competent examiners make use of sound tests such as the Stanford-Binet and

Wechsler scales, many of the reservations about mental testing noted earlier in this chapter are lessened.

In summary, it should be noted that the concept of intelligence is central to considerations of the nature of mental retardation. The considerable scientific and professional effort that has been made in the definition and measurement of intelligence has unquestionably clarified the many subtle issues regarding the nature of mental retardation. IQ scores, however, cannot infallibly stamp children as mentally retarded. A formal and well-conducted intellectual examination is no more than a sample of a child's behavior. Intellectual assessment is very much like taking a child's temperature; it gives information about body temperature at a given moment in time. The presence of a high temperature may be an indication of other problems. The presence of a low IQ score may also be an indication of other problems, even of mental retardation. Children, nonetheless, change and develop over time, and intellectual abilities and IQ's can also change and develop over time. The IQ as measured at any given time is only one of several important considerations in the diagnosis and treatment of mental retardation.

Classification of Mental Retardation

Perhaps the first scientific attempt to classify mentally retarded individuals was made by J. E. D. Esquirol, the great French psychiatrist of the nineteenth century (Blanton, 1975). Esquirol (1838) grouped the retarded into the major classes of *idiots* and *imbeciles,* using the presence of speech in the latter as the basis of distinction between the two classes. Esquirol's use of a functional behavior, namely speech, as a criterion of classification foreshadowed the more sophisticated systems of classification that now use measured intelligence and adaptive behavior as the basis of classification.

In giving the WISC-R, the psychologist should be certain the child clearly understands the instructions. Important, too, in the assessment of the test results and the determination of the child's needs are the psychologist's observations of the child's behavior while taking the test.

Since adaptive behavior has not as yet been subjected to the history of rigorous validation that has been the case with the measurement of intelligence, classification systems continue to reflect the importance of measured intelligence as the key factor in the consideration of mental retardation. When children are classified according to levels of measured intelligence, the following categories are typically employed:

Profound retardation: measured IQ below 20 (Dependent);
Severe retardation: measured IQ between 21 and 35 (Dependent);
Moderate retardation: measured IQ between 36 and 50 (Trainable);
Mild retardation: measured IQ between 51 and 65 (Educable);
Borderline retardation: measured IQ between 66 and 80.

Borderline retardation has been eliminated as a category of classification by the American Association for Mental Deficiency, whereas it is still used as a category in the DSM-II of the American Psychiatric Association. The new edition of the APA manual (DSM-III) is expected in the near future, and it is likely that the category of borderline retardation will be eliminated from the definition of mental retardation. The Fifth Edition of the AAMD manual (Heber, 1959) had included a category of borderline, but the Sixth Edition stressed the criterion *significantly subaverage* and eliminated the category of borderline retardation. The direction of current thinking in this matter is clearly to tighten criteria by which a child can be labeled mentally retarded. These changes, if and when they are accepted by school systems, will surely have a significant effect in reducing the numbers of children who have traditionally been assigned to special education classes for the educable mentally handicapped (Filler, Robinson, Smith, Vincent-Smith, Bricker, & Bricker, 1975). In relation to the above categories, it should also be noted that IQ ranges for each category may vary slightly, depending on the particular test being used for assessing IQ; this is due to slight statistical differences between such tests as the Stanford-Binet and the Wechsler tests.

A system of classification based on measured IQ is a very practical and useful approach to the classification of retarded children for purposes of education and behavioral types of intervention. In the particular case, however, measured IQ is only one criterion, and *low intelligence itself is an insufficient criterion for the diagnosis or labeling of a child as mentally retarded;* the adaptive behavior criterion is equally important in the evaluation of a child's functioning. Children who are retarded in intellectual functioning but not retarded in terms of their adaptive behavior should *not* be classified as mentally retarded, whatever their level of measured IQ might be. Case Study 8.1 gives ample evidence of the importance of thorough diagnosis before classifying a child as mentally retarded.

INCIDENCE AND ETIOLOGY

Discussion of the causes of mental retardation and the numbers of children affected very much depends on the manner in which mental retardation is defined. Since standards for the definition of subaverage intellectual functioning have been changing and since criteria have been made more restrictive

GRACE AND VIRGINIA: A CASE OF MISIDENTIFICATION

SAN DIEGO (AP)—Grace and Virginia Kennedy, 6-year-old identical twins regarded as severely retarded for most of their lives, are actually bright children who developed their own private language, speech therapists say.

The twins' gibberish is their way of communicating with each other, therapists at Children's Hospital discovered.

The hospital said that investigators now know that Grace calls Virginia "Cabengo," while Virginia calls Grace "Poto."

The rest of their speech is still a mystery to outsiders, but the girls chatter rapidly when they are together.

"Dug-on, haus you dinikin, du-ah," Grace said to Virginia while they played with their dollhouse.

"Snup-aduh ah-wee die-dipana, dihabana," Virginia replied.

Speech therapists Alexa Romain and Ann Koeneke hope to find out what the girls are saying and publish their findings of this rare case.

"The girls talk to each other in what we call idioglossia, or twin speech," said Ms. Romain. Persons with the condition pronounce words so badly that they appear to be speaking a secret language.

"The development of this kind of language has been found to occur in very rare instances among twins who have had no other contact with peers—other children," she said. "There is very little in medical literature about it."

The girls had seizures shortly after their birth, and until recently they were treated as if they were severely retarded.

They never learned to speak English, or German, their mother's native language.

However, researchers said the girls know four languages. They understand English and German with good comprehension, although they do not speak either one. In addition to their private language, the girls have learned sign language as part of therapy.

From Associated Press (July 23, 1977)

with the addition of an adaptive behavior criterion, it may be that, in the future, fewer individuals will be assessed as mentally retarded and that the causes of mental retardation will likewise be in need of reassessment. The discussion that follows reflects current available knowledge.

The Incidence of Mental Retardation

It is usually estimated that some 3 percent—over 6,000,000 individuals—of the general population of the United States will be classified as retarded at some point during their lifetime. The Report of the President's Panel on Mental Retardation (1962) estimated that 5,400,000 children and adults in the United States are mentally retarded and that each year 126,000 babies are born who at some time in their lives will be diagnosed as mentally retarded. With increases in the general population, current estimates indicate that 135,000 children born each year in the United States will eventually be diagnosed as mentally retarded (Cytryn & Lourie, 1975). In practice, this would mean that in this country there are currently about 1,500,000 children under age 18 diagnosed as retarded.

Estimates of incidence, however, seldom make distinctions between the categories of severity of retardation. The combined categories of moderate, severe, and profound probably represent no more than one-sixth of the entire population of retarded individuals; the mildly retarded represent some five-sixths (Clark & Rosen, 1973). In the same way, the distribution of retarded youngsters in the general population differs in various age groups. During pre-school years, only 1 percent of the population is diagnosed as retarded, since only the more severe cases are identified. As children enter school, the likelihood of being identified as retarded increases because of more astute observation and increasing demands for intellectual and social performance in the school setting. After the school years, the incidence of retardation in the general population drops considerably because many of those who had been diagnosed as mentally retarded in school blend unnoticeably into the general population (Cytryn & Lourie, 1975). In terms of numbers, therefore, the highest incidence of mental retardation occurs during the middle school years when large numbers of children are identified as borderline or mildly retarded. One must wonder, of course, whether a considerable proportion of such youngsters are labeled retarded solely on the basis of low test scores on IQ tests rather than on the basis of both intellectual ability and adaptive behavior. It might well be expected that the current, stricter definitions of mental retardation will in time significantly affect estimates of incidence, reducing the number of children labeled as retarded.

The Causes of Mental Retardation

The question of causation in mental retardation remains a highly controversial issue. Although there are over 200 known causes of mental retardation, all too frequently the cause or causes in a given child remain obscure or undetermined. In many cases, children who are identified as mildly retarded do not show any clear-cut evidence of organic causation. In this regard, the experts themselves are divided on the issue of whether such retardation is caused by subtle genetic influence or by environmental influences such as psychosocial disadvantage, poverty, inadequate nutrition, family instability, lack of adequate educational opportunities, or unstimulating infant environments.

Discussion of the causes of mental retardation requires a review of major medical findings. There has been an extensive history of medical research in the causes of mental retardation, and an understanding of the possible causes is essential to every worker in the field. The AAMD (1973b) reviewed the causes of retardation in terms of nine major categories: infections and intoxications; trauma or physical agent; metabolism or nutrition; gross brain disease; unknown prenatal influence; chromosomal abnormality; gestational disorders; following psychiatric disorder; and environmental influences. A brief discussion of each of these categories follows.

Infections and intoxications

There are several identified ways in which infections and intoxications cause irreversible brain damage associated with mental retardation. Prenatally, *rubella* (German measles) that infects the mother during the first month of pregnancy may produce abnormalities in 50 percent of the fetuses so infected. A mother who has *syphilis* may infect the fetus, passing on a variety of disorders in the newborn, including blindness, deafness, and mental retardation; fortunately, penicillin has proven to be a very effective treatment of syphilis, and treatment of the mother with penicillin during pregnancy can also treat the infected fetus successfully. Postnatally, viral, bacterial, or parasitic infections of the infant may cause *encephalitis,* an inflammation of the brain, with retardation as a possible consequence.

Trauma or physical agent

This category refers primarily to brain damage associated with extreme difficulties in labor and delivery. *Complications during birth* (such as malposition of the infant for delivery or disproportion between the size of the infant and the cervical opening) may produce brain damage that is not evident until the child reaches school age. *Anoxia,* or loss of oxygen, sometimes caused by the wrapping of the umbilical cord around the infant's neck, may also cause retardation. *Childhood accidents* involving cerebral assault or prolonged loss of consciousness can also cause brain damage associated with retardation.

Metabolism or nutrition

Metabolic problems due to hereditary defects account for only a small percentage of the cases of mental retardation, but the study of these disorders has provided valuable lessons in the prevention and treatment of retardation by known organic cause. The metabolic disorder that has received the most attention is *phenylketonuria (PKU),* first identified by Folling in 1934. PKU is a congenital deficiency in which natural controls for the excessive build-up of phenylalanine, an amino acid, are lacking. The excessive production of phenylalanine in the infant's system produces brain damage that can result in severe mental retardation, including seizures and other neurological abnormalities. Since the discovery of PKU, screening methods have been developed that include urinalysis and compulsory blood tests at birth. Early detection of PKU is extremely important, since a diet management program (in which the child is required to avoid foods containing phenylalanine) before 3 months of age greatly enhances the prospect of normal development. Although the frequency of PKU is probably no more than one case in every 10 to 20 thousand births, the study of PKU has served as a model for research in other metabolic disorders. Success in the treatment of PKU has fueled the hope that further medical breakthroughs are possible in other areas of mental retardation.

Another well-known metabolic disorder is *cretinism,* or *congenital hypothyroidism.* This condition is due to diminished production of thyroid secretions and can be prevented if identified early in life and treated with thyroid extract. If untreated in infancy, mental retardation and physical features such as dwarfism, coarse skin, large tongue, and malformation in the position of the eyes are almost inevitable.

Although PKU and hypothyroidism are probably the best known of the metabolic disorders, more than 50 distinct metabolic deficiencies are known to cause mental retardation, and research in this area is still in its infancy.

Difficulties in adequate nutrition can also affect relationships between the body's biochemistry and the functioning of the brain. Gross malnutrition during infancy and early development is known to have an adverse effect on normal intellectual development. Severe malnutrition can stunt brain growth and produce significant lowering of intellectual ability (Kaplan, 1972). Protein deficiencies in the diet of the mother during pregnancy, as well as in the diet of the infant, have been identified as specific causes of mental retardation. Although the relationship between nutrition and intellectual functioning has not been fully clarified, inadequate nutrition is known to be a significant cause of mental retardation.

Gross brain disease

The category of gross brain disease as a set of causes for mental retardation includes a large number of hereditary disorders that are not well understood. *Huntington's chorea,* for example, is marked by seizures, spasmodic movements (or rigidity without such involuntary movements), progressive retardation, and death. The onset seldom occurs before 4 years of age, but more commonly first symptoms do not occur until 30 to 50 years of age. *Tuberous sclerosis,* or *epiloia,* is characterized by the presence of tumors throughout the brain and other parts of the body, such as the heart or kidneys. Although the severity of this disease varies, mild to severe retardation is inevitable. There is no known treatment for the disease itself.

There are a number of physical diseases that affect the functioning of the brain, thus causing mental retardation. The relationship between brain damage and intellectual functioning, however, is highly complex and poorly understood. There are cases in which intellectual functioning is quite normal despite evidence of considerable damage to the brain; on the other hand, seemingly slight damage to the brain is often associated with severe mental retardation. Continued research is clearly necessary to cast further light on the relationship between brain damage and mental functioning.

Unknown prenatal influence

There are a number of conditions known to occur before birth for which the specific etiologies are unknown. Such congenital conditions include cerebral malformations (deformities in brain structure), cranial anomalies (malformation of the head structure), and cranial-facial anomalies (malformation of both the head and face). *Craniostenosis,* for example, is a condition in which cranial sutures close prematurely, producing an abnormally shaped head, increased pressure on the brain, and some degree of brain damage; although retardation is not inevitable, many such children are severely retarded. *Macrocephaly* refers to an enlargement of the head, most frequently caused by *hydrocephalus,* an excess of cerebrospinal fluid within the brain structure; not all cases of hydrocephalus produce macrocephaly, but macrocephaly is almost always associated with a severe degree of retardation. *Microcephaly,* a rarely occurring phenomenon, is a condition involving an abnormally small cranium and impairment in the development of the brain. Although accurate statistics are not available, it is likely that a large percentage of institutionalized, severely retarded persons are individuals afflicted with congenital anomalies of the brain, head, and face.

Chromosomal abnormality

Abnormalities in the number or structure of chromosomes can be caused by ingestion of drugs by parents, natural mutations of genes, radiation, and a host of other factors whose influence remains unknown. The most widely known chromosomal abnormality is *Down's syndrome,* sometimes referred to as *mongolism.* This condition was first described by Langdon Down (1866); the Mongoloid facial features of these youngsters prompted Down to refer to the condition as "mongolian idiocy." It is interesting to note that Down assumed this condition represented a reemergence of a more primitive evolutionary status, which he erroneously believed to be occupied by the Mongolian race (Blanton, 1975).

It is now known that Down's syndrome is caused by an abnormal chromosomal relationship that alters patterns of growth and development. Normally, a person has 46 chromosomes (23 matching pairs) in every body cell. A child with Down's syndrome typically has an extra chromosome in the twenty-first pair, creating a total of 47 chromosomes. Since the twenty-first pair of chromosomes is actually 3 chromosomes instead of 2, the condition is sometimes called *trisomy 21.* Exhibit 8.1 shows the abnormal chromosomal relationship of trisomy 21.

EXHIBIT 8.1

DOWN'S SYNDROME AND THE TRISOMY OF CHROMOSOME 21

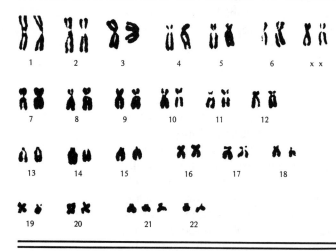

This picture of chromosomes shows an aberration involving the trisomy of chromosome 21. Most cases of Down's syndrome reveal 47 instead of the normal complement of 46 chromosomes.

Down's syndrome is the most commonly occurring form of mental retardation that is known to be due to a specific organic cause. On the average, one child in every 640 live births has Down's syndrome (Smith & Wilson, 1973). The condition can occur in any family, regardless of race, socioeco-

The hand structure characteristic of some children with Down's Syndrome can present complications in physical dexterity. The boy shown here appears to have overcome these difficulties while completing a complex block-building project.

nomic class, or education of parents. For young mothers, the risk of having a child born with Down's syndrome is rather small, but the risk increases with the age of the mother. The unusual patterning of physical characteristics that typifies children with Down's syndrome makes these youngsters easily identifiable. Although few of these children have all the characteristics typical of this syndrome, the following features are common: slanting of the eyes; speckling of the iris of the eye; abnormally thick eyelids; flat, broad face and nose; thickened tongue; short, broad neck; stubby fingers. The number of physical features bears no relationship to the degree of retardation in the child. The range of mental retardation in Down's syndrome varies, but the majority of these children are in the moderately retarded range.

There are, of course, many other types of chromosomal abnormalities that cause mental retardation. Down's syndrome, however, is by far the most common and the most widely known. With the exception of Down's syndrome, the actual number of children whose retardation is caused by chromosomal abnormality is rather small. There is considerable research in this area, despite these small numbers, because of the scientific hope that a key can be discovered that will enable geneticists to locate critical enzymes in the genetic structure (Cytryn & Lourie, 1975).

Gestational disorders

Still another set of factors that can cause mental retardation involves abnormality in the gestational period, or length of pregnancy. The normal human gestation period is a 40-week pregnancy from the first day of the last menstrual period. It is not only the length of the pregnancy itself but also the weight of the infant that is the major concern. Infants who weigh less than

2500 grams (5 pounds 8 ounces) are called "low birth weight infants." Even a full-term infant with low birth weight raises concerns about possible health issues. Retardation, of course, is not an inevitable consequence of premature birth or low birth weight; nonetheless, low birth weight infants require highly specialized postnatal care and should be carefully followed throughout their early development.

Following psychiatric disorder

Another possible cause of mental retardation can be the presence of severe psychiatric disorder during the developmental period. Children who are emotionally disturbed for extensive periods, particularly during the crucial stages of early childhood, may be deprived of the normal sources of intellectual and social development. The relationship between severe psychiatric disorders in childhood (e.g., childhood schizophrenia and early infantile autism) and mental retardation remains, nonetheless, obscure for a number of reasons. First, it is difficult to know which condition causes the other; it may well be that the same set of causes produces both the emotional disorder and the mental retardation in some children. Second, the causes of childhood psychoses are far from obvious, with the possibility that either psychogenic factors or organic factors, or both, are operative. Third, the possible effects of psychiatric disorder on intellectual development are almost impossible to assess.

Environmental influences

The various types of organic causes described above account for a rather small percentage of the entire population of retarded persons. It is believed that only 20 to 25 percent of the total retarded population have abnormal medical findings caused by clear-cut organic conditions (Garrard & Richmond, 1975). The vast majority of children who are identified as retarded do not give evidence of organic symptoms. This is particularly true of the mildly retarded, who, as we have noted, represent some five-sixths of the total population of mentally retarded persons. Although subtle genetic influences or as yet unknown causes may be significant in this regard, there is considerable evidence implicating environmental influences as the major cause of mental retardation.

The most significant set of sources related to retardation as caused by environmental influences is the child's very cultural and familial background. The 1973 revision of the AAMD manual described this condition as "retardation due to psychosocial disadvantage." This condition has been previously described as "cultural-familial mental retardation" (Heber, 1959), "familial mental deficiency" (Allen, 1958), "exogenous mental deficiency" (Strauss & Lehtinen, 1947), and "subcultural mental deficiency" (Lewis, 1933). Each of these designations underlines the notion that the retardation is caused by environmental factors that are "outside" of the child rather than organic factors that are "inside" the child's brain or biochemical constitution.

Although hereditary lower intelligence may well be a significant cause of this condition, some type of **sociocultural deprivation** is typically identified as causative. Sociocultural deprivation can include many individual causes or a combination of causes: genetically low intelligence in the child's family, low socioeconomic status, lack of stimulation in the mother-child relationship, poor housing, lack of adequate education and social training, inadequate medical care, hunger and malnutrition, low achievement motivation, racial discrimination, emotional instability of parents, and parental or family disharmony.

One set of factors that is receiving increasing attention in this regard involves the variables of infant stimulation and maternal deprivation. Many investigators have underlined the important relationship that exists between maternal stimulation of the infant and normal development (Barbero & Shaheen, 1967; Bowlby, 1951; Powell, 1974; Spitz, 1945; Suran & Hatcher, 1975). These studies, and many others, have sought to examine the relationship between environmental stimulation in infancy and normal development of the child. In these studies, the lack of adequate stimulation of the infant is seen to be an important causative factor in the retardation of both physical and mental development; maternal deprivation or prolonged isolation of the infant may well cause life-long retardation as well as severe emotional disorder.

Our knowledge of the precise mechanisms involved in environmental influences such as maternal deprivation or lack of infant stimulation remains somewhat tentative and uncertain, but the importance of environmental factors as significant causes of mental retardation cannot be underestimated. Retardation associated with sociocultural deprivation represents a tragic waste of human potential. As we shall see later in this chapter, the situation is even more tragic when it is considered that many cases of sociocultural retardation can be prevented through intensive intervention into the social conditions of disadvantaged populations.

DIAGNOSIS AND IDENTIFICATION

Our discussion of the causes of mental retardation makes it clear that it is far from a homogeneous category of special childhood, and as indicated earlier, it would be far more accurate to speak of "the mental retardations." Differing types of mental retardation can be extraordinarily distinct from each other in terms of cause, severity, prognosis, and the type of intervention possible. The diagnosis and identification of actual or possible retardation in the individual child remains a complex and often uncertain process. Children are identified as retarded in different ways, depending upon the age of the child at diagnosis and the severity of the child's disability.

Identification at Birth

The most pronounced cases of mental retardation are due to genetic-biological causes and can be quite evident by the presence of clear-cut organic or physiological signs. Children with Down's syndrome, for example, can frequently be identified by examination of physical characteristics. Newborns in hospitals are conventionally examined by a pediatrician shortly after birth, and many of the more severe forms of mental retardation can be detected at this time. Blood tests for the presence of phenylketonuria (PKU) are mandatory for hospital births. Since correct diet management in children identified with PKU can prevent the onset of retardation, early screening for this metabolic disorder is extremely important.

The pediatric examination at birth should be routinely conducted. When a handicapping condition is identified at birth, however, it is often quite difficult to convey such a diagnosis to parents in an accurate but empathic fashion. If the examining physician feels that there is the slightest possibility that the diagnosis may not be accurate, he/she may shrink from the awesome responsibility of bearing such unfortunate information to the parents. When physicians are not extremely sensitive to this issue, they may unconsciously set up a cycle of false hopes or inaccurate expectations in the parents by minimizing the importance of early findings or by maintaining that only further tests can confirm the condition. Of course, there are no tests that have been developed to test IQ level in the newborn. Standardized neurological examinations to assess reflexes and basic behaviors currently constitute the most advanced approach to the assessment of the child's behavior (Brazelton, 1973). If findings at infancy are ambiguous, the parents should be advised of this fact with the understanding that the infant will have to be followed for the first several years of life until adequate assessment is possible.

Identification During Late Infancy or Preschool Years

In the great majority of children who are eventually diagnosed as mentally retarded, it is impossible to detect any signs of potential retardation in the newborn. In the first few years, children who are slow in the acquisition of motor and language skills frequently raise concerns about retardation in the minds of parents or relatives. Diagnostic evaluation for retardation during the first few years of life should include physical examination by a pediatrician, neurological examination by a child neurologist, and psychological examination by a child psychologist. Because of the uncertain and highly variable nature of physical, motor, and language development during the first few years of life, diagnosticians seldom risk firm predictions of retardation, even in the older infant. Although excellent developmental tests have been recently constructed, such as the Bayley Scales of Infant Development (1969), these tests tend to sample sensorimotor bases of intelligence and adaptive behavior and typically are poor predictors of later IQ's (Bayley, 1970; McCall, Hogarty, & Hurlburt, 1972). By the late preschool years, however, children who test below the mildly retarded range and demonstrate deficits in adaptive behavior are typically identified as mentally retarded, and early placement in special education programs becomes the primary form of intervention.

Identification During School Years

The great majority of children who are identified as retarded are youngsters in the mildly retarded range who demonstrate deficits in intellectual ability and adaptive behavior in response to the demands of formal education. Case Study 8.2 gives an example of a child who was identified as retarded in this manner. In most cases of this type, it is the teacher who begins raising questions about the child's adequacy, and it is the teacher who serves as the source of referral for more formal evaluation. Such formal evaluations by school nurses, psychologists, and social workers frequently precede continuing evaluations by the multidisciplinary staffs of child guidance and child development clinics.

223
Diagnosis and
identification

CASE STUDY 8.2

JANICE: A MILDLY RETARDED CHILD

Janice, age 10 years 6 months, lived with her mother (age 31), father (age 34), and sister (age 6), and was referred for a diagnostic evaluation by the third-grade teacher at the parochial school she had attended since first grade. Despite repeating second grade, she had continued to lag behind younger children in her third-grade class. Janice's parents, Mr. & Mrs. O., shared the school's concerns about Janice's inability to learn and were also concerned about her tendency to daydream, shyness in social situations, and inability to engage easily in conversations.

Interview with Parents

Mr. and Mrs. O. had been married for 12 years. They described a happy marriage with few conflicts and open communication. Mr. O., a high-school graduate, had worked his way up from a janitor to a machinist and had been with the same company for 12 years. He had had little contact with his own parents since the age of 18, when he had left his father's rural farm in West Virginia to move to an industrial city in the North. Mr. O. stated that he had not been a good student in school, had been forced to remain in school by his parents, and had left home as soon as he had graduated from high school. Mrs. O., one of ten children, was born and raised in Chicago. She had completed two years at a commercial high school specializing in bookkeeping; she, like her husband, had been a poor student. She had worked for two years after school but had not worked in a formal job since she met and married Mr. O.

Both parents described Janice as a wanted child. It had been Mrs. O's first pregnancy—full-term and without complications. Labor and delivery had been normal. Janice weighed 7 pounds 6 ounces at birth. She sat alone at 7½ months, took her first steps at 11 months (somewhat earlier than is usual), said her first words before 1 year, was easily toilet trained at 3 years, and seemed to be achieving developmental milestones at a normal rate. She did have difficulty learning to ride a bike, however, and had always had poor table manners. Janice had been a physically healthy child throughout her childhood. Her parents had little concern about the normality of her development until she began school. Although she had difficulties in the first grade, she was passed into second grade for compassionate reasons. During the second grade, her difficulties in learning became even more pronounced, and she was retained in second grade. After two years in second grade, she was passed to third grade but continued to have difficulty with second-grade work. Janice's parents had had school difficulties during their respective childhoods and were very concerned that their child do well in school.

Diagnosis

Neurological examination of Janice produced no positive findings. Evidence of any organic damage was lacking. The neurologist felt, however, that Janice was very immature during the examination and that her behavior was inappropriate for her age. The neurologist suggested that emotional problems might well be causing her learning difficulties.

The psychologist noted that Janice was an unkempt child, with ill-fitting clothes, uncombed hair, and crumbs from a recently eaten cookie still on her chin.

WISC-R RECORD FORM

Wechsler Intelligence Scale for Children—Revised

WISC-R PROFILE

Clinicians who wish to draw a profile should first transfer the child's scaled scores to the row of boxes below. Then mark an X on the dot corresponding to the scaled score for each test, and draw a line connecting the X's.

	Year	Month	Day
Date Tested	74	7	31
Date of Birth	64	1	29
Age	10	6	2

	Raw Score	Scaled Score
VERBAL TESTS		
Information	7	3
Similarities	5	3
Arithmetic	7	4
Vocabulary	17	3
Comprehension	8	5
(Digit Span)	(4)	(2)
Verbal Score		18
PERFORMANCE TESTS		
Picture Completion	16	8
Picture Arrangement	13	6
Block Design	8	4
Object Assembly	16	7
Coding	27	5
(Mazes)		
Performance Score		30

	Scaled Score	IQ
Verbal Score	18	60
Performance Score	30	73
Full Scale Score	48	65

*Prorated from 4 tests, if necessary.

Many inappropriate behaviors were noted during testing: she laughed uncontrollably when successfully completing a puzzle, demonstrated contorted facial expressions when confused, and puffed up her cheeks when she grew tired of the testing. She showed severe problems in concentration.

On the Wechsler Intelligence Scale for Children-Revised (WISC-R), she achieved a Verbal Scale IQ of 60, a Performance Scale IQ of 73, and a Full Scale IQ of 65, which placed her in the mildly retarded range of intellectual ability. All of her subtest scores on the WISC-R were below the normal range (the scaled scores have a mean of 10 and a standard deviation of 3).

On projective tests, Janice gave evidence of very little mental energy. Her responses to projective tests were all impoverished and extremely limited. She was overly sensitive, easily irritated, and had little understanding of others. Thus, Janice was diagnosed as a child who was currently functioning within the mildly retarded range. This diagnosis was based on the actual measurement of intellectual functioning by formal testing, on con-trolled observations of limited social adaptation, and on her inability to learn in school through conventional methods of instruction.

Treatment

It was suggested to the parents that Janice be placed in an advanced EMH class where she could receive more individualized attention suited to her level of functioning. It was further suggested that the parents be seen for several sessions of counseling to help them work through the shock and disappointment of the diagnosis, as well as to help them manage their own interventions with their daughter in a growth-oriented fashion. Periodic evaluations at intervals of 12 to 18 months were recommended in order to monitor Janice's continued development and to help plan for her education and livelihood. All recommendations were accepted by the parents.

At the beginning of the next school term, Janice was transferred from her parochial school to an EMH class in the public school system. Janice seemed to respond to this placement with "a sigh of relief." Academic expectations were geared to her known level of functioning, and she was helped to learn at her own pace. Her EMH class had only eight students, with one special education teacher and one teacher's aide. There was ample opportunity for individualized attention to Janice's difficulties in learning. There was also an emphasis on helping Janice acquire social skills, such as grooming, manners, self-care, and conversation.

In counseling, Mr. & Mrs. O. were helped to accept the nature of Janice's limitations, but were also encouraged to expect continuing development. Despite Janice's slow rate of mental and social growth, the counseling psychologist helped the parents discover several areas in which they could assist their daughter. For example, because of Janice's "shyness," her mother and father frequently allowed her to spend much time daydreaming by herself. This cycle of shyness and daydreaming was altered by having the mother and the father, respectively, structure a half hour of Janice's free time in interactional activities, such as helping her mother wash dishes or reading a picture book with her father. Helping the parents identify ways to become more involved with their daughter proved to be a very effective form of intervention.

Janice is now completing her first full year in EMH and is scheduled for a psychological reevaluation. Depending on the results of this reevaluation, she may remain in EMH placement or be moved to an ungraded classroom where she could also receive tutorial help. Her response to EMH placement, as well as her parents' response in seeing themselves as having a beneficial influence on their daughter's learning and social adaptation problems, hold forth hopes that Janice can demonstrate considerable improvement in academic and social competence.

It should be emphasized that diagnostic evaluation with the child who is identified as retarded is not a "one-shot" affair. Intellectual ability and adaptive behavior are not fixed and immutable capacities, and the retarded child needs repeated evaluation so that the level and object of intervention can be geared to the child's changing abilities. Some youngsters may give evidence of a decrease in ability, and in such cases it is also important to adjust expectations to the child's current capacities. At the same time, the diagnosis of mild mental retardation is far from final, and continuing evaluation is necessary, especially during the developmental period: it is not unusual in clinical practice to find IQ gains of 10 to 20 points in the mildly retarded youngster who is placed in an intense intervention program. It is also important to remember, however, that intervention is only selectively successful, and dramatic increases in tested IQ do not occur automatically with special intervention. The effect of intervention (*nurture*) on native ability (*nature*) remains a puzzling and controversial issue, and current clinical practice stresses the responsibility of the examining clinician for repeated assessment during the developmental period.

DEVELOPMENTAL CONSEQUENCES

Anyone who has had experience in working with retarded children knows only too well that the most subtle accidents of birth and infancy can condemn children to lifetimes of unrealized potential. An awesome fact of mental retardation is the simple statistic that the vast majority of retarded children are substantially handicapped throughout their lifetimes. Recognizing that such conditions function as life-span disabilities, Congress in 1969 passed Public Law 91-517, the Developmental Disabilities Services and Construction Act. This law was intended to assist the Secretary of Health, Education, and Welfare in proposing and implementing services for the lifelong needs of special children, but it also sanctioned a specific meaning for the notion of "developmental disability":

Developmental disability *means a disability attributable to mental retardation, cerebral palsy, epilepsy, or another neurological condition of an individual found by the Secretary to be closely related to mental retardation or to require treatment similar to that required for mentally retarded individuals, which disability originates before such individual attains age eighteen, which has continued or can be expected to continue indefinitely, and which constitutes a substantial handicap to the individual. (Developmental Disabilities Act, 1969)*

Mental retardation is not synonymous with developmental disability, and the term "developmental disability" is a legal definition for funding purposes. The passage of the Developmental Disabilities Act, however, has brought significant legal and social attention to the needs of the retarded. Neisworth and Smith (1974) pointed out that the term "developmental disability" has been instrumental in underlining the fact that children who are substantially deficient in locomotive, communicative, adjustive, or intellectual functioning are typically in need of lifelong assistance. Hobbs (1975) noted: "The concept of developmental disability has one inherent virtue: it recognizes a certain community of service needs by persons who have long-enduring handicaps of early onset and who require sustained assistance in both childhood and adult life" (p. 84). The concept of developmental disability will not replace the more specific, although global, category of mental retardation, but the extensive developmental consequences of mental retardation are well served by descriptive terms that represent retardation in a dynamic, rather than in a static, fashion.

Cognitive and Educational Factors

Since mental retardation is specifically a retardation in the development of intelligence and adaptive behavior, the most specific consequences of this disorder involve its effects on the child's ability to learn and to progress educationally. The learning capacities of retarded children have been studied extensively and from various perspectives. For our purposes, it will be sufficient here to review relevant conclusions regarding the effects of degree of retardation on general learning potential (see Exhibit 8.2). Since some 75 to 80 percent of retarded children are identified as mildly retarded, the majority of the retarded population is **educable** and able to function independently as adults. Children in the moderately retarded range are **trainable;** although they typically cannot learn to read and write, they have the potential for unskilled employment under supervision. Educational programs for the retarded are typically described as EMH (educable mentally handicapped) or TMH (trainable mentally handicapped), based upon the child's capacity for cognitive and educational achievement.

Retarded children learn in basically the same fashion as normal children. Retarded children, however, acquire information at a slower pace than is true of normal children. Mental retardation implies, in essence, a slow rate of mental growth. Although there are a variety of reasons to account for the slower rate of learning in retarded children, educators must be especially sensitive to two areas of cognitive functioning within the retarded child: memory and attention.

EXHIBIT 8.2

227
Developmental
consequences

EDUCATIONAL ACHIEVEMENT AMONG THE MENTALLY RETARDED

Degree of Mental Retardation	Potential for Educational Achievement	Potential for Adult Functioning
Mildly retarded: IQ approximately 51-65	"Educable"; capable of 3rd to 6th grade educational achievement; able to read and write and use basic mathematics	Able to be independent personally and socially; able to be self-supporting; frequently lose identification as retarded and blend into "normal" population
Moderately retarded: IQ approximately 36-50	"Trainable"; capable of kindergarten through 3rd grade achievement; typically not able to read and write	Able to be employed in unskilled occupations if supervision available; typically incapable of independent living or marriage
Severely retarded: IQ approximately 21-35	Able to acquire some self-care skills; able to talk and express self; unable to acquire any academic skills	Need permanent care from family or society; some are capable of performing simple chores under total supervision
Profoundly retarded: IQ approximately 20 or lower	Unable to speak; some are capable of self-ambulation but many remain bedridden throughout their lives	Incapable of any self-maintenance; require permanent nursing care

Research has indicated that retarded children have more substantial *short-term and long-term memory deficits* than normal children of the same chronological age (Gardner, 1971; Hyatt & Rolnick, 1974; Weisberg, 1971). Difficulties in retaining material already learned seem more pronounced for more abstract material than for more concrete information. Such memory problems may well be due to the fact that retarded children do not "rehearse" as they are learning. Educational intervention is typically more effective, therefore, if learning is programmed in organized clusters with time-out for rehearsal of new material in order to assist in storing information that is being learned. Since retarded youngsters have deficiencies in past learning, special efforts are required to help them overcome memory deficits and engage in more successful learning strategies.

A second area of importance in the learning processes of retarded children involves *difficulties in focusing and maintaining attention* (Estes, 1970; Hagan & Huntsman, 1971; Tarver & Hallahan, 1974). Retarded children frequently do not know what it is that they are expected to learn in a given learning situation; helping them focus attention on relevant aspects of the learning problem will usually facilitate learning and performance. It should also be remembered that for the retarded, many previous learning situations have been ineffective and unsuccessful. This fact may well contribute to lags in attention. Learning and performance in retarded children can be fostered by encouraging them to focus and maintain attention.

Personal and Social Factors

Historically, many myths have arisen regarding the personalities of the retarded. Perhaps the most prevalent stereotype of the retarded is that of a blissful, trusting child who remains joyfully unaware of the complexities of life. This stereotype lends itself to a variety of beliefs, namely that retarded persons are happy doing useless activities, that they lack powerful emotions, that they have no sexual urges, and that they are contented with merely minimal attention from their caretakers. Recent research has indicated, however, that such supposed personality and social characteristics of the retarded have little do to with their intellectual ability (MacMillan, 1971; MacMillan & Keogh, 1971; Zigler, 1971a, 1971b); rather, they are the result of specific environmental experiences and expectations to which the retarded have been subjected.

One of the presumed effects of limited intellectual ability, for example, was thought to be *rigidity,* the tendency to be inflexible in learning situations and by consequence to take greater enjoyment in monotonous and repetitive tasks. Although this is a complicated research issue, findings tend to indicate that such rigidity is a function of social deprivation rather than limited intellectual ability. Children who are institutionalized are more socially deprived than noninstitutionalized youngsters; therefore, they are highly motivated for supportive adult attention and more willing to work at monotonous tasks in order to receive supportive adult attention (Zigler, 1971a, 1971b).

A second factor that contributes to unfortunate stereotypes of the re-

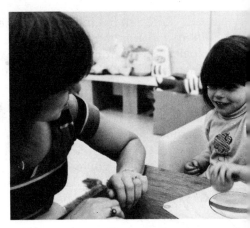

Personal attention and warm reassurance can do much to motivate mentally retarded children in their development. Here, a visually-impaired and hydrocephalic girl practices with a peg board to improve her motor skills; a boy receives guidance in matching/drawing tasks, and a preschooler responds to individual encouragement in learning object matching.

tarded involves the area of *motivation and expectation of failure.* Several studies have shown that retarded children tend to experience more failure than normal children and that retarded children, therefore, learn to expect the experience of failure (MacMillan, 1971; MacMillan & Keogh, 1971). The expectation of failure sets up a cycle that affects the child's motivation. When retarded children do not experience themselves as able to achieve, they become passive, lose their initiative, and become overly dependent upon others to tell them what to do. This series of environmental experiences tends to reinforce popular misconceptions that the retarded are, by nature, easily manipulated and must be told what to do.

A third factor of particular concern in the personal and social development of retarded children involves *self-concept and social acceptance.* Retarded children are frequently subjected to teasing and isolation by their normal peers, and social experiences of this kind can have seriously adverse consequences on the child's self-esteem and very sense of self. Much of the research in this area has attempted to assess the respective effects of special versus regular class placement on self-concept and social acceptance. Research findings have been ambiguous, but all of these studies tend to underline the fact that self-concept in the retarded child is very much a function of social acceptance (Gampel, Gottlieb, & Harrison, 1974; Gottlieb & Budoff, 1973; Goodman, Gottlieb, & Harrison, 1972; Mayer, 1966; Monroe & Howe, 1971). Retarded children do not feel innately inferior; rather their sense of adequacy is a function of the socializing experiences to which they have been exposed. Thus a number of issues related to the personal and social characteristics of retarded children are currently being rethought, and research is attempting to control for such factors as social deprivation, feelings of being different, and experience of academic failure.

PREVENTION AND INTERVENTION

Prevention and intervention currently offer considerable promise in the area of mental retardation. Many authorities in this field are of the opinion that the potential for prevention and intervention is totally untapped and that coming generations will witness exciting and dramatic opportunities to create better lives for the retarded. Rapid advances in genetics and behavioral engineering, combined with new social programs that wage war on poverty and ignorance, have created a climate of optimism and expectation for those who are involved with the mentally retarded. It is a cautious optimism that dominates this field, however, for seasoned professionals know only too well the disappointment that follows upon unrealized hopes. Assistance for the retarded has nonetheless become a critical social issue supported in many sectors that lie beyond those directly affected by it. We find today a renewed investment in traditional perspectives held by highly regarded educators and therapists of the past—Itard, Montessori, Seguin, Howe—combined with the development of more current conceptualizations of the retarded. The problems of the retarded child are no longer viewed as a curse from God but rather as a complex medical-educational-psychological-social challenge capable of being solved. The helping process for the retarded child takes place on many fronts, including primary prevention, medical intervention, psychological intervention, and social and educational intervention.

Primary Prevention

Perhaps the most prominent notion in the entire field of mental retardation is that many of the manifestations of mental retardation are preventable. Prevention, of course, is one of the current "buzzwords" in contemporary health circles, but in mental retardation the concept of primary prevention has become more than a promise that creates false hopes. **Primary prevention** refers to the establishment of medical and social programs that seek to alter the conditions responsible for the development of any disability or illness. On the medical level, a heightened awareness of the importance of adequate prenatal care now makes it possible to decrease the risks involved in pregnancy, labor, and delivery. Effective prenatal care can now prevent or reduce the risk of prematurity, Rh incompatibilities between the mother and child, vitamin and diet deficiencies, and infections. In addition, children who are delivered *at risk* can now be provided with neonatal care that can be extremely effective in reducing postnatal factors responsible for retardation.

One of the more exciting approaches in this respect involves the establishment within hospitals of "stimulation programs" designed to promote the development of low-birth-weight or high-risk infants (Barnard, 1973; Brown & Hepler, 1976; Powell, 1974; Scarr-Salapatek & Williams, 1973; Williams & Scarr, 1971). These programs have been oriented toward a variety of preventive measures, including training of mothers in infant stimulation, placing ribbons on infants in incubators in order to make them more physically appealing to staff who interact with them, and follow-up care with both mothers and infants. Such programs tend to provide only brief intervention, and even though the effects of such intervention may be somewhat temporary, these studies have brought significant attention to the possibilities of preventive intervention.

Heber, Garber, and Falender (1973) have shown the dramatic possibilities that exist through more extensive efforts at prevention. Working with a group of poverty-level inner-city parents, these investigators enrolled infants between 3 months and 6 months of age in extensive stimulation programs that continued throughout the preschool years. The focus here involved both the parents and the child, and the results were gratifying. Children enrolled in the program showed stabilized intellectual superiority of 25 to 30 IQ points compared to children from similar backgrounds who had not been enrolled in the stimulation program.

Such efforts at primary prevention strongly support the need for more far-reaching intervention than just preventive medicine. The proportion of mentally retarded children who are retarded by reason of identifiable organic causes is relatively small compared to the number of youngsters who are retarded because of cultural deficiencies, understimulating environments, parental ignorance of adequate childrearing approaches, and the abject poverty in which many families exist. Comprehensive prevention of mental retardation must necessarily include massive social changes that address the lack of adequate standards of living and education among large segments of the disadvantaged population. In the absence of such massive social changes, however, programs of the type described above provide exciting and productive opportunities for prevention among the culturally disadvantaged.

Medical Intervention

There are no surgical procedures or miracle drugs known to be effective in actually increasing intellectual ability or adaptive behavior. In general, medical intervention is directed primarily toward the prevention or correction of organic conditions that can cause mental retardation rather than toward the actual remediation of retardation in children who are identified as retarded. It has already been noted that certain organic conditions known to be causal factors in mental retardation can be successfully managed when identified early. Mental retardation in PKU can be prevented if a low phenylalanine diet is introduced early in infancy. Hypothyroidism, which is known to produce mental retardation and cretinism, can also be managed successfully with the institution of thyroid extract treatment in the first 6 months of life. The medical management of PKU and hypothyroidism provide striking examples of the kinds of breakthroughs that are possible with continuing medical research.

Surgery offers another form of medical intervention. Hydrocephalus, for example, can be treated by a surgical procedure involving the insertion of a shunt that directs excess cerebrospinal fluid away from the brain. Successful surgery with hydrocephalic conditions can thus reduce the possibility of brain damage, thereby preventing mental retardation that may follow upon brain damage. With or without surgical intervention, a child may be hydrocephalic without being brain-damaged and without being mentally retarded.

In short, the current trend in medical research centers on the early identification and treatment of organic conditions that cause mental retardation rather than on the treatment of retardation itself.

Psychological Intervention

Psychological approaches to the treatment of the retarded child range from counseling and psychotherapy with parents to psychotherapy and behavior modification with the child. Each of these formats of psychological intervention may have various goals and rationales.

Parent counseling

Counseling the parents of a retarded child is a vital part of the intervention program. Chapter 14 will focus more extensively on this issue, but it must be noted here that the parents' reaction to a diagnosis of retardation can be a crucial factor in the effectiveness of other interventions with the child. Grief, guilt, and shattered hopes typically characterize the response of parents to the discovery that their child is actually or potentially retarded. Counseling, therefore, includes the major goals of helping parents identify and accept their feelings, air their grief and/or anger, and understand the actual reasons, if known, for their child's retardation. It is not unusual for parents to believe that the child's condition is a punishment for some parental misdeed of the past or to believe that the true cause of the retardation is some secret defect within one or both of the parents. As such, sound and accurate information regarding the possible reasons for the child's condition are very important in helping the parents adjust positively.

Equally important, the counselor should be sensitive to the parents' experience of the situation and be a source of advice and guidance regarding the management of the child. In the case of the severely retarded child, the parents may well be highly ambivalent about the decision to keep the child or to give him/her up for institutionalization. The sensitive counselor does not force personal biases in this regard, but rather attempts to help the parents determine what is best both for them and for the child. Counseling should also include advice and information about the sources of help, the existence of relevant community agencies that work with the retarded, educational alternatives, and what, in general, the parents might expect of the future.

In some cases, the stress that is involved in discovering that one's child is retarded may activate other personal problems in one or both of the parents. In these instances, individual psychotherapy or marital psychotherapy may well be indicated. The goals of psychotherapy in such cases are not technically different from the goals of psychotherapy for anyone who is experiencing problems in living or coping with stress.

Psychotherapy with the retarded child

It is indeed unfortunate that many clinicians fail to recognize the potential utility of psychotherapy for the retarded. Because the retarded are often limited in verbal abilities, the more traditional forms of "talk therapy" are regarded by many therapists as inappropriate for retarded individuals. The retarded nonetheless experience many of the problems typically treated in conventional therapy—for example, poor self-concept, inadequacy in interpersonal relationships, difficulties with parents or peers, and problems in impulse control. Although psychotherapeutic approaches may well require considerable modification in working with the retarded child, there is increasing evidence that psychotherapy for retarded children is both possible and desirable.

Leland and Smith (1965, 1972) described rather unique approaches via play therapy, in which the overall goal of increasing the child's ability to think can be flexibly adapted to the needs and levels of the individual child. The Leland and Smith approach begins with such basic goals as fostering self-awareness through the use of play materials designed to meet the child at his/her own level of experience. Although play therapy approaches of this kind have not been subjected to adequate empirical investigation, their use with retarded children indicates that basic changes are taking place in the way that psychotherapists view the possibility of assisting the retarded.

Group therapy for the retarded is also becoming increasingly recognized as a viable form of treatment, especially for children who have been placed in institutions. Sternlicht (1966), Mowatt (1970), Slivkin and Bernstein (1970), and Borenzweig (1970) all attested to the clinical usefulness of group therapy with retarded children. Group therapy is seen as an economical and fruitful approach to improving social and communication skills, relieving anxiety, decreasing feelings of isolation and uselessness, and providing a sense of companionship and camaraderie. The goals of group treatment of the retarded, therefore, differ little from the goals of group psychotherapy with individuals of normal intelligence. Mowatt (1970), for example, used a group therapy approach in which the mothers of retarded children were seen together in group therapy at the same time that the children were themselves involved in group therapy. This approach provided opportunities for the mothers to share their anxieties, to learn from the experiences of others in similar situations, and to receive feedback regarding the management of their retarded child. Grossman (1972) went even further in an interesting study in which the brothers and sisters of retarded youngsters were seen in group therapy to help them deal with the problems associated with having a retarded sibling. These novel approaches to psychotherapy are ample evidence that clinicians are demonstrating a greater degree of awareness and involvement in the psychological problems of both retarded children and their families.

Behavior modification with the retarded child

The behavior therapies have been generally viewed as a genuine advance in the enhancement of the developmental potential of the retarded. Since the behavioral approach tends to minimize the importance of cognitive processes such as intelligence and to focus instead on more directly observable behaviors, many investigators feel that behavior modification is ideally suited to the problems of the retarded child.

Kerr, Meyerson, and Michael (1965) demonstrated one of the ways that behavioral principles could be applied to the problems of a severely retarded, institutionalized child. A 3-year-old girl who was mute, emotionally disturbed, and severely retarded was placed in a shaping program intended to stimulate language production. In a few brief hours of therapeutic contact, the child was producing spontaneous vocalizations in response to the therapist's verbalizations. Despite the fact that this child remained severely retarded, the ability to vocalize represented a genuine advance in her developmental potential.

Girardeau and Spradlin (1964) introduced a token economy program for a group of adolescent girls whose IQ's ranged from 20 to 50. By giving tokens that could be used in vending machines when the girls performed a number of specified desirable behaviors, the researchers found that motivation for improved behavior increased significantly in the state institution in which the girls lived.

Giles and Wolf (1966) focused on self-care skills and attempted to toilet train 5 severely retarded boys in a residential setting by the use of positive reinforcers for successful toileting and aversive stimuli for soiling. These investigators reported positive results with all subjects, and methodologies of this type are now in regular use for toilet training institutionalized retardates.

For the severely retarded who live in institutions, the use of behavior modification procedures has been particularly important because it is able to

*In a preprimary class for retarded chil-
dren, the rewards of playing a number
bingo game can be a strong incentive for
the players to practice a number of
skills—including number and color recognition and attending skills, such as sitting
in one's chair and following directions.*

change the focus of institutionalization from custodial care to treatment. Behavioral approaches are also being applied with increasing frequency to the
noninstitutionalized retarded. One of the more exciting approaches in this
regard involves training parents to act as behavior therapists for their own
retarded children (O'Dell, 1974; Tavormina, 1974; Watson & Bassinger, 1974).
In a typical program of this kind, the parents observe a trained therapist working with their child. The parents are then trained to observe and record
behavior accurately and provided with basic instruction in the various tech-
nologies of reinforcement. The behavior therapist then serves as the consultant
to the parents as they systematically attempt to increase the behavior capacities of their child. In this manner, the use of behavioral approaches for the
retarded child offers a varied and economical type of intervention frequently
not possible in the more traditional psychotherapies.

Both psychotherapy and behavior modification are currently well represented as clinically relevant forms of intervention with the retarded youngster.
The emphasis of these techniques has not been to improve intellectual functioning specifically, but rather to increase the child's adaptive behavior. In
this respect, psychological forms of intervention show great promise despite
the fact that the available research literature is fraught with many methodological problems. Selectively applied, parent counseling, psychotherapy, and be-

havior therapy have demonstrated a number of socially relevant prospects for treatment of the retarded child.

Social and Educational Intervention

Although medical and psychological forms of intervention can make a useful contribution, these aspects of the helping process touch only a small percentage of retarded children. More extensive intervention services for the retarded are provided by social and educational programs, and the blending of these programs often makes them indistinguishable. Both social and educational intervention will be considered here under the rubrics of institutionalization, environmental manipulations, vocational training and rehabilitation, and special education.

Institutionalization

In the eyes of many, the institutionalization of retarded persons has become one of the great social crimes of the modern era. Large, understaffed, state institutions originally conceived as a means of providing custodial shelter and humane care for those who could not care for themselves have become notorious for substandard conditions, inhumane treatment, violations of basic human rights, and punitive attitudes by untrained staff and supposed caretakers. In many cases, children who are assigned to such institutions are simply "thrown away" to become victims of aggression and contempt (Blatt, 1970; Blatt & Kaplan, 1966; Braginsky & Braginsky, 1971). Because of such conditions, many health professionals have concluded that institutionalization no longer represents a viable form of care for the mentally retarded.

It should be recalled, however, that the first institutions for the retarded were intended to serve as centers for education and training. The shift to purely custodial care in institutional settings came about only gradually and to a large extent because of public apathy and disinterest. Inability to realize overly zealous treatment expectations certainly helped dampen the hopes of many professional workers, and gradual moves toward custodial rather than rehabilitative service was in time accepted by staff members as a matter of course. The eugenics movement that occurred in the early part of the twentieth century made totally fallacious arguments citing hereditary retardation as the principal cause of criminality, prostitution, poverty, alcoholism, and a whole host of social ills. More contemporary thinking, of course, identifies such social ills as very likely causes of retardation, rather than vice versa, but the association of retardation with these social evils created fear of the retardate in the general public. It was an easy step to turn institutions into places of incarceration intended to protect the public from the supposed evils of the retarded.

Today, concepts of institutionalization have come full circle. The general public has once again become aware that retarded persons pose no social threat but must themselves be protected from social victimization. The nature of institutions for the retarded is undergoing a significant change in conceptualization, and the primary goals of institutionalization are once again being seen as education, rehabilitation, and training rather than custodial care and protection of the community.

Current thinking in the field of mental retardation is marked by two specific attitudes toward institutionalization: (a) it should be prevented whenever possible, and (b) when necessary, it should occur in small, community-based residences. In many cases of mild or moderate retardation, sufficient services exist within the community to make institutionalization unwarranted and undesirable. The prospects of a more normal life for a retarded youngster are greatly enhanced when the youngster is part of a functioning family unit which is sensitive to the child's deficiencies but which expects appropriately socialized behavior. On the other hand, when institutionalization is necessary—because of the severity of handicap or the lack of a nurturing family—a homelike residential setting is advocated as a more benign environment than large, impersonal institutions. Current residential settings for the retarded should stress a comfortable atmosphere with as normal a life as possible. Although neighborhood residents frequently object to the placement of a residence for the retarded in their midst, such arrangements are currently considered the placement of choice for the good of the retarded child. With some 200,000 retarded children now in institutional placement (Cytryn & Lourie, 1975), the shift toward smaller, community-based residences cannot be accomplished overnight. In time, however, it is likely that traditional institutionalization will be limited solely to the bedridden and profoundly retarded who require custodial care.

Environmental manipulations

The provision of adequate social environments for the retarded is currently considered to be one of the most critical factors in effective treatment. The question of environmental manipulation, of course, is intimately connected with the problems of institutionalization versus home care and large institutions versus small, residential settings. The qualitative, normalizing nature of the child's environment is more and more being viewed as the critical variable in a retarded child's development. As increasing research indicates that much of the apparently maladaptive behavior of the retarded is due not so much to limited intelligence as to environmental experiences and expectations, the nature of the child's environment becomes a key factor in the selection of possible treatment approaches. Although a variety of research strategies have been used in this regard, Tizard and his associates in England and Skeels, Skodak, and their associates at the University of Iowa have conducted independent studies that dramatically demonstrate the importance of the environment as a critical factor in the development of the retarded child.

In a famous study now known as the "Brooklands experiment," Tizard (1962) showed that institutionalized, moderately retarded children could make significantly positive changes in social-emotional maturity, intelligence, and human relationship skills when regularly exposed to normal amounts of attention and social stimulation. In another study, Tizard (1964) removed a group of retarded children from an overcrowded institution and placed them in small residential settings; these children showed significantly greater verbal and social development than a control group who remained in the large institution.

The close relationship between nurturing and environmental stimulation and mental growth processes was dramatically underlined by the Iowa studies begun in the late 1930s. Skeels and Skodak and their associates conducted a number of studies of the benefits that surrogate mothers and foster parents might have for retarded children as compared to the nonnurturing atmosphere of typical institutional placement (Skeels, 1966; Skeels & Dye, 1939; Skeels & Harms, 1948; Skodak, 1939; Skodak & Skeels, 1949). Skeels' early work was based on the observation of two 1-year-old girls who were transferred from an orphanage to an institution for the retarded because they appeared to be profoundly retarded. In the state institution, they were cared for with great affection by adolescent girls who were themselves inmates and retardates. Continued and repeated testing of these infants demonstrated that they achieved and maintained intellectual development and behavioral capacity within the normal range. This clinical observation gave rise to more controlled studies that yielded similar findings. Although these studies are complex and touch on many controversial factors, such research strongly suggests that intellectual and social functioning is greatly enhanced when retarded children are placed in favorable environments that provide adequate quantity and quality of nurturance.

A number of variables complicate efforts of social programs seeking to place retarded youngsters in favorable home environments such as foster families or small residential settings. It is difficult to obtain adequate foster placement for many retarded children, and it is equally difficult to develop adequate residential services staffed by well-qualified and compassionate aides and therapists. The realities of economics and politics often interfere with the best-intentioned funding practices, and the provision of adequate and stimulating environments for the retarded is unquestionably a costly enterprise. Despite the fact that stimulating and stable nurturing relationships appear to be a crucial variable in the healthy development of retarded children, such environments are all too frequently lacking for large numbers of children who are identified as retarded.

Vocational training and rehabilitation

One of the central goals of education is to help the student acquire the skills necessary to lead a productive and self-supporting existence. In the past, the education of the retarded child all too often showed negligible results because of an emphasis on academic skills. The education of retarded children, particularly in the adolescent age range, is shifting more and more toward the acquisition of vocational skills with concomitant emphasis on the importance of such training. A significant part of a person's self-esteem is tied to ability to be engaged in productive work that enables one to lead an independent life, or at least a less dependent life. Many professionals who deal with retarded persons must struggle to avoid a patronizing attitude because they often encounter the retarded in dependent, nonproductive situations. The large majority of retarded persons, however, are capable of self-supporting, productive work. Tizard and O'Connor (1950a, 1950b) changed much of the thinking about the productivity of the retarded when they reviewed the research demonstrating the considerable success of various training programs to help the retarded obtain functional employment.

There is a need, of course, for a continuum of vocational-rehabilitative services for the retarded (Morgenstern & Michal-Smith, 1973). Some retarded persons need little more than vocational assessment and some counseling before they can enter the job market. Others need more direct assistance in identifying possible jobs, as well as active help in obtaining and maintaining employment. Vocational or prevocational training is now available in most metropolitan areas both through state and federally funded grants and through many business enterprises that recognize the retarded as potentially good employees.

One of the more significant forms of training in this regard has come to be known as the **sheltered workshop.** The sheltered workshop can be either one step in a retarded individual's progress toward independent living and employability or a lifetime living and working circumstance for those who cannot function in total independence. The sheltered workshop typically exists in cooperation with private industry and provides unskilled work such as box-making, packaging, and assembly. Retarded persons in this setting benefit from continued supervision and assistance, and, at the same time, have a degree of useful activity that is far more meaningful than simply being cared for in a custodial fashion. The education of the retarded, of course, can be much more fruitfully conducted if long-range planning toward eventual employment and independent living (or quasi-independent living) begins early in a retarded child's educational curriculum.

Special education

The history of the education of the mentally retarded in the United States is associated with the special school or the special class, and throughout the

Through the teaching of varied projects in ceramics, woodworking, and candle-making, prevocational departments for the mentally retarded can focus on developing work attributes that will prepare the retarded adult to go into a sheltered workshop program. Among the basic goals are attributes basic to any job— applying oneself to the task at hand, getting along with fellow workers, and doing a job from beginning to end.

first half of the current century, segregated education for the retarded was simply taken for granted (Blanton, 1975). In the past decade, the segregation of retarded youngsters (more particularly the borderline or mildly retarded) into residential schools, special day schools, and/or special classes has been challenged by court decisions as well as current educational philosophies of *mainstreaming* and *normalization*. Parent groups have become particularly active in insisting that retarded children receive equal and even regular educational opportunities. One of the intentions of the Education of All Handicapped Act (Public Law 94-142), of course, is to facilitate optimum mainstreaming of retarded and other special children who can benefit from regular classroom placement. The determination of regular or special placement for the retarded remains controversial, and a review of some of the more relevant research may help shed light on the nature of the difficulties.

Generalizations regarding the superiority of regular versus special placement for the retarded are compounded by the fact that available school practices do not easily lend themselves to research in this area. A satisfactory experimental design to investigate this problem would require that children who are otherwise comparable be separated completely into regular and special classes for several years; if other relevant variables were adequately controlled, perhaps it would be possible to obtain data on the effectiveness of competing educational strategies. It would likely be difficult to obtain subjects for such research, however, because many parents might feel that their child was being treated unfairly by placement in one or the other of the programs. In short, well-controlled and reliable studies of this type are extremely difficult to execute.

The problem is further compounded by disagreement regarding the relevant criteria for measuring success. Is increase in measured intelligence the best criteria? Is social adjustment the best criteria? Is academic achievement the best criteria? Perhaps even more important than any of these is the underlying issue of whether the retarded should be trained in the more conventional academic skills that may well be useless to them in terms of their future livelihood rather than receive training in vocational areas that are more directly related to the conduct of a productive life.

Problems of this nature make it extremely difficult to draw sensible conclusions from the existing research. Johnson (1962) concluded that research showed better achievement for students in regular classrooms but better social adjustment for students in special classrooms. This conclusion seems to have taken a foothold in the literature and is mildly supported by several subsequent studies. Goodman et al. (1972) and Gottlieb and Budoff (1973), for example, found that mildly retarded students in special classes seem to have more positive self-concepts than their peers in regular classes who are perhaps more often isolated and teased by classmates. On the other hand, Gampel et al. (1974) found that mildly retarded children in regular classes demonstrated more adequate social behavior than did peers who were in special classes. In short, the issue of mainstreaming or special placement for the retarded is a complex one, and research in this area is currently too scanty to allow for adequate conclusions.

When properly funded and competently executed, educational intervention can dramatically affect the development of children identified as actually or potentially retarded. The work of Heber and his associates (Heber & Garber, 1971, 1974; Heber, Garber, & Falender, 1974) in the "Milwaukee Project" is perhaps the best-known example of a complete program of educational intervention. This program has been a model for the application of varied educational interventions with children who are at risk for sociocultural retardation.

The study originally began with a survey of the most poverty-ridden area in the city of Milwaukee; this survey indicated that mothers with IQ's below 80 (half the sample tested) accounted for 80 percent of the children with IQ's below 80. In short, this data indicated that in low socioeconomic groups, the lower the IQ of the mother, the greater the probability that the child would have a low IQ. Heber hypothesized, therefore, that maternal IQ might well be a critical variable in the causation of sociocultural retardation among poor children. The Milwaukee Project began by selecting 40 infants born during a given year of mothers known to have IQ's of less than 75. These infants were placed in experimental and control groups with intervention focusing on the experimental group. Intervention consisted of multiple efforts, including infant stimulation programs begun at home and preschool education at the Infant Education Center in Milwaukee; the mothers were also assigned for habilitation at the Infant Education Center. The major focus of the intervention, however, was a five-day-a-week, seven-hour-a-day, year-round educational experience at the Infant Education Center until the children entered the first grade. The results of this study have been most gratifying, with the experimental children demonstrating a 20- to 30-point IQ advantage over the control children. Since the great majority of children who eventually are placed in special classes are youngsters whose retardation stems from no known organic pathology and more likely derives from sociocultural deprivation, the Milwaukee Project points to the efficacy of extensive preschool intervention as a critical aspect in the helping process. Important, too, is the stimulus provided by the Milwaukee Project for genuinely experimental approaches to educational intervention in this area.

Legal and Ethical Issues in Mental Retardation

In the past few decades, great strides have been made by handicapped individuals and organizations of handicapped persons in securing equal status before the law. The civil rights movement of the 1960s provided considerable impetus for the handicapped as well, but many are convinced that the surface has just been scratched. The discrimination and deprivation of equal justice for the retarded is an even more complex problem because the retarded typically lack the social sophistication to recognize the ethical and legal problems that they experience. The rights of the retarded are usually best articulated by spokespersons and organizations who have a vested interest in mental retardation. Several statements or "bills of rights" have appeared recently in this regard; one of the best is that written by the Assembly of the International League of Societies for the Mentally Handicapped and is reproduced in Exhibit 8.3.

Of the problems that touch directly on the rights of the retarded child, the right to a fair psychological assessment is an area that needs scrutiny by

EXHIBIT 8.3

241
Prevention and
intervention

DECLARATION OF GENERAL AND SPECIAL RIGHTS OF THE MENTALLY RETARDED

Whereas the universal declaration of human rights, adopted by the United Nations, proclaims that all of the human family, without distinction of any kind, have equal and inalienable rights of human dignity and freedom;

Whereas the declaration of the rights of the child, adopted by the United Nations, proclaims the rights of the physically, mentally or socially handicapped child to special treatment, education and care required by his particular condition.

Now Therefore

The International League of Societies for the Mentally Handicapped expresses the general and special rights of the mentally retarded as follows:

Article I

The mentally retarded person has the same basic rights as other citizens of the same country and same age.

Article II

The mentally retarded person has a right to proper medical care and physical restoration and to such education, training, habilitation and guidance as will enable him to develop his ability and potential to the fullest possible extent, no matter how severe his degree of disability. No mentally handicapped person should be deprived of such services by reason of the costs involved.

Article III

The mentally retarded person has a right to economic security and to a decent standard of living. He has a right to productive work or to other meaningful occupation.

Article IV

The mentally retarded person has a right to live with his own family or with foster-parents; to participate in all aspects of community life, and to be provided with appropriate leisure time activities. If care in an institution becomes necessary it should be in surroundings and under circumstances as close to normal living as possible.

Article V

The mentally retarded person has a right to a qualified guardian when this is required to protect his personal wellbeing and interest. No person rendering direct services to the mentally retarded should also serve as his guardian.

Article VI

The mentally retarded person has a right to protection from exploitation, abuse and degrading treatment. If accused, he has a right to a fair trial with full recognition being given to his degree of responsibility.

Article VII

Some mentally retarded persons may be unable, due to the severity of their handicap, to exercise for themselves all of their rights in a meaningful way. For others, modification of some or all of these rights is appropriate. The procedure used for modification or denial of rights must contain proper legal safeguards against every form of abuse, must be based on an evaluation of the social capability of the mentally retarded person by qualified experts and must be subject to periodic reviews and to the right of appeal to higher authorities.

ABOVE ALL—THE MENTALLY RETARDED PERSON HAS THE RIGHT TO RESPECT.

From the International League of Societies for the Mentally Handicapped (1969) everyone involved with retarded youngsters. The psychological assessment of retarded children—perhaps more accurately of children who are diagnosed as retarded on the basis of such assessment—can make major differences in the type and quality of education that the child receives, in the perception of the child by teachers and other relevant professionals, and even in the child's own self-concept. It has been shown, for example, that when children are identified as retarded, teacher expectations regarding their academic potentials frequently decrease (Guskin & Spicker, 1968). Educational and psychological assessors, therefore, must be sensitive to the possibility of sentencing a child to a cycle of inappropriate expectations and inadequate education.

In the matter of institutionalization, the AAMD (1973d) has attempted to define a retarded person's *right to live in the least restrictive appropriate environment* as well as the *right to privacy and to protection against exploitation, demeaning treatment, or abuse.* The AAMD has also sought to define the *right to fair compensation for labor* (1973a), which can easily be violated in an institutional setting.

A much more controversial area involves the use of extraordinary life-saving procedures for infants and children who are profoundly retarded and likely to require lifelong custodial care. The AAMD (1973c) has taken a firm position in this regard: "It is the position of the American Association on Mental Deficiency that the existence of mental retardation is no justification for the terminating of the life of any human being or for permitting such a life to be terminated either directly or through the withholding of life-sustaining procedures" (p. 66). The problem is a painful and complex human dilemma, and it is well that organizations for the retarded speak so forcefully and unambiguously in favor of protecting the rights of the retarded. Decisions to withhold life-sustaining procedures are typically made by persons other than the retarded persons who are affected, and it is important that a clear and direct definition of the rights of the retarded be available to parents and families and to courts who may be asked to intervene in conflicts between physicians and families.

The *protection* of the rights of the retarded child, of course, is a step beyond the issue of defining rights and refining social conceptions of the retarded child. The statement of rights by responsible organizations represents an important first step in eventual protection of rights by the courts. At the same time, the protection of the rights of the retarded child requires sensitive vigilance on the part of professionals, parents, and organizations serving the retarded. The lessons of history indicate only too well that public opinion regarding the retarded is fickle and subject to the mood of the times. The protection of human rights must be secured by law rather than by the court of public opinion.

SUMMARY

1. The definition of mental retardation currently includes the criteria of significantly subaverage intellectual functioning as well as deficits in adaptive behavior, learning, and social adjustment.

2. Recent trends in the social and psychological aspects of mental retardation have been to tighten the criteria by which children can be labeled as mentally retarded.

3. Tests of intelligence must be used cautiously in the diagnosis of retardation, and the child's total functioning must be taken into account in the process of diagnosis.

4. It is estimated that 3 percent of the general population of the United States will be classified as retarded at some point in their lifetimes.

5. The causes of mental retardation include both organic factors (such as infections, metabolic disorders, physical trauma, brain disease, unknown prenatal influences, chromosomal abnormalities, gestational disorders, and psychiatric disorders) as well as environmental factors (such as low socioeconomic status, lack of stimulation in the mother-child relationship, racial discrimination, low achievement motivation, lack of adequate education and social training, and family disharmony).

6. The great majority of children are identified as retarded during their school years in response to difficulties in meeting academic demands; these children are typically in the mildly retarded range.

7. Learning processes in retarded children do not differ substantially from normal peers; retarded children learn at a slower pace than normal children and frequently have difficulties in the retention of learned material and in maintaining attention to the learning process.

8. Personal and social factors that distinguish retarded children from normal peers tend to be learned rather than innate; these involve such issues as social deprivation, lack of social acceptance, and the expectation of failure.

9. The most dramatic breakthroughs in the area of intervention have focused on the prevention of retardation in children who are identified as being at risk, due either to organic causes or environmental causes.

10. Medical intervention in mental retardation is geared toward reducing or eliminating the organic condition that might produce the retardation.

11. Psychological, educational, and social intervention in mental retardation is geared toward stimulating intellectual, personal, and social skills.

12. Considerable advances have been made in recent years regarding the definition and protection of the rights of the retarded.

Children with Learning Disabilities

*Reeling and writhing, and the different branches of arithmetic—
ambition, distraction, uglification, and derision. Mysteries, ancient
and modern, with seaography. Drawling, stretching, and fainting in
coils. Laughing and Grief.*

Lewis Carroll, *Alice in Wonderland* (1865)

AN INTRODUCTION TO LEARNING DISABILITIES

Sensitive and dedicated teachers have long been aware that certain children
encounter extreme difficulties in the process of learning. The reasons why
seemingly normal children have severe problems in education have been quite
obscure for many years, and at times such youngsters have been identified
as "slow learners" or "stubborn students." Unfortunately, it was not unusual
for such children to be considered mentally retarded or even emotionally
disturbed. Until relatively recent times, educators and other professional colleagues lacked an adequate frame of reference or means of understanding that
some children experienced a kind of disability that was specific to the very
process of education. As the demands of mass education placed more and
more children squarely in the midst of rigorous and organized education,
however, it became increasingly clear that many children of otherwise average
intelligence and normal emotional make-up could not learn elementary
materials that other youngsters acquired with relative ease. Through several
decades of experience with such children, the concept of learning disability
has gradually evolved.

Still, the notion of learning disability remains a poorly understood and
highly controversial description and categorization of a child's problems with
education. Beneath this broad, descriptive designation lie a host of equally
controversial categories of exceptionality: minimal brain dysfunction or minimal brain damage, developmental hyperactivity or hyperkinetic impulse disorder, perceptual-motor handicaps, congenital word blindness or developmental dyslexia, and many more imposing and multisyllabic characterizations
of learning problems. Confronted with the proliferation of so many diagnostic
categorizations of learning difficulties, many educators have come to question
whether such conditions actually exist in real children. A "doubting Thomas"
may well wonder whether education has not taken a step backward from the
days when certain children were classified as "slow learners" or "stubborn
students." Despite the many complexities in understanding the concept of
learning disability, however, this relative latecomer to the categories of special
childhood is valid and necessary in assisting children who have an often
elusive form of disability. Whatever confusion exists within the field of learn-

ing disabilities, the basic problem in learning-disabled children is an incapacity to learn through normal and conventional channels. This incapacity can be specific or more general; whatever, it presents the learning-disabled child with a problem that can potentially threaten the entire fabric of his/her educational experience.

DEFINITION AND CLASSIFICATION

To begin to understand children who are described as learning disabled, we must first recognize that the general category of "learning disability" is not a unitary concept and does not represent a homogeneous group of children. Learning-disabled children can be quite different in terms of their learning problems; for example, one learning-disabled child might have an extremely high activity level that renders him/her almost uncontrollable in the classroom, while another child might be quite compliant but have a specific difficulty in learning how to read. It would be wise for the reader, therefore, to wonder at the outset whether learning disabilities can be understood as a single clinical entity or whether the concept is merely an umbrella that covers a multitude of very different kinds of children.

The Definition of Learning Disabilities

There can be no doubt that the term "learning disability" currently includes vastly different populations of children. Because of this fact, many educators and psychologists feel that the concept has little value as a general category of special childhood. It is argued that children should not be described as "learning disabled" but should be described solely in terms of their *specific* learning difficulties, such as "reading disability." Those who favor the concept of learning disabilities as a general category do not maintain that it is a single, defined syndrome but rather that "it is the learning disability that constitutes the basis of homogeneity of this group of handicapped children" (Johnson & Myklebust, 1967, p. 8). Learning-disabled youngsters may differ in many critical educational and psychological characteristics, but in some way they share a common problem involving their inability to learn according to normal channels.

Whatever the specific nature of a particular child's learning difficulty, the notion of a general category has had the effect of distinguishing the child's difficulty from other categories of exceptionality—such as mental retardation, blindness, deafness, physical health impairments, and emotional and behavioral problems. In point of fact, current definitions of learning disability tend to exclude other identifiable conditions of special childhood from the very category of learning disabled. Given the considerable controversy regarding the kinds of problems that should be excluded from and included in the category of learning disability, a review of the many facets of this issue would take us far beyond the scope of this discussion.

Recent congressional action attempted to clarify the definition of learning disability for the purpose of funding school programs:

*The term "children with specific learning disabilities" means those chil-
dren who have a disorder in one or more of the basic psychological
processes involved in understanding or using language, spoken or written, which disorder may manifest itself in imperfect ability to listen,
think, speak, read, write, spell or do mathematical calculations. Such disorders include such conditions as perceptual handicaps, brain injury,
minimal brain dysfunction, dyslexia and developmental aphasia. This
term does not include children who have learning problems which are
primarily the result of visual, hearing or motor handicaps, or mental
retardation, or emotional disturbance, or of environmental disadvantage.
(From Public Law 91-230, Section 602-15, April 13, 1970)*

This definition makes two important points that are central to the definition
of learning disabilities: *(a) learning disabilities involve a difficulty in one or
more of the modalities of learning* and *(b) learning disabilities do not include
learning problems that are caused primarily by other special conditions.*

Types of Learning Disabilities

Attempts to classify children as learning disabled suffer from the theoretical
confusion and interprofessional disputes that mark the field of learning disability. In clinical practice, professionals tend to follow the dominant practice
and thinking of their respective professions. Physicians conduct physical and
neurologic examinations and tend to state their findings in organic terms, such
as minimal brain dysfunction. Psychologists conduct tests of intellectual functioning (verbal abilities and perceptual-motor abilities) and tend to state their
findings in psychological terms, such as perceptual-motor deficit. Educators
tend to assess achievement level and learning modalities and therefore tend
to state their findings in terms of specific disabilities, such as reading disability.

In short, the field of learning disabilities is not yet sufficiently integrated
at the professional level to have achieved a comprehensive system of classification that adequately represents the major orientations of respective professionals who work with learning-disabled youngsters. While recognizing the
need for an integrated system of classification, our review will reflect the
current practices of relevant professional disciplines. As such, we will discuss
the classification of (a) minimal brain dysfunction, (b) perceptual-motor disabilities, and (c) psycholinguistic or language disabilities.

Minimal brain dysfunction (MBD)

The term **minimal brain dysfunction** (MBD) is a widely used diagnostic classification for children who present a wide array of possible signs, symptoms,
and behaviors. The concept of MBD has a complicated history involving clinical and research interest in the behavioral consequences of damage to the
brain and central nervous system. Adolph Meyer (1904), a leading psychiatrist
and neurologist of the early twentieth century, reported that individuals who
suffered cranial lesions experienced long-term behavioral effects such as poor
concentration, irritability, slowness of thought, forgetfulness, impulsive behavior, and easily induced fatigue. Though Meyer made no specific connection
to learning disability per se, it is clear that such behaviors would impair learn-

ing; as such, Meyer's early work set the stage for the consideration of brain damage as a possible causal factor in learning disabilities.

Kurt Goldstein (1942) published a significant study of the aftereffects of brain injuries sustained by German soldiers during World War I. Goldstein noted that brain-damaged soldiers demonstrated continuing inability to deal with abstract concepts or to differentiate between a figure and its background, as well as an incapacity to maintain attention or to control emotions. Goldstein's work had the effect of solidifying the presumed relationships between such behaviors and actual damage to the brain.

Though Meyer and Goldstein inferred relationships between such behaviors as perceptual problems, distractability, forgetfulness, and inability to control emotions, on the one hand, and damage to the brain, on the other, their subjects were, in both cases, *adult* patients who had sustained *identifiable* damage to the brain. It still remained to be seen if a similar relationship occurred in children.

This was accomplished through the work of Alfred A. Strauss and his colleagues (Strauss & Kephart, 1955; Strauss & Lehtinen, 1947; Werner & Strauss, 1941) at the Cove Schools in Racine, Wisconsin, and Evanston, Illinois. Specifically, Strauss attempted to distinguish the behavior of those children whose retardation was presumably due to an external cause (namely, brain injury) from those children whose retardation was due to cultural-familial causes. It should be pointed out, however, that in most of Strauss' cases there was no independent evidence of brain damage. Despite these difficulties in identifying children who actually suffered identifiable brain damage, Strauss concluded that it was possible to identify in children certain behaviors as a presumed function of brain damage; these behaviors included difficulties in perception, very high activity levels, distractibility and poor attention span, impulsive behavior, and emotional instability. This description of a constellation of behaviors soon came to be known as the *Strauss syndrome*, or *brain-injured syndrome*. The definition of the brain-injured child as described by Strauss and Lehtinen (1947) is worth repeating here:

> a . . . *child who before, during, or after birth has received an injury to or suffered an infection of the brain. As a result of such organic impairment, defects in the neuromotor system may be present or absent; however, such a child may show disturbances in perception, thinking, and emotional behavior, either separately or in combination. These disturbances prevent or impede a normal learning process. (p. 4)*

Strauss' work marked the first clear statement that unidentified but presumed injuries to the brain in children can produce a variety of problems that interfere with processes of normal learning. Strauss did not use the terms "learning disability" or "minimal brain dysfunction," but his theory of subtle brain damage had laid the basis for a way of understanding a complex of varying behaviors that interfered with normal learning. Since these children described by Strauss did not present clear evidence of identifiable brain damage, it became popular to describe the supposed syndrome as "minimal" brain damage or "minimal" brain dysfunction. This terminology has gained wide acceptance among physicians who favor the assumption of an organic cause to explain disordered behavior. It should be noted that *many physicians view minimal brain dysfunction as an equivalent term for learning disabilities rather than as a particular type of learning disability.*

Throughout the 1950s, the notion of minimal brain dysfunction was used increasingly to explain many different types of behavior. In an important paper, Clements and Peters (1962) listed ten major characteristics of children who were diagnosed as having minimal brain dysfunction:

Hyperactivity
Specific learning deficits in the presence of normal intelligence
Perceptual-motor deficits
Impulsivity
Emotional instability
Short attention span
Coordination deficits
Distractibility
Unclear neurological signs
Frequently abnormal EEG's

Although the data is not sufficient to lend itself to firm conclusions, research has not supported the notion of MBD as a unitary syndrome with the characteristics listed by Clements and Roberts. Routh and Roberts (1972) examined 89 children between the ages of 6 and 13 who had been referred to a university clinic because of poor school performance. These youngsters were given a battery of psychological and neurological tests designed to assess the most frequently noted symptoms of MBD. Analysis of the data failed to find sufficiently significant relationships among the purported symptoms of MBD to justify the notion that these symptoms actually appear together often enough to constitute a unitary syndrome. The authors concluded that their data were "somewhat damaging to the idea of such a syndrome" (p. 313). Crinella (1973) also administered an extensive battery of neuropsychological tests to 90 children, 19 of whom had known brain damage, 34 of whom had been independently diagnosed as having MBD, and 37 of whom were a control group of children functioning at an above-average level. Crinella found no evidence for a specific and unitary MBD syndrome. Some of the data indicated, for example, that the MBD children were quite unlike the children with known brain damage, thus casting doubts on the notion of minimal brain damage as an adequate construct to explain the variety of behaviors supposedly displayed by these children. Further research is clearly needed in this area, but in the meantime MBD continues to enjoy considerable popularity as a means of describing many children who have learning and behavioral difficulties in the classroom.

Perceptual-motor disabilities

Perception is a process by which an organism is aware of the objects, qualities, or events stimulating the sense organs. The term **perceptual-motor** typically refers to the process of visual perception and the coordination of visual perception with motor behavior. Difficulties in learning can occur if a child experiences disturbances in either perceptual modalities (such as the inaccurate perception of forms, including numerals and the alphabet) or in motor modalities that depend on visual perception (such as difficulty in correctly copying a figure). Perceptual-motor processes are clearly central in conventional classroom learning, and theory and research in the field of learning disabilities has emphasized their importance as key factors in a child's education. Difficulties in this area constitute one of the major identified forms of learning disability.

Children who are atypical in perceptual-motor functioning often cannot be identified except by formal psychological and/or educational testing. The diagnosis of perceptual-motor deficit is usually based on standardized testing situations in which the child is required to respond to a particular type of stimulus. For example, when an examiner asks a youngster to copy a stimulus figure of certain proportions, many children with perceptual-motor disabilities give immediate evidence of their problems. Some children not only demonstrate marked inability to produce accurately the stimulus drawing (see Exhibit 9.1) but also engage in unusual behaviors, such as strange posturing

EXHIBIT 9.1

**EXAMPLE OF DIFFERENCES IN FIGURE-COPYING BETWEEN
A NORMAL CHILD AND A PERCEPTUALLY HANDICAPPED CHILD**

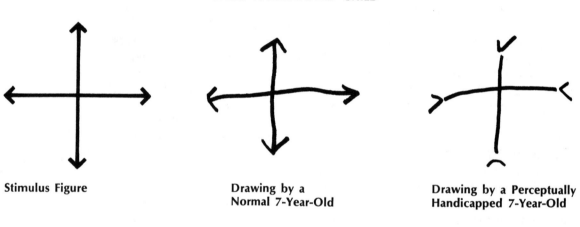

Stimulus Figure   **Drawing by a
Normal 7-Year-Old**   **Drawing by a Perceptually
Handicapped 7-Year-Old**

or guiding the writing hand with the other hand. Clinical and educational experiences of this sort have been instrumental in bringing attention to the problem of perceptual-motor disabilities, and many investigators have studied such disabilities from a variety of viewpoints.

Kephart (1960) was one of the first investigators to conceptualize learning disabilities in terms of perceptual-motor deficits and to recommend a program of intervention based upon the remediation of such deficits. Kephart maintained that the child's first normal learning experiences involve the acquisition of motor skills (e.g., crawling, standing, walking). These early motor activities are presumed to create patterns of movement or motor generalizations which, in turn, form the basis of the child's developing perceptual structures. Perceptual-motor disabilities, therefore, are understood to be a function of some form of maldevelopment. Thus, according to Kephart, a perceptual-motor disability represents the lack of an appropriate fit between motor experience and perceptual experience. Kephart further assumed the presence of a cause-and-effect relationship between perceptual disabilities and lack of achievement in specific academic areas (see Exhibit 9.2). Briefly stated, Kephart noted that basic perceptual-motor skills such as drawing and copying figures are the prerequisites of more advanced skills such as writing and reading; he further assumed that children who have difficulty in reading and writing may well benefit from specialized assistance that seeks to correct the more basic perceptual-motor problem.

Barsch (1965) took a slightly different approach and emphasized deficits in movement efficiency as the basis of learning disabilities. He gave the name *movigenics* to the study of patterns of movement that produce learning efficiency. Seeing children as moving beings in a spatial existence, Barsch assumed the need for visual, auditory, tactual, and kinesthetic experiences as the basis for efficient learning, and his "movigenic curriculum" is designed to maximize such experiences in education.

Getman (1965), an optometrist, developed an approach that relies heavily on vision as an explanatory variable in learning difficulty, maintaining that "vision is a derivative of numerous sensorimotor systems within the total operational organism" (p. 51). Getman established an extremely elaborate model to explain the development of what he termed the "visuomotor complex" in the individual child. This model includes the postulation of a step-by-step acquisition in development of innate response systems, general motor systems, special motor systems, ocular motor systems, speech motor systems, and visualization systems as the building blocks of perception. Essentially, Getman maintained that the visuomotor complex (or perceptual-motor behavior) is itself learned and that these abilities form the basis of future learning.

In 1964, Frostig began with the clinical observation that many children who had difficulties in learning demonstrated disabilities in visual perception on various psychometric instruments. In developing her own tests—known as the Marianne Frostig Developmental Tests of Visual Perception (Frostig, Lefever, & Whittlesey, 1964)—Frostig attempted to differentiate the various types of visual perceptual abilities involved in common learning experiences. This differentiation of the various abilities involved in visual perceptual behavior forms the basis of Frostig's diagnostic and treatment approaches to the learning-disabled child.

In summary, it should be noted that perceptual-motor disabilities are considered by many investigators to be the major type of learning disability. Kephart, Barsch, Getman, and Frostig—though influenced by the earlier work of Strauss—have moved Strauss' formulations away from brain damage and more directly into the direct analysis of perceptual-motor behavior. For the past few decades, perceptual-motor approaches have been a powerful influence in understanding and explaining a wide variety of academic difficulties among the learning disabled. In effect, children with perceptual-motor disabilities have captured most of the attention of workers in the field of learning difficulties.

EXHIBIT 9.2

KEPHART'S ANECDOTE ON READING AND PERCEPTUAL-MOTOR DEFICITS

A mother and her ten-year-old son were required to travel 120 miles to meet a clinic appointment. As they were driving down the interstate highway at 70 miles an hour, the youngster suddenly said, "All the cows in that field have a collar like my dog." At 70 miles an hour the mother had only been able to see a herd of cows and was not able to identify any one animal, let alone a specific aspect of any animal. She, therefore, predictably and understandably, delivered to the youngster a discussion on the advisability of differentiating between truth and fancy and not permitting one's imagination to run wild.

Arriving at the clinic, the mother recounted the story of the cows. The clinician suggested that it would be interesting to note what there was about these cows that prompted this response from the child. Therefore, on the return trip, the mother stopped the car at the proper point and carefully inspected the herd of cows. Then she saw that this was a registered herd and each cow wore a leather collar with its pedigree number stamped on it.

Had an incident similar to this one occurred in a school situation, the tendency might have been to commend the youngster for his powers of observation. The excellent visual differentiation would have been noted and the extraordinarily high level of visual performance would have been commented on. Seldom would it have been suspected that the real reason why the child saw the collar was because he was unable to see the cows. To see a cow requires the organization of perceptual elements—horns, legs, tails, etc.—into an integrated whole which represents an animal and in which no part can exist independent of the others. This very dominance of the whole which is characteristic of form perception, however, obscures the details. The normal individual tends to see wholes rather than details because these details are integrated into and subserved by an organized whole. The organization is what is important to us and we overlook the detail in our concern for the whole. Such integration of perceptual elements into a whole was not possible for this child and thus the apparent superiority of visual performance was, in fact, an evidence of a visual-perceptual handicap.

It has proved impossible to teach this child to read. Flash cards, phonics, remedial reading techniques, all have been to no avail. When his response to the cows is seen in the light of an inability to form perceptual wholes and as a weakness in form perception, his difficulties in reading are understandable.

None of us could read if we had to deal only with the details of the print. We read by organized wholes which subsume the details and hence we pay little attention to the nature of the details. The difficulty of proofreading meaningful material illustrates the extent to which we overlook details in the interest of forming meaningful wholes. The youngster described, however, has only details; he has very few wholes with which to deal. It is not surprising, therefore, that reading proved impossible for him. It also becomes logical to suppose that, if his perceptual problem could be relieved, reading might become less difficult.

From Kephart (1968, pp. 9–11)

Psycholinguistic, or language, disabilities

Another major type of learning disability involves the area of language and the cognitive processes upon which language is based. Disabilities in this area are frequently described as **psycholinguistic disabilities** or, more simply,

language disabilities. The importance of language disabilities within the general field of learning disabilities has been underemphasized primarily because the field has been dominated by concerns in the perceptual-motor areas of learning. It goes without saying, of course, that many kinds of learning are dependent upon the child's ability to use language and to manipulate verbal symbols. In many respects, sensitivity to problems of language disabilities were not evident until the more sophisticated development of the science of *linguistics,* which is the study of the function and nature of human language.

The three major types of language disabilities are (a) inner language disorders, (b) receptive language disorders, and (c) expressive language disorders. **Inner language disorders** involve the preverbal ability to internalize and organize experiences. For example, a child may have difficulty organizing concrete experiences with a general concept, such as the sound of rustling leaves with the general concept of "wind." **Receptive language disorders** involve difficulties in the process of understanding verbal symbols. For example, a child may understand the meaning of a word used in one context but not in another; in such a case, the word "running" may make sense when applied to a track athlete but not to water "running" from a spigot. **Expressive language disorders** involve difficulties in producing spoken language; children with expressive language disorders tend to avoid the use of words in communicating and may rely extensively on pointing and gesturing or overusage of certain words that have become comfortable. The study of language disabilities is currently gaining in interest among linguists, speech therapists, special educators, psychologists, and language pathologists.

Theoretical Issues in the Definition and Classification of Learning Disabilities

As we have indicated, the study of learning disabilities is still in its beginnings, and major issues remain perplexing. Perhaps the central problem in this field is how best to understand what a learning disability is, and there is active disagreement among the experts in this most basic of issues. Educators and many psychologists tend to view learning disabilities in the two major categories of perceptual-motor disabilities and language disabilities. Physicians frequently favor the diagnosis of minimal brain dysfunction as a catchall classification for all forms of learning difficulty. We have discussed these three major types of learning disability, but as the field develops and has more extended opportunity to examine itself, a much more sophisticated system of classification is likely to emerge.

One of the most important functions of the science of learning disabilities is to understand why certain children have severe difficulties in acquiring basic academic skills in reading, writing, spelling, arithmetic, and so forth. The tendency has been to seek explanations at a level of causation removed from the actual skill itself. Thus, the dominant positions in the definition and classification of learning disabilities have taken the view that children have difficulty in reading, 'riting, and 'rithmetic because of minimal brain dysfunction, perceptual-motor deficits, or hidden language problems. Each of these views seeks explanations in undetermined aspects of central nervous system functioning,

OPEN ISSUE

A 10-year-old girl in the fourth grade is having learning problems in school. On an academic achievement test, she is found to be 3 years behind grade level in reading ability. On the basis of formal testing, she is identified as having a learning disability in the area of reading skills. The technical term for reading disability is dyslexia, *or developmental dyslexia, and the reading-disabled child is said to be* dyslexic.

But what is the nature of this learning disability known as "dyslexia"? Is it a manifestation of subtle neurological damage, or is it merely a problem in acquiring relevant educational skills? There are two vastly different approaches to the understanding of dyslexia, and the term is therefore used in two very different senses.

The classical understanding of dyslexia has its origin in the 1860s, when a number of patients were described by British physicians as being unable to comprehend printed and written words following an injury to the brain. In 1877 Kussmaul used the term *caecitas verbalis,* or word blindness, to describe the condition of inability to read the written word despite the intactness of vision. The term dyslexia gradually came into use to describe such conditions, and developmental dyslexia came to be a diagnostic description for children who had difficulty acquiring reading skills. In this classical view, the term dyslexia is restricted to children of adequate intelligence and cultural background who are sufficiently motivated to read but cannot. The inability to read is presumed to be a function of cerebral immaturity or maldevelopment of the central nervous system, and a child is considered dyslexic only when the presumption of such neurological dysfunction seems warranted.

There is another, very different, view of dyslexia. This more recently derived position does not make any presumptions regarding the presence of neurological dysfunction as the cause of the reading disorder. In this broader view of dyslexia, any child who is significantly underachieving in the acquisition of reading skills can be described as dyslexic. The cause of the reading disorder can be quite varied, including such factors as low intelligence, cultural disadvantage, lack of motivation, lack of stimulating home environment, emotional problems, and dislike for schooling, as well as presumed neurological dysfunction.

The differences in conceptualizing the nature of dyslexia cause confusion in the field and, at times, unnecessary concern to parents. When parents are informed that their child is dyslexic, they may well presume that he/she has some form of disease or "thing" that causes the reading deficit when, in fact, the child may simply dislike school and refuse to work. Similar problems take place when other technical names are applied to academic deficits: dysgraphia (writing deficit), dysorthographia (spelling deficit), dyscalculia (arithmetic deficit), or dysphasia (language deficit). At present, however, we are in a state of flux: there is no consensus as to what really constitutes a reading disability, spelling disability, writing disability, arithmetic disability, language disability, or any other type of learning disability.

and they are currently under a severe challenge, primarily from behaviorally oriented psychologists (see Hallahan & Kauffman, 1976).

From a strict behavioral viewpoint, problems in learning are best understood in terms of their observable behaviors and the observable relationships that exist between the behavior and significant events in the environment. Explanations beyond the scope of the behavior and the environment that controls the behavior are not actively sought. As such, minimal brain dysfunction and perceptual-motor problems are less relevant explanations of learning problems than are the specific behaviors involved in a specific academic difficulty. Behaviorists in the field of learning disabilities favor the notion of *specific academic deficits* as the most meaningful focus in the science of learning disabilities. The behaviorists would limit the focus, therefore, to the actual areas of academic difficulty, such as reading disability, writing disability, spelling disability, and arithmetic disability. In the same way, minimal brain dysfunction might be seen as a problem in hyperactive behavior or poor concentration behavior. From a behavioral standpoint, it makes no difference whether a child with a reading disability is mentally retarded, emotionally disturbed, or disabled in terms of perceptual-motor behavior. The important issue is the reading disability itself.

INCIDENCE AND ETIOLOGY

Because of the disagreements regarding the nature and definition of learning disabilities, it is virtually impossible to gain accurate estimates of prevalence. The Bureau of Education for the Handicapped estimates that there are 1,375,000 learning-disabled children in the United States (Craig, 1976). Other estimates place the incidence as high as 7,500,000 children under the age of 18 (Brutten, Richardson, & Mangel, 1973). Differences in the definition of learning disability clearly produce wide variations in estimates of prevalence.

Some investigators maintain that learning disabilities are the most pervasive medical problem in the United States, affecting 5 to 20 percent of the nonretarded population (Tarnopol, 1971). Hyperactivity, for example, is regularly reported as the most common referral reason in the practice of child psychiatry (Chess, 1960; Wender, 1973); it is estimated that 7 percent of all school-age children are hyperactive (Renshaw, 1974) and that some 200,000 children in the United States are receiving drug treatment (amphetamines) to control hyperactivity (Krippner, Silverman, Cavallo, & Healy, 1973). These are staggering figures for any form of childhood disorder, and the various forms of learning disability clearly pose problems of considerable magnitude.

Causation in the field of learning disabilities is poorly understood but actively debated. As early as 1937, Samuel Orton, one of the first recognized authorities on reading disability, took the position that mixed dominance (namely, right-eyed and left-handed preference or left-eyed and right-handed preference) was inherited and caused reading disability (Orton, 1937). More recently, Ross (1976) suggested that the cause of reading disability is difficulty in selective attention. Causation for a specific disability such as reading problems, therefore, may run the gamut from hereditary traits to poor training. In fact, the state of the science of learning disability is such that we really don't know what causes learning disability in either its specific or more generalized forms.

Hirsch (1970) suggested eight major categories of possible causes for learning disabilities:

Minimal brain damage
Mixed dominance or mixed laterality

Traditional visual anomalies
Developmental abnormalities
Intellectual deprivation
Psychological disorders
Genetic causation
Teaching methodology

None of these categories has been clearly substantiated as a major cause of learning disabilities, and our knowledge at this point is not sufficient to risk a hypothesis as to which of these possible causes may be more significant than others. As such, these categories of causation are best understood as suggested directions for research rather than generally accepted facts.

DIAGNOSIS AND IDENTIFICATION

The diagnosis and identification of learning-disabled children is currently a complex and, all too frequently, uncoordinated process. Since learning disability is primarily an educational problem, the most relevant specialists in the diagnosis should be the clinical educator or school psychologist. In practice, however, many professionals become involved in the diagnosis and identification of learning-disabled children, and these include the pediatrician (where there is the possibility of minimal brain dysfunction), the optometrist (where there is the possibility of perceptual-motor disorders), the psychiatrist (where there is concern about emotional problems), and the clinical psychologist (where there are behavioral difficulties or questions about intellectual adequacy). Each of these professionals might have a very different view regarding the nature of learning disability, and for these reasons the diagnosis and identification of learning-disabled children is often more complicated than seems necessary.

The Problem of Late Identification

Despite the prevalence and significance of learning disorders, the identification of the learning-disabled child in the school system remains very much a trial-and-error phenomenon. The assessment of a potential or actual learning disorder in a particular child requires extensive individual testing and examination, and the current state of the art would make mass screening procedures prohibitively expensive. Thus, in most instances, children are identified as learning disabled only when they have been exposed to a sufficient degree of school contact, and teachers and school personnel have become aware of problems in the child's behavior or response to teaching. It is not unusual for a child to be in formal schooling for several years before it becomes apparent that there is need for a formal evaluation of either learning or conduct problems. This is especially true when the learning disorder is specific to a particular area; for example, a child may not be identified as having a reading disability until the youngster has been in school for several years and has shown little progress in reading. Thus the very discovery of a reading disability usually means that a student is already several years behind grade-level in reading—a situation that necessarily involves a series of unsuccessful experiences before identification of the problem can conventionally be made. In other words, the more specific forms of learning disability require a "period of gestation" in which normal accomplishment fails to take place. At the same time, such disabilities require formal and often sophisticated means of assessment as a condition of effective identification. Case Study 9.1 gives an example of this "backdoor method" by which learning disabilities are frequently identified; this case study also illustrates the common clinical experience of identifying learning disabilities in children who are referred because of more general concerns with schooling and conduct.

CASE STUDY 9.1

WILLIAM: IDENTIFICATION OF A CHILD WITH A PERCEPTUAL-MOTOR LEARNING DISABILITY

William was an 11-year-old boy in the sixth grade of a suburban school. His family had moved recently to the school district; he had spent his first five years at a school in the metropolitan system, where he was reportedly a good student with few problems. Teacher reports from his fifth-grade teacher revealed some concern about his abilities in spelling and arithmetic. Since entering the sixth grade in the suburban system, he had been identified as a mild behavior problem, talking to other children while the teacher was speaking, rebelling against the teacher's discipline, and regularly refusing to turn in both classroom and homework assignments. Neither the teacher nor the parents understood this apparent change in William's behavior, and his parents were concerned that William was "paying us back for moving to the suburbs."

Psychological Evaluation
William was of tall and slender build, with a mildly ungainly appearance. He appeared to be an alert and intelligent young man who was quite capable of taking care of himself. He was well aware of the purpose of the evaluation, and although mildly suspicious of the examiner in the first interview, he subsequently revealed an inclination to speak honestly and candidly about his school difficulties. Although he felt that he had sometimes been unfairly treated and mis-

understood by his previous teacher, he harbored little resentment toward school and showed good capacity for viewing his difficulties in school in an objective fashion. William was quite skilled verbally, he related well to the examiner, and rapport was soon established.

William was given a number of tests, including the WISC, the Developmental Test of Visual-Motor Integration (Beery-Buktenica), the Wide Range Achievement Test, the Bender-Gestalt, the Rorschach, the Thematic Apperception Test (TAT, 8 cards), and the Sentence Completion Test. On all tests, William was diligent and hardworking; he was motivated toward achievement and was easily ego-involved by the challenge of a testing situation. There were dramatic differences, however, in his capacity to perform verbal tests as opposed to nonverbal tests. On verbal tests, William appeared immensely challenged and involved, and his problem-solving postures were quite appropriate; on nonverbal tests, he was easily confused and became aimless and anxious. This evidence of differential functioning was substantiated by the results of all testings.

On the WISC, William achieved a Verbal Scale IQ of 120, a Performance Scale IQ of 90, and a Full Scale IQ of 107. Verbal skills were in the superior range, whereas nonverbal skills were at the lower end of the average range. The disparity between verbal and nonverbal skills was consistent and quite debilitating. William's visual memory and visual perceptual-motor abilities were much less advanced than auditory/verbal channels were, representing a learning disability of some magnitude.

On the Beery, William achieved a visual-perceptual-motor integration age equivalent of 9 years 4 months, some 2 years behind his chronological age level. The Bender-Gestalt, which requires an even greater degree of perceptual-motor organization than the Beery, likewise revealed serious deficits in perceptual-motor abilities.

William's learning disability manifested itself on the Wide Range Achievement Test as follows: reading—grade norm of 6.3; spelling—grade norm of 4.2; arithmetic—grade norm of 4.2. Spelling and arithmetic are learning areas that depend heavily on intact visual memory and visual organization, and they were therefore the areas most affected by William's disability.

Projective personality tests indicated that William was a well-integrated youngster who did not display any significant degree of emotional disturbance. There was no evidence of any emotional overlay that could be attributed to previously undetected learning disability. It would seem that his previous schooling experiences had been very supportive and that his teachers had instinctively responded quite appropriately to his learning problems. With the transfer to a new school, William's learning problems had become more apparent to him as he found himself considerably behind his peers in certain areas. The mild behavioral and discipline problems reported in his new school very likely represented William's response to the anxiety associated with his increasing awareness of his inability to manage certain areas of learning. It could be expected that the identification of his learning problems and appropriate assistance would forestall the development of further behavior or discipline difficulties.

Recommendations

The examiner felt that William was in need of special remedial help in both spelling and arithmetic. Since William was well-integrated in his current classroom, and since he had excellent verbal/auditory skills, it was considered best both for his educational growth and for his interpersonal growth that he remain in his regular classroom. As such, it was recommended that William be placed in a supplementary itinerant program that could provide special tutorial assistance in spelling and arithmetic.

In some situations, it is possible to identify a learning disability on the basis of sensitive observation by a skilled teacher or on the basis of scores obtained on mass-administered achievement tests. Discrepancies in the child's learning modalities or actual levels of achievement in different areas may be an important clue to an underlying learning disorder. At other times, gross behavioral difficulties or conduct problems may mask a learning disorder that has been unsuspected by teachers or other school personnel. The clear identification of a learning disability, however, typically requires a referral by teacher or parent to a school or clinical psychologist, a neurologist, a clinical educator who specializes in assessment, or a speech pathologist. Such referrals can be made to professional personnel who are connected with the school system or to professionals in private practice or in various types of child clinics. Since pure cases of specific learning disabilities are much rarer than cases of mixed disabilities, or attendant conduct problems or emotional problems, in most situations a multidisciplinary evaluation is necessary in order to assess competently and correctly the nature of a child's disorder. This form of assessment requires specific types of tests sensitive to the presence of learning disabilities.

Formal Assessment of Learning Disabilities

It has already been noted that many children with learning disabilities may not be identified until they have already established a history of school failure or academic deficiency. There is obviously a significant advantage in early identification of potential learning disorders in that a child can be spared much of the frustration that can be involved in false expectations regarding learning

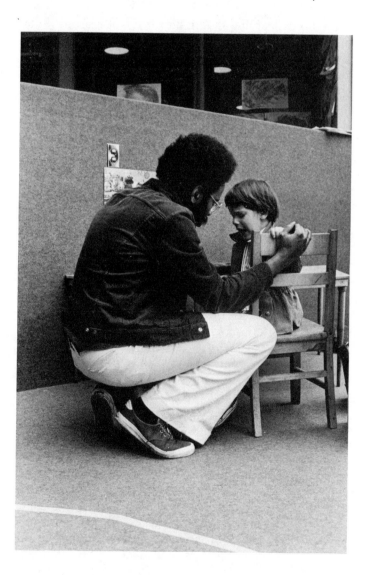

Continuing conduct problems may mask a learning disorder that is the reason for the child's frustration. In such cases, it is wise to refer the child to a specialist who can diagnose such a possibility.

potential. The early identification of a potential learning disorder enables school personnel to plan educational experiences that maximize the child's strengths and that also provide an atmosphere of understanding for deficits which become apparent in the child's developing educational repertoire. The establishment of screening devices for the identification of learning difficulties can thus provide the opportunity for needed services during the critical formative years of a child's education. At the same time, formal evaluations of suspected learning disorders through psychometric assessment can be effective in clarifying the nature of a presumed difficulty and distinguishing a learning disorder from other childhood disabilities such as mental retardation, emotional disturbance, and so forth. Our discussion will focus on screening devices and psychometric testing.

Screening devices

Because of the complex nature of learning disabilities, it is not reasonable to anticipate the development of a screening instrument that might be effective in identifying all potential disabilities. A meaningful screening instrument requires both ease of administration and economy of time and expense. A "crystal ball" of this kind for the field of learning disorders is like chasing a rainbow. Nonetheless, important strides have been taken in developing screening instruments for specific purposes.

Slingerland (1969) has contributed a prereading screening procedure that can be used with first-graders to assess potential reading disorders. Tests like Slingerland's are oriented toward the assessment of a child's readiness for academic learning in specific areas of school achievement, and they are generally considered to be excellent screening instruments for the early identification of academic deficiencies. Similar screening batteries have been developed by Jansky and De Hirsch (1972) and Satz and Friel (1974). These batteries have excellent predictive validity in discriminating, at the kindergarten level, both potentially good readers and potentially poor readers. In the Satz and Friel screening instrument, the kindergarten test battery consists of such items as finger recognition, letter naming, visual form discrimination, and visuomotor skill. A follow-up study conducted, at the conclusion of the second grade, on 474 boys from the original kindergarten sample correctly identified 82 percent of the disabled readers and 88 percent of the good readers (Satz, Friel, & Rudegair, 1974). Benton (1976), however, noted that such formal screening batteries have not been demonstrated to be any more effective than evaluations based on intelligence tests or the intuitive assessments of kindergarten teachers.

One of the most widely used screening devices is Frostig's Developmental Tests of Visual Perception (1964). Standardized on 2100 children between the ages of 2½ to 9 years, the Tests are designed to screen potential difficulties specific to the area of visual perception, such as abilities in eye-hand coordination, figure-ground relationships, shape constancy, space position, and spatial relationships. For example, on the Position in Space subtest, the child is shown an object in a particular position and is then asked to choose the similarly positioned object from a number of different choices displaying the object in a variety of positions. Since the test is well-standardized, it offers excellent norms to compare a given child's performance. The test is considered to be an excellent screening device for visual-perceptual problems, but many educators consider it of little help in identifying problems in reading, writing, spelling, and arithmetic.

Pediatricians and child neurologists have also become interested in developing screening procedures for generalized learning disabilities. A promising screening instrument in the identification of early school failures is the Meeting Street School Screening-Test, which is being developed at the Meeting Street School Children's Rehabilitation Center (Denhoff & Tarnopol, 1971). This test is a brief neurological examination used with the 6- to 7½-year-old child. It consists of a series of items, including balance (standing straight for 15 consecutive seconds), fine motor coordination (touching the tip of the little finger to the nose with eyes closed two times), and motor speech (opening and closing the mouth smoothly five times). Denhoff and Tarnopol maintain that the immature performance of these skills beyond the age of 7 is an excellent indication of potential academic difficulty. In a standardization study with this screening examination, "it was possible to predict with 89 percent accuracy that 19 percent of 355 normal first-grade children would fail either the first or second grade" (Denhoff & Tarnopol, 1971, p. 75). Although this approach may not screen specific problems, it shows promise as a general screening device.

Psychometric testing

From the standpoint of formal psychometric testing, a learning disability can be operationally defined as a significant discrepancy between a child's actual level of achievement and the achievement expected of that child at his/her chronological age. Psychometric testing, therefore, offers a quantitative approach to the assessment of the child's current level of functioning in the various areas of learning. In the most obvious sense, the learning-disabled child is presumed to be of normal intelligence, so it is not the lack of intelligence that interferes with the capacity to learn; thus, one of the first steps in the assessment of a possible learning disability must include formal testing of the child's intellectual level. Another assumption regarding the definition of learning disability is that the child is not acquiring academic skills at grade expectancy or at the normal rate; thus, a second important component of psychometric testing includes the formal assessment of the child's academic achievement. A third assumption in the definition of learning disability is the notion that specific modalities of learning are affected by the presumed disability; thus, the third central component of psychometric testing includes methods of assessing specific modalities of learning. As such, psychometric testing of the child who is *at risk* for learning disability must include: (a) assessment of intellectual potential, (b) assessment of achievement level, and (c) assessment of various modalities of learning.

Intelligence testing. The major purpose in the intellectual assessment of the child with suspected learning disability is to rule out the possibility of mental retardation and to establish the fact of normal intellectual ability. In addition to this basic purpose, an individually administered intelligence test, such as the Wechsler Intelligence Scale for Children–Revised (WISC–R), can be helpful in specifying the nature of a child's learning disorder. The major types of intellectual ability tested by the WISC–R include verbal abilities and nonverbal or performance abilities. Wide discrepancies in the scores of a subject on these differing scales can provide valuable information about the nature of possible learning disorders. In addition, discrepancies among the various subtests of the Verbal and Performance Scales can give clues that specific modalities of learning are affected by the presumed disability. For example, a child who scores in the average or above-average range on all subtests except Block Design (a test of visual-motor coordination) and Coding (a test of eye-hand motor coordination) may well be giving evidence of a perceptual-motor disability. Used in this way, intelligence tests can not only indicate a child's level of intellectual ability but also point toward areas of cognitive functioning that may be involved in the learning disability itself.

Achievement testing. It has now become conventional practice in education to conduct routine tests of achievement at various points in a child's education. There are a number of well-standardized and easily administered tests for this purpose. An excellent example of an achievement test of specific areas of academic progress is the Wide Range Achievement Test (Jastak & Jastak, 1965). The WRAT, as it is affectionately known, tests in the areas of reading (word

Though this child's learning disability seems obvious, thorough psychometric testing is a key to developing the best educational program to fit his needs.

recognition), spelling, and arithmetic; the number of items correctly answered on each of these subtests is then translated into grade equivalents that provide the actual measures of achievement. The merit of achievement testing is, of course, that by comparing a given youngster to national norms of expected achievement, the possibility of subjective bias is eliminated. Small discrepancies between actual grade level and achieved grade equivalents may not be meaningful, but a youngster who achieves several years behind grade level raises relevant concerns regarding his/her educational progress.

Assessment of learning modalities. Another approach to the assessment of learning disabilities is to isolate and measure the underlying abilities or discrete psychological functions that are basic to the process of learning. A test of this type requires a theoretical model about the learning process, and such models tend to be far from comprehensive in that they emphasize certain aspects of learning to the neglect of other aspects. An example of a very good test and sound theoretical model in this regard is the Illinois Test of Psycholinguistic Abilities (ITPA) (Kirk, McCarthy, & Kirk, 1968), which attempts to measure learning in terms of receptive processes, organizing processes, and expressive processes. The ITPA is thus a series of subtests that attempt to measure the following abilities:

a) *Auditory reception*—"the ability to understand auditory symbols such as verbal discourse";
b) *Visual reception*—"the ability to gain meaning from visual symbols";
c) *Auditory association*—"the ability to relate concepts presented orally";
d) *Visual association*—"the ability to relate concepts presented visually";
e) *Verbal expression*—"the ability to express concepts verbally, i.e., vocally";
f) *Manual expression*—"the ability to express ideas manually";
g) *Grammatic closure*—"the ability to make use of the redundancies of oral language in acquiring automatic habits for handling syntax and grammatic inflections";
h) *Visual closure*—"the ability to identify a common object from an incomplete visual presentation";
i) *Auditory sequential memory*—"the ability to reproduce from memory sequences of digits of increasing length";
j) *Visual sequential memory*—"the ability to reproduce sequences of nonmeaningful figures from memory" (Kirk & Kirk, 1971, pp. 23–24).

The clear advantage in a test such as the ITPA resides in the power of the test to specify learning strengths as well as learning weaknesses and thereby provide a basis for planning the child's educational needs.

DEVELOPMENTAL CONSEQUENCES

Our knowledge of the developmental consequences of learning disorders remains sparse and hypothetical. It is only within the past few decades that children with learning disabilities have gradually come to be identified as a specific population of special children. In the past, these youngsters were often considered to be mildly retarded, behaviorally disturbed, or emotionally disturbed. There is not yet a collection of adequate scientific literature examining the developmental characteristics of learning-disabled children, and for this reason much that we say here must be viewed as preliminary and suggestive. We will examine two specific psychological aspects of learning disabilities, namely, underachievement and emotional overlay.

Psychological Aspects of Underachievement

One of the primary characteristics of learning-disabled children is academic underachievement. Academic underachievement occurs when a child's actual achievement lags behind the achievement level expected of a child of his/her chronological age. As we have seen, achievement level is typically measured by standardized tests. Another measure of achievement level, however, takes place more quietly and less objectively. It is the child's own inner measure of value and worth that is associated with his/her success or failure in the educational experience. This measure is based on the child's unique experiences: being called on in class and not knowing the answer; being handed a written assignment and not knowing what the questions mean; being given a test and finding oneself confused; being teased by peers; or being corrected by teachers.

Children who have had a series of frustrating school experiences because of undetected learning disabilities frequently develop ways to cope. They may label themselves "dumb"; they may learn to expect little of themselves; or they may think they are inferior. It is difficult to measure and identify these early coping responses in young children, but the effects of frustrating school experiences on self-esteem and sense of adequacy should be considered foremost among the adverse psychological consequences of learning disabilities (Abrams, 1973).

Some investigators are of the opinion that certain children are predisposed to experience school as a failure phenomenon. Liss (1955) described such problems as a separate class of learning disabilities and used the term "affect or functional psychic disabilities" as a distinct rubric of classification. Liss felt that this condition could exist with or without a specific learning disability, because it was primarily a problem in the child's emotional development. Other researchers have noted that children may well develop personality problems as a response to various aspects of the learning process. In such cases, these problems are viewed as psychological inhibitions about knowing and growing up (Gardner & Sperry, 1974). There are a variety of psychological factors that may consciously or unconsciously interact with school experiences to produce a condition of underachievement: (a) the family may need to have a child appear stupid or slow; (b) the child may not wish to excel more than the parents; (c) the family environment may be too chaotic to allow the child to study at home; (d) underachievement may be a means by which a child can retaliate against parents who press too strongly for achievement; (e) the child's energies may be overcommitted in dealing with family conflicts so that little time is left for school. Case Study 9.2 pre-

BART: A CASE OF READING DISABILITY
AND PSYCHOLOGICAL UNDERACHIEVEMENT

Bart K., a 13½-year-old boy, was referred to a child guidance clinic because of a history of academic problems. It was reported that Bart had consistently performed well below average in academic work, shown difficulty concentrating, and was considered to be the "class clown." Having completed the seventh grade at a Catholic parochial school, Bart was, for the fourth summer in a row, taking summer school classes in reading to help prepare him for the next school year.

Bart presented a slightly different version of his school problems. "It's the teachers," he said. "How can you learn when they make fun of you and won't help you? One time in English class, I asked the teacher 'What's a verb?' He said, 'Sit down, Bart. We covered that a long time ago.' How are you going to learn when they treat you like that?" Bart summed up his problem as follows: "I know I'll never get anywhere with my brain. I ain't real quick, and the teachers ain't helping me any."

A tall youngster nearing six feet, Bart was a well-mannered and neatly dressed young man who was nervous about making a favorable impression. It was clear that his main interests were not in school but in sports, and his parents confirmed that he was an excellent athlete. Bart volunteered, "When I grow up, I'm going to play sports for a living or join the Coast Guard like my Dad did."

Interview with Bart's Parents
Bart's parents were a handsome couple in their mid-forties who had run a family-owned tavern for many years. Mr. K. admitted to having been alcoholic until seven years previously. "Haven't had a drink since Bart started school," he vowed, "so it's not my drinking that caused the problems." Bart's father was tall and muscular, and he admitted to being a strict disciplinarian. "If Bart comes home a minute late, I ground him for a week. If that doesn't work, I lay him across the bed and give it to him with the strap. I'm firm with him so that

can't be the problem either." At the same time, Mr. K. admitted that he and Bart had a very affectionate relationship and that Bart was never deprived of anything that he needed: "If he comes to me and asks, I'll give him whatever he needs."

Mrs. K. admitted that she became easily aggravated and yelled a lot at Bart, but she did not feel that this caused any problems. "I've read a lot on hyperactivity, and I think he's got it. He can't control his mind enough to center on anything. That's the problem." Neither of Bart's parents had completed high school, but they were very respectful toward Bart's school and his teachers; they refused to side with Bart against his teachers. The parents impressed the examiner as lacking insight into Bart's problems and into themselves.

Psychological Evaluation
On the WISC, Bart received a Verbal Scale IQ of 115 (above average range), a Performance Scale IQ of 122 (superior range), and a Full Scale IQ of 118 (above average range). On the Developmental Test of Visual Motor Integration, Bart functioned at the level of a 16-year-old boy, some 2½ years in advance of his chronological age. None of the tests revealed any signs of organic difficulties, neurological dysfunction, or perceptual-motor deficits. Despite this lack of positive findings, Bart functioned 3 years behind grade level expectancy in reading skills, 4 years behind in spelling skills, and 2 years behind in arithmetic.

On projective tests of personality functioning, Bart perceived himself as childlike and dependent; he felt fortunate whenever anyone treated him well. He had a very poor image of himself and considered himself to be a "dumb" child. Bart also demonstrated a total inability to express any negative feelings about his father, whom he regarded as a powerful figure of authority. On Card 7BM of the Thematic Apperception Test (a card that depicts a young man and an older man speaking with each other), Bart told the following story:

"The young guy did something wrong and the old guy is telling him from his own experience that what he did was wrong. It looks like the young guy is saying to himself, 'What does this old guy know?' After a while, the old guy convinces the young guy that what he did was wrong. The young guy feels embarrassed and does what the old guy tells him to do."

In this story, Bart appeared to be talking about himself and his father. Because he perceived his father to be so powerful, he was unable to assert himself with his father and tended to displace his anger onto the school situation. He felt that he was treated poorly in school and said so because it was safe for him to dislike school. He did not feel safe to dislike things about his father and, in fact, strongly identified with his father. It was safer for Bart to believe that he was a dumb child who was misunderstood and treated badly in school than to deal appropriately with issues in his home life.

Treatment

The findings were shared with the parents, who rejected a recommendation for family therapy. However, the parents did accept a recommendation for tutoring, and Bart was referred to a clinical educator who was also skilled in interpersonal matters. The tutor worked with Bart in terms of his school problems (which pleased the parents) as well as his problems in self-concept and expression of feelings (which pleased Bart). In the next year, Bart was less of a problem in school and began making better academic progress as a function of his "tutoring."

---

sents an example of a youngster with a reading disability who displayed problems in self-esteem and adequacy as a function of both the reading disability and the family dynamics.

Emotional Overlay

In addition to the academic and psychological aspects of underachievement, one of the most serious problems faced by children with learning disabilities is the possibility of disruption of normal social and emotional development. The term **emotional overlay** is used to describe *adverse emotional and behavioral problems that develop as a function of a learning disorder*. The term "overlay" stresses the concept that the emotional and behavioral problems are literally superimposed on the learning disability. In many cases of this sort, the child is thought, on the one hand, to be primarily a behavior problem who is aggressive with peers, unresponsive to conventional management by teachers, antagonistic toward authorities; or, on the other hand, the child tends to engage in immature behavior, playing the role of the class clown and constantly seeking attention from teachers and peers. Thus, emotional overlay may manifest itself either as a conduct-behavior problem or as an emotional problem.

We have noted that children who cannot learn at the same pace as their peers, despite the presence of normal or above-average intelligence, are required to cope with many difficult issues often beyond their budding maturity. The inability to learn easily can breed anxiety, frustration, and anger toward the learning situation. It can create disappointment on the part of parents and misunderstanding on the part of teachers. It can expose one to ridicule from peers. It can assault one's developing sense of pride and self-esteem. The longer that a learning-disabled child remains in school without being properly identified, understood, and appropriately helped with the learning disability, the greater the likelihood of possible adverse emotional consequences.

The problem of emotional overlay in the learning-disabled child can be particularly detrimental during adolescence. There is now an imposing degree of evidence implicating learning disabilities as a primary factor in the school dropout rate during adolescence (Edelman, Allen, Brown, & Rosewater, 1974). Increasing concern among authorities in the field is being directed at the cycle in which the academically defeated adolescent resorts first to nonproductive behavior, then to delinquent behavior, and then to criminal activities (Meier, 1976). Obviously, learning disabilities do not *cause* delinquency and criminal behavior; during adolescence, however, the school experience can be an important source of positive self-esteem, conduct regulation, peer approval, and social direction. In the presence of a negative school experience, the adolescent is more vulnerable to the nonproductive behavior that can serve as the first step to delinquency or criminal activity.

One of the more interesting studies of learning disability and emotional overlay is a longitudinal study by Werner and Smith (1977). They followed a group of 600 children from infancy to 18 years of age on the Hawaiian island of Kauai; 88 percent of this group were still available for study at 18 years of age. Some 3 percent of the original group had been diagnosed at age 10 as learning disabled. The researchers found that 80 percent of this learning-disabled group demonstrated continuing academic underachievement and attendant problems of truancy, absenteeism, and a high incidence of repetitive acting-out behavior that led to sexual misconduct in girls and problems with law enforcement agencies in boys. They found that the rates of contact with community treatment agencies were nine times as high for this learning-disabled group as for control subjects in the rest of the population. This is a striking set of findings that raises serious concerns about the relationships between learning disabilities of various sorts and the problems of emotional overlay and delinquency. If this problem has been underestimated in the past, it will likely become increasingly difficult to ignore the considerable social import of learning disorders on children's behavior.

INTERVENTION

Intervention with learning-disabled children occurs in a variety of ways but is mainly a function of the manner in which learning disabilities are understood and defined. Physicians who consider learning-disabled children from the diagnosis of minimal brain dysfunction are likely to rely on drug therapy to reduce activity level and distractibility. Psychologists and educators who view learning disabilities as perceptual-motor deficits will likely seek forms of treatment that enhance perceptual-motor functioning. Psychologists and educators who view learning disabilities as specific academic deficits will likely attempt to improve skills in the direct area of the deficit. Thus, there are a number of different treatment approaches to learning-disabled children—some quite accepted and some quite controversial. At the same time, certain treatments considered acceptable in some quarters, such as medicine, may be highly controversial in other quarters, such as education, and vice versa. Since the category of learning disability is a relative newcomer to the classifications of special childhood, treatment approaches are less established than is the case with other special conditions that have a more extensive history of professional intervention. The two major classes of intervention in learning disabilities originate from medical perspectives and psychoeducational perspectives, and we will review intervention in terms of these respective approaches.

The Medical Therapies

Medical conceptualizations of learning disabilities assume that such children suffer undetermined but nonetheless real neurological problems that interfere with normal learning. Typically, such problems are understood to involve the syndrome of minimal brain dysfunction with the focal symptoms of hyperactivity, distractibility, and impulsivity. The general intent of medical intervention is to reduce symptoms that interfere with the learning process by treating the underlying neurophysiology of the symptoms. Current forms of medical intervention include drug therapy, megavitamin therapy, diet management, and neurophysiological retraining.

Drug therapy

In an extensive review of the literature, Stevens (1977) concluded that within medicine, the most widely used approach to the treatment of minimal brain dysfunction is the use of *psychostimulant drugs* (drugs that stimulate the central nervous system and have the effect of reducing activity level in children). Currently, methylphenidate (Ritalin) is used more often than the second choice, dextroamphetamine (Dexedrine), because it seems to produce fewer side effects (Krager & Safer, 1974).

In terms of administration, there appears to be considerable variation in procedures, but a typical therapeutic regimen tends to follow that outlined by Eisenberg (1972): the child begins with a minimal dosage (5 milligrams of Dexedrine or 10 milligrams of Ritalin) given daily at breakfast. If no improvement results, the dosage is increased in similar increments at two- or three-day intervals. A second dosage may be added at lunchtime. A daily maximum dosage would be 40 milligrams of Dexedrine or 80 milligrams of Ritalin. Eisenberg reported that two-thirds to three-quarters of hyperactive children can be expected to improve significantly through this treatment approach.

Although Dexedrine and Ritalin have been the most widely used psychostimulant drugs, other central nervous system stimulants include caffeine and magnesium pemoline (Cylert). These psychostimulants, as well as imipramine (an antidepressant drug) and phenothiazine (a major tranquilizer), have been used with varying degrees of success in reducing activity and distractibility. Caffeine, for example, was used by Schnachenburg (1973) in a pilot study of 11 children who had previously developed side effects on Ritalin. On an activity level rating scale, these children demonstrated similar ratings on caffeine and Ritalin, and both caffeine and Ritalin induction produced significantly reduced activity level when compared to a no-drug condition. Other studies using lower dosages of caffeine failed to document its effectiveness as compared to Ritalin or Dexedrine (Conners, 1975; Garfinkel, Webster, & Sloman, 1975).

One of the central concerns with any form of drug therapy is the problem of side effects. The most frequently noted side effects of the stimulant drugs are insomnia and loss of appetite, and these are known to occur more frequently with Dexedrine than with Ritalin. These side effects are usually short-term and tend to occur at the onset of administration of a drug. They must be carefully monitored, however, and if they persist, the dosage is reduced or the child is placed on another drug.

Of greater concern in the use of drugs is the question of long-term side effects. There is relatively little empirical research on this matter, but several potentially serious findings have emerged. Several studies have identified increased heart rate as a result of the stimulants (e.g., Aman & Werry, 1975). An initial study by Safer, Allen, and Barr (1972) reported growth inhibition in children who were taking methylphenidate (Ritalin) for more than three years. A follow-up study showed a gain in growth rate following termination of drug treatment, even exceeding the expected level of recovery (Safer & Allen, 1976). Although drug therapy for children diagnosed as suffering from MBD continues to expand, it remains a controversial form of intervention that raises spectres of a generation of drugged children being unwillingly brought into conformity.

The most significant reason for the dramatic expansion of drug therapy has come from numerous reports of its effectiveness with children. The most favorable of these place the long-term success rate of methylphenidate in the reduction of hyperactivity at over 80 percent effectiveness (Hoffman, Engelhardt, Margolis, Polizos, Waizer, & Rosenfeld, 1974; Schain & Reynard, 1975). Other summaries are more cautious, suggesting that 35 to 50 percent of hyperactive children show dramatic improvement, 30 to 40 percent show moderate benefit, and 15 to 20 percent show no benefit (Safer & Allen, 1976).

Three major concerns regarding the use of drugs with hyperactive children must nonetheless be noted: (a) the majority of stimulant drug studies are plagued by weaknesses in experimental design that raise concern about the accuracy of findings (Wiens, Anderson, & Matarazzo, 1972); (b) the question of potentially damaging long-term side effects has not been adequately explored to the point that these drugs can be guaranteed as safe; and (c) the relationship between drug effects and actual enhancement of learning ability remains obscure. In this final regard, data from a recent study of hyperactive children taking Ritalin showed that while clinical observers noted improvement in the children's behavior, the children showed no gains on actual achievement measures (Rie, Rie, Stewart, & Ambuel, 1976). Despite these concerns, however, drug therapy has become the treatment of choice among the majority of pediatricians and child psychiatrists who treat hyperactive children.

Megavitamin therapy
A highly controversial approach that has received considerable publicity is **megavitamin therapy,** a form of treatment that involves massive doses of vita-

mins. Megavitamin therapy has not been exclusive to the field of learning disabilities, and has been advocated as a possible cure for a variety of physical and psychiatric ailments. Perhaps the person most closely associated with this approach is Linus Pauling, an internationally known chemist from the University of California. In recent years Pauling has received much notoriety for his support of Vitamin C in the prevention of the common cold and similar maladies. Pauling views megavitamin therapy as a branch of orthomolecular medicine in general and of orthomolecular psychiatric therapy in particular.

Pauling (1968) defined this new treatment approach as follows: "Orthomolecular psychiatric therapy is the treatment of mental disease by the provision of the optimal molecular environment of the mind, especially the optimum concentration of substances normally present in the human body" (p. 265). The administration of vitamins in large amounts is considered by Pauling (1968) to produce "optimum molecular concentrations" beneficial to both mental functioning and behavior. Megavitamin therapy has been attempted with a wide variety of psychiatric problems, including seriously disturbed schizophrenic children, as well as children with learning disabilities. The paper that fueled the notion of megavitamin therapy for learning-disabled children was written by Cott (1971) and gave the impression that megavitamin therapy for learning-disabled children was a substantiated and highly effective form of treatment.

In point of fact, biochemical approaches of this sort require many years of careful investigation before claims of treatment effectiveness can be substantiated. There has been a paucity of research using megavitamin therapy with learning-disabled youngsters, and it is much too early to evaluate the potential effectiveness of this form of treatment (Silver, 1975). Unfortunately, megavitamin therapy has at times been presented in the popular media as a cure-all, and parents of learning-disabled youngsters frequently make specific requests for this form of therapy. Despite the excitement generated, however, megavitamin therapy remains a highly unsubstantiated form of intervention with learning-disabled youngsters.

Diet management

Another treatment approach that has received much controversial attention is the reported attempt to reduce hyperactivity by the management of diet. Feingold (1975) maintained that artificial colors and flavors that are added to foods may be an active ingredient in the causation of hyperactivity. He advocated controlled diet management that restricted intake of such food additives as a means of preventing and reducing hyperactivity. Since controlled studies of the effectiveness of this technique have yet to be published, it is impossible to evaluate the demonstrated or potential utility of this approach.

Neurophysiological retraining

Treatments based on neurophysiological retraining are also controversial and will require more extended comment. The theory and treatment methods of Doman-Delacato have probably fired the most heated arguments in the treatment of learning disabilities in the past quarter century. Although there are several different versions of neurophysiological retraining, the Doman-Delacato method has claimed the greatest degree of effectiveness and has evolved as a fully developed treatment procedure.

The Doman-Delacato method found its inspiration in the work of Temple Fay, a respected Philadelphia neurosurgeon and one of the founders of the American Academy for Cerebral Palsy. Late in his career, Fay became interested in the treatment of brain-injured patients, and in the 1940s and 1950s he published extensively on procedures for the remediation of brain injury in children and adults. Wolf (1968) noted that Fay's theories form the basis of the treatment procedure that came to be known as the Doman-Delacato method, but Fay himself was never involved in any of the controversial claims of effectiveness. Glen Doman, a physical therapist, and Carl Delacato, an educational psychologist, worked with Fay in Philadelphia; when Doman helped found the Norwood Rehabilitation Center, Fay became one of the consultants. In 1963, the Center was reorganized and became the Institute for the Achievement of Human Potential, with Doman as director and Delacato as associate director (Hallahan & Cruickshank, 1973).

The Doman-Delacato method assumes a standard medical interpretation of learning disability—that is, it assumes that underlying neurological dysfunction is the basis for learning dysfunction. This approach further presumes, however, that the source of neurological dysfunction is a defect in *neurological organization* that occurs because the child fails to pass properly through a proper sequence of developmental stages in which central nervous system factors are activated through normally developing behavior. The treatment consists of an extensive array of exercises intended to stimulate normal brain activity. These exercises include crawling about on the floor, manipulating certain body patterns in the child, stimulating senses to increase body awareness, and so forth.

The Doman-Delacato method has met with considerable popularity and acceptance by the general public, but it has been widely criticized by medical, psychological, and educational professionals. The tenor of these criticisms has involved such issues as claims for cures in the absence of adequate controlled research, claims for rapid and conclusive diagnosis, promotional methods that induce guilt in parents if they fail to use the method, inflexible regimens for the identified patient that impose unnecessary hardships on other family members, the alleged universal applicability of the theory, and the general lack of supporting research evidence. Although much of the debate regarding the "neurological organization" hypothesis of Doman-Delacato has lessened in the past decade, this approach to treatment continues to have its staunch supporters and detractors. In the continuing absence of supporting research evidence, however, the efficacy of the Doman-Delacato method must remain questionable.

The science and the art of medicine require that the effectiveness of various treatment approaches be subjected to the rigid scrutiny of demonstrable evidence. In the biomedical and behavioral sciences, it is expected that treatment methods will be subjected to experimental testing so that the effectiveness of procedures can be openly evaluated by both professionals and the general public. In the medical treatment of learning disabilities, drug therapy alone has undergone rigorous experimental investigation; unfortunately, many drug studies have been poorly conducted in terms of experimental design, and poor research can be more misleading than no research. Medical treatments of learning disabilities currently function at the level of a clinical art rather than an established science, but drug therapy is clearly the most advanced in its attempts to develop a body of supporting evidence.

Psychoeducational Therapies

There are an extensive number of treatment approaches to the learning-disabled child that are based on psychological and educational perspectives. A thorough review of this extensive literature would be beyond the scope of this discussion, and this review will focus on the areas of behavior modification, perceptual-motor training, and educational intervention.

Behavior modification

In recent years, behavior modification has been increasingly applied to a variety of learning problems. Space does not permit discussion of the wide variety of these applications, but an examination of the behavioral approaches to hyperactivity will illustrate the general nature of behavioral procedures in the area of learning disabilities.

On a theoretical basis, behavioral psychology does not subscribe to the medical model that views hyperactivity as one of the significant symptoms of minimal brain dysfunction. Rather, hyperactive behavior is understood to represent a class of responses having different and varied causes but maintained by a number of identifiable environmental consequences. In short, hyperactivity is thought to be a behavior that is inadvertently reinforced in subtle ways by parents, teachers, peers, and others. This hyperactive behavior is considered to be incompatible with the attentive behavior that is necessary in learning. The general treatment approach, therefore, involves procedures that seek to reinforce attentive behavior and to extinguish disruptive and highly active behavior.

A number of studies have reported a high degree of success with such procedures. For example, a token system that paired a material reinforcer with an auditory and visual stimulus (a light and a buzzer) successfully reduced movement and destructive behavior in 6 hyperactive children (Doubros & Daniels, 1966). Pihl (1967) attempted to reduce hyperactivity by increasing the amount of time that hyperactive subjects spent sitting in their seats; a panel of lights flashed as seconds in the chair were counted, and accumulated seconds in the chair earned points that could later be exchanged for money or privileges. This procedure was successful in reducing out-of-seat behavior in a 14-year-old hyperactive boy and a 7-year-old boy with brain damage. Twardosz and Sajwaj (1972) reduced out-of-seat behavior in a 4-year-old boy by using a prompting technique and by putting X's on a piece of paper worn about the boy's neck; the X's served as visible signs of the boy's progress, and the boy was also rewarded with praise and tokens that could be exchanged for candy and trinkets.

Behavioral approaches to reducing hyperactivity have been quite ingenious in the development of gadgetry to control activity level. One of the most recent innovations in this regard is the biomotometer, a portable electronic device which simultaneously measures the child's activity level and provides an auditory feedback signal to the subject. The biomotometer consists of a small electronic box, the size of a package of cigarettes, that is worn about the waist and measures activity level by the angular displacement of mercury switches stored in the box; an ear plug delivers a "beep" signal to the subject if the subject becomes overactive. This simple auditory feedback mechanism helps the child identify activity level in process, and the biofeedback offers the prospect of self-control. Preliminary research with this device has been quite promising as a means of controlling hyperactivity. Schulman, Stevens, Suran, Kupst, and Naughton (1978) reported significant improvement in the activity levels of a hyperactive 11-year-old boy and a hyperactive 11-year-old girl who were conditioned "live" in the classroom setting. The results of this early study suggest that the biomotometer may prove to be a useful instrument for the reduction of hyperactivity in school-aged children.

These studies, and others too numerous to review, report consistent success with reducing hyperactive behavior and increasing attentive behavior. Behavior modification, therefore, is increasingly being viewed as a safer alternative to medication of the hyperactive child. A number of studies have been done comparing the effectiveness of conditioning techniques with that of stimulant medication in the treatment of hyperactivity. In a study with three hyperactive subjects previously on medication, a token reinforcement system (involving check marks on an index card exchanged for material reinforcers) was used to reduce hyperactivity in the classroom (Ayllon, Layman, & Kandel, 1975). Results indicated that the subjects made better academic progress under the token system as compared to their performance while on medication. A variety of other studies under slightly different conditions also support the view that behavioral techniques represent a viable alternative to drug therapy for hyperactivity (e.g., Gittelman-Klein, Klein, Abikoff, Katz, Gloisten, & Kates, 1976).

It should be pointed out, however, that behavioral treatments are typically limited in application to a small number of children and often require extraordinary efforts on the part of the trainer or investigator. Such demands on the use of professional time may be significantly decreased as new generations of educators are trained in the application of behavioral principles to conventional classroom settings. Behavioral approaches to learning disabilities are based on sound rationale, rigorous experimental study, and specificity of orientation that make them highly appealing as a set of treatment procedures for the learning-disabled child.

Perceptual-motor training

Educators and psychologists who conceptualize learning disabilities from the viewpoint of perceptual-motor deficits typically assume that the most effective form of treatment for learning disabilities involves the enhancement of perceptual-motor functioning. In his book, *The Slow Learner in the Classroom,* Kephart (1960) proposed specific exercises presumed to be useful in strengthening various aspects of perceptual-motor functioning—among them, walking a narrow balance rail, tracing figures on templates, and using chalkboards for learning. These activities placed important emphasis on perceptual-motor development, and such efforts encouraged the establishment of very specific approaches to perceptual-motor development.

An excellent example of a specific program of perceptual-motor training is the one developed by Frostig (Frostig & Horne, 1964; Frostig & Maslow, 1973). This packaged program seeks to remediate deficiencies in perceptual-motor abilities assessed by the Frostig Developmental Test of Visual Perception and is based on the five diagnostic subtests of the Frostig test: namely, eye-hand motor coordination, figure-ground, form constancy, position in space, and spatial relations. The training program consists of a series of workbook exercises in these areas.

Children who complete the Frostig training program usually show marked improvement in perceptual-motor skills when measured by retesting on the Frostig Developmental Test of Visual Perception. Research, however, does not support the supposition that enhancement of perceptual-motor skills increases the child's achievement in specific academic areas such as reading. Anderson (1972), for example, followed 33 second-graders identified as having perceptual-motor deficiencies and reading problems. These youngsters received 16

Devices such as the one shown here can be helpful in training children to correctly perceive figures. As the child traces the figure, a beeping sound can let him know immediately if he is incorrectly copying the figure.

weeks of daily training in the Frostig program while a control group received similar amounts of tutoring without the specifics of the Frostig program. Children in the Frostig program did not show more significant improvement in reading ability than the control group youngsters. Anderson interpreted the findings to mean that the improvement shown in both groups was a function of additional teacher attention rather than the specifics of the particular program. Controlled research studies of this type question the relevance of elaborate perceptual-motor training programs in assisting the child's progress in basic academic areas. The burden of proof continues to reside with the advocates of such programs.

Educational intervention

Although children with learning problems have always posed difficulties to educators, the concept of learning disabilities has not had an extensive history in education. It is, perhaps, premature to compare various educational approaches with respect to effectiveness of intervention. Education clearly needs a period of gestation that allows for innovative programming and experimentation with new procedures. Educators are still struggling with the search for providing the most effective education for the many different types of children who give evidence of learning disability. Should there be special schools for learning-disabled children? Should there be special classes within regular schools? Should such youngsters be mainstreamed and provided with itinerant personnel or tutors? The field of learning disabilities is a microcosm of the social issues and philosophies of education that are debated throughout the field of special education.

Although a consensus regarding the most effective forms of educational intervention is still lacking, individualized instruction with the learning-disabled child frequently produces rapid improvement in areas of academic deficiency. Once the nature of a child's disability has been identified, teachers can more confidently program instruction to meet the child's needs. Instruction should be directed at the child's identified ability level and gradually increased in difficulty as the child's skills develop. Minskoff (1975) provided a number of guidelines for teaching the learning-disabled child, including such instructions as providing small steps in a graduated sequence of learning, directing remediation to the child's individual rate of progress, making the content of remedial methods and materials of social value to the child, and building the possibility of a transfer of skills and experiences directly into the teaching situation. There is no substitute for sensitive and skilled instruction, and teachers of children with learning deficiencies tend to develop a variety of techniques for motivating the child and bringing excitement into the learning process.

This review of the field of learning disabilities has included both established positions and controversial points of view. From differences in conceptualization of the problem to highly varying approaches to treatment, there is little in this area of special childhood that is not subject to honest criticism. It should be apparent to the reader that the presence of disparate viewpoints in this field is very much a function of the fact that both medicine and education have a considerable stake in the diagnosis and treatment of learning-disabled children. Among the conditions of special childhood, learning disability alone is so circumscribed by the process of education that such children may experience little or no difficulty in areas other than education. Educators, perhaps rightly, take a proprietary interest in the learning-disabled child, and they feel that significant advances in this field are likely to derive from psychoeducational perspectives rather than from medical interests. Physicians, on the other hand, are conscious of a growing number of children referred to them with the apparent characteristics of "minimal brain dysfunction," and they increasingly view learning disability as an organic problem in need of medical intervention. Parents are understandably confused by the confusion inherent in the state of the field, and a parent's best resource at this time is to become knowledgeable about the controversies that plague the entire area of learning disabilities.

Although the student may justifiably wonder whether such interdisciplinary disputes are merely ways of firing the passions of professional chauvinism, the presence of such active disagreement must be viewed as a healthy sign. Disagreements of this sort tend to encourage careful thinking and solid research, thus serving the needs of both the parent and the individual child. In the next few decades there are likely to be major shifts in the conceptualization of learning disabilities. The field is still very young and has not as yet had ample opportunity to examine itself. In order for a field of study to grow and prosper, it must sift through its sources and winnow its traditions, saving the relevant and the original while discarding the impractical and the outmoded. The field of learning disability has not had sufficient time to review its own history and to assess its own traditions; in the same way, it has not had an adequate basis of experience with the learning-disabled child. In the coming years, such experience will surely provide more confidence in diagnostic and treatment procedures.

SUMMARY

1. The basic problem in learning-disabled children is an incapacity to learn through normal and conventional channels.
2. Learning disabilities do not include learning problems that are caused by other special conditions, such as mental retardation, physical disability, or emotional disturbance.
3. The diagnosis of minimal brain dysfunction (MBD) presumes that unidentified injuries to the brain account for the presence of learning disabilities in otherwise normal children.
4. Perceptual-motor disabilities include difficulties with visual perception and/or difficulties in the coordination of visual perception with motor behavior.
5. Psycholinguistic learning disabilities involve difficulties in the area of language and the cognitive processes upon which language is based.
6. Estimates of the prevalence of learning disabilities in children under 18 range from 1,375,000 to 7,500,000; some investigators feel that learning disabilities are the most pervasive medical problem in the United States.
7. The causes of learning disabilities are very poorly understood, but they could include such disparate factors as maldevelopment of the brain and poor teaching.
8. From a psychometric standpoint, a learning disability can be operationally defined

as a significant discrepancy between a child's actual level of achievement and the achievement expected of a child at his/her chronological age.

9. Learning disabilities can be identified by intelligence tests, achievement tests, and tests of specific learning modalities.

10. One of the unfortunate consequences of learning disabilities is the potential for disruption of normal social and emotional development; the term "emotional overlay" is used to describe the adverse emotional and behavioral problems that may develop as a function of a learning disorder.

11. Many children who are diagnosed as having minimal brain dysfunction respond favorably to drug therapy; the continued use of drugs with children, however, may produce long-term side effects, and drug therapy is currently a highly controversial issue.

12. A variety of behavior modification techniques have been shown to be effective in altering behaviors that are incompatible with learning in the classroom.

13. Since the concept of learning disabilities is a relative newcomer to the categories of special childhood, there is, as yet, a lack of consensus regarding the most effective forms of educational intervention.

CHAPTER TEN

Gifted Children

True democracy demands that every child, whether superior, average, or inferior in ability be given the fullest opportunity to develop to the limit of his [her] mental capacity. It is the gifted child, more than any other, who has hitherto lacked this opportunity.

Lewis M. Terman (cited in Seagoe, 1975, p. 80)

GIFTED CHILDREN AS SPECIAL CHILDREN

It is easy to understand the unique needs of most special children and to feel a genuine concern for their welfare. We can readily understand the frustrations that speech- and hearing-disabled children experience as they try to communicate. Blind and physically handicapped children make us painfully aware of our taken-for-granted abilities to walk and care for ourselves. Retarded youngsters clearly require special educational provisions in order to learn basic skills. It is precisely because these children have problems so clearly requiring special treatment and educational programs that tremendous progress has been made in providing them with medical, psychological, educational, and social intervention.

By contrast, the child with unique abilities or talents rarely arouses the same levels of awareness or concern. Frequently, the extremely bright child is taken for granted, or made the subject of unusual demands and pressures for perfect performance when recognition of special abilities does occur. Similarly, the creative child is often viewed as a stubborn nuisance, or as rebellious and arrogant. Special interests or talents in art, music, or athletics are often interpreted as signs of lopsided development by well-meaning parents or teachers. Such pursuits are, therefore, often shunted aside in order to promote "well-balanced" or "normal" development.

In cases where educational systems have made attempts to identify children with special intellectual or creative abilities, questions have been raised regarding the fairness or equality of special treatment. In misguided attempts at assuring equal treatment, special educational programs for the gifted have often been viewed as elitist and undemocratic.

As a consequence of these sundry misconceptions and misunderstandings, gifted children have typically received little in the way of special programming to facilitate development of their skills. Instead, they have more often encountered frustration and boredom when placed in situations where neither teachers nor curriculum offer the challenges they need to develop their full potentials. Such failures on the part of society to provide adequate educational programming may lead to immeasurable loss of talent. While such loss is always tragic for the individual, it is no less so for our rapidly changing society, where problems can only be solved through the intelligent and wise use of technology and sociopolitical structures and through the creative search for ways of improving the quality of life for all its citizens.

DEFINITION OF GIFTED CHILDREN

A necessary first step in the study of gifted children is the development of a clear conception of what giftedness means. On one level it seems self-evident that a gifted child is a bright child, one who shows high intelligence or unusual talent. Anyone with eyes and ears can recognize such ability when it is present. However, in order to develop meaningful educational programs for gifted children, clearer definitions are needed so that such children can be identified early and provided with educational experiences that precisely match their needs. Such precision is important so that expectations may be geared to the child's abilities while recognizing the child's limitations. There is little point in making unrealistic demands of even the most talented child, since the only likely outcomes will be anxiety, frustration, resentment, and a damaged self-concept. Furthermore, effective identification is also important in recognizing those children who may give an impression of unusual ability without being able to learn and develop at an accelerated rate. Again, misidentification of normal children as gifted is likely to produce developmental problems.

The importance of adequately defining giftedness as a precursor to identification has led to a multiplicity of definitions. Those definitions that are very broad and nonspecific offer little direction for accurate identification. The National Society for the Study of Education, for example, defined giftedness as "consistently remarkable performance in any worthwhile line of endeavor" (1958, p. 19). Though recognizing the inadequacy of his definition as a guide to recognizing the gifted child, Barbe (1961) nevertheless suggested that "the gifted child is *one who possesses potential creative leadership ability*" (p. 10). Still other definitions refer to giftedness as "a very high level of academic aptitude, either demonstrated or potential" (Durr, 1964, p. 16) or "superior ability to deal with facts, ideas, or relationships" (Kirk, 1972, p. 109).

In sharp opposition to these broad, nonspecific definitions are those that narrowly limit giftedness to performance above a specified level on a particular intelligence test. Typically, such definitions call for achievement of an IQ score of 130 or above on a test such as the Stanford-Binet or the Wechsler Intelligence Scale for Children-Revised. While these definitions offer direction in identifying gifted children in a clear and operational fashion, they are narrow in scope and restricted in applicability. Definition in terms of an IQ score inevitably excludes such factors as special talent in music, art, mechanics, leadership, creativity, and so on. Giftedness, by these definitions, tends to be equated largely with verbal problem-solving ability. Furthermore, definition in terms of an IQ score is impractical in application because it should be framed in terms of individually administered tests of intelligence, which are prohibitively expensive for use as screening devices.

A broader but more practical definition of giftedness was presented to

Congress by the Commissioner of Education (Marland, 1972) for the United States Office of Education (USOE). Simultaneously inclusive, specific, and practical, this definition suggests that *gifted and talented children are those who exhibit outstanding ability or talent in a variety of areas—including general intelligence, specific aptitudes, creativity, leadership, artistic ability, or athletic talent—and who have been identified as possessing such ability by professionally qualified individuals* such as teachers, psychologists, or others with special training in the area of the child's special talent. Whenever possible, professional judgment should be supplemented by objective indices such as psychometric tests or product and performance evaluations.

Several aspects of this definition are worth emphasis. *First, specific identification of gifted and talented children is explicitly made a matter for professional evaluation and decision.* The use of arbitrarily specified IQ scores is replaced with flexible professional judgment based on the best available objective measures of ability or talent. The most effective identification techniques include a combination of standardized intelligence tests, standardized achievement tests, assessment of products or performance, and the use of rating scales that explicitly identify commonly observed performance characteristics of gifted children (Gallagher, 1975).

A second important aspect of the above definition of giftedness *is the explicit recognition that it may encompass many more kinds of talents and abilities in addition to academic or verbal aptitude.* For example, musical precocity is a special ability worthy of identification and development. The same is true of talent in the graphic or performing arts or in athletics. Recognition is given to the fact that outstanding ability comes in a variety of forms and may require a variety of specific programs. Equally significant is the clear reference to creative ability as a form of giftedness. Sidestepping the fruitless controversy over the relative importance of high intelligence as opposed to creativity, the USOE definition recognizes both as requiring careful nurturance and conservation.

On the basis of this definition, the USOE estimated that 3 to 5 percent of

Early identification and encouragement of children with special abilities can be important in helping them reach their talent's potential.

an unselected population will likely exhibit some combination of talents requiring special educational provisions for full development. This kind of estimate can be useful to the teacher or administrator in assessing the efficacy of identification programs. It also indicates in concrete terms the magnitude of the problem facing our educational system, since 5 percent of the elementary and secondary school population is equivalent to slightly over 2.5 million children and adolescents. The gifted among very young children and preschoolers would add considerably to this figure.

IDENTIFICATION OF GIFTED CHILDREN

Although interest in individuals of special ability has been noted in all ages, the scientific study of gifted children did not really begin until Francis Galton (1822–1911) published *Hereditary Genius* in 1869. Galton took as subjects for his study nearly 1000 eminent British men who had lived between 1768 and 1868. His subjects included statesmen, soldiers, scientists, writers, poets, artists, and ministers. Galton investigated the close relatives of these subjects to determine the frequency of eminence among this related group. Galton's group of 977 men had 332 close relatives as eminent as themselves. Statistically, one would expect only one relative to achieve the same degree of eminence in a randomly selected group of 977 men. On the basis of his study, Galton developed a theory regarding the heritability of genius and concluded that intellectual ability is largely inherited. While Galton's conclusion remains controversial even today, his study marks the beginning of systematic efforts to identify gifted individuals.

Working at about the same time, the Italian scientist Cesare Lombroso (1835–1909) investigated the popular notion that genius is closely related to insanity. In 1891 Lombroso published *The Man of Genius,* in which he concluded, using a case study method, that genius is a marked aberration from the normal and akin to other mental aberrations. While important in its application of the case study method to identification of unusual ability, Lombroso's work has had the unfortunate effect of perpetuating the belief that where giftedness exists, it is likely to be marred by emotional instability (Lichtenstein, 1971; Martindale, 1971). Despite considerable evidence to the contrary, this stereotyped conception of the unusually bright or creative individual remains widespread even today.

Another major study, similar in conception to those of Galton and Lombroso, was conducted by Catherine Cox (1926). Though much more refined in execution than earlier biographical studies, Cox still relied heavily on published accounts of the lives of eminent men as sources of data. Using developmental norms as a guide, Cox and her colleagues were able to estimate the IQs of these famous men (see Exhibit 10.1) and also to develop a series of character ratings. Statistical analyses of character ratings for 300 geniuses yielded a trait profile characteristic of youthful geniuses who achieved eminence. These men were at or above the average for individuals of normal intelligence on 67 positively valued traits, including sense of humor, self-

EXHIBIT 10.1

283

Identification of
gifted children

ESTIMATED IQs OF A GROUP OF EMINENT MEN

As part of her study of the early mental traits of the gifted individual, Catherine Cox and her associates used extensive biographical material to develop IQ estimates for a large sample of eminent men. Cox's methodology involved a comparison of current developmental norms with biographical data recorded for her subjects to estimate intelligence. Though it does not constitute "proof" of any contention, Cox's study provides interesting insights into the relationships between achievement and ability.

Name	Field of Eminence	IQ Estimate
John Adams	Statesman	145
John Quincy Adams	Statesman	165
Johann Sebastian Bach	Musician	140
Francis Bacon	Philosopher	155
Ludwig van Beethoven	Musician	140
Napoleon Bonaparte	Soldier	140
Samuel Taylor Coleridge	Writer	165
Charles Darwin	Scientist	140
Charles Dickens	Writer	155
Goethe	Writer	200
Alexander Hamilton	Statesman	140
Thomas Jefferson	Statesman	150
Immanuel Kant	Philosopher	145
G. W. Liebnitz	Philosopher	190
John Stuart Mill	Philosopher	170
Wolfgang Mozart	Musician	155
Rembrandt	Artist	135
Wm. T. Sherman	Soldier	135
Leonardo da Vinci	Artist	150
Voltaire	Writer	180
George Washington	Statesman	135

From Cox (1926)

esteem, fondness for companionship, impulsive kindness, trustworthiness, common sense, physique, sense of justice, and physical bravery. However, they were higher than average on several traits, including an occasional liability to extreme depression, a tendency to quick anger, and unconventionality.

On the basis of her massive investigation, Cox concluded that the youthful genius had a superior heredity and environmental advantages; that he manifested genius at an early age; and that later eminence was a function not only of high intelligence but also of persistence of motivation and effort, self-confidence, and great strength and force of character. Altogether, Cox's study is a fascinating rebuttal to stereotyped conceptions of the historical genius.

Though the biographical studies of Galton, Lombroso, and Cox are interesting and provocative, the watershed of knowledge regarding the development and identification of gifted children is the monumental longitudinal study begun by Lewis M. Terman (1877–1956).

In 1921 Terman undertook a massive study of slightly more than 1500 gifted children selected from a total school population of about a quarter million southern California children. His method of selection involved a series of steps beginning with teacher nominations followed by group and individual intelligence tests. The majority of subjects selected for inclusion in the study had achieved IQ scores above 140 on the 1916 Stanford-Binet Intelligence Test; a small group of 62 subjects scoring between 135 and 139 were also included. Upon checking his identification and selection procedures, Terman estimated that he had effectively located approximately 90 percent of the gifted children in the schools sampled.

Terman's subjects were studied from a variety of perspectives. In addition to extensive psychometric testing, anthropometric measurements were taken, as well as medical and family histories, educational histories, and standardized achievement tests. Subjects of the original study have been followed throughout their lives, and several volumes have been published reporting the achievements and life adjustment of these gifted individuals.

The results of Terman's studies have served as a point of departure for much of the subsequent research on gifted children. While it is impossible to do justice to the depth and richness of these investigations, some of the major findings are worth highlighting.

In regard to the identification of gifted children, Terman reported that the most adequate identification procedures must include some form of psychometric testing, preferably including an individually administered intelligence test. Terman felt unaugmented teacher reports were unreliable; he even concluded that, "if you are allowed only one method of locating the highest IQ in a classroom, your chance of getting the right child is better if you merely look in the class register and take the youngest child than if you trust the teacher's judgment!" (1947, p. 6). This was true despite definite instructions to teachers to take into account children's ages. Teacher errors in identifying gifted children stemmed from a failure to consider the importance of the relationship between mental age and chronological age. While more adequate class placement makes this kind of conclusion less tenable today, judgments of ability level based on classroom performance alone are still likely to be in error (Gallagher, 1975), and any observer must be cautious in the unaided assessment of children's abilities.

Failure to identify and correctly place gifted children was typical in the schools where Terman found his subjects. Of children with IQs of 135 or more, at least half were capable of schoolwork two years beyond the grade in which they were placed (Terman, 1947). The situation Terman described is not too far removed from current educational practices, and it is estimated that fewer than 4 percent of gifted and talented children receive the educational services they need for optimal development (Lyon, 1976–77).

Terman's research provided guidelines for the identification of gifted children that remain relevant and viable today. While no single factor is by itself adequate, *identification of gifted children should include some combination of: (a) group and individual intelligence testing, (b) educational achievement, (c) family history, and (d) observation of physical, personality, and social characteristics.* This last factor is particularly relevant in view of extensive information available regarding developmental characteristics of gifted children.

CHARACTERISTICS OF GIFTED CHILDREN

One of the significant aspects of the early studies of gifted children conducted by Terman and his associates was the emergence of a clear descriptive picture of the gifted child. Stereotyped for generations as timid, bookish, physically weak, homely, and unpopular, the gifted child was perceived in the popular mind as an object of derision as well as secret envy. However, Terman found a different picture in reality.

For nearly every trait measured, the gifted group was superior to individuals of normal intelligence (Terman, 1925; Terman & Oden, 1947). This superiority might have been expected in educational achievement, breadth of interest, and literary and mathematical skills. However, it also extended to physical health, size, appearance, energy, trustworthiness, modesty, self-awareness, and emotional stability. Follow-up studies of the gifted group conducted between 1950 and 1952 indicated that, compared to the general population, the gifted live longer, enjoy better health, show higher educational and occupational achievement, have happier marriages, and in general are more productive (Terman & Oden, 1959).

The most recent follow-up of Terman's gifted group was conducted in 1972 when the average age of the subjects was 62. At this point in their lives, these subjects felt that they had experienced great joy in living and found satisfaction in their family lives and occupations (Sears, 1977).

Subsequent research has only partially confirmed the findings of the original Terman studies. One of the primary shortcomings of the original research was a failure to sort out the relative contributions of heredity and

On the whole, the gifted read earlier, more intensively, and more selectively than their peers.

superior socioeconomic background in understanding the superior achievement of gifted children. When socioeconomic status is controlled, some of the marked differences between gifted children and children of normal ability appear less pronounced or even disappear. Physical superiority is one such difference (Laycock & Caylor, 1964). However, in other areas, such as emotional stability and social adjustment, the superiority of gifted children has been repeatedly confirmed (Newland, 1976).

A variety of studies have suggested or confirmed that gifted children are characterized to a greater degree by good emotional adjustment and mental health (e.g., Hollingworth, 1942); superior social adjustment and popularity (Gallagher, 1966); greater responsibility, social interest, social commitment, flexibility, psychological maturity, tact, realism, and independence (Marland, 1972). The gifted read earlier, more intensively and more selectively than their peers (Terman & Oden, 1959). They show a wider range of interests and special aptitudes. In an extensive review of the existing research, French (1964) summarized basic characteristics commonly found in gifted children. These are listed in Exhibit 10.2.

In brief, the gifted appear to be precisely what the term implies—a group of individuals who are especially advantaged in confronting and mastering the challenges of life in every sphere. As does every human being, they confront many problems in developing and in meeting the tasks of life, but they are especially well-equipped to resolve these problems.

DEFINITION AND IDENTIFICATION OF CREATIVE CHILDREN

The study of gifted children must include a discussion of creativity, a talent that is closely related to, and yet distinguishable from, high intellectual ability. Though research on creative children is rife with contradictory trends and conclusions, some consistencies have emerged over the years, and these contribute to a more complete picture of children with special abilities. Though recognition of intellectually gifted children has posed a variety of problems to the educator, these are minor compared to the complexity of identifying creative children. In the first place, there are no generally agreed upon definitions of creativity. We will here adopt a common definition of **creativity** as a capacity to restructure the world in unusual conceptual terms. Some researchers prefer to speak of "genius" or "originality" (Ashby & Walker, 1968), while others speak of "divergent thinking abilities" (Guilford, 1956, 1959). Still others view this elusive ability as "ideational fluency," a facility in producing numerous and varied associations of ideas or concepts (Mednick, 1962; Wallach, 1970).

In addition to the lack of any generally accepted definition of creativity, there is tremendous disparity in approaches to identifying the creative child and understanding the characteristics underlying creative ability or associated with it in the individual child. In order to understand and evaluate conclusions that have been offered regarding creative children, it is important to discuss key research efforts.

EXHIBIT 10.2

287

Definition and
identification of
creative children

CHARACTERISTICS OF GIFTED CHILDREN

In examining the literature on gifted children, J. L. French developed the following list of characteristics, which have been repeatedly observed in various research studies. In examining these characteristics, it is important to remember that no child consistently manifests all of them. The observer is searching for the child who *often* exhibits *many* of them.

1. Superior physique as demonstrated by above-average height, weight, coordination, endurance, and general health;

2. Longer attention span;

3. Learns rapidly, easily, and with less repetition;

4. Learns to read sooner and continues to read at a consistently more advanced level;

5. More mature in the ability to express himself/herself through the various communicative skills;

6. Reaches higher levels of attentiveness to his/her environment;

7. Asks more questions and really wants to know the causes and reasons for things;

8. Likes to study some subjects that are difficult because he/she enjoys the learning;

9. Spends time beyond the ordinary assignments or schedule on things that are of interest to him/her;

10. Knows about many things of which other children are unaware;

11. Is able to adapt learning to various situations somewhat unrelated in orientation;

12. Reasons out more problems since he/she recognizes relationships and comprehends meanings;

13. Analyzes quickly mechanical problems, puzzles, and trick questions;

14. Shows a high degree of originality and often uses good but unusual methods or ideas;

15. Possesses one or more special talents;

16. Is more adept in analyzing his/her own abilities, limitations, and problems;

17. Performs with more poise and can take charge of the situation;

18. Evaluates facts and arguments critically;

19. Has more emotional stability;

20. Can judge the abilities of others;

21. Has diverse, spontaneous, and frequently self-directed interests.

From French (1964, pp. 58–59)

Research on Identification of Creative Children

J. P. Guilford can be credited with the earliest programmatic investigations of creativity. Through elaborate experimental procedures, he devised a model of intellectual functioning in which different abilities were identified and reduced to specific components. Guilford proposed that intellectual ability could be understood in terms of several distinct intellectual operations. These include **convergent thinking,** which involves "thinking toward one right answer, or toward a relatively uniquely determined answer" (Guilford, 1959, p. 151). The term "convergent thinking" derives from the fact that intellectual operations converge on a predetermined correct answer, such as arriving at the solution of an arithmetic problem, completing a logical syllogism, or discovering the identity of the murderer in a mystery novel.

Another intellectual operation, **divergent thinking,** is "a type of thinking in which considerable searching about is done, and a number of answers will do" (Guilford, 1959, p. 151). This is the type of thinking a chef might use in trying to improve a recipe, or an architect might employ in trying to relate function, aesthetics, and cost in the design of an office building. Divergent thinking does not lead to a single, correct problem solution; rather, it opens up novel ways of conceiving the world, identifies new problems, and leads in directions that could not be predicted prior to the thinking itself. *Divergent thinking is the basis of creative problem solving.*

Guilford and his associates devised a number of measures to identify and study divergent thinking, and these have served as the mainspring for much subsequent investigation of creativity. However, though Guilford's research has had tremendous *heuristic* (research-producing) impact, subsequent research has not always supported the confidence researchers initially placed in the Guilford tests or structure of intellect theory. An extensive and thoughtful review of research using the Guilford structure of intellect model and related creativity tests was conducted by Wallach (1970). Examination of many studies

Creative individuals enjoy the challenge and intensity of projects that involve divergent thinking, in which "considerable searching about is done."

and reanalysis of the data from some prompted Wallach to conclude that, with the exception of ideational fluency, Guilford's so-called creativity tests do not really measure anything other than general intelligence as assessed by traditional IQ measures.

This conclusion has two important implications. First, there *is* an identifiable process distinguishable from general intellectual ability. This process may be described as *ideational fluency*, "the ability to generate—within a limited time—ideas that will fulfill particular requirements . . ." (Wallach, 1970, pp. 1213–14). Second, most of the conclusions and inferences of creativity research based on the Guilford model and tests are called into question. Much of this research has attempted to show that creativity is independent of intellectual ability and that creative individuals exhibit personality and intellectual characteristics different from the intellectually gifted. If indeed, as Wallach suggested, Guilford's tests measure much the same abilities as intelligence tests, then such distinctions must be viewed as artificial and, perhaps, meaningless.

Another important research tradition in the study of creativity has grown from the work of Getzels and Jackson (1962) in identifying creative children. Like Guilford, these investigators devised a number of techniques for identifying creative ability and based their research program on these techniques. For example, Getzels and Jackson asked subjects to give as many definitions as possible for common words such as "bark" or "bolt." Creative ability was inferred from the number of associations and the number of categories into which definitions could be grouped. Another of their tests was borrowed from Guilford and required subjects to think of as many uses as possible for an object (e.g., uses for a brick or a toothpick). Subjects producing many and unusual uses for these objects were viewed as creative. Getzels and Jackson believed that the ability to respond to tasks like these was independent of intellectual ability as measured by traditional intelligence tests.

On the basis of their research, Getzels and Jackson concluded that (a) at higher levels of intelligence, creativity and IQ are independent; (b) high-IQ students are better known and liked by their teachers than high-creativity students; (c) high-creativity students are less success oriented than their high-IQ counterparts; (d) high-creativity students are less socially conforming and more independent than high-IQ students.

However, these conclusions must be viewed as highly tentative on the basis of extensive technical criticism leveled at Getzels and Jackson's research methodology. Thorndike (1963) suggested that no clear evidence was presented indicating the independence of creativity measures from general intellectual ability. Cronbach (1962) pointed to the fact that the creativity tests had no external validation whatever. This means that there was no evidence to support the belief that they were measuring creativity except for the fact that Getzels and Jackson said they were. Wallach (1970) suggested that, since no evidence was produced to show that the creativity tests measured anything other than intelligence, it is reasonable to conclude that differences between high-IQ and high-creativity children stemmed from the fact that the so-called creativity tests were simply poor IQ tests that gave erroneous estimates of intelligence.

Despite these flaws, the Getzels and Jackson research has been important in highlighting the importance of creativity as a subject for investigation and in stimulating further research (Gallagher, 1966). One such study was that of Wallach and Kogan (1965). Using a sample of children with a broad range of intellectual ability, these researchers were able to demonstrate a clearer distinction between intelligence and creativity than had been previously shown. Comparing various combinations of intellectual and creative ability levels, these researchers confirmed some of the Getzels and Jackson findings regarding intellectual and personality characteristics. In the following section some of the personality characteristics that have repeatedly been observed in highly creative individuals will be discussed.

Before going on, however, it is important to emphasize that research is not an endeavor with clear beginnings and conclusions. As the above discussion has made clear, all conclusions must be viewed as tentative and subject to verification. This does not mean that action must always await certainty, but rather that a healthy skepticism is critically important for the student of behavior. Research findings must be used cautiously, but it is important that what is known be used in developing better educational programs for both gifted and creative children.

Characteristics of Creative Children

Bearing the above cautions in mind, a variety of characteristics of creative individuals have been observed in enough different contexts to warrant consideration.

Beyond a given minimum level of intelligence, creativity becomes important in contributing to an individual's academic performance (Wallach, 1970; Yamamoto, 1964). This minimum level of intelligence has frequently been specified as an IQ of 120 (e.g., Torrance, 1962b), the equivalent of superior intellectual ability. It also appears fairly certain that a critical component of what is termed creativity is the ability to produce large numbers of associations to a given fact, idea, or problem (Mednick, 1962; Wallach, 1970). By implication, it is evident that creativity becomes a characteristic that is only quantitatively different from person to person. That is, people can be viewed as more or less creative, but the processes underlying creativity are not categorically present or absent. They are present in all people to some degree.

Furthermore, it also seems likely that individuals can be assisted in developing ideational fluency (Mednick, Mednick, & Mednick, 1964; Mendelsohn & Griswold, 1964; Wallach, 1970). Put differently, this means that instructional sets or training can affect the extent of an individual's ability to produce creative responses.

With several research leads suggesting the possibility of distinguishing individuals exhibiting unusual creative abilities, a number of investigators have turned to the study of the personality of the creative person.

Torrance (1962a) identified 84 characteristics that have been attributed to the creative individual. Among others, these include adventuresomeness, altruism, disorderliness in habits, determination, strong convictions, independence in judgment, emotionality, a preference for being alone, a questioning attitude, self-assertiveness, a sense of humor, speculativeness, tenacity, versatility, and a willingness to take risks.

Taylor and Holland (1964) described the creative individual as more able to toy with ideas and to engage in fantasy than less creative peers. The creative person also has an ability to sense problems, a capacity to be puzzled, broadly diffused rather than focused attention, and a tendency to be verbally superficial.

The creative individual has been variously described as valuing a sense of humor (Gallagher, 1966), having wild or silly ideas (Torrance, 1962b), confident and self-acceptant (MacKinnon, 1962), self-aware (Torrance, 1962b), dominant, adventurous (Drevdahl & Cattell, 1958), and intuitive (Barron, 1963). Altogether, the picture that emerges is one of an individual who is highly competent intellectually as well as being socially aware, personally insightful, and highly ethical.

Obviously individuals with these qualities are highly valuable in any society. Though it is still unclear whether these personality characteristics emerge from creative abilities or whether they are the medium in which creativity flourishes, it is evident that creativity itself is valuable and should be fostered. Like intellectual giftedness, creativity is a valuable natural resource to be encouraged and developed.

DEVELOPMENTAL CONSEQUENCES

Despite controversy in many specific areas, it is a clear and unequivocal fact that gifted children—whether extremely intelligent or highly creative—are better equipped than most children to solve the inevitable problems that life poses. Nevertheless, gifted children do experience problems in living that can best be resolved through special educational programs or through professional intervention in the form of counseling or psychotherapy.

Like all children, unusually talented youngsters often confront issues that arouse deep anxiety. In some ways, the acute sensibilities of gifted children make them especially likely to experience the pain and anxiety that other children might more readily deny or repress. The social awareness and personal insight that characterize gifted children can also serve to intensify typical developmental problems stemming from relationships with parents, peers, and teachers.

Relationships with Parents

Parental relations may be problematic for the gifted child on several levels. Failure on the part of parents to recognize their child's exceptionality may lay the groundwork for a long series of frustrating experiences as they continue to treat the child according to chronological rather than mental age. This is not meant to imply that parents should treat the very bright child as though the youngster were several years older. On the contrary, the gifted child cannot escape the physical and emotional limits imposed by chronological age. Rather, adequate recognition of a child's abilities may help parents be sensitive to the peculiar frustrations that attend a marked age-ability discrepancy. For example, the youngster who is appropriately prohibited from some activities because of age may have difficulty recognizing the need for limits because of his/her clear comprehension of a situation. Parents need not yield in their responsibilities, but they might be well advised to be sensitive and to empathize with the child's frustration and resentment.

Parents must also remain aware that the articulate, clever, insightful youngster is, nevertheless, a child whose judgment may be influenced as much by shortsighted impulsiveness as any other youngster. The ability to "talk a good fight" does not mean the gifted child is really capable of assuming responsibilities that may be desired desperately. As in every other area of child-rearing, it is crucial for parents to try to develop a real knowledge of their child's abilities and limits, and then to give the child room to develop without abdicating their responsibility to set limits.

In some cases parents of gifted youngsters may resent the special abilities of their child (Gold, 1965). They may be envious of the child's abilities or they may perceive a conflict with and threat to their own value system in the child's abilities or independence. In such cases, professional counseling may be of help in resolving conflicts or, at least, in helping the child cope more adequately.

In other families, the parents may have pressing economic problems limiting their ability to maximize opportunities for their child. The family may need the direct assistance of the youngster in earning money or be unable financially to provide opportunities not available within the public school system. Some families may not even recognize the existence or importance of the child's gifts (see Case Study 10.1). This is particularly tragic since evidence indicates that early appropriate stimulation can improve intellectual functioning in culturally disadvantaged groups (Gallagher, 1966). Conversely, evidence

CASE STUDY 10.1

LARRY: THE BOY FROM VENUS

Larry, age 13, was brought for evaluation by his parents who were concerned about his unusual "habits." Upon examination it became clear that Larry's "habits" consisted of an extensive series of strong compulsive behaviors. Larry became anxious whenever he discovered an open doorway or open cabinet door. Prior to going to bed at night Larry had to touch each object in his bedroom and to stand facing in each direction. Larry also continually cleared his throat, though he attempted to be unobtrusive about this. He was extremely concerned that homework assignments be done perfectly and would rework an assignment several times until it was flawless. On

one occasion he succeeded in doing a perfect paper after several attempts and then accidentally spilled a soft drink on the paper. At this he flew into a rage, broke a lamp and kicked a hole through a wall before he regained control.

Larry's parents attempted to "help" him by trying to "break him of his habits." They would intentionally leave doors open and insist that he not touch them. They would ridicule him and try to convince him of the foolishness of his behavior. When they found that they could not succeed in helping Larry, they sought professional help.

Upon his first meeting with the psychologist, Larry related easily and spontaneously. A tall, slender, and handsome youngster, he was also physically awkward and always appeared to be surprised at finding his hands and feet where he did not expect them.

Larry spoke easily about his "habits." He was concerned about them and about the fact that he could not restrain himself from them. He recognized that he was chronically anxious and complained about having so many worries, ranging from his "habits" to social injustice in his community, tense international relations, and the arms race. Larry was also concerned about the fact that he had no real friends and found that most of his peers were unreliable, petty, and selfish. His attempts to make friends were pathetically awkward and painfully genuine. Larry plunged into the diagnostic and treatment procedures eagerly and curiously. Intellectual examination indicated that he had an IQ between 145 and 155.

In treatment, Larry made rapid progress in developing awareness of the relationship between his habits and periods of heightened anxiety. After several sessions Larry developed enough confidence in his therapist to make a startling admission. He felt he had originally been born on Venus and was currently living with a foster family here on earth! Exploration of this apparent delusion indicated that Larry did not really believe he was from another planet. Rather, he enjoyed fantasizing about a family from another planet that was far more sophisticated than his own blue-collar parents.

Though he loved his parents—was in fact rather dependent on them—Larry felt that they could not understand his interests, his ambitions to become a scientist, his concern about social problems. Factually, Larry's parents were poorly educated and had little understanding of his school experiences or his intellectual ability. By contrast, his "Venusian" family would understand thoroughly his interests in astronomy and chemistry, and he was sure that Venus did not have the kind of social problems that plague earthlings.

For a long period Larry was reluctant to give up his fantasy. However, as he entered high school, he found youngsters with a broader range of abilities, some of whom had interests similar to his own. He began to make friends and develop social confidence. He found his classes interesting and threw himself enthusiastically into his studies. Discussion of his experiences in therapy helped Larry recognize that his compulsions were ways of dealing with anxiety and that desperate isolation from family and peers had given rise to his intricate fantasy about a Venusian family. As he developed greater confidence, Larry was less chronically anxious. He gradually developed greater assertiveness and confidence and slowly began to relinquish his "habits." Therapy was terminated on a timetable set up by Larry. A Christmas card received a year after termination indicated that Larry was making a good adjustment.

---

also indicates a progressive deterioration of functioning in the absence of adequate environmental stimulation (Deutsch & Brown, 1964).

Relationships with Peers

Peer relations can also be a source of problems for highly intelligent or creative youngsters. For the most part, gifted children are popular and socially adept. Nevertheless, the gifted child is typically several years in advance of age-mates in intellectual development and interests. Such a discrepancy can easily lead to problems in interpersonal relations, particularly during pre-adolescent and adolescent years when group pressures for conformity are at a peak.

It is all too easy for the bright or creative youngster to alienate peers in an eagerness to demonstrate unusual abilities. The gifted youngster may experience intense conflicts between a sense of integrity and a highly developed personal ethical system on the one hand, and a desperate desire to be liked and accepted on the other. One unfortunate resolution of this conflict that is occasionally selected is an attempt to hide special abilities and talents behind a mask of mediocrity.

Relationships with Teachers

Surprisingly, many of the problems arising from parental and peer relations are combined in the gifted child's experiences with teachers. Like parents, teachers may impose expectations and demands that are incongruent with the child's ability level. Teachers, particularly, are prone to experiencing personal gratification in a student's achievements. This is one of the rewards of teaching. However, in those cases where teacher gratification takes precedence over the child's developmental interests, then the situation is amiss. Adequate teacher training can help forestall this kind of problem.

In some situations, teacher attitudes toward the gifted may be negative. The gifted child may pose a threat to the teacher who feels insecure intellectually. Searching questions, refusal to be satisfied with platitudes, incessant curiosity may all serve as irritants to a teacher who is unsure of the answers or uncomfortable admitting ignorance. In such cases the child may be discouraged from asking questions, put off with inadequate answers, chided for being arrogant or immodest, and even ridiculed (Thomas, 1973).

In an interesting study Jacobs (1972) assessed teacher attitudes toward the gifted. As a first step in developing an attitude assessment instrument, he selected a number of statements regarding gifted youngsters and presented them to a variety of subjects. He first compared the responses of teachers of gifted children with the responses of a group of high-school dropouts, assuming that dropout attitudes would be more negative. He found this to be the case. However, when comparing the attitudes of teachers of the gifted, high-school dropouts, and then all kindergarten and first-grade teachers of an entire school district, he came to the remarkable conclusion that the attitudes of kindergarten and first-grade teachers were more similar to those of high-school dropouts than to those of teachers of the gifted. According to Jacobs, gifted children arouse as much discomfort as do retarded and other special children. The question remains, however, Why do the gifted arouse resentment? No clear answers exist to this question but it is likely that some combination of distorted stereotypes, misunderstanding, suspicion, envy, and even fear make it difficult for many people to understand or empathize with gifted and creative children. After all, special education for the gifted is simply another case of the "rich getting richer." The fact that all our lives are enriched by the wise use of talent is difficult to demonstrate concretely.

Regardless of reasons, the gifted child may be confronted with lack of understanding, demands that are too low or too high, and resultant conflict and anxiety. Yet these problems all exist at a personal level, and there is some possibility that the gifted youngster—by definition a talented problem solver—can work out alternative ways of coping and satisfaction.

There is little the youngster can do, however, to cope with an educational system that persists in its refusal to develop adequate programming. Fortunately, a few attempts have been made at developing creative programming for creative and bright children. Though educational programs for the gifted are far from adequate in availability, scope, imagination, or public commitment, options do exist that are worth reviewing.

EDUCATIONAL INTERVENTION

Recognition of the need for special intervention and educational approaches unique to the needs of gifted children has led to a variety of program innovations. Some of these involve little modification of the regular school program. Others require major administrative and organizational changes along with implementation of curricular innovations. In every case the question of primary importance must be, Do the gifted benefit from special educational provisions? An expensive program without significant outcomes is worthless. Minor innovations leading to substantial changes in scope and rate of learning can be critically important. As in most other areas, the evidence suggests that quality programming is expensive, but positive outcomes in student motivation and commitment to learning justify the support required.

Enrichment

Probably the least expensive and most prevalent intervention mode employed in the education of gifted and talented children is enrichment. Basically, **enrichment** consists of providing special materials and/or activities designed specifically for children who can master the regular curriculum at an accelerated pace.

Individual attention and guidance can do much to foster a gifted child's growth.

Specific enrichment activities may take a variety of forms. One of those that often occurs in the absence of any formalized program is an increased amount of individualized attention to the gifted student. Because such children can be rewarding students, some teachers become invested in their intellectual development, sharing interests, suggesting readings, and discussing abstract issues. In many ways this kind of relationship is almost ideal in that it replicates a traditional master-apprentice relationship in which knowledge is transmitted, questions and curiosity are encouraged, intellectual commitment is developed, rewards are personal and immediate, and ethical values and personal qualities are modeled.

Gallagher (1966, 1975) suggested that *enrichment activities should assist the student in learning to relate and evaluate facts and ideas, to think originally, to work through complex problems and issues, and to apply understanding to new situations and new people.* A good student-teacher relationship can meet all these objectives. This is especially true in situations where the teacher is explicitly aware of the student's ability and has administrative support in enriching the student's school experience.

Unfortunately, these ideals are often impeded by the realities of the classroom situation, with demands on teacher time and resources. Often there is little administrative support or recognition for teacher efforts, and, in fact, special efforts to work with gifted children may produce accusations of favoritism. Further, there is no systematic way of ensuring that the teacher's abilities and interests match those of the student.

The same sort of relationship can occur in more formalized enrichment programs. Where these exist they typically involve provisions for the availability of challenging materials; encouraging the student to assume responsibility in the classroom and in the school at large; encouraging hobby and interest development; extracurricular activities such as clubs, field trips, and science experiments; and use of individual and small group projects.

Unfortunately, many enrichment programs appear to be largely well-meant exhortations and do not include specific curricular modifications for the gifted. Instead, they "encourage" and "provide opportunities." In evaluating the substance of an enrichment program Kough (1960) suggested that every classroom teacher in a school should (a) be able to identify the gifted children in his/her classroom, (b) be able to identify the specific enrichment activities available for each child, and (c) have available resource persons trained in the education of gifted children for consultation.

Research on the outcomes of enrichment activities does not yield clear evidence in support of such programs (Marland, 1972). This is not to imply that such programs be abandoned. On the contrary, there is often little more available for the gifted. Rather, the teacher must clearly recognize that responsibility for implementation of enrichment activities is almost completely a function of teacher time, energy, interest, and patience.

Ability Grouping

Ability grouping is a self-explanatory concept and simply refers to removal of gifted children from heterogeneous classroom settings to classrooms composed of children with similar ability levels. In some cases, grouping may be done within the self-contained classroom with independent groups of students working at different rates of progress.

Examining the latter option first, it does not appear that grouping within the classroom is particularly effective (Marland, 1972). Often it means no more than more work at the same level rather than horizontal enrichment of the curriculum or actual acceleration of learning.

The special classroom provides opportunities for actual acceleration and horizontal expansion of the curriculum. Thus, if a student has completed material on the geography of a region ahead of classmates, the teacher may work with the student on subsequent units or expand his/her experiences horizontally with study of the history, social customs, famous people, or traditions of the region. The special classroom also provides greater likelihood that enrichment activities will really occur, since the teacher's time is not devoted to a variety of planning responsibilities at different levels.

Ability grouping may take several forms. Ability groups may be constituted on either a full- or a part-time basis. Criteria for selection of students may relate to overall intellectual ability or to a specific aptitude such as science or music or literature. Grouping may occur within a single school if enrollment is large, or students from several schools may be transported to a single school within a district. Special groups may meet during regular school hours, or they may meet on an extracurricular basis. It is interesting to note, incidentally, that gifted students do not appear to mind extra meetings outside of school hours for enrichment activities (Musgrove & Estroff, 1976–77).

Probably more than any other educational modification for the gifted,

Science classes are but one area in which creativity can be promoted as pupils work toward analyzing relationships and seeking possible solutions.

ability grouping has aroused considerable controversy. For the most part, arguments do not stem from a firm basis in research but rather reflect the interests, opinions, and biases of educators, parents, and the public. While many specific arguments have been advanced both pro and con in relation to ability grouping (Hildreth, 1966), most of these reduce to two basic issues. On the positive side, special ability grouping provides the gifted student with more opportunities, challenges, teacher competence and attention, peer stimulation, and independence. On the negative side, special ability grouping is seen as fostering elitism, parental pressure, and limited contacts with normally functioning students.

The ultimate arbitrator of such controversy should always be the research evidence that has been accumulated. In the case of ability grouping, however, research does not provide clear guidelines. On the basis of her review of research in this area, Hildreth (1966) concluded that ability grouping appears to produce "slightly greater academic achievement in comparison with instruction of the bright in regular classes" and as yet has produced no evidence of "any lasting harmful effects" (p. 320). However, this is hardly an enthusiastic endorsement of special classrooms and special schools for the gifted. The critical variables in effective education remain the skilled teacher and an imaginative curriculum. Nevertheless, grouping of gifted students can maximize the effects of teacher and curriculum by permitting greater flexibility and more time for planning, individualized attention, greater depth of study, and promotion of creativity.

Acceleration

A third widely used option for providing better education for the gifted youngster is **acceleration.** Most people are familiar with acceleration in the form of "grade skipping" in which a bright child is promoted beyond the grade level appropriate to chronological age. The major objection to this practice has been the fact that grade skipping places the gifted youngster with other children who are physically, emotionally, and socially more mature. To some extent, at least, this is a specious argument, since the bright child also tends, on the whole, to be more advanced in these spheres as well.

Acceleration can maximize a student's intellectual potential, maintain interest and motivation, permit earlier entrance to high school, college, or graduate studies and earlier embarkation on a career, and be fiscally sound, since acceleration results in the savings of large sums of money. Reviewing the research on acceleration, a number of investigators agreed that there is no evidence of negative effects either intellectually, socially, or emotionally from moderate educational acceleration of the gifted (Cutts & Mosely, 1957; Durr, 1964; Gallagher, 1966; Gold, 1965; Terman & Oden, 1947). Exhibit 10.3 summarizes various educational alternatives for the gifted.

Promoting Creativity

In addition to specific program modifications to match educational experiences to the abilities of very bright students, a number of suggestions have

EXHIBIT 10.3

299
Educational
intervention

EDUCATIONAL ALTERNATIVES FOR THE GIFTED

1. *Early admission:* The unusually bright youngster may be admitted to kindergarten, first grade, high school, or college prior to reaching the usual chronological age for admission.

2. *Acceleration:* The bright youngster may be allowed to skip grades or be double promoted. In ungraded classes the child may proceed at his/her own pace. At the secondary level, the adolescent may be allowed to take a heavier than normal course load or to take summer courses.

3. *Enrichment:* The gifted child in the regular or special classroom may be given opportunities to use special materials or to do special projects. Enrichment may be horizontal, exposing the child to a wider than usual variety of materials related to the topic of study; or there may be vertical enrichment, providing greater depth and intensity of study.

4. *Ability grouping:* Special classes or special schools may be developed to group bright students together, thereby permitting greater realization of the child's potentials.

5. *Special extracurricular programs:* These programs may be organized after school hours, on Saturdays, or during the summer, and they may take the form of workshops, seminars, and special projects (such as publishing a newspaper).

6. *Advanced placement:* Many colleges now permit students to demonstrate competency in required areas by means of examination or review of credentials. Some colleges have cooperative arrangements whereby students may earn college credits while still in high school.

7. *Independent study:* A bright student may opt to work in an area of interest under the supervision of a teacher. Together, they map out an area of investigation, and the student then pursues the study with minimal contact with the instructor. This may take a variety of forms, ranging from musical or artistic productions to scientific experimentation.

8. *Itinerant teachers:* The itinerant teacher with special training in education of the gifted may spend some time working with gifted groups in several schools throughout a district, or the teacher may assume the role of consultant to the classroom teachers or to school administrators.

9. *Seminars:* A single school or a district may organize periodic seminars bringing gifted students together with specially trained teachers or experts in a specified field.

10. *Community sponsors:* Interested individuals may be recruited from the community to work with students who have expressed interest and talent in the area of the sponsor's expertise.

Adapted from Educational Research Service (1975, pp. 5–7)

been offered that are specifically directed toward promoting creativity in the classroom. Unlike enrichment, ability grouping, or acceleration, these ideas are typically framed in terms relating to classroom practices and teacher techniques. For example, one manual for teachers of primary grade children emphasizes the importance of stimulating the child's awareness of the sensory environment and asking questions about experiences rather than providing information and answers (Castro Valley School District, 1963). Other suggestions derive from an analysis by Wallas (1926) that divides the creative process into stages of (a) preparation, (b) incubation, (c) illumination, and (d) verification. This scheme recognizes that a period of observation and incorporation

OPEN ISSUE

Are special educational programs for the gifted really necessary? In view of the pressing needs of physically, intellectually, and emotionally impaired children, is it not wiser and more humane to devote limited resources to the care of these special children? After all, gifted and creative children are better able to cope with inadequacies in the educational system than any other group of youngsters. Chances are good that they will achieve adequately regardless of whether special programs are provided for them.

On the other hand, gifted and creative children may be viewed as a precious natural resource to be developed and used in finding ways to improve the quality of life for all. Viewed in this way, perhaps the wisest use of limited financial resources is to use them to foster and enhance the development of intellectually and creatively talented youngsters, for it is precisely these individuals who may ultimately develop the medical, psychological, and educational techniques and approaches that will prevent or minimize the handicapping effects of developmental disabilities.

These issues may be reduced to a single basic question: What is the wisest allocation of wealth and resources within the context of our educational system? Should we devote monies and energy primarily to care for those who are disabled, or should we also be careful to invest a significant portion of our resources in the future development of human services through programs for the gifted? To date, the question remains open to debate.

must precede creative output. Subsequently, incorporated knowledge is processed outside of direct awareness until the individual appears rather suddenly to perceive the solution to a problem. This is the familiar "Aha!" or "Eureka!" experience.

Creative work inevitably requires a laborious process of verification. The implications of this analysis include an awareness on the part of the teacher that the child needs exposure to a wide variety of experiences along with encouragement to analyze those experiences on a personal level. In addition to providing an environment rich in stimulation, the teacher must also permit the developing child latitude and flexibility in organizing and understanding experiences. *The child will need time to reflect, to fantasize, and to play with ideas in an atmosphere of openness and acceptance.* As the child develops creative insights and ideas, the teacher must be prepared to acknowledge and reward these with enthusiastic interest and encouragement. Finally, the teacher can, by example, foster the self-discipline the child will need in order to evaluate and apply newfound ideas and insights.

In a provocative analysis, Moustakas (1967) suggested that these very experiences are often undervalued in contemporary society and missing from the creative child's educational experiences. Freedom in following areas of interest is often restricted in deference to a lesson plan or schedule or to rigid curricular requirements. Children are often discouraged—both by society and by the teachers who implement its standards—from exploring their own internal experiences. Introspection is little valued. Desensitization to oneself and others occurs in deference to requirements for conformity and efficiency. In such a context, creativity must wither.

Perhaps more than any other investigator, E. Paul Torrance has attempted to provide parents and educators with ideas and suggestions to stimulate creative thinking in the home and in the classroom (1962, 1963). Torrance suggested that teachers can and should provide opportunities for creative behavior through the kinds of questions asked, the kinds of projects assigned, the problems posed for discussion, and the provision of latitude for individually initiated experiments and learning projects. Torrance further suggested that teachers learn to be genuinely respectful of unusual questions and ideas, but also to create "thorns in the flesh" for students by highlighting inconsistencies, disturbing elements, and defects in traditional thinking. Finally, the teacher must be willing to forestall criticism or evaluation of creative work.

Perhaps even more important than specific techniques, however, is the attitude the teacher brings to the classroom of the gifted child. Genuine learning and creativity can only occur in an atmosphere of tolerance, openness, and mutual respect.

SUMMARY

1. Gifted children were defined as those children who show outstanding ability or talent in a variety of areas, including general intelligence, specific aptitudes, creativity, leadership, artistic ability or athletic talent, and who have been so identified by professionally qualified individuals.

2. Identification of gifted children should be done on the basis of individualized assessment procedures by professionally qualified personnel.

3. Contrary to popular stereotypes, gifted children are emotionally well-adjusted, socially skillful, physically healthy, and psychologically mature.

4. Creativity is a capacity to restructure the world in unusual conceptual terms. Various researchers have discussed this capacity in terms of ideational fluency, originality, and divergent thinking.

5. Creative children tend to be adventuresome, altruistic, emotional, private, assertive, humorous, and flexible.

6. Gifted and creative children occasionally develop problems in relation to teachers, parents, and peers because of their unusual abilities and related personality characteristics.

7. Special educational programs for the gifted often take the form of enrichment programs, ability grouping, and acceleration.

8. Fostering of creative talent is often a matter of individual encouragement on the part of invested and understanding teachers.

PART FOUR

Children with Emotional and Behavioral Differences

CHAPTER ELEVEN

Children with Personality Problems

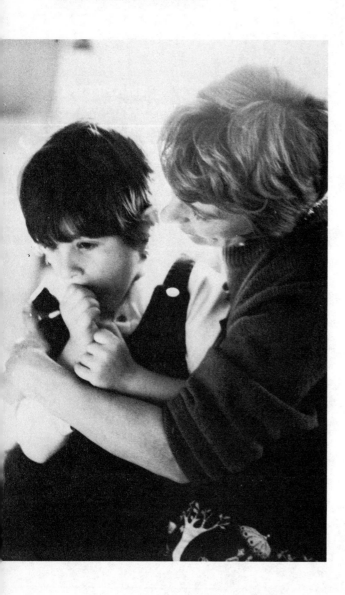

Methought I walked a dismal place
  Dim horrors all around;
The air was thick with many a face,
  And black as night the ground.

I saw a monster come with speed,
  Its face of grimmliest green,
On human beings used to feed,
  Most dreadful to be seen.

I could not speak, I could not fly,
  I fell down in that place,
I saw the monster's horrid eye
  Come leering in my face!

Amidst my scarcely-stifled groans,
  Amidst my moanings deep,
I heard a voice, "Wake! Mr. Jones,
  You're screaming in your sleep!"

Lewis Carroll, "Horrors" (1850)

THE MYTH OF THE HAPPY CHILD

Adults delight in speaking of childhood as a carefree time of life, and many look back longingly to a period in which their only concerns were play, toys, and holidays. Pressed by daily concerns about work problems, financial pressures, marital tensions, and difficulty in finding satisfaction and contentment, many view childhood with wistful nostalgia and children with envy.

In fact, such idyllic childhoods exist only in adult imagination. Realistic recollection must include more than dimly remembered play and toys, and childhood is at least as often a period of anxiety, tension, awkwardness, anger, guilt, and confusion. Childhood is a period of eager anticipation, yes. But it is also a period of fearful apprehension. It is a time of buoyant confidence, but also a time of feeling miserably inadequate and dependent. It is a time of growing assertiveness, but also a time of guilty suppression of anger and jealousy. Childhood truly is a time of play and toys, but just as surely a time of fearful monsters, murky dangers, and horrors.

It is critically important to balance nostalgic images with less pleasant reality in order to be really able to understand and empathize with the experiences of children. Without such balance it is easy to develop distorted conceptions of childhood that lead to misunderstanding and confusion about the things children feel and the things they do.

Misconceptions about childhood can have a number of undesirable consequences. In some cases, the myth of the happy child may prompt parents to feel resentment about their own childhood experiences if they were less than idyllic, and they may then attempt, vicariously, to achieve satisfaction by ensuring that their own children will never experience the fears or resentment they felt. In other cases, adult myths about childhood may lead to excessive anxiety as parents note that their children do not seem to be as happy and carefree as they "should." The mythology of childhood just as easily extends to many professionals as well, so that classroom teachers, physicians, and psychologists might easily become concerned about "symptoms" that may be no more than reflections of the normal tensions of development. While it is clearly important to recognize and treat developing problems as quickly as possible, professionals less often realize that premature diagnosis and treatment can have negative effects.

Iatrogenic Disorders

Unrealistic concern for a child's happiness can lead to iatrogenic disorders. Literally, an *iatrogenic disorder* is a problem that is produced by efforts to prevent or treat a presumed or actual disorder or disease. Specifically in relation to special children, iatrogenic disorders may arise from premature diagnostic labeling or attempts at treatment (Stuart, 1970). For example, a transient tensional outlet such as rocking behavior in a youngster may lead to a search for other "symptoms" and subsequently to a "diagnosis." The outcome of such efforts may be anything but desirable if adults then begin to view the child as "disturbed" and in need of "treatment." Parental anxiety is then created or intensified, and normal parental reactions may become stilted and artificial as parents fear doing or saying the wrong thing. Classroom teachers and other adults may become sensitized to any unusual behaviors. Eventually the child may begin to develop some awareness that things are amiss, and adult anxieties may become the spur for the child to develop a concept of self as different or inadequate.

Research Evidence and the Mythical Happy Child

The sequence of events outlined above is not at all farfetched or unlikely. The fact is that during the course of normal development, most children exhibit a variety of behaviors that, under appropriate circumstances, could be considered characteristic of disturbed development. Studies by Rema LaPouse and Mary Monk (1958, 1964) have clearly indicated that a variety of behaviors traditionally viewed as indicative of emotional disturbance occur in large numbers of children. These investigators studied the behavior of nearly 500 children, ages 6 to 12, randomly selected from the population of Buffalo, New York. Interviews with the mothers of these children revealed that more than 40 percent of the children exhibited seven or more fears and worries. Bedwetting was reported in 17 percent of the children; 28 percent experienced nightmares; nearly 50 percent were described as overactive.

These data might lead one to conclude that Buffalo has an unusually large number of disturbed children or that emotional disturbances in children are of epidemic proportions. However, analyses of their data led LaPouse and Monk to conclude that "increased age is associated with a decreased prevalence of behavior deviations in school-aged children. This is consistent with the thesis that such deviations occur as transient developmental phenomena" (1964, p. 446).

In a similar study, John Werry and Herbert Quay (1971) attempted to obtain prevalence rates for behavior commonly found in child guidance clinic populations. These investigators asked teachers to report on the behavior of 926 boys and 864 girls, virtually the entire kindergarten through second-grade population in Urbana, Illinois. Werry and Quay obtained findings similar to those reported by others, indicating that symptoms of emotional disturbance are quite high in the general population and, therefore, of limited diagnostic utility when applied without other criteria. For example, nearly 23 percent of the boys in this study exhibited odd or bizarre behavior; nearly 50 percent were restless and unable to sit still; 39 percent were self-conscious and easily embarrassed; 46 percent were annoying and disruptive; 23 percent were tense and unable to relax. Among the girls in this sample, 39 percent were easily embarrassed and self-conscious; 41 percent were shy and bashful; 33 percent lacked self-confidence; 32 percent were hypersensitive and easily hurt; 17 percent were anxious and generally fearful.

In a somewhat different vein, David Bauer (1976) conducted a study of changes in children's fears with increasing age. Fearfulness is often used as a criterion of emotional disturbance, and Bauer's study is of interest here because reanalysis of his data indicates that randomly selected groups of kindergartners, second-graders, and sixth-graders all exhibit a surprisingly high number of fears. Specifically, of a total of 54 children interviewed, 39 percent reported a fear of bodily injury; 43 percent reported fears of monsters and ghosts; 50 percent reported bedtime fears; and 65 percent reported frightening dreams.

Taken together, studies such as these indicate clearly that the "myth of the happy child" is indeed a myth. Many children experience a variety of fears and worries; many exhibit behavior that is problematic for themselves and/or irritating to others. Nevertheless, most children do outgrow these behaviors. Before deciding that any individual child is in need of treatment, it is critically important to develop and employ a variety of criteria that converge to indicate that a problem *really* exists.

Indiscriminate diagnosis and treatment of what may only be transient developmental phenomena are just as dangerous in their potential to produce iatrogenic disorders as is the denial of problems that really do exist.

DEFINITION AND CLASSIFICATION

In view of the fact that many behaviors traditionally viewed as symptomatic of personality or conduct disorders occur in normally developing children, how, then, does one recognize situations in which there is genuine cause for concern and intervention? There is no simple answer to this question. Inevitably, the decision that a given child exhibits problems warranting professional intervention is a difficult one for parent or teacher. In many cases, diagnosis presents problems for the psychologist or psychiatrist as well. There are several reasons for the difficulties that exist in deciding that the behavior of a child is abnormal.

For one thing, children do not often have an awareness of the possibility that what they are experiencing may differ from the experiences of others. Piaget has aptly termed this inability to adopt different frames of reference "egocentricity." Thus, on a subjective level, the disturbed child may simply have no awareness that personal experiences are unusual, and therefore no awareness that help is either needed or available.

At the same time, younger children typically do not have adequate verbal labels for internal experiences. Without such labels, the child is unable to describe subjectively felt anxiety, depression, or resentment. Complicating matters still further, in many cases the problem in question is one that others have in dealing with the child rather than subjectively felt discomfort. This is particularly true of disorders in which the child behaves destructively or exhibits aggression toward others. It is not uncommon in such cases that the child even actively resists attempts to help. Yet another problem stems from the fact that behavior is continually changing during the course of development and, as noted previously, many symptomatic behaviors are no more than transient tensional outlets. To all these difficulties one may further add the wide variability in rates of development, broad time ranges for the achievement of developmental tasks, and wide variance in the kinds of behavior that are accepted or encouraged depending on sociocultural background and economic status. Finally, it is also important to recognize that the decision that a given child is exhibiting genuinely disturbed behavior is also a function of prevailing diagnostic systems that contain many inherent weaknesses and are subject to wide variation in interpretation. The decision that a child is developing abnormally is a difficult one, indeed.

Criteria for Recognizing Personality Problems

Despite the many difficulties mentioned above, some guidelines have been developed that form the basis of clinical judgments regarding the interpretation of symptomatic behavior. Typically, such guides have evolved empirically in clinical practice and do not have clear-cut foundations in research. Nevertheless, the teacher or clinical specialist can make better recommendations and decisions regarding referral or treatment by considering symptoms within the context of the child's total developmental pattern.

Taken together, a number of criteria constitute a broad definition of personality problems or, as they have been traditionally termed, **neuroses.** The critical consideration in evaluating symptomatic behavior is the *overall direction* of a child's development (A. Freud, 1965). That is, a given behavior or series of behaviors may be indicative of genuine disturbance if it occurs within the context of slowed developmental progress or overall regression in the child's adaptive capacities. Occasional disruptive behavior, however, within the context of adequate developmental progress and social adjustment need not create undue alarm in parent or teacher.

In addition, Kessler (1972) suggested several more specific criteria helpful in diagnosing the existence of a problem. The *frequency* of a given behavior that is disruptive or disturbing should be evaluated. An occasional nightmare does not warrant the alarm that would be appropriate in the case of sleep disturbances occurring several times a week. The *age of the child* in relation to the symptoms must be considered. Frequent sleep disturbances in a 2 or 3 year old are not as likely indicative of a problem as they are in an 11 or 12 year old. Another factor to be considered is the *number of symptoms* the child exhibits. The more symptoms, the more likely it is that a pervasive and serious problem exists. Some symptoms, of course, create more social problems than others, and the *degree of social disadvantage* occasioned by the symptoms should be carefully examined. Fear of dark rooms may be problematic, but a fear of going outside the home without mother's presence is obviously incapacitating. The degree of subjective discomfort reported by the child is also a factor warranting consideration. Though it is often difficult to assess accurately, careful observation and conversation with the child should provide some indication of the *amount of subjective anxiety or unhappiness* the child feels. In fact, it may be more useful to think of the child's discomfort in terms of the degree of happiness–unhappiness rather than in terms of internal conflict, ambivalence, or various other clinical concepts (Shaw, 1966). Kessler also suggested consideration of the difficulty encountered in changing the behavior in question. If a symptom is extremely *resistant to efforts at producing change,* or if it persists long after age-appropriate disappearance, chances are it will reflect the existence of problems warranting professional intervention.

Classification of Personality Problems

In contemporary psychology and psychiatry, the terms "personality problem" and "neurosis" are often loosely defined and mean little more than the commonly used notion of "emotional disturbance." At the same time, however, several formal classification systems—for example, the DSM-II of the American Psychiatric Association (1968) and the 1966 proposed classification system of the Group for the Advancement of Psychiatry (GAP)—have been developed that offer a variety of distinctions among these broad diagnostic categories. As a result of varying usage, it is often difficult for the nonprofessional to understand the bases of distinction among different diagnostic categories or the implications of different terms. Problems with terminology and classification also plague professionals and interfere with clear communication and mutual understanding. Briefly, the development of an adequate diagnostic nomenclature has been a longstanding problem in child mental health. Consider the following example:

> *A child is referred to a mental health specialist because of poor academic performance despite high potential as indicated by aptitude or achievement tests. Upon investigation it becomes apparent that this youngster*

has a long history of nocturnal enuresis (bed-wetting), fear of the dark, and apprehensions about being separated from the parents. Additionally, the investigator notes a longstanding history of bronchial asthma. In interviewing the child, it appears that there is a tendency for the youngster to be overly compliant and dependent on the interviewer, and this pattern of dependency is confirmed by the parents who also note that the child spends most of the time watching television and appears to be fearful of engaging in competitive games or interactions with other children.

The complex of symptoms described here is typical of many youngsters in that disturbances of functioning appear in several different areas and give an impression of pervasive maladjustment. Depending on the theoretical orientation of the diagnostician, the relative severity of the various symptoms, parental acceptance of particular kinds of behavior as "normal" or "abnormal," and the concerns of those making the referral, diagnostic decisions may take any of several forms.

If the sleep disturbance, fear, and general apprehensiveness are emphasized, then a consideration of "psychoneurotic disorder, anxiety type" would be appropriate, since subjectively experienced anxiety is the major characteristic of neurotic disorders (Kaplan, 1971). Such a diagnosis would reflect the view that sleep disturbances and fearfulness are direct expressions of intense, subjectively experienced anxiety. Generally, intense, free-floating anxiety or anxiety in conjunction with specific symptomatic features characterizes "neurotic" disorders.

However, if the diagnostician focused on the longstanding passive and dependent behavior as more important aspects of the child's functioning, a diagnosis of "personality disorder, overly dependent personality" (Group for the Advancement of Psychiatry, 1966) would be a possible diagnostic classification. The use of the term "personality disorder" implies a pattern of adjustment in which anxiety is not quite as prominent a feature as in neuroses. Instead, the child develops coping strategies that minimize anxiety, but do so at the expense of assertive, independent behavior. Crystallized symptoms may not be as evident, but the child appears to be immature, behaving in such a fashion that satisfactions and mature development are limited.

If the asthmatic attacks appear to be prominent in the child's development, the diagnostician might consider a diagnosis of "psychophysiological disorder, respiratory type." Finally, focusing on bed-wetting as a primary problem could lead to a diagnosis of "special symptom, enuresis."

It is important to recognize that these diagnostic possibilities do not have any necessary implications regarding the competence of the diagnostician, the nature of the disorder, or the best course of treatment. Rather, the classification systems reflect a long history of clinical experience and a tendency to structure thinking within familiar categories.

Does available research evidence support this traditional usage?

Research Evidence on Diagnostic Categories

As early as 1946, Hewitt and Jenkins reported that examination of case records and statistical analyses revealed only three major symptom clusters in disturbed children, which they termed "socialized delinquency," "unsocialized aggressive behavior," and "overly-inhibited behavior." Somewhat later Himmelweit (1953) concluded that his research on symptom patterns warranted only two broad diagnostic categories termed "conduct problems" and "personality problems." These early studies implied that there was sufficient variability and overlap in the symptom patterns exhibited by disturbed children that attempts to distinguish more than two or three broad categories lead to artificial distinctions and an unfounded complexity in available classification systems.

More recently, Peterson (1961) had 28 teachers rate the behaviors of 831 kindergarten and elementary-school children. Peterson used normal children because of his interest in obtaining a large sample of subjects and justified this

Children with personality problems are characteristically withdrawn and apprehensive. Special efforts to calm their anxiety and draw them out of themselves are important first steps in helping such children.

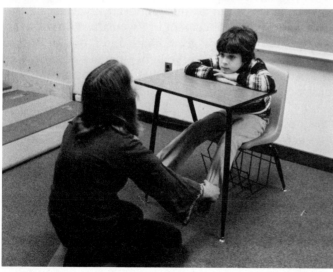

sample selection on the basis of the assumption that nonorganic and non-psychotic disorders are simply extremes of behavior found in most normal children. Peterson analyzed teacher ratings and decided that his results warranted the use of two broad diagnostic categories: a "conduct problem" category—in which impulses are expressed to the dismay of others in the child's environment—and a "personality problem" category—in which impulses are inhibited, and the child exhibits anxiety and subjective "suffering."

Quay, Morse, and Cutler (1966) asked teachers to rate the behaviors of 441 children in public-school classes for the emotionally disturbed. Using the problem-behavior rating scale developed by Peterson (1961) as a basis for teacher ratings, these investigators felt that three factors adequately described their population. One of these, "conduct problems," included such behaviors as defiance, irritability, impertinence, and boisterousness. A second factor, "inadequacy-immaturity," included such behaviors as laziness, dislike for school, sluggishness, and poor attentiveness. A third factor was similar in composition to "personality problems" as described by earlier investigators. Children exhibiting personality problems tended to be self-conscious and to feel inadequate, inferior, and anxious; they were fearful, shy, and depressed.

Achenbach (1966) recorded symptoms and biographical data from case histories of 300 male and 300 female children exhibiting psychiatric problems. Analysis of his data led him to subsume most behaviors in his sample of children under two major factors, "externalizing" and "internalizing" behaviors. Externalizers exhibited such behaviors as disobedience, lying, stealing, fighting, truancy, sexual delinquency, quarrelsomeness, inadequate guilt feelings, and destructiveness. Internalizing children tended to show nausea, pains, headaches, phobias, stomachaches, fearfulness, obsessions, nightmares, shyness, crying, depression, worrisomeness, self-consciousness, and withdrawal.

In reviewing these and other studies, Wolff (1971) concluded that complex diagnostic systems broken down into specific symptom syndromes were inadequate because of the amount of variability and overlap in the behavior of real children. Overall, the weight of evidence militates against the use of traditional diagnostic systems such as that of the American Psychiatric Association and that of the Group for the Advancement of Psychiatry. Such systems do not accurately reflect the behavior of any given child, and they can lead to preconceived notions of educational and psychotherapeutic remediation. Their persistence is explained largely by the fact that they are familiar and comfortable. Yet one must question whether this is adequate justification for their continued use.

The approach to diagnosis and classification that we will take is that suggested by empirical research. In this chapter we will discuss personality problems in children, and we will subsume under this heading problems that have traditionally been classified as childhood neuroses, psychophysiologic disorders, and special symptoms. The key to understanding children with these problems is the recognition that, among a diversity of symptoms, there is an undercurrent of anxiety, inhibition, apprehension, depression, and internalization. In Chapter 12 we will examine conduct disorders and aggression characterized by externalization.

The decision to ignore traditional terminology and classifications is important in breaking down theoretical conceptions that do not conform to the behavior of real children. However, it also creates significant difficulties in developing realistic estimates of the incidence of personality problems.

As we noted previously, some behaviors falling within the broad category of personality problems occur in as many as 50 percent of young children. However, if we were to apply the various criteria for distinguishing personality problems from transient developmental phenomena, these figures would be considerably reduced. While the specific behaviors might not be "normal," the child exhibiting them would, nevertheless, be developing normally. Thus, the research of Peterson, LaPouse and Monk, and others do not help in estimating the incidence of personality problems, since they are based on normally developing youngsters.

Using data based on the traditional category of psychoneurosis, estimates have been made that between 8 and 10 percent of children seen in various treatment settings would fit within this category (Rosen, Bahn, & Kramer, 1964). However, this estimate is derived from observations of children observed in clinical settings and is not really applicable to the general population. Furthermore, the category of psychoneurosis is too narrow and would exclude some personality problems. The Joint Commission on the Mental Health of Children (1970) estimated that between 8 and 10 percent of the children in this country exhibit "emotional problems," but though this estimate is applicable to all children, it is too inclusive and would encompass several groups of children in addition to those with personality problems. Even an estimate by the Bureau of Education (Craig, 1976) that 2 percent of school-age children exhibit problems of sufficient severity to warrant professional intervention is not really helpful, since it includes only children in school, and only those whose problems are so severe that special educational attention is needed. What is more, this estimate would encompass both personality problems and conduct disorders. About all that can be said with some probable accuracy is that between 2 and 10 percent of the children in this country exhibit personality problems serious enough to warrant professional intervention.

Another problem that arises from the decision to avoid traditional classification systems is simply that of deciding how to approach a discussion of behavioral disturbances. Dealing with symptomatic behaviors as they really appear in individual children forces us to face the full complexity of disturbances in behavior. Neat conceptual explanations no longer fit conveniently with the fact that disordered behaviors do not present themselves in the form of coherent "symptom syndromes." Thinking must be reordered to correspond with the way children are, rather than reconceptualizing behavior to fit theoretical notions. As such, it becomes virtually impossible in a single chapter to encompass all the personality problems that one may encounter in classroom or clinic; and it becomes necessary to decide selectively to discuss certain representative problems in enough detail to allow critical evaluation of causation and treatment of personality problems. Later in this chapter we will discuss several examples of personality problems that have been traditionally viewed as "neurotic disorders," "psychophysiologic disorders," or as "special symptoms." Specifically, these will include, respectively, phobic and anxiety reactions, ulcerative colitis, and nocturnal enuresis (bed-wetting). We will examine each of these problems from a psychoanalytic point of view and from the perspective of contemporary social learning theory, since these are the major explanatory frameworks for understanding personality problems. The final sections of this chapter will be directed toward an examination of treatment approaches in home, classroom, and clinician's office.

Perspectives on the Etiology of Personality Problems

The most widely prevalent theoretical framework for understanding personality problems for the past fifty years has been psychoanalysis or one of a variety of psychodynamic theories derived from it. However, in recent years, findings from the experimental psychologist's learning laboratory have gained increasing currency as applications have been developed in the treatment of personality problems. As noted in previous chapters, the theoretical controversy is often vigorous and heated. At this point in time, the student interested in clinical applications—the remediation of personality problems in children— would be wise to recognize that both perspectives, as well as many others, can contribute importantly to helping the special child. Increasing flexibility among different theoretical positions is beginning to suggest that some differences, at least, are more apparent than real, and many points of agreement can be found.

Psychoanalytic Perspectives

Psychoanalytic theories of the etiology of neurotic disorders are founded on several critical assumptions. Perhaps the most basic of these is that personality problems are understood to be the outcome of a dynamic interplay of motivational forces and counterforces in the ongoing development of the child. Second, it is assumed that behavior is the external manifestation or sign of this interplay. That is, observable symptoms in the child reflect internal and largely unconscious conflicts. These conflicts inevitably reduce to the issue of whether wishes for immediate impulse gratification may be fulfilled or whether, because of familial and social restrictions, the impulses must be excluded from awareness and defended against potential expression. It is the latter course that is typically followed, and Freud termed this process of excluding unacceptable thoughts from awareness "repression."

As a result of internalization of social standards and self-imposed sanctions for violation of these standards, internal conflicts assume a critical role in development. The stage is set for ongoing warfare between various aspects of the individual's personality. In most cases, the developing personality is capable of resolving these internal conflicts in an environment that, hopefully, keeps sources of instinctual excitation to a minimum. However, in other cases the conflict becomes unmanageable either because the child lacks the resources to integrate instinctual demands with reality limitations and the insistent pressures of conscience or because the environment overstimulates the child and causes incessant demands for instinctual gratification.

It is in these cases that the child's attempts to repress instinctual demands often fail, and forbidden impulses threaten to force themselves into consciousness. At such points, small amounts of anxiety (*signal anxiety*) warn of impending danger and additional defensive behaviors are mobilized to avoid awareness of the impulses and resultant conflicts. It is these defensive behaviors, or the anxiety that occurs when they fail, that constitute the core features of neurotic personality problems.

Anna Freud has suggested that this sequence of (a) conflict, (b) anxiety, (c) defense against anxiety, (d) compromise attempts at conflict resolution, and (e) symptom formation is applicable to the understanding of neuroses in general. The specific symptom picture that develops in the individual child is a function of constitutional characteristics, environmental circumstances, the relative effectiveness of various defense mechanisms in reducing anxiety, and fixations in psychosexual development. In summary, psychoanalytic theory views personality problems as the consequences of internal, unconscious conflicts over impulse expression leading to the development of anxiety, defense mechanisms, and observable symptoms.

Social Learning Perspectives

Some of the basic assumptions of social learning perspectives were discussed in Chapter 2 and will be only briefly reviewed here. The basic assumption of the social learning/behavioral approach is that personality problems should be understood as samples of the individual's behavior rather than as signs of underlying disorder. In essence, the symptom is the disorder. Further attempts at explanation on the basis of inferences about unconscious conflicts, fixations, and so forth are viewed as superfluous and misleading. Instead, attempts are made to arrive at an understanding of personality problems through a *functional analysis of behavior* in terms of antecedent conditions and response consequences. In other words, what stimulus conditions can be observed that regularly precede or accompany the symptomatic behavior, and what are its outcomes? Answers to these questions can be framed in terms of a variety of phenomena observed in classical (respondent) conditioning, operant (instrumental) conditioning, and modeling or social learning.

A second important assumption of the social learning perspective is that *behavior should be observed empirically, with a minimum of inference and without the limits imposed by a theoretical framework that may lead one to see what is expected and to ignore what exists.* As a result, each child is viewed in a highly individualized fashion, and functional analyses of one child's behavior are not applicable to any other child.

A further implication of this assumption is that diagnostic labels may obscure the reality of a child's problems more than they illuminate those problems. Consequently, any use of diagnosis beyond the broadest empirically defensible categories is unwarranted. In instances where there is some purpose to the use of diagnostic labels, these should be viewed as purely descriptive and not as explanatory.

OPEN ISSUE

Freud's classic report of the case of Little Hans, a 5-year-old boy with a severe phobia for horses, has been a model for psychodynamic theories of childhood personality problems. Hans' fear of horses —which eventually generalized to a fear of even going outside—was seen as the behavioral symptom of underlying, unconscious conflicts. In essence, Freud believed that Hans feared his father's retribution because of Hans' unconscious desire to displace his father in his mother's affections. Hans' fear of horses was simply a symbolic expression of his unconscious fear of his father.

Watson's research into classical conditioning of a fear response in a young child indicated that fears might be learned in associative fashion. Watson used Little Albert as his subject and demonstrated that Albert developed a phobia for a small laboratory animal when Watson paired presentation of the animal with a sudden, unexpected, loud noise.

In many respects, the cases of Little Hans and Little Albert capsulize the controversies between psychodynamic and social learning theories as explanations of personality problems in children. These controversies extend to treatment approaches as well as theories of causation, and clinical and research evidence has been presented on both sides. However, issues in science are not argued away. Rather, thoughtful analysis and continued research will eventually indicate the most useful directions in understanding and treatment of personality problems in children.

Finally, it is also assumed that personality problems are continuous with normal behavior. There are no sharp dichotomies nor qualitative differences between normal and so-called neurotic behavior. Both are lawful, and both are understood within the framework of the same explanatory principles. The behavior of any child is viewed as the outcome of interactions between hereditary-constitutional factors and life experiences.

In addition to psychoanalytic and social learning perspectives on personality problems, there are a variety of other approaches to understanding these disorders. However, most of these are variations on one or the other basic themes we have sketched here and do not provide essentially different points of view. In discussing examples of specific kinds of personality problems, we will use psychoanalysis and social learning theory as basic frames of reference.

DIAGNOSIS AND IDENTIFICATION

The recognition of behaviors that constitute personality problems is simple enough, since these behaviors are easily observed and familiar in the behavior of most children. However, the decision that a given behavior is, in fact, serious enough to warrant intervention is quite a different matter and requires careful and thorough diagnostic evaluation. Virtually all children are fearful of one thing or another. The decision that the fear is of sufficient intensity and impairs the child's development, however, can be difficult. Similarly, most children are anxious at one time or another, but there are no clear demarcations between normal anxiety and a problematic anxiety reaction. Adequate diagnosis demands the careful application of the specific criteria outlined earlier to determine whether a given behavior is symptomatic of a personality problem and requires professional intervention. In the following sections we will describe the behavioral characteristics of several personality problems and examine specific theoretical notions regarding the causation of these problems.

Phobic Reactions in Children

Probably the most widely studied disorders of childhood are **phobic reactions,** in which children exhibit intense, irrational fears of specific objects or events. In a recent review of research in the area of phobic disorders, Miller, Barrett, and Hampe (1974) defined a *phobia* as a particular kind of fear that is (a) disproportionate to the realities of a situation, (b) cannot be controlled voluntarily, (c) causes avoidance of the feared situation, (d) persists over a long period of time, and (e) is maladaptive. Within the context of this definition, virtually any object or event can become the occasion for a phobic reaction. Rachman and Seligman (1976), for example, report one case in which an individual developed an extremely powerful fear of chocolate and another in which the patient showed an unreasonable fear of vegetables. However, cer-

The severe anxiety of this young Polish girl is apparent, both in her eyes and in her drawing—a depiction of the war she lived through, World War II.

tain kinds of phobias appear to be more common than others, and a distinction is warranted among the most prevalent phobic responses in children: fears of physical injury, fears of abandonment or separation from parents, fears of natural events, and fears of social situations such as school (Miller, Barrett, & Hampe, 1974; Poznanski, 1973).

Because of its high prevalence rate, school phobia has been more widely studied than other phobic reactions. Varying estimates of the incidence of school phobia have been offered ranging from 1 percent (Miller, Barrett, Hampe, & Noble, 1972) to as high as 8 percent of the general population (Kahn & Nursten, 1962). There is little question that it is the most frequent phobic reaction observed in children, constituting 69 percent of a sample of phobic children (Miller et al., 1972).

Several investigators have attempted to determine whether there are observable consistencies in the behavior of school-phobic children. One distinction is between more acute as opposed to chronic manifestations of school phobia. Kennedy (1965, 1971) called these, respectively, Type I and Type II school phobias.

In Type I school phobias the phobic reaction is typically a first episode, has an acute onset, and occurs on a Monday following an illness the previous Thursday or Friday. Type I school phobia occurs most often in the lower grades. Diagnostic study usually reveals that the child has expressed some concerns about death and that the mother's health is in question or, at least, the child thinks there is some problem. The parents of these children are characteristically well-adjusted and have good communication, although the father is often competitive with the mother in household management.

There are several important differences in Type II school phobias. In these disorders the onset is more gradual and, typically, the episode in question is the second or third occurrence. Type II school phobias occur more often in the upper grades, and the parents characteristically show adjustment problems themselves and have poor communication patterns. In these families the parents are difficult to work with and show little understanding of the child's fear or their own role in it.

Hersov (1960) suggested at least three distinguishable types of school phobics, basing his distinctions on the child's behavior patterns at home and at school and on parental behaviors. In one pattern, the child is timid at school but demanding at home, with an overindulgent mother and a passive father. In a second pattern, the child is obedient at home and timid at school, with an overcontrolling mother and a passive father. In a third pattern, the child is willful at home and friendly at school, with an overindulgent mother and a firm father. This distinction does not necessarily contradict the findings of Kennedy, but it does highlight the importance of family factors in the genesis and maintenance of school phobias.

A variety of explanations have been offered regarding the etiology of school phobias. Typical psychoanalytic views suggest that school phobia is a reflection of the child's anxiety at separating from the mother with whom there is a longstanding hostile-dependent relationship. The child's fear of school is seen as a result of fear of separation from the mother, which, in turn, stems from anxiety over the mother's welfare because of repressed hostility toward her and unconscious death wishes. An alternative psycho-analytic explanation (Fenichel, 1945) suggests that fear of school may reflect fear of learning, triggered by the content of a school topic that arouses anxiety related to repressed impulses.

Veltkamp (1975) also suggested that the school phobic child is really afraid of separation from the mother because their relationship is simply overly close and dependent, without necessary implications of underlying, repressed hostility. The child's fears of separation are strengthened by a mother who is equally uncomfortable with separation. The mother's need for intimacy with the child may be a substitute for a poor marital relationship, or the mother may be attempting to compensate for repressed resentment of the child (Levy, 1966); or the mother may simply be duplicating the kind of parental relationship she had with her own mother.

Leventhal and Sills (1964) developed a conception in which school-phobic children are seen as overestimating personal abilities and overvaluing themselves. However, there is also a marked sensitivity to threat and a tendency to use helplessness to maintain the self-image. Additionally, the mothers of such children cooperate in the maintenance of the child's pre-ferred self-image, and both parents dedicate themselves to gratifying the child's infantile demands. When such children encounter threat in the school situation—such as a change in schools, a return after an illness, an episode leading to embarrassment, or actual or fantasied failure in school—they avoid school in favor of the home situation where the preferred self-image may be maintained.

Actually, these notions are not incompatible with behavioral conceptions of school phobia. Yates (1970), for example, suggested that the parents, and particularly the mother, serve as important sources of social reinforcement for the child, particularly during early stages of development. As a result, the child becomes overdependent and fearful of separation from the parents. Home is viewed as a safe, rewarding place; by contrast, school is seen as insufficiently rewarding or as anxiety-arousing because of teacher demands or traumatic experiences with peers. While other children find alternative sources of reinforcement, peer support, and self-esteem in school, the school-phobic child sees nothing there but danger.

From this perspective, the school phobia is learned as a classically condi-tioned response in which one or several stimuli in the school environment become associated with heightened anxiety or in which separation from mother and home itself becomes a cue for the experience of anxiety. If the child is allowed to avoid school because of this intense anxiety, the avoidance is thereby reinforced and the phobia intensified.

While treatment approaches will be discussed in a later section, there is sufficient distinction in treating school phobias that separate discussion is warranted. Virtually all authorities agree that it is important that the school-phobic child be returned to the school environment as rapidly as possible. Eisenberg (1959) for example, considered this critically important for several reasons: (a) missing school means missing work and falling behind classmates; (b) it also means a backlog of homework to be made up; (c) there is necessity for explaining absence to peers; (d) additional attention received at home is difficult to give up; (e) the child often receives reinforcement of fears by over-concerned adults and, in fact, the very fact of being allowed to remain at home gives some substance to the child's fears.

Kennedy (1971) outlined a "rapid treatment program" for certain school-phobic children in which the parents kindly, but authoritatively, insist that the child attend school. Parents are reassured that Type I school-phobic children always recover, and the transient nature of the disorder is stressed. Thus reassured, most parents are able to take the child to school matter-of-factly; leave the child with school authorities despite tears, nausea, vomiting, and so forth; and ignore later complaints about how bad school was. Parents are instructed only to reinforce the child's attendance and ignore complaints or apprehensive statements. The patterned consistency in the behavior of school-phobic children and their parents helps the clinician predict most of the variables in the child's behavior and in the home situation and helps considerably in assuring parents that they are following the right course. In the meantime, support from teachers and clinical personnel in the school can simultaneously reassure the child that everything will be all right. However, such support must be given sparingly and judiciously, and with emphasis on the child's ability to face fears. Using this kind of highly structured treatment approach results in dissipation of fear in most Type I school-phobic children within three to four days. (Exhibit 11.1 is a detailed outline of this treatment approach.)

Naturally, not all school-phobic children respond readily to this approach to treatment, and not all phobias are as clearly understood as school phobias. However, the basic paradigm that views phobic reactions as learned fear responses that are maintained by the anxiety reduction in avoiding the phobic object appears to be accurate, and approaches to treatment derived from this paradigm promise success.

Anxiety Reactions in Children

Anxiety reactions in children as well as adults are manifested by an experience of intense, diffuse anxiety not associated with specific objects or situations. In this respect, these personality problems represent a clearly different set of symptoms from phobic reactions, though both phobic and anxiety reactions can be observed simultaneously in some children.

Both physiological and psychological symptoms comprise the anxiety reaction. In addition to experiencing chronic worrisomeness and apprehension, the child may also experience frequent nightmares and/or other sleep disturbances; stomach disturbances; respiratory problems; and periodic attacks of acute discomfort, including heart palpitations, hyperventilation, urinary frequency and urgency, trembling, and sweating. On occasion episodes of giddiness or uncontrollable laughing may also be observed. Children with anxiety reactions may be tense, irritable, overreactive, and hypervigilant to any threat in the environment. Some children exhibit preoccupation with bodily functioning and are easily frightened and disorganized by experiences that do not really hold any threat. Such an attitude has been termed "cowardliness with regard to living" (Anthony, 1971).

EXHIBIT 11.1

321

Diagnosis and
identification

RAPID TREATMENT PROGRAM FOR SCHOOL PHOBIA

1. Have the father take the child to school. These fathers are not unkind, and they can show authority when necessary.

2. Have the principal or attendance officer take an active part in keeping the child in the room.

3. Allow the mother to stand in the hall if she must or to visit the school during the morning, but do not allow her to stay.

4. Stressing the following points, conduct with the parents a structured interview designed to give them sufficient confidence to carry out the therapeutic program even in the face of considerable resistance from the child:

Lead the interview. The confidence of the parents is greatly increased by the interviewer's verifying the history rather than taking it. Correctly anticipating 7 out of 10 variables within a family structure is well-calculated to induce full cooperation.

Be optimistic. Stressing the transient nature of the difficulty, the dependable sequence of a difficult Monday, a somewhat better Tuesday, and a symptom-free Wednesday, tends to lighten the depression of the parents regarding their child's unwillingness to go to school.

Emphasize success. Type I cases always recover. Ninety percent of the Type I phobics stay at school most of the first day. Along with optimism, comes a slight mobilization of hostility, which helps the parents to follow the plan.

Present the formula. Simply but directly with repetition for emphasis, outline a plan for the parents to follow assuming that it is the end of the school week by the time of the referral and that the interview with the parents is conducted on Thursday or Friday.

Do not discuss in any way school attendance over the weekend. There is nothing a phobic child does better than talk about going to school. Don't discuss phobic symptoms. Simply tell the child Sunday evening, "Well, son, tomorrow you go back to school."

On Monday morning get the child up, dressed, and ready for school. Give the child a light breakfast to reduce the nausea problem. Have the father take the child matter-of-factly off to school. Don't ask him how he feels or why he is afraid to go to school or why he doesn't like school. Simply take him to school. Turn him over to the school authorities, and go home. If the child's therapist has not seen the child the previous week, he may see him after school on the first day.

On Monday evening, compliment the child on going to school and staying there, no matter how resistant he has been, no matter how many times he has vomited, cried, or started to leave. If he has been at school for 30 minutes on Monday, progress is being made. Tell the child Monday evening that Tuesday will be much better and make no further mention of the symptom.

Tuesday can be expected to be a repetition of Monday, but with everything toned down considerably. On Tuesday evening, encourage and compliment the child strongly for doing so much better.

Wednesday should be virtually symptom-free. Wednesday evening with considerable fanfare, give a party for the child in honor of his having overcome his problem.

The child himself should be seen only briefly by the child therapist and only after school hours. The content of the interview should be stories which stress the advantages of going on in the face of fear—how student pilots need to get back into the air quickly after an accident and how important it is to get right back on the horse after a fall.

From Kennedy (1971, pp. 48–50)

What are the sources of such disruptive anxiety? As in the case of phobic disorders, the answer to this question depends on theoretical perspective.

For the psychoanalyst, initial sources of anxiety lie in traumatic experiences during the birth process that serve as precursors of all later anxiety. During the course of development, anxiety stems from perceived dangers in the real world. This is termed *objective anxiety,* and it serves an important adaptive function in warning the developing child of potential dangers. However, in some cases anxiety appears without adequate justification in reality or is totally out of proportion to the perceived sources of danger. In these cases Freud and others have suggested that anxiety must be understood as an outcome of impulse repression and subsequent fear that the impulses may become uncontrollable and overwhelm the personality. This fear that impulses may overwhelm the controls of the personality is termed *neurotic anxiety.* Environmental situations that serve as sources of excitation of repressed impulses, therefore, may trigger periods of acute anxiety.

In other instances there may be no particular external excitation stirring repressed impulses, but instead there may be a weakening of censorship functions and repressive energy again leading to potential impulse expression. This is the case in sleep disturbances such as nightmares or fear of falling asleep. During sleep, the controls that operate to maintain repressions are relaxed, with the result that partial expression of impulses occurs in disguised form in dream symbols. These partial expressions then stimulate anxiety and lead to waking and reinstitution of vigilance against internal impulses.

In *night terrors,* in contrast to nightmares, anxiety is not experienced in awareness, since the child does not waken but rather behaves in a trancelike state, exhibiting symptoms of terror and failure to recognize people in the environment. The child appears to be engaged in a hallucinatory episode and acts as though he/she is actually seeing and hearing dangers in the environment. Eventually the episode subsides, the child returns to comfortable sleep, and upon waking there is no recall of the episode.

In contrast to detailed psychoanalytic conceptions regarding the origins of anxiety reactions and sleep disturbances, behavioral theory has had little to say regarding the origins of such disturbances beyond the assertion that anxiety is a conditioned fear response. That is, the association of fear with previously neutral cues leads to a state in which these cues can elicit a fearful response through a process of classical conditioning. This process occurs regularly during the course of normal development and constitutes the basis for the development of a conscience and for socialization generally. In fact, as we will see in Chapter 12, the absence of such conditioning is viewed as an important element in the development of conduct disorders.

However, some children appear to be born with constitutionally high levels of emotional arousability or anxiety. In these children anxiety becomes too easily associated with a wide variety of cues and forms the basis for numerous avoidance responses. Since these avoidance responses often succeed in reducing anxiety, and since anxiety-reduction is reinforcing, these responses eventually become strong habits that are highly resistant to extinction. A similar process with greater situational specificity was discussed in relation to the development of phobic reactions.

Thus a combination of respondent and operant conditioning paradigms effectively explains the genesis of pervasive anxiety responses in the individual child and the maintenance of avoidance responses. The anxious child perceives threat everywhere because so many cues have become functionally related to anxiety, and the child is in a more or less continual state of emotional arousal. Shyness, withdrawal, and timidity can all be understood as conditioned avoidance responses in such a chronically and generally fearful child. Some of these factors are illustrated in the case of Holly K. (see Case Study 11.1).

CASE STUDY 11.1

HOLLY: A CHILDHOOD ANXIETY REACTION

Holly K., age 7, was initially brought to a community child guidance clinic for evaluation because she was "scared of her own shadow." Mr. and Mrs. K. complained that Holly had always been rather dependent, clingy, and fearful, but in the past six months, her pervasive fearfulness had become unbearable for the parents.

Although she usually attended school willingly enough, Holly could not tolerate any other separations from her parents and would become panic-stricken if she learned that her parents were going to leave her with a baby-sitter. Holly had few friends and did not play outside at all. Instead, from the time she returned home from school and on weekends, she would follow her mother around the house engaging in casual chatter. Bedtime was also a problem. Holly would try a variety of tactics to delay bedtime, and then insist that one of her parents stay with her until she was asleep. She also insisted that a room light be left on in her bedroom. Frequently, she would awaken in the middle of the night frightened by a nightmare and crawl into her parents' bed. Mr. and Mrs. K. finally decided to seek professional consultation because Holly was also beginning to exhibit some resistance to going to school.

Mr. and Mrs. K. were a young, well-educated couple, and Holly was their only child. Mrs. K. was solicitous and overprotective of Holly, and she readily admitted this, believing that Holly would not be so fearful if she were a better mother. Mr. K. was quite despondent over Holly's infantile behavior and feared that she would grow up to have severe emotional problems. Generally, however, Mr. and Mrs. K. supported each other and had a good relationship.

An interview with Holly was scheduled, and she proved to be a bright, attractive child who was comfortable with adults and able to relate easily. However, she was also somber, and discussion with her focused on her many concerns and fears. Holly was reassured that she had little to be fearful about and that the clinic staff would be able to help her with her "problems," which were another source of concern for her. In many respects, Holly appeared to have tuned in to her parents worries and was also beginning to feel there was something wrong with her.

Subsequent consultation with Mr. and Mrs. K. was arranged in the form of series of behavior management instruction sessions. Mr. and Mrs. K. were reassured that they were adequate parents and did not harbor "unconscious resentment" of Holly as they had been led to believe by some reading they had done on their own. Instead, they were told that Holly was picking up their apprehensions and uncertainty and that they were inadvertently reinforcing her apprehensiveness. In several role-playing episodes, Mr. and Mrs. K. were shown how to react to Holly's fears with more confidence in their and her ability to manage such fears. They were instructed to ignore specific aspects of Holly's fearful behavior and to reward her with liberal praise and attention for grown-up behavior. Holly's parents were also helped to set up a reward system in which Holly could earn several special outings with them by spending several periods of increasing length with a baby-sitter.

Mr. and Mrs. K. were relieved to see that their concern and solicitousness were simply occurring at the wrong times and reinforcing Holly's own fears about the world and herself. They left the initial consultation almost buoyantly, and after three additional consultation sessions felt that Holly's behavior had "changed 1000 percent." Follow-up interviews at three and six-month intervals indicated that Holly was doing well. She was out of the house more and enjoyed playing with friends her own age. She did not mind staying with a baby-sitter, and the parents were even arranging to spend a weekend away. Holly's nightmares had gradually faded without any particular efforts to deal with them. Rather than resisting school, Holly was even eager to leave on some mornings when special activities were planned.

For sleep disturbances specifically, behavioral psychologists might hypothesize that such disturbances simply reflect chronically high anxiety levels without any implications regarding unconscious conflicts as sources of such anxiety. Naturally, sleep itself may become a cue or stimulus for anxiety as a consequence of previous sleep disturbances, so that a pattern develops in which anticipation of sleep increases anxiety and thereby increases the probability of further sleep disturbances (Blackham & Silberman, 1975). As is the case with psychoanalytic formulations, further research is needed to substantiate these notions.

Psychophysiological Reactions in Children

Psychophysiological reactions are those in which there is a demonstrated or presumed relationship between chronic, stress-related emotional arousal and the eventual appearance of physiological symptoms. Familiar examples of such disorders include bronchial asthma, migraine headaches, obesity, peptic ulcers, and a variety of skin reactions such as rashes and hives.

A number of explanations have been developed that attempt to demonstrate the mechanisms whereby psychological arousal eventuates in physiological symptoms. These include: (a) the conception that genetic vulnerability of a specific organ system predisposes the individual to respond to emotional arousal with a deterioration in the functioning of that system; (b) the belief that physiological arousal of specific organ systems may become associated with specific external cues via classical conditioning, leading to eventual deterioration of a given organ system as a result of repeated arousal; (c) the belief that particular psychological characteristics predispose the individual to related arousal in specific organ systems as, for example, in the assumption that inhibition of anger leads to gastric secretions eventuating in peptic ulcers; (d) the conception that fixation at particular levels of psychosexual development eventuates in deterioration in symbolically related organ systems.

At this point there is not sufficient evidence for a definitive understanding of the roles of personality characteristics, genetic-constitutional factors, or environmentally produced stress in the etiology of psychophysiological reactions. As in previous sections, we will examine in more detail an example of a specific disorder, ulcerative colitis, which exemplifies some of the issues and approaches that have evolved in attempting to understand psychophysiological disorders.

Ulcerative colitis is an intestinal inflammation that leads to periodic appearances of chronic diarrhea, bloody stools, loss of appetite, weight loss, and sometimes intestinal pain. Clinical examination usually reveals changes in the mucous lining of the lower intestine, with ulceration in severe cases (Finch, 1971). *It is important to recognize that there is no question about actual physiological involvement in the symptomatology of psychophysiological reactions,* and in some cases the severity of the disorder may be of life-threatening proportions. This is true in ulcerative colitis (Broberger & Lagercrantz, 1966).

Several investigators have described the existence of a specific constellation of psychosocial factors in colitis patients, including passivity, general inhibition, submissiveness, and dependency (Prugh & Jordan, 1971). Additional personality characteristics that have been noted or hypothesized are the existence of unconscious conflict, depressive mood, and disturbances of family interaction (Feldman, Cantor, Soll, & Bachrach, 1967).

Writing from a psychoanalytic perspective, Spitz (1951) suggested that psychophysiologic reactions (including ulcerative colitis) may stem from maternal rejection, compensatory overpermissiveness, oscillation between hostility and overprotectiveness, or emotional deprivation. In other words, the child is experiencing maternal rejection either directly in the form of overt resentment, or in the form of compensatory overprotection. Another psychoanalytic hypothesis is that of Fenichel (1945), who suggested that the colitis patient experiences unconscious anal impulses that are in continual conflict with social demands for bowel retention. The simultaneous pressures toward impulsive elimination and compulsive bowel retention eventually create intestinal disturbances.

A more plausible model has been developed by Minuchin, Baker, Rosman, Liebman, Milman, and Todd (1975) who have developed a conception of colitis and other psychophysiological disorders as the outcomes of family dysfunctions. A child who is physiologically vulnerable to a specific organic dysfunction confronts a rigid, overprotective family environment that enmeshes the child in patterns of conflict avoidance. Within this family structure, the child may be put in a position in which self-expression leads to alienation of one parent or the other, or in which the child is used as an ally in parental conflicts. Either situation leads to chronic stress. The actual development of a specific symptom picture is a function of family history and organization that lead to differential responsiveness to particular physical illnesses. Thus, a family that is sensitive to gastrointestinal disturbances for one reason or another may reinforce the appearance of such symptoms in a child. A conception of psychophysiological reactions as the outcome of family dysfunction is gaining some currency among contemporary theorists (Cermak, 1973; Luban-Plozza & Comazzi, 1973; Selvini-Palazzoli, 1970), but clear evidence supporting these conceptions has still to be developed (Werry, 1972).

A more likely viewpoint comes from behavioral and social learning theorists who suggest that ulcerative colitis is the possible outcome of multiple causative factors, including constitutional vulnerability, developmental experiences, psychosocial climate, and possible conditioning of gastrointestinal reflexes as responses to stressful situations (Prugh & Jordan, 1971).

Altogether, evidence demonstrating the psychological causation of ulcerative colitis, as well as other psychophysiological reactions, must be interpreted cautiously. In concluding his review of research in this area, Werry (1972) offered the following interpretive guidelines: (a) there is no evidence that so-called psychophysiological disorders are *necessarily* outcomes of maladjustment or family problems; (b) there is some evidence that in some disorders, several causative agents may be operative, including familial and environmental stresses; (c) the absence of known physical etiology should not by itself be construed as implying psychological causation. The fact is that psychophysiological disorders may well be caused by physiological processes so subtle that medical research has not yet discovered them. A good example of this is research suggesting that ulcerative colitis may be the result of an autoimmune process (McDermott & Finch, 1967) in which the body develops antibodies that destroy normal colonic bacteria, which leads to the development of colitis symptoms. In other words, colitis may result from the operations of antibodies that immunize the organism against normal bacterial processes.

Nocturnal Enuresis in Children

In a historical survey of nocturnal enuresis (bed-wetting), Glicklich (1951) noted that the problem was discussed in the first pediatrics text, written in the sixteenth century, in a section entitled, "Of Pyssying in the Bedde." In addition to its quaintness, this historical note emphasizes clearly the fact that the problem is an age-old one that continues to plague countless children.

While formal definitions of **nocturnal enuresis** vary regarding frequency of occurrence and ages at which children should be completely dry at night, most investigators agree that the essential feature of the disorder is involuntary bed-wetting in the absence of demonstrable organic disorder (Werry, 1972). Because of disagreement as to when a child should be completely dry at night, prevalence estimates vary. Nevertheless, several investigations suggest that nocturnal enuresis occurs in as many as 20 percent of normal five and six year olds (Jones, 1960; Oppel, Harper, & Rowland, 1968; Sears, Maccoby, & Levin, 1957).

The problem of nocturnal enuresis is, thus, an important one, and it affects many children and families. However, the question must also arise as to whether a problem occurring with such high frequency constitutes or indicates by itself the presence of a personality problem. As noted in the opening pages of this chapter, we are coming to a more realistic appraisal in which enuresis may be viewed as an isolated immaturity—a failure in habit development—or it may be viewed as part of a larger pattern of personality problems. However, contrary to the view of only a few years ago, its presence is no longer considered a sufficient indicator, by itself, of the presence of disturbed emotional development.

For example, an influential study by Gerard (1939) suggested that enuresis is typically one symptom of a neurotic syndrome characterized by anxiety, nightmares, recurrent dreams, passivity, and self-deprecation. This kind of thinking stemmed directly from the early writings of Freud (1905) who suggested that enuresis represented a nocturnal seminal emission and was a substitute for forbidden masturbation. Fenichel (1945) agreed that nocturnal enuresis provided autoerotic pleasure and was an unconscious equivalent of masturbation. However, there is no evidence supporting the notion that enuresis is *prima facie* evidence of emotional disturbance nor that it inevitably represents unconscious masturbatory impulses.

Enuresis has also been viewed as indicative of neurological disturbance, genitourinary disease, delayed development, allergic reactions, unusually deep sleep, and failure in adequate habit development (Bindelglas, 1975). Actually, each of these alternative explanations has been implicated in some cases of nocturnal enuresis. For this reason it is important that medical factors be considered and ruled out before alternative explanations are considered. Approximately 10 percent of enuretics suffer from some form of organic dysfunction (Yates, 1970).

Currently, the conception of enuresis as a failure in habit development appears to have wide support and has led to effective forms of treatment. Basically, this conception views awakening in response to urinary urgency as a classically conditioned response. That is, originally, bladder pressure is an unconditioned stimulus leading to the unconditioned reflex response of urination. Through conditioning the child learns the conditioned response of waking to bladder pressure and then urinates appropriately.

Where this conditioned response is not learned, the child urinates while asleep and may or may not then waken. Treatment has taken the form of using a bed pad mechanically wired to sound a bell or buzzer immediately upon contact with moisture. Thus, as soon as the sleeping child begins to urinate, an electrical circuit is completed sounding a bell or buzzer and waking the child. This so-called "bell and pad" method of dealing with enuresis has been available at least since 1938, when it was invented by Mowrer and Mowrer. Extensive research has demonstrated it to be an effective approach to treatment (Bindelglas, 1975; Taylor & Turner, 1975; Young & Morgan, 1973); and Yates (1970) summarized research on conditioning treatment of enuresis as "extremely gratifying" with estimates of success rates as high as 90 percent.

More recently, Azrin, Sneed, and Foxx (1974) developed what they feel is an even more effective approach to eliminating nocturnal enuresis with a procedure that includes the bell and pad, but also includes: (a) consumption of large amounts of fluid to increase the child's need to urinate; (b) waking the child hourly during the night; (c) teaching the child to waken to mild stimuli; (d) practice in toileting; (e) reinforcement for appropriate nighttime toileting; and (f) helping the child become more aware of the dry versus wet condition. Exhibit 11.2 outlines this "dry-bed procedure."

On the whole, current evidence suggests that, while nocturnal enuresis may be a component of a larger pattern of personality problems or neurosis,

DRY-BED PROCEDURE

I. Intensive training (one night)
   A. One hour before bedtime
      1. Child informed of all phases of training procedure
      2. Alarm placed on bed
      3. Positive practice in toileting (20 practice trials)
         a. child lies down on bed
         b. child counts to 50
         c. child arises and attempts to urinate in toilet
         d. child returns to bed
         e. steps a,b,c, and d repeated 20 times
   B. At bedtime
      1. Child drinks fluids
      2. Child repeats training instructions to trainer
      3. Child retires for night
   C. Hourly awakenings
      1. Minimal prompts used to waken child
      2. Child walks to bathroom
      3. At bathroom door (before urination), child is asked to inhibit urination for one hour (omit for children under 6)
         a. if child could not inhibit urination
            i. child urinates in toilet
            ii. trainer praises child for correct toileting
            iii. child returns to bed
         b. if child indicated that he could inhibit urination for one hour
            i. trainer praises child for his urinary control
            ii. child returns to bed
      4. At bedside, the child feels the bed sheets and comments on their dryness
      5. Trainer praises child for having a dry bed
      6. Child is given fluids to drink
      7. Child returns to sleep
   D. When an accident occurred
      1. Trainer disconnects alarm
      2. Trainer awakens child and reprimands him for wetting
      3. Trainer directs child to bathroom to finish urinating
      4. Child is given Cleanliness Training
         a. child is required to change night clothes
         b. child is required to remove wet bed sheet and place it with dirty laundry
         c. trainer reactivates alarm
         d. child obtains clean sheets and remakes bed
      5. Positive Practice in correct toileting (20 practice trials) performed immediately after the Cleanliness Training
      6. Positive Practice in correct toileting (20 practice trials) performed the following evening before bedtime

From Azrin, Sneed, & Foxx (1974, p. 150)

it may also be the result of organic dysfunction in about 10 percent of the cases encountered. In the absence of organic deficits, it is more likely that enuresis is a failure of habit development, which may occur totally independently of a pattern of severe personality disturbance. There is strong evidence, however, indicating that elimination of enuresis has the result of improving overall emotional adjustment (Geppert, 1953; Lovibond, 1964; Mowrer & Mowrer, 1938). This finding suggests that at least in some cases, emotional problems may be the result rather than the cause of enuresis.

DEVELOPMENTAL CONSEQUENCES

From the foregoing discussion it is evident that personality problems may take a wide variety of specific forms or be manifested in pervasive adjustment difficulties. They may be extremely serious and debilitating or relatively mild. In some cases, personality problems persist in recognizable patterns over time, while in others symptoms shift and change from one age to another. For these reasons it is difficult to specify the concrete developmental consequences of personality problems with any precision. However, there are some consistencies among personality problems that we have also noted. These include higher than average levels of anxiety and apprehensiveness, shyness and timidity, extreme dependency on parents and other adults, inhibition, and passivity. These children often have high levels of aspiration and equally high levels of guilt and depression if they do not live up to their own or others' expectations. While we cannot make specific predictions regarding the development of these youngsters, certain consequences are, in a general way, more likely than others.

Conceptual Abilities and Educational Achievement

There is no systematic relationship between the emergence of personality problems in children and intellectual ability. However, in some youngsters timid, passive behavior and dependency do interfere with adequate utilization of potential. Learning is an active enterprise that requires initiative and energy. If a child is unrealistically perfectionistic and fearful of making a mistake, learning is inevitably hampered and, often, the youngster expends more energy in self-recrimination than in active learning. Furthermore, apprehensiveness and anxiety inhibit curious exploration of one's world, and the fearful child is often threatened by the possibility that learning will bring with it demands for activity and performance. The child with personality problems is not adventuresome, and learning is surely an adventure.

As a result of these characteristics, it often happens that youngsters with personality problems are perceived by teachers and others as shy and backwards. In many cases, they are fearful of speaking in class or reading aloud. Often tests and examinations are occasions for sheer panic and freezing. And in still other instances, fantasy and daydreaming become escapes from the threatening reality of teacher expectations and peer competition. Thus, while children with personality problems are no different in ability from others, there are often differences in actual performance.

In some instances, children with personality problems actively compensate for their fearfulness in interpersonal situations by withdrawing into books and study. In so doing they find an area of personal worth and achievement but without direct competition with more aggressive classmates. At the same time, such youngsters thrive on adult attention, and certainly academic achievement is a sure road to parent and teacher praise. In these cases, youngsters do find important sources of gratification and self-esteem; however, it is often at the expense of adequate interpersonal development. Occasionally, too, a teacher inadvertently reinforces such timidity by emphasizing the child's difference from "rowdy" peers, but this only serves to increase alienation and loneliness in many cases.

It is important for any child to develop a balance between academic achievement, self-confidence with adults and peers, and active, curious exploration of the world, but children with personality problems have particular difficulty achieving such balance.

Personal and Social Factors

As in the case of educational development, apprehensiveness and anxiety are key factors leading to problems in personal and social development. The child with personality problems is often uncomfortable with self and uncomfortable with others. There is rarely an easy, spontaneous sense of liking others and being liked by them. On the contrary, the child with personality problems fears that others will be critical and rejecting, and this fear often provokes the kind of rejection that is expected. The world is perceived as threatening, and the child with personality problems consequently behaves in a manner that is constantly defensive and self-protective even when there is no realistic occasion for fear.

The overall result of such an orientation to self and others is excessive timidity and shyness in interpersonal relations. Fearful of others' opinions and actions, the child with personality problems often refrains from participating in social events, and if forced to participate by parents or teachers, often behaves in a clumsy, awkward fashion that makes others uncomfortable and provokes ridicule or rejection. While patient understanding might help such youngsters in social situations, adults and peers often lose patience quickly and become critical. Unfortunately, such responses only reinforce the child's anxieties and demonstrate that he/she was right to be apprehensive in the first place.

The child with personality problems is acutely aware of others' reactions and too often bases self-evaluation on the opinions of others. As a result, it is difficult for the child to form a healthy self-concept and a feeling of being able to cope with most life situations. Instead, a defeatist attitude often develops along with feelings of worthlessness and self-criticism. Most of us are familiar enough with periods of dejection and apprehension to have a fleeting sense of what such children live with constantly.

There is a circularity, too, in the development of children with personality problems. Fearfulness leads to avoidance of competitive situations and peer relations. Avoiding them then makes them appear even more formidable so that the youngster becomes even more fearful and apprehensive. It is not at all surprising that, under such circumstances, early social awkwardness and apprehension lead to increasing discomfort and avoidance of social interactions. Furthermore, social inadequacy often reinforces the child's sense of worthlessness and unacceptability.

Though the prognosis for improvement in the personal and social adjustment of these youngsters is good with treatment (Robins, 1972), there is no evidence that these patterns of development improve without environmental changes that stimulate changes in self-concept. Without intervention, problems in social relations and self-acceptance appear to persist through adolescence and into adulthood, though the specific symptom patterns may change over time (Abe, 1972; Robins, 1972; Waldron, 1976). Thus it is critically important that intervention occur if the child with personality problems is to develop into a self-acceptant adult who is comfortable with self and others. Without intervention, anxiety, apprehensiveness, self-criticism, hypersensitivity, and dependency are likely to persist and become manifest in a variety of specific problematic behaviors.

Most children experience situations in which they feel shy and timid. If, however, they allow these feelings to keep them constantly isolated from others, then their healthy development is impeded, as they have little chance of enhancing their self-concept.

INTERVENTION

The importance of theoretical conceptions regarding the origins of personality problems becomes apparent when one is faced with decisions regarding appropriate educational programs, teacher roles, and psychotherapy. It should be evident at this point that a view of personality problems as symptomatic manifestations of anxiety arising from unconscious conflict and repressed impulses will inevitably lead to a different conception of remediation than a viewpoint that understands the symptoms as the problem with no further inferences about unobserved or unconscious events. The following sections will outline some of the educational and therapeutic implications of the two major theoretical positions regarding the origins of personality problems.

Psychoanalytic Theory: Educational and Therapeutic Implications

Psychoanalytic approaches to education and psychotherapy are aimed not only at symptom removal, but also at resolving the presumed conflicts that cause the symptoms. Very much as a physician attempts to treat the infectious agents that give rise to a fever, the psychoanalyst attempts to treat the presumed conflict that gives rise to a phobia or an anxiety reaction or a psychophysiological reaction. This approach has been termed the "medical model" of psychological disorder because of its similarity to approaches that have been so effective in medicine. However, there are several subtle implications of the medical model underlying psychoanalysis.

Most importantly, there is the obvious implication that psychological disorders fall largely within the realm of medical intervention by physicians trained in psychiatry and/or psychoanalysis. This means that treatment, for all practical purposes, is restricted in applicability because of the tremendous time and expense involved in the painstaking uncovering and interpretation of unconscious conflicts.

The corollary of this first implication is that ancillary remedial approaches in home or classroom are "second best" and less likely to be successful than traditional methods of dream analysis, free association, and interpretation of unconscious material. There are also implied suggestions of lack of responsibility on the part of the "patient," and hints that parental mishandling is a major causative factor in the development of the disturbance.

A further implication of the medical model is that removal of symptoms without analysis of underlying conflicts will lead to "symptom substitution." That is, one symptom will simply be replaced by another unless the underlying "cause" is discovered and removed. Despite the fact that no evidence exists to support this belief, it remains firmly entrenched in the minds of professionals and laypersons alike.

Because personality problems are viewed within the framework of the medical model, genuine treatment is typically assumed to occur only within the context of specified therapeutic sessions with a highly specialized and highly trained mental health professional. Treatment sessions with a social worker, psychologist, or psychiatrist may be scheduled from one to several times per week and extend over a period of up to several years. The role of the teacher in the regular classroom or the special classroom is essentially viewed as supportive, with the teacher attempting to provide an acceptant, nonthreatening atmosphere and gently setting behavioral limits. The teacher also acts as an observer and reporter, providing additional sources of information for the therapist.

However, "real treatment" is presumed to occur within the therapeutic relationship, and to require traditional forms of verbal psychotherapy or play therapy as outlined in Chapter 4. The roles of parents and teachers in the treatment of personality problems are, at most, secondary.

Social Learning Theory: Educational and Therapeutic Implications

As indicated in previous sections, social learning and behavioral approaches operate from the assumption that personality problems are the result of interactions between hereditary-constitutional factors and experience. Depending on the nature of personal experience, the child may fail to learn responses that are important, may learn responses that are detrimental, or may learn the wrong responses to particular stimuli (Ross, 1974). In the child exhibiting personality disturbances, it is often the case that anxiety responses are learned too readily and to too many stimuli, while assertive social responses are not adequately learned. In still other cases, as in enuresis, there is a failure to learn necessary responses.

Within this context, a behavioral approach further assumes that everyone in the child's environment—whether intentionally or inadvertently, willingly or unwillingly—is a potential teacher. Faulty teaching and learning may create personality problems; but, by the same token, more adequate teaching may be a key to correcting them.

A social learning perspective demands that there be a thorough analysis

These pictures of children labeled either "emotionally disturbed" or "behaviorally disordered" show them interacting with their teachers or counselors. An important goal of their therapy program involves their learning to receive and give affection, and slowly to control themselves.

of the circumstances that maintain the child's problems and subsequent intervention in the natural environment to change those circumstances. Thus parent and teacher become as important in therapeutic efforts as psychologist or psychiatrist, since it is either the parent or teacher who will typically carry out recommended plans or programs in day-to-day interactions with the child. In some instances, of course, therapeutic efforts may still demand highly specialized skills, but even in these cases parents and teachers remain key members of the behavior change team.

In treating personality problems, the focus is on individual symptomatic behaviors that become targets for change efforts. Thus, for example, if shyness is a problem, efforts may be made to develop situations so that social interactions become more reinforcing and less threatening to the child. If nonspecific anxiety is a primary problem, efforts may be made to increase the child's self-confidence and assurance of ability to cope through a number of specific techniques. In the case of phobic reactions, the child might be helped to relax in the presence of feared stimuli or to observe others interacting with the feared object in a nonfearful way.

The many techniques that have been developed and reported in the research literature are too extensive to be reviewed here. Instead, a few examples of the treatment of personality problems will be presented to illustrate the kinds of approaches employed.

O'Connor (1969) asked teachers to select the most socially withdrawn children in their classes, and then observed the social behavior of these children to validate teacher assessments. These children were exposed to a film depicting groups of nursery-school children interacting in a positive and rewarding fashion. A control group of children observed a film depicting several circus animal acts. Subsequent to this treatment, children were again observed in the classroom setting. Results indicated that, while control children showed no change in frequency of interactions, children exposed to the modeling experience showed marked increases in social activities. In fact, in postexperimental sessions, the behavior of these children was similar to that of nonisolates in the classroom. In this study, modeling alone without further intervention had significant impact on the social withdrawal of young children.

Kirby and Toler (1970) increased the social interaction of a shy, withdrawn youngster by the simple expedient of having the child pass out candy to other children in a nursery school. Subsequently, this youngster developed much more sociable, assertive behavior in relation to peers.

Leitenberg and Callahan (1973) asked parents of nursery-school and kindergarten children whether their children were afraid of the dark. Children fearful of the dark were selected as participants in this study and pretested by asking the children to go into a darkened room as part of a game; a child entering the room could win a prize. Each child was then shown the room and asked to enter it, close the door, and remain inside as long as possible without being afraid. Each child was told to come out of the room if frightened. Subsequent to this pretest condition, children were trained by asking them to enter a darkened room to earn a prize. On each session during which they could increase the time they stayed in the room, they could earn an additional prize. Following this simple training, youngsters dramatically increased the amount of time they could spend in a darkened room without being frightened. A control group showed no change.

Clement (1970) reported the treatment of a boy who was disturbed by recurrent nightmares of being chased by a big, black bug; these nightmares in turn led to sleepwalking. In this case, the mother was used as a therapist, and an attempt was made to condition waking as a response to the nightmare by having the mother wake the child whenever she observed thrashing movements as though the boy were having a nightmare. After waking the child, the mother had him hit and tear pictures of the frightening bug. This treatment was successful in eliminating the problem.

Straughan (1964) used modeling and direct coaching to teach a mother to interact with her 8-year-old daughter in such a fashion as to increase the girl's spontaneity and reduce her fearfulness and timidity. Parent modeling with coaching was successful in increasing spontaneous and assertive behavior.

Lazarus (1960) used a desensitization procedure in the treatment of a boy who had a phobia for automobiles. Discussions with the child initially avoided mention of cars, but gradually mention of other motor vehicles and then cars were introduced while the child was enjoying chocolates. Eventually, the child watched comfortably as accidents with toy cars were enacted, was able to sit with the therapist in a stationary automobile, and by the seventeenth therapy session was able to ride in a car with a stranger.

Lazarus and Abramovitz (1962) used a method termed "emotive imagery" to deal with phobic responses in children. Similar to the procedure outlined above, the nature and magnitude of the child's fears were determined. The child was then instructed to think about a favorite hero while the therapist introduced mention of items far removed from the phobic object, gradually mentioning more feared items. If the patient felt any discomfort at any time, a signal was given to the therapist, and the child was instructed to think about heroic adventures. This procedure was effective in rapid elimination of phobic reactions in young children.

In all these examples, it is important to note the reliance on familiarity with principles of learning and conditioning combined with careful analysis of the child's problem. Use of these procedures requires understanding of the learning process, careful and precise observation, and creativity in applying principles of learning to the elimination of the problem. This is by no means a simple procedure. However, it does not require training in esoteric techniques nor specialized degrees. While the indiscriminate and thoughtless attempt to apply social learning and behavioral approaches to the treatment of children's problems should be discouraged, the careful use of such approaches in consultation with others means that many more children can be helped—without the stigma so often attached to clinical diagnostic labels. Within this framework, parents and teachers become as important in the elimination of children's problems as psychologist and psychiatrist.

While personality problems in children do not strike us with the force and impact of other childhood disabilities, they are perhaps the cause of as much pain, suffering, and loneliness as any other impairment we know. They affect every area of the child's development and often lead to tremendous waste in the form of unexploited abilities and talents. Children with personality problems do not usually bother us. Instead, they suffer in silence and live quiet, fearful lives. It is important that parents and teachers recognize such children and not assume that a docile child is necessarily a happy child. This is often a difficult task, since such youngsters do not always demand our attention in a forceful way. Nevertheless, the sensitive teacher and concerned parent can do much to help such youngsters realize their potential, and often through straightforward approaches that have proven remarkably effective.

SUMMARY

1. Contrary to popular stereotypes, childhood is often a time of anxieties, fears, and tensions, and it is important to be able to sort out these normal tensions from genuine personality problems.

2. Diagnostic evaluation of personality problems in children requires careful evaluation of such factors as the child's overall development, the frequency of problematic behavior, the child's age, the number of problems present, the developmental consequences of the problem, and the extent of the child's discomfort.

3. Research evidence suggests that the categories of personality problems and conduct disorders encompass most of the problematic behaviors in children and are more accurate than traditional diagnostic systems.

4. Personality problems may be viewed as external symptoms of inner conflicts or as manifestations of faulty learning experiences.

5. Phobic reactions are intense irrational fears of specific objects or events.

6. Anxiety reactions in childhood are characterized by intense, free-floating apprehension, tension, and fearfulness in regard to living.

7. Psychophysiological reactions result when chronic emotional arousal leads to the development of medical problems.

8. Nocturnal enuresis is a frequently occurring symptom that has been treated successfully within a learning-based orientation.

9. Personality problems may have negative consequences in the child's educational achievement and interpersonal relations.

10. The most common intervention approaches are psychodynamic psychotherapy and behavior therapy.

11. Social learning theory indicates that teachers and parents can be important change agents in the development of children with personality problems.

Children with Conduct Disorders

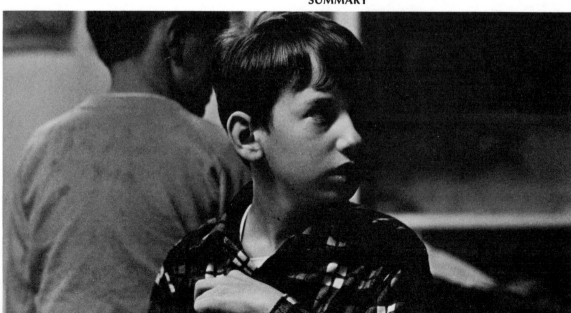

"Stop thief! Stop Thief!" There is a passion for hunting something *deeply implanted in the human breast. One wretched breathless child, panting with exhaustion; terror in his looks, agony in his eyes, large drops of perspiration streaming down his face, strains every nerve to make head upon his pursuers; and as they follow on his track, and gain upon him every instant, they hail his decreasing strength with still louder shouts, and whoop and scream with joy. "Stop thief!" Ay, stop him for God's sake, were it only in mercy!*

Charles Dickens, *Oliver Twist* (1837–38)

AN INTRODUCTION TO CONDUCT DISORDERS

In 1899 in Illinois, the first juvenile court law was enacted "to regulate the treatment and control of dependent, neglected, and delinquent children." Under the leadership of such individuals as John Peter Altgeld and Julia Lathrop, a reform movement gained sufficient impetus to achieve unanimous approval of the Illinois state legislature for the establishment of a court whose sole function would be to act as a chancery court, a court charged with the responsibility of ensuring the welfare of those in its charge as opposed to adjudicating criminal responsibility. Other states rapidly followed suit in producing legislative systems and procedures to keep youngsters from entering the criminal court system.

Thus the juvenile courts were not designed to determine the guilt or innocence of youngsters but to oversee their welfare either by placing them under the supervision of the courts, by placing them in foster homes, or by committing them to reform institutions. Though designed with the welfare of children in mind, the establishment of the juvenile court system also had the effect of avoiding issues regarding the rights of children. The juvenile courts did not involve adversary proceedings between state and defendant, and the importance of safeguarding the constitutional rights of children did not arise. All decisions were presumed to have the welfare of children as the central concern of all involved. This kind of approach had the ironic consequence that, since the establishment of the juvenile court system, children and adolescents have often been subjected to treatment approaches that—if applied to adults—would constitute clear violations of constitutional rights.

Nevertheless, despite the many weaknesses and shortcomings of the juvenile court system, these early legislative actions did have several important consequences: (a) juvenile offenses were removed from the realm of criminality and the adult penal system; (b) society at large was forced to recognize the complexity of causes leading to antisocial behavior in children and adolescents, and (c) dozens of social reformers and scientists launched investigations into the roots of conduct disorders and delinquent behavior.

In this chapter we will explore the broad areas of behavior encompassed by the original legislation that established the juvenile court system. It is important to note at the outset that categories and labels are often arbitrary and used for the sake of convenience in research and discussion. It is not always clear in the case of an individual child whether patterns of behavior can be termed simply personality problems or conduct disorders. Either of these categories may overlap the other, and both may overlap one or several other descriptive groupings outlined in other sections of this book. After studying the conceptions derived from research and clinical experience, it is always imperative to return to the reality of the individual child who does not necessarily conform to theoretical conceptions. As Leo Kanner has noted, "The children haven't read those books" (1969, p. 2).

DEFINITION AND CLASSIFICATION

Because the concept of *delinquency* is basically a legal notion implying deviance from cultural norms and/or legal restrictions, it is of little help in gaining insight into developmental problems. At the same time, it has been an important idea in stimulating and shaping research for more than seventy years, and it cannot be avoided altogether. However, no attempt will be made here to formulate or to adopt a formal definition of "delinquency." We will use the term in its popular sense to refer to any behavior of a child or young adolescent that violates the legal standards of the community.

A more useful concept from the standpoint of understanding the individual child is that of **conduct disorder,** which encompasses any behavior of a developing youngster that causes difficulty or disruption in the child's relationships with parents, family, teachers, or the larger community—including law enforcement agencies. This definition would include such diverse forms of behavior as vandalism, teenage prostitution, and theft. No distinction is made here between conduct disorders and delinquency, since the only real distinction between the two is a matter of legal definition. Stated differently, a child who is chronically aggressive or who steals is exhibiting a conduct disorder. Whether the child is also delinquent depends on the moral standards of the community and on whether the child is apprehended by legal authorities. Children who do not come to the attention of the police and the courts are not formally delinquent, but they may very well be acting in ways that are clearly indicative of problems in socialization and ethical development that fall within the scope of the broader concept of conduct disorders. For the purposes of this discussion, the two terms will be used interchangeably, since legal distinctions are less important in this context than characteristics of psychological and social development.

As noted in Chapter 11, there is ample research justification for this inclusive grouping of a wide variety of disturbing behaviors under the heading of conduct disorders, since such behaviors often occur together in clusters in the real child and since they reflect greater difficulty in interpersonal relations than in the child's ability to cope with anxiety. In other words, the present discussion is concerned with "externalizing problems" as opposed to the "internalizing problems" discussed in Chapter 11.

Specifically, the kinds of behavior implied by the use of the term "conduct disorder" include restlessness, destructiveness, lying, stealing, aggressiveness manifested in quarreling, fighting, swearing, disobedience and defiance, disinterest in school, truancy, sexual promiscuity, prostitution, substance abuse, and running away (Werry & Quay, 1971). It is obvious, of course, that most of these behaviors can also be classified as delinquent—to the extent that they bring the child into direct conflict with the law. Nonetheless, the concept of conduct disorder, though broader, is also more aptly descriptive, since it does not presume that a given child has been accused or apprehended in connection with a crime. The behaviors in question may be ranged along a continuum from mild to extremely severe, and only arbitrary designations distinguish fighting from assault, taking from stealing, lateness from curfew violation, and sex for favors from sex for money.

INCIDENCE AND ETIOLOGY

It is the very problem of trying to distinguish the psychosocial concept of conduct disorder from the legal concept of delinquency that complicates the task of estimating the incidence of conduct disorders or of understanding causative factors. Thus, for example, the Joint Commission on the Mental Health of Children (1970) estimated conservatively that 11 percent of American children will appear in juvenile court by the age of 19. At the same time, however, there is also evidence that unrecorded delinquency is extensive (Short & Nye, 1958), and that apprehension of youngsters for delinquent behavior is as much a function of community size, racial or ethnic background, and socioeconomic status as of the actual delinquent act itself. When the concept of delinquency is broadened beyond contact with police or courts to include other forms of disruptive behavior, estimates of conduct disorder jump to as high as one in every five American children (Feldhusen, Thurston, & Benning, 1973).

In investigating the causes of conduct disorders, a number of theoretical explanations have been developed. These have ranged from ideas that disruptive behavior is genetically determined to others that imply that conduct disorders are understandable exclusively in environmental terms. In recent years, however, theories implying exclusive causation by heredity or environment or any single factor have fallen by the wayside, and it is evident that multiple causative factors have to be examined in an interactive context. In the following sections we will examine a variety of theoretical notions and then attempt some synthesis of these ideas.

Physical Constitution and Conduct Disorders

The attempt to explain conduct disorders as a consequence of heredity and constitutional endowment is ancient, indeed. One can readily find speculations about human conduct and the "bad seed" concept of delinquent behavior throughout history. Hippocrates, for example, suggested that the delinquent individual possesses a choleric, irascible temperament and is prone to impulsive, aggressive behavior. Centuries later, Cesare Lombroso, an influential Italian criminologist, also believed that the "criminal type" is born predisposed to engage in antisocial behavior.

Within this century important support has been given to a constitutional approach to understanding delinquent behavior by the research of Sheldon and Eleanor Glueck. The Gluecks first reported the findings of a major longitudinal study of conduct disorders in their book, *Unraveling Juvenile Delinquency* (1950). Beginning in 1948, the Gluecks undertook extensive investigations of background, personality, and physical characteristics of 500 delinquent and 500 nondelinquent boys.

In their report the Gluecks clearly acknowledged the importance of environmental factors in understanding delinquent behavior. The 500 delinquent youngsters they studied came from underprivileged areas in Boston that were characterized by physical deterioration, poverty, and antisocial deviance. The Gluecks felt certain that the physical and social dilapidation of these neighborhoods were important negative influences leading to the development of conduct disorders. However, one major fact made any totally environmental explanation of delinquency untenable: the 500 nondelinquent boys were selected from the same neighborhoods. With social environments the same for both groups of youngsters, it became clear that explanations of deviant behavior had to go beyond the social decay characteristic of urban slums.

The Gluecks also acknowledged the instability of family life in the backgrounds of delinquent youngsters and presented a picture of rather erratic, impulsive, unstable family backgrounds. At this point, discrepancies emerged in their research. While all the boys in their study came from similar socioeconomic backgrounds, instability was more characteristic of the home lives of delinquent youngsters. Such instability was indicated by higher frequencies of parental delinquency, psychological disturbance, alcoholism, forced marriages, divorce, poverty, confusion in household maintenance, conflicting standards of behavior between parents, maternal laxness, paternal overstrictness, large families, overcrowding, inconsistency in discipline, and, in the Gluecks' terms, a generally "slipshod" approach to family life.

However, the most important finding to emerge from this massive study—perhaps because it runs counter to the mainstream of theories regarding the origins of conduct disorders—was the evidence of physical-constitutional differences between delinquents and nondelinquents. Overall, there were differences in the general physical makeup or physique of the two groups of boys. The delinquent youngsters exhibited (a) sturdier physical build, (b) better integrated or more harmonious physical structure, and (c) more masculine bodily makeup than their nondelinquent counterparts.

Despite the fact that the delinquent and nondelinquent boys had been matched along a number of important dimensions—including race, age, socioeconomic background, and neighborhood—clear differences in physique persisted, with delinquent boys exhibiting a more muscular, rugged, well-knit type of physique. This body type had earlier been termed a "mesomorphic physique" by W. H. Sheldon (1940) and correlated with such behavioral traits as aggressiveness, high energy level, emotional insensitivity, and a tendency to resort to physical action when tense or frustrated. Further, the youngsters with mesomorphic physiques did not show constraints against antisocial behavior and were not submissive to authority, timid, or fearful (Glueck & Glueck, 1968).

It is important to note that the Gluecks did not suggest that body type is a direct cause of delinquency. On the contrary, the relationship between physique and delinquency is a complex one, and the Gluecks hypothesized that constitution may make delinquent behavior more functional and effective for a youngster developing within the context of social deprivation and family instability. That is, the mesomorphic youngster may, because of physical advantage, be able to find rewards in antisocial behavior while lacking the social inhibition involved in learning to adhere to the dictates and sanctions of society. While a timid, fearful child may be too apprehensive about possible punishment to violate social sanctions and be unable physically to get away with much, the aggressive mesomorph, by contrast, may find violations of social norms or legal restrictions exciting, achievable, and satisfying. It is interesting to note in this regard that some research evidence supports the notion that delinquents perceive risks differently than nondelinquents and find risk-taking behavior exhilarating and enjoyable (Claster, 1967).

Neurological Problems and Conduct Disorders

Though still highly controversial and with much conflicting evidence, there is sufficient data available to warrant mention of the possibility that conduct disturbances may be related to neurological disorders (e.g., Berman, 1972; Beshai, 1971; Critchley, 1968; Ishihara & Yoshii, 1971). Berman (1972) pointed to behavioral similarities between children with presumed minimal brain damage and children with conduct disorders as suggestive of similar causation. These behavioral similarities include hyperactivity, short attention span, impulsivity, low frustration tolerance, inability to delay gratification, irritability, and aggressiveness. Even more direct evidence is presented in research indicating that a sample of juvenile delinquents exhibited evidence of a specific learning disability (dyslexia) in 60 percent of the cases studied (Critchley, 1968).

Despite the provocative nature of such findings, however, the issue of neurological involvement in the etiology of conduct disorders is largely presumptive and inferential. Little direct evidence is yet available, but the area is a potentially fertile one for future research.

Social Causes of Conduct Disorders

The primary social milieu in which the child develops is the family. Consequently, in searching for the social origins of conduct disorders, the family must be the initial focus of study. One of the most consistent findings of extensive research on the origins of delinquent behavior is that the delinquent youngster is more likely to come from a home broken by divorce or separation than the nondelinquent child (Anderson, 1968; Glueck & Glueck, 1962, 1968; Sanders, 1976). However, the key factor related to the development of a conduct disorder is not the fact of divorce, but rather the absence of adequate parental control of the child's behavior (Glueck & Glueck, 1962). Thus, the child often fails to develop appropriate standards of behavior because these are not, in fact, either taught directly or modeled in the home. Furthermore, lack of adequate parental control can also reflect parental delinquency and emotional disturbance (Glueck & Glueck, 1962; West, 1973; Wilson, 1975). Taken together, these various findings indicate that the delinquent child often comes from a home characterized by parental conflict that often eventuates in divorce, absence of prosocial standards of behavior in the parents as evidenced by high rates of parental delinquency, and failure to communicate standards of behavior to the child (Hirschi, 1969).

Research has also repeatedly linked conduct disorders to low family income, large family size, and erratic management of finances (Glueck & Glueck, 1962; West, 1973; Wilson, 1975). While the research evidence is not as clear in the following area, it is possible to link parental instability to these family characteristics in the background of the child. It seems evident that the behavioral instability and impulsivity that result in parental delinquency and high divorce rates may also explain—at least partially—large family size and financial instability.

In addition to problems arising from unstable family structure and absence of appropriate parental control, further social factors relating to the appearance of delinquent behavior include the influences of neighborhood and peer group.

So-called "structural theories" of delinquency approach this problem from an environmentalist perspective and emphasize the importance of social class variables as causative factors. From this perspective, delinquency is understood as a result of membership in lower socioeconomic classes, which leads to social deprivation and blockage of aspirations for achievement. Delinquent youngsters respond to this frustration by rejecting the normative standards of the society they cannot enter and by rebelling against that society angrily through crime and violent expression of frustration or by entrance into criminal activities as an alternative opportunity structure (Cloward & Ohlin, 1960).

A complementary conception understands delinquency as a consequence of *social anomie,* an absence or rapid shifting of societal norms and values. Thus the delinquent is seen as coming from deprived segments of society that respond to conditions of deprivation with such rapidly shifting value structures that the developing youngster does not really have an opportunity to observe and internalize a coherent set of values and standards for self-regulation of behavior. Strong support for this hypothesis comes from repeated observations that the incidence of delinquency is highest in urban neighborhoods undergoing rapid population transitions and changes from more affluent, stable residents to poorer, more transient residents (McCartney, 1974).

A further consequence of living under conditions of economic and cultural deprivation is a narrow restriction in socialization opportunities.

Potentially delinquent youngsters live under circumstances in which specific patterns of association are favored: namely, association with others who engage in socially deviant activities or criminal behavior. These associations can lead to the learning and incorporation of deviant behavioral patterns eventuating in a delinquent life-style. Sutherland and Cressey (1974) theorized that delinquent behavior is learned within the context of small groups that view violation of the law as more functional than adherence to it. These groups characteristically form on the basis of neighborhood associations and contacts, and directly teach antisocial values and even techniques for committing crimes.

This kind of "subcultural deviance" may or may not be associated with psychological disturbance, but is basically independent of such disturbance. That is, it is quite possible that the youngster developing in a deviant subculture may be psychologically healthy and well-adjusted, but well-adjusted to a socially deviant group such as a neighborhood gang or a criminal reference group.

Altogether, there is strong research evidence suggesting that environmental approaches to understanding the development of conduct disorders

Growing up in an environment where socially deviant behavior is frequent and accepted can be a potent factor in later delinquent behavior.

are accurate and valuable. However, it still remains unclear as to why certain individuals developing within the context of a disturbed family and a deteriorating environment actually develop conduct disorders while others develop into well-socialized, contributing members of the community.

Psychological Development and Conduct Disorders

Still another approach to understanding the causation of conduct disorders is offered by psychological and psychiatric investigators. Psychodynamic theorists have long been interested in delinquent behavior, viewing it as the outcome of defects in conscience development along with the presence of internalized conflicts. In children with weak character structures arising either constitutionally or from damaging life experiences, aggressive behavior may simply represent direct discharge of the tension associated with unconscious impulses by acting out of the impulses. In other words, the delinquent child is acting out behaviorally those impulses that cannot be defended against successfully by other means (Bettelheim & Sylvester, 1949, 1950). At times, social factors also become prominent, and delinquent behavior may be the outcome of faulty conscience development where the child internalizes parental standards, but the parents themselves exhibit defects of character, glaring lapses of conscience, or moral contradictions. In these instances, parental impulses may be satisfied through the child's behavioral expression (Beres, 1958; Johnson, 1949). In other words, a child with generally adequate conscience development who engages in certain forbidden behavior may be acting out parental impulses as well as internal ones.

Alternatively, delinquent behavior may represent a desire for punishment in an individual with deep-rooted, unconscious feelings of guilt (Abrahamsen, 1960). In these cases, the individual is said to engage in socially deviant behavior in order to elicit punishment from others to assuage unconscious guilt arising from internalized, unconscious conflict. In still other instances, delinquent behavior may be understood as "identification with the aggressor"; a child may internalize the behavior patterns of a harsh, punitive parent and express violent aggression toward others (Spitz, 1958).

Erikson (1968) saw delinquent behavior as the possible outcome of negative identification. The developing adolescent, engaging in experiments with self-definition and attempting to resolve a psychosocial identity crisis, may identify with a socially deviant hero who represents a resolution of internalized unconscious conflicts.

Taken together, these conceptions indicate that conduct disorders and delinquent behavior cannot be understood in any simple fashion. Rather, they represent a variety of individual attempts to resolve internalized conflicts or failures in adequate conscience development.

Still other psychological perspectives understand social deviance as the outcome of learning processes. In other words, conduct disorders and delinquency can be understood within the context of operant learning conceptions. The delinquent child is simply a youngster whose disruptive or socially unacceptable behavior has been reinforced directly or inadvertently. In a deviant subcultural group, it is easy to understand a process whereby a youngster may win peer approval and acceptance by engaging in behavior that the larger culture rejects. Thus, if daring and courage are valued by the peer group, a youngster may win social approval by defying a teacher or engaging in a theft. In other instances deviant behavior is self-rewarding, as when a child takes something impulsively without any subsequent recriminations or only long-delayed punishment. In this case the behavior itself is rewarding in its outcomes and likely to be repeated. Parents may inadvertently reward deviant behavior by their approval of aggressiveness, daring, or defiance; or reward may be more direct as parents actively support a child's flouting of social standards.

Modeling is another vehicle by which a child learns particular patterns of behavior. As a child observes others engaging in norm-violation or aggressive behavior without punishment or even with rewarding consequences, the likelihood of such behavior is increased (Bandura, 1965, 1969).

Naturally, a child living within a context of social deprivation and differential patterns of association with peers already engaged in delinquent behavior is likely to experience both modeling influences and direct reinforcement for unacceptable or illegal behavior.

AN INTEGRATIVE MODEL OF CONDUCT DISORDERS

When several different theoretical perspectives offer persuasive explanations for a particular behavior, then it is likely that each has some important insights that should be considered. Research evidence and clinical experience suggest that each of the perspectives reviewed here briefly may further our understanding of delinquent behavior. Consequently, it is important to try

Within the warm and structured setting of a group home for troubled girls, these adolescents will be reinforced for socially acceptable behavior and will thus have the promise of developing more adaptive behavior patterns and a sense of self-worth.

to integrate these conceptions to come to a clearer understanding of the multiple forces that impinge on the individual to produce conduct disorders.

Enumeration of research findings indicates that conduct disorders are associated with (a) conditions of socioeconomic deprivation, (b) family disorganization, (c) faulty learning experiences, (d) hereditary and constitutional factors, and, possibly, (e) neurological disorder.

Is there a way of integrating these diverse perspectives? Extensive reviews of research literature by Eysenck (1964, 1975) and Franks (1961) supported the viewpoint that individuals exhibit constitutional differences that are important in understanding socially deviant behavior. While these investigators did not explicitly subscribe to the typology espoused by the Gluecks, they did describe characteristics in some individuals that are similar to the characteristics of the mesomorphic youngster (Eysenck, 1965). Specifically, Eysenck suggested that certain individuals exhibit high levels of emotionality, which he termed "neuroticism." At the same time, and independently, some individuals exhibit great difficulty in forming conditioned responses and unusual ease in the extinction of such responses when formed. Eysenck termed this characteristic "extraversion." The combination of emotionality and difficulty in forming conditioned responses leads to a situation in which a youngster is likely to engage in impulsive, erratic behavior without the capacity to learn readily from the consequences of such behavior (Eysenck, 1976).

Stated differently, the child exhibiting a conduct disorder seems to have difficulty in learning the self-control that is a key part of appropriate social development. While the normally developing child also engages in socially unacceptable impulsive behavior, parental scoldings or punishments cause sufficient anxiety that the child avoids such behaviors on subsequent occasions. This is not the case with the delinquent youngster who does not form the conditioned avoidance responses that are an important component of conscience (Yates, 1970).

Children with serious conduct disorders often have problems with self-control, and their temper outbursts may be frequent and seemingly undiminished by scoldings or punishments.

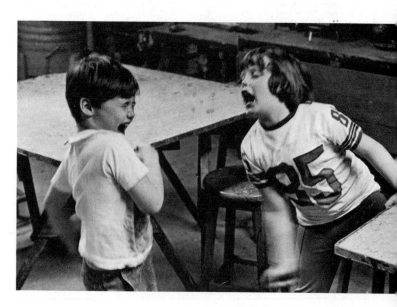

Thus the child with a conduct disorder or delinquent behavior has difficulty incorporating impulse restraints that other children learn rapidly as the result of conditioned associations between specific unacceptable behavior and anxiety.

A further complicating factor arises in situations where socially forbidden behavior is capable of providing reinforcement. Situations often arise in which a forbidden behavior brings immediate reinforcement, while punishment does not occur until some time later. Puppies trained in such a fashion are curiously delinquent in character; they exhibit behavioral indications of anxiety—suggesting recognition that the behavior is forbidden—along with simultaneous impulsive indulgence in the punished behavior (Solomon, 1964; Solomon, Turner, & Lessac, 1968).

To summarize, the potential delinquent exhibits higher than average levels of neuroticism and extraversion that impede the formation of anxiety responses in relation to prohibited behavior, and on occasion experiences reinforcement of such behavior.

Conditions of social deprivation further complicate the picture by introducing experiences of chronic or repeated frustration and patterns of differential association with deviant subcultural groups (such as delinquent gangs or, more often, adolescent peer groups trying to establish autonomy from adult control). Early research by John Dollard and Neal Miller suggested that frustra-

---

OPEN ISSUE

Traditional childrearing advice has it that failure to exercise firm discipline—often thought of in terms of corporal punishment—will result in "spoiling" a child. Defiant, unruly, aggressive behavior must be dealt with quickly and firmly regardless of underlying reasons. Otherwise, a child will develop without appropriate respect for adults or willingness to abide by social norms and legal standards.

On the other hand, parents and teachers often receive professional advice suggesting that too much discipline or too stringent discipline will produce adults who are rigidly conforming, inhibited, and withdrawn. A child who is forced to comply with external demands of parents and other authority figures may deny significant aspects of his/her own personality and experience intense conflicts between what is felt to be right and what others say is right.

As a result of these different approaches and philosophies, parents and teachers often waver back and forth between lenience and harshness in trying to determine some middle ground in disciplinary practices. And, as is so often the case, research conclusions can be uncovered that support virtually any position. Periodic reports in the popular press depict the positive effects of "get tough" programs in different communities where a school, the police and courts, or a parent-teacher organization begin to enforce stringent disciplinary measures, sometimes including physical punishment. Other reports suggest understanding and acceptance are the keys to reducing conduct problems. There are at present no simple answers to this open issue.

tion often elicits aggression as a dominant response pattern (Dollard, Doob, Miller, Mowrer, & Sears, 1939; Miller, Sears, Mowrer, Doob, & Dollard, 1941). Much subsequent research was directed toward demonstrating this relationship, and a large body of supporting data was amassed. However, contemporary research has indicated that a variety of other factors must also enter into an understanding of aggressive behavior, including differential reinforcement of aggressive responses and modeling effects (Bandura, 1969). It is in relation to modeling that differential patterns of association become more clearly understandable as causative factors.

Essentially, then, aggressive responses may be understood not only as consequences of frustration and emotional arousal, but also as outcomes of material or social reinforcement through goal attainment or removal of interpersonal obstacles, or as consequences of observing models whose aggressive behavior is either not punished or actually rewarded. Aggression and anti-social behavior may thus be learned in a variety of ways.

An additional consistent finding that should be considered has to do with the family background of the delinquent or disruptive youngster. In view of the factors thus far reviewed, it should be evident that, for a child born into a family disrupted either through divorce or emotional instability, it is unlikely that he/she will learn the avoidance responses that constitute an important part of socialization. Put more concretely, it is unlikely that the child will encounter the consistent discipline or social education that permits the development of discriminations regarding socially acceptable or prohibited behavior. In simplest terms, the child is not taught right from wrong in a fashion that permits the consistent, fine distinctions and self-control which constitute socialization. Further, inconsistent patterns of reward and harsh punishment often do no more than teach the child that aggression and violence are functional and useful. Modeling influences directly teach the youngster the useful effects of aggression. The parent who says, "I'll teach *you* to hit," and then proceeds to administer harsh physical punishment is literally administering a lesson in aggression.

To summarize, it appears likely that conduct disorders result from the confluence of constitutional vulnerability, inadequate family background, social deprivation, and the interaction of these with classical and instrumental conditioning and modeling effects. Conduct disorders consist of behavior that is learned by a predisposed individual encountering conditions of poverty, frustration, poor peer models, and inadequate family structure. Exhibit 12.1 portrays this complex interaction graphically. Within this framework, conduct disorders should be modifiable if appropriate preventive or corrective experiences can be provided. In a later section we will explore approaches applicable in the home and the classroom that have offered promise of effective remediation of conduct disorders.

DIAGNOSIS AND IDENTIFICATION

The importance of understanding the etiology of conduct disorders becomes particularly evident in relation to developing an adequate developmental

EXHIBIT 12.1

351
Diagnosis and
identification

FACTORS INVOLVED IN THE CAUSATION OF CONDUCT DISORDERS

**Constitutional
Predisposing Factors**

Mesomorphic body structure
Emotional instability
(neuroticism)
Difficulty in forming conditioned responses (extra-
version)
Possible neurological dysfunction in some individuals

Psychological Factors

Difficulty developing adequate
self-control (problems in formation of adequate condi-
tioned anxiety responses
inhibiting impulsive be-
havior)
Reinforcement of aggressive
behavior
Modeling influences from
peers, media
Identification with poor parental models
Desires for attention/possibly
desires for punishment
Chronic frustration leading to
aggressive responses

Environmental Factors

Social and economic deprivation
Differential patterns of association with delinquent peers
Chronic frustration of educa-
tional/economic aspirations
Absence of adequate opportunity structure

Family Factors

Parental conflict, divorce
Disorganization within family
Impulsive, unstable parents
Inconsistent, harsh disciplinary
practices
Neglect by parents—emotional
rejection
Poor parental models who
themselves engage in delin-
quent behavior patterns
Parental alcoholism, drug abuse

diagnosis. In understanding an individual child, we must be able to make distinctions between aggressive behavior and normal assertiveness, between defiance of authority and healthy independence, between disruptiveness and energetic initiative. In some cases, these distinctions pose no problem, and the existence of a genuine conduct disorder is readily recognized. However, in younger children prior to the development of rather consistent behavior patterns, it is often difficult to determine whether a problem does, in fact, exist. At the same time, it is precisely during earlier developmental periods that it is critically important to recognize emerging problems and to develop intervention strategies before socially maladaptive patterns of behavior emerge.

While several attempts have been made to develop diagnostic assessment techniques predictive of conduct problems and delinquency, these techniques have typically been unsuccessful (Venezia, 1971). The *complex interactions among the child's personality and behavior, parental characteristics, and social environment preclude any simple approach to diagnostic assessment, particularly in younger children.* Instead, it is critical to understand the child as the focus of a variety of forces that may interact with emerging personality characteristics and result in disordered behavior and even delinquency.

To achieve this kind of understanding, it is essential that diagnostic study begin with an examination of the child, but extend well beyond into exploration of parental characteristics, interactions within the family, quality of the neighborhood environment, and the child's relationships in school and in the local neighborhood.

Key factors in the diagnostic study of the child include assessment of the kinds and frequencies of problematic behavior in relation to the child's age. For example, occasional truancy in a 10-year-old is evidently more problematic than the same problem in an adolescent; however, anything more than occasional truancy is cause for concern for a youngster of any age. Similarly, we expect an adolescent to be occasionally defiant as a step in asserting growing independence; however, a consistently defiant elementary-school child may be developing patterns that will later become seriously problematic.

Of equal importance in the diagnosis is an assessment of the child's ability to relate to others with spontaneity, trust, and genuine affection. Difficulty in forming relationships characterized by trust and mutuality may lead to chronic interpersonal problems and an inability to empathize with others. Furthermore, the youngster must value the acceptance and affection of others in order for them to influence development and serve as social reinforcers. In this respect, it is particularly important to assess the youngster's ability to relate to adults and respond to authority in a reasonable fashion. Delinquency-prone youngsters exhibit particular difficulty in handling the demands of authority figures, often responding with angry submission or explosive defiance.

Problems in any of these areas may interact with parental behavior in such a manner as to increase the probability of conduct problems. Thus, for example, if parents are careless or rejecting, there is little basis for a suspicious youngster to develop a sense of trust or to value adult acceptance. Harsh punishment or frequent criticism are further alienating behaviors that are often found among parents of youngsters with conduct disorders.

The diagnostic assessment must further view these factors within the context of the neighborhood and school environments. A youngster with problems in several of the above areas may, nevertheless, encounter peers and teachers who respond positively and serve as strong role models, and who also are important reinforcing agents. If these models are unavailable, or if available models themselves are disturbed or delinquent, the probability of disturbed behavior in the child is even further increased.

In some respects, the diagnostic study of the child exhibiting behavior problems must be viewed in an additive sense. That is, the more of the above factors that are problematic, the greater the likelihood that the child will eventually develop chronically disturbed behavior patterns or delinquency.

EXHIBIT 12.2

353
Developmental
consequences

INDICATORS OF CONDUCT DISORDERS AND DELINQUENCY PRONENESS

1. Home supervision limited; lack of parental interest or involvement; only one parent in the home; home life characterized by disorganization; conflict between parents; emotional disturbance, criminal behavior, alcoholism, or drug abuse in one or both parents.

2. Socioeconomic deprivation; qualifies for subsidized school lunch or breakfast programs; family receiving public assistance.

3. Dislike of school; problems with school authorities; truancy; history of detentions, suspensions; unexcused absences, class cuts; defiance of teachers; refusal to complete assignments.

4. Difficulties in educational achievement; failure of one or more school subjects; reading below grade level; older than classmates because of grade retentions.

5. Patterns of association with delinquent peers; gang involvement; early use of drugs or alcohol; minor police involvement.

6. Early history of neurological dysfunction or learning disabilities; impulsive behavior patterns; below average to average intellectual ability.

7. Emotional instability; erratic behavior patterns; easily angered; unable to accept responsibility; rigidly independent or overly conforming.

No single characteristic by itself is indicative of a conduct disorder or proneness to delinquent behavior; the more factors present, the greater the probability of chronic behavior disturbance.

Based in part on Powell (1975)

Exhibit 12.2 summarizes a number of variables that should be considered in the diagnostic assessment of youngsters with behavior problems.

In cases where a youngster is exhibiting isolated problematic behaviors, the diagnostic process should result in recommendations to parents and/or teachers for specific intervention plans to remedy these behaviors. However, in cases where a number of diagnostic indicators are simultaneously present in the child's personality and environment, more pervasive intervention strategies become necessary and may require simultaneous plans to work with the child, the family, and teachers. In some instances, the diagnostic process may reveal that the child's life circumstances are so pervasively disturbed that foster home or institutional placement are the only realistic alternatives. Wherever possible, however, such drastic measures should be taken only where all other attempts have failed to produce changes in a child's behavior.

DEVELOPMENTAL CONSEQUENCES

As in the case of personality problems, it is difficult to distinguish the symptoms of conduct disorders from their developmental consequences. Thus, for example, poorly socialized behavior is a broad, defining characteristic of conduct disorders, but it is also an ongoing developmental consequence. Likewise, disturbed relationships with parents are symptomatic of a conduct disorder but can also be viewed as an ongoing developmental characteristic. Distinctions between symptoms and developmental consequences in the case of conduct disorders are largely artificial and will be made only to focus attention on two important areas, educational achievement and interpersonal relations.

Conceptual Abilities and Educational Achievement

While there is no solid evidence to indicate differences in intellectual ability between children with conduct disorders and normal children, a number of characteristics in the former are significant in impeding educational progress. Prominent among the behaviors that characterize children with conduct disorders are disobedience, defiance of authority, disruptiveness, irresponsibility, attention seeking, and boisterousness (Quay, 1972). None of these is likely to endear a child to teachers, and children with conduct disorders display school problems very early in their school careers. Unwilling to submit to teacher authority and unable to control impulses, these children have much difficulty in the regular classroom. Frequently, and understandably, they alienate their teachers and create problems in classroom control. As a consequence, patterns of interpersonal friction develop so that the child comes to resent every attempt of the teacher to exert control or authority while the teacher, on the other hand, becomes sensitive to potential infractions that might go unnoticed in another child. In this way the stage is set for the development of resentment of the learning process and a general aversion to the school experience. Chronic problems with school authorities and truancy are frequent consequences.

Within this context of continual tension between child and school, learning itself is impeded, and failure to learn further intensifies aversions to school. The result, often, is frequent truancy and eventual dropping out of school. Failure to learn, truancy, and dropping out of school, in turn, usually mean that the youngster will have limited opportunities to find satisfying or meaningful work. Resulting frustration and anger often set the stage for embarkation on a more intensive antisocial career. Indeed, the presence of a conduct disorder in childhood is often predictive of adolescent delinquency and adult criminality (Quay, 1972; Robins, 1972).

Problems in educational achievement, therefore, are important consequences of conduct disorders and lead to further alienation from the mainstream of society.

Personal and Social Factors

Children with conduct disorders are irritable, quarrelsome, destructive, aggressive, and deficient in normal guilt feelings (Quay, 1972). The presence of these characteristics, along with those discussed in the previous section, inevitably lead to extensive and intense interpersonal problems. Beginning with defiance of parental authority and disobedience, children with conduct dis-

*For children who are unwilling to submit
to teacher authority or unable to control
impulses, further problems will likely en-
sue as the continuing tension between
teacher and pupil impedes learning itself.*

orders display an inability to get along with most people. Within the family,
relationships are characterized by continual struggles for control punctuated
by outbursts of anger and aggression. As we noted earlier, the parents of
delinquent youngsters themselves may display problems in self-control and
adequate socialization. Confronted by a child who creates further tension
within the family, parents often give vent to their own impulses in the form of
harsh physical punishment. The young child has little defense against parental
anger and often responds by displacing his/her own anger against siblings or
peers. With little ability to empathize with others, the child behaves in callous
fashion, and impulses are restrained only when the fear of punishment out-
weighs potential gratifications. In some instances even punishment is inadequate, and the child behaves impulsively regardless of the consequences.

As the child develops, there is increasing likelihood that disobedience
and impertinence will give way to assaultiveness and crime, and the child with
a conduct problem becomes an adolescent delinquent.

Though relationships with peers may be somewhat less problematic than
those with parents or other authority figures such as teachers or police, there
is nevertheless difficulty in peer relations. The child with conduct problems is
usually unable to consider the consequences of behavior or to empathize with
the feelings of peers. As a result, peer relationships are often characterized by
shallowness and attempts at mutual exploitation. There is little depth or loyalty
in such relationships.

There is an exception to this pattern in the behavior of some youngsters who, though technically delinquent, do not share many of the characteristics we have been discussing. In these youngsters poor environmental background may lead to delinquency and crime, but within the context of an adequately developing personality. In these cases loyalty exists, but it is misplaced. Empathy is possible, but only with members of one's own gang. In essence, the child is adequately socialized but within the context of an antisocial gang culture.

More often, however, youngsters with genuine conduct problems do not develop patterns of healthy interpersonal relationships and are incapable of genuine intimacy founded in mutual respect and consideration. The sad fact of the matter is that such youngsters usually do not develop beyond a stage of egocentric impulsivity and, in the majority of cases, exhibit similar patterns into adulthood (Robins, 1972). Frank's development (Case Study 12.1) is typical of such youngsters.

CASE STUDY 12.1

FRANK: FROM CONDUCT DISORDER TO DELINQUENCY

Frank was 11 years old at the time of his first referral for psychological services. That referral culminated a series of detentions, suspensions, and a parent conference for unruly school behavior, defiance, stealing, fighting, and truancy. None of the disciplinary measures tried had been successful, and during the parent conference Frank's mother reported that she was unable to control him at home, where he was aggressive and disobedient. In addition to these problems, neighbors reported that Frank had made sexual advances to their daughters and were insisting that the school take measures to control him.

At home Frank's mother had tried, unsuccessfully, to instill some sense of obedience through scoldings and repeated severe spankings. By the time of the referral, however, she had abandoned this approach, since Frank had struck back at her on several occasions. The mother had no support in her disciplinary efforts; Frank's father had abandoned the family 18 months earlier and had not been heard from since. In addition, Frank's mother resented school and neighbor complaints, since these implied that she was not an adequate mother. In fact, this was the case: she took little interest in her children and explicitly rejected Frank because his behavior created problems for her.

The school had little more success in controlling Frank than did his mother, and it appeared that there was no way to control him: punishment made him more resentful, and he felt that school administered rewards and privileges were "baby stuff." Referral to the school psychologist was made in the hope that some keys could be found to reversing the patterns of Frank's behavior.

The psychologist found Frank to be a handsome, well-built youngster. However, this was about all the "information" he was able to obtain, since Frank refused to speak during their meetings together. After three sessions of silence on Frank's part, the psychologist suggested that a long-term psychotherapy relationship might be more effective in helping Frank to become more trusting in another person. Psychotherapy was undertaken by a social worker on the school staff, but despite assurances of confidentiality, Frank refused to speak to him either. In fact, during the first psychotherapy interview, Frank turned his chair toward the wall and did not speak a single word. This pattern persisted through an additional eleven interviews, and therapy was terminated.

There was no change in Frank's behavior as a result of these efforts, and school authorities persisted in disciplinary efforts that had previously been unsuccessful. Thus Frank's school career consisted largely of disruption, punishment, and failure to learn. However, up to the time of graduation from elementary school, Frank managed to avoid problems with the police, and school authorities had little recourse but to live with his behavior.

Both Frank and his teachers were relieved at his graduation. There was little change in high school; typical patterns of truancy, fighting, and the like persisted until, finally, Frank's thefts escalated, and he was apprehended for stealing a car. A second car theft occurred while Frank was awaiting a juvenile court hearing for the first theft, and Frank was referred again for psychiatric evaluation. Frank was more communicative this time and told the psychiatrist to "F—— off." The juvenile court judge saw little alternative but to commit Frank to a juvenile home for a minimum period of two years.

Upon arrival at the boys' home, Frank was explicitly informed by houseparents about their expectations and the consequences of failure to conform to rules. Opportunities were available for earning rights and privileges through a system of earning points for a variety of chores and responsibilities. Privileges included access to television programs, activities, and sports. In addition, group contingencies were also in effect so that peers could lose privileges if they responded to Frank's disruptiveness. The consistent application of clearly stated rules and contingencies rapidly convinced Frank of the advantages of conformity, and disruptive behavior declined. In addition, Frank appeared to form several friendships with other boys, and he was less sensitive to restrictions imposed by houseparents and others.

At this point Frank is still in the boys' home and apparently adjusting reasonably well. Whether such adjustment will persist upon his eventual return to home and community is still questionable.

INTERVENTION WITH CONDUCT DISORDERS AND DELINQUENCY

Attempts to treat the child with a conduct problem or to rehabilitate the adolescent delinquent have taken a variety of forms ranging from simple punishment through administration of medication and psychotherapy. Punishment has rarely been effective in inducing permanent change, and medications have not yet been discovered that can induce empathy or develop self-control. While psychotherapy has often been attempted in the treatment of conduct disorders, it has less often been successful (Robins, 1972). Consequently, our discussion of intervention approaches will focus on behavioral techniques. Though still limited in effectiveness, these offer the most promise of being able to facilitate pervasive behavioral change on a long-term basis.

Dealing with Conduct Problems in the Classroom

There is no way that the classroom teacher can *directly* affect the social inequities that produce poverty and deprivation. There is relatively little within the teacher's capabilities for changing patterns of association that a youngster may have in the community, and it is not possible to eliminate the reinforcing consequences of disruptive behavior outside the classroom. There is absolutely nothing the teacher can do to modify constitutional endowment or possible neural defects.

Nevertheless, the classroom often appears to be the key situation that can

lead eventually to constructive change in child and adolescent conduct disorders. For one thing, the teacher is often the first individual who becomes
aware of the existence of a problem. The observant teacher can be alert for
such factors as a home broken by separation or divorce, lack of adult supervision, socioeconomic background of the family, the child's reading ability,
progress in school, dislike for school and defiance of school authorities,
truancy, and disciplinary actions—all of which have been used as predictors
of potential delinquency (Powell, 1975). Upon noting such predictive patterns,
the teacher can initiate intervention measures on the part of parents and other
school personnel. It is also the teacher who is in a critical position to develop
a positive relationship with a youngster and perhaps become a more adequate
role model than delinquent peers.

One way in which the teacher can establish such a relationship is by
providing rewarding, successful experiences in the classroom and in extracurricular activities. Such experiences, in turn, can often have a positive effect
on the youngster's negative self-concept, which produces self-definition in
antisocial terms. In other words, the fact that a large proportion of delinquent

*In working with a problem child, it is
important to provide her with an opportunity to be heard without recrimination.*

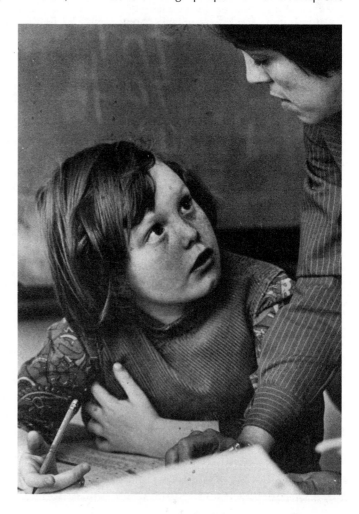

youngsters have poor school records and little interest in academic areas leads eventually to a conception of the entire academic experience as threatening and punishing. Thus the child often develops a self-concept based on defiance of the entire school experience. Hirschi (1969) described a sequence in which (a) poor academic performance leads to (b) dislike of school which, in turn, stimulates (c) rejection of all school authority, and eventuates in (d) the commission of delinquent acts. If the teacher is resourceful enough to structure the school experience so that the incipient delinquent can have positive, self-enhancing experiences, the process of withdrawal from the educational system may be slowed or even reversed.

In addition to providing academic success and affirmation of the youngster's self-worth, Powell (1975) suggested that the teacher can provide careful and highly structured educational freedom for the youngster to develop and pursue personal interests. Specific training in self-direction and control can also be initiated, and the youngster's efforts in these directions rewarded. The teacher can ensure basic skill mastery by recognizing deficiencies and working to correct them. The problem child—as well as other children—is often aware of inadequacies in reading, writing, and mathematics. It is also possible to explore and encourage the child's extracurricular interests. Finally, the teacher is in a position to provide the child with an opportunity to be heard without recrimination.

Naturally, all these steps require tremendous investments of time and energy, but the teacher is in a key position to encourage change and growth in the child, and is often the only person who can make such investments.

Behavior Modification in the Classroom

In combination with the measures outlined above, the teacher may also structure classroom experiences through the use of behavioral intervention strategies based on research findings in operant conditioning, modeling, and behavioral counseling.

While behavioral strategies are the subject of considerable controversy in relation to the modification of conduct problems, there is sufficient evidence of their effectiveness that the classroom teacher should be aware of approaches that have been used in various settings with predelinquent and delinquent youngsters (Braukmann, Fixsen, Phillips, & Wolf, 1975).

One area of importance that has already been mentioned has to do with teaching self-control procedures to youngsters exhibiting disruptive behaviors. Drabman, Spitalnik, and O'Leary (1973) undertook to train a group of eight disruptive 9- and 10-year-olds placed in an "adjustment" class to correctly evaluate and control their own behavior. All of these children had been described as very disruptive by their teachers, and all were at least a year behind age level in reading skills—indicators of potential delinquent development. Change procedures were initially undertaken in an after-school reading remediation class that met for one hour daily, for which parental cooperation was enlisted to assure their boys' attendance at least four days per week. During the sessions, a combination of token reinforcement and teacher praise was used to develop accurate self-evaluation of behavior in initial phases of the study. Students were rewarded with tokens for accurate matching of their own evaluations of their behavior with their teachers' evaluations. Eventually, teacher praise for correct matching replaced tokens, and then teacher checking of student self-evaluations was itself eliminated. During the last twelve days of this fifty-eight day study, all checking was discontinued, and students were awarded the number of tokens they felt they deserved. General praise for honest self-evaluation was continued.

The results of this study indicated that token reinforcement administered in conventional fashion was successful in reducing disruptive behavior and increasing academic behavior. More importantly, these youngsters learned accurate self-evaluation and honest reporting. "On occasion, they might even say, 'I was bad but I'm honest'" (p. 330). Further, the program maintained appropriate behavior even after teacher checking was discontinued. These investigators noted an additional interesting outcome: apparently teacher praise for appropriate behavior served to initiate imitation by students; that is, the youngsters themselves modeled their behavior after their teachers and praised appropriate behavior in their classmates. The students themselves no longer wanted to be bothered by peer disruption. Altogether, academic skills were improved, and there was increased participation in academic activities. It appears possible that improved academic performance itself became reinforcing for these youngsters. This study illustrates the potential applicability and utility of behavioral strategies in modifying conduct disorders and impeding the potential development of more serious disruptive behavior.

In another study (Becker, Madsen, Arnold, & Thomas, 1967), teachers were asked to select students exhibiting "severe" behavior problems. After initial baseline recording of the frequency of problem behaviors prior to any intervention, it was concluded that these youngsters exhibited inappropriate behavior interfering with learning approximately 72 percent of the time. Subsequently, teachers were instructed in specific classroom strategies: (a) classroom rules were stated explicitly and repeatedly; (b) inappropriate behaviors were to be ignored; (c) punishment for inappropriate behavior was administered in the form of withdrawal of approval; and (d) teacher praise and attention were made contingent on appropriate social behavior incompatible with disruptive behavior. A posttreatment assessment indicated that disruptive behavior had decreased from 72 percent of the time to 19.5 percent of the time.

In attempting to sort out the effective aspects of this program, Madsen, Becker, and Thomas (1968) discovered that knowledge of rules in itself did not change behavior, but teacher praise administered contingent on good behavior combined with ignoring inappropriate behavior appeared highly effective.

The studies we have reviewed so far highlight several of the key elements of applied behavioral technology in classroom situations. These elements include: (a) specification of target behaviors to be changed in explicit, unambiguous terms; (b) collection of baseline data or frequency counts of target behavior prior to any intervention; (c) planned intervention using positive reinforcement (tangible rewards, tokens, praise, privileges, attention) administered contingent on the occurrence of specified behaviors; (d) extinction of undesirable behaviors through *nonreinforcement*. It is critically important in regard to this last point to remember that *even negative attention (punishment) can be rewarding to some children and can maintain undesirable behavior.*

Another approach that has found frequent application in the treatment of conduct disorders and delinquency is *contingency contracting*, a procedure in which mutual behavioral expectations are explicitly stated in contract form, along with explicit statement of contingencies for compliance or noncompliance. In a major study of the application of behavioral techniques in naturally occurring settings, Tharp and Wetzel (1969) clearly demonstrated the utility of contingency contracting. Typically, such contracts are negotiated between teacher and student or between parent and child. The contract contains explicit statements regarding privileges and responsibilities, reciprocal obligations, and accountability procedures (Stuart & Lott, 1972). It is interesting to note here that, while behavioral contracting is a useful procedure, its effectiveness may be as much a function of initiating communications during the negotiation process as of the contract itself. Further, Stuart and Lott noted that the skill of the contractor is extremely important in opening and maintaining such communication.

Eitzen (1975) explored the effectiveness of behavioral technology as a means of altering the attitudes of delinquent youngsters so that they approximate the attitudes of nondelinquents. Subjects in this study were 12- to 16-year-old boys living in a community based home for delinquent boys (Achievement Place). Although the Achievement Place program has been successful in achieving behavioral improvement (Phillips, 1968; Phillips et al., 1971), Eitzen was interested in determining whether attitudinal changes accompany behavioral improvement. Attitude scales were administered to boys at the beginning of their stay at Achievement Place and at several points

Working together toward a goal, such as this clean-up project, can help these boys learn both a sense of responsibility and better patterns of interacting with others.

thereafter, including a final administration at the end of the program. Eitzen's results showed that there were significant changes in attitudes of delinquent youngsters in the program, with greatest changes in improved self-esteem and a sense of personal control of behavior. The significance of Eitzen's study is its clear demonstration that behavioral changes can produce attitudinal changes. While we normally think that our attitudes influence our behavior, it is important to recognize that behavioral change can change the way we think. *Behavior can influence attitudes.*

Sulzbacher and Houser (1968) employed group contingencies to control disruptive classroom behaviors. These investigators announced to students that a special ten-minute recess was to be instituted, but the recess would be eliminated for each day on which specified disruptive behaviors occurred. The group contingency immediately reduced the frequency of undesired behaviors. Further, the attention often elicited from peers for undesirable behavior was eliminated, since the entire group would lose the special privilege if they sustained the behavior by attending to it. Sulzbacher and Houser felt the procedure they employed was advantageous because it did not require extra equipment, alteration of classroom routine, or large investments of teacher time. Yet the procedure was highly effective in modifying classroom behavior and also in using the natural social consequences of peer attention to unacceptable behavior.

The several studies reviewed here represent only a sampling of a wide array of behavioral tools that can be important in controlling the classroom behavior of youngsters exhibiting various conduct disorders. There is no simple formula, however, in terms of which these techniques can be summarized, and teachers have sometimes made the mistake of believing that effective change can be implemented through the rote application of behavioral formulas. *The effective use of behavioral technology demands that programs should always be carefully developed and individualized to suit the requirements of the individual child and the classroom situation.* Further, behavioral approaches are inherently empirical: failure to produce change simply implies the necessity for improving the program rather than deciding that the child is incorrigible.

It has been noted that behavioral technology is little more than the application of common sense. Nevertheless, common sense is more often honored in the breach than the observance, and the effective use of behavior modification requires careful observation, precise measurement, thoughtful and creative development of programs, and familiarity with the growing body of research in this area. It is also important to recognize that behavior modification is not a cure-all for conduct problems, and much careful research needs to be done to understand the circumstances under which certain procedures work and, equally important, to understand why they fail.

Dealing with Conduct Problems in the Home

In addition to being a key figure in the recognition and modification of conduct disorders, the teacher is often in a position to facilitate parental awareness of such problems, and parents often turn to the classroom teacher as a resource in managing their children's behavior. In providing parents with assistance, the teacher may act as a referral source, encouraging the family to seek assistance at a community agency. The teacher may also initiate referral procedures within the school system, seeking the input of social worker, psychologist, guidance counselor, and speech and reading specialists.

More directly, however, the teacher may be an important source of ideas for parental management of a youngster's behavior (Gardner, 1976). For example, the teacher may help the parents establish academic and behavioral objectives that can then be encouraged both at home and at school. Consultation may be provided for behavior management procedures to be carried out at home, and even more directly, specific behavior modification programs may be designed for cooperative use at home and at school.

Behavioral approaches to modifying conduct problems in the home do not differ, in principle, from those employed in the classroom. Initially, it is useful for the teacher to explain to parents that disruptive behavior is often learned and may be inadvertently maintained by circumstances or by the very intractability of the child's responses. Consequently, it is important to try to analyze and understand the circumstances that may be sustaining the undesirable behavior. It is also important that no blame or criticism be implied in discussions with parents, since such implicit criticism will likely disrupt efforts to help the parents gain control over the child's behavior (and since such criticism is often unfounded and unwarranted anyway).

However, none of these steps will be particularly useful if the teacher has no concrete assistance to offer. Consequently, familiarity with approaches and techniques is important.

In an early study, Wahler, Winkel, Peterson, and Morrison (1965) demonstrated that mothers could be trained as effective behavior therapists for their own children. In the case of Eddie, age 4, the mother reported—and observations confirmed—that the child was extremely stubborn and negativistic. Interactions between Eddie and his mother were limited largely to spankings, scoldings, threats, and pleading on the part of the mother to get Eddie to behave. She was frustrated by his defiance and felt he often misbehaved simply to make her angry.

Eddie's behavior was clearly indicative of the existence of a conduct problem. What is more, the nature of interactions between Eddie and his mother were quite similar to the kinds of interactions often depicted between parents and older children exhibiting predelinquent behavior. Eddie's mother was taught to respond differentially to his behavior, ignoring oppositional behavior and responding enthusiastically to cooperation. In addition, a punishment contingency was eventually developed in which Eddie was removed from any toys or social interactions as a consequence of oppositional behavior. This kind of punishment is often referred to as *time-out from positive reinforcement*. More specifically, Eddie was to be left in his room for a period of five minutes following negative behavior; if tantrums or other negative behavior occurred during the time-out period, the period was extended until undesirable behavior terminated.

By the end of twenty training sessions with Eddie and his mother, disruptive behavior had been largely eliminated and replaced by cooperative interactions. Studies by Hawkins et al. (1966) and Zeilberger et al. (1968) provided similar conclusions regarding the effectiveness of parent training.

In a broader study conceived along similar lines, Alexander and Parsons (1973) undertook to analyze the family interactions that served to maintain delinquent behavior in youngsters; to improve family communication patterns so that communications would be characterized by more clarity and precision; and to provide instruction in contingency contracting procedures based on clearer communication patterns. Families participating in this study were selected from cases referred by a juvenile court system and included youngsters between ages 13 and 16 who had been arrested or detained for delinquent behavior, and their families.

Specific interventions in this study included: (a) differentiation of rules from requests; (b) systematic use of social reinforcement; (c) development of a manual providing instruction in the use of behavior modification based on a popular primer by Patterson and Gullion (1968); (d) implementation of token economy programs. According to Alexander and Parsons, their study clearly demonstrated the effectiveness of a properly designed and explicit family treatment program for delinquent youngsters and their parents.

Kifer, Lewis, Green, and Phillips (1974) also focused attention on communication processes among predelinquent youngsters and their parents. These investigators developed a training procedure in which parent-child pairs were presented with a conflict situation and then instructed to consider the most acceptable solutions from a list of options given to them and the consequences of each option. Following discussion of options and consequences, a simulation situation was presented and approached along the lines practiced in discussion sessions.

In examining behaviors of parents and children during these sessions, Kifer and his associates identified several response classes. These included: (a) *complete communications*—statements of a position along with requests for reciprocal statement of the other's position; (b) *identification of issues*—statements explicitly pinpointing conflictual issues; (c) *suggestions of options*—statements of possible alternatives that might lead to conflict resolution; (d) *compliant agreements*—statements in which one person simply yielded to the position of the other; (e) *negotiated agreements*—compromise positions different from the original position of either party. Results of this procedure of problem statement, clarification, and negotiation produced substantially greater amounts of negotiation, with generalization to situations other than those in which training had occurred. These investigators felt that their research provided "evidence that relatively inexpensive procedures can be developed that change parent-child interaction during conflict situations from disagreement to negotiation and agreement" (Kifer et al., 1974, p. 364).

Other studies have demonstrated that parents can effectively manipulate their children's behavior to produce either "good" or "bad" behavior, depending on the requests of experimenters (Johnson & Lobitch, 1974); that parents can be taught to be aware of and control attention contingent on either desirable or undesirable behavior (Herbert & Baer, 1972); and that parents can effectively implement home-based token economy programs to produce cooperative behavior in their children (Christophersen, Arnold, Hill, &

Quilitch, 1972) or implement cooperative programs with school authorities (Todd, Scott, Bostow, & Alexander, 1977).

In a comprehensive review of behavior modification in the remediation of conduct disorders and delinquency, Braukmann et al. (1975) concluded that an "educational model" that views deviant behaviors as learned is more useful than the traditional "medical model" that views such behaviors as symptoms of underlying pathology. Behavior modification approaches appear to be more direct, efficient, and effective in bringing about measurable improvement. It is also important to note that behavioral approaches have wider applicability and can be employed in home and classroom with appropriate training of parents and teachers, as well as in the office of psychologist or psychiatrist.

Nevertheless, despite promising evidence of effectiveness, it is also necessary to sound a cautionary note and indicate that follow-up studies leave much to be desired (Emery & Marhalin, 1977), and much research has yet to be done in order to develop increased effectiveness, efficient training procedures for intervention personnel (including parents and teachers), and tools for increasing permanency and generalization of changes that are implemented. With these cautions in mind, behavioral technology may be viewed as an important tool in the repertoire of teacher, social worker, psychologist, and other professionals concerned with the adequate development of youngsters exhibiting conduct disorders.

SUMMARY

1. The establishment of the juvenile court system removed conduct disorders from the realm of criminality and prompted research into the complex causes of conduct disorders and delinquency.
2. The concept of conduct disorder includes any behavior that disrupts the child's relationship with family, school, or the larger community and differs from delinquency only in that the latter is a legal rather than a psychological concept.
3. The causes of conduct disorders include constitutional predisposing factors, poor family environment, socioeconomic deprivation, faulty learning, and, possibly, neurological dysfunction.
4. The diagnosis of conduct disorders is a complex process and must involve evaluation of the child's personality and behavior, parental interactions, and neighborhood milieu.
5. Developmentally, conduct disorders and delinquency often lead to educational problems and disruption of important interpersonal relationships.
6. Intervention strategies for dealing with conduct disorders include efforts by teachers to modify educational practices and classroom environment, and efforts by parents to modify family interaction patterns and disciplinary practices in the home.

Children with Psychoses

... I must try not to feel more sorry for myself than for Noah, but some days I forget.

At that time he was four years old. He was neither toilet trained nor could he feed himself; he seldom spoke expressively; his attention span was almost nil; he rarely played with toys at all; he never came when he was called by name; he was almost always lost in a world whose activities consisted solely of thread-pulling, lint-picking, blanket-sucking, spontaneous giggling, inexplicable crying, eye-squinting, finger-talking, wall-hugging, circle-walking, bed-bouncing, head-nodding, and body-rocking.

From Josh Greenfeld, *A Child Called Noah* (1972, pp. 97–98)

AN INTRODUCTION TO CHILDHOOD PSYCHOSIS

The importance of the study of childhood psychosis is not a function of the prevalence of the disorder. On the contrary, childhood psychoses occur infrequently. Despite their infrequency, however, the psychoses of childhood have consumed tremendous amounts of time and money spent on research and treatment. There are several reasons for this interest. First, the study of a disorder that arises so early in development, with such pervasive consequences, promises to shed light on critical processes and mechanisms of normal child development and to highlight the basic needs of children. It is also hoped that understanding of these developmental problems will permit the discovery of effective treatment approaches or preventive measures that will even further reduce their occurrence.

Most importantly, however, direct contact with a psychotic child inevitably and indelibly impresses the observer with the total human devastation that is meant by psychosis. No other human behavior is so removed from the range of normal experience or so difficult to understand. Case Study 13.1 demonstrates the tragic nature of these disorders.

For many people psychotic children are so totally incomprehensible in the bizarreness of their behavior, the intensity of their emotions, and the totality of their human isolation, that they experience fear and revulsion in the presence of such children. Such responses are human and understandable. We often fear what we do not know and understand. Fortunately, many others experience genuine compassion and professional commitment to the treatment and education of these lonely, tormented children who rarely enter our world. As so often happens, human tragedy also prompts human development, and the psychotic child is today less often abandoned or destroyed

CHARLES: "HE LIVES IN A WORLD OF HIS OWN"

Charles N. was brought by his mother on February 2, 1943, with the chief complaint: "The thing that upsets me most is that I can't reach my baby."

Charles was born on August 9, 1938. He was a planned and wanted child. He sat up at 6 months; at 14 months "he stood up and walked one day." As a baby, he was "slow and phlegmatic." He would lie in his crib "almost as if hypnotized." Thyroid extract medication had no effect.

He was the oldest of three children. Mr. N., a high school graduate clothing merchant, was described as a "self-made, gentle, and placid person"; his relatives were said to be "ordinary, simple people." Mrs. N., "of remarkable equanimity," had a successful business record, running a theatrical booking office. Her "dynamic and forceful" mother had done some writing and composing. Mrs. N. had a brother, a psychiatrist, who had great musical talent, a sister who was "very brilliant and psychoneurotic," and a sister who was referred to as "the Amazon of the family."

The mother prefaced her story thus: "I am trying hard not to govern my remarks by professional knowledge which has intruded in my own way of thinking now." In this she succeeded. This is a brief abstract of her report: "His enjoyment and appreciation of music encouraged me to play records. When he was 1½ years old, he could discriminate between symphonies. He recognized the composer as soon as the first movement started. He would say 'Beethoven.' At about the same age, he began to spin toys and lids of bottles and jars by the hour. He would watch it and get excited and jump up and down in ecstasy. Now he is interested in reflecting light from mirrors and catching reflections. When he is interested in a thing, you cannot change it. . . . The most impressive thing is his detachment and his inaccessibility. He lives in a world of his own where he cannot be reached. No sense of relationship to persons. He went through a period of quoting another person; never offers anything himself. His entire conversation is a replica of whatever has been said to him. He used to speak of himself in the second person, now he uses the third person at times. . . . He is destructive; the furniture in his room looks like it has hunks out of it. He will break a purple crayon into two parts and say, 'You had a beautiful purple crayon and now it's two pieces. Look what you did.' . . . He developed an obsession about feces, would hide it anywhere (for instance, in drawers), would tease me if I walked into the room: 'You soiled your pants, now you can't have your crayons!' . . . As a result, he is still not toilet trained. He never soils himself in the nursery school, always does it when he comes home. The same is true of wetting. He is proud of wetting, jumps up and down with ecstasy, says; 'Look at the big puddle he made.'"

Charles was a well-developed, intelligent looking boy, who was in good physical health. When he entered the office, he paid no attention to the people present. Without looking at anyone, he said: "Give me a pencil," took a piece of paper from the desk and wrote something resembling a figure 2 (a large desk calendar prominently displayed a figure 2, the day was February 2). He had brought with him a copy of *Readers' Digest* and was fascinated by a picture of a baby. He said: "Look at the funny baby," innumerable times, occasionally adding: "Is he not funny? Is he not sweet?" When the book was taken away from him, he struggled with the hand that held it, without looking at the person who had taken the book. When he was pricked with a pin, he said: "What's this?" and answered his own question: "It is a needle." He looked timidly at the pin, shrank from further pricks, but at no time did he seem to connect the pricking with the person who held the pin. When the *Readers' Digest* was put on the floor and a foot placed over it, he tried to remove the foot as if it were a detached and interfering object, with no concern for the person to whom the foot belonged. . . .

He did not respond to being called and

did not look at his mother when she spoke to him. When the blocks were removed, he screamed, stamped his feet and cried: "I give it to you!" (meaning: "You give it to me").

Charles was placed at the Devereux Schools on February 10, 1943. Early in 1944, he was removed, spent 3 months (from March to June) at Bellevue Hospital; was admitted on June 22, 1944, to New Jersey State Hospital at Marlboro; transferred to Arthur Brisbane Child Treatment Center on November 1, 1946; transferred to Atlantic County Hospital, February 1, 1951; transferred to the State Hospital at Ancora on October 14, 1955. He is still there, now 32 years old. This means that he has been a State Hospital resident from the age of 5 years and 10 months. Inquiries by the Clinic, if responded to at all, yielded meager general statements about continuing deterioration. One note of December 1953, said something about "intensive psychotherapy." The last note, dated December 23, 1970, said: "This patient is very unpredictable in his behavior. He has a small vocabulary and spends most of the time singing to himself. He is under close observation and is in need of indefinite hospitalization."

From Kanner (1971, pp. 134–36)

or left to exist for empty years in institutions that exaggerate personal isolation.

DEFINITION AND CLASSIFICATION

The term **childhood psychosis** is a broadly inclusive one. Loosely, it refers to a *pattern of child behavior that is essentially characterized by failure to recognize, understand, or respond appropriately to people or objects in the environment.* More specifically, the psychotic child is recognized most often by extreme seclusiveness and withdrawal along with bizarre behavior and inappropriate emotional response. While such descriptions may be a useful preliminary introduction to the psychotic disorders of childhood, however, they provide little assistance in distinguishing psychotic behavior from severe neurotic behavior, or from some manifestations of severe learning disabilities or retardation. Nor are such broad descriptions useful in developing differential diagnostic statements to distinguish among different types of psychotic disorder.

In order to understand these severe disturbances of childhood, it is essential to begin with a few clarifying notions. In the first place, it is important to recognize that psychotic symptoms may, in many cases, result from severe organic trauma. Infection or injury may lead to central nervous system damage and eventuate in behavior that is indistinguishable from those psychotic disorders that do not have a specifiable cause. These *organic psychoses* can be caused by vascular problems, infections, tumors, or externally induced injuries such as ingestion of toxic substances, severe head injury, or burns (Bollea, 1971).

More often, however, discussions of psychotic disorders are limited to those that have *no clearly identifiable organic etiology.* Though there is considerable controversy as to the cause of these disturbances, tangible evidence of central nervous system dysfunction is lacking. For this reason these disorders have traditionally been distinguished from the organic psychoses. This is not meant to imply that there may not someday be clear evidence of subtle genetic or biochemical causation of psychotic disorders; in fact, contemporary research is pointing increasingly in this direction. However, for the time being conclusive evidence is not yet available.

The psychotic disorders to be discussed here are characterized by:

> . . . *severe and continued impairment of emotional relationships with persons, associated with an aloofness and a tendency toward preoccupation with inanimate objects; loss of speech or failure in its development, disturbances in sensory perception; bizarre or stereotyped behavior and motility patterns; marked resistance to change in environment or routine; outbursts of intense and unpredictable panic; absence of a sense of personal identity; and blunted, uneven or fragmented intellectual development. In some cases, intellectual performance may be adequate or better, with psychotic disorder confining itself to other areas of personality function. (Group for the Advancement of Psychiatry, 1966, p. 251)*

It is important to note here that, while these disorders may be distinguished into several more specific syndromes, there is wide variability in the number of subgroups proposed and disagreement as to the appropriateness of different grouping systems. Some authorities use only the broad category of psychosis and ignore distinctions among specific syndromes (Bomberg, Szurek, & Etemad, 1973). Others use early infantile autism as synonymous with childhood schizophrenia and distinguish from these only organic psychoses (Ornitz, 1973). Still others insist that autism is distinct from childhood schizophrenia, and that these two categories constitute the major diagnostic subdivisions (Rimland, 1974; Rutter, 1974).

This diagnostic confusion arises from the fact that there are a wide variety of symptoms characteristic of childhood psychosis and wide variability in the symptoms present in individual children. It is quite difficult to specify characteristics that are both necessary and sufficient to diagnose a specific type of psychotic disorder, and that are simultaneously distinguishable from other psychoses. The persistence of terminological confusion has led to continual controversy and lack of precision in research findings. Nevertheless, the confusion exists and must be dealt with.

In this chapter we will maintain two major diagnostic subgroups for descriptive purposes: childhood schizophrenia and early infantile autism.

Childhood schizophrenia will be defined as a severe disorder of childhood characterized by some combination of extreme interpersonal isolation; noncommunicative use of speech; repetitive body movements (including rocking, hand-flapping, or posturing); self-injurious behavior; regression in behavior; abnormal responses to light or sound; problems in feeding, sleeping, or toileting; abnormal fears or lack of fears; and delusional or hallucinatory behavior (Creak, 1961; Hingtgen & Bryson, 1972; Rimland, 1964; Rutter, 1974; White, DeMyer, & DeMyer, 1964; Wolff & Chess, 1964).

While many of these same characteristics may be observed in autistic children, a diagnosis of **early infantile autism** should be reserved for cases in which the disorder appears prior to 30 months of age and is characterized by "a profound and general failure to develop social relationships; language retardation with impaired comprehension, echolalia [echoing of words or phrases], and pronominal reversal; and ritualistic or compulsive phenomena" (Rutter, 1974, p. 329). Additionally, distinctions between early infantile autism and childhood schizophrenia have been noted in a large body of research literature, and some of these will be discussed in relation to incidence, etiology, and diagnosis.

INCIDENCE AND ETIOLOGY

The Joint Commission on the Mental Health of Children (1970) estimated the incidence of psychotic disorders in children to be .6 percent, six cases per 10,000 children. Using census figures available in 1970, this would mean that there were approximately 350,000 psychotic children in the United States at that time. This estimate is slightly higher than that arrived at by Treffert (1970), whose data indicated an incidence rate of five cases of childhood psychosis per 10,000 children, including 3.1 cases of childhood schizophrenia per 10,000 children. These figures are in essential agreement with the findings of Lotter (1967) who studied incidence rates of childhood psychosis among English children. Averaging the findings of several incidence studies, Hanson and Gottesman (1976) estimated that approximately four of every 10,000 children suffer from some form of childhood psychosis.

Incidence estimates for early infantile autism are even lower. Rimland (1974) estimated the incidence rate of early infantile autism to be 10 percent of the incidence of childhood schizophrenia, or about five cases per 100,000 children. Treffert estimated that fewer than one in 10,000 children could be accurately diagnosed as autistic.

Despite the evident inconsistencies in these incidence estimates, however, several factors emerge clearly. First, childhood psychoses occur infrequently. Second, there is some agreement that childhood schizophrenia occurs much more frequently than early infantile autism. Third, a number of studies (including those cited above) point consistently to higher incidence rates in males (Hingtgen & Bryson, 1972). Male children are two to four times more likely to develop childhood psychosis than females.

With these basic incidence estimates in mind, we can proceed to an examination of causative factors in childhood psychoses. Because of important differences between childhood schizophrenia and early infantile autism, we will consider etiological research separately for each group.

Etiology of Childhood Schizophrenia

In view of the massive problems in deciding what childhood schizophrenia *is,* it is hardly surprising that there is considerable controversy regarding its causes. At one time or another, a variety of theories about the origins of childhood schizophrenia have been scientifically "fashionable." However, most theories of the origins of childhood psychosis can be categorized either as "nurture" theories, emphasizing environmental causes (particularly parental mishandling of the child); "nature" theories, emphasizing biological dysfunction; or "nature/nurture" theories, suggesting that a constitutionally vulnerable infant who encounters environmental stresses will develop overt symptoms (DeMyer, 1975). Each approach currently has proponents who argue heatedly for the validity of their viewpoint. At this point in time, the weight of evidence appears to favor "nature" theories of the etiology of childhood schizophrenia. However, the question is far from closed, and many researchers are attempting to fill the wide gaps in our understanding.

Theories of environmental causation

One prominent representative of the "nurture" viewpoint is J. L. Despert, whose clinical experiences led her to the conclusion that weakening of the family structure in contemporary society, role reversal between husband and wife, and unconscious rejection of an unwanted child combine to produce tremendous anxiety in the developing youngster (1968, 1970). More specifically, Despert stated that "instinctive motherliness is being smothered in the material wealth of modern life" (1970, p. 248), and children no longer receive the security, guidance, love, and behavior limits that are characteristic of more traditional cultures. Consequently, Despert saw parents and children as beset with conflicts and ambivalence that create tension, role confusion, and mutual resentment. These conflicts weaken the family and set the stage for failure of adequate ego development and emotional disturbance in the child.

Bowen (1960), Weakland (1960), and others have viewed the schizophrenic child as the ultimate scapegoat of chronic tensions and conflicts within the entire family system. Schizophrenia is seen as the outcome of unbearable anxiety created by contradictory demands and messages to the

It may be that psychotic children, unable to cope with a hostile, confusing world, withdraw from human contact and defend themselves through isolation, stereotyped mannerisms, and attempts to maintain constancy in the environment through compulsive rituals.

child on the part of one or both parents. The child may be a victim of parental anger displaced from a spouse, or parental conflicts with their own parents may be reenacted in their relationship with the child. The result is that the child is made the object of parental anger and rejection.

Confused by an apparently hostile world and unable to cope, the child withdraws from human contact and defends against unbearable anxiety through isolation, stereotyped mannerisms, and attempts to maintain constancy in the environment through compulsive rituals. On occasion, anxiety breaks through these defenses in the form of uncontrolled panic or terrifying hallucinations; sometimes the child even acts out parental hatred through self-injurious behavior.

At this point, however, the question must be asked whether these disruptions in the child's relationships with the parents are sufficiently destructive to cause the total personality disintegration encountered in schizophrenia. The answer, increasingly, appears to be "No." Extensive research has failed to demonstrate any consistent differences in family interaction patterns between families of schizophrenic and nonschizophrenic children (Frank, 1965; Jacob, 1975). The fact is that current research in the area of childhood schizophrenia suggests biological defects as the primary etiological agents in this disorder. Exhaustive reviews of available research by Bender (1971a, 1971b), Goldfarb (1970), Werry (1972), and White (1974) highlight research efforts that may be leading toward resolutions of major questions regarding both childhood and adult schizophrenia.

Research findings on biological causation

One of the consistent research findings that suggests that childhood schizophrenia originates in some form of biological impairment is the high frequency of complications in the pregnancy and birth of infants later diagnosed as childhood schizophrenics (Hingtgen & Bryson, 1972; White, 1974). Gittelman and Birch (1967) studied detailed case histories of 97 schizophrenic children. In 83 children for whom complete information was available, 35 had mothers who had experienced complications during pregnancy or delivery. Of the total group of 97 cases, 75 percent exhibited either moderate or severe neurological dysfunction.

Pollack and Woerner (1966) reviewed and summarized five studies dealing with complications in pregnancy or delivery of children later diagnosed as childhood schizophrenics. They found a higher incidence of prenatal complications in childhood schizophrenics than in normal controls, including toxemia, vaginal bleeding, and severe maternal illness during pregnancy. While prematurity was not a differentiating factor, there appeared to be a higher incidence of complications during other pregnancies in mothers of schizophrenic children, including higher frequencies of spontaneous abortions and stillbirths.

Similar findings were reported by Taft and Goldfarb (1964) in a study in which "blind ratings" of the histories of schizophrenic children, their normal siblings, and normal controls revealed significantly more prenatal and perinatal complications in the schizophrenic group than in other groups. Terris, LaPouse, and Monk (1964) studied large samples of birth records of schizophrenic and unselected children and again found higher rates of previous stillbirths and spontaneous abortions in mothers of schizophrenic children.

Repeated findings of prenatal complications and/or complications during delivery suggest that childhood schizophrenia may be a manifestation of subtle neurological damage and, therefore, similar etiologically to such disorders as minimal brain dysfunction (Hingtgen & Bryson, 1972; White, 1974).

Evidence of neurological abnormalities. In addition to significantly higher rates of pregnancy and delivery complications, investigators have also found a higher incidence of neurological symptoms in schizophrenic children. These two classes of events would be expected to correlate with each other, and the fact that they do serves as mutually supportive evidence of biological causation.

Lauretta Bender (1947, 1956, 1971b) has been particularly forceful in her arguments for a neurological basis in the etiology of childhood schizophrenia. She has pointed particularly to the fact that disturbances of functioning in childhood schizophrenics are pervasive and affect virtually all spheres of development and behavior, including automatic functions such as breathing and digestion, perception, thinking, motor activity, language, emotions, and social behavior. In addition, schizophrenic children show a higher incidence of "soft" neurological signs than other children.

"Soft" neurological signs are diagnostic indicators of possible neurological dysfunction; they are not conclusively indicative of nervous system damage, however, and may stem from other causes. The kinds of "soft" signs that Bender has found convincing include "whirling" (that is, turning the body with outstretched hands either spontaneously or in response to passive turning of the child's head), hypotonia (reduced muscle tone), and choreiform movements (twitching or dancing movements).

In a particularly impressive study employing neurological signs, Barbara Fish and others (Fish, Shapiro, Halpern, & Wile, 1965; Fish, Wile, Shapiro, & Halpern, 1966) were able to select three children vulnerable for schizophrenia from a group of sixteen infants at one month of age. Fish began to note such signs as deviations in consciousness, movement patterns, muscle tone, and vestibular regulation (ability to right, or balance) as early as the first day after birth. Follow-up studies at several intervals confirmed her original predictions of infant vulnerability.

William Goldfarb (1961) administered neurological tests to a sample of children selected for presence of schizophrenic symptomatology and absence of gross neurological abnormality. In comparing the performance of these children with a group of normal controls, Goldfarb found schizophrenic children to be inferior on all indicators of subtle neurological dysfunction, including tests of visual-motor coordination, muscle tone appraisal, the whirling test, postural and righting reflexes, and the "finger-to-nose" test.

White (1974), Werry (1972), and Goldfarb (1971) independently reviewed large numbers of electroencephalographic (brain wave) and neurological studies, and all reached similar conclusions: despite the absence of indisputable evidence (such as that provided by postmortem tissue studies), high rates of pregnancy and delivery complications, pervasive deviations in biological functions, and the presence of many "soft" neurological signs suggest that childhood schizophrenia is, in fact, somehow related to central nervous system damage or dysfunction.

Evidence of genetic factors. In addition to increasingly clear evidence of neurological impairment, a number of intriguing studies suggest important genetic factors are also involved in the etiology of childhood schizophrenia.

One of the most recent thorough reviews of genetic factors in schizophrenia is that of Gottesman and Shields (1972). These investigators studied a sample of schizophrenic patients selected from same-sex twin pairs, born in the Maudsley and Bethlem Royal Joint Hospital between 1948 and 1964, who had survived until at least age 5. Their final sample consisted of 24 *monozygotic* (identical) twins and 33 same-sex *dizygotic* (fraternal) twins, all diagnosed as schizophrenic. Briefly, these investigators found *concordance* rates of 42 percent and 9 percent, respectively, for monozygotic and dizygotic twin pairs. That is, in 42 percent of the sample of diagnosed schizophrenics having monozygotic twins, the monozygotic twin had also at some time received the same diagnosis.

Severity of illness was also found to be systematically related to the likelihood that the co-twin would develop schizophrenia. Severe schizophrenia in the *proband* (selected twin) was associated with increased likelihood of schizophrenia in the co-twin. Examination of environmental variables failed to reveal any greater abnormality in living situations where both twins were concordant for schizophrenia as opposed to situations where they were discordant—data suggestive of the priority of genetic endowment over environmental variables in the etiology of schizophrenia. Gottesman and Shields also observed that, in cases where the twin pairs were discordant for schizophrenia, the schizophrenic twin was more submissive during development. A curious but unexplained incidental finding was the observation that twin pairs discordant for schizophrenia were also discordant for handedness, while those pairs concordant for schizophrenia were also concordant for handedness.

In addition to reporting the results of their own research, Gottesman and Shields also presented thoughtful methodological evaluations of earlier genetic studies. In every major study reviewed, monozygotic concordance rates were higher than dizygotic concordance rates. These included reports by Rosanoff et al. (1934), Kallmann (1946), and Inouye (1961). Naturally, the implication of higher concordance rates in monozygotic pairs is that genetic variables account for the greater similarity in monozygotic than in dizygotic pairs.

In an interesting variant of traditional twin studies Pollin, Stabenau, Mosher, and Tupin (1966) elected to observe only monozygotic twin pairs *discordant* for schizophrenia. In this way they were able to limit genetic variation in identical monozygous twins and to focus specifically on environmental and experiential variations. Observations of five families led to several consistent findings: the schizophrenic twin in each pair weighed less at birth, was perceived by parents—and particularly by mothers—as vulnerable, and was the focus of anxiety, attention, and involvement by the parents. The schizophrenic twin was also observed to have developed more slowly, to be more docile and compliant, and to be less competent than the nonschizo-phrenic co-twin. Furthermore, these patterns tended to persist from birth onward. In each of the five cases, the mother had experienced a strong conscious fear that she or the infant or both would die shortly after birth. These results, of course, demonstrate clearly that, whatever genetic mechanisms might be involved in the causation of childhood schizophrenia, they operate subtly and interact with the child's life experiences.

In another investigation Pollin, Allen, Hoffer, Stabenau, and Hrubec (1969) studied a large sample of twins inducted into the armed forces. Of 80 monozygotic twin pairs found, 14 percent were concordant for schizophrenia; of 146 dyzygotic pairs found, 4 percent were concordant for schizophrenia. These findings are consistent with most other concordance studies.

Evidence of biochemical factors. While there is a relatively long history of genetic research on schizophrenia that has produced a relatively consistent body of findings, the same cannot be said for biochemical research. Although studies have been plentiful, problems in diagnosis and adequate research design have prevented the development of any firm conclusions. However, some research results are suggestive.

Bernard Rimland (1973), for example, reported some success in the use of megavitamin treatment of nearly 200 psychotic children in the United States and Canada, and he has consequently speculated on the role of genetically induced inordinate needs for massive quantities of certain nutrients.

S. A. Mednick (1970) suggested that prenatal and perinatal complications, frequent in the history of childhood schizophrenics, may induce anoxic damage to specific brain areas that regulate blood supplies of certain hormones. An oversupply of these hormones, in turn, might create a state of continual hyperarousal in schizophrenics and interfere with the normal transmission of neural impulses.

Other studies (Seller & Gold, 1964; Gold, 1967) have analyzed the cerebrospinal fluid of schizophrenic children and found that it contained components involved in the stimulation of seizure activity in experimental animals. While many similar studies have been conducted, there are no consistent patterns at present that point to key biochemical mechanisms in the genesis of childhood schizophrenia. Altogether, biochemical leads remain highly tentative and still require extensive investigation (Goldfarb, 1970).

Summary of etiological research

In this brief review we have only sampled the massive research literature in the area of childhood schizophrenia. However, even this brief sampling is adequate to suggest several tentative conclusions. First, there appears to be little substantive evidence to support "nurture" theories of the causation of childhood schizophrenia. There are no systematic differences between the parents of schizophrenic children and the parents of normal children, nor is there evidence of specific patterns of parenting behavior or family interaction (Hingtgen & Bryson, 1972; White, 1974). Second, a large number of research studies point to some form of central nervous system damage or dysfunction in schizophrenic children, although the site of such impairments cannot presently be specified. Third, there is also consistent evidence that genetic factors may play a role in the etiology of childhood schizophrenia, probably through their effects on neurochemical metabolic processes. However, the specific nature of these processes remains unclear and must be subjected to extensive study.

Etiology of Early Infantile Autism

As we noted earlier, distinctions among specific subgroups of psychotic disorders remain controversial. Nevertheless, there is evidence that childhood schizophrenia and early infantile autism are sufficiently distinct categories to warrant separate treatment. These distinctions become particularly evident in discussions of etiology, where several specific notions of the causation of early infantile autism have been suggested.

Theories of environmental causation

Early infantile autism, or *Kanner's Syndrome,* was first described by Leo Kanner in 1943. At that time Kanner described a number of symptoms characterizing his initial group of eleven children, but he emphasized most particularly their *profound withdrawal from human contact* and their *obsessive desire for the maintenance of sameness in the environment.* In addition to these critical characteristics, Kanner noted striking consistencies in the family backgrounds of autistic children. The parents of these children were characterized by high intelligence and unusual achievement. In addition to exceptional intellectual ability, early research suggested that the parents of autistic children were emotionally cold, aloof, and reserved in their interactions with others, including their children. Rather than relating to others easily, Kanner noted that the parents of autistic children were preoccupied with abstractions and intellectual pursuits and had comparatively little interest in people. Later research (Kanner, 1949) indicated that rates of mental illness among parents and blood relatives of a larger sample of 100 autistic children were strikingly low, about one-third of what one might expect in the population at large. Divorce rates were also unusually low. Rimland's review of the literature on autism in 1964 led him to support Kanner's descriptions.

These early descriptions led inevitably to speculations that lack of adequate parenting—*emotional refrigeration* as it has been termed—was a primary factor in the genesis of early infantile autism (Eisenberg, 1957; Eisenberg & Kanner, 1956). Stated briefly, this conception implied that very early in life—during the first months after birth—the infant encounters a world that fails to provide adequate warmth, support, love, and nurturance. As a consequence, the child never enters into contact with other people and remains emotionally isolated from the very earliest moments of life.

Kanner (1965) later denied that he intended this kind of interpretation of his description of the parents of autistic children; indeed, in his original article Kanner had stated that "these children have come into the world with innate inability to form the usual, biologically provided affective contact with people" (1943; reprinted in Kanner, 1973, pp. 42–43). However, the "epidemic environmentalism" (Friedman, 1974) that occurred during the 1950s and

1960s led many theorists and clinicians to view parental deficiencies as the source of childhood disorders. The notion of parental etiology of autistic disturbances presumed that any disorder occurring so early in life must be a function—in one way or another—of radical aberrations in maternal behavior.

One of the most outspoken proponents of this point of view has been Bruno Bettelheim (1967). Drawing upon his extensive clinical experience with psychotic children, Bettelheim attempted to integrate clinical observations with psychodynamic theory into a theory of the etiology of early infantile autism. Bettelheim explored in detail the mutual dependency and interaction of mother and infant during the first hours of life, and suggested that these first hours are a critical period in establishing basic patterns of interaction with others and attitudes toward the world. Without denying the possibility of genetic/organic vulnerability in autistic children, Bettelheim nevertheless argued that these early experiences—particularly in relation to feeding—may be so disastrous as to preclude the child's development of normal patterns of interaction or relatedness to the world.

According to Bettelheim, observations of normal infants indicate typical anticipatory responses to the mother as early as the fourth feeding and no later than the fourteenth feeding. The absence of such responses is an indication that a problem may be developing. In some cases anxiety or maternal resentment of the child may preclude adequate mutuality in the mother-child interaction.

> If things go wrong because such anticipatory behavior is not met by an appropriate response in the mother, the relation of the infant to his environment may become deviant from the very beginning of life. Thus an infant's later fighting against or autistically withdrawing from the world may be caused by what happens so early in life that unless the first few feedings have been carefully observed, it may seem to be the consequence of inborn behavior. (Bettelheim, 1967, p. 395)

In a few cases, Bettelheim believed the interference of a nurturant, supportive father may provide the infant with protection from the negative effects of maternal inadequacy. More often, however, according to Bettelheim, both parents resent the child and wish he/she did not exist. Protectively, the child withdraws into a fortress of isolation, but since there is no development of a self, there is really nothing to protect.

A number of researchers have supported the notion that inadequate parental handling is a key factor in the genesis of autism. Alan Ward (1970), for example, suggested that at least some autistic children may experience a home environment that is so "nonnurturant, unstimulating, and unpatterned (unpredictable) that the child has no recourse but to develop whatever patterns of behaviors he can organize by himself. . . . The lack of stimulation may result from either the physical absence or the psychological absence of a mothering figure" (p. 361).

It is important to emphasize that few investigators have ventured a hypothesis that maternal behavior is exclusively the cause of autism. Virtually all "nurture" theories have allowed for the possibility that innate deficiencies exist in the child's psychological or genetic makeup (Bettelheim, 1967; Mahler,

1952; Ward, 1970). However, the case study material they have presented and their discussions of clinical and theoretical issues have been such that parental behavior inevitably has received major emphasis, with only passing allusions to "constitutional defects" or "inadequate stimulus barriers" in the child.

The unfortunate result of such misplaced and highly speculative emphasis has been that "a witchhunt developed not too commonly seen in the counseling rooms of physicians and psychologists. Parents of autistic children were clearly blamed for the behavior of the autistic child; their detachment and inability to relate (though unproved) were viewed as the behavioral parent of the severe symptomatology" (Friedman, 1974, p. 6).

As in the case of theories of childhood schizophrenia, theories regarding the origins of early infantile autism can be viewed as "nurture" theories, "nature/nurture" theories, and "nature" theories (DeMyer, 1975). Having sketched the basic outlines of several "nurture" theories, we will now turn to a few of the "nature" theories.

Theories of biological causation

Beginning most clearly with the publication in 1964 of Rimland's *Infantile Autism,* research efforts into the biological correlates of early infantile autism gained momentum. A number of researchers began to see autistic symptoms as possible outgrowths of disturbances in genetic endowment, neurological integrity, or biochemical functioning.

As Rimland summarized his position sardonically: "We are not saying that psychogenesis is an imaginary influence; we are merely saying that there appears to be no evidence that it is anything but imaginary" (1964, p. 51). Drawing together a number of observations regarding the symptomatology of autistic children and typical family characteristics, Rimland concluded that the broad variety of symptomatic behavior could be traced to one focal disability: *"The child with early infantile autism is grossly impaired in a function basic to all cognition: the ability to relate new stimuli to remembered experience"* (1964, p. 79). For example, this kind of impairment could reasonably explain the autistic child's failure to relate to or imitate others. One cannot relate in the absence of familiarity, and imitation presupposes the capacity to integrate inner and outer perceptions, past and present perceptions. Similarly, amazing feats of rote memory that have occasionally been noted along with deficits in conceptual ability in autistic children are understandable, since rote memory and form perception require no conceptual or integrative ability; rather they require only the retention of discrete stimuli. Concern with preservation of sameness and stereotyped behaviors may be desperate attempts by the child to maintain order and familiarity in an experiential universe that is virtually random, since there is no meaningful integration of experiences.

What is the source of this impairment in ability to relate present and past experiences? Rimland speculated that the problem stemmed from damage occurring immediately after birth to a brain structure involved in the regulation of incoming sensory information. More recently, however, Rimland (1973, 1974) has begun placing greater emphasis on possible neurochemical factors in the genesis of autism. In either case, however, he has emphasized that research evidence accumulates ever more strongly in favor of a "nature" theory.

While agreeing that autism is caused by some form of impairment or dysfunction in the nervous system, other theorists have speculated about alternative explanations of the cause of this impairment. For example, Ornitz and Ritvo (1976) explored the potential role of problems in serotonin metabolism. **Serotonin** is a neurohumor or chemical mediator in the transmission of neural impulses. Although there are no clear results from research conducted thus far, there is suggestive evidence that autistic children have higher levels of blood serotonin than normal control subjects matched for age (Yuwiler, Geller, & Ritvo, 1976; Yuwiler, Geller, Ornitz, Saeger, & Plotkin, 1970). This research direction is also intriguing because serotonin metabolism has been implicated as a possible factor in the etiology of schizophrenia in adults (e.g., Domino, 1969). However, while there is widespread confidence that serotonin metabolism plays some role in the development of adult schizophrenia, its role is unclear, and "some researchers believe that schizophrenia is due to too little serotonin, while other researchers blame too much serotonin" (Arieti, 1974, p. 455). Needless to say, there is even less certainty regarding the role of this neurohumor in infantile autism, where research on it has begun more recently.

Apart from neurochemical considerations, however, examination of the symptomatology of autism led Ornitz and Ritvo (1968a, 1968b) to postulate a defect in the child's ability to integrate perceptual experiences with each other or with motor behavior, and an inability to modulate sensory input and behavior (Ornitz, 1973). While the specific mechanisms differ from those proposed by Rimland, these researchers appear to be converging on a deficiency in integration or modulation of experiences as the key to understanding autistic symptomatology.

Another view of the etiology of autism was offered by Austin DesLauriers and Carole Carlson (1969), who focused their attention on the total interpersonal isolation of the autistic child. Noting similarities between the total withdrawal of the autistic child and the artificial isolation that has occurred in "sensory deprivation" experiments, DesLauriers and Carlson speculated on other possible similarities. *Sensory deprivation experiments* involve the creation of artificial conditions of human isolation by restricting the sensory input available to adult human subjects. After prolonged periods of sensory deprivation, adults begin to experience drastic impairments in cognitive and emotional functioning, including discontinuity in thoughts and perceptions, and impairments in learning capacity, memory, emotional control, and physical coordination. They even exhibit ritualistic and repetitive behavior.

The parallels between the behavior of isolated adults and autistic children are striking. Intrigued with the notion of sensory deprivation as a possible factor in the etiology of autism, DesLauriers and Carlson looked for *naturally occurring* instances of reduced sensory input, since experimentation with children in these areas is obviously impossible. Two areas of research were suggestive. Early studies of infants reared in institutions (Spitz, 1945) showed that under conditions of reduced stimulation, infants exhibited behaviors similar to those of autistic children. Additionally, blind children have been observed to exhibit what some investigators have termed "blindisms," manneristic behaviors similar to behavior often found in autistic children. Further searches of the literature on sensory deprivation revealed that under conditions of reduced sensory input, individuals attempt to structure their experiences and impose meaning on their existence through, among other activities, compulsive rituals (Bruner, 1961; Ruff, Levy, & Thaler, 1961).

At this point it seemed very likely to DesLauriers and Carlson that a key factor in understanding the genesis of autistic behavior lay in tremendously reduced sensory input similar to that occurring under conditions of sensory deprivation. Yet the question remained as to why this condition occurred. One obvious speculation that others had offered related to possible inadequate parenting by aloof, cold, intellectual parents. A tempting explanation. However, since early observations of the parents of autistic children, much research had shown that these parents do not differ in any significant respects from other parents in personality or childrearing practices (Kolvin et al., 1971; Pitfield & Oppenheim, 1964; Rutter et al., 1967).

Reviews of neurophysiological research led DesLauriers and Carlson to suspect, as had others, that impairments in brain functions might create conditions under which autistic children experience reduced sensory input and/or emotional responsiveness. The hypothetical mechanisms underlying problems in reduced sensory input and emotional responsiveness are complex, and we will not go into details here. However, these mechanisms are capable of explaining why the autistic child may fail to enter the interpersonal world: because external events are incapable of affecting him/her emotionally, and because his/her behavior does not bring experiences of emotional pleasure from the responses of others, the child is unable to form interpersonal bonds or to develop a sense that behavior can change the environment. In the normal course of events, the behavior of an infant elicits enthusiastic, affectionate responses from parents and others. These responses are reinforcing to the infant and bring about heightened probability of recurrence. Without the capacity for experiencing pleasurable emotions in connection with a given response, however, the child cannot learn, cannot form attachments, cannot imitate. In short, the autistic child is left isolated by defects in neurological functioning.

The final line of research we will mention suggests that early infantile autism is a *cognitive defect* involving, primarily, comprehension and use of language (Rutter, 1971, 1974). With a primary defect in ability to understand and use language, the autistic child is impaired in capacity to form relationships, ability to learn by normal means, and ability to integrate experiences from the environment in a meaningful way. Without such experiences, the child resorts to self-stimulatory behavior and compulsive rituals. When language is present, it is usually phonologically correct, but carries no meaning and is noncommunicative.

Recent research (Ornitz, Guthrie, & Farley, 1977) supports the notion of cognitive, linguistic deficits in autistic children. These researchers compared information on the development of normal and autistic children with an average age of approximately 4 years. Among these children, only 16.1 percent of the autistic youngsters were using single words at the same age as more than

79 percent of normal children. However, Ornitz and his associates also found significant motor deficits in autistic children and suggested that an adequate theory must account for more than language and cognitive deficits. They felt that such a theory will eventually demonstrate the importance of biological impairment in the etiology of autism.

Summary of etiological research

Our review of environmental and biological theories of the causation of early infantile autism suggests that once-popular notions regarding parental mishandling as the primary causative factor in autism are on the wane. By contrast, convincing evidence is accumulating that autism is the result of central nervous system impairments resulting from prenatal or perinatal damage. The nature of such impairments is far from clear, but the progress made thus far has been exciting, and investigators from many disciplines ranging from psychiatry and neurology through experimental psychology are beginning to fit together pieces in an important developmental puzzle.

DIAGNOSIS AND IDENTIFICATION

As noted earlier, problems in the diagnosis of childhood psychosis have been a major impediment to progress in understanding these disorders. On the face of it, it would appear a rather simple matter to recognize disorders of such pervasiveness and severity. However, the fact is that *psychoses resulting from injury or infection are descriptively quite similar to autism and childhood schizophrenia.* Furthermore, many severely retarded children develop behaviors which are symptomatically similar to psychotic disorders but which are secondary to limited intellectual ability. Finally, childhood psychoses can—and typically do—co-exist with retardation. The diagnostic question is Which is the primary disorder? That is, are the symptoms in a given child a result primarily of psychotic disturbance that limits intellectual functions, or do primary intellectual limitations lead to psychotic symptoms? The answer to this diagnostic question is important if we are to develop an adequate understanding of the nature and causes of childhood psychoses.

One of the earliest systematic attempts to develop a diagnostic system for differentiating between schizophrenic and autistic children and for distinguishing them from other impaired youngsters was developed by Rimland (1964). Using an extensive diagnostic checklist (now commonly referred to as *Form E-1*) Rimland differentiated between autism and schizophrenia on the basis of symptomatology, onset, parental characteristics, and course of the disorder. Exhibit 13.1 summarizes the kinds of items included in Form E-1. Subsequently, Rimland modified his initial instrument with Forms E-2 and E-3, and more recent research has suggested that it is possible consistently to distinguish autism and childhood schizophrenia (Rimland, 1971).

Other investigators have also developed systems for differential diagnosis (DeMyer, Churchill, Pontius, & Gilkey, 1971), and many are now convinced, as a result of such studies, that autism and schizophrenia are clinically distinct entities (Rutter, 1974). On a research basis, these distinctions have been im-

EXHIBIT 13.1

383
Diagnosis and
identification

DISTINCTIONS BETWEEN AUTISM AND CHILDHOOD SCHIZOPHRENIA

1. *Onset and course.* Childhood schizophrenia appears to follow a period of normal development, whereas autism is usually present "from the beginning of life."

2. *Health and appearance.* Autistic children are usually described as having excellent health and being physically attractive. Schizophrenic children typically exhibit poor health from birth and are physically less attractive.

3. *Electroencephalography.* Autistic children tend to have normal EEG's, whereas as many as 80 percent of schizophrenic children exhibit EEG abnormalities.

4. *Physical responsiveness.* Autistic children do not adapt their bodies to those holding them. Schizophrenic children have been noted to "mold" to adults.

5. *Autistic aloneness.* Autistic children are withdrawn emotionally and indifferent to others. Schizophrenic children more typically elicit a sympathetic response.

6. *Preseveration of sameness.* An insistence on maintenance of sameness in the environment that characterizes autistic children is not observed in childhood schizophrenics.

7. *Hallucinations.* Schizophrenic children are observed to exhibit hallucinations and delusions. These are absent in autistic children.

8. *Motor performance.* Autistic children are characterized by fine and gross motor dexterity and grace. Schizophrenic children show gross motor awkwardness and poor coordination and balance; both groups of children are observed to twirl and spin small objects.

9. *Language.* Affirmation by repetition, pronominal reversal, metaphoric language, and part-whole confusion are all typical of the language usage of the autistic children but are not seen in schizophrenic children.

10. *Idiot savant performance.* These kinds of unusual abilities within the context of delayed development are often found in autistic children but only rarely in schizophrenic children.

11. *Personal orientation.* Schizophrenic children often appear to be disoriented, confused, anxious. Autistic children, by contrast, are unoriented, detached, disinterested.

12. *Conditionability.* Childhood schizophrenics condition easily, but in autistic children conditioned responses are difficult to establish and easily extinguished.

13. *Twins.* An unusual number of twins with autism have been reported to have high rates of monozygosity. Schizophrenic twins show more typical rates for mono- and dizygosity.

14. *Family background.* Families of autistic children are characterized by high intelligence, emotional stability, and low divorce rates. Family backgrounds of schizophrenic children appear more typically to be average or inadequate.

15. *Familial mental disorder.* Parents and grandparents of autistic children show strikingly low rates of mental disorder. In schizophrenic children there is a strong familial tendency that results in higher rates of disorder among the parents and grandparents than in the general population.

Adapted from Rimland (1964, pp. 67–76)

---

portant and have permitted the development of key generalizations in understanding. For example, on the basis of initial differential diagnosis of autistic children, DeMyer (1975) compared groups of autistic, retarded, and normal youngsters. She found that there were no differences in parental handling of these three groups of children, with one major exception: the parents of subnormal children provided less stimulation than either the parents of autistic or normal children. Further, the parents of autistic children were no more intellectualizing than the other parents and did not exhibit any greater amount of psychological disturbance. In another study of differential diagnosis Davids (1975) distinguished between autistic and other psychotic children and confirmed an earlier report (Rimland, 1964) that there is a higher proportion of Jewish families with autistic children. By itself, the significance of this kind of result is questionable, but it is the gradual integration of many isolated bits of information that eventually produces understanding of developmental problems.

On an individual level, however, the significance of differential diagnosis is less clear. There is at present no specific treatment approach unique to autism or childhood schizophrenia. However, distinctions between childhood psychoses and other disorders remain important and are generally easily made. Exhibit 13.2 details the variety of symptoms characteristic of childhood psychoses. On the basis of differential diagnosis of childhood psychosis from retardation without psychosis, organic psychosis, and severe, nonpsychotic disturbance, more adequate treatment plans can be developed.

DEVELOPMENTAL CONSEQUENCES

Severe emotional disturbance in children is pervasive and affects virtually every aspect of development. As we noted earlier in discussion of definition and etiology, childhood schizophrenia may interfere with basic functions such as breathing and digestion, motor behavior, intellectual development, linguistic development, interpersonal relations, emotional responsiveness, or all of these simultaneously. Similarly, early infantile autism may affect all aspects of the child's development. In fact, it is the unusual case in which more than one or two isolated bits of the child's developing personality are left untouched. Nevertheless, two key areas of development are worth special emphasis: intellectual and educational achievement and interpersonal factors.

Conceptual Abilities and Educational Achievement

Perhaps the single point of agreement among all authorities in regard to childhood psychosis is the *dismal prognosis for improvement*. This is particularly true in relation to cognitive development. While psychotic children occasionally show normal intellectual development, in the overwhelming majority of cases, rating scales and intelligence tests yield estimates of intellectual functioning in the retarded range (Hingtgen & Bryson, 1972; DeMyer, 1975; Ornitz, Guthrie, & Farley, 1977; Rutter, 1974). Though there is somewhat greater variability in intellectual functioning among schizophrenic youngsters, it is only in rare instances that a psychotic child is ever able to function in a normal school setting; and even with special educational provisions, the ability to function at or near normal levels is quite unusual.

In a later section we will examine educational approaches in detail, but

EXHIBIT 13.2

SYMPTOMS OF CHILDHOOD PSYCHOSIS

Interpersonal Behavior

Fails to develop social responses; avoids eye contact; withdraws from people

Does not anticipate being picked up

Treats people as objects

Does not play with other children

At times may cling in panic but without real recognition of other person

Appears to be deaf; does not respond to speech

Does not imitate others

Sometimes extremely aggressive, but in an impersonal fashion

Prefers to be alone

Sometimes stiff, aloof when held; sometimes "melts" into holding person

Speech and Language Behavior

Fails to develop speech; mute

When speech is present, it is not used to communicate

Speech phonologically accurate, but meaningless

Speech simply "echoes" or "parrots" what others say

Does not use pronoun "I"

Talks in different voices; whispers

Does not understand speech

Affirmation by repeating statement or question

Empty repetition of phrases

Reversal of pronouns

Odd intonations, voice tone

Islets of normal intellectual functioning

Unusual abilities in rote memory

Sometimes capable of performing unusual intellectual feats

General retardation in intellectual functioning

Sensory and Motor Behavior

Repetitive, rhythmic body movements

Crib rocking and/or head-banging

Spinning, jumping, whirling, flapping, twiddling objects

Strange grimaces, twitching

Hallucinations

Food fads

Self-injurious behavior

Insensitive to pain

Abnormal responsiveness to lights, sounds, or colors

Ritualistic play and mannerisms

Tries to maintain sameness in physical environment

Disrupted by change in routine or environment

Sometimes well coordinated physically; sometimes extremely awkward

Problems in sleeping, feeding, toileting

Abnormal fears or lack of fears

these efforts must be understood as attempts to maximize available potentials. The likelihood of normalizing intellectual functioning in psychotic children is virtually nonexistent within the context of available treatment and educational techniques.

Personal and Social Factors

In discussing the developmental consequences of sensory impairments, physical disabilities, retardation, personality problems, and other conditions of special children, it was always possible to begin with the basic presumption that the child has some awareness of him/herself as a person even during early stages of development. It is not at all clear that we can presume such awareness in children who exhibit severe psychotic disorders. One aspect of development in psychotic children that has occasionally been studied is development of body awareness and body image (Hingtgen & Bryson, 1972). Research results indicate that some psychotic youngsters, with a great deal of training, are able to develop some limited awareness of their own bodies. Curiously, however, there is virtually no research attempting to delineate the psychotic child's psychological self-awareness. Bettelheim (1967) noted that the failure to use first-person pronouns may reflect a denial of the self, but other investigators typically do not even touch on the issue of self-awareness in young psychotic children. During the course of development, the picture appears to change somewhat in psychotic individuals who have been exposed to treatment or educational intervention, and behavior sometimes appears to imply self-awareness. In a few cases, the individual is able to speak and think in reference to an emergent "self."

For the most part, however, research has focused on "social" behavior without reference to subjective self-awareness. Investigations in this area again reflect severe limitations developmentally. Psychotic children rarely relate to or interact with other children or adults in a spontaneous manner, though they can be trained to interact in somewhat mechanical fashion. Reports of normal social development even with intensive intervention are rare.

Problems in interpersonal responsiveness are particularly evident within the family context. Parents of autistic youngsters report that from the earliest weeks, their children failed to show any responsiveness or awareness of others. Though schizophrenic children appear, initially, to respond to others, they do not characteristically exhibit normal patterns of relatedness with awareness and concern for the experiences and feelings of others. As psychotic symptoms become more evident, even this minimal relatedness typically dissipates. In a few psychotic children, abnormal dependence on the mother has been noted, but again without a sense of mutuality in the relationship.

Aberrations in responsiveness are, of course, devastating to parents who search eagerly for evidence of social awareness in their children. Failing to find such normal responses, the parents often discontinue their efforts to stimulate and relate to the child. In some instances, bizarre behavioral aberrations, self-injurious behavior, and aggressiveness further alienate parents. On occasion, the psychotic child will make contact with a teacher or some other caregiver, but the strange behavior and emotional isolation of psychotic children make such encounters infrequent.

The sad fact of the matter is that *social development in psychotic children is minimal* (Hingtgen & Bryson, 1972), *and even where some social awareness develops, it is limited in quality and extent.*

INTERVENTION

Students often experience puzzlement at what must seem the pedantry of researchers. In the absence of clear evidence, why is so much energy expended in debates regarding subtle diagnostic and etiological questions? Why do investigators not work together toward effective therapeutic approaches, instead of engaging in heated controversy over whether or not autism is something different from childhood schizophrenia or whether primary etiological factors are parental behavior or genetic-biological constitution?

Actually, the answer is quite simple. As in so many areas of physical or psychological aberration, treatment approaches follow on an understanding of the causes of a problem. This is in no way a necessary relationship. In fact, in many cases treatment of disorders has proceeded independently of etiological understanding. Consider the remedial approaches to learning disabilities, for example. Even at the present time, there is no clear understanding of the underlying mechanisms leading to the various forms of this disability. Nevertheless, educational approaches have been developed that are often highly effective in compensating for a poorly understood problem.

In many other instances prevention and treatment have had to wait for the discovery of the etiology of a disorder. In still other cases, even a clear understanding of etiology has not produced therapeutic effects. This would be the case, for example, in various forms of mental deficiency, such as Down's Syndrome.

In the case of psychotic disorders of childhood, however, despite the lack of a clear understanding of etiology, theories of causation do affect modes of treatment. Unfortunately, *none* of the various treatment approaches have had notable success in leading to improvement, and *the prognosis for the psychotic child is very poor indeed.* Nonetheless, it is often possible to reduce the severity of certain symptoms and sometimes to assist the child in the development of basic skills. Because even these small gains are important in improving the condition of psychotic children and easing the problems of those who care for them, it is important to review the major therapeutic approaches. These include traditional psychodynamic psychotherapy, behavior modification, and chemotherapy and orthomolecular treatment approaches. Typically, the distinctions among treatment approaches are not as hard and fast in practice as they are in theory. The wise therapist is a pragmatist and does not ignore any treatment opportunities because of theoretical biases. For the psychotic child, a considered eclecticism incorporating the findings and techniques of medicine, psychology, education, neurology, chemistry, and genetics promises the most likely improvement.

Psychodynamic Psychotherapy

Psychodynamic theory views childhood psychoses as, in one way or another, the result of early experiences within the family. The child's relationship with the mother is often seen as a critical factor in causing the child to withdraw defensively from anxiety-arousing contacts with others. Symptoms are viewed as defenses that help the child avoid intimacy, reduce anxiety, and develop a sense of order and security in a frightening world.

If this is the case, then treatment must logically be directed toward reducing anxiety and helping the child cope more effectively with reality. This is more or less the premise upon which Bruno Bettelheim based his treatment approaches with psychotic children. In several moving books (1955a, 1955b, 1967), Bettelheim reported the intensive efforts of many staff members to help individual children.

Psychodynamic treatment of this type is conducted in a residential setting and apart from the parents. Typically, the course of treatment lasts several years. The child is seen in individual psychotherapy with professional therapists, but equally important is constant contact with trained houseparents, teachers, even household staff. In fact, in this kind of **milieu therapy**— in which the total environment is designed to promote growth—contacts with nonprofessional personnel may even be more important than a few hours spent with a therapist. The general orientation of all personnel in a therapeutic residential setting is toward helping the child begin to feel and then to understand that the world is not necessarily a destructive or frightening place. In an accepting fashion, the child is allowed to begin again to experience those impulses and feelings that had once seemed to threaten total destruction. Very slowly, and without forceful intrusion, the child is encouraged to form rela-

The general orientation of all personnel in a therapeutic residential setting is toward helping the psychotic child begin to feel and then to understand that the world is not necessarily a destructive or frightening place.

tionships with people who are tolerant but firm, loving but not engulfing, understanding but not frighteningly omniscient. Through gradual interpretation of behavior and fantasies, the child is helped to understand the sources of conflictual, ambivalent feelings and their relationship to behavior that often seemed to have controlled the child instead of being controlled. Always, the main direction is toward helping the child gradually understand and gradually cope. Whether treatment is conducted on an outpatient basis, in day-treatment centers, or in total residential facilities, the basic assumptions remain those of psychodynamic theory, with an attempt to understand the unconscious forces controlling behavior. Although not an important part of Bettelheim's approach, simultaneous treatment of one or both parents is usually encouraged (Berlin, 1973; Wald, 1973; Wilson, 1968).

I. N. Berlin also subscribes to a psychodynamic perspective in the treatment of childhood psychosis. Berlin (1973) suggested that psychotherapy may be most useful through its effects on family members other than the disturbed child. In his view, the child's progress is often blocked until key conflicts are worked out by the parents, particularly by the mother. Often such conflicts are unconscious parallels to the child's own problems regarding infantile needs for nurturance and gratification. Naturally, if parental conflicts lead to behavior that communicates resentment or anxiety to the child, such conflicts must be resolved if the child is to progress while remaining a part of the family.

Sybille Escalona (1964) operated from the following presumption:

> . . . what has been done to a human being can be undone. Thus we believe that if a maladjusted child can experience—in his relation to the therapist—some of the gratifications and the sense of continuity and stability which he lacked in his earlier life, if he can be helped to remember and understand events which were traumatic to him, and if his misconceptions about human affairs can be interpreted in terms of his needs, then normal processes of ego development can be resumed, and the object of psychotherapy will have been achieved. (p. 54)

In practice, play is used as a therapeutic medium through which the child is helped to express unconscious fears and conflicts. Escalona termed this *expressive psychotherapy.* Equally important to Escalona in the treatment of psychotic children is *suppressive therapy,* in which the child is helped to suppress and control certain thoughts and fantasies that are presently acted out and constitute the basis of the psychotic symptoms. The therapist must use professional skill and knowledge of the child to decide which of these two modes is more important at any given point in the therapeutic process.

Behavior Modification

In recent years the research literature has been flooded with reports of behavioral techniques in the treatment of psychotic children (Margolies, 1977; Schopler, 1976). Generally, these approaches have been less ambitious than traditional individual psychotherapy or child analysis. Rather than working toward "improved adjustment" or "increased ego strength" or related global therapeutic objectives, approaches derived from research on operant learning are typically quite specific in the outcomes sought. This kind of orientation has two consequences. In the first place, outcomes are more easily assessed, and the techniques employed can, therefore, be readily evaluated. At the same time, however, dramatic changes are rarely noted in overall behavior, and those changes that do occur are seen by some as robotlike responses to external stimulus control. Bettelheim suggested that approaches of this sort reduced autistic children "to the level of Pavlovian dogs" (1967, p. 410).

There seems to be little point in entering this kind of controversy between proponents of psychodynamic as opposed to behavioral approaches. As noted earlier, treatment of psychotic disorders is a pragmatic business, and thoughtful eclecticism is the most useful approach. Furthermore, psychotic children and their parents derive little benefit from such debates. Instead, where reduction of symptoms is claimed, it is worthwhile to examine the claims and see what can be learned.

The basic assumptions and techniques of behavioral approaches to treatment have been discussed earlier. At this point, only one further general statement need be made in order to clarify the applicability of behavioral approaches to psychotic disorders. Although early advocates of behavior modification made assumptions regarding parental behavior as a major etiological factor in childhood psychoses (Ferster, 1961), there is absolutely no necessity for such an assumption. *Behavioral techniques may be effective regardless of the etiology of the disturbance if they can be shown to effect changes in behavior.* In other words, evidence suggesting that childhood psychotic disorders may have genetic or biochemical sources does not negate the possibility that operant learning techniques may be helpful in establishing absent behaviors (such as language or social responsiveness) or in eliminating excessive behaviors (such as self-stimulation or self-detructiveness). Treatment must be evaluated on the basis of whether or not specified changes in behavior can be made.

In a comprehensive review of research conducted between 1961 and 1968, Leff concluded that "behavior modification techniques may be extremely useful tools in the education and rehabilitation of psychotic children" (1968, p. 406). In addition, these techniques often lead to relatively rapid change, do not require the direct involvement of highly trained professionals, can be taught to parents, teachers, and others who have direct contact with the child, and do not necessitate the construction of a complex theoretical structure that ascribes responsibility for the child's problems to the parents.

In a wide-ranging variety of treatment reports, behavioral techniques have been effective in reducing self-injurious behavior (Baroff & Tate, 1968); increasing imitation (Hingtgen, Coulter, & Churchill, 1967); teaching basic speech skills (Lovaas, 1966); establishing social responses (Lovaas, Schaeffer, & Simmons, 1965); increasing attention span (Marr, Miller, & Straub, 1966); extinguishing tantrums (Patterson & Brodsky, 1966); and teaching letter and word recognition (Hewett, 1964). It should be noted that many of these reports are studies of only one or a few children rather than large-scale investigations. However, it should also be noted that these are only examples. Additional studies with similar conclusions have been conducted in each of the areas specified. It should also be noted that a large number of the behavioral studies employ what has been termed an *ABAB,* or *reversal experimental design.*

A reversal design is one in which a target behavior is subjected to an initial period of baseline counting prior to intervention. This results in a determination of the average frequency of the behavior in question. Subsequently, behavioral intervention is implemented while frequency rates are observed. If the rates of the behavior change, then it appears that the treatment has been effective. However, it is also possible that extraneous variables may have affected the behavior. In order to establish clearly that functional control of the behavior has been established, the intervention is then suspended with a return to conditions prevailing at the time the original baseline was taken—most often with the result that the behavior returns to its original frequency. Having changed and then reestablished the target behavior, the final step is to reintroduce the intervention. This is an extremely powerful demonstration that one understands and can manipulate the critical elements controlling the occurrence of a specified behavior.

In a recent review of literature describing educational applications of behavioral intervention strategies, Gallagher and Wiegerink (1976) developed several guidelines for teachers of autistic children. Most importantly, they suggested that training of autistic children should follow developmental guidelines. That is, tasks that normally occur early in development should take priority in remedial training of a given child. For example, if imitation is a prerequisite to the development of speech, then training should first be directed toward the establishment of imitative skills, and only later should

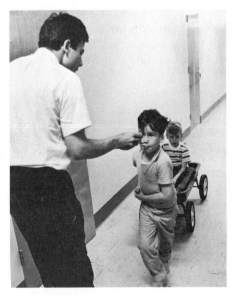

These two autistic boys were enrolled in an intensive behavior therapy program at the UCLA Neuropsychiatric Institute. Here the boys receive immediate positive reinforcement in the form of food for their participation in simple tasks such as ball tossing and pulling a wagon.

work begin on speech development. Additionally, it is important for the teacher of psychotic children to be aware of the impact of sensory stimuli and either reduce sensory input or regulate it carefully to facilitate learning.

General evaluations of the outcomes of behavioral treatment of childhood psychoses have been positive but cautious. Werry, for example, concluded his review of behavioral treatment in childhood psychosis with the statement that this approach shows "promise" (1972, p. 211). However, he added that behavioral approaches do not normalize psychotic youngsters. Similarly, Rimland (1974) noted that the main contribution of behavioral intervention is that it helps the psychotic child establish controls essential for entrance into structured educational programs.

In a review of treatment efforts with severely disturbed autistic children, Lovaas, Koegel, Simmons, and Stevens-Long (1973) found that (a) behavioral methods can effect decreases in inappropriate behaviors and increases in appropriate speech, play, and nonverbal social behaviors; (b) some children exhibit spontaneous social interactions and use of language after about eight months of treatment; (c) intelligence and social quotients do improve somewhat during treatment; (d) follow-up studies showed that, where parents had been trained in behavioral methods, improvements continued. In evaluating their experiences with behavioral approaches, Lovaas et al. stated that:

> . . . many of the procedures we have described are not new, but bear striking similarities to those described by Itard ("The Wild Boy of Aveyron") and by Sullivan (in Gibson's "The Miracle Worker") and recently by Clark ("The Siege"). We are especially struck by the similarity in their willingness to use functional consequences for the child's behaviors, the meticulous building of new behaviors in a piece-by-piece fashion, the intrusion of the education into all aspects of the child's life, the comprehensive, hour-by-hour, day-by-day commitment to the child by an adult, etc.
>
> So the principles we employ are not new. Reinforcement, like gravity, is everywhere, and has been for a long time. The principles can be used to the child's advantage or they can be used against him. What is new in behavior therapy is the systematic evaluation of how these principles affect the child. It is not the content of behavior therapy that is new but its research methodology. In that sense we have an immense and often unappreciated advantage over those who preceded us; the methodology enables us to contribute in a cumulative manner psychological treatment. (1973, pp. 163–64)

Stevens-Long and Lovaas (1974) noted cautiously that behavioral approaches are effective in modifying the behavior of autistic children and are important in maintaining an optimistic view toward the future: "The assumption is always that behavior is modifiable, only our own ignorance prevents us from being of greater help" (p. 202).

Chemotherapy and Orthomolecular Treatment

In view of the strong evidence pointing toward a genetic-neurochemical etiology of the psychotic disorders of childhood, the greatest promise of adequate treatment—and perhaps eventually prevention—comes from the bio-chemical laboratory. At this point in time, the promise has not yet been realized and as much confusion and controversy exist in this area as in psychological approaches to treatment. Nonetheless, beginnings have been made, and some data have been reported and are worth consideration.

One of those who has taken a cautious approach to the use of drugs in the treatment of psychotic children is Goldfarb (1970, 1971). Goldfarb suggested that, while not curative in any sense of the word, medication can have the effect of reducing various symptomatic manifestations of the psychotic disorder. Medication can be helpful in reducing anxiety, increasing attention span, and reducing hyperactivity.

Connell (1966) suggested that pharmacotherapy is an important part of the treatment program for psychotic children—provided certain guidelines are observed. These include initial administration of medication at low levels, with gradual increase until the desired effects are achieved without undesirable side effects. This observation implies awareness of the wide range of individual variation in children's responses to drugs. It is also important to consider the child's response to the form of medication, and to allow for individual variation in preference for tablets or liquids. Finally, Connell pointed out that it is critically important not to use physical force to induce the severely disturbed child to take medications.

Fish (1960) described more than ten years of clinical experience in the use of medication in the treatment of psychotic and severely disturbed children. Among a subgroup of 20 children, she observed that drugs provided some help for children who had not responded at all to psychotherapy. This subgroup included all the most disturbed children in her sample. Others responded to combinations of medications and other forms of treatment.

Fish emphasized the critical importance of close and continuous monitoring of the effects of medication, and the utility of explaining to children who are able to understand the likely effects of the medication. Another aspect of the clinical use of medication that is often neglected is the importance of securing parental understanding and cooperation in the administration of the medication. Fish found that maternal attitudes toward medication were often important in furthering understanding of the mother-child interaction. In addition, Fish (1976) felt optimistic that early use of medications in cases where infants vulnerable to psychotic disorders can be identified may be helpful in preventing the debilitating effects of such symptoms as withdrawal, self-stimulation, and self-destructiveness, and thereby facilitate more normal learning and socialization.

Eisenberg (1968) was critical of the frequency with which physicians use medications in lieu of alternate forms of treatment, but he recognized the usefulness of drugs—providing careful principles are followed. Connors (1972) was cautious in his evaluation of the efficacy of pharmacological treatment, but ultimately felt that drugs can be useful in the control of symptomatology and in making the child more responsive to educational and other treatment efforts.

On a more experimental level, several investigators have been involved in the exploration of the effects of lysergic acid diethylamide (LSD) in the treatment of childhood psychoses. Abramson (1967) reviewed several studies and reported that administration of LSD was effective in reducing stereotyped behavior and increasing positive contacts with adults. Bender (1966) administered LSD to 50 autistic and schizophrenic children between 4 and 15 years of age and found no untoward side effects. She reported positive changes in mood, appearance, responsiveness, and perception.

Mogar and Aldrich (1969) reviewed seven drug studies in which psychedelic agents were administered to psychotic children. Their review indicates that children receiving these medications exhibited greater involvement with therapists, increases in emotional responsiveness to adults, increases in speech behavior in previously mute children, and decreases in ritualistic, stereotyped behavior. Altogether, the effects of psychedelic drugs with psychotic children has opened new leads for future research.

An alternative approach, also founded in biochemical research, is that offered by Pauling (1973), Osmond (1973), Rimland (1973, 1974), and others. These investigators believe that wide variations in individual biochemistry deriving from genetic variations lead to consequent variations in optimal concentrations of nutrients. As a result, undetected individual vitamin deficiencies may lead to localized cerebral deficiency diseases and psychotic symptomatology. Treatment is therefore based on administration of large doses of certain vitamins to correct these hypothesized deficiencies.

Rimland (1973) reported that popular accounts of the use of megavitamin therapy with adult schizophrenics prompted numbers of parents of psychotic children to attempt independent experimentation with administration of large doses of water-soluble vitamins to their children. Several parents corresponded with Rimland and reported encouraging results with their experiments, prompting him to do a more systematic survey of parents of psychotic children to gather more extensive data. Intrigued by positive reports by a number of parents and physicians, Rimland reviewed formal research reports of the use of vitamins in treating various childhood disorders, including psychoses. Unable to find any reports of negative effects, he decided to undertake his own research on the effectiveness of megavitamin treatment with psychotic children:

> A group of 300 children was given a combination of vitamins including B_1, B_2, B_6, folic acid, niacinamide, and vitamin C. The study lasted 24 weeks. Parents were given schedules of vitamin administration to follow and were also required to make behavioral reports on standard schedules. A no-treatment period was included prior to the end of the study to determine effects of discontinuation. Preliminary analyses of data indicated definite improvement in 45.3 percent of the cases studied and possible improvement in 41 percent. No improvement was reported for 10.5 percent, and deterioration was reported for 3.1 percent.

Even with numerous methodological problems, Rimland viewed the results as encouraging, and he and others continue to pursue this line of investigation.

Despite promising leads in several areas, however, the fact remains that *there are no consistently or generally effective approaches to intervention with psychotic children.* Occasional reports of symptom reduction, increases in social responsiveness, and elimination of self-injurious or bizarre behavior are exciting, but they do little to alter the overall prognosis for childhood

OPEN ISSUE

Megavitamin therapy involves the administration of massive doses of specific nutrients to children in an attempt to reduce the frequency or intensity of psychotic behavior patterns. Often associated with dietary and nutritional fads both in the minds of laypersons and professionals, megavitamin therapy is an extremely controversial approach to the treatment of childhood psychoses. Despite the fact that an authority as eminent as Bernard Rimland has suggested that megavitamin treatment is at least worth exploration and has himself reported research in this area, most professionals remain not just skeptical but rather openly hostile to this approach to treatment.

In the face of such widespread resistance, research has proceeded extremely slowly and tentatively. Occasional promising reports are dismissed, and little programmatic follow-up research is conducted. In some respects, the issue is not really open at all, since investigators in this area often risk their professional credibility within the scientific community.

Caution, skepticism, and a demand for repeatable results are hallmarks of the scientific endeavor. But so are exploration of new areas and open discussion of controversial ideas. In view of the massive human suffering so clearly evident in childhood psychosis, can we afford to overlook any leads? Despite its unusual nature and lack of a clear rationale, megavitamin therapy deserves, at least, open hearing and discussion, and the status of an open issue.

psychosis. The unfortunate truth is that at this point in time, *the futures of psychotic children are bleak at best*. And yet, even this gloomy statement is a far cry from conditions that existed in the recent past and that still exist in isolated cases. Psychotic children are no longer locked away and left to grow for years without attempts at education and training. Intensive treatment efforts have been shown to produce some change, and a growing number of individuals are committing themselves professionally to the treatment of psychotic children.

SUMMARY

1. Childhood psychosis is a condition characterized by failure to recognize, understand, or respond appropriately to people or objects in the environment.
2. Research supports a distinction between organic psychoses, childhood schizophrenia, and early infantile autism as major types of childhood psychoses.
3. The causes of childhood schizophrenia have been sought in parental mishandling, neurological abnormalities, genetic factors, and biochemical abnormalities.
4. Early infantile autism was once thought to result from parental mishandling, but current research increasingly points toward some form of neurological impairment as the primary causative factor.
5. Differential diagnosis of childhood schizophrenia and early infantile autism has been shown to be possible in a number of research investigations.
6. The developmental consequences of childhood psychosis are pervasive and severe, usually leading to chronic impairment through the life span.
7. The prognosis for childhood psychoses is still very poor despite rapid research advances.
8. Therapeutic intervention takes the form of psychodynamic psychotherapy, behavior modification, and administration of antipsychotic medication.

Applications to Special Children

CHAPTER FOURTEEN

Special Parents

Each parent has a dream of what his child will be, and it takes time to realize that a child is not a dream but a person in his own right.

The parent may be the best kind of person he can be, but the final product is not entirely within his control no matter how much of his life he devotes to the children.

Group for the Advancement of Psychiatry (1973, pp. 43–44, 99)

PARENTAL EXPECTATIONS

While awaiting the birth of a child, prospective parents experience a wide range of emotions. In most cases there is eager anticipation and excitement as parents plan for the child's birth. Often there is a sense of increased closeness between the parents and a feeling of fulfillment. Usually, prospective parents also experience some anxiety regarding the process of birth itself and potential problems that may arise, but these are kept in the background as parents anticipate what their child will be like. Always, there are expectations about the kind of person the child will eventually become; and prospective parents are notorious dreamers as they await the birth of a child who represents a lifetime of potential. Even in cases where the pregnancy was unwanted or where the parents are experiencing conflict or financial stress, expectations nevertheless develop regarding the unborn child.

In most cases parents wish for their children the happiness that they have had and freedom from faults and flaws that they see in themselves. They expect that their children will experience a better world—perhaps even help shape that world. Most parents also expect that family life will conform to a personal fantasy that grows both from their own experiences and from images conveyed in the mass media. Often this expectation "is that in normal family life there is no trouble" (GAP, p. 35).

In fact, this is rarely the case. There are inherent developmental reasons for expecting periods of tension, defiance, and conflict as the growing child and adolescent eventually begins to recognize and test his/her autonomy. Nevertheless, when such emotional upheavals do occur, they often prompt parents to experience a sense of disappointment, guilt, and failure. Unfortunately, in some cases parental expectations focus entirely on such disappointments or on the burdens and responsibilities inherent in having and raising children. Other parents may focus on the inevitable restrictions in their lifestyle that accompany parenthood. Often these kinds of expectations accompany unwanted pregnancies.

The point of this discussion of parental expectations is simply to underscore the fact that *parenthood has a unique meaning for each father and mother, and that one's role as a parent is bound up with the motives and expectations one brings to parenthood.* For most parents there is a reasonably good likelihood that some expectations can be fulfilled. And these constitute part of the joy of parenthood. Even when expectations are drastically modified, such modifications occur over long periods of years, and parents and children have the opportunity gradually to adjust to each other's expectations without abrupt changes or painful disappointments (Gorham, Des Jardins, Page, Pettis, & Scheiber, 1975).

In sharp contrast to these typical experiences, it is the tragedy of parents of special children that few, if any, expectations may ever be fulfilled. The limitations of special children inevitably limit the satisfactions of their parents, whose fate it is to experience anguish, frustration, ambivalence, guilt, and a host of painful emotions.

For many parents of special children there are rewards, too, and these should not be minimized. Special children can be a source of joy and love, and they can bring a sense of meaning and greater depth of understanding to their parents. But for many of these parents, life becomes a series of fears, anxieties, crises, and ongoing desperation.

THE CONCEPT OF THE SPECIAL PARENT

The problems of special children naturally elicit different kinds of emotional responses and coping behaviors on the part of their parents. Nevertheless, the fact that problems exist in their children's development means that these parents will share certain common emotional experiences. Thus a **special parent** may be defined simply as any parent of a special child. Yet, while defining special parenthood on the basis of shared experiences, there are some differences among groups of special parents that result in different coping problems and different emotional experiences. Though many of their experiences are similar, there are some differences between the problems encountered by parents of physically disabled youngsters and those encountered by parents of intellectually impaired children. Even more pronounced are contrasts between the experiences of these parents and those of parents of emotionally disturbed children, whose difficulties are compounded by a sense that, in some way, they may be intimately involved in and responsible for their children's problems. A further distinction must be made between parents of emotionally disturbed children and those parents whose own disturbances lead to neglect, exploitation, and abuse of their children.

Because of the complexity of these issues, it is necessary to draw somewhat arbitrary distinctions among groups of parents; most particularly, it will be necessary to discuss in detail parents of emotionally disturbed children and neglectful and abusive parents who are themselves emotionally disturbed. Both these groups of parents, in a very real sense, constitute groups apart by virtue of the kind of understanding—or lack of understanding—that they receive from the professionals who work with them.

However, it is critical to remember that reality seldom adheres to textbook distinctions and desires for neatness. Groupings made for ease of discussion should not be allowed to obscure the fact that parents of special children share many common experiences. In the following sections, we will discuss first the experiences of parents of physically disabled and retarded children. While we will discuss these groups of parents separately to emphasize certain aspects of their experiences, it is important to remember that, in reality, they share many of the same experiences in coping with their children's impairments. We will also discuss parents of emotionally disturbed children who experience many difficulties in coping with their children's problems, but who must also deal with child-care professionals whose theories often suggest—implicitly or explicitly—that parents are directly responsible for emotional problems in their children. Our review of extensive research evidence regarding parental behavior and emotional disturbance will, hopefully, provide a realistic perspective for understanding parents of emotionally disturbed children.

The differences in experiences among these groups of parents are important, but they should not obscure the fact that they all share very tangibly a sense of tragedy and loss; many experience a sense that their children's lives and their own lives have been irrevocably spoiled.

PARENTS OF PHYSICALLY DISABLED CHILDREN

Physical disabilities may range from severe motor problems that leave a child completely nonambulatory and totally dependent to problems that are manifested only in motor awkwardness or difficulties in verbal expression. Sensory impairments may be partial or complete and may lead to varying levels of difficulty in adjustment. Because of the wide variety of forms such problems may take, and because of gradations in degree of severity, parents of physically impaired children may experience a wide range of reactions.

Paradoxically, and depending on parental expectations, severe physical problems may be more easily accepted than mild impairments. The clear-cut nature of severe disabilities leaves little room for parental distortion or denial, and forces a more immediate adjustment. Further, parents are able to adjust their expectations to the severity of the child's impairment and are more readily able to understand and communicate about the child's limitations (Ross, 1972).

In some cases, parents with very high expectations for their child may find their dreams and fantasies disrupted by even mild impairments, while others may be able comfortably to accept the most severe defects (Zuk, Miller, Bartram, & Kling, 1961). Religious beliefs, socioeconomic status, educational background, and the presence or absence of extended family and community supports are only a few of the additional variables that interact with severity of the child's disability to influence parental reactions. Thus, while degree of impairment is an important factor, it is difficult to predict whether parents will be able to adjust more adequately to mild or severe problems.

Another factor of importance in the course of parental adjustment to a child's impairment is the way that parents become aware of the problem. In

Parents' expectations can come to a sudden halt when their newborn infant's very life is in danger. This may be but their first step down the often frustrating and difficult road of special parenthood.

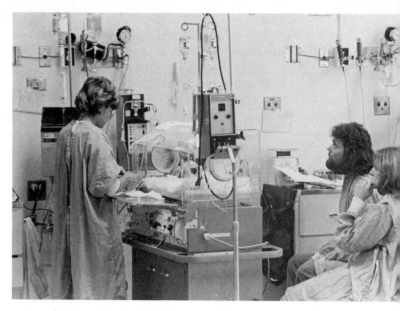

some instances, the presence of an impairment is evident immediately after birth. At other times, the existence and severity of a disability may not become apparent for some time. Again, although it is difficult to predict the kind of adaptive response parents will develop, the way in which they become aware of the problem will affect attitudes toward the child and toward themselves and their relationship.

Regardless of the severity of a child's problem or the immediacy of parental awareness, virtually all parents of special children experience a number of common reactions and adaptive patterns. These may include grief and mourning, anger, depression, denial, and ambivalence; and finally—it is to be hoped—adaptation and growth.

The Experiences of Grief and Mourning

The initial reaction to diagnosis of a physical impairment—whether it occurs immediately after birth or later in development—is some measure of shock. Upon initial diagnosis, however, the severity of the condition is often difficult to estimate clearly and, often, easy for parents to deny. As the child fails to develop normally, outright rejection of diagnostic statements becomes less possible, and parents respond with grief and with what might be described as a mourning response (Solnit & Stark, 1961). Yet the terms "grief" and "mourning" do not completely capture the essence of the difficult experience of recognizing a child's handicap.

> It is not like having a death in the family, when people come together to grieve and draw comfort from the presence of friends and family. Learning that one's child is "not normal" is a lonely experience; having such a child tends to thrust the parents outside the mainstream of help, comfort, and advice. Uncommon problems cannot be shared with next-door

neighbors. Friends and relatives feel, and often are, ill qualified to advise or assist. The usual sources of professional help, like one's physician, may seem inappropriate. The [parents themselves] may feel some alienation from the "normal" world . . . . (Gorham et al., 1975, p. 156)

Individuals counseling parents of disabled youngsters note that parents often describe experiencing fantasies that the child they had expected is dead and not the same child actually born to them. In effect, this is precisely the case. Expectant parents fantasize about the development of their child and, in some respects, begin to think about certain traits and qualities as characteristic of the child. Most parents share this kind of fantasy experience and, in fact, most have to modify their dreams to fit reality during the course of the child's development. However, parents of special children must compress these modifications in their thinking into a period of months or even days. The shock is massive. In attempting to incorporate knowledge of a child's disability, parents may poignantly describe now-lost toys, plans for shared experiences that will never occur, disrupted school and career hopes, and even marriages and grandchildren that will not happen. In a few cases, parents even abandon previously chosen names upon learning of a child's disability, as though the child they had expected were dead and another had taken its place.

During this initial period of adjustment to a diagnosed impairment, many parents also experience a strong sense of guilt, as though in some way they were responsible for the child's defect. The sources of profound guilt feelings are many. For one thing, socialization practices in our society are frequently based on the induction of guilt feelings; any experience that implies failure—such as giving birth to an impaired child—may also become an occasion for feelings of guilt and self-condemnation. Further, as parents experience negative emotions of disappointment and anger, ambivalent feelings toward the child may give rise to additional guilt feelings. The relationship between sexual behavior and conception may also elicit guilt feelings: parents who feel that sexual behavior is immoral may come, irrationally, to view the child's defect as retribution for their sins. In still other instances, the child may be the result of an unwanted pregnancy, or attempts at aborting the pregnancy may have been unsuccessful; in either case guilt feelings result (Covert, 1964; Love, 1970; Ross, 1972). However, underlying all of these possible explanations for parental guilt is the basic fact that "having conceived the child, parents feel responsible for every aspect of his [her] being" (Covert, 1964, p. 61).

Dealing with Anger and Depression

In addition to grief and mourning, many parents also experience and express intense anger. In some, the anger is nonspecific and finds outlet in relations with grandparents, friends, spouse—anyone who tries to provide comfort. Depending on their religious beliefs, some parents may experience anger toward a god or fate that has unjustly given them a damaged child. Some parents report feelings of intense anger toward normal children they know. It is as though the very normality of other children exaggerates the parents' hurt and disappointment in their own child.

Almost invariably, anger is eventually directed toward medical personnel who are seen as responsible for damaging their child or who have failed in sensitivity and understanding of the parents' needs during initial periods of shock and grief. While such anger may be a projection of the parents' feelings toward their child (Ross, 1972), it may also be a justifiable and realistic response to the kind of treatment parents actually receive. Hospital personnel—from physicians through nursing staff—are often discomfited by the birth of an impaired child, and their anxieties may provoke embarrassing blunders, well-intentioned but callous advice, or insensitivity to what parents are feeling. It is the unusual nurse or physician who has had any preparation for helping parents deal with their pain. Medical training does not include preparation for dealing with the intense emotions parents experience on learning of an impairment in their child. Gorham et al. (1975) also pointed to the fact that physicians may experience personal discomfort at having to present parents with a painful diagnosis; as a result, they may retreat into distant professionalism or make a hasty referral so that they will not have to deal either with the child or parents. Unfortunately, parents of special children rarely encounter the kind of assistance they need to cope with their emotional pain and the problems they face in helping their child. As a result, they often develop mistrust of professional personnel and long-lasting bitterness.

In some parents, angry outbursts alternate with periods of profound depression and hopelessness. A sense of despair may engender apathy toward the child and the world at large. Most parents do not remain long in this kind of mood. The demands of caring for a special child and supporting one's spouse through a period of emotional despondency prohibit prolonged passive depression.

Denial as a Coping Mechanism

At some time during this period of early adjustment to awareness of a child's impairment, most parents attempt to cope with their anxiety and despair by means of denial. In some cases, denial manifests itself in conceptions of diagnosticians as inept and mistaken. Unable to face the reality of a child's impairment, parents may reject diagnostic and prognostic statements. Well-meaning relatives and friends may complicate matters by attempting to comfort and reassure the parents, thereby supporting parental denial. Anecdotes and recollections about "a child just like yours" suddenly appear, almost always a child who "just grew out of it" in a short time. The parents of a special child are attuned to anything that offers hope, and occasionally they will fixate on such anecdotes to bolster their attempts to deny the painful reality of the child's condition.

Sometimes denial results in a period of "doctor shopping," and parents seize on any discrepancies in diagnostic statements to bolster their hopes. Again, medical and professional personnel sometimes contribute to coping difficulties because of their own uncertainty or their reluctance to confront parents with a distressing diagnosis and prognosis. Statements regarding the child's condition may be hedged and circuitously guarded. Conversely, the parents may receive information in blunt, shocking terms that they are only too ready to deny and interpret as a function of professional incompetence. It is interesting to note here, parenthetically, that people are often advised to seek several opinions when facing a serious problem requiring medical or other professional advice. Yet when parents of special children engage in such behavior, it is typically viewed as a failure to face the child's disability realistically. This is not to deny that in many instances parental "doctor shopping" is, in fact, a refusal to face reality; but it may also be a realistic attempt to find confirmation of opinions that will shape the child's entire life.

While parental trips from doctor to doctor may be attempts at denial, inefficient service delivery systems can also contribute to the phenomenon of going from one doctor to another (Gorham et al., 1975). In many instances, diagnostic procedures are uncoordinated and unrelated to treatment efforts. The family physician or pediatrician, suspecting an impairment, may refer the family to another medical or professional specialist more competent to deal with the suspected problem. This specialist may, in turn, seek consultations from psychologists, speech therapists, special educators, and so on. The perspectives of different professions frequently lead to variations in diagnostic impressions and labels. The parents may end up with a bewildering array of diagnostic impressions and no one to integrate and interpret them. From among the various labels, parents may, in resisting acceptance of the child's disability, select those that are most innocuous.

A further service delivery problem stems from the fact that, although a variety of diagnostic services are available, treatment services for the special child may be more difficult to find. This problem is summarized in the aphorism that "many will test, but few will treat." Receiving diagnostic impressions without offers or opportunities for remediation services, parents have little recourse but to begin again by seeking other diagnostic impressions. Often the process may be repeated several times, with each diagnosis eventuating in disappointment regarding realistic treatment possibilities.

In recent years, integrated diagnostic and intervention services are beginning to replace fragmented service delivery systems. While this is certainly a desirable improvement, professional practice—even in these settings—often neglects a critical function: bringing parents into the decision-making process in relation to their own child. While professionals compare opinions and recommendations, parents are characteristically informed only of the end results. Unaware of professional disagreements or alternative modes of understanding their child, the parents are not really able to make informed decisions on the basis of all available information. Furthermore, their input is often viewed as inessential or too emotion-laden to be really useful. But is it possible to make recommendations and decisions about a child's life without active parental involvement at every step?

It is hardly surprising that parental attempts at denial persist through bewilderment, confusion, disagreement, and exclusion from some of the most critical decisions they will ever face. The importance of ongoing parental involvement in all aspects of the diagnostic process—along with ongoing supportive counseling and interpretation—simply cannot be overemphasized. Parents are not outsiders in their children's lives. Yet, all too often, this process of parental involvement is neglected, and the omission contributes to parental reliance on unrealistic and nonfunctional coping techniques.

In some cases, parents of special children attempt to deny the presence of a problem by magnifying small signs of developmental progress into major milestones. A small change in the child's condition may serve as a spur for the parents to engage in frenzied remediation attempts, despite the absence of real evidence that the child can profit from these efforts. Inevitably, too, where people desperately cling to hope, charlatans and quacks appear and foster unrealistic hopes. In one recent instance, for example, parents of Down's Syndrome children were offered hope that a certain medication would reverse the physical and intellectual characteristics of this genetic disorder.

More often, however, legitimate practitioners find that parents are prone to distort the implications of experimental research or new treatment approaches. Hopeful parents may grasp at the most tentative statements regarding treatment possibilities to bolster a shaky denial system. Special children may be subjected to intensive remediation exercises or other therapeutic regimens on the basis of a newspaper report or a magazine article of ongoing research. Hopes are renewed repeatedly only to be repeatedly shattered. Usually, the pain engendered by denial is more problematic than the pain avoided by it, and the search for miracles ends.

Yet, it is important that parents maintain realistic hope. Without it, the child's handicap may be magnified unrealistically; appropriate treatment efforts may be abandoned; parents may come to expect less of the child than he/she is capable of accomplishing. The balance between outright denial of a child's problems and initial depression upon recognition of those problems is delicate, yet it must be maintained if the child is to develop optimally.

Parental Ambivalence

Perhaps the most widely shared experience among parents of special children—indeed of all parents—is that of ambivalence. No parent is uniformly loving and giving toward his/her children. On the contrary, though parental

Though this little girl will be in a cast for some time because of a congenital dislocation of her hips, her impairment is correctable, and it would be a mistake to treat her as though she were seriously handicapped. While the cast is on, the best course for her mother is to be patient and loving, to help when her daughter needs assistance, and, most of all, to provide her with as many normal experiences as possible.

feelings toward their children are predominantly positive, all parents some-times experience feelings of anger and resentment toward their children. Such ambivalent feelings are particularly problematic for parents of develop-mentally disabled children.

For one thing, the extreme dependency of the severely impaired child demands continual, intensive care. Parents cannot deny the needs of their child who, in many cases, may not be even minimally self-sufficient. For example, the nonambulatory physically disabled child may need to be carried from place to place; toileting may be an unrealistic goal for children who are unable to move independently; in some cases, physically disabled children may need to be fed. All parents share these experiences of having to carry, diaper, and feed their children. But for many parents of physically disabled children, these burdens do not disappear as the child grows taller and heavier. On the contrary, such tasks only become increasingly difficult.

Further, a disabled child may limit and restrict parental activities and satisfactions, since he/she cannot be left alone and since parent substitutes are often reluctant to care for a special child. Apart from the limitations necessi-tated by physical care, the problems of severely disabled children may also impose heavy financial burdens. In fact, there is virtually no aspect of family life that is not affected by the presence of the special child.

Unceasing demands for care and nurturance often engender parental resentment and anger. These feelings in turn can lead to guilt and self-con-demnation in most parents who wish to experience themselves as loving and caring and who do, in fact, love their child. Add to this complex of emotions a basic pity for a child who is in no way responsible for his/her condition, and one begins to sense the emotional turmoil experienced by special parents.

Complex, confused emotions can lead in several directions. Some parents begin to focus on the negative, burdensome aspects of their lives as parents and begin to experience increasing resentment. Occasionally, such resentment takes the form of overt rejection and hostility toward the child. Such rejection may appear as neglect, or it may be expressed more directly in criticism, impatience, ridicule, or anger. On occasion, rejection is evident in a parent's unrealistic demands for the disabled child to develop and perform, and in pressures exerted to force this development. In some instances, a therapeutic regimen will be adhered to in such rigid fashion that, in effect, it constitutes punishing behavior toward the child. In other cases, stringent disciplinary standards will be imposed by a rejecting parent, and the child's inability to adhere to these standards provides tangible reasons for the resentment the parent experiences.

Regardless of the form it takes, rejection is eventually destructive both for child and parents. Disagreements regarding childrearing practices may occur as one parent has higher expectations than the other. Parents may argue about whether to discipline the disabled child or how to discipline; they may argue about the realism of expectations; they may accuse each other of being at fault for the child's disability or disagree about whether or not the child should be placed in a residential institution. They may argue about whether or not to have other children. In one study (Boles, 1959), it was discovered that mothers of cerebral-palsied children reported significantly higher amounts of marital conflict than mothers of normal children. In such cases, blaming parents is all too easy for professionals who have the safety of emotional distance. An empathic understanding of the parents' struggles and the misery that may lead to rejecting attitudes is essential, but much more difficult to achieve.

In contrast to the rejecting parent, other parents may respond to their ambivalent feelings in a compensatory fashion. Denying any resentment, they become overprotective and self-sacrificing. In some cases, rejection and over-protection even alternate in the same parents. However, just as rejection may produce debilitating effects in the child's development, so may overprotection lead to negative effects in the form of *infantilizing,* or "babying," the child. Thus, for example, a parent may try to anticipate the child's every need and avoid any possible frustration. However, this kind of behavior may prevent the child from using residual abilities to the fullest. In some cases marital conflict may develop as one parent or the other sacrifices spouse and family for the special child.

As in the case of rejection, overprotection must be understood empathically rather than judgmentally. Overprotection may be an attempt to restitution on the part of a parent who experiences a profound sense of guilt and personal inadequacy for having produced a defective child.

Parental Adaptation and Growth

The day-to-day problems of caring for the special child make it very easy for parents to focus on the negative aspects of their lives. Disappointed, exhausted by the child's needs for special care, apprehensive about the child's future and their own—it is hardly surprising that many special parents become discouraged, resentful, even bitter. What is surprising is the fact that so many special parents are able to cope with these problems at all; yet they do. And many are able to find a definite sense of joy and meaning in the small accomplishments of their children and in their own participation in those accomplishments.

The professional literature is filled with discussions of the defenses and maladaptive behavior exhibited by parents of special children. Yet one is hard-pressed to find discussions of the endurance, emotional strength, and humor of the special parent. These characteristics do exist and, in many respects, are as typical as the reactions discussed in previous sections. Fortunately, a few reports are beginning to demonstrate that living with a handicapped child can have rewards as well as pains and can lead to personal growth and greater maturity (Grossman, 1972; Holt, 1958).

To obtain some sense of the positive, adaptive reactions of special parents to their problems, one must turn to the parents themselves. David Melton, the father of a special child, wrote:

> In the hundreds of parents of brain-injured children whom I have met, I have not encountered the guilt-ridden neurotics that I am led to expect from articles which are frequently found in educational and medical periodicals. If parents are, indeed, guilt-ridden, I find that they hide it very well. . . . I believe that in the parents of brain-injured children whom

I meet, I am privileged to witness humanity's finest hour. I see a strength in these people, a strength born of great sorrow and discipline. . . . I see families function as families should: as a unit composed of individuals, with individual needs. (Melton, 1972, pp. 29 ff.)

In her survey of special parents, Gorham—herself a special parent—encountered responses such as the following:

As the parent of [a special] child, I want neither pity nor admiration of my "self-sacrifice, patience, love, nobility," and all the other mouthings. I want understanding of the problems by more people, and enough concern on society's part to provide the necessary pressure, at whatever level, so that these children can obtain the proper education and therapy needed to give them a real chance in life. . . . Incidentally, when people tell me how marvelous I am, I have one of two answers: "But I am the mother" or "If not I, who then, and if not now, when?" Usually there is no response. (Gorham et al., 1975, p. 167)

Professionals often interpret such statements as indicative of underlying resentment projected onto society or as denials of the parents' emotional reactions to their special children. In turn, special parents have begun to reject these appraisals as they examine themselves and find, that while they have many problems, they are, nevertheless, coping.

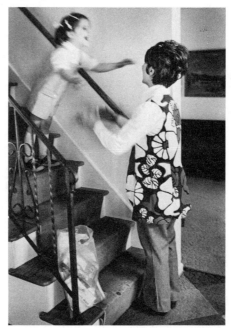

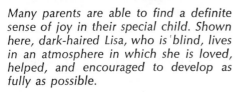

Many parents are able to find a definite sense of joy in their special child. Shown here, dark-haired Lisa, who is blind, lives in an atmosphere in which she is loved, helped, and encouraged to develop as fully as possible.

A later section of this chapter will examine approaches to helping the special parent cope, but it should be made quite clear that, for the most part, this help is offered to basically adequate parents who have confronted tragedy that is difficult for most people to share and understand. Special parents receive praise, blame, sympathy, admiration, ostracism, encouragement, and countless other reactions that only complicate their emotional situation. Rarely do they experience nonjudgmental, nonadvisory understanding of their pain and their struggle to cope.

PARENTS OF INTELLECTUALLY IMPAIRED CHILDREN

Parents of mentally retarded children share many of the experiences already described in relation to parents of physically disabled youngsters. In cases of congenital and perinatal causation of retardation, parents may be made aware of the child's handicap immediately after birth. In such situations, reactions of shock and grief occur immediately upon learning of the child's diagnosis. In a larger number of cases, however, the presence of a retarding condition is not apparent at birth, and recognition of intellectual limitation comes more slowly.

In these latter cases, the parents gradually become aware of missed developmental milestones as the child develops over a period of several years. Walking, talking, independent feeding, and toileting are all delayed. Developmental tasks accomplished by a normal child within a period of months may stretch over a period of several years in the retarded child. With growing awareness of the child's limitations, these special parents also often exhibit grief, guilt, denial, resentment, and ambivalence. And, more often than not, they cope.

In addition to a variety of similar emotional reactions, parents of intellectually and physically impaired children face certain common problems. For example, both groups of special parents must make decisions regarding whether to provide home care for their children or institutional placement. Both must assess the impact of the special child on other family members. Both must face questions regarding the allocation of financial resources and care of their children after their deaths.

However, parents of mentally retarded children must also cope with certain unique problems, including difficulty in recognizing the existence of retardation in some cases and difficulty in dealing with the responses of relatives, friends, and the local community. These major issues warrant separate discussion.

Recognition of Mental Retardation

While severe and profound levels of retardation are readily recognizable, it may be quite difficult for parent or professional to recognize or to understand the child who is moderately or mildly retarded, especially during the first several years of life. Frequently, parents mistake limitations in ability for stubbornness. The mildly retarded child, especially, comes to be seen by parents and by others as a "bad" child who is uncooperative and lazy. Except in cases of severe retardation, parental misunderstanding of their child's abilities can lead to intense resentment, conflict, and rejection because of the lack of any apparent reason for the child's failure to develop normally. As in the case of parents of physically disabled children, such instances of mild or moderate impairment are often more difficult for parents to cope with than instances of severe impairment, since expectations are unclear and confused (Miller, 1958).

Even as parents become more clearly aware of limitations in their child's intellectual abilities and dispense with such unfortunate labels as "slow," or "stubborn," or "lazy," their expectations may not match their child's abilities. In some cases, overestimation of their child's potential may lead the parents to make inappropriate demands and to exert pressures that only foster resentment in the child and disappointment in themselves. Equally problematic is underestimation of the child's ability, since this imposes limitations on the extent to which parents help the child actuate potentials.

Conflicts arising from unclear expectations of the retarded child are further intensified in families that believe strongly in our society's characteristic emphasis on the value of success in competitive endeavors.

> *Our emphasis on physical and intellectual prowess causes a retarded child to represent a threat to the self-esteem of his parents, placing them at a distinct disadvantage in facing many of life's routine experiences. In the "backyard" comparison of infant development and achievement, these parents have few sources of gratification and many sources of anxiety and embarrassment. (Begab, 1966, p. 72)*

Thus the upwardly mobile, middle-class family experiences the retarded child as threatening to the values around which they have organized their lives. This is not to imply that the special child is necessarily resented or rejected—though that may be true in some families—but rather to emphasize the intense conflicts engendered in all family members by the presence of a child whose abilities and limitations are unclear and confusing.

Dealing with Reactions of the Community

The same unclear conceptions of the limits of the mildly or moderately retarded child that make parental understanding difficult serve to complicate parental relationships with extended family members and with neighbors and the community at large (Ross, 1972). Parents frequently receive criticism for being too lenient or for being too demanding; for being neglectful or for being overprotective. The parents' own unhappiness and frustration may go unrecognized as others attempt to work out—through the retarded child—their own prejudices toward people who are different. "Well-meaning" friends may suggest institutionalization as the only possible course. Others may imply that institutionalization is tantamount to abandonment and inconceivable for parents who love their child. The special parent is advised that, with enough effort, he/she can normalize the retarded child; but this is difficult to reconcile with advice that one should not sacrifice spouse and siblings to the retarded child's needs. As with the physically disabled child, there is no lack of advice or suggestions—only a lack of empathic understanding.

Stereotyped conceptions of the retarded youngster often prompt other parents to withdraw from contact with parents of a special child. "Feelings of aversion and nonacceptance toward the retarded still characterize public thought and discourage families from social contacts. Neighbors stare and make unkind, if unwittingly so, comments; complain about the retarded child's behavior; and refuse to let their normal children play with him" (Begab, 1966, p. 76). Though these reactions stem from a curious mixture of fear, ignorance, prejudice, and projection, they nevertheless do lead to an intensification of parental feelings of guilt, shame, and ambivalence. Understanding the sources of prejudice against their children does not necessarily make it easier for special parents to cope with the feelings elicited by prejudice. In fact, as Aronson (1972) suggested, an attempt to understand and integrate the prejudicial attitudes of others may lead the victims of prejudice to even more negative and derogatory self-perceptions.

It is particularly curious to note that stereotypical conceptions of the retarded child and related fears often seem to focus on concerns about sexual behavior. Ross (1972) suggested that such fears may arise from behavior that really represents an attempt to win affection and acceptance on the part of some retarded youngsters. Though sexual curiosity and experimentation among children and adolescents are often taken for granted in today's society, the retarded youngster can expect no such tolerance. Retarded males are often suspected of being sexually hyperactive and potentially assaultive, and retarded females are viewed as naively promiscuous. The fact is that these individuals are rarely sexually assaultive or objects of sexual exploitation (Begab, 1966), and where problems do occur they more likely result from poor judgment rather than from intentional violation of social standards. The fact that such fears persist despite strong evidence to the contrary suggests that much anxiety regarding sexual behavior among the retarded stems from adult projections and conflicts.

In contrast to typical fears and anxieties, the fact is that opportunities to develop adequate sexual information and to develop satisfying relationships with the opposite sex seem almost systematically denied retarded individuals. It seems plausible to hypothesize that the occasional problems that do occur arise from curiosity and lack of information and instruction.

Dealing with Reactions of Siblings

One of the major themes that runs through the literature on physically and intellectually impaired children is the examination of the effects of the special child on his/her siblings. Generally, the focus of clinical and research investigations has been on the potential negative effects of the impaired child on siblings, and the outcomes of such investigations have pointed to a wide variety of potential problems. Perhaps the most pervasive problem is a tendency on the part of the special parent to neglect normal siblings of the retarded child (Adams, 1966; Covert, 1964; Farber, 1962; Love, 1970; Ross,

1972). The extreme dependency of the handicapped child elicits strong parental concern and attempts to compensate for the handicap through extra attention and nurturance. To a limited extent, such attention is appropriate and, in the case of severe limitations, may be essential. However, it can easily happen that parents begin to rearrange aspects of family life to meet the needs of their special child; little attention may be paid to more capable and independent siblings, and expenses associated with the care of the special child may limit the opportunities given to siblings. In extreme cases, the entire family may be sacrificed in a misguided attempt to protect and care for the special child.

Another problem observed in parents of mentally retarded children is the development of compensatory aspirations and expectations for normal siblings (Schild, 1971). Parents may come to expect their normal children to be more independent, understanding, tolerant, and generous than is reasonable. The normal sibling may be obliged—implicitly or explicitly—to accomplish at a higher level than is possible for him/her.

The limitations of the special child may also create difficulties for normal siblings, as they experience embarrassment about and shame of the special sibling in relationships with their peers (Love, 1972). This is particularly true of the young adolescent sibling who is already experiencing doubts about social acceptability, and who fears that a retarded brother or sister may be an additional source of stigmatization. Compounding this reaction are feelings of guilt because the normal sibling feels ashamed or embarrassed; the normal sibling may even feel guilt because of his/her normality (Schild, 1971). In some instances, normal siblings identify with the special child and come to view themselves as defective (Grossman, 1972); or they may begin to fear a hereditary taint. Again, these problems can be intensified by the typical conflicts and anxieties of adolescence.

In families where the normal sibling is expected to assume a major portion of the responsibility for the care of the retarded child, the situation is potentially disastrous. Schoolwork and social activities may have to be neglected if the normal sibling is viewed as responsible for the welfare of the special child. Occasionally, parents explicitly communicate the expectation that the normal sibling will assume responsibility for the care of the special child—even after the parents' death. In such instances, resentment and guilt may develop to such an extent that the normal sibling develops clearly maladaptive emotional and behavioral response patterns.

It should be evident, of course, that none of these problems *must* occur. Many families are able to adapt successfully to the stresses created by the presence of a special child. Begab (1966) suggested that concern for the welfare of the normal sibling may be exaggerated by well-meaning professionals, and that the reactions of siblings are largely reflections of parental reactions. Studies by Holt (1958) and Graliker, Fishler, and Koch (1962) indicated that *the majority of normal siblings are able to adjust to the presence of a special child in the family without major emotional disturbance.* An important study went even further in suggesting that the siblings of the special child may even benefit from their experience with a handicapped brother or sister (Grossman, 1972). In this study of 83 normal siblings of a retarded child, Grossman found that many siblings benefited from their contacts with a retarded brother or sister. In summarizing her findings, Grossman concluded that

> . . . those who had benefited had a greater understanding of people, more tolerance of people in general and handicap in particular, more compassion, more sensitivity to prejudice and its consequences, more appreciation of their own good health and intelligence than many of their peers who had this experience (of a retarded sibling) as well as a sense that the experience had drawn the family closer together. (pp. 93–94)

The Issue of Placement

At one time or another in their lives, virtually all parents of moderately and severely disabled children must deal with the question of whether or not to place their special child in a residential institution. There is, perhaps, no more painful issue than this for the special parent. Apart from the obvious difficulty of separating from a loved one, the issue is complicated by guilt and feelings that the child is being abandoned. Parents struggle to sort their motives and feelings, and they wonder: Is placement in the best interests of the child? Are we simply being selfish? Can we continue to cope? What of our other children? Will their futures be damaged by keeping the child at home? Will our marriage be permanently spoiled by keeping the child at home? Will he/she be well cared for? Will there be people to give him/her love? Will our child miss us? Hate us? Unfortunately, there are few guidelines that can help parents in struggling with these questions. What is more, changes in professional and community attitudes further complicate the parents' dilemma.

Though there are still physicians and other professional personnel who recommend placement as a matter of course for all moderately and severely retarded or disabled children, it is becoming increasingly difficult to maintain the view that special children should be placed in institutions for their own protection and happiness and the well-being of the family (Robinson & Robinson, 1976). It is equally possible that a warm family and community atmosphere may be the most desirable setting for healthy, normalized experiences and optimal development of the intellectually impaired child (Love, 1972).

A number of research investigations have uncovered variables relating to family decisions to institutionalize retarded children. For example, working-class families are more likely to institutionalize than are upper-class families (Farber, 1962); males are more likely to be institutionalized than females (Sabagh & Windle, 1960); the child's position in the birth order of the family is related to likelihood of placement, with youngest children least likely to be placed (Graliker, Koch, & Henderson, 1965); perhaps most important is the family's perception of its ability to cope with the special child and its sense of disruption (Wolf & Whitehead, 1975).

However, research findings are of little help to individual parents as they face their own placement decisions. In these cases, it is important that parents be helped to sort out their feelings and then be supported in the kind of decision they make. Whether, objectively, the decision appears to be right or

415
Counseling parents
of physically
disabled and
intellectually
impaired children

wrong, contradictory opinions from people outside the family cannot facilitate reintegration or future adjustment. The family's struggle to come to a decision is not facilitated by recommendations or advice, but by sensitive counseling toward self-understanding and self-acceptance regardless of the decision eventually made.

COUNSELING PARENTS OF PHYSICALLY DISABLED AND INTELLECTUALLY IMPAIRED CHILDREN

Counseling approaches to parents of special children have traditionally been oriented toward helping them resolve a variety of emotional conflicts that are, by implication, more or less maladaptive and neurotic. Professional personnel often make the patronizing assumption that parents of a special child inevitably require assistance in accepting and living with their child because they are unaware of their unconscious conflicts and deep-seated resentments (Matheny & Vernick, 1970). While such assumptions may be apt in some cases, it is important that those working with parents of special children adopt realistic rather than stereotyped attitudes. This means that each parent must be understood as an individual who is coping with his/her child's disabilities within the context of personal abilities, needs, emotional strengths, and a host of sociocultural and interpersonal factors.

It is foolish to assume that all special parents need assistance in coping, that in-depth exploration of parental emotions is always necessary, or that parents who reject such assistance are manifesting difficulties in accepting their children. At the same time, however, it is important to recognize parental needs when they exist. Those who work with special parents must be attuned to parental expressions of need and be prepared to respond to parents as unique individuals rather than as people who experience predetermined sets of problems.

Counseling with special parents should always be based on honest, direct, nontechnical sharing of diagnostic information and the likely developmental consequences of the child's impairment. Where such information is unclear or questionable, these qualifications should be shared frankly with parents along with the reasons for uncertainty. However, parents should not be placed in the position of having to reassure the diagnostician because of his/her personal uncertainty. Rather, diagnostic impressions should be presented with appropriate certainty and qualification as dictated by the outcome of the diagnostic process.

It is also important that the counselor be sensitive to parental responses and not overwhelm parents with too much or too technical information. At the same time, concern for the parents should not lead the counselor to hedge on his/her impressions or to present a falsely optimistic prognosis. Confronting a child's impairment is a difficult experience both for the parents and for the counselor, but it is the counselor's professional responsibility to help the parents cope with their emotional reactions, not to evade them. It is also important for the counselor to avoid judgment of the parents' reactions. There is no good or bad or right or wrong way to confront personal tragedy.

SUGGESTIONS FOR PROFESSIONALS

1. Have the parent(s) involved every step of the way. The dialogue established may be the most important thing you accomplish. If the parent's presence is an obstacle to testing because the child will not cooperate in his presence, the setup should include a complete review of the testing procedure with the parent. . . .

2. Make a realistic management plan part and parcel of the assessment outcome. Give the parents suggestions for how to live with the problem on a day-to-day basis, with the needs of the child, the capacities of the family, and the resources of the community all considered. Let the parents know that you will suggest modifications if any aspect of the management plan does not work.

3. Inform yourself about community resources. Give the parents advice on how to go about getting what they need. Steer them to the local parent organization.

4. Wherever possible, make the parent a team member in the actual diagnostic, treatment, or educational procedures. It will give you a chance to observe how the parent and the child interact.

5. Write your reports in clear, understandable, jargon-free language. . . . the parent *must* be as well informed as you can make him. Information that he does not understand is not useful to him. The goal is to "produce" a parent who understands his child well enough to help him handle his problems as he grows up.

6. Give copies of the reports to parents. They will need them to digest and understand the information in them; to share the information with other people close to the child; and to avoid the weeks or months of record-gathering which every application to a new program in the future will otherwise entail.

7. Be sure the parent understands that there is no such thing as a one-shot, final, and unchanging diagnosis. . . .

8. Help the parent to think of life with this child in the same terms as life with his other children. It is an ongoing, problem-solving process. Assure him that he is capable of that problem solving and that you will be there to help him with it.

9. Be sure that he understands his child's abilities and assets as well as his disabilities and deficiencies. . . .

10. Warn the parent about service insufficiencies. Equip him with advice on how to make his way through the system of "helping" services. . . . Tell him that his child his a *right* to services. . . .

From Gorham et al. (1975, pp. 183–84)

The parents will attempt to cope to the best of their ability. The counselor may be able to assist by providing an atmosphere in which the parents can explore their reactions without fear of criticism and with awareness of the counselor's confidence in their concern and ability as parents. The counselor should also be conversant with community resources available to the parents and with legislation affecting their child's rights.

Perhaps most importantly, within the context of professional expertise and professional competence, the counselor should have "an understanding heart, the rare gift bestowed upon those who can look at a parent sitting across the desk and believe that 'But for the grace of God, there sit I'" (Murray, 1969, p. 16). It is crucial here to keep in mind that maudlin sympathy or overidentification with the problems of the parents does not help; rather,

EXHIBIT 14.2

417

Parents of
emotionally
disturbed children

SUGGESTIONS FOR PARENTS

1. You are the primary helper, monitor, coordinator, observer, record keeper, and decision maker for your child. Insist that you be treated as such. It is your *right* to understand your child's diagnoses and the reasons for treatment recommendations and for educational placement. No changes in his treatment or educational placement should take place without previous consultation with you.

2. Your success in getting as well informed as you will need to be to monitor your child's progress depends on your ability to work with the people who work with your child. You may encounter resistance to the idea of including you in the various diagnostic and decision-making processes. The way you handle that resistance is important. Your best tool is not the angry approach. Some of your job will include the gentler art of persuasion. Stay confident and cool about your own abilities and intuitions. You know your child better than anyone else could. . . .

3. Try to find, from among the many people whom you see, a person who can help you coordinate the various diagnostic visits and results.

4. Learn to keep records. . . . Such documentation for every step of your efforts to get your child the service he needs can be the evidence which finally persuades a program director to *give* him what he needs. No one can ever be held accountable for conversations or meetings with persons whose names and titles you do not remember, on dates you cannot recall, about topics which you cannot clearly discuss.

5. Make sure that you understand the terminology used by the professional. Ask him to translate his terms into lay language. Ask him to give examples of what he means. Do not leave his office until you are sure you understand what he has said. . . .

6. Ask for copies of your child's records. . . .

7. Read. Learn as much as you can about your child's problem. But do not swallow whole what you read. . . .

8. Talk freely and openly with as many professionals as you can. Talk with other parents. Join a parent organization. . . .

9. Stay in close touch with your child's teacher. . . .

10. Listen to your child. It is *his* point of view that he is giving you, and on that he is an expert.

11. Work hard at living the idea that differentness is just fine—not bad. Your child will learn most from your example. Help him to think of problems as things that can be solved if people work at them together.

From Gorham et al. (1975, pp. 184–86)

---

what is needed is a capacity for realistic understanding and empathy from a competent professional. Exhibits 14.1 and 14.2 provide important suggestions for parents and professionals in working together for the welfare of the special child.

PARENTS OF EMOTIONALLY DISTURBED CHILDREN

The single most important factor in understanding the parents of emotionally disturbed children is the prevalence among helping professionals of theoretical concepts that suggest parental pathology as the primary etiological factor in the development of emotional problems in children.

Unlike other special parents whose responses are seen as consequences of living with a disabled child, the parents of the emotionally disturbed child are often viewed as contributing to the development of the disturbance. In some cases, this is a valid conception, and one can trace developmental aberrations in the child to specific parental behavior or modes of interaction. Abuse and neglect are examples of disturbances of parenting behavior that often result in severe emotional or behavioral problems in children. In many other cases, however, parents are presumed to have caused their child's emotional problems without any evidence to support such a presumption. Parents of emotionally disturbed children are often confronted—directly or indirectly—with implications that their own neurotic conflicts in relation to their child have impaired any chance that the child will develop normally. While all special parents experience a sense of loss and sorrow, parents of emotionally disturbed children must additionally face the notion that they may have failed as parents and ruined their children's lives. As we will see, there is little research evidence to support this notion as a blanket assumption.

It is easy to blame parents for their children's problems. It is equally easy to believe that parents always do their best and cannot be held responsible for problems in their children. Unfortunately, reality is complex rather than convenient, and easy impressions do not contribute to realistic understanding. We will summarize a variety of concepts and perspectives, each of which may have some validity in understanding the unique experiences of specific parents and their children. Then we will review available research evidence on the relationships between parental behavior and childhood disturbances and present an interactional model of parent-child relations.

Theories of Parental Causation

Simple common sense as well as psychological theory, clinical experience, and research evidence all indicate that there is an important relationship between the emerging personality of the child and the child's experiences with parents (Bandura, 1971a; Bandura & Walters, 1963; Sears, Maccoby, & Levin, 1957; Whiting & Child, 1953). Parental styles of communication and expression of affection, parental values, disciplinary and educational attitudes, presence or absence of parental conflict, and simple modeling are only a few of the ways in which parents influence the development of their children. *There is no question regarding the importance of parental influence on the emotional and behavioral development of children.*

Rather, questions regarding parental involvement in the development of emotional disturbances in children must focus on parental attitudes toward children, the presence or absence of parental pathology as a necessary or sufficient condition for childhood disturbance, and on whether mistakes or distortions in parenting behavior lead inevitably to disturbance. Further questions relate to the role of the child in the development of faulty interaction patterns in the family and to the basic question of the child's inherent vulnerability to psychological disturbance. These questions should guide consideration and evaluation of the theories and research findings discussed in the following sections.

Parental rejection

Most theories of parental causation of emotional disturbance in children are elaborations of the assumption that parental rejection disrupts normal patterns of nurturance essential for healthy psychological development in the child. Bruno Bettelheim (1967), for example, suggested that maternal emotions may be sensed and may disrupt the mother-child relationship during early interactions in nursing. While Bettelheim acknowledged the importance of the "mutuality" that exists in the mother-child interaction, it is nevertheless easy to form the impression from his writings that it is rejecting attitudes—conscious or unconscious—in the parents that initiate and perpetuate emotional disturbance in the child (Bettelheim, 1955a, 1955b, 1967).

Bettelheim's view of the way in which emotional disturbance develops

During periods of special stress, nurturance is important for a child's healthy development. If parental support and assistance are missing, anxiety may grow and contribute to subsequent emotional problems.

during such basic interactions as nursing is similar to concepts suggested by Harry Stack Sullivan (1953), who believed that in earliest contacts, an anxious or rejecting mother communicates her anxiety to her infant. For the infant, these experiences of maternal anxiety lead to the development of self-defensive measures to avoid threats to security. These defensive processes involve distortions in the child's perception and experience of the world. In fact, the child's anxiety may be so intense that certain experiences are totally rejected and never really incorporated into the developing self, while other experiences form the core of negative self-feelings and a concept of the self as "bad."

A related formulation of the development of severe emotional disorder was proposed by Fromm-Reichman (1948), who developed the concept of the **schizophrenogenic mother,** a dominant and binding parent who simultaneously rejects her child emotionally and induces severe anxiety in the child. The schizophrenogenic mother is a powerful, controlling woman who prevents normal development in her child because of her intense needs to control others' lives (Despert, 1970). Such a mother tends also to be a perfectionist in her own behavior and to demand similar qualities in others. She often chooses a husband who can never meet her demands or resist her control. Retreating passively into isolation from the rest of the family, he leaves his wife to oversolicitous, all-enveloping concern for her child. The child is tantalized by the promise of having all needs fulfilled without effort, but simultaneously resents the mother's excessive control. In the end, the child succumbs and retreats from the outside world to the security promised by an all-powerful, all-gratifying mother whose hatred and resentment are masked from herself and from the rest of the world behind a facade of concern.

Anna Freud (1970) suggested that severe anxiety may also be induced as a result of more direct rejection by a mother who is unwilling to assume a maternal role. "The reasons for the unwillingness may be external ones; financial difficulties, lack of their own home or of space, the burden of too many earlier children, or illegitimacy of the relations with the child's father" (Freud, 1970, p. 379). In some cases, rejection may stem from serious internal conflicts regarding sex role and an unconscious rejection of femininity. For these mothers, rejection is inextricably bound up with long-standing neurotic problems that were themselves engendered by deficient parenting.

Rejection may take a variety of behavioral forms. It may be the basic motivation leading some mothers to seek *physical separation* from their children. In some mothers, rejection may appear instead as *psychological aloofness* in which little interest is shown in the child's activities or concerns. In other instances, rejection is evident in *inconstancy of feelings* as the mother's level of investment in her child appears to be fickle and capricious. From moment to moment, the mother may alternately experience intense overconcern, resentment, unconcern, and so on. *Neglect* and *abuse* are further direct manifestations of rejection. These forms of behavior are sufficiently important to warrant more detailed discussion below.

Overprotection

In some cases, a mother defends against awareness of unacceptable, unconscious resentment toward her child by becoming oversolicitous. In a sense, she disavows any possible resentment toward her child through her involvement with every aspect of the child's existence. Levy (1966) termed this *guilt-provoked overprotectiveness.* However, because such solicitousness is prompted by unconscious resentment, the child is ultimately damaged anyway through interference with normal patterns of growth and development.

In his extensive study of maternal overprotection, Levy described other kinds of unconscious distortions that lead to excessive involvement with the child. For example, *pure overprotection* may arise from prolonged anticipation of the birth of a child, or in "naturally maternal" women whose behavior as mothers is a primary source of self-esteem. In still other instances, overprotection may be a maternal reaction to a severe injury or illness in the child, which prompts extreme anxiety and caution regarding the child's health.

It is important to recognize that an understanding of underlying motives is often difficult to attain through superficial analysis. Instead, one must use a few kinds of behavior as definitions of maternal overprotection apart from unconscious motives. These behaviors include either overpermissiveness or an excess of control, excessive contact with the child, infantilization, or prevention of independent behavior. Any of these behaviors, singly, or in combination, may lead to disturbance in the child.

Neglect

As indicated earlier, neglect is a behavioral manifestation of parental rejection. **Child neglect** is defined by failure on the part of parents to provide for the child's basic physical needs, safety, and reasonable socialization. In contrast to certain forms of psychological rejection, neglect is not difficult to recognize. It is characterized by failure to feed children adequately or to provide foods that meet basic nutritional needs, ignorance of basic health care practices, inattention to health problems, failure to dress children or to provide reasonable clothing, leaving children unattended or unsupervised for prolonged periods of time, failure to ensure school attendance or to provide standards of social behavior. "If the behavior of neglecting parents toward their children could be summed up in one word, that word would be indifference" (Young, 1971, p. 31).

In some instances, parental indifference and neglect result from resentment of the child's dependency and needs for care. In her extensive study of neglected children and their parents, Leontine Young (1971) found that neglect is often a function of parental immaturity. Neglected themselves as children, neglecting parents are unable to see beyond their own needs for nurturance and immediate impulse gratification. As a result, there is an absence of planning and elemental routines. No thought is given to meal planning or to economic planning, reflecting, respectively, an inability to think a few hours ahead or to think ahead about the family's future welfare. Neglecting parents have neither a sense of adequacy nor an ability to control their lives. "Drowned in their own needs, they are concerned with 'I want' not with 'I do'" (Young, 1971, p. 32). •

Often, this pattern of parental indifference, passivity, and isolation is passed on from generation to generation. Social conditions that encourage passivity—poverty, ignorance, lack of opportunity—further contribute to perpetuation of this pattern. Rejected as individuals, neglected children are in many respects also rejected by the society that permits them to grow in hunger, filth, ignorance, and disorder. The neglected child experiences the acute pain of an empty, pointless existence, but society also pays a price (see Exhibit 14.3).

In a smaller number of cases, neglect may be a consequence of severe neurotic or psychotic disturbances in parents. In families where one or both parents exhibit severe emotional disturbance, neglect of the child may be a by-product of such disturbance rather than an outcome of rejection of the child. The various symptoms of disorder exhibited by a parent may lead to an inability to attend to the needs of the child or to a distortion in the parent's conception of those needs, or even to a kind of role reversal in which a dependent, inadequate child comes to care for an even more dependent parent.

Abuse

Though often confused on a commonsense level, there are sharp differences between the psychological organization and behavior of abusive parents and

EXHIBIT 14.3

CHILDREN OF NEGLECT

In her study of abused and neglected children Leontine Young presents a vivid picture of the costs of neglect to children themselves and to society at large:

... More than anything else they are searchers—searchers for strength, concern, consistency, searchers for affection, order, and security. In that search they may be appeasing or defiant, withdrawn or belligerent, sullen or flippant. Some of them, like their parents, detach themselves from feeling, from attachment to anyone, and seek in a futile indulgence of transient impulses a way out of their empty world. Others substitute dreams and live on fantasy.

With indifference and confusion at home, subject frequently to social isolation and ridicule from schoolmates, without access to that protected and prosperous world they see flicker across the movie screens, they have little reason to trust, little incentive to struggle for something better, little strength or structure to set a goal or direction. They tend to be followers, not initiators, easily discouraged, frequently hostile, often sug-

gestible. The energy of youth is frittered away in all directions because they begin with defeat. Beneath the manifest behavior lies for most of them the deep layer of sadness that is so often present in those deprived of childhood.

A child expressed it in poetic words. She was eight and had already known desertion by her mother, rejection by her aunt, a weary succession of sterile boarding houses used by her mother or aunt as a convenient place to leave her. Removed from their care by the court, she was living in an institution. She was usually in trouble, fighting with other children, stealing their finery, defying authority. She was also very bright. One day her caseworker asked her what she wanted to be when she was grown. Her face shadowed and her answer was simple. "I don't want to be." When her caseworker questioned, she replied patiently, "You don't understand. I don't want to be. When I was very little I went once to a lake. I wondered what it would be like to fall in. I still think about it."

From Young (1971, pp. 24–25)

neglectful parents. While neglectful parents are often oblivious to their children's needs, abusive parents, by contrast, typically exhibit serious emotional disturbance leading to what could be considered malignant control over their children.

In a comprehensive clinical study of sixty families in which abuse had occurred, Steele and Pollock (1974) gathered extensive information on the characteristics of abusive parents. These investigators found that abusive parents seemed to constitute a cross-section of families in our society in terms of socioeconomic level, education, occupational level, age, and intelligence. A variety of religious and ethnic backgrounds were represented in their sample. A wide range of complex diagnostic patterns also emerged, again without a clear prevalence of particular forms of emotional disturbance in the parents. However, Steele and Pollock did find several consistencies that suggested that a breakdown of maternal affectional and nurturance patterns over several generations is at the core of many instances of abuse.

> *Without exception in our study group of abusing parents, there is a history of having been raised in the same style which they have recreated in the pattern of rearing their own children.... All had experienced a sense of intense, pervasive, continuous demand from their parents. This demand was in the form of expectations of good, submissive behavior, prompt obedience, never making mistakes, sympathetic comforting of parental distress, and showing approval and help for parental actions. (Steele & Pollock, 1974, p. 97)*

There is also general agreement that abusive parents tend to be socially isolated, suspicious, distrustful of others, and possessive of their children (Elmer, 1967; Steele & Pollock, 1974; Young, 1971). Several investigators have independently developed typologies (groupings) of abusive parents (Fontana, 1973; Gil, 1970; Merill, 1962). Bearing in mind the caution that typologies are ways of organizing thinking rather than accurate reflections of reality in any single case, let us look at one typology. Vincent Fontana (1973) suggested six distinguishable groups of child abusers: emotionally immature, neurotic and psychotic, mentally deficient or uninformed, disciplinarian, criminal/sadistic, and addicts.

Emotionally immature parents, afraid to face the demands of adulthood, turn to their children for love and protection. Cast in the role of caretaker, the very young child is inevitably bound to fail and disappoint the immature parent. In so failing, the child becomes subject to the wrath of the disappointed and frustrated parent.

Neurotic and psychotic parents impose their distorted concepts of reality on the child. Often they impute characteristics and motives to a child who cannot conceivably function in a fashion that presumes purpose and sophistication far beyond any child's capacity. In such cases, the battered child may be accused of wishing to destroy the parents' marriage or of hating the parent(s); another child may be viewed as intentionally tormenting the parent with misbehavior or stubbornness; still another child may be brutalized for acting in a sexy, provocative manner. "[I]t is one of the main characteristics of the emotionally undernourished or imbalanced parent that he or she assumes in the child an adult capacity for organized, purposeful behavior; behavior that is at odds with the parents' needs" (Fontana, 1973, p. 65).

Mentally deficient or uninformed parents do not necessarily exhibit the pathological distortions found in other parents. Rather, they exemplify a caricature of more prevalent childrearing behaviors. These parents have high expectations for child behavior and impose such expectations at unrealistically early ages. This is illustrated by abusive mothers who use physical punishment with children under 6 months of age or who expect a child to know right from wrong by 12 months of age (Wittenberg, 1973). These gross distortions of childhood abilities often precipitate anger as ignorant parents expect independent feeding or toileting many months before any child would be able to perform such functions.

Fontana also described a group of parents that he labeled *disciplinarians*. For these parents, firm discipline—which to them is achieved only through corporal punishment—must be imposed lest the child develop into a monster. When reproached for abusive behavior, such a parent

> is astonished or appears to be. First, it is his right to bring up his child as he pleases. Second, he is only trying to do the very best he can to "teach respect," "straighten the kid out," "wallop the nonsense out of him," "make him grow up to be a useful citizen." These individuals claim not to understand why severe physical punishment is not acceptable or effective. What was right for their parents was right for them. After all, look how well they turned out. (Fontana, 1973, p. 69)

Fortunately, Fontana's last two types of parents—*criminal/sadistic parents* and *addicts*—are rare enough to constitute only a small portion of abusive parents. In both cases, abuse is a consequence of severe personality disorders. The child's only function in the lives of such parents is as an object of abuse, a victim to be tormented as the parent feels tormented by life.

Few children are able to survive intense conditions of abuse without severe psychological disturbance. Many, of course, do not survive at all.

Family conflict

In recent years, studies of parental etiology of emotional disturbance in children have come to focus on the complete family unit rather than on just the parent(s). Lidz et al. (1965), for example, agreed with Anna Freud and others that rejection of the child is important in the genesis of emotional disturbance. However, Lidz proposed that such rejection arises as a consequence of **marital schism,** overt marital conflict in which the parents experience mutual hatred and an inability to resolve their interpersonal difficulties. In such families, children are exposed to continual, overt, intense antagonism between the parents. They live in an atmosphere of argument, threats of separation or divorce, mutual parental defiance, undercutting of authority, and, sometimes, physical violence. The children become potential allies courted by one parent for use against the other, or they may be used as weapons to hurt the marital partner.

Problems may also stem from **marital skew,** a situation in which the serious psychopathology of one parent dominates the household organization (Lidz, 1965). For example, a dependent, weak partner might find support in the cruel, domineering behavior of the spouse. Such families do not exhibit overt conflict. Rather, potential conflict is hidden behind masks of concern and cooperation. However, the anger that seeps through this facade creates anxiety in the child; further, a sense of unreality and distortion is experienced because the child can never really identify the reasons for his/her anxiety.

Descriptions of maritally skewed families are closely akin to observations by Bateson, Jackson, Haley, and Weakland (1969) who suggested that some families communicate contradictory messages at various communicative levels. This **double-bind theory** of severe emotional disturbance is complex and subtle· It includes the following components: (a) a repeated experience between two persons, one of whom is the "victim" of the double-bind; (b) a message communicated to the victim to do or not to do something under threat of punishment; (c) a second message communicated simultaneously but at a different communicative level and conflicting with the first message; and (d) a third message that prohibits the victim from escaping from the situation or commenting on it.

For example, a child might be taught that it is important to express feelings honestly while implicitly being taught by example that "nice" people do not get angry. Or alternatively, a child might be exposed to sexually seductive behavior by a parent who criticizes indications of sexual curiosity. In still another case, a child might be told that it is extremely important to do well in school, but find that his/her parents show more enthusiasm and interest in another youngster's athletic achievements. Eventually, the child learns to perceive the universe in double-bind patterns so that the complete set of components of the double-bind becomes superfluous. "Almost any part of a double-bind sequence may then be sufficient to precipitate panic or rage. The pattern of conflicting injunctions may even be taken over by . . . hallucinatory voices" (Bateson et al., 1969, p. 134).

As a result of experiencing simultaneous contradictory messages, the child experiences confusion and anxiety but is unable to resolve this confusion, since some of the messages are never communicated clearly or directly in the first place. Furthermore, unlike adults caught in similar uncomfortable situations, the child cannot simply withdraw or rebel or comment on the double-bind because of utter dependence on the victimizing parent. In brief, the child is placed in a situation of irreconcilable confusion in which punishment inevitably occurs either overtly or psychologically through rejection or experiences of guilt. Continued existence in this kind of family context leads to deterioration of the child's ability to cope.

A closely related theory has been proposed by researchers who insist that the family must be viewed as a unit or even as a single organism (Ackerman, 1958, 1968; Bowen, 1960). Psychological disturbance in a child is understood as a symptomatic expression of a disordered family system. Thus, for example, aggressive behavior in a child is only an expression of pervasive problems that affect the relationships of all family members. If the child is treated alone, family problems will not change, and if the child improves, chances are that some other member of the family system will then develop symptoms.

As in other theories we have reviewed, this approach, too, views the causation of childhood disturbance in *unidirectional fashion*. That is, the influence of causation is seen as going in only one direction—from parent to child—and the parents are seen as causing the problems in their children. Bowen (1960), for example, suggested that parental conflict in most of the families he had observed began within the first few days or weeks of marriage, and led ultimately to the development of psychiatric disorder in the identified child patient.

Research on Family Interaction and Psychopathology

Thus far, our discussion of parents of emotionally disturbed children has focused on clinical experience and theoretical concepts that suggest that childhood problems result from faulty parenting. This perspective has several important consequences. First, there is the inevitable implication that parents of emotionally disturbed children are responsible for their children's pathology. Furthermore, there is the implication that childhood disturbances are not simply the result of parental mistakes, but rather that parental resentment and rejection arising from the neurotic conflicts of the parents have created the problems. These implications of parental causation have further important consequences in the attitudes of professional personnel toward these special parents. In many cases, parents are directly and explicitly blamed for the child's problems. In many more cases, the blame is not explicit. Instead parents are confronted with subtle suggestions that they have failed; often their behavior is overinterpreted; their statements are not believed or are perceived as pathological distortions of reality; their behavior and attitudes are forced into theoretical frameworks that may have little to do with the reality of their own unique relationship with their special child. Finally, there is a general intensification of parental anxiety. Believing that they have damaged their child, these special parents become overanxious about any parenting behavior. They blame themselves and they blame each other. Not infrequently, the imputed pathology really does begin to develop in an atmosphere of constant tension and self-blame.

Because of these consequences of experiential and theoretical statements regarding parental etiology of childhood disturbance, it becomes important to examine the research evidence relating to such statements in order to develop a realistic and balanced understanding of these special parents.

Research findings

Frank (1965) conducted an extensive review of research reports relating patterns of family interaction to the development of psychopathology in children. Typically, these investigations involved collection of data by means of case histories, psychiatric interviews, psychological testing, or direct observation of family interaction. As might be expected, Frank encountered extensive variability in the methodological adequacy of these studies. Few of them met such basic criteria as employing control groups of matched families without disturbed children or using procedures for minimizing the effects of experimenter expectations. Despite evident methodological problems in this research, however, Frank discovered that many investigators had offered conclusions regarding their research. Often such conclusions have been incorporated into further theoretical literature and have resulted in the kinds of theories we reviewed in the previous section. However, taken as a whole, Frank was unable to see any clear directions in the body of research relating parental behavior to psychopathology in children. He concluded that there was no consistent evidence that parental problems are the major cause of childhood problems.

In a later review of research literature investigating the theory that family problems cause schizophrenia, Fontana (1966) discounted most of the research as being virtually worthless because of gross methodological problems. According to Fontana, the only studies worth examining are those that use some form of direct observation of family interaction as the major source of evidence. Limiting his review to research employing direct observation techniques, Fontana stated that:

> Four general findings are consistently supported by the few methodologically adequate research studies reviewed here: (a) there is no evidence for the proposed "schizophrenogenic" pattern of dominant mother–passive father, (b) there is little support for the proposed interaction between parental dominance pattern and premorbid adjustment of patients, (c) there is more conflict between the parents of schizophrenics . . . than between the parents of normals, and (d) communication between parents of schizophrenics . . . is less clear than it is between parents of normals. (1966, p. 225)

Extensive research has led to few tenable conclusions. What is more, even those conclusions that receive some support do not speak to the assumption that parents directly cause problems in their children in unidirectional fashion. In spite of the suggestion that families of schizophrenics exhibit more conflict and less clarity in communication, there is, as yet, no research that has determined whether such behaviors lead to the development of child disorders, result from the disorders, or are simply tangential characteristics arising from unidentified factors. Hetherington and Martin (1972) concluded their extensive review of theoretical and research literature with similar deprecations of the methodology employed in studies of the origins of childhood disturbance. In addition, they pointed to the artificiality of separating social learning experiences, broad social forces, traumatic experiences, or constitutional factors. "Although any one of these factors may initiate a developmental process, unidirectional causality quickly gives way to an interactive process between the child and other family members" (1972, p. 72).

Lachar (1975) confined his review of experimental literature to an examination of the family interaction patterns of psychotic children. Lachar categorized 91 studies into the areas of general family characteristics, parental characteristics, and interactional patterns in the families of psychotic children. While he pointed to some provocative results, he nevertheless summarized his research by indicating that it is impossible to develop conclusive generalizations. Among the results that Lachar felt were suggestive are the following: (a) families of psychotic children are present in disproportionate numbers in the upper socioeconomic levels; (b) approximately one-quarter of the parents of psychotic children are moderately or severely disturbed (leaving three-quarters who are not); (c) parents of psychotic children function at a higher intellectual level than either parents in general or parents of nonpsychotic, disturbed children; (d) childrearing attitudes of psychotic parents are similar to those of nonpsychotic parents of deviant children; (e) interactional patterns in families with psychotic children differ from those without deviant children and include more conflict and disequilibrium; (f) mothers of psychotic children are more unhappy with their lot than are their husbands.

In examining these results, it is again evident that no statements can be made regarding etiology. None of the results suggest that parental disturbance or marital conflict are primary causative factors in the development of emotional disturbance in children. Even more interesting is the fact that several of the results cited by Lachar would be equally applicable to parents of physically or intellectually impaired children. As noted earlier, parents of impaired children exhibit more personal problems and more marital conflict than control groups of parents of normal children.

In summarizing his review, Lachar stated—as did Frank ten years earlier—that there are tremendous difficulties inherent in research into family interaction in the families of disturbed children, and he likewise called for greater methodological sophistication.

Finally, Jacob (1975) also conducted a comprehensive review of studies of patterns of interaction in families of disturbed and normal children. Confining his discussion to more sophisticated studies using direct observation methodology, Jacob concluded that "family interaction studies, although based on a potentially sound methodological strategy, have not yet isolated patterns that reliably differentiate disturbed from normal groups" (p. 56).

Research problems
The question that obviously arises from these several reviews is why, after more than fifty years of intensive research into the etiology of childhood psychopathology, have researchers failed to develop any viable conclusions? Perhaps this question can be answered in two ways. The first has to do with the *basic problems inherent in empirical research into the relationships between interpersonal behavior and psychopathology*. For example, one has always to confront the basic issue of diagnostic reliability or consistency. That is, do different researchers and clinicians define diagnostic terms in the same ways? One need only refer to the variety of uses of terms such as "neurosis" or "psychosis" to see that there is a good deal of inconsistency in the application of diagnostic labels.

Going beyond the question of diagnostic reliability, one has then to devise adequate observational techniques that can provide some reasonable focus or point of reference for deciding which, among a virtual infinity of potential behaviors, one is going to study. As Fontana (1966) suggested, it is difficult to know where to begin. Going further yet, reasonable control procedures have to be developed to assure comparability among various diagnostic groups and normal subjects; simultaneously, experimenter biases must also be controlled. Even if these obvious problems can be overcome, one has then to face the question of whether identifiable parental behaviors or patterns of interaction relate to childhood disturbances in an identifiable fashion. That is, are parental behaviors causes that lead to pathology or outcomes that arise from living with a disturbed child? The only possible approaches to answering this question are in analogue research with animals or in longitudinal research with humans. Ultimately, the latter of these two alternatives is the only means of developing definitive and satisfying conclusions.

The second answer to the question of why research conclusions in this area are still questionable is *the fact that most research has, at some point, been generated by a theoretical model that assumes a unidirectional relationship between parental behavior and childhood pathology*. This problem has already been mentioned in passing, but it needs emphasis. The experience of clinicians has generally suggested that parental problems cause childhood problems. In a clinical setting this appears to make good sense, since one is confronted by parents and children with crystallized problems, and since parents are generally more able to make intentional changes in their behavior. However, this point of view often ignores the reality of developmental processes and denies the legitimacy of parental statements about their behavior and the growth of their child. Without denying the fact that, in many instances, parents do in fact cause problems in their children, it is also imperative that normal functioning in parents be recognized and accepted when it exists. And, as the research suggests, it exists more often than not. A realistic appraisal of parental behavior and attitudes toward children in the unique context of a given family structure is absolutely critical. Naive assumptions of universal parental malignancy whenever childhood problems are diagnosed have no basis in reality; over the years such assumptions have created anxiety and guilt in already troubled families and have not furthered the cause of understanding and remediation.

An Interactional Model

It is only recently that an interactional model has begun to develop greater currency (though Freud long ago called for such an approach). This model suggests that we cannot search for simple causes in parental behavior that lead predictably and regularly to childhood disturbance. Instead, investigation must begin afresh by examining the possibility that childhood disturbances *and* parental problems stem from multiple causes and develop interactively.

Nearly twenty years ago, Murray Sidman (1960) suggested that disturbed behavior is an outcome of the same orderly principles that apply to all behavior; but it is only in recent years that a number of theorists are beginning to apply this concept in their understanding of emotional disturbance. This kind of perspective makes no assumptions about the necessity of parental disturbance or severe overt or covert family conflict as prior conditions to the development of disturbance in the child. There is no question that disturbed parents and disturbed marriages can—and often do—eventuate in disturbed behavior in children. What is questionable is the assumption that such parental behavior is either necessary or sufficient to produce emotional disturbance.

An interactional viewpoint recognizes the importance of the child's effects on the parents as well as their effects on the child (e.g., Bell, 1968; Harper, 1975). Maladaptive behavior is seen as a consequence of inappropriate patterns of response and reinforcement, perception and interpretation, which develop mutually between parents and children. For example, a child may fail to develop language appropriately because initial attempts at verbalization were not effective in producing responses from parents too involved in their own conflicts. However, it may also be the case that parental approaches to a child were diminished because of the child's lack of response to parental attention. Parents may then begin to experience conflicts between themselves as they experience increased tension because of the child's failure to develop normally and as they disagree about ways of understanding or handling the situation.

In addition to recognizing that parents and children serve as mutual sources of stimulation and reinforcement, an interactional viewpoint also recognizes the importance of the child's constitutional endowment as a variable that affects the parent-child interaction system. A steadily growing body of research indicates that children are constitutionally different in emotionality, sociability, and activity level (Hetherington & Martin, 1972).

One major study of constitutional variables in child development was conducted by Thomas, Chess, and Birch (1968). These investigators conducted a longitudinal study of 136 children who were examined at three-month intervals until the age of 18 months, at six-month intervals until the age of 5, and at yearly intervals thereafter. The 85 families of the children were also studied intensively to determine relationships between childrearing attitudes and

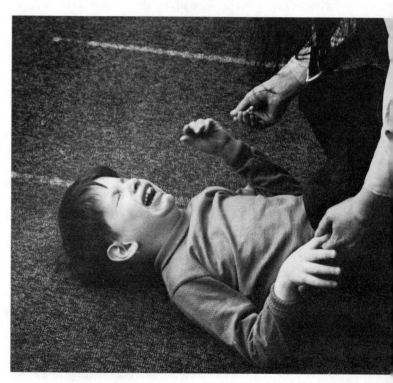

This autistic boy's aversion and rejection of contact with others will no doubt affect the way his parents interact with him.

EXHIBIT 14.4

431
Parents of
emotionally
disturbed children

TEMPERAMENTAL CHARACTERISTICS OF INFANTS AND CHILDREN

The research of Thomas, Chess, and Birch (1968, pp. 19–24) indicated that infants and young children can be characterized in terms of a variety of response patterns that are largely consistent for each child. These categories of reactivity include:

1. *Activity level:* the amount of general movement exhibited by the child during all activities including sleep.

2. *Rhythmicity:* the regularity of biological functions, including bladder and bowel habits, rest and sleeping patterns, eating patterns.

3. *Approach or withdrawal:* the child's initial response pattern to new stimuli, including people.

4. *Adaptability:* the ease or difficulty the child has in adjusting to new and different situations.

5. *Intensity of reaction:* the strength of the child's responses to positive or negative stimuli.

6. *Threshold of responsiveness:* the level of the child's sensitivity to various stimuli.

7. *Quality of mood:* the child's general feeling state expressed in positive or negative emotional behavior.

8. *Distractibility:* the ability of environmental stimuli to interfere with ongoing behavior.

9. *Attention span:* the child's capacity to attend to given environmental stimuli or to persist in ongoing purposeful activity.

---

actual practices. Forty-two of the children exhibited behavioral/emotional disturbances during the course of the study and received intensive psychiatric evaluations. Results of this study indicated that the children exhibited consistent temperamental differences along a variety of dimensions, probably as a result of constitutional predispositions. Exhibit 14.4 summarizes the results of this important research.

These temperamental differences in both normal and disturbed children may influence the nature of the child's interactions with the environment and may, in turn, be influenced by the interactions.

> *In fact and in theory . . . environment and temperament are not completely independent entities. Environment and temperament not only interact, but they also can modify each other. A parent's attitudes toward and practices with a specific child may reflect preexisting, long-standing aspects of the parent's personality structure. But, these attitudes and practices may also be reactive and reflect a response to the temperamental characteristics of the given child. (Thomas et al., 1968, pp. 73–74)*

Both normal and disturbed behavior in children must be viewed as the outcome of multiple influences, some of which stem from parental behavior and some of which the child brings to the parent-child interaction. *Any attempt to attribute the primary causation of disturbed child behavior to parents or assumptions that child disturbance cannot be treated without first treating presumed parental pathology must be viewed as injudicious.* Such assumptions are not supported by growing research evidence of genuine parent-child mutuality and reciprocity. Parents do influence their children.

But children also influence parental physiology, motor patterns, eating habits, attachment and nurturance behavior, sexual behavior, communication, and personality (Harper, 1975).

In focusing on observed behaviors and patterns of parent-child interaction, and also in their applications of normal behavioral principles to an understanding of disturbed behavior, many behaviorally oriented investigators reject the notion that pathology breeds pathology. Instead, well-functioning families may foster maladaptive behavior depending on specific interactional circumstances, or, conversely, poorly functioning families may not necessarily prohibit the development of healthy behavior in their children. The risk of developmental disturbance is seen both as a function of environmental circumstances and as a function of the child's basic vulnerability or invulnerability to these circumstances (Anthony, 1974). From this point of view, the search for individual, unidirectional pathogenic forces is fruitless. Theory is abandoned in deference to observation.

Every set of parents brings to their marriage their own unique personalities, products of their own physiological endowments and life experiences. However, these individuals do not interact in a vacuum, but rather in the context of social, cultural, and economic conditions. Their mutual adjustment or failure to adjust is partly a function of their status within the larger system. Changes in sex roles and views of marital functions, acceptability of divorce or alternative forms of marriage, different understandings of the value and role of children, increased social mobility, modifications in the forms of nuclear and extended families—all these and many more variables have an impact on the marital pair and, indirectly, on the way they interact with their children.

While theoretical systems that permit interpretation and convenient understanding of behavior might be more satisfying intellectually and easier to comprehend, they rarely present adequate reflections of reality. Where pathology exists, explanations for it are not likely to exist in simple terms.

In addition to offering hope of more useful research conclusions, an interactional approach is a beginning toward alleviating unnecessary guilt and self-reproach so characteristic of the special parents of the emotionally disturbed child. More importantly, an interactional approach directs therapeutic efforts specifically at problematic interactions between parents and children rather than in the direction of traditional, circuitous, and time-consuming analyses of presumed parental and family pathology.

COUNSELING PARENTS OF DISTURBED CHILDREN

The previous discussion should have made it clear that any attempt to reduce counseling or psychotherapy with special parents of emotionally disturbed children to a single approach or formula can only be characterized as naive. Presumptions that parents are invariably in need of psychotherapeutic intervention must be discarded. Instead, treatment of the parent-child system must be based on careful, objective observation and understanding. Where there is evidence that parental pathology has been a contributing factor in the development or maintenance of childhood disturbance, then treatment should be recommended for the parents either individually or as a couple. If diagnostic study indicates the existence of interlocking family pathology such that changes in the system will be necessary to effect changes in any individual member, then a recommendation for family treatment is indicated. However, it may also be the case that the parents need only reassurance or guidance in the management of the child or, perhaps, extensive instruction in certain aspects of parenting, or even assistance in communicating more clearly. The point is that counseling should be predicated on a clear understanding of the nature of the child's problem and the role of the parents in relation to the child. Empathic understanding, not only of the child's suffering but also of the parents' anxieties and guilt as well, is a first step in attaining the kind of perspective that will facilitate effective treatment.

Professional intervention with special children depends to a very great extent on the active cooperation and support of their parents. Enlisting such support requires that child-care professionals be sensitive to the needs and problems that parents have in understanding and coping with their children's problems. Research evidence increasingly indicates that traditional assumptions and generalizations must be discarded. Parents need individualized understanding and assistance that addresses their unique circumstances and enables them to optimize their own development as persons and to meet the needs of their special children.

SUMMARY

1. While all parents develop expectations of what their children will be like, it is the experience of parents of special children that many of these expectations may never be fulfilled.
2. Most special parents share many common experiences, but certain experiences are especially associated with parenting physically disabled children, mentally retarded children, and emotionally disturbed children.
3. Parents of physically disabled children often experience grief and mourning, anger, depression, denial, ambivalence, adaptation, and growth.
4. Parents of mentally retarded children must cope with the problems of recognizing that retardation exists, dealing with community reactions, dealing with the reactions of siblings, and dealing with the critical issue of placement.
5. Counseling with special parents must be oriented toward a realistic understanding of their unique needs and emotions.
6. Parents of emotionally disturbed children are often faced with explicit or implicit beliefs that they have caused their child's problems.
7. Theories of parental causation of emotional disturbance in children usually include such factors as parental rejection, overprotection, neglect, abuse, and family conflict.
8. Research findings do not support any universal notion of parental causation of emotional problems in children.
9. A reasonable approach to the relationship between parental behavior and childhood emotional disturbance is an interactional model based on extensive empirical research and on an understanding of the unique experiences of each family as its members interact with each other and influence each other's development.

CHAPTER FIFTEEN

Special Education and the Schools

by Alfred Hirshoren

Inherent in the philosophy of democracy is the doctrine that every child is entitled to an education to the limit of his capacity. "All men are created equal" is a phrase so often used that it has become almost trite. Yet it is always meaningful. All are equal before the law, equal in their claim to freedom, equal in their right to learn if not in their capacity to learn.

Democracy is, therefore, committed to the principle of education for all, regardless of race, creed, or abilities. . . . The education of exceptional children represents an attempt on the part of the school to furnish equal opportunity to individuals who differ in physical, mental, and social characteristics. It is a logical application of the truth that "all men are created equal."

National Society for the Study of Education (1950, pp. 3–4)

THE NATURE OF SPECIAL EDUCATION

Throughout this text, a number of intervention procedures have been discussed in relation to special children, not the least of which has been education. Of all the agencies that touch on human services to children, the school is the one that has the potential and the mandated responsibility to provide services to all children. Since the role of the school is so important in the lives of special children, it is only right that we devote a chapter to this very important aspect of intervention.

In the recent past, many children were often legally excluded from school if they were considered to be too handicapped to attend or, in the opinion of an expert of some type, they were too handicapped to profit from the available school program (Burton, 1971). Other children did not attend school for other reasons, including frequent moves and the economic need, as perceived by the family of the child, to earn a wage, albeit small, rather than attend school. The schools often conveniently closed their eyes to the fact that these children were not attending school by not enforcing mandatory school attendance laws. The goal of recent legislation, to be discussed later in this chapter, is to ensure that all children will have an education to as near the limits of their ability as possible, regardless of their handicaps. Though this goal is yet to be attained, development of new programs and approaches to the education of exceptional learners is evident.

Early chapters of this book focused on child development and the nature of special children and youth, which formed the foundation for understanding the deviations in child growth and development that were discussed in detail in the chapters which followed. As noted in Chapter 5, in considering these deviations it is important to understand that the terms "disability" and "handicap" do not mean the same thing. Myopia (nearsightedness), for example, is a common visual *disability*, but—with corrective lenses—it should not be a *handicap* nor should it require special educational provisions. Likewise, paraplegia is a physical disability but not necessarily an educational handicap: it may require an alteration in the physical environment but not in the educational program and methodology for the child, except for the physical education program. The educable mentally retarded child who is continually frustrated by the regular class curriculum has an educational handicap. This child does need a different educational program. So does the gifted child, who may be bored and therefore unresponsive to the regular class program and, because of this boredom, needs a special stimulating environment or program. Not all special children need the educational interventions noted in Chapter 4, but for those who do, special education is available.

Special education, itself, has been called "an enriched form of general education . . . in so far as it makes use of specially trained educational personnel who are aware of the application of methodological advances in education and of technological equipment to offset certain types of handicap" (UNESCO, 1974). In an even broader sense, special education can be considered to be any systematic instructional program that strives for optimal functional ability of special children and youth and seeks to improve their overall status. This can range from toilet training for the school-aged child who has not acquired adequate bladder and bowel control to nurturing of divergent thinking for the gifted child. Such a definition of special education is consistent with recent federal and state legislative mandates and court decisions that explicitly state that "each child of school age (will be provided with) a free and suitable publicly-supported education regardless of the degree of the child's mental, physical or emotional disability or impairment" (*Mills* v. *District of Columbia Board of Education*, 1972).

In this chapter we will look at the growth of special educational services for special children from its beginnings in New England in residential institutions for a few children with sensory handicaps to its current attempts to provide the needed educational programs for all special, or exceptional, children. The major legal decisions and the law that defines the national purpose for special education will also be highlighted. Teaching strategies and individual educational programs needed to meet the needs of special children will then be considered, as will the needs of the culturally different child.

THE GROWTH OF SPECIAL EDUCATION

During the nineteenth century, public school education programs were just being established throughout the United States. Special education was limited primarily to the training school or asylum, an approach developed in France and brought to the United States by European physicians and educators (Aiello, 1976). These were residential institutions. Samuel Gridley Howe, a physician and humanitarian, started educational institutions for the blind, retarded, and deaf in the Commonwealth of Massachusetts. Thomas Gallaudet, after study-

ing at the National Institute for Deaf-Mutes in Paris, established the first residential school for the deaf in this country in Hartford, Connecticut, in 1817.
Edouard Seguin, a French physician, emigrated to the United States and, with
the help of individuals such as Samuel Gridley Howe, opened the first residential state institution developed around an educational program for the mentally
retarded in Syracuse, New York. Unfortunately, Seguin promised more than
he could deliver. He believed that the physiological method he had developed—which included movement training, sensory stimulation, and speech
and educational instruction—would cure the retarded, and much public support was obtained with that hope. Though he failed on that count, he nevertheless did have a lasting influence on special education.

Further growth of special education programs had to wait for the enactment of compulsory school attendance laws by each state. Rhode Island in
1840 was the first state to pass such a law. Similar action was soon taken by
most of the other states. As Lloyd Dunn noted, "This really was the first time
that educators were faced with the question of what to do with the less able
youngsters. With the advent of these laws the tracking, sorting, and categorizing of exceptional children began a very significant event" (quoted in Aiello,
1976).

The twentieth century witnessed the development and translation into
English of the Binet-Simon Intelligence Scale, the growth of the child study
movement, and the concomitant growth of special education. These events of
the nineteenth and twentieth centuries brought with them the start of long
overdue programs designed specifically for exceptional children (see Exhibit
15.1).

The growth of services to the handicapped and gifted in the public
schools has been more or less steady, with increasing enrollments since 1922,
the first year for which data are available. The numbers of children enrolled in
special education programs for selected years are indicated in Exhibit 15.2. In

EXHIBIT 15.1

===

YEARS IN WHICH CLASSES FOR THE EXCEPTIONAL WERE FIRST INSTITUTED

The deaf	1869	Boston
Unruly or truant boys	1874	New York City
The mentally handicapped	1896	Providence
The blind	1896 (or 1899)	Chicago
Orthopedics	1899 (or 1900)	Chicago
Speech defective	1908	New York
The pretuberculosis or malnourished	1908	Providence
Epileptics	1909	Baltimore
The partially sighted	1913	Roxbury (Mass.), Cleveland
The hard of hearing	1920	Lynn (Mass.), Rochester, (New York)

Wallin (1955, pp. 18–19)

EXHIBIT 15.2

ENROLLMENT OF EXCEPTIONAL CHILDREN IN SPECIAL PROGRAMS: 1922 to 1975 (FIGURES IN THOUSANDS)

Year[1]	Total	Visually Handi-capped	Aurally Handi-capped	Speech Impaired	Crippled and Special Health Problems	Emo-tionally and Socially Mal-adjusted	Mentally Retarded	Other Handi-capping Condi-tions	Gifted	Learning Dis-abilities	Multi-Handi-capped
1975[5]	7,886	39	95	1,850	235	230	1,250	126	(NA)	235	13
1970[2]	3,158	24	78	1,237	269	113	830	33	481		
1966	2,106	23	51	990	69	88	540	22	312		
1963 *[3]	1,682	22	46	802	65	80	432	12	215		
1958	890	12	20	490	52	29	223		52		
1953	497	9	16	307	29	(NA)	114		23		
1948	378	8[4]	14[4]	182	50[4]	15	87[4]		21		
1940	314	9	13	126	53	10	98		3		
1936	297	7	9	117	48	13	100		3		
1932	164	5	4		40	14	75		2		
1930		(NA)	(NA)	23	32	10	(NA)				
1927		4	4				52				
1922			3				23				

* Denotes first year for which figures include Alaska and Hawaii.

NA—Not Available

1 Beginning 1958, data as of February; earlier years, data for school year ending.

2 Estimated on the basis of State reports to the U.S. Office of Education (See *Digest of Educational Statistics,* 1972, table 34.)

3 Beginning 1963, includes residential schools.

4 Includes Hawaii.

5 Source: Statistical Abstract of the U.S., 1976.

From U.S. Department of the Census (1975)

the thirty-one years between 1932 and 1963, enrollment in special education programs increased by 1,518,000 children; in the seven years between 1963 and 1970 enrollments increased almost as much—1,476,000 children; and in the five years between 1970 and 1975 the increase in enrollment was more than 150 percent of the enrollment of the previous thirty-eight years.

Although the increase in the delivery of educational services to exceptional children is impressive, only 38 percent of exceptional children were receiving special education in 1968. By 1975 programs had increased to include 50 percent of exceptional children in special programs. Even though 88 percent of the mentally retarded, 82 percent of the speech impaired, and 71 percent of the physically handicapped were enrolled in at least minimal special education programs by 1975, many children still had unmet educational needs. The surprising fact is that services to the hearing-impaired and emotionally disturbed had barely improved in terms of the percentage of children served in over forty years. Seventy-five percent of hearing-impaired children, 80 percent of emotionally disturbed children, and about 40 percent of visually impaired children were not being adequately served as of 1975. In addition, fewer than 20 percent of children with learning disabilities and fewer than 42 percent of children with multiple handicaps were obtaining special education services. Programs for the gifted enrolled fewer than half of the eligible children. By 1980, as a result of the enactment of The Education for All Handicapped Children Act (Public Law 94-142), all handicapped children and youth between the ages of 3 and 21 in need of special education services are to have those services available.

THE SCOPE OF THE PROBLEMS OF SPECIAL EDUCATION

In order to plan adequate and economical programs for children in need of special education services, it is necessary to have some fairly reliable indication of the prevalence of each of the handicapping conditions in school-age children. As of 1977, no national census of the prevalence of handicapping conditions in school-age children has been done. Most prevalence figures are educated guesses, often based on limited population samples. Other estimates are based on statistical extrapolations, such as the prevalence estimates for the mentally retarded and the gifted. Other variables involved in prevalence determination include regional variations, rural versus urban location, ages surveyed, sex distribution, and whether cross-sectional or longitudinal methodologies were employed (Hirshoren, Schultz, Manton, & Henderson, 1970). The most accepted set of prevalence estimates of exceptional children are those developed by The Bureau of Education for the Handicapped (BEH). By applying these prevalence figures to the estimated 1978 school-age population, one can obtain an estimate of 6,792,500 children who would be eligible for special education programs. This is a conservative estimate because it does not include handicapped children between the ages of three and five, handicapped youth between the ages of 18 and 21, or gifted children. With these groups included, estimates exceed 10,000,000 children and youth who would benefit from being included in some type of special education program.

These estimates, while they may be valid for the nation and for all children of school age, may not be applicable to a specific community or state, or for children of a specific age. Williams (1977), for example, found that though the prevalence estimates for the state of Georgia for educable mentally retarded children was 2.894 percent (which is very close to the national prevalence estimate), regional prevalence estimates ranged from 1.170 percent to 5.357 percent. Using the national prevalence estimate of 3 percent would have overestimated the number of retarded children in one part of the state and seriously underestimated the number in another part of the state. Williams also found that the prevalence rate in the secondary school was 1.71 times greater than in the elementary school. In all likelihood, similar studies done in other states would find similar results.

The special children are there waiting to be served. The resources of the educational community are being mobilized to meet the needs of these children, but there is a lack of adequately trained special educators to provide the needed instructional programs, especially in the areas of the hearing-impaired, emotionally and socially maladjusted, learning-disabled, and multi-handicapped children. The very important role of the federal government in promoting programs to improve resources for these special children will be discussed in the next section.

Federal Involvement

Federal involvement in special education dates from the early 1920s. Initially, it was limited to the compilation and dissemination of statistics about existing programs. Later efforts also included the promotion of more adequate programming, both in quality and quantity. The first major legislative proposal that affected the education of the handicapped was the Cooperative Research Act (P.L. 83-531), which, though approved by Congress on July 26, 1954, was not funded until 1957. Approximately two-thirds of the $1 million appropriated was earmarked to be spent on research relating to the education of the mentally retarded (Martin, 1968). Other legislation of this era was to promote the training of leadership personnel (P.L. 85-926) in special education and the expansion of services to the deaf. In the mid-1960s legislation permitting grants to states for preschool, elementary, and secondary school handicapped children was enacted (P.L. 89-313 and P.L. 89-750). Public Law 89-750 also created the Bureau of Education for the Handicapped and earmarked specific funds for the handicapped. Subsequent bills in the Ninetieth and Ninety-First Congress attempted to expand services and make them available to more and younger handicapped children.

Two landmark legal decisions gave important cues that education was about to enter a new era. In the first case, *The Pennsylvania Association for Retarded Children (PARC)* v. *The Commonwealth of Pennsylvania* (1971), the courts ruled that "Expert testimony . . . indicates that all mentally retarded persons are capable of benefiting from a program of education and training . . . therefore every retarded person between the ages of six and twenty-one years . . . shall be provided access to a free public program of education and training appropriate to his capacities. . . ." In the second case, *Mills* v. *The Board of* of Columbia shall provide to each child of school age a free and suitable publicly supported education regardless of the degree of the child's mental, physical or emotional disability or impairment. Furthermore, defendants shall not exclude any child resident in the District of Columbia from such publicly supported education on the basis of a claim of insufficient resources."

Despite these court decisions, up until very recently fewer than 60 percent of all handicapped children have been receiving the educational programs they have needed. This situation is rapidly changing as a result of the passage, in 1975, of Public Law 94-142, titled The Education for All Handicapped Children Act. This piece of major legislation calls for the implementation of the principles cited in the introductory quote to this chapter. It is worthwhile to repeat a part of that quote here. "Democracy is . . . committed to the principle of education for all, regardless of race, creed, or abilities. . . ." P.L. 94-142 calls for "a free, appropriate public education, which emphasizes special education and related services designed to meet . . . [the] unique needs" of all handicapped children between the ages of 3 and 21. It also attempts "to assure that the rights of the handicapped and their parents and guardians are protected." Because of its importance, portions of this law are abstracted in Exhibit 15.3.

EXHIBIT 15.3

YOUR RIGHTS UNDER THE EDUCATION FOR ALL HANDICAPPED CHILDREN ACT—P.L. 94-142

State and Local Plans (§613 and 614)*
To be eligible for money under P.L. 94-142, a state must continue to submit annual state plans (or amendments to earlier plans to BEH [Bureau for the Education of the Handicapped] *and* local school districts must submit a detailed plan to their SEA [State Education Agency]. These plans must show how the SEA and LEA [Local Education Agency] will conform to the major requirements of the law. In addition to the requirements with which the state plan . . . must demonstrate compliance, the following specific requirements must be met:

1) *Full Services Goal* (§612(2), 612(3))— a "free appropriate public education" must be available to all handicapped children . . . ages 3–21 by September 1, 1980, unless, with regard to 3–5 year olds and 18–21 year olds, "inconsistent" with state law. States must place a priority in

the use of their funds under this Act on two groups of children: 1) handicapped children who are *not* receiving an education, and 2) handicapped children with the most severe handicaps, within each disability, who are receiving an inadequate education.

2) *Due Process Safeguards* (§612(5)(A), 614(a)(7), 615)—As of October 1, 1977, the policies and procedures describing due process safeguards available to parents and children in any matter concerning a child's identification, evaluation, or placement in an educational program must include:
a) prior notice to parents of any change in their child's program and written explanation in their primary language, of the procedures to be followed in effecting that change;
b) access to relevant school records;
c) an opportunity to obtain an independent evaluation of the child's special needs;
d) opportunity for an impartial due process hearing which must be con-

* Section numbers cited here refer to the appropriate authority within the Act.

ducted by the SEA or local or intermediate school district, but in no case by an employee "involved in the education or care of the child." In any hearing, parents have the right to be accompanied by a lawyer or any individual with special knowledge of the problems or special needs [of] children, the right to present evidence, to confront, compel and cross-examine witnesses, and to obtain a transcript of the hearing and a written decision by the hearing offcer. Parents have the right to appeal the hearing decision to the SEA and, if they are still dissatisfied, the SEA ruling in federal or state court;

e) the right of a child to remain in his/her current placement (or, if trying to gain initial admission to school, in the regular school program) until the due process proceedings are completed; and

f) the designation of a "surrogate parent" to use the procedures outlined above on behalf of children who are wards of the state or whose parents or guardians are unknown or unavailable.

3) *Least Restrictive Alternative* (§612-(5)(B), 614(a)(1)(C)(iv), 614(a)(7))—handicapped children, *including children in public and private institutions,* must be educated as much as possible with children who are not handicapped.

4) *Non-Discriminatory Testing and Evaluation* (§612(5)(c), 614(a)(7))—the tests and procedures used to evaluate a child's special needs must be racially and culturally non-discriminatory in both the way they are selected and the way they are administered, must be in the primary language or mode of communication of the child, and no one test or procedure can be used as the sole determinant of a child's educational program.

5) *Individualized Educational Plans* (§612(4), 613(a)(11), 614(a)(5))—written individualized educational plans for each child evaluated as handicapped must be developed and annually reviewed by a child's parents, teacher, and a designee of the school district. The plan must include statements of the child's present levels of educational performance, short- and long-term goals for the child's performance, the specific educational services to be provided the child, and specific criteria to measure the child's progress. Each school district must maintain records of the individualized education plan for each child.

6) *Personnel Development* (§613(a)(3), 614(a)(1)(C)(i))—a comprehensive system to develop and train both general and special education teachers and administrative personnel to carry out requirements of this law must be developed by the state, and each local school district must show how it will use and put into effect the system of personnel development.

7) *Participation of Children in Private Schools* (613(a)(4), 614(a)(6))—free special education and related services must be provided for handicapped children in private elementary and secondary schools if the children are placed or referred to private schools by the SEA or local school districts to fulfill the requirements of this law. The SEA must assure that private schools which provide programs for handicapped children meet the standards which apply to state and local public schools, and that handicapped children served by private schools are accorded all the same rights they would have if served in public schools.

From The Children's Defense Fund (1976, pp. 4–6)

A parallel piece of legislation concerned with civil rights is Section 504 of the Rehabilitation Act of 1973, the Civil Rights Act for Handicapped Persons, which makes it illegal for the schools or any other public or private organization which receives federal funds to discriminate *in any way* against handicapped persons. Special steps must be taken by those programs or agencies that have federal funding to ensure that handicapped individuals have the opportunity to "learn, work, and compete on a fair and equal basis."

Programming to Meet the Needs

As a rule of thumb, approximately 20 percent of the people in a community are of school age at any given time. Of this number, approximately 12 to 14 percent could be classified as exceptional learners. Using these prevalence figures, it becomes obvious that in smaller school districts, there would be insufficient numbers of children with certain types of low-incidence handicaps to develop an adequate program for them. A city such as Plains, Georgia, with a population of less than 5,000, or Athens, Ohio, with a population of about 25,000, would be too small to provide enough programmatic options to meet the needs of many exceptional learners. Smaller rural communities would be even less able to provide an adequate program. In fact, based on the estimates in Exhibit 15.4, it would probably be difficult for a community with a population much smaller than 100,000 to provide a comprehensive program for *all* exceptional learners.

To plan for the needs of special children in these smaller communities, a number of agencies have been started for the purpose of combining resources in several communities to form cooperative special education programs through which children can receive services. Known by a variety of titles—for example, Boards of Cooperative Educational Services (BOCES) in New York, Cooperative Education Service Agencies (CESA) in Georgia, Joint Agreements (Illinois)—these agencies are able to combine the financial and programmatic resources of several school districts. In so doing, they can provide the variety and depth of services needed for special education so that the educational needs of all children can be realistically attended to without causing an unrealistic financial burden to any one school district.

EXHIBIT 15.4

**ESTIMATED NUMBER OF SCHOOL-AGE
HANDICAPPED CHILDREN FOR COMMUNITIES OF VARIOUS SIZES**

	Percent of Population	Population of Community				
		25,000	50,000	100,000	250,000	500,000
Visual	.22*	11	22	44	110	220
Hearing	.57	28	57	114	285	570
Speech	3.50	175	350	700	1,750	3,500
Orthopedic	.50	25	50	100	250	500
Behavioral	2.00	100	200	400	1,000	2,000
Mental retardation	3.00	150	300	600	1,500	3,000
Learning disabled	2.50	125	250	500	1,250	2,500
Multiple handicapped	.06	3	6	12	30	60
	12.35	617	1,235	2,470	6,175	12,350

* BEH figures from Craig (1976)

In keeping with the provisions of The Education for All Handicapped Children Act, it is the responsibility of the public schools to place each special child in as normal an educational environment as possible, consistent with the child's ability and the limitations imposed by the handicap. Such placement is known as the **least restrictive environment (LRE)** for that special child at that time. In general, the regular classroom is considered to be the least restrictive environment possible for a special child within the public schools. This regular class placement, which has been called the **mainstream** by some, can provide the most adequate models of age-appropriate behavior and interaction with peers, as well as an educational environment believed to be more conducive to learning for most children. **Mainstreaming,** however, involves not only the placement of the special child in the regular classroom with nonhandicapped peers but also *the addition of whatever supportive services are needed to ensure a successful educational experience.* This is an important point to remember. The mandate of P.L. 94-142 is to provide the fullest, most nurturing educational environment for each special child. If combining the skills of both regular and special education can provide such an environment, the mandate to do so is clear. While many special children can spend at least some portion of the school day in the regular class, some will require an alternate placement because of their special needs.

A well-accepted and very practical way of looking at possible educational placements is the **Special Education Placement Cascade,** developed by Maynard Reynolds (1962, 1976). This cascade is a series of optional placements in the schools. Any of these placements may be the least restrictive environment for a special child *at some time,* depending on the needs of the child *at that time.* The eight placement options (shown schematically in Exhibit 15.5) are:

a) *The regular classroom without any specialized services:* Considered to be the least restricted placement, this is the placement in which most children receive their education.

b) *The regular classroom with consultative assistance:* In this placement the child remains in the regular classroom, but the teacher obtains help via consultation from special personnel. The purpose here is to help the teacher alter the regular classroom environment to better serve the special child.

c) *The regular classroom with assistance by itinerant specialists:* In this placement direct services are provided to the child either individually or in small groups scheduled to meet several times per week. This type of service is exemplified by the speech therapist or special reading teacher. The child is still being served in the regular classroom on an almost full-time basis.

d) *The regular classroom plus resource room help:* Such a placement might be of value to provide services to a child with a moderate reading problem or learning disability. Though the child remains a member of the regular classroom, he/she spends a portion of each day in the resource room for special instruction aimed at ameliorating his/her problem.

e) *The regular classroom plus part-time special class:* An educable men-

EXHIBIT 15.5

THE SPECIAL EDUCATION PLACEMENT CASCADE

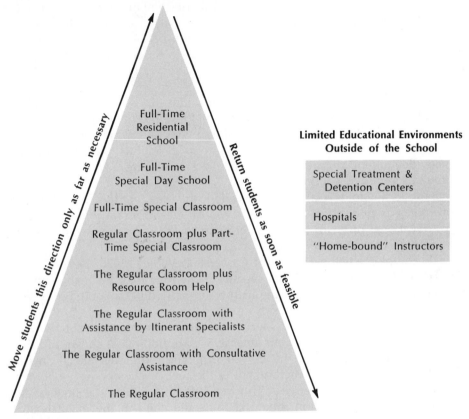

Move students this direction only as far as necessary

Return students as soon as feasible

Full-Time
Residential
School

Full-Time
Special Day School

Full-Time Special Classroom

Regular Classroom plus Part-
Time Special Classroom

The Regular Classroom plus
Resource Room Help

The Regular Classroom with
Assistance by Itinerant Specialists

The Regular Classroom with Consultative
Assistance

The Regular Classroom

**Limited Educational Environments
Outside of the School**

Special Treatment &
Detention Centers

Hospitals

"Home-bound" Instructors

From Reynolds (1962)

tally retarded child might benefit from such an arrangement. The child, because of his/her slow rate of learning, receives academic instruction in the special class but is able to participate with age peers in other aspects of the program in which academic ability is not a major factor.

f) *The full-time special classroom:* This is a more restricted educational environment than those listed above, but it is still in a regular school building. In this placement all of the child's day is spent in a special educational program, but some contact with nonhandicapped children is possible. Such placement is very appropriate, for example, for a young child with seriously impaired hearing, where the program emphasis throughout the day is on language development.

g) *The full-time special day school:* This placement is similar to the full-time special class above, but it is in a separate building that does not include nonhandicapped children. Frequently, ancillary services (such as physical or occupational therapy or other treatments not found in the public schools) are part of the program for the child. Children in this placement need a more structured educational placement, but they are still able to live in their homes in the community.

h) *The full-time residential school:* This placement represents the most restricted educational placement in which it is not advisable for the child to live at home. Such a placement is considered appropriate for a seriously emotionally disturbed child, where structure needs to be emphasized throughout the child's waking day.

The remaining three placements are not educational, although education is usually part of the program. The focus of these programs may be medical treatment—as in hospital schools for children with severe physical disabilities; special social/behavioral rehabilitation—as in residential facilities for disturbed, delinquent children; or basically custodial care—as in facilities for profoundly retarded children.

Basic to Reynolds' Placement Cascade is the idea that *the child should be moved only as far as necessary from the regular classroom to obtain the necessary educational program and then returned to the regular classroom or to a less restricted environment as quickly as possible.*

To complement the Placement Cascade, Reynolds (1976) developed the **Cascade of Services.** Basic to this cascade is the idea that, for many children, the services can be brought to the learner in many different settings, *without moving the child.* No type of service need be limited to only one type of placement. While some highly specialized types of services might be better provided in more restricted environments, we are finding, as shown in Exhibit 15.6, that many services can be moved from the more specialized environment to the less restricted environment of the regular classroom—*without impairing the quality of the service.* This movement of services facilitates a very important goal of education today: keeping the child in the mainstream of general education.

In order to provide this environment, we need to reconsider the philosophy and curricula that are currently followed in preparing teachers to work in the schools. While it is not necessary for every teacher to be a special education teacher, it *is* necessary for every teacher to be able to *assist* in providing quality educational programs to all children, regardless of their intellectual, educational, social, or physical status. Successful mainstreaming experiences for children will require special education and regular education teachers, along with support personnel, to work together, as has seldom been done in the past. Such efforts will require coordination of teaching materials and methods, and continuing evaluation of both the child and the program. These efforts will undoubtedly be more costly than previous special education programs, but the long-term gains to be realized will, it is hoped, justify the added expenditure.

In the midst of the challenges ahead for the field of education, it is wise to reemphasize the intention behind the mandate of P.L. 94-142: to provide an education that meets the unique needs of each special child. Though the simple goal might seem that of mainstreaming every child into the regular classroom, this may not always be the best educational path for every child.

EXHIBIT 15.6

THE CASCADE OF SERVICES

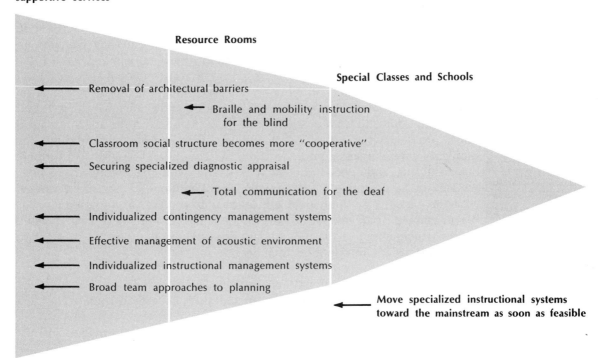

**Regular classrooms, shops,
and laboratories with
supportive services**

Resource Rooms

Special Classes and Schools

← Removal of architectural barriers

← Braille and mobility instruction
for the blind

← Classroom social structure becomes more "cooperative"

← Securing specialized diagnostic appraisal

← Total communication for the deaf

← Individualized contingency management systems

← Effective management of acoustic environment

← Individualized instructional management systems

← Broad team approaches to planning

← **Move specialized instructional systems
toward the mainstream as soon as feasible**

From Reynolds (1976)

Cruickshank (1977) cautioned that the available research with learning-disabled children does not warrant the integration of many exceptional children into the regular class. "The fact of the matter is that in terms of current educational practice, the *'least' may more often be the most restrictive* place for learning-disabled children to receive their education" (p. 193). Hapeman (1977) expressed the concern that mainstreaming efforts have "the potential of erasing 75 years of gains made for visually handicapped children and their parents" (p. 36). There is the peril that in the rush to institute mainstreaming programs, "the 'mainstreaming' may be distorted and result in offering children with handicaps less intensive education than they require" (Martin, 1977, p. 46).

We need to keep in mind that the goal is to help children obtain an appropriate education—regardless of their handicap. Mainstreaming is only one option for placement for that education. It is not the best option for *all* special children. Quality teaching can take place in a great variety of settings. The first responsibility is to the child, not the setting.

SPECIFIC PROGRAM MODIFICATIONS

Teachers have used lesson or teaching plans as organizational aids for their instructional programs for some time. Each lesson plan usually contains information on the objectives of the instruction, the materials to be used, the mode of presentation, the mode of response, the instructional sequence, and the method of evaluation. In working with exceptional learners, modification of lesson plans developed for the regular class may be necessary. The extent to which modifications are needed depends, of course, on the specific educational problems manifested by the child. These problems should be the subject of careful assessment undertaken by school psychologists, educational diagnosticians, and special education teachers. Once the findings have been assessed by all personnel working with the exceptional learner and discussed with the parents, an **individual educational plan (IEP),** as required by P.L. 94-142, should be developed for the child. While no specific form is dictated for the development of the IEP, the law does require that certain information be provided. This information includes:

a) the current educational achievement levels;

b) the annual educational goals, including short-term instructional objectives;

c) a statement detailing the educational services to be provided and the extent to which each child will be able to participate in regular educational programs;

d) the anticipated date for the initiation of these services and the expected length of time that these services will be provided;

e) the appropriate objective criteria and evaluation procedures, with at least annual schedules for determining if the instructional objectives are being achieved.

By law, an IEP must be developed for each child in a special education program. The IEP must be approved in writing by the parents or guardians. They have the right not to approve the testing, placement, and/or special program for their child(ren). They also have the right to an "impartial due process hearing" that may be carried beyond the school district to state or federal courts if they are not satisfied with what the public school proposes for their special child.

In deciding the IEP for a particular child, a number of areas of consideration are relevant: the child's levels of development in the motor, cognitive, psychosocial, and educational areas; previous school experience; special environmental needs; and the special education needs. If the decision is to keep the child only in the special class at this time, the special education teacher will be responsible for the total instructional program. If the child is to spend some portion of his/her day in the regular class and part of the day in a special program, a close working relationship, with assigned educational responsibilities, between special and regular teachers is crucial for the child's well-being. No one can reasonably expect regular classroom teachers to implement highly specialized educational programs for all exceptional children, but one can expect that they will promote the children's being part of the class and participating in school and school-related functions. It is hoped that the teacher will also tutor the exceptional learner when the schedule permits. The regular classroom teacher should maintain continuing contact with the special teacher, speech therapist, and other persons who have some responsibility for providing continuing services to the special child.

A detailed discussion of teaching methods developed for special children is well beyond the scope of this book. Nevertheless, there is a good deal that a regular classroom teacher can do to adapt the program to better meet the educational needs of the special child. In this section, a number of these educational adaptions will be outlined.

Children with Sensory Impairments

Until relatively recently, children with major sensory impairments usually obtained the greater part of their education in special schools if they lived in a larger city, or in a boarding school under state control if they were from a smaller community or rural area that had no local special school. We have now come to realize that with adequate school resources, many of these children can be educated in the regular school through the help of a special teacher and an adequately equipped resource room. This is in keeping with the current emphasis on the least restrictive environment.

The hard-of-hearing child

The hard-of-hearing child has a mild-to-moderate hearing loss that can limit the extent to which the child can profit from the usual instructional program in the classroom. Nevertheless, this child's educational program will emphasize helping the child obtain maximum value from whatever hearing remains.

a) *Educational objectives:* The objectives of instruction will be quite similar to those objectives for hearing children. Nevertheless, it is important to keep in mind the limited language ability that is the result of the hearing impairment. Speech therapy may also be needed.

b) *Materials to be used:* No great adjustment will be needed, but visual aids should be used wherever possible to supplement and clarify auditory stimuli. Again, the language limitations must be kept in mind.

c) *Mode of presentation:* Here again, no great adjustment will be needed for most hard-of-hearing children, but auditory presentation is enhanced when it is supported by visuals. Precise enunciation is a must.

d) *Mode of responding:* When the signal is adequately received, hard-of-hearing children respond quite similarly to hearing children.

e) *Instructional sequence:* Added attention will be needed in the areas of vocabulary development and reading.

There are many things that a regular classroom teacher can do to ease the situation for the hard-of-hearing child in the regular class. Philip Schmitt (n.d.) of Gallaudet College suggested a number of modifications:

a) Seat the child where he/she can read the teacher's lips and easily follow class procedures. The child's better ear should be toward the teacher and the class. The hearing-impaired child should sit where he/she does not face the light while attempting to lipread.

b) During class discussions, encourage the hearing-impaired child to face the individual who is speaking. Allow roving privileges—moving around the room during various activities so that he/she can readily follow what is happening.

c) Speak naturally. Do not shout or raise your voice, especially if the child wears a hearing aid. Avoid exaggerated or overemphasized speech.

d) Avoid visual distractions while speaking and make sure you are facing and have the attention of the hearing-impaired child.

e) Since a moving person is more difficult to lipread, stand in one place when dictating or spelling words.

f) Try to use grammatically complete sentences to give the hearing-impaired child contextual cues and provide a richer language model. With some children it is better to use simple, fairly short sentences, but make sure they are structurally and functionally complete.

g) If the child misinterprets, rephrase the question or statement rather than just repeating it. You may have used words the child could not lipread because of poor visibility or lack of familiarity with the words.

h) Encourage the child to ask for repetition when what has been said is not fully understood.

i) Ask both hearing-impaired and hearing students to repeat directions for the benefit of the entire class.

j) A matter-of-fact attitude toward the handicap will help, and it will be reflected by the children in the class.

k) Provide cues, such as some familiarization with new vocabulary, prior to the lesson.

With few exceptions, the educational prognosis for the hard-of-hearing child is good. Remedial instruction will probably be needed to help the child in the areas of speech and language development and reading. If a hearing aid has been prescribed, it is important for the child's education that it be worn and that the batteries be fresh.

The educationally deaf child

As was discussed in Chapter 5, the age at which deafness occurs is a critical factor. A child who becomes deaf before adequate language is developed— usually age 5 or 6—has a very severe language deficit that results in a severe educational disability. Educational retardation of from 2 to 5 years is not uncommon in these children. It is important, therefore, that such children begin a special educational program as soon as the hearing problem is discovered; this program should continue throughout the child's school career.

a) *Educational objectives:* Because the educationally deaf as a group are significantly educationally retarded, it will be necessary to prepare educational objectives consistent with the child's functional level rather than with chronological age or ability level. Much special help will be needed in the areas of language and vocabulary development and in communication skills.

b) *Materials to be used:* The materials need to be adjusted for the level of functioning. Especially with the educationally deaf, visual aids should be used.

c) *Mode of presentation:* Because the major pathway for the development of language is blocked, emphasis must be on visual presentation. If auditory presentation is used, an interpreter skilled in manual communication should be available. Help in taking notes may be needed.

d) *Mode of response:* Vocal responding should be encouraged but, depending on the age when the deafness occurred and on the child's speech development, it may be difficult to comprehend. Many deaf individuals prefer to communicate through an interpreter or in writing.

e) *Instructional sequence:* Much attention should be placed on language and vocabulary development and on reading. The school must assist the deaf child in developing social skills. Bertness (1976) reported that providing manual communication skills for hearing children in the Tacoma schools resulted in the development of a buddy system in which fifth-grade hearing students teamed up with one or two younger deaf children to help them with their schoolwork and to help involve them in school activities.

In programming for the educationally deaf child, Vernon and Prickett (1976) emphasized that giving hearing aids to deaf children, placing them in regular classes—even with preferential seating—and giving them two or three periods a day with a special teacher is, at best, inadequate. They stated that

When he was in sixth grade, this boy with a serious hearing loss moved from a school for the deaf to a regular middle school where students can move freely from working as individuals to working with neighbors, with teacher assistance readily available. Now in eighth grade, he continues to work seriously and effectively, enjoying the challenges of learning and interacting with his peers.

the most able of the deaf children "may get from 5 percent to 20 percent of what the teacher says when the teacher's lips can be seen" (p. 6). To further compound the problem, most deaf children are severely educationally retarded and will not be able to read the textbooks used. Vernon and Prickett advocated the use of *The Holcomb Plan,* which was developed and operates in the Newark, Delaware, school system. In this Plan, the deaf child is placed in a mainstream program "only when he[/she] has a tutor-interpreter who interprets into sign language what the regular classroom teacher says" (p. 10). In addition to interpreting, the tutor-interpreter also tutors the deaf child in that class, thus providing a good deal of support for the deaf learner.

The speech-impaired child

More children have speech problems than any other single handicap. Though needed classroom modifications are usually minor, all teachers need to have some understanding of speech problems in children in order to facilitate the work of the speech therapist and, just as important, in order to create an understanding classroom environment for the speech-impaired child.

a) *Educational objectives:* If the speech handicap is the only problem that the child manifests, the educational objectives will be the same as for other children.

b) *Materials to be used:* In general, no modifications will be needed. In those cases where different materials are needed, they should be suggested by the speech therapist.

c) *Mode of presentation:* No modifications will be needed.

d) *Mode of response:* Depending on the type of speech problem, minor modifications in how the child is expected to respond may be necessary. Oral communication should be encouraged.

e) *Instructional sequence:* No major revisions will be needed for speech-impaired children.

Unfortunately, children have learned from the Saturday morning cartoons on television that speech disorders are something at which they laugh. Now, with the teachers' help, they must learn to be patient and accepting in their reactions to their classmates who have speech problems. The teacher has to provide a climate in the classroom in which the child with a speech problem feels free to talk. This is especially important for the child who stutters and who may go to great lengths to keep from talking.

The partially sighted child

Most partially sighted children will receive the bulk of their education in the regular class. Special care will be needed to help these children make maximal use of whatever remaining vision they have. With minor variations (to be discussed below), the regular class does present the least restrictive environment for most partially sighted children.

a) *Educational objectives:* The educational objectives for partially sighted children will generally be the same as for sighted children, with the addition of **mobility training,** that is, teaching them to use their remaining vision to maneuver around the classroom, school, community, and other environments.

b) *Materials to be used:* It may be necessary to obtain magnifiers and text

453
Specific program
modifications

materials printed in large type, which are available from the American Printing Home for the Blind in Louisville, Kentucky, as well as from a few commercial publishers. Audio materials, such as Talking Books, may also be needed. Some use may also be made of *compressed speech,* a new tape-recording technique in which the nonessential aspects of speech are omitted, thus providing the material to be played without distortion and permitting more material to be listened to in a shorter span of time. Cassette recorders may be used by the students to facilitate note-taking. Tactual aids, such as relief maps, may also be helpful. Pencils with soft, black lead and black nylon tip pens are preferred for writing.

c) *Mode of presentation:* No great adjustment will be needed for most partially sighted children. The visual channel will still be used, but greater use of the auditory mode of presentation will be necessary.

d) *Mode of response:* Instead of writing responses, some children learn to type. Otherwise no major differences need be expected in the mode of responding.

e) *Instructional sequence:* The instructional sequence for partially sighted children does not differ markedly from that for normally sighted children. Mobility training and typing are usually added to the program. It should also be kept in mind that reading either magnified print in regular books or special large-type books is a somewhat slower process than the reading of regular size type. As such, it is important to allow the partially sighted child more time to complete his/her work.

Eye glasses and magnifiers will need to be checked routinely for adjustment and to have the lenses cleaned. It often helps partially sighted children to vary tasks between those requiring near-point vision and those requiring far-point vision, for example, seat work and working from material on the board. The child should also be permitted to rest his/her eyes whenever necessary. Pelone (1957) recommended that "creative or free-hand art work [be used] between activities that require intensive eye work" (p. 36). Legibility in handwriting should be stressed. Some teachers have found that permitting the child to write larger than average makes the task somewhat easier. Large, soft, white chalk should be used at the blackboard because it makes a heavier, whiter line that is easier to see.

The educationally blind child
Except for the fact that the visual channel is not functional for educational purposes, educationally blind children function quite well in school.

a) *Educational objectives:* Educational objectives for blind children will remain relatively unchanged from those for sighted children. Major changes will be in the addition of independence training, including mobility training and skill in the use of specialized media.

b) *Materials to be used:* Use should be made of audio materials available from several sources. It is even possible to obtain specially recorded texts for the blind (from Recordings for the Blind, 215 E. 58th St., N.Y., N.Y., 10022). The Library of Congress, Division for the Blind and Physically Handicapped, Washington, D.C., is able to provide materials in braille, as well as disc and tape recordings of adult, adolescent, and juvenile books and periodicals.

Brailled music and instructional texts are also available. It is also necessary for blind children to learn to use the typewriter, braille writer, and braille slate and stylus. So that other children in the classroom are not disturbed by the sounds, earphones should be used with the disc players and tape machines.

c) *Mode of presentation:* Obviously, the visual mode is nonfunctional for the educationally blind child. The auditory and tactile modalities will be the primary senses through which the educationally blind child will learn. Since hearing is the major learning modality, the noise level in the room should be regulated.

d) *Mode of response:* Like the partially sighted, the blind learn early to use the typewriter to communicate in writing with the seeing world. Other major modifications in how the blind child communicates are not needed.

e) *Instructional sequence:* Braille reading or listening to recordings are relatively slow ways to obtain information. Therefore, more time needs to be provided for the educationally blind learner to do the required reading and listening.

The regular classroom teacher can do a number of things to help a blind child in the classroom, including instructing classmates on how to act as a guide for the blind child. Guides are especially important until the blind child learns the geography of the classroom and the adjacent areas. It is also important to have a guide available in case of an emergency or fire drill. The best guide provides an elbow for the blind classmate to hold rather than trying to steer by pulling and pushing the blind classmate. Care should also be taken not to move furniture around in the classroom without informing the blind child. Verbal warning should be given when it appears that there are obstacles, such as open or closed doors or other objects in the way. The teacher should also provide the blind student with storage space near his/her desk for storage of the special equipment and materials that are frequently needed.

The child with physical health disorders

In Chapter 7, the great variety of classifications involved in describing the many physical health disorders was discussed. As one might expect, the need

Braille books and typewriters are a central part of any blind child's entry into the world of print. Here, in an open classroom, a blind child does an assignment using both—while an interested classmate looks on.

for special education services varies for these children, and the least restrictive environment might range from the regular classroom to a bed in a medical facility. Whatever the case, educational decisions must involve medical and other health professionals, as well as special and regular educators.

a) *Educational objectives:* The educational objectives may depend on factors other than the physical handicap. Because many of these children will have had repeated and prolonged absences from school for medical treatment, they may be significantly behind in academic performance. It is of importance to remember that many physically handicapped children may have a second or even third handicap, such as speech problems and mental retardation, in addition to the physical disorder. Educational objectives can best be developed through careful consultation among the special education personnel, the regular class teacher, and the medical personnel involved with the child.

b) *Materials to be used:* Here too, for some children with physical health disorders, the materials used need be no different from those used with the balance of the class. For others, major adaptions of materials may be needed, such as special stand-up desks (which can be moved into the classroom) or

As so many bicyclists have found, a basket is a useful accessory—and no less so for the child who must use a walker.

specially adapted typewriters for the child with weak muscles or serious fine motor problems. Here again, the materials needed by a particular child are best determined in consultation with the attending physician, the special education personnel, and the regular classroom teacher.

c) *Mode of presentation:* No major changes in the mode of presentation may be necessary. However, a recent study (Fassler, 1970) indicated that some cerebral-palsied children function somewhat better under reduced auditory input.

d) *Mode of response:* This will depend on the nature of the physical health disorder. For most of the children it will not differ significantly from that for the nonhandicapped child.

e) *Instructional sequence:* Because of the time lost from school and obvious limitations, the sequence may require more time and directed teaching to complete.

The major school-related difficulties encountered by children with physical health disorders may not be educational in nature. The need is frequently to create a barrier-free environment that permits an entry into the educational system. The problem may begin with getting the child out of the home, into a suitable vehicle, and into the school. At the school there may be other problems—such as narrow doorways, stairs to be negotiated, and toileting facilities that have not been adapted to the specific needs of the physically handicapped. As required by P.L. 94-142, architectural barriers are currently undergoing modification to permit the handicapped to enter into the regular educational environment.

Even in a barrier-free environment, however, the extent to which a physically handicapped child will be able to enter into a school program in which mainstreaming is emphasized depends on factors such as the severity of the handicap, the abilities the physically handicapped child does have, and the social-emotional adjustment made by the child and family to the problems. Though it is true, as Kirk (1972) pointed out, that the learning process for physically handicapped children is the same as for children who are not crippled, concomitant speech and neuromotor handicaps and the greater need for more ancillary services suggest that assignment to a program should be done only after a very careful study—by a team of professionals—of both the child and the available programs. If the problem is primarily one of locomotion, placement in a mainstream program needs to be considered. It is only when the educational needs of the child become very complex that a special class program as the least restricted placement needs to be considered. When medical services are required on a continuing or on-call basis, a special school or hospital school may be the placement of choice.

Because a child's appearance is often not a good indicator of his/her physical condition, it is important that close contact be maintained with medical personnel familiar with the child and his/her problems. A boy with pseudohypertrophic muscular dystrophy may actually appear to be very well-muscled, when in fact the muscle tissue is being replaced with fatty tissue. Children with cystic fibrosis do not appear to be handicapped and may be considered to be bothersome and generally inattentive by the uninformed (Edgington, 1976).

Children with cognitive differences—the mentally retarded, the learning-disabled, and the gifted—make up the largest and most diverse group of special children. Every teacher, regardless of grade, will have children with at least mild cognitive differences in his/her class. Frequently, the teacher is not aware that a child is "different" until someone labels the child as having some exceptionality. As was noted in Chapter 3, the use of labels can have a pejorative effect on the child and on the program provided to the child. It is especially important to keep this in mind when working with children with cognitive differences: the goal, as for all children, should be the least restrictive—but most suitable—educational environment for the child at any particular time. The teacher should watch for any changes in the child's performance that might indicate that a change in the child's educational program is warranted.

The educable mentally retarded child

Most educable mentally retarded (EMR) children should be able to benefit from at least a partial placement in the regular classroom. Emphasis needs to be placed on what the child can accomplish, not on what the child can't accomplish. Practical application of the skills learned in the classroom to real-life situations should be emphasized.

a) *Educational objectives:* Not to expect academic performance from EMR children is to create a self-fulfilling prediction because the tendency

These girls are in a special class that groups "mentally handicapped" pupils according to their learning deficits. The prime goals are to help them overcome their learning difficulties and prepare them to return to the regular classroom as soon as feasible. Here they are learning to recognize some common items under a microscope.

would be not to present the work to the children. The learning performance of EMR children placed in the regular classroom with resource room help should overlap that seen in low-achieving regular class students (MacMillan, 1977). Emphasis should also be placed on career education and prevocational to vocational training and social-personal skills.

b) *Materials to be used:* Again, for the most part, materials similar to those used for the low-functioning group should be appropriate.

c) *Mode of presentation:* While major changes should not be anticipated, the level of presentation must correspond to the EMR student's level of functioning, not the grade level in which the student is placed. Repetition will probably be necessary.

d) *Mode of response:* Though it may be necessary to adjust expectations to the level at which the child can achieve, no major changes need be anticipated.

e) *Instructional sequence:* More time will be needed to complete some of the work. Instructional steps will need to be smaller than for the other children in the class. Anticipate the need for more practice for the development of new skills.

It is important for the classroom teacher to be aware that many children who are of educable mentally retarded ability will, because of past experiences and past failures, have secondary problems, such as poor frustration tolerance and low self-esteem. If the objectives and expectations are reasonable and if ample time to practice developing skills is provided, learning should take place. Many of the social and personality characteristics attributed to the mildly retarded are the result of poor instruction techniques that do not adjust the demands of the environment to the child's ability.

The trainable mentally retarded child
Regular classroom modifications for the trainable or moderately mentally retarded child are not included in this section since, as Burton (1976) noted, although mainstream placement for trainable mentally retarded (TMR) children has been used in some programs, "their best interests have not usually been met through this arrangement; and this is, perhaps, the least desirable alternative for a program" (p. 171). Depending on the age of the child and the administrative structure of the school district, the least restrictive educational environment for a trainable mentally retarded child is probably the special class housed within the public school or possibly the special center, which is still part of a public school program. Such centers frequently house several classes for different age groups and often include a sheltered workshop program for the older adolescent TMR. Ancillary services, such as speech therapy and health services, are frequently available in the special center.

The severely and profoundly retarded child
The subject of the education of severely and profoundly retarded children has been misinterpreted by many well-intentioned people. All handicapped children—regardless of degree of handicap—are entitled to public education at the expense of the tax-supported public schools. This is mandated. Also mandated is that each child receive his/her education in the least restricted en-

vironment consistent with the child's abilities. Nowhere is mainstreaming ordered. It is probable that the least restricted educational environment for severely and profoundly retarded children is in a separate facility within the community (Burton & Hirshoren, 1978). The educational program for severely and profoundly retarded would focus on sensory-motor development, physical mobility and coordination, self-care skills, language development, and social behavior. It is also important to keep in mind that the majority of the severely and profoundly retarded children will have multiple handicaps requiring the services of medical specialists, physical and occupational therapists, psychologists, speech and hearing specialists, and social workers.

The learning-disabled child

Learning disabilities in children are a significant problem for many teachers. At this point in time, it is impossible to say for certain whether the learning problem is inherent in the child, the result of faulty teaching, or an interaction between some problem in the child and an instructional program that is not suited to the child. Deciding the cause of a specific learning disability (SLD), however, is much less important than deciding on the educational program to help the child overcome the learning disability. The least restrictive environment for these children is the regular classroom with accompanying resource room instruction.

a) *Educational objectives:* The child with mild-to-moderate specific learning disabilities generally should be expected to complete the objectives of the regular class; however, it will be necessary to consider the effect of the SLD on the child's learning and to permit the child latitude in meeting the objectives. It should be possible for the SLD child to obtain special tutoring to assist him/her in meeting the objectives.

b) *Materials to be used:* Despite the many gadgets and pieces of paraphernalia available in school supply catalogs—which claim to be especially designed for children with specific learning disabilities—there is no evidence that much of this material or equipment is effective (Bleil, 1975). Certainly, the use of audiovisual aids may assist the teaching and learning of the SLD child, but this statement would be as true for most children. Whatever materials are used, they should be adjusted to the level at which the child is functioning.

c) *Mode of presentation:* Depending on the learning disability, it may be necessary to modify the way assignments or materials are presented. For instance, if the learning disability appears to be in the visual area, it may be necessary to record assignments on a cassette tape or to have the child tell what he/she understands the assignment to be after reading the directions, so that the teacher can be sure that the child understands what he/she is expected to do.

d) *Mode of response:* Here, too, adjustments may be needed. If the child has difficulties with writing, a typewriter might be used; or the child could record his/her responses so the teacher could listen to them. At the same time the child is permitted to use compensatory methods of responding, it is important that remedial instruction in the deficit area be underway so that eventually a normal mode of response could be anticipated.

e) *Instructional sequence:* Because of the very nature of specific learning disabilities, it may be necessary for the instructional sequence to be altered. Repeating some sequences to make certain they are overlearned may help assure the child's success in a later learning situation. The instructional sequence must be carefully planned to assure that the opportunity for learning takes place.

Remedial education should be developed to suit the specific learning needs of each child. Often these children have learned over a period of several years that they cannot do certain tasks. The first job of the teacher is to convince a child that a task can be mastered. The judicious use of task analysis, coupled with positive reinforcement, frequently helps. Task analysis involves breaking a skill into a graduated series of subskills that are easier to learn. The difficulty level should increase gradually as the child masters each of the skills. Often children cannot see the relevance of certain learning skills. The teacher should provide the opportunity for the child to use these newly mastered skills in some new way, possibly around the home or other non-school setting. This helps provide for what some educators call *transfer of training.*

The gifted child

Many teachers find gifted children to be as difficult to work with as many of the other special children. Because of the tendency of the gifted to question so many things, many carefully developed lessons have been side-tracked into a digression. It is not uncommon for teachers to talk of gifted children as being disturbances in the classroom. Special planning is necessary to help make school a more meaningful experience for these children.

a) *Educational objectives:* Gifted children should be able to complete the usual objectives in the regular class in less time, especially if they are allowed to use self-paced programmed instruction. Less drill is needed. It will be neces-

The least restrictive environment for a learning-disabled child is usually the regular classroom with resource room instruction that focuses on overcoming the specific learning difficulty.

sary to provide enrichment activities and/or some form of acceleration to permit them to complete formal schooling at an earlier age, depending on the design of the instructional program. With care, objectives relating to divergent thinking and creativity can be added to their program.

b) *Materials to be used:* The usual materials are a good starting place. Because gifted children generally enjoy going beyond the obvious, it is well to have enrichment materials available. A good library is indispensable. Also of value are science experiments, which assist in the teaching of research skills.

c) *Mode of presentation:* No adjustment is needed.

d) *Mode of response:* No adjustment is needed.

e) *Instructional sequence:* The instructional sequence will be completed in less time by the gifted. Depending on the school policy, some form of acceleration or meaningful enrichment is needed to make school a worthwhile experience for these children. They do not need more of the same to keep them busy. Gallagher (1975) presented some helpful suggestions to the teacher who wants the classroom structured to encourage creativity among gifted students. He suggested that teachers:

— *Organize and base the curriculum on the teaching of concepts rather than facts.*

— *Allow more individual assignments of projects under competent supervision.*

— *Bring students into contact with the maximum talent and knowledge available in the teaching staff.*

— *Follow the general philosophy that "Truth is something to be sought for, rather than something that will be revealed." (pp. 254–55)*

Gallagher added that teachers need more competence in content areas, as well as a better understanding of how gifted children develop and how to teach to stimulate their talents.

Gifted children represent a potential national resource. Though programs for the gifted are not mandated by the Education for All Handicapped Children Act, it would be very short-sighted of a school district not to provide this program. It would be tantamount to saying that we need less than the best-trained minds to assume the leadership positions of this country.

Children with Mild-to-Moderate Behavior Disorders

It is the rare classroom that does not have some children with conduct disorders or personality problems. The conduct disorder syndrome is the most common behavior disturbance seen among these children, and it is also the most troublesome to teachers. While children with personality problems are less troublesome, they often suffer intense anxiety. Regardless of the diagnostic category in which a child may be placed, the educational program must be realistically adapted to the classroom context (Kavale & Hirshoren, 1977).

a) *Educational objectives:* Frequently the fear of failure is at the root of the way a child behaves or misbehaves in school (Glasser, 1969). It is important that the teacher attempt to program success into the child's program without appearing to patronize the child. The educational objectives developed for the nonhandicapped child are appropriate, with the addition of specially developed objectives in the area of social and emotional development.

b) *Materials to be used:* The same materials used with the nonhandicapped will be appropriate. Morse (1970) recommended that self-tutoring devices be used. These devices are often successful instructional aids "when personal interaction is too difficult" (p. 302). The use of charts that show improvement and progress reports are often of value as motivating tools. Contingency contracts and other behavior-management materials may also be of value.

c) *Mode of presentation:* No special adjustments should be needed.

d) *Mode of response:* No adjustments anticipated.

e) *Instructional sequence:* The instructional sequence and rate should approximate that for the nonhandicapped child. Extra time may be required to include programming for corrective work in the affected areas.

The behaviors exhibited will range from mild, attention-seeking acting-out behavior to overly shy and withdrawn behavior. Obviously the needs of the children will vary. It is of major importance to consider what may be reinforcing the child for a given behavior within the classroom. It may be impossible to discover, or it may be something over which the teacher has no control. Remember though, something in the environment is reinforcing the negative behavior in the classroom. To discover what it is is the beginning of developing control.

For reasons of safety, it is sometimes necessary for a teacher to intervene and stop a child from behaving in a certain way before someone is hurt or before the child loses the last vestiges of self-control. Generally, however, it is better for the misbehavior to be ignored by the teacher, as well as by the other children in the class. The latter is not an easy task to accomplish. At the same time, attention and praise, as well as other forms of reinforcement, should be provided when the child is behaving appropriately. Instructions should have clear, unambiguous directions so that they are easily understood—the child should know specifically what he/she is expected to do. Behavioral expectations should also be clear—the consequences of both appropriate behavior and inappropriate behavior should be clearly defined. Activities for the child should be in keeping with his/her level of social development, achievement level, academic ability, and interest level if they are to be effective. Gearheart and Weishahn (1976) suggested a number of basic techniques that can help in managing students with behavior problems. These are listed in Exhibit 15.7.

Children with Severe Behavior Disorders or Psychoses

Severely disturbed children—like other severely and profoundly handicapped children—are entitled to an education at public expense. Because of the high degree of supervision and structure needed by these children, the initial program should be one in which educational skills are secondary to needed social/rehabilitative skills. These needs can best be provided for in a residential facility, where twenty-four hour programming is available. Hopefully,

EXHIBIT 15.7

463

Specific program
modifications

FIRST AID FOR THE TEACHER

The following are some basic techniques that can help in managing misbehavior in the regular class. This is not meant to imply that they will be the "answer" to your problem. They are techniques... found to be helpful in the classroom.

1. Stop misbehavior in time. Do not wait until the situation is totally out of hand before stopping it. Stop the act before you become angry and lose control or before the whole class gets into the act.

2. Program for a variety of changes. Activities with a great deal of manual emphasis are more likely to succeed than heavy doses of desk work.

3. Make tasks clear and orderly and give the child time to complete one task before beginning another. A troubled child needs to know what is expected of him in an activity. He needs closure on one activity before he can freely and without frustration move onto a new task. Insist that the student complete an activity. Be sure that the task is on the student's ability level and that he understands the directions.

4. Comment positively when the student is attending appropriately to a task. Let him know you know he is working constructively. Praise him. Smile.

5. Establish limits and maintain consistent, clear ground rules. This structure gives the student the necessary backbone to function successfully in the class. He needs to know what is appropriate or inappropriate. He needs to know what the consequences of his behavior will be. Be consistent in following through with legitimate consequences. Threats and bribes will not work.

6. Manage transitional times with quieting down periods between two activities. Take the time to allow a child to slow down from one activity, such as physical education, to be ready for another activity, such as reading.

7. Set up filler corners, activity centers a child can go to when he has completed required activities. These can be media corners or game corners.

8. Set up a quiet corner where a child can go to be alone, to cry, or to calm down. The corner should not be used for punishment; rather it should be a place to gain control. If a child needs to be sent to the quiet corner, send him calmly and quickly. He is to stay in the corner until *he* feels able to return and behave responsibly. Do not set a time limit. Let the student decide when *he* is in control of feelings and behavior.

9. Plan for anger breaks; give a distraught, anxious, or angry student a chance to swim laps in a pool, run laps around a track, beat pillows, hit a punching bag, throw bean bags at a wall, pedal an exercise bike, jump rope, or pound clay. Follow this anger break by providing activities that trigger a heavy dose of laughter; then, arrange for a quiet period.

10. Provide success: be sure the material is relevant, interesting, and appropriate for the child.

Steps that are *inappropriate* for helping a troubled student include the following:

1. Using brute force: "You hit me, I'll hit you back!"

2. Accusing the student of misbehaving. You are, in a sense, forcing the child to lie to save face.

3. Comparing the student's behavior with that of his peers.

4. Arguing—you cannot win an argument with a student. Usually, you both lose.

5. Embarrassing the student in front of his peers.

6. Removing the student from activities he does well and enjoys doing.

7. Ridiculing the student for his mistakes or misbehavior.

From Gearhart & Weishahn (1976, p. 169)

as progress is made in shaping the child's social behavior, less restrictive educational placements could be made.

A Caveat

In attempting to structure a school program to provide the least restrictive environment for each child, there is a temptation to overuse those teachers who appear to be more receptive to working with special children. Such a practice could lead to the existence of a few classrooms that are unofficially designated as the "mainstream classes." But this would merely result in the development of a different type of special class, hardly reflecting the spirit inherent in the idea of placing each child in the least restrictive environment consistent with the needs of the child. Whichever placement is chosen for a special child, it should result from a complete study of the social, educational, psychological, and physical needs of that child. The results of these evaluations need to be discussed not only by the staff who assessed the child, but also by those regular educators and special educators who are or will be working with that child *and* the parents as well. Resulting recommendations must consider the child and the teachers, as well as the services necessary, to increase the probability that the school experience will be beneficial for the child.

EDUCATING THE CULTURALLY DIFFERENT

The culturally different, or disadvantaged, or deprived, or underprivileged; or the educationally disadvantaged; or the low socioeconomic children, or ghetto children, or barrio children, or poor minority children . . . have always been there but, until relatively recently, have been pretty much ignored by the schools of this country. Usually, they have left school at the first opportunity—often before the legal departure age—to become part of the pool of unskilled labor who maintain a marginal existence.

In 1965, Title I of the Elementary and Secondary Education Act was enacted (P.L. 89–10). The specific aim of this legislation has been to improve the educational achievement of over 9 million children who are, by definition, "educationally deprived." The children served by compensatory education programs funded by this act are *socioeconomically deprived,* as determined by the annual family income and also by their failure to achieve at a reasonable level in school. According to the 1970 census, of the 59 million children in the United States, "8.7 million come from families with incomes under $5,000 a year, 400,000 of these attended nonpublic schools. Four million were from families which earned less than $3,000 a year—but of these 757,000 did not attend any school" (National Advisory Council on the Education of Disadvantaged Children, 1973, p. 7). According to this census, 28 percent of black children, 75 percent of Spanish-American children, 20.7 percent of American Indian children, and 4.4 percent of white children attending school came from families with an income of less than $3,000 a year. These children and youth, for the most part, have been alienated from the schools. The values espoused by the schools have not been those that have been meaningful or important or even understandable to many of these children. This lack of meaningfulness, obviously, is a major social problem, but the schools, as a community agency, have a definite responsibility in preparing children and youth to better cope with the structure of society in a positive way and to better meet their own socioeconomic and biological needs.

The approaches to this problem of school alienation have been on at least three fronts, with varying degrees of success: the home, preschool programs, and programs during the school years.

Programs for the Home Environment

Because there is convincing evidence that the home environments in which many children live serve to inhibit rather than nurture their intellectual development during their early years (Deutsch, 1964, 1965; Hunt, 1964; Karnes & Zehrbach, 1975), the area of parent education is of importance. Schaefer (1972), after reviewing research on parent-training programs, concluded that these programs are effective as a supplement to preschool programs and even as an alternative to preschool programs. Lillie (1975) noted that there are at least four major areas in which systematic planning is needed to assure a successful parent education program: social and emotional support, exchanging information, parent participation, and improving parent-child interactions.

We know from the popularity of books on childrearing and the number of adult education groups concerned with parenting that many parents have feelings of inadequacy or at least self-doubt regarding their own ability as parents. In addition to these anxieties and doubts, many parents may have guilt feelings, stemming from the resentment they frequently feel toward their children because of the responsibilities and restrictions having a child brings. The middle-class parent is usually better able to find the books, groups, or experts to provide help than is the socioeconomically disadvantaged parent. Lillie noted that in parent programs for the disadvantaged, the purpose of **social and emotional support** is "to reduce anxieties . . . and feelings of inadequacy, and to provide socially stimulating activities which increase positive feelings about the family unit as well as the parent's feelings toward themselves as competent parents" (p. 9). Not only is help available from the program staff but, possibly of more importance, help is also available from other sets of parents who may have had similar problems or concerns with which they successfully dealt. Group meetings can be a powerful aspect of any parent education program.

Exchanging information is the second main area noted by Lillie. The goals in this area include helping the parents understand the purposes, objectives, and day-to-day aspects of the program; understanding how the program applies to their child and what the child does in the home; and obtaining background information on the child and further encouraging the parents to discuss how the program appears to be affecting the child at home. Methods that may be used to foster the exchange of information include notes, forms to be completed, newsletters, and phone calls, as well as personal interviews. One important point of the exchange aspect should be emphasized. In the past such activities have frequently resulted in a "talking to" rather than in a "talking with." The goal, obviously, is the latter.

The third area, **parent participation,** attempts to involve the parents in some aspect of the ongoing program. Parent participation not only provides needed help for the program but, more importantly, it provides the opportunity for the parents to observe other adults interacting with children in ways that may be new to them. That is, the staff and other parents may serve to model new and frequently more growth-enhancing ways for parents to interact with their children. Parent participation provides the opportunity for these new interaction patterns to be practiced under supervision. Once used and found successful, these newly learned methods of interacting may become part of the store of behaviors the parents use with their own children. Such activities instill in the parents a feeling of belonging to and of being responsible for a part of the program. Their children are not only consumers of the program, but they—the parents—are the providers of part of the program, which serves to enhance their feelings of self-worth.

The fourth area, **improving parent-child interactions,** which is really the end-result of the total program, helps develop those skills that "improve the effectiveness of parents as teachers and 'rearers' of their child[ren]" (p. 11). Lillie noted that in addition to those skills that promote general development of the child, skills are also needed in helping the parents use everyday experiences to promote social and emotional development and encourage linguistic growth in their child. In addition, they need skills in using the available community resources to foster their child's well-being and learning.

Programs for the Preschool Years

As the child grows older, it becomes possible to further enlarge his/her world. Now other adults and groups of children can enter the child's life as part of an organized preschool and kindergarten program in which formal instruction becomes the focus. This is the second approach to the education of the culturally different child.

> It includes motivating the child to find pleasure in learning. It involves developing the child's ability to attend to others and to engage in purposive action. It includes training the child to delay gratification of his desires and wishes and to work for rewards and goals which are more distant. It includes developing the child's view of adults as sources of information, and ideas, and also as sources of approval and reward. Through such development the child changes his self-expectations and his expectations of others. (Bloom, Davis, & Hess, 1965, p. 15)

Few areas in education have been anticipated with such great hope (Bloom, 1964; Hunt, 1964; Silberman, 1964) and dismissed as such a failure (Averch et al., 1972; Circirelli et al., 1969; Jencks et al., 1972) as the preschool education program Head Start. This dismissal, however, appears to be unwarranted. Brown (1977), in a reexamination of the studies that allegedly found Head Start not to be effective, noted that the studies ignored small cumulative effects. He noted that several studies that were first interpreted to be critical of the Head Start program must, upon reexamination, be considered to support the program. The criticism seems more justly directed toward the need for careful planning and structure of the Head Start programs: the gains made by children in well-structured programs far outweigh the lack of progress by children in less-structured programs.

A few of the noteworthy Head Start programs include the Academic Preschool developed in Champaign, Illinois, by Carl Bereiter and Siegfried Englemann. This program emphasizes the directed teaching of early academic skills using a highly structured approach. Bereiter and Englemann developed specific, limited educational goals, which served as the basis for the instructional program. Although critics have accused users of this approach of "force feeding" and criticized the program as an academic pressure cooker, the children appear to have benefited (Bereiter & Englemann, 1966). Another program of note is the Ypsilanti Perry Preschool Project (Weikart, 1967). This program developed a cognitively oriented curriculum based on the theories of Jean Piaget. Basic to this program is the development of logical modes of thought in the child. Many of the materials and activities used in this program are basically the same as found in most nursery school programs, but they were used in a more specific way in line with the theoretical orientation of the program. As a result of the program, most of the children were able to obtain greater benefits from the regular elementary school program (Ryan, 1974). The emphasis in these and many other successful preschool programs is on "Learning to Learn" (Bloom et al., 1965), which really means helping children attain a sense of pleasure in learning, developing attending skills, and being able to delay gratification, as much as it is on language development and cognitive development.

Programs During the School Years

There are now data indicating that gains made in preschool compensatory education programs can be maintained if the children receive a continuing

Getting an early "headstart" in the pleasure of learning and relating concepts, these youngsters are learning to distinguish self from others by drawing and cutting out life-size figures of themselves.

program, similar to Head Start in goals, during the school years (Seitz, Apfel, & Efron, 1977). Some of these continuation programs are known as "Follow Through." Many of these compensatory education programs for children of elementary-school age are concerned with developing a higher level of educational functioning in the basic skills, especially in reading. To this end many programs emphasize remedial reading. These programs, using such special material as programmed reading and reading labs—along with small group instruction by trained, enthusiastic teachers—have been able to have an impact on the reading performance of thousands of the children in the compensatory programs (Annual Reports, National Advisory Council on the Education of Disadvantaged Children, 1973, 1974, 1975, 1976). McCormick (1975) provided several examples of Follow Through projects. A few of them are:

a) the *Engelman-Becker Model for Direct Instruction,* which focuses on an accelerated rate of instruction of academic skills that builds upon the skills the child has and relies heavily on drill and repetition;

b) the *Tucson Early Education Model,* a process-oriented program that stresses "learning to learn";

c) the *English as a Second Language Model,* built on using bilingual education in reading and oral-language development.

Like the Head Start programs, most of the Follow Through programs involve the family to some degree. Preliminary evaluations of the Follow Through programs are at this point encouraging and warrant continuation (Emrick, Sorensen, & Stearns, 1973; Abelson, Ziegler, & DeBlasi, 1974). Some of the successful instructional techniques include cross-age tutoring, in which older children who are in the upper grades but who are poor readers are used to tutor younger children in reading. It appears that the older children get additional practice in reading, as well as an improved self-concept in acting as tutors; the younger children experience improved reading performance. McCormick (1975) indicated that both the younger and the older children benefit from such instruction. Team teaching, individualized instruction, and the use of programmed instruction have all been successfully used in Follow Through programs.

Other programs have been concerned with the plight of children of migrant farm workers. In 1974 approximately 380,000 migrant children in 49 states were enrolled in compensatory programs (National Advisory Council, 1975). These 380,000 children represented approximately 70 percent of the migrant children eligible for special programs at that time. And the problem is still with us. Most of these children are enrolled in elementary level programs; only a small percentage are in secondary level programs. The school dropout rate is very high; many children never reach the secondary school because they join their parents to work in the fields. It has been found that 60 percent of the workers do not speak English and that, for many of the children, English is used only as a second language. Further complicating the situation is the fact that the average time spent at any one camp site is 25 to 28 days, which means that there is very little continuity to formal education, even if the children of migrant workers continue to go to school.

The fact that many school programs are not relevant to the children is attested to by the high rate of truancy seen in many schools, especially in urban centers (Daugherty & Rudd, 1967). Among possible explanations for this high rate of truancy is that the program is of little interest to the child. This may be because he/she cannot experience success in the activities or that the goals of the school, as reflected in the curriculum, are too remote and the instruction too verbal and abstract. Successful programs select material appropriate for the child's current level of functioning, stress overlearning and differential practice, and provide carefully sequenced and well organized material (Ausubel, 1963).

Special education has grown into a program of educational services designed to meet the educational as well as the social and physical needs of all special children. As a result of the passage of the Education for All Handicapped Children Act, the new emphasis is on developing programs specifically for each child in the least restrictive educational environment consistent with the child's needs within the educational structure. Whenever possible, special children will now be placed in the regular classroom—the mainstream of education—for at least a portion of the day, with the addition of whatever services are needed to make the placement a productive one for the child.

The future of these new programs within special education depends on their proven effectiveness in the years to come. While the promise of a better education for the handicapped and the gifted is the goal, the final word on the efficacy and value of these educational programs for special children still awaits critical research evaluation.

SUMMARY

1. Special education for exceptional children has been an aspect of the services offered by the public schools since the latter half of the nineteenth century, but as late as 1975 only 50 percent of all exceptional children were enrolled in special education programs.

2. As a consequence of the passage by Congress of the Education for All Handicapped Children Act in 1975, all special children between the ages of 3 and 21 are to have special education services available to them by the 1980 school year.

3. Because it is difficult for a smaller community to provide the array of needed services and educational alternatives for all special children, cooperative programs that include several communities are being widely developed.

4. Special education programs need several placement alternatives so that the programs can offer each special child the least restrictive educational placement based on the educational and social goals for the individual.

5. Mainstreaming is the least restrictive of all possible special educational placements, but mainstreaming is not appropriate for all handicapped children.

6. Teaching strategies and individual educational programs must be developed to meet the special needs of each exceptional child.

7. Though not considered exceptional children, culturally different children are frequently in need of special educational attention.

8. Compensatory programs for culturally different children have been developed, with varying degrees of success, at the preschool level, as well as the elementary and secondary levels.

9. Programs that foster parent involvement and education have been an integral part of the overall programs for culturally different children.

CHAPTER SIXTEEN

Child Advocacy and Services for Special Children

We can, Will we?

We can markedly reduce mental retardation, developmental disabilities, infantile or early childhood mental illness. Will we? We can either prevent or intervene early into a wide variety of learning and behavior disorders of childhood. We can alter educational patterns to enhance learning and promote problem solving skills in school. Will we? We can work effectively with parents to help them help their own children to learn. We can show parents how to assume responsibility for reducing children's psychotic symptoms and disability from a wide variety of neurophysiologic disorders noted shortly after birth. Will we? We can change patterns of health and mental health care and provide neighborhood advocacy for children and families. Will we? We can reduce crime, delinquency, drug and alcohol abuse. We can eliminate poverty and reduce racism. Will we?

Norman V. Lourie & Irving N. Berlin (1975, p. 311)

INTRODUCTION

In the closing decades of the twentieth century, the provision of adequate services for the needs of special children is increasingly becoming a matter of political and legal action. Significant changes have occurred in our very views of childhood itself, of healthy child development, and of the nature of intervention programs needed to help children—especially special children—achieve maturity and reach their full human potential. In the present century there has been a growing realization that children have special needs and must be extended certain protections of their rights if the opportunity for optimal development is to be achieved. But the challenge ahead is that of implementing recognition into action.

Many service delivery systems have their roots in previous generations that were less sensitive to the child as a person, and established systems often resist change. Organized political and legal actions are increasingly viewed as the most effective tool to temper public indifference and/or bureaucratic ineptitude. More and more frequently, child advocates are promoting the rights of children in the courtroom: to date, the results have been mixed, but the dedication of today's child advocates promises a brighter future.

In the final analysis, the issue of adequacy and continuity of services for special children seems very much dependent upon persistent, organized efforts for such services. In this concluding chapter, we will address three major concerns related to providing services: the problems in current service delivery systems for special children, the status of children's rights, and the nature of child advocacy.

PROBLEMS IN SERVICE DELIVERY SYSTEMS

As we have seen throughout this book, a wide variety of services are possible for the particular needs of specific populations of special children. Our approach has been to review those forms of direct clinical services that are currently practiced in the diagnosis and treatment of the problems of special childhood. We have seen that these services include such varied forms of intervention as special education administered by a state or local board of education, surgical procedures administered by children's hospitals, residential placement services administered by state departments of children and family services, and psychotherapy or behavior therapy provided by a private practitioner or child guidance clinic. In this section we will take a slightly broader view of services for special children and attempt to provide a general overview of the problems facing service delivery systems.

There are many different kinds of organizations that foster or provide services for special children. A **service delivery system** is simply any organization or organized set of procedures by which some form of service is made available to the public. Service delivery systems typically provide a specific type of service, such as administrative, medical, legal, educational, social, or psychological. Service delivery systems can function at the national, state, and local levels; they may be public (publicly legislated and publicly funded) or private (voluntary and privately funded). Lourie (1975a) estimated that between 400 and 500 different federal grant programs flow downward to state and local governments and providers of services. This vast network of services for special children is beset by a number of problems and relevant criticisms (Collins, 1975; Lourie, 1975a).

First, many programs for children are institution-centered rather than child-centered. This is perhaps the major "illness" of all bureaucracies: as institutions evolve and become entrenched, they tend to serve themselves rather than the goals for which they were founded and funded. Consider the following example. A program is started to serve the needs of mentally retarded children. The first phase of the program is to provide diagnostic services, and a number of staff are hired who are skilled in psychological testing. The program begins by providing psychological testing services for children who are suspected of being mentally retarded. Difficulties consequently arise in the establishment of the treatment phase of the program. Instead of intensifying efforts at developing the treatment phase, the administration and staff of the program simply settle back and continue to provide diagnosis without treatment. Service arrangements all too frequently tend to be oriented to the needs of the professionals, administrative staffs, and interest groups who provide or support service rather than those for whom the service is intended.

A second problem of service delivery systems is that they are frequently fragmented and tend to compete with each other for the same public tax dollar. For example, in many metropolitan areas, there may be several service agencies that provide outpatient psychotherapy for emotionally disturbed children. Each of the agencies serves a limited number of clients, and centralization of the services would be much less costly. Despite this knowledge, the agencies continue to fight for their own lives and submit grants for support of services that are clearly unnecessary for the community and merely redupli- cate the programs of competing agencies. In the same way, new service sys- tems are frequently created without awareness of existing services or needs. Such programs typically fail to evolve a comprehensive service, so that only one aspect of a child's needs is addressed.

A third problem of service delivery systems is that they often tend to be unresponsive to genuine needs. On the one hand, only a small percentage of the target population is typically served; on the other hand, those members of the target population that need the services most badly are often screened out. For example, a residential treatment program may be established in a poverty area to provide treatment for adolescents who come from broken homes and disruptive families. The adolescents who need this service the most—namely those from the most chaotic family situations—typically display behavior problems that are difficult to manage and treat. The program, there- fore, may find it easier to serve adolescents who come from more intact families and who are less difficult to control. Thus, there is often a tendency among service organizations to "serve safe risks" deliberately.

Fourth, most service providers do not view the child as existing in a distinct series of developmental stages. Although developmental continuity should be a distinguishing feature of children's programs, programs are in- frequently planned to follow the child throughout the developmental period. For example, a particular program may be funded to provide a maximum of two years of residential treatment for adolescents with conduct disorders; it is known that most of the children who complete the program cannot be re- turned to their families of origin. When sixteen-year-olds are accepted, they are eighteen at the completion of the program and can be moved directly to independent living. When thirteen-year-olds are accepted, however, they are only fifteen at the completion of the program. Many of the residents will have used up their funding and be inappropriately referred to inadequate foster placements where treatment gains are quickly lost. A program that does not account for the child as a developing, dependent being does not serve the child's needs.

Fifth, service programs tend to avoid evaluation of the effectiveness of their own services. Follow-up and evaluation of effectiveness are critical in the discovery of what works and what doesn't work. Administrators of pro- grams may fear that evaluation of effectiveness may actually demonstrate in- effectiveness of service, which in turn might reduce or eliminate funding. Fortunately, federal agencies that provide funding seem increasingly inclined to require ongoing program evaluation. Title III of Public Law 94-63 (1975), for example, requires that federally funded community mental health agencies conduct a continuing evaluation of the effectiveness of programs. This law mandates the use of an amount not less than 2 percent of the annual operat- ing expenses of the agency for the purpose of evaluation and further requires that the program measure its effectiveness in meeting the actual mental health needs of the area (Koocher & Broskowski, 1977).

Sixth, all services for special children are weakened by the absence of a national strategy to implement programs for the health, education, and welfare of children. In the absence of an integrated strategy, four separate streams of federal activity operate independently of each other: a child health institute of research within the National Institutes of Health (National Institute of Child Health and Human Development); grants to the states for maternal and child health services (Medical Services Administration); various types of services for children identified as handicapped, disabled, or exceptional (Bureau of Education for the Handicapped); and various types of diagnostic and treatment services for children who are on welfare (Health Services Administration) (Steiner, 1976). The separateness of these four distinct forms of federal involvement tends to create situations in which the left hand does not know what the right hand is doing. There is currently no administrative or legislative mechanism for bringing these different levels of federal involvement under a single, comprehensive agency.

Many other criticisms, of course, can be leveled at service delivery systems for special children, but those mentioned above tend to strike at the very heart of the problem. In the main, bureaucratic difficulties tend to hinder the establishment of comprehensive, responsive services for all special children. (Exhibit 16.1 presents but one outcome of such bureaucratic diffi-

EXHIBIT 16.1

RULE BACKFIRES ON HANDICAP AID

A Board of Education program to help parents learn to cope with infants with severe hearing and vision problems is in danger of being wiped out because of a new federal law to ensure education for handicapped children.

For five years, the parent-infant program at Skinner Elementary School, 111 S. Troop St., Chicago, Illinois, has been a haven for parents facing the sudden shock of knowing that their babies can't hear or see or have other severe physical or mental problems. The program serves 69 infants—from 8 months to 3 years of age.

Mothers bring their youngsters twice a week to the school. A teacher works with the child in simple learning exercises with the mother first observing, then joining in.

Ernest Boyer, United States commissioner of education, hailed the program as "a model for the nation" during a visit to Skinner a few weeks ago.

Ironically, what threatens the parent-infant classes is a federal law, "The Education for All Handicapped" measure, that is supposed to ensure educational opportunities for all children.

"The law is great, but it doesn't apply to us," said Mrs. Albert Bryant, coordinator of the parent-infant program.

The law requires schools to provide "a free and appropriate education" for all handicapped children and young people from ages 3 through 21. In the past, schools sometimes turned away children with severe handicaps because the schools supposedly did not have the facilities and teaching abilities to educate them.

But the new law starts with the age of 3 and does not provide for use of funds for infant programs. Neither is there any state law enabling schools to use state or local funds for the small children.

Arthur M. Shapiro, Skinner's principal, said legislatures in other Midwestern states—Wisconsin, Michigan, Iowa, and Minnesota among them—have passed bills permitting programs for children under 3. But not Illinois.

Skinner's parent-infant program is receiving $300,000 in federal funds this school year, but no money can be used after July 1, Shapiro said....

Parents in the Skinner program say the classes have been a godsend in helping infants begin the long road toward learning to live with their handicaps. By the age of 3, when they enter the regular programs for handicapped pupils, they may have mastered many basic self-help and communications skills, and come from happy, secure homes because the parents have learned how to cope with them, Shapiro said.

A year ago, Patricia Higuet was struggling to cope with her son, Raymond, now 2, who has a severe hearing problem. "He should have been talking, but he wasn't," she said. "He was afraid of being with another person. We didn't know how to handle him."

But through Children's Memorial Hospital, she heard about the Skinner program. "Now he is able to communicate," she said. "He can make sounds and gestures. He can tell us what he wants."

The program has monthly meetings for parents with experts in pediatrics to discuss the unique problems of handicapped infants. Teachers visit homes at least monthly to see how well mothers are applying the lessons.

From C. B. Banas, *The Chicago Tribune*, February 6, 1978

culties.) Despite these difficulties, of course, many individual programs or communities develop outstanding service systems. And yet, the problems that exist in services for special children tend to underline the fact that children in contemporary America lack a representative voice in the control of their own destinies.

CURRENT STATUS OF CHILDREN'S RIGHTS

Attempts to define and implement the rights of children have met with varying degrees of unbounded enthusiasm and cautious alarm. Assertions of children's rights are frequently threatening to adult caretakers; they also pose timely and costly implications for public policy. The passage of The Education for All Handicapped Children Act (P.L. 94-142), for example, has been the bane of many educators and educational administrators because the Act requires extensive changes in the ways that school systems respond to the educational needs of special children; under the new law, the rights of special children to equal educational opportunity are more specifically defined and more adequately safeguarded.

In this respect, however, the Joint Commission on the Mental Health of Children has noted:

> We believe that every American child has the right to a mentally healthy life of well-being and effectiveness. If we are to fulfill this right, we must face squarely the social crises of our times and commit ourselves to radical social change. (1973, p. 8)

The question of radical social change is disturbing to many Americans, and the implication of the Joint Commission is that attitudes toward children's rights may well prove to be as difficult to change as the social conditions that underlie many of the problems of special children. In the following sections, we will examine the status of children under the law and review the empirical research regarding attitudes toward children's rights.

The Status of Children Under the Law

The legal rights of children to special services remains an area of conflict and confusion. As Goldstein, Freud, and Solnit (1973) observed:

The child is singled out by law, as by custom, for special attention. The law distinguishes between adult and child in physical, psychological, and societal terms. Adults are presumed to be responsible for themselves and capable of deciding what is in their own interests. Therefore, the law is by and large designed to safeguard their right to order their personal affairs free of government intrusion. Children, on the other hand, are presumed to be incomplete beings who are not fully competent to determine and safeguard their interests. They are seen as dependent and in need of direct, intimate, and continuous care by the adults who are personally committed to assume such responsibility. (p. 3)

Neither philosophically nor legally are children recognized as having rights to do anything about their own lives. The best that they can do is await the actions of well-intentioned adults on their behalf. This powerlessness of children under the law has been called "the last relic of feudalism" (Wald, 1974).

The legal rights of special children are being grudgingly defined on an issue-by-issue and case-by-case basis. A number of these rights are being prosecuted at this writing, and some very significant issues currently stand before local and state courts. Polier (1976) discussed four significant rights issues currently needing legal clarification.

The first of these involves the right of a child deprived of freedom "under the name of treatment" to receive *appropriate* treatment. This issue is particularly relevant for special children placed in institutional treatment facilities for the mentally retarded or the behaviorally disturbed, or in special schools for the blind or the deaf. When children are placed in such facilities, they have a right to actual treatment for their disabilities, rather than mere custodial care alone. The special child is a developing being, and treatment facilities must make every effort to ensure the integrity of the child's development.

The right of the special child to an education is now a matter of law. Here a parent meets with teachers to provide input into the planning of an individual educational program for her child.

477
Current status of
children's rights

The second issue involves the right of a child to be protected from cruel and unusual punishment in the name of treatment. Children who are placed in institutions for the emotionally disturbed, the mentally retarded, or the physically disabled frequently present problems of control and behavior management. Staff in such institutions must be prevented from aggressive and intrusive forms of control, such as solitary confinement or the use of chemotherapy without medical supervision. When children are difficult to manage, there is a tendency to view them as "inmates" rather than as "patients." Special children who are placed under such circumstances are simply defenseless.

A third issue involves the right of the child to receive services within his/her own state and as close to home as possible. This right falls under the general issue of "least restrictive placement." When a state does not have a particular type of service, the state has the duty to develop the service rather than commit the child to the services of another state. Removing the child from his/her loved ones and community can impede the child's development unnecessarily.

The last issue involves the need to defend children against a host of possible violations of their right to equal protection under the constitution. Some of these violations include such factors as exclusion from voluntary agencies on the basis of sex, race, or religion; state licensing of services that are discriminatory; and failure to provide equal opportunities for foster placement as a function of color or cultural difference. The role of the courts in advancing the rights of children who need special services cannot be underestimated. The courts have the power to direct correction of injustices within child service systems. There are signs, however, that the courts do not always welcome the advocacy of children's rights. Exhibit 16.2 gives an example of the kind of setbacks that can occur when cases are pressed to the Supreme Court.

Research on Attitudes Toward Children's Rights

There has been a paucity of research regarding attitudes affecting the rights of children. Several papers have commented on the status of current research and the difficulties inherent in conducting such research (Hyman, Petruzzi, & Schlossman, 1976; Kamerman, Kahn, & McGowan, 1972), but few studies have attempted direct assessment of attitudes toward the rights of children. Two studies that have done so have revealed some interesting data. Actual research seems to indicate that attitudes regarding the rights of children may well be less negative than most professionals have supposed to be the case.

Wrightsman, Rogers, and Percy (1975) developed a conceptualization of children's rights, as well as a scale for measuring attitudes toward such rights. These authors first defined five broad classes of rights currently being advocated for children: rights to care, rights to health and safety, rights to education and information, economic rights, and legal-judicial-political rights. They then categorized these rights under two major orientations: a nurturance orientation (stressing the provision by society of beneficial privileges, experiences, and environments) and a self-determination orientation (stressing the child's capacity to exercise control over relevant aspects of his/her life). A 300-

SUPREME COURT REFUSED TO RULE IN CHILDREN'S RIGHTS CASE

On May 16, 1977, the Supreme Court refused to render a judgment in an important children's rights case, *Bartley v. Kremens*. In this case, the State of Pennsylvania was accused of having violated due process clauses of the Constitution by committing five children to state mental institutions with both the approval of the parents and a certifying physician *but against the consent of the children involved.*

The Supreme Court voted 7 to 2 against deciding the case, stating that a new state law and new state regulations governing confinement had made the case impossible, in its present form, to decide. The result of this "decision not to decide" was to annul the decision of a lower court "that children, like adults, are entitled to legal representation and to other procedural safeguards" (*New York Times*, May 22, 1977).

Justices William J. Brennan, Jr., and Thurgood Marshall dissented, stating that the majority had shirked its responsibility to render a decision. Child advocates may well see this decision by the Court as a setback to the children's rights movement and may find the decision "further evidence (if any is needed) that the secret and sometimes not-so-secret target of all reactionaries is the dangerous subversive called Child" (*Behavior Today*, May 30, 1977, p. 7).

item questionnaire based on the five classes of the rights of children aged 10 to 14 was then given to four different groups: high-school juniors and seniors, undergraduate education majors, undergraduate liberal arts majors, and school teachers attending summer school classes. The findings supported the hypothesis that nurturance orientation and self-determination orientation were two distinct classes of rights. Two significant group differences were found. High-school students held less favorable attitudes toward the nurturance rights of children and more favorable attitudes toward self-determination rights of children, and females were more likely to endorse nurturance rights than males. Perhaps the most interesting finding was that the adolescent group endorsed more strongly the right of self-determination for children than did the other groups in this study.

Suran and Lavigne (1977) compared the attitudes of parents and various groups of health care professionals toward two different bills of rights for children in hospital settings: the bill of rights developed by the National Association of Children's Hospitals and Related Institutions (NACHRI) and a locally developed bill of rights for a children's hospital. Each respondent rated statements drawn from the respective bills from "strongly agree" to "strongly disagree." A high level of agreement for both bills was found for all groups, but the local bill was significantly preferred. Attending and resident physicians were significantly lower in agreement than most other groups on 11 of the 32 statements surveyed; and they disagreed most strongly on statements involving rights—such as the child's right to privacy when being examined, the child's right to consent to care, the child's right to have an immediate, understandable diagnosis from a physician. Despite the strong disagreement of physicians to certain rights of child patients that might alter common medical practice, there was a higher level of endorsement for the rights of children in medical settings than the researchers had originally expected. In view of the far-reaching implications of such rights, one might well expect far greater opposition by those so directly involved in the care of hospitalized children.

Research involving attitudes toward children's rights is clearly still in its infancy. Although the presumption of opposition to the rights of children must be well taken, radical social change in this regard may be less necessary than was predicted by the Joint Commission on the Mental Health of Children. Let us now examine the nature of child advocacy.

CHILD ADVOCACY

Because of the many difficulties involved in the delivery of services to special children, as well as the often confusing nature of children's rights under the law, child advocacy has become a growing necessity in contemporary society. The term "child advocacy" is increasingly being used to describe both the concept itself and the range of activities involved in identifying the unmet needs of children, as well as in rectifying existing abuses of children's rights. Since one of the central goals of advocacy is to stimulate public response to identified needs and abuses, there is considerable public confusion regarding the meaning and intentions of the child advocacy movement. Child advocacy is, in fact, a wide-ranging movement that has several meanings and that functions at different levels. In this section we will review both the concept and the current types of child advocacy.

The Concept of Advocacy

In the general sense, an *advocate* is someone who pleads the cause of another or who defends or maintains a particular cause or proposal. As a general movement, **child advocacy** can be defined as any social, political, or legal action that is intended to achieve a better life for children from infancy to adulthood (Lourie, 1975b). Although many of the actions of child advocates are expressly directed to the needs of special children, child advocacy itself is a broader movement that applies to all children.

An example of one form of child advocacy was introduced at a forum of the Colorado Juvenile and Family Court. A recommendation of this forum was to appoint a responsible member of the community to function as the child advocate: "the advocate primarily would be the day-to-day protector in the community of the child's rights in nearly all areas of child concern. He would step in when the child's liberty or health is jeopardized, whenever he is deprived of a home, schooling, medical care, property rights, entitlements or benefits, or is subject to involuntary treatment" (Epstein, 1971, p. 6). In this sense, advocacy involves the designation of a representative within the community who exercises responsibility to protect the civil and personal rights of the child. It is interesting to note that this concept of the child advocate is not significantly different than that of the "tithingman" advanced in seventeenth century New England (see Chapter 1). While societies change, the needs of children remain the same.

At the national level in 1970, the Joint Commission on the Mental Health of Children proposed sweeping recommendations, urging all levels of government to act as advocates for children by expanding existing services of a supportive, preventive, or remedial nature as well as fostering research in the area of child development and the remediation of the problems of childhood. The Joint Commission urged the establishment of a *national advocacy system* spearheaded in the Office of the President but extending its influence downward to various health, social, and educational services throughout the country. Advocacy in this sense intends to define and propagate a national mentality that would service the needs of all children, but especially the needs of the handicapped or disadvantaged.

Child advocacy, therefore, is as much an attitude of mind as it is a form of concerted action on behalf of children. Advocacy groups have been formed for such diverse causes as children's nutritional needs, monitoring the rights of poor and minority children, and advocating the needs of particular populations of special children. In a broad sense, every effort on behalf of a child or the needs of children is an advocacy effort. In fact, so many forms of advocacy have come into existence that in 1971 the Department of Health, Education, and Welfare established a National Center for Child Advocacy. Attempting to limit the concept of advocacy, the National Center has endorsed the distinction between child welfare and child advocacy. *Child welfare* is a form of intervention whose primary concern is the child's family or surrogate family; *child advocacy* is a form of intervention whose primary concern is the set of secondary institutions surrounding the child—such as schools, programs of special education, service agencies, and juvenile courts (Kahn, Kamerman, & McGowan, 1972). The concept of advocacy in contemporary America is still developing, however, and will likely undergo considerable change and clarification in the next few decades.

Current Forms of Child Advocacy

There are several forms of child advocacy especially relevant to special children. Since advocacy for special children involves social, political, or legal action on behalf of special children, these forms of child advocacy can be thought of as strategies to bring about more favorable conditions for special children. Knitzer (1976) discussed five distinct strategies of child advocacy: case advocacy, class action litigation, monitoring, legislative advocacy, and administrative advocacy.

Case advocacy

Case advocacy functions in the interest of a specific child and seeks to secure for the child those services to which the child is entitled. The objectives of case advocacy include such issues as gaining or increasing existing rights, services, or resources; developing new rights, services, or resources; and preventing or limiting the client's involvement with inappropriate or ineffective services (Grosser & McGowan, 1975; McGowan, 1973). The child advocate who serves as the day-to-day protector of children in a given community would be an example of case advocacy in action. Most forms of legal action

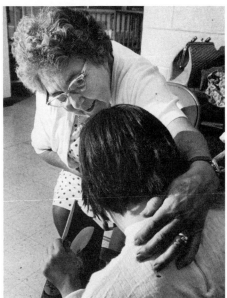

An RSVP volunteer encouraging a cerebral palsied boy in his painting, a foster grandparent comforting a disturbed child, a teacher guiding a retarded child toward the delight of discovery—each can be an advocate for special children. Perhaps most inspiring can be the advocacy of special children themselves—like the deaf youths shown above left who can grow into the advocates of the future.

on behalf of a particular special child would also constitute a form of case advocacy.

Case advocacy, however, also involves a series of efforts that are directed toward bringing attention to the rights of special children. The National Information Center for the Handicapped (a project of the Bureau of Education for the Handicapped), for example, publishes a newsletter that is intended to inform the parents of special children about issues relevant to their child. With the passage of Public Law 94-142, an entire issue of the newsletter (*Closer Look*, Fall 1977) was directed to informing parents of their rights under the new law. Exhibit 16.3 gives an example of the kind of advice *Closer Look* provides to parents so that they might act as case advocates for their children.

Class action litigation

Legal action on behalf of a class of children is a form of advocacy in which the courts are used to promote change. Class action litigation for special children can be invoked for a variety of purposes: to remove children from mental institutions when there is the appearance that they have been committed by parents as a punitive action; to secure services for special children who have been excluded from public schools; to remove children from special classes that parents consider to be inappropriate. In many instances, the use of class action litigation can be a critical method of defining or enforcing children's rights. One of the better known examples of this fact is *PARC* v. *Pennsylvania* (1971), in which the parents of special children questioned the constitutionality of school policies and practices that excluded certain special children from a public education. The court ruled that all special children have a right to public education and mandated the state of Pennsylvania to provide appropriate public education for all special children. This decision in the state courts was an important step in defining those rights that eventuated in Public Law 94-142, the Education for All Handicapped Children Act (Lippman & Goldberg, 1973).

Monitoring

A monitor is simply someone who "watches over something or someone" (Knitzer, 1976). The purpose of monitoring in child advocacy is to hold systems accountable for rights to service that have already been defined and upheld by law or legal action. In *PARC* v. *Pennsylvania*, for example, the court actually appointed a team that would oversee the eventual implementation of its ruling regarding the right to public education. In most cases, the courts are unable to oversee such rulings, so monitoring becomes an important function of parent groups and child advocacy organizations.

Legislative advocacy

Legislative advocacy seeks to ensure that laws themselves are appropriate to the needs and rights of children. Those who are involved with the needs of children must be willing to bring pressure to bear at both federal and state levels in order to ensure the adequacy of legislation that affects rights to critical services. Public Law 94-142 is a splendid example of the central importance of legislation as a means of addressing the needs of special children.

EXHIBIT 16.3

483
Child advocacy

DUE PROCESS IN A NUTSHELL

[The following is] a quick review to keep in mind the main steps involved in due process. Each of these steps reinforces your right to stay on top of decisions about your child.

1. You must receive notice in writing before the school system takes (or recommends) any action that may change your child's school program. Notice in writing is also required if a school refuses to take action to change your child's program.

2. You have the right to give—or withhold—permission for your child to be: tested to determine whether or not he requires special education services (identification); evaluated by specialists to determine what his educational needs are (evaluation); placed in a specific school program to meet his needs (placement).

3. You have the right to see and examine all school records related to the identification, evaluation and placement of your child. If you find that certain records are inaccurate or misleading, you have the right to ask that they be removed from your child's file. Once removed, they may *not* be used in planning for your child's placement.

4. If you do not agree with the school's course of action at *any* point along the way, you have the right to request an impartial due process hearing. This means that you can initiate a hearing to protest any decision related to identification, evaluation or placement of your child.

5. If you fail to win your case, you have the right to appeal the results of the due process hearing to the State Department of Education; and you can appeal to the courts if you lose your case at the state level.

Calling for a due process hearing is your right, but remember that it can be an exhausting process. Before going this route, be sure you have tried to settle differences through every other means— by being as persuasive as possible in meetings with teachers, the principal, special education administrators. If you know that you're up against a brick wall, and you're sure that a due process hearing must be held to resolve conflicting points of view, then you must prepare your case as thoroughly as possible. Be sure to get help from an advocacy group or a lawyer who is familiar with education law and procedures in your state, or an experienced parent. (According to law, the school system must tell you about sources of free or low-cost legal aid. Ask for this information.)

Know your rights at a hearing:

- The hearing officer must be impartial, may not be employed by the school district or involved in the education of your child.
- You have the right to legal counsel (which includes the advice and support of any advocate, not necessarily a lawyer); to examine witnesses; present evidence; ask questions of school spokespeople; obtain a record of the hearing and all of its findings.

NOTE: Write directly to the superintendent of schools in your district to request a hearing. Hearings must be held not later than 45 days after requested. State Departments of Education must review appeals within 30 days.

From *Closer Look* (Fall 1977, p. 3)

There are many strategies to achieve needed legislation, of course, but one of the most important is the lobby. Lobbying is the direct participation in the political process to achieve desired ends. Knitzer (1976) cautioned that lobbies can be a torturous experience because of the immense costs that are involved;

OPEN ISSUE

Class action litigation can be a two-edged sword when it pits interest groups against each other. In some cases, class action litigation intended to benefit a particular group of special children can have adverse effects on another group of special children. This is precisely what took place in California regarding the issue of placement of children in special education classes for the educably mentally handicapped (EMH).

As Mercer and Richardson (1975) reported, up until 1969, California, as did most states, had a program whereby children who tested below a specific intelligence criterion were typically recommended for placement in EMH classes. In 1969, however, a class action suit was filed on behalf of Mexican-American children, charging that intellectual assessment procedures used by the State Board of Education were culturally biased and that Mexican-American children were being misdiagnosed and unfairly placed in EMH classes (*Diana et al.* v. *State Board of Education,* 1969). In response to this class action, a bill that sought to lower the criterion for placement in EMH classes was introduced into the state legislature. The proposal would have had the effect of eliminating placement in EMH classes for the great majority of Mexican-American children who had been previously diagnosed as educably mentally handicapped. At the same time, however, it would also have eliminated many Anglo-American children from these classes. A number of Anglo-American parent organizations were outraged and opposed this suggested lowering of the criterion for EMH placement; they felt that their children who were classified as EMH were properly placed, and they viewed the EMH placement as a desirable and necessary service.

A settlement was negotiated in this case. The settlement, in effect, involved agreement to a more flexible criterion in which the unanimous consent of the involved parties was the key factor in any special education placement decision.

Similar class action litigations continue to be brought in many states, as well as California, involving the assessment of minority children with conventional testing procedures. Many black and Latino spokespersons view conventional assessment instruments as culturally biased and discriminatory. In some cases (e.g., *Larry P. et al.* v. *Wilson Riles et al.,* 1972), the courts have upheld the contention that intelligence tests are culturally biased and tend to discriminate against minorities. In California, alternate plans are being devised to assist students who would have been previously classified as EMH on the basis of psychological and intellectual assessments. Students who have difficulty coping with school demands because of cultural or socioeconomic differences will no longer be labeled EMH. Rather, they will be given individualized instruction, resource rooms, and other supplementary programs, while remaining within regular classes (Mercer & Richardson, 1975). Thus, despite the controversies involved, class action litigation can still serve the interests of all special children.

---

she also noted, however, that children's lobbies have been formed at the state level in California and at a regional level in western Pennsylvania. Efforts to form a national children's lobby have proven to be ineffective to date (Steiner, 1976).

Administrative advocacy

Administrative advocacy is directed at those who administer governmental agencies and services. Administrators are frequently in a position to make decisions of considerable consequence. Although most government programs have guidelines that limit the personal decision-making process, administrative officials must still be held responsible by and to their constituencies. In a state Department of Children and Family Services, for example, the assignment of funds for specific programs and services is often a function of *awareness* of need, access to responsible officials, and outright political pressure. Child advocates can be most effective in voicing the needs of particular populations of special children and orchestrating public pressure on administrators to be responsive to defined needs.

CLOSING REMARKS

Those of us who have been raised in the midst of the great American dream maintain optimism that all things can be accomplished. We believe that medical, biomedical, psychological, and educational research will one day be effective in preventing and curing all forms of childhood disabilities. We believe that with grit and determination the life of any special child can be made better. We believe that there is reason to work hard for the accomplishment of such ends.

And yet, it must be admitted that there is no unified strategy of intervention that has been developed for special children. We are frequently effective with a given child or with a group of children. Nonetheless, we lack a master plan. As Steiner (1976) pointed out: "Children's issues are too often the province of social reformers and child-welfare workers whose support for an increased public role in children's lives invariably shows enthusiasm, compassion, and a sense of mission but is less frequently accompanied by specific and tested plans for implementing their goals" (p. 241).

An effective strategy of intervention with special children requires coordinated planning in research, training, and services at the federal level. In the absence of a federal strategy, coordination of services within the individual states remains problematic and uncertain. Direct services at the community and local levels can only suffer from federal and state obscurities in the planning and administration of services for special children. Though the needs of some individual children may be met, many children will remain unserved.

The fact that many children are not being served should be less a reason for discouragement than a spur to greater accomplishment. Although effective intervention with particular populations of special children dates back several centuries, special childhood as a field of study for the relevant helping professions is still in its infancy. The most exciting discoveries lie ahead.

The future holds great promise. The signs are on the horizon. Medical breakthroughs in the prevention and treatment of many organic disorders that threaten the integrity of children's bodies are but a step away. Basic knowledge of the essentials of healthy psychological development mounts daily in the professional and scientific journals and is increasingly available to concerned parents. Educational approaches to special children now offer a variety of possible interventions to suit the specific needs of the individual child. Carefully developed social programs have demonstrated, at least with limited populations, that the adverse effects of poverty, prejudice, and ignorance can be negated as relevant factors in a child's development.

The promise of the future, however, must be tempered with the lessons of the past. Children are defenseless beings. In times of trouble, they suffer first and most. A society that lacks a vigorous philosophy of humane care for its offspring will inevitably abandon the needs of the powerless in its own struggle for survival. Contemporary America is at a turning point in history. Grudgingly, but with increasing clarity, the special child—indeed all children— are being defined by courts throughout the land as genuine persons with rights to equal protection under the law.

Those who work with special children must be guided by this sensitivity to the child as a person, as an equal. Itard knew it instinctively when he first encountered the Wild Boy of Aveyron. William Howe knew it to be the central issue when he undertook to teach the deaf-mute Laura Bridgman. No matter how damaged or disordered a child might appear to be, the child's personhood cannot be questioned. The real issue with special children is how much of their potential will be realized.

SUMMARY

1. A service delivery system is an organization or organized set of procedures by which some form of specific service (medical, psychological, educational, social, legal, administrative) is made available to the public.

2. Some of the more central problems with current service delivery systems for special children include: institution-centered rather than child-centered programs, fragmentation of services, lack of response to genuine needs, lack of a developmental perspective, lack of adequate evaluation of effectiveness, and absence of a national strategy to implement programs for the health, education, and welfare of children.

3. Among the more pressing legal issues facing special children, the following are most significant: the right of a child deprived of freedom "under the name of treatment" to receive appropriate treatment; the right of the child to be protected from cruel and unusual punishment in the name of treatment; the right of the child to receive services within his/her own state and as close to home as possible; the right to equal protection under the constitution.

4. Although there has been a paucity of research regarding attitudes toward children's rights, some studies suggest that opposition to changes in children's rights may be less intense than might be supposed.

5. Child advocacy can be defined as any social, political, or legal action that is intended to achieve a better life for children from infancy to adulthood.

6. The most common types of child advocacy are case advocacy, class action litigation, monitoring, legislative advocacy, and administrative advocacy.

Glossary

Ability grouping. Refers to removal of children from heterogeneous classroom settings to classrooms composed of children with similar ability levels.

Academic underachievement. Occurs when a child's actual achievement lags behind the achievement level expected of a child of her/his chronological age.

Acceleration. Promoting a bright child beyond the grade level appropriate to his/her chronological age.

Accommodation. Piaget's term for the process of modifying existing patterns of motor behavior to cope with different conditions.

Acquired hearing loss. Hearing disability developed any time after birth.

Activity group therapy. A form of group psychotherapy in which the interactions of the group members are organized around specific activities, such as crafts or games. *See* **Group therapy.**

Administrative advocacy. Advocacy directed at those who administer governmental agencies and services.

Advanced placement. Allowing bright students to demonstrate competency in required areas by means of testing or review of credentials.

Advocate. Someone who pleads the cause of another or who defends or maintains a particular cause or proposal.

Amplification. Intensification of sound through mechanical or electrical means.

Anacusis. *See* **Total hearing loss.**

Anal stage. A psychodynamic concept introduced by Freud describing the psychosexual stage in which the infant focuses libidinal energy on the anal area and the mastery of processes of elimination.

Animistic. Attributing to inanimate objects the characteristics of life.

Anoxia. Loss of oxygen.

Anxiety reaction. The experience of intense, diffuse anxiety not associated with specific objects or situations. *See* **Psychoneurotic disorder/anxiety type.**

Aphasia. Disability in use of words.

Articulation disorders. Speech errors in which the child omits or distorts word sounds, substitutes one word sound for another, or adds irrelevant sounds to words.

Assessment procedures. Procedures that facilitate the diagnostic process, including standardized observation methods of demonstrable validity and reliability.

Assimilation. Piaget's term for the process of receiving information and stimulation from the environment.

Association. Process through which central nervous system mediating processes relate encoding and decoding and permit use of linguistic symbols.

Atropinization. Aspiration of the eye with an alkaloid drug (atropine) used in treating cataracts.

Audiologist. A specialist in the assessment of hearing functions and hearing impairments.

Audiometer. Primary hearing assessment device that permits the controlled presentation and measurement of sounds.

Automatic sequential capacities. Individual's capacity to retain and automatically execute acceptable grammatical habits.

Baseline. Frequency of a target behavior measured under specific, naturally occurring conditions prior to treatment intervention.

Behavioral pharmacology. *See* **Psychopharmacology.**

Behavioral play audiometry. Used for children with limited language. The child is conditioned to make structured play responses when presented with sounds through a set of earphones.

Behavior therapy. The application of scientifically derived principles of experimental and social psychology to the alleviation of human problems; views behavior as a function of antecedent conditions and consequent events.

Bilateral hearing impairment. Impairment affecting both ears.

Blindisms. The self-stimulating, directionless, rhythmic movements often typical of blind children.

Braille. A touch system involving embossed points used for reading and writing. Consists of 63 characters that are alphabetical, numerical, and grammatical.

Case advocacy. Support in the interest of a specific individual, seeking to secure the services to which the individual is entitled.

Case assignment nursing. Use of a single nurse in providing for the complete care of a given patient.

Cataract. Cloudiness in the lens of the eye that prevents passage of light through pupil to retina.

Central auditory hearing loss. Hearing loss involving neurological damage in the cerebral cortex that interferes with the perception, organization, and comprehension of sounds.

Cerebral malformations. Deformities in brain structure occurring at or before birth.

Chancery court. A court charged with the responsibility of ensuring the welfare of those in its charge.

Chemotherapy. The treatment of organic dysfunction by the use of biochemical agents.

Child abuse. Physical and/or psychological harm to a child by the parents or other caretakers.

Child advocacy. The range of social, political, and legal activities involved in identifying the unmet needs of children and in rectifying existing abuses of children's rights.

Child advocate. A representative within the community who exercises responsibility to protect the civil and personal rights of the child.

Child development. A series of typically patterned and predictable changes that foster a child's ability to cope with and master the external environment.

Childhood psychosis. A pattern of child behavior that is essentially characterized by failure to recognize, understand, or respond appropriately to people or objects in the environment.

Childhood schizophrenia. Category of psychosis characterized by combination of isolation, noncommunicative speech, repetitive body movements, self-injurious behavior, regression in behavior, abnormal fears, delusional or hallucinatory behavior, or problems with bodily functions.

Child life programs. Educational programs for hospitalized children in which the goals include academic instruction as well as play therapy, occupational therapy, recreational therapy, and activity therapy.

Child psychiatrist. Physician specializing in the diagnosis and treatment of childhood psychological disorders.

Child welfare. A form of intervention in which primary concern is the child's family or surrogate family.

Choreiform movement. Twitching or dancing movements; a neurological soft sign.

Chromosomal abnormality. A deviation in the number or structure of chromosomes.

Chronic. Term for a condition that cannot be easily or completely cured and is therefore long-standing in duration.

Class-action litigation. Court action on the behalf of a class of individuals.

Classroom consultant. Clinical professional who aids the teachers and school in the educational management of the special child.

Clinical audiological testing. Assessment of hearing capacity conducted by an audiologist using an audiometer.

Clinical child psychologist. Individual holding a Ph.D. in psychology and specializing in the diagnosis and treatment of children's psychological and developmental disabilities.

Clinical method. The application of generalized scientific data to the actual assessment, treatment, and care of the individual.

Clonic blocks. Type of stuttering involving repetitions of words or speech sounds.

Cluttering. Speech that is excessively rapid, erratic in rhythm, slurred, garbled, or unintelligible.

Cognitive model. A view of child development, such as Piaget's, that stresses the importance of knowledge acquisition and information processing in the child's overall development.

Compliant agreement. One of several response classes, involving statements in which one person simply yields to the position of the other.

Compressed speech. A tape-recording technique that omits the nonessential aspects of speech; used for partially sighted children.

Concrete operations. Piaget's fourth stage of child development in which the child begins to use mental operations to reason about things without any genuine capacity to abstract or to generalize.

Conduct disorder. Any behavior of a developing youngster that causes difficulty or disruption in the child's relationships with parents, family, teachers, or the larger community.

Conductive hearing loss. Hearing loss involving malfunction in the transmission of sounds from the auditory canal to the inner ear. Often successfully treated medically or surgically.

Congenital hearing impairment. Hearing disability present at birth either as a result of hereditary factors or problems during intrauterine development.

Congenital hypothyroidism. *See* **Cretinism.**

Contingency contracting. A procedure in which mutual behavioral expectations are explicitly stated in contract form along with an explicit statement of contingencies for compliance or noncompliance.

Contingency management. A set of procedures designed to change an individual's behavior through the use of a change agent who associates certain reinforcers with specific behaviors of the individual.

Convergent thinking. Process by which intellectual operations converge on a predetermined correct answer, e.g., completing a logical syllogism.

Coping behavior. Describes the many responses of children and families to the stress represented by chronic health problems and other continuing disabilities.

Cosmetic disability. A condition that predominantly affects physical appearance.

Cranial anomalies. Malformation of the head structure, occurring at or before birth.

Cranial-facial anomalies. Malformation of both the head and face, occurring at or before birth.

Craniostenosis. Condition in which cranial sutures close prematurely, producing an abnormally shaped head and some degree of brain damage.

Creativity. The capacity to restructure the world in unusual conceptual terms.

Cretinism. A condition caused by diminished production of thyroid that, if untreated, results in distorted physical features and mental retardation. Also known as *congenital hypothyroidism.*

Crib-O-gram. A diagnostic instrument that objectively measures auditory capacity by monitoring basic physiological responses.

Critical stage hypothesis. Suggests that speech is a function of maturational changes in the central nervous system that occur at critical stages of infant development.

Cross-age tutoring. Use of older children in the upper grades who are poor readers to tutor younger children in reading.

Cystic fibrosis. A progressive disease of the pancreas.

Day school. A school that keeps a child in his/her family while still providing specially trained teachers; the child does not live at the school but merely attends on a daily basis.

Deaf. An individual who has a hearing loss greater than 75 to 80 decibels in the better ear.

Decibel (dB). Unit for measuring the loudness of perceived intensity of a sound; used as a means of classifying the degree of functional hearing.

Decoding. Using language to express meaning.

Defense mechanism. Unconscious method of dealing with anxiety-arousing situations or threats to self-esteem.

Delinquency. Any behavior of a child or young adolescent that violates the legal standards of the community.

Developmental delays. An observed disparity in a child's actual development and the expected age levels at which specific critical behaviors typically occur.

Developmental diagnosis. Pioneered by Gesell, the assessment of a child's behavior patterns by means of a physical examination, a detailed health history, and a parent interview.

Developmental disability. A disability attributable to mental retardation, cerebral palsy, epilepsy, or another neurological condition closely related to mental retardation which is present by age 18, can be expected to continue, and constitutes a substantial handicap.

Developmental milestones. *See* **Norms of development.**

Deviation IQ. Procedure whereby each subject's performance on an intelligence test is compared only with that of other individuals in the same age range of the standardization sample.

Diagnosis (as a process). The comprehensive study of an individual based on findings derived from assessment procedures.

Diagnostic label. A term from a classification system used as a means of categorizing a person's condition or behavior.

Differential diagnosis. The precise specification that a given set of symptoms is indicative of one disorder rather than another.

Disability. Defect in physical makeup or functioning that can be specified and described objectively; impairment.

Disciplinarians. Term used for parents who feel that firm discipline, achieved only through punishment, must be imposed lest the child develop into a monster.

Divergent thinking. Process that opens up novel ways of conceiving the world, identifies new problems, and leads in directions that could not be predicted prior to the thinking itself; the basis of creative problem solving.

Dizygotic twins. Fraternal twins.

Double-bind theory. The communication by the parent of contradictory messages at various communicative levels, which leads to confusion and anxiety in the child.

Down's Syndrome. Also known as mongolism; a chromosomal abnormality that alters patterns of growth and development; these children usually function in the moderately retarded range.

Dysphemia theory. The belief that stuttering is an outcome of undetected organic dysfunction.

Early admission. Admitting the unusually bright youngster into school prior to reaching the usual chronological age for admission.

Early infantile autism. Category of psychosis characterized by early onset, profound failure to develop social relationships, language retardation, and ritualistic or compulsive behavior.

Educationally blind. Term for a child who cannot make use of vision for the purpose of learning, even if the child has a small degree of residual vision.

Egocentrism. Individual's lack of awareness of anything beyond himself or herself; self-centeredness.

Electroretinogram (ERG). Instrument that records the eye's response to light.

EMH (educable mentally handicapped) programs. Programs for retarded children described as educable.

Emotionally immature parents. Parents unable to face the demands of adulthood and who turn to their children for love and protection.

Emotional overlay. Applies to adverse emotional and behavioral problems that develop as a function of a learning disorder.

Emotional refrigeration. Lack of adequate parenting, manifested by coldness and aloofness to the child.

Encephalitis. Inflammation of the brain.

Encoding. Understanding language.

Enrichment. Programs providing special materials and/or activities designed specifically for students who can master the regular curriculum at an accelerated pace.

Epigenetic principle. Erikson's principle that development follows a patterned course, with specific physical and social components giving rise to integrated functioning.

Epiloia. *See* **Tuberous sclerosis.**

Esophogeal speech. Type of speech learned by laryngectomy patients by means of exhalation of breath through the esophagus.

Etiology. The cause of an illness or disorder.

Expressive aphasia. Type of aphasia characterized by the inability to find the correct word, to express an idea, or to communicate verbally.

Expressive language. Spoken language.

Expressive language disorders. Difficulties in producing spoken language.

"Expressive" psychotherapy. Child is helped to express unconscious fears and conflicts through play.

Extinction. Nonreinforcement of the maladaptive target behavior, which operates to decrease that behavior.

Family therapy. A form of psychotherapy in which several or all of the members of the identified patient's family are brought together for treatment; the entire family system rather than the individual patient are considered to be the object of intervention.

Field of vision. Angle of vision.

Formal operations period. Piaget's fifth stage of child development in which the child learns to reason in the manner typical of adult thought, namely with abstractions and deductions.

Foster placement. Placement of a child with a family other than the natural family.

Functional vision efficiency. The way in which an individual uses the vision he/she has.

Genital stage. A psychodynamic concept introduced by

Freud describing the psychosexual stage in which the adolescent's libidinal satisfaction focuses on heterosexual genital stimulation and sexual intercourse.

Gestation. Period of pregnancy.

Gifted children. Children who exhibit outstanding ability or talent in a variety of areas and who have been identified as possessing such ability by professionally qualified individuals.

Group therapy. A form of psychotherapy in which individuals with similar problems are treated together in a group; the interactions between the members of the group are considered to be a critical element of the treatment.

Guilt-provoked overprotection. An excessive involvement with every aspect of the child's existence; prompted by unconscious rejection in the parent.

Handicap. Potential limitation in functioning that may arise when obstacles imposed by physical disability interfere wtih optimal development.

Haptic tests. Tests that assess intelligence by relying on touch perception.

Hard of hearing. An individual who has a hearing loss of less than 75 to 80 decibels in the better ear.

Heuristic. Research producing.

High-risk register. A listing of various medical factors associated with increased risk of a specific disability. Used for early identification of infants who have a higher probability of a disability; includes prenatal, perinatal, and postnatal conditions.

Homebound instruction. Short-term education provided at home by an itinerant teacher when a child has been released from the hospital but cannot yet return to school.

Hospitalism. The observed effects of maternal and emotional deprivation due to hospitalization of young children.

Huntington's chorea. An hereditary brain disease marked by seizures, spasmodic movements, progressive retardation, and eventual death.

Hydrocephalus. An excess of cerebrospinal fluid within the brain structure, often producing macrocephaly.

Hypotonia. Reduced muscle tone; a neurological soft sign.

Iatrogenic effect. "Doctor produced"; an unforeseen consequence of treatment efforts by a professional agent.

Ideational fluency. The ability to generate—within a limited time—ideas that will fulfill particular requirements.

"Identity crisis." A psychodynamic concept introduced by Erikson that describes the adolescent period of transition marked by confusion and experimentation in the individual's sense of self and social role.

Incidence. The frequency and distribution of an illness or disorder.

Individual educational plan. A modified lesson plan based on the inter- and intra-individual differences manifested by the exceptional child.

Inner language disorders. The inability to internalize and organize experiences using verbal or linguistic symbols.

Intelligence. The capacity to learn; the sum total of knowledge acquired by an individual; the ability to adjust or to adapt to the total environment.

Intelligence quotient. Child's performance score on an intelligence test presented as a ratio of chronological age (CA) to mental age (MA).

Interactive theory. A theory that views maladaptive behavior as a consequence of inappropriate patterns of response and reinforcement, and perception and interpretation, which develop mutually between parents and children.

Intervention. The application of professional skills to maintain or improve a child's potential for ongoing healthy development.

Intuitive period. Piaget's third stage of child development (4th through 7th years) in which the child begins to involve an initial capacity to give reasons for his/her beliefs or actions.

Itinerant teacher. A specially trained educator who provides individual assistance to a child for specific periods during the normal school schedule.

Juvenile court. Chancery court for the juvenile delinquent.

Lalling. Articulation disorder in which the *r* and *l* sounds are distorted.

Language disorder. Disorder involving a central nervous system dysfunction that impedes the comprehension or use of words.

Laryngitis. Voice disorder in which the larynx is inflamed as a result of respiratory infection, resulting in hoarseness.

Latency period. A psychodynamic concept, introduced by Freud, that describes the psychosexual stage prior to adolescence in which the child's libido is thought to be largely repressed and diffused.

Learning disabled. A broad category of children who share a common problem involving their inability to learn through normal channels. These learning problems result from a difficulty in one or more of the modalities of learning and are not problems caused by other conditions.

Learning theory. An approach to child development that views the increasing elaboration of observable behavior in the course of development as a continuing formation of relationships between stimuli and responses.

Least restrictive environment. Educational or therapeutic environment as similar to normal educational or developmental environment as possible that provides structure or services necessary to the optimal development of the special child.

Legally blind. Term for visual acuity that is no greater than 20/200 in the better eye or when field of vision is 20 degrees or less.

Legislative advocacy. Advocacy that functions to ensure the adequacy of legislation which affects rights to critical services, such as a national children's lobby.

Libido. Psychosexual energy.

Linguistics. The scientific study of the nature and function of human language.

Lisping. Articulation disorder in which one sound is substituted for another.

Macrocephaly. Enlargement of the head, frequently caused by hydrocephalus and almost always associated with severe retardation.

Mainstream education. Provision of educational programs for the special child while keeping him/her in a regular classroom setting.

Management. Process of coordinating and monitoring various aspects of intervention.

Manual training methods. Use of sign language or finger spelling for individuals with hearing loss.

Marital schism. Overt marital conflict in which the partners experience mutual hatred and an inability to resolve their difficulties.

Marital skew. A situation without overt conflict, but in which the serious psychopathology of one parent dominates the household organization.

Maturation. The physical growth of children; a type of growth that is governed by inherent physical processes.

Maturational model. Gesell's view of child development, which sees growth in the child as governed by naturally occurring and regulating processes innate to the maturing nervous system, of which increasingly complex behavior is the observable expression.

Mediation. In social learning theory, an unseen, inner process inferred to be intervening between an observed stimuli and an observed response.

Medical model. An approach to the helping process that is based on traditional medical practice of intensive diagnostic study followed by treatment that is related to the diagnostic findings. In the treatment of psychological problems, a framework that views maladaptive behavior as symptomatic of an underlying illness.

Megavitamin therapy. A form of treatment that involves the administration of massive doses of vitamins.

Mental age. A measure of determined mental ability based on the child's success in passing a series of tests ordered in difficulty at various age levels.

Mental retardation. A condition in development involving subnormal or significantly subaverage intellectual functioning and deficits in adaptive behavior or impairment of learning and/or social adjustment.

Mental status examination. Examination of intellectual, emotional, behavioral, social, and general personality dimensions.

Mesomorphic physique. A muscular, rugged physique found by some researchers to be accompanied by such behavioral traits as aggressiveness, a high energy level, emotional insensitivity, and a tendency to resort to physical action when frustrated.

Mild hearing loss. Hearing loss in which the individual cannot hear sounds below 30 decibels.

Milieu therapy. A form of residential treatment that involves careful planning of the physical and social environment, aimed toward optimum development of the patient.

Minimal brain dysfunction. Presumed damage to the brain and central nervous system resulting in a wide array of possible signs, symptoms, and behaviors.

Mixed dominance. Condition whereby neither cerebral hemisphere coordinates muscular activity; thought to occur because of hereditary factors or attempts to change handedness.

Mixed hearing loss. Hearing impairment in the conduction of sounds *and* sensorineural damage.

Model. Viewpoint based on distinct premises, providing a specific guide for understanding something.

Modeling. In social learning theory, learning by watching others (i.e., models) do things. Also known as imitation or vicarious learning.

Moderate hearing loss. Hearing loss in which the individual cannot hear sounds below 50 decibels. Hearing aid is needed if individual is to learn adequate *receptive* and *expressive* language.

Mongolism. *See* **Down's Syndrome.**

Mobility training. Encouragement and training for blind children in moving from place to place safely.

Monozygotic twins. Identical twins.

Motor disability. Condition that interferes significantly with motor function either directly or indirectly.

Movigenic curriculum. Providing visual, auditory, tactual, and kinesthetic experiences to maximize efficient learning.

Movigenics. Study of patterns of movement that produce learning efficiency.

Multiple-response recorder. Instrument that monitors variations in respiration and motor responses to determine whether or not a sound has been heard.

Multiply handicapped. A classification of special children having two or more different disabilities, each of which may require different types of intervention.

Natural voice level. Refers to the middle of the tonal range readily producible by a given individual; a function of physical voice musculature.

Needling. Traditional treatment of cataracts, which involves breaking up the substance of the crystalline lens of the eye with a knife needle.

Neglect. Failure on the part of parents to provide for the child's basic physical needs, safety, and reasonable socialization.

Negotiated agreements. One of several response classes, involving compromise positions different from the original position of either party.

Neoplasms. Tumors or abnormal growths.

Neurological soft signs. Behavioral indications of possible neurological dysfunction; includes whirling, hypotonia, and choreiform movements.

Neurosis. Personality problem related to subjectively experienced anxiety; child may exhibit fearfulness, shyness, and self-consciousness; also called *psychoneurosis.*

Neurosurgery. Surgery for disabling conditions of the brain and spinal cord.

Neurotic and psychotic parents. Parents who impose their distorted conceptions of reality on the child, imputing unrealistic characteristics and motives to the child.

Neurotic anxiety. Anxiety stemming from the fear that impulses may overwhelm the controls of the personality.

Neuroticism. High level of anxiety that may be constitutional.

Night terrors. Occur when a child experiences anxiety and terror while asleep, but cannot remember the experience upon awakening.

Nocturnal enuresis. Involuntary bed-wetting in the absence of demonstrable organic disorder.

Noncategorical therapeutic preschool. Day school operated by child clinic or hospital, providing programs based on level of social development.

Nondirective play therapy. A type of play therapy in which the therapist seeks to create an atmosphere of unconditional acceptance of the child.

Norms of development. Empirically identified age levels at which infants and children are typically able to perform various critical behaviors (such as sitting up, crawling, walking, using language, etc.); also called *developmental milestones.*

Objective test. Test using a clearly structured series of questions, calling for responses that can be categorized as right or wrong (usually ability and achievement tests).

Objectivity anxiety. Anxiety stemming from perceived dangers in the real world.

Operant behavior. A voluntarily emitted response within an organism's behavioral repertoire that operates on its environment.

Operant conditioning. A form of learning in which the probability of a behavior is increased by associating the behavior with a specific consequence. This type of learning can be used to treat specific behavior problems. Also known as *instrumental conditioning.*

Operational thought. Piaget's term for the mental ability to relate experience to an organized and meaningful whole.

Optacon. A reading aid consisting of a small electric camera that translates printed material into sharp pulsations to one's fingertips.

Opthalmologist. A physician specializing in the diagnosis and treatment of eye disorders.

Opthalmoscope. Instrument used in examining the interior structure of the eye.

Optometrist. A licensed specialist in vision who is trained in the art and science of vision care.

Oral stage. A psychodynamic concept, introduced by Freud, that describes the psychosexual stage in which the infant's libidinal energy is almost totally directed toward oral gratification.

Organism. A living entity governed by natural laws of biological functioning.

Organic trauma. Trauma caused by infection or injury, possibly leading to central nervous system damage.

Orientation. A method of teaching appropriate head and facial movements, in conversation, to the blind.

Orthopedic surgery. Surgery for problems of the skeletal system.

Otolaryngology. Medical specialty dealing specifically with the ears, nose, and throat, and concerned with the potential physical relationships between speech and hearing disability and with the linguistic consequences of deafness.

Parental management. The use of contingency management procedures by the parent(s) of a special child.

Partially sighted. Term for an individual with sufficient functional vision efficiency to utilize vision for the chief avenue of learning.

Pediatric evaluation. Assessment procedure that includes health history and physical examination, based on established developmental norms.

Pediatric neurologist. A physician specializing in the diagnosis and treatment of children's nervous system disorders.

Pediatric psychology. A specialty of clinical psychology designed to meet the psychological needs of children for whom medical care has been indicated.

Pediatrician. Physician specializing in the prevention and care of childhood medical problems.

Perception. Process by which the organism is aware of the objects, qualities, or events stimulating the sense organs.

Perceptual-motor deficit. Condition involving lack of appropriate fit between motor experiences and perceptual experiences.

Perceptual-motor training. Treatment involving specific exercises presumed to be useful in strengthening various aspects of perceptual-motor functioning.

Perinatal conditions. Conditions occurring during delivery.

Phacoemulsification. A method of breaking up cataracts with the use of a low-frequency ultrasonic needle.

Phallic stage. A psychodynamic concept, introduced by Freud, that describes the psychosexual stage in which the child discovers the genital area as the major source of libidinal pleasure.

Phenylketonuria (PKU). A congenital deficiency in which natural controls for the excessive buildup of phenylalanine are lacking.

Phobic reaction. Disorder in which individual exhibits intense, irrational fears of specific objects or events.

Physical health disorder. Any identified physical health problem that requires intensive medical attention or hospitalization, cannot be easily and completely cured, and places severe demands on the individual's ability to lead a normal life.

Play therapy. A form of psychotherapy in which play is the medium by which the therapist helps the child resolve inner conflicts and tension.

Positive reinforcement. Any stimulus event that, when following an organism's response, increases the strength or frequency of that response.

Postnatal (or neonatal) conditions. Conditions occurring after birth.

Preconcepts. Piaget's term for the child's beginning ideas or notions about the properties of things.

Preconceptual period. Piaget's second stage of child development in which the child forms beginning ideas (preconcepts) about the properties of things in the environment.

Prenatal conditions. Conditions present before birth by reason of genetics or complications during pregnancy.

Primary prevention. The establishment of medical and social programs that seek to alter the conditions responsible for the development of any disability or illness.

Primary reinforcement. Reinforcement that results in the reduction of a primary drive, such as hunger.

Profound hearing loss. Hearing loss in which the individual cannot hear sounds below 100 decibels. Individual cannot hear ordinary language sounds accurately, even with amplification.

Prognosis. The likely course or outcome of an illness.

Projective test. A type of test that presents the individual with a highly ambiguous and unstructured stimulus (such as an inkblot) to elicit a highly subjective and personal response (which must be interpreted and evaluated by an expert).

Psychodynamic model. View of human behavior as a function of inner, unconscious mechanisms of motivation.

Psycholinguistic disabilities. Learning disabilities in the area of language and cognitive processes upon which language is based.

Psychological evaluation. Evaluation that explores patterns of development and current behavior, usually through the use of psychological tests.

Psychological parent. A legal-psychological term for a person who, on a continuing basis, fulfills the child's psychological needs for a parent, as well as the child's physical needs.

Psychometric testing. A quantitative approach to the assessment of the child's current level of functioning through the use of standardized psychological tests.

Psychoneurotic disorder/anxiety type. Personality problem characterized by sleep disturbance, fear, and general apprehensiveness. *See* **Anxiety reaction.**

Psychopharmacology. The study of the use of drugs to induce psychological effects on mental functioning, behavior, and emotional responsiveness. Also known as *behavioral pharmacology.*

Psychophysiological reaction. A disorder in which there is a demonstrated or presumed relationship between chronic, stress-related, emotional arousal and the eventual appearance of physiological symptoms.

Psychosocial model. Erikson's series of psychosocial stages, each of which offers the child an opportunity to work out a conflict between inner needs and social requirements.

Psychostimulant drugs. Drugs that stimulate the central nervous system and have the effect of reducing activity level in children; used to treat minimal brain dysfunction.

Psychotherapy. The planned management of an interpersonal patient-therapist relationship, which is intended to relieve the patient's initial distress and to enhance overall developmental processes.

Punishment. Any stimulus event presented consequent on a response that decreases the strength or frequency of that response.

Rating scale. A type of subjective test in which one individual rates another individual on a series of descriptive statements that estimate the frequency or intensity of certain characteristics or types of behavior.

Receptive aphasia. Type of aphasia whereby the ability to comprehend spoken language is impeded.

Receptive language. Ability to understand language.

Receptive language disorders. Difficulties in the process of understanding verbal symbols.

Reconstructive surgery. The surgical repair of physical abnormalities.

Rehabilitation. Intervention procedures that seek to restore a child to normal or optimal functioning following illness or injury.

Reinforcer. Any specific environmental event that strengthens the tendency of a response to occur again.

Reliability. The degree to which standardized observations are consistent; the extent to which individuals earn the same relative scores each time a particular test is given.

Remediation. Process aimed at correcting deficits in skills and abilities.

Representational capacities. Individual's use of language in mediating the meaning of linguistic symbols.

Repression. Excluding unacceptable thoughts from consciousness; a psychoanalytic term.

Residential placement. Placement in an institution.

Residential school. A type of school in which the child lives on a full-time basis and which typically provides extensive services for a particular population of special children.

Resource room. A special class available to the child while mainstreaming the majority of the child's educational program.

Respondent conditioning. A type of learning first demonstrated by Ivan Pavlov in which an unconditioned stimulus is paired with a conditioned stimulus to produce a conditioned response. This type of learning can be used to treat specific behavior problems. Also known as *classical conditioning.*

Response events. The overt and covert activities of the individual.

Retinoblastoma. A malignant tumor of the retina that usually arises in infancy and can cause blindness.

Retrolental fibroplasia. One of major perinatal causes of blindness. Known to occur when excessive oxygen is administered in premature births; causes growth of fibrous tissue behind lens of eye.

Reversal experimental design. Three-step procedure involving baseline counting of target behavior before intervention is initiated, frequency counting during intervention, and frequency counting upon return to conditions prior to intervention.

"Rooming in." Service by which parents can remain with their ill child during the hospitalization.

Schizophrenogenic mother. A dominant and binding mother who simultaneously rejects her child emotionally and induces severe anxiety in the child; powerful, perfectionistic mother.

School psychologist. Individual holding a master's degree in psychology and state certification.

Scientific method. Systematic observation under experimental or naturally occurring conditions to gather data that can describe common characteristics and aid in predicting patterns of behavior.

Screening devices. Assessment instruments for detecting problems in large groups of individuals; characterized by ease of administration and economy of time and expense.

Secondary reinforcement. Reinforcement that results in the reduction of social drives for approval and affection; social reinforcement.

Self-contained classroom. Special classes in the normal public school for children with similar disabilities, aimed at providing responsive, therapeutic education.

Self-report inventory. A type of subjective test in which the individual evaluates as true or false a series of statements as applied to the self.

Self-tutoring devices. Mechanical educational devices used by some behavior-disordered children when personal interaction is too difficult.

Sensorimotor period. Piaget's first stage of child development in which infants gain experience through their senses and absorb these experiences into evolving patterns of motor behavior.

Sensorineural hearing loss. Hearing loss that involves some degree of physical damage to the auditory nerve or to the nerve endings of the inner ear. Usually cannot be corrected medically.

Sensory compensation. An unsupported hypothesis that blind individuals have superior tactile and auditory senses to make up for loss of vision.

Sensory disability. Condition that interferes with vision, hearing, or speech.

Serotonin. A neurohumor or chemical mediator in the transmission of neural impulses.

Service delivery system. An organization or organized set of procedures by which some form of service is made available to the public.

Severe hearing loss. Hearing loss in which the individual cannot hear sounds less than 80 decibels and unable to develop adequate receptive and expressive language without professional intervention.

Sheltered workshop. A form of employment for the retarded that typically exists in cooperation with private industry and provides unskilled work under supervision.

Signal anxiety. A psychoanalytic term referring to small amounts of anxiety that warn against potential danger of repressed impulses breaking into consciousness.

Simultaneous language acquisition. Training method employing simultaneous presentation of verbal stimulus and manual communication or sign.

Slit lamp. Instrument that emits a narrow beam of light useful in the examination of frontal portions of the eye.

Snellen chart. A standardized series of letters, numbers, or symbols used to measure visual acuity that, in testing, is read from a distance of 20 feet.

Social anomie. An absence or rapid shifting of societal norms and values.

Socialization. The general process by which an individual acquires the beliefs, skills, values, behavior patterns, and other characteristics considered appropriate for a particular society. To the learning theorist, learning situations critical in the individual's personality formation.

Social intervention. Intervention that involves placement of the individual in a special environment.

Social reinforcement. See **Secondary reinforcement.**

Social worker. A professional with a master's degree in social work (M.S.W.) who is specially trained in managing the provision of a variety of social services; many social workers are also trained psychotherapists.

Special children. Children for whom the presence of a physical, psychological, cognitive, or social factor makes difficult the realization of their needs and full potential. Also referred to as *exceptional, disabled, handicapped, impaired,* or *dysfunctioning* children.

Special school. A type of school that attempts to provide extensive intervention for the needs of a particular population of special children, such as a school for the blind.

Special education. A form of educational intervention involving appropriate facilities, specialized methods and materials, and specially trained teachers.

Special education teacher. Individual trained and certified to use specific educational methods with special children.

Special parent. A parent of a special child.

Speech disability. An impairment of effective verbal communication to the extent that the intelligibility of spoken language is reduced.

Speech pathologist. A specialist in the diagnosis, assessment, and treatment of speech and language disorders.

Speech reading. A method of reading what a person is saying by looking at their lips.

Standardization. Uniformity achieved when conditions of observation are held constant across a large number of subjects, who are presumed to be representative of the group for whom the test is intended to be used.

Stimulation programs. Hospital programs designed to promote the development of low-birth-weight or high-risk infants.

Stimulus events. The many chemical, physical, biological, and social events that act upon the individual.

Strauss syndrome. A condition that results from injury or infection of the brain, impairing normal learning processes.

Stuttering. Problem in the sequential timing of speech, caused by a disability in breathing control while speaking; consists of repetitions of words, hesitations in speech, and prolongation of speech sounds.

Subcultural deviance. Delinquent behavior learned within the context of small groups that feel violating the law is more functional than adhering to it.

Subjective test. A test designed to gather information about a given individual's attitudes, feelings, perceptions of self and others, and behavior.

"Suppressive" psychotherapy. Therapy in which the patient is helped to suppress and control certain thoughts and fantasies that are presently acted out and constitute the basis of psychotic symptoms.

Symptom substitution. Psychoanalytic theory that one symptom will simply be replaced by another unless the underlying cause is discovered and removed.

Symptom syndrome. Constellation of symptoms characteristic of an illness or disorder.

Target behavior assessment. Diagnostic procedure that relies on the direct observation and measurement of precisely defined behaviors, without inference as to the meaning of that behavior.

Team approach. Pooling and coordinating the different skills and services needed in the diagnosis and treatment of the special child.

Telescopic lens. Optical aid that increases the visual angle and makes an object appear larger than it really is because the image that falls on the retina is enlarged.

Therapy. The treatment of an illness or disabling condition.

Time-out. A behavioral management procedure that involves removal of all positive reinforcement consequent upon oppositional behavior.

Tithingman. In 1670s Massachusetts, a community member charged with monitoring the behavior of children and parents with respect to each other. Similar to contemporary "child advocate" as a protector of children's rights.

TMH (trainable mentally handicapped) programs. Programs for retarded children described as trainable.

Token economy. System in which symbolic rewards (tokens) given for predetermined appropriate behavior can be exchanged for tangible reinforcers, such as food or money.

Tonic blocks. Type of stuttering involving the prolongation of sounds and hesitations between sounds.

Total hearing loss. Hearing loss in which the individual cannot hear anything more than noise-type sensations. Technically known as *anacusis*.

Toxemia. An abnormality associated with the presence of toxic matter in the blood.

Tracking. A means of grouping children with similar educational needs into homogenous classes.

Tuberous sclerosis. Hereditary brain disease characterized by the presence of tumors throughout the brain and other parts of the body, resulting in mild to severe retardation. Also known as *Epiloia*.

"Tunnel vision." Reduced field of vision; only a narrow band is perceived.

Turner's syndrome. A chromosomal anomaly in which the major symptoms involve dwarfism, infantile sexual development, and webbed neck.

Ulcerative colitis. An intestinal inflammation that leads to periodic appearances of chronic diarrhea, bloody stools, loss of appetite, weight loss, and sometimes intestinal pain; a psychophysiologic reaction.

Unilateral hearing impairment. Impairment affecting only one ear.

Validity. The extent to which a test accurately measures what it is intended to measure.

Verbalism. Tendency of blind children to verbalize excessively or to use speech confidently about objects that they have not really experienced and do not really understand.

Vestibular regulation. Ability to right or balance oneself.

Visual acuity. Measure of the accuracy of distance vision compared to normal vision.

Visual disability. A condition of visual loss in children who, after all possible correction, continue to have severe limitations in vision and are handicapped in their school programs.

Visual-perceptual deficit. Deficit involving lack of appropriate fit between visual experience and perceptual experience.

Voice disorders. Impairment of tone, inflection, or volume of speech.

"Wanted" child. A legal-psychological term meaning one who receives nourishment and affection on a continuing basis from at least one adult.

References

ABE, K. Phobias and nervous symptoms in childhood and maturity: Persistence and associations. *British Journal of Psychiatry*, 1972, *120*, 275-83.

ABELSON, W. D., ZIEGLER, E., & DeBLASI, C. L. Effects of a four-year follow-through program on economically disadvantaged children. *Journal of Educational Psychology*, 1974, *66*, 756-71.

ABRAHAMSEN, D. *The psychology of crime.* New York: Columbia University Press, 1960.

ABRAMS, J. Learning disabilities. In S. L. Copel (Ed.), *Behavior pathology of childhood and adolescence.* New York: Basic Books, 1973, 300-23.

ABRAMSON, H. A. The use of LSD (d-Lysergic Acid Diethylamide) in the therapy of children. *Journal of Asthma Research*, 1967, *5*, 139-43.

ACHENBACH, T. M. The classification of children's psychiatric symptoms: A factor-analytic study. *Psychological Monographs*, 1966, *80* (Whole No. 615, 1-37).

ACKERMAN, N. W. *The psychodynamics of family life.* New York: Basic Books, 1958.

ACKERMAN, N. W. The role of the family in the emergence of child disorders. In E. Miller (Ed.), *Foundations of child psychiatry.* New York: Pergamon, 1968.

ADAMS, M. Siblings of the retarded and their problems and treatment. Paper presented at the 90th Annual Conference of the American Association of Mental Deficiency, Chicago, May 1966.

ADAMS, M. A. A hospital play program: Helping children with serious illness. *American Journal of Orthopsychiatry*, 1976, *46*, 416-24.

ADELSON, E., & FRAIBERG, S. Gross motor development in infants blind from birth. *Child Development*, 1974, *45*, 114-26.

ADVISORY COMMITTEE ON THE EDUCATION OF THE DEAF. The handicap of deafness. In R. L. Jones (Ed.), *Problems and issues in the education of exceptional children.* Boston: Houghton Mifflin, 1971.

AIELLO, B. Especially for special educators. A sense of our own history. *Exceptional Children*, 1976, *42*, 244-52.

ALEXANDER, J. F., & PARSONS, B. Short-term behavioral intervention with delinquent families: Impact on process and recidivism. *Journal of Abnormal Psychology*, 1973, *81*, 219-25.

ALLEN, G. Patterns of discovery in the genetics of mental deficiency. *American Journal of Mental Deficiency*, 1958, *62*, 840-49.

ALTSHULER, K. Z. Studies of the deaf: Relevance to psychiatric theory. *American Journal of Psychiatry*, 1971, *127*, 11-23.

ALTSHULER, K. Z. The social and psychological development of the deaf child: Problems, their treatment, and prevention. *American Annals of the Deaf*, 1974, *119*, 365-76.

AMAN, M. G., & WERRY, J. S. Methylphenidate in children: Effects upon cardiorespiratory functioning. *International Journal of Mental Health*, 1975, *4*, 119-31.

AMERICAN ASSOCIATION ON MENTAL DEFICIENCY. Guidelines for work by residents in public and private institutions for the mentally retarded. *Mental Retardation*, 1973, *11*, 59-62. (a)

AMERICAN ASSOCIATION ON MENTAL DEFICIENCY. *Manual on terminology and classification in mental retardation* (Rev. ed., H. J. Grossman, Ed.). Washington, D.C.: American Association on Mental Deficiency, 1973. (b)

AMERICAN ASSOCIATION ON MENTAL DEFICIENCY. The right to life. *Mental Retardation*, 1973, *11*, 66. (c)

AMERICAN ASSOCIATION ON MENTAL DEFICIENCY. Rights of mentally retarded persons. *Mental Retardation*, 1973, *11*, 56-58. (d)

AMERICAN FOUNDATION FOR THE BLIND. *The Pine Brook report.* New York: Author, 1954.

AMERICAN PSYCHIATRIC ASSOCIATION. *Diagnostic and statistical manual of mental disorders* (2nd ed.). Washington, D.C.: American Psychiatric Association, 1968.

ANASTASI, A. Psychological testing of children. In A. M. Freedman, H. I. Kaplan & B. J. Sadock (Eds.), *Comprehensive textbook of psychiatry* (Vol. II). Baltimore: Williams & Wilkins, 1975.

ANDERSON, R. E. "Where's Dad?" Paternal deprivation and delinquency. *Archives of General Psychiatry*, 1968, *18*, 641-49.

ANDERSON, W. F. The relative effects of the Frostig program, corrective reading instruction, and attention upon the reading skills of corrective readers with visual perceptual difficulties. *Journal of School Psychology*, 1972, *10*, 387-95.

ANNUAL REPORT TO THE PRESIDENT AND THE CONGRESS/ *1973: America's educationally neglected.* Washington, D.C.: National Advisory Council on the Education of Disadvantaged Children, 1973.

ANNUAL REPORT TO THE PRESIDENT AND THE CONGRESS/ *1974 Title I: Expanding educational growth.* Washington, D.C.: National Advisory Council on the Education of Disadvantaged Children, 1974.

ANNUAL REPORT TO THE PRESIDENT AND THE CONGRESS/ *1975.* Washington, D.C.: National Advisory Council on the Education of Disadvantaged Children, 1975.

ANNUAL REPORT TO THE PRESIDENT AND THE CONGRESS/ *1976.* Washington, D.C.: National Advisory Council on the Education of Disadvantaged Children, 1976.

ANTHONY, E. J. Neuroses of children. In A. M. Freedman & H. I. Kaplan (Eds.), *The child: His psychological and cultural development* (Vol. 2). New York: Atheneum, 1971, 105-43.

ANTHONY, E. J. The syndrome of the psychologically invulnerable child. In E. J. Anthony & C. Koupernik (Eds.), *The child in his family: Children at psychiatric risk.* New York: John Wiley & Sons, 1974.

APGAR, V., & STICKLE, G. Birth defects: Their significance as a public health problem. *Journal of the American Medical Association*, 1968, *204*, 408-15.

APLEY, J., & MacKEITH, R. *The child and his symptoms.* Philadelphia: Davis, 1968.

ARIETI, S. *Interpretations of schizophrenia.* New York: Basic Books, 1974.

ARONSON, E. *The social animal.* San Francisco: W. H. Freeman, 1972.

ASHBY, W. R., & WALKER, C. C. Genius. In P. London & D. Rosenhan (Eds.), *Foundations of abnormal psychology.* New York: Holt, Rinehart and Winston, 1968.

ASHCROFT, S. C. Delineating the possible for the multihandicapped child with visual impairment. *Sight-Saving Review*, 1966, *36*, 90-94.

ASHCROFT, S. C., HALLIDAY, C., & BARRAGA, N. *Study II: Effects of experimental teaching on the visual behavior of children educated as though they had no vision.* Washington, D.C.: U.S. Office of Education, 1965.

AUSUBEL, D. P. A teaching strategy for culturally deprived pupils: Cognitive and motivational considerations. *The School Review*, 1963, *71*, 454-63.

AVERCH, JR., H. A., et al. *How effective is schooling: A critical review and synthesis of research findings.* Santa Monica: The Rand Corp., 1972.

AXLINE, V. *Play therapy.* Cambridge, Mass.: Riverside Press, 1947.

AXLINE, V. The eight basic principles. In M. Haworth (Ed.), *Child psychotherapy.* New York: Basic Books, 1964.

AYLLON, T., & AZRIN, N. H. *The token economy: A motivational system for therapy and rehabilitation.* New York: Appleton-Century-Crofts, 1968.

AYLLON, T., LAYMAN, D., & KANDEL, H. J. A behavioral-educational alternative to drug control of hyperactive behavior. *Journal of Applied Behavior Analysis*, 1975, *8*, 137-46.

AZARNOFF, P. Mediating the trauma of serious illness and hospitalization in childhood. *Children Today*, July-August 1974, 12-17.

AZRIN, N. H., SNEED, T. J., & FOXX, R. M. Dry-bed training: rapid elimination of childhood enuresis. *Behaviour Research and Therapy*, 1974, *12*, 147-56.

BAILEY, J. S., WOLF, M. M., & PHILLIPS, E. L. Home-based reinforcement and the modification of predelinquents' classroom behavior. *Journal of Applied Behavior Analysis*, 1970, *3*, 223-33.

BANDURA, A. Influence of models' reinforcement contingencies on the acquisition of imitative responses. *Journal of Personality and Social Psychology,* 1965, *1,* 589-95.

BANDURA, A. *Principles of behavior modification.* New York: Holt, Rinehart and Winston, 1969.

BANDURA, A. (Ed.). *Psychological modeling: Conflicting theories.* Chicago: Aldine-Atherton, 1971. (A)

BANDURA, A. Psychotherapy based on modeling principles. In A. E. Bergin & S. L. Garfield (Eds.), *Handbook of psychotherapy and behavior change.* New York: Wiley, 1971. (b)

BANDURA, A. Behavior theory and the models of man. *American Psychologist,* 1974, *29,* 859-69.

BANDURA, A. The ethics and social purposes of behavior modification. In C. M. Franks & G. T. Wilson (Eds.), *Annual Review of Behavior Therapy* (Vol. 3). New York: Brunner/Mazel, 1975.

BANDURA, A., & HUSTON, A. C. Identification as a process of incidental learning. *Journal of Abnormal and Social Psychology,* 1961, *63,* 311-18.

BANDURA, A., ROSS, D., & ROSS, S. A. Transmission of aggression through imitation of aggressive models. *Journal of Abnormal and Social Psychology,* 1961, *63,* 575-82.

BANDURA, A., ROSS, D., & ROSS, S. A. Imitation of film-mediated aggressive models. *Journal of Abnormal and Social Psychology,* 1965, *66,* 3-11.

BANDURA, A., & WALTERS, R. H. *Social learning and personality development.* New York: Holt, Rinehart and Winston, 1963.

BARBE, W. B., & STEPHENS, T. M. (Eds.). *Educating tomorrow's leaders.* Div. of Special Educ., Ohio Dept. of Educ., 1961.

BARBERO, A., & SHAHEEN, E. Environmental failure-to-thrive: A clinical view. *The Journal of Pediatrics,* 1967, *71,* 639-44.

BARKER, R. G., WRIGHT, B. A., MEYERSON, L., & GONICK, M. R. *Adjustment to physical handicap and illness — A survey of the social psychology of physique and disability* (Bulletin 55). New York: Social Science Research Council, 1953.

BARKER-LUNN, J. C. *Streaming in the primary school: A longitudinal study of children in streamed and nonstreamed junior schools.* Slough, England: National Society for Educational Research in England and Wales, 1970.

BARNARD, K. *A Program of Stimulation for Infants Born Prematurely.* Paper presented at the meeting of the Society for Research in Child Development, Philadelphia, March 1973.

BAROFF, G. S., & TATE, B. G. The use of aversive stimulation in the treatment of chronic self-injurious behavior. *Journal of the American Academy of Child Psychiatry,* 1968, *7,* 454-60.

BARRAGA, N. C. *Increased visual behavior in low vision children.* New York: American Foundation for the Blind, Research Series No. 13, 1964.

BARRAGA, N. C. Utilization of sensory-perceptual abilities. In B. Lowenfeld, *The visually handicapped child in school.* New York: John Day, 1973.

BARRON, F. *Creativity and psychological health.* Princeton, N.J.: D. Van Nostrand, 1963.

BARSCH, R. H. *A movigenic curriculum.* Madison, Wis.: Bureau for Handicapped Children, 1965.

BATEMAN, B. D. *Reading and psycholinguistic processes of partially seeing children* (Research Bulletin No. 8). New York: American Foundation for the Blind, Jan. 1965.

BATEMAN, B. D. Reading and psycholinguistic processes of partially seeing children. *Council for Exceptional Children Research Monograph,* 1963, 1-46 (Series A, No. 5).

BATESON, G., JACKSON, D. D., HALEY, J., & WEAKLAND, J. Toward a theory of schizophrenia. In A. H. Buss & E. H. Buss (Eds.), *Theories of schizophrenia.* New York: Atherton Press, 1969. (Originally published in *Behavioral Science,* 1, 1956, 251-64.)

BAUER, D. H. An exploratory study of developmental changes in children's fears. *Journal of Child Psychology and Psychiatry,* 1976, *17,* 69-74.

BAUMANN, M. K. Psychological and educational assessment. In B. Lowenfeld (Ed.), *The visually handicapped child in school.* New York: John Day, 1973.

BAYLEY, N. *Bayley scales of infant development: Birth to two years.* New York: The Psychological Corporation, 1969.

BAYLEY, N. Development of mental abilities. In P. E. Mussen (Ed.), *Carmichael's manual of child psychology.* New York: Wiley, 1970.

BECKER, W. C., MADSEN, C. H., ARNOLD, C. R., & THOMAS, D. R. The contingent use of teacher attention and praise in reducing classroom problems. *Journal of Special Education,* 1967, *1,* 287-307.

BEGAB, M. The mentally retarded and the family. In I. Philips (Ed.), *Prevention and treatment of mental retardation.* New York: Basic Books, 1966.

BELL, R. Q. A reinterpretation of the direction of effects in studies of socialization. *Psychological Review,* 1968, *75,* 81-95.

BENDER, L. Childhood schizophrenia: Clinical study of one hundred schizophrenic children. *American Journal of Orthopsychiatry,* 1947, *17,* 40-55.

BENDER, L. Schizophrenia in childhood: Its recognition, description and treatment. *American Journal of Orthopsychiatry,* 1956, *26,* 499-506.

BENDER, L. D-Lysergic Acid in the treatment of the biological features of childhood schizophrenia. *Diseases of the Nervous System,* 1966, *7,* 43-46.

BENDER, L. Alpha and omega of childhood schizophrenia. *Journal of Autism and Childhood Schizophrenia,* 1971, *1,* 115-18. (a)

BENDER, L. The nature of childhood psychosis. In J. G. Howell (Ed.), *Modern perspectives in international child psychiatry.* New York: Brunner/Mazel, 1971. (b)

BEREITER, C., & ENGELMANN, S. *Teaching disadvantaged children in the pre-school.* Englewood Cliffs, N.J.: Prentice-Hall, 1966.

BERES, D. Vicissitudes of superego functions and superego precursors in childhood. *Psychoanalytic Study of the Child,* 1958, *13,* 324-51.

BERGMAN, T., & FREUD, A. *Children in the hospital.* New York: International University Press, 1965.

BERLIN, I. N. Simultaneous psychotherapy with a psychotic child and both parents: The reversal of mutism. In S. A. Szurek & I. N. Berlin (Eds.), *Clinical studies in childhood psychoses.* New York: Brunner/Mazel, 1973.

BERLIN, I. N. We advocate this bill of rights. In I. N. Berlin (Ed.), *Advocacy for child mental health.* New York: Brunner/Mazel, 1975.

BERMAN, A. Neurological dysfunction in juvenile delinquents: Implications for early intervention. *Child Care Quarterly,* 1972, *1,* 264-71.

BERTNESS, H. J. Progressive inclusion: One approach to mainstreaming. In J. B. Jordan (Ed.), *Teacher, please don't close the door.* Reston, Va.: Council for Exceptional Children, 1976.

BESHAI, J. A. Behavioral correlates of the EEG in delinquents. *Journal of Psychology,* 1971, *79,* 141-46.

BETTELHEIM, B. *Love is not enough: The treatment of emotionally disturbed children.* New York: Free Press, 1955. (a)

BETTELHEIM, B. *Truants from life: The rehabilitation of emotionally disturbed children.* New York: Free Press, 1955. (b)

BETTELHEIM, B. *The empty fortress: Infantile autism and the birth of the self.* New York: Free Press, 1967.

BETTELHEIM, B., & SYLVESTER, E. Physical symptoms in emotionally disturbed children. *Psychoanalytic Study of the Child,* 1949, *3/4,* 353-68.

BETTELHEIM, B., & SYLVESTER, E. Delinquency and morality. *Psychoanalytic Study of the Child,* 1950, *5,* 329-42.

BIJOU, S. W., & BAER, D. M. *Child development I: A systematic and empirical theory.* New York: Appleton-Century-Crofts, 1965. (a)

BIJOU, S. W., & BAER, D. M. *Child development II: The universal stage of infancy.* New York: Appleton-Century-Crofts, 1965. (b)

BIJOU, S. W., & GRIMM, J. A. Behavioral diagnosis and assessment in teaching young handicapped children. In T. Thompson & W. S. Dockens (Eds.), *Applications of behavior modification.* New York: Academic Press, 1975.

BINDELGLAS, P. M. The enuretic child. *The Journal of Family Practice,* 1975, *2,* 375-80.

BINET, A., & SIMON, T. Méthodes nouvelles pour le diagnostic du niveau intellectuel des anormaux. *Année Psychologique,* 1905, *11,* 191-244.

BIRCH, J. W., TISDALL, W. J., PEABODY, R., & STERRETT, R. *School achievement and effect of type of size on reading in visually handicapped children* (U.S. Office of Education Cooperative Research Project No. 1766). Pittsburgh: University of Pittsburgh, 1966.

BLACK, F. O., BERGSTROM, L., DOWNS, M., & HEMENWAY, W. *Congenital deafness: A new approach to early detection of deafness through a high risk register.* Boulder, Col.: Colorado Assoc. University Press, 1971.

BLACKHAM, G. J., & SILBERMAN, A. *Modification of child and adolescent behavior.* Belmont, Calif.: Wadsworth, 1975.

BLACKMAN, L. S., & HEINTZ, P. The mentally retarded. *Review of Educational Research,* 1966, *36,* 5-36.

BLAKE, J. N. *Speech, language, and learning disorders: Education and therapy.* Springfield, Ill.: Charles C. Thomas, 1971.

BLANTON, R. L. Historical perspectives on classification of mental retardation. In N. Hobbs (Ed.), *Issues in the classification of children* (Vol. I). San Francisco: Jossey-Bass, 1975.

BLATT, B. *Exodus from pandemonium.* Boston: Allyn & Bacon, 1970.

BLATT, B., & KAPLAN, F. *Christmas in purgatory: A photographic essay on mental retardation.* Boston: Allyn & Bacon, 1966.

BLEIL, G. Evaluating educational material. *Journal of Learning Disabilities,* 1975, *8,* 12-19.

BLOCH, E. L., & GOODSTEIN, L. D. Functional speech disorders and personality: A decade of research. *Journal of Speech and Hearing Disorders,* 1971, *36,* 295-314.

BLOOM, B. S. *Stability and change in human characteristics.* New York: Wiley, 1964.

BLOOM, B. S., DAVIS, A., & HESS, R. *Compensatory education and cultural deprivation.* New York: Holt, Rinehart and Winston, 1965.

BOLES, G. Personality factors in mothers of cerebral palsied children. *Genetic Psychology Monographs,* 1959, *59,* 159-218.

BOLLEA, G. Acute organic psychoses of childhood. In J. G. Howell (Ed.), *Modern perspectives in international child psychiatry.* New York: Brunner/Mazel, 1971.

BOMBERG, D., SZUREK, S., & ETEMAD, J. A statistical study of a group of psychotic children. In S. Szurek & I. N. Berlin (Eds.), *Clinical studies in childhood psychoses.* New York: Brunner/Mazel, 1973.

BORENZWEIG, H. Social group work in the field of mental retardation: A review of the literature. *Social Service Review,* 1970, *44,* 177-83.

BORNSTEIN, B. Clinical notes on child analysis. *Psychoanalytic Study of the Child,* 1945, *1,* 151-66.

BOWEN, M. A family concept of schizophrenia. In D. D. Jackson (Ed.), *The etiology of schizophrenia.* New York: Basic Books, 1960.

BOWLBY, J. Maternal care and mental health. *Bulletin of the World Health Organization,* 1951, 355-534.

BRADLEY, C. The behavior of children receiving Benzedrine. *American Journal of Psychiatry,* 1937, *94,* 577-85.

BRAGINSKY, D., & BRAGINSKY, B. *Hansels and Gretels: Studies of children in institutions for the mentally retarded.* New York: Holt, Rinehart and Winston, 1971.

BRAGINSKY, B., BRAGINSKY, D., & RING, K. *Methods of madness: The mental hospital as a last resort.* New York: Holt, Rinehart and Winston, 1969.

BRANNON, J. B. Linguistic word classes in the spoken language of normal, hard-of-hearing, and deaf children. *Journal of Speech and Hearing Research,* 1968, *11,* 279-87.

BRANNON, J. B., & MURRAY, T. The spoken syntax of normal, hard-of-hearing, and deaf children. *Journal of Speech and Hearing Research,* 1966, *9,* 604-10.

BRAUKMANN, C. J., FIXSEN, D. L., PHILLIPS, E. L., & WOLF, M. M. Behavioral approaches to treatment in the crime and delinquency field. *Criminology,* 1975, *13,* 299-331.

BREMNER, R. H., BARNARD, J., HAREVEN, T. K., & MENNEL, R. M. (Eds.). *Children and youth in America: A documentary history* (Vol. I: 1600-1865). Cambridge, Mass.: Harvard University Press, 1970.

BREMNER, R. H. et al. (Ed.). *Children and youth in America: A documentary history* (Vol. II: 1866-1932). Cambridge, Mass.: Harvard University Press, 1971.

BROBERGER, O., & LAGERCRANTZ, R. Ulcerative colitis in childhood and adolescence. *Advances in Pediatrics,* 1966, *14,* 9-54.

BROPHY, J. J. Psychiatric disorders. In M. A. Krupp & M. J. Chatton (Eds.), *Current medical diagnosis and treatment.* Los Altos, Calif.: Lange, 1974.

BROWN, B. Long-term gains from early intervention—an overview of current research. Paper presented at the meeting of the American Association for the Advancement of Science, Denver, Col., Feb. 23, 1977.

BROWN, J., & HEPLER, R. Care of the critically ill newborn. *American Journal of Nursing,* 1976, *76,* 578-81.

BROWN v. BOARD OF EDUCATION, 347 U.S. 483 (1954).

BRUNER, J. The cognitive consequences of early sensory deprivation. In P. Solomon (Ed.), *Sensory deprivation.* Cambridge, Mass.: Harvard University Press, 1961.

BRUTTEN, M., RICHARDSON, S. O., & MANGEL, C. *Something's wrong with my child.* New York: Harcourt Brace Jovanovich, 1973.

BURLINGHAM, D. Some notes on the development of the blind. *Psychoanalytic Study of the Child,* 1961, *16,* 121-45.

BURLINGHAM, D. Hearing and its role in the development of the blind. *Psychoanalytic Study of the Child,* 1964, *19,* 95-112.

BURLINGHAM, D. Some problems of ego development in blind children. *Psychoanalytic Study of the Child,* 1965, *20,* 194-208.

BUROS, O. K. (Ed.). *Mental measurements yearbooks* (2 vols.) (7th ed.). New Jersey: Gryphon Press, 1972.

BURTON, T. A. Mental health clinic services to the retarded. *Mental Retardation,* 1971, *9,* 38-40.

BURTON, T. A. *The trainable mentally retarded.* Columbus, Ohio: Charles E. Merrill, 1976.

BURTON, T. A., & HIRSHOREN, A. The focus of responsibility for education of the severely and profoundly retarded. *Psychology in the schools,* 1978, in press.

CALNAN, M., & RICHARDSON, K. Speech problems in a national survey: Assessments and prevalence. *Child: Care, Health, and Development.* 1976, *2,* 181-202.

CAMPBELL, J. D. Illness is a point of view: The development of children's concepts of illness. *Child Development,* 1975, *46,* 92-100.

CARROLL, L. Horrors. In: *The Complete Works of Lewis Carroll.* New York: Vintage Books, 1976. (Originally published, 1850.)

CASTRO VALLEY SCHOOL DISTRICT. *The challenge: A guide for teachers of gifted children, K-3.* Alameda County School Dept., 1963.

CERMAK, I. Family crisis and psychosomatic illness. *Psychotherapy and Psychosomatics,* 1973, *22,* 250-54.

CHESS, S. Diagnosis and treatment of the hyperactive child. *New York State Journal of Medicine,* 1960, *60,* 2379-85.

CHESS, S. *An introduction to child psychiatry.* New York: Grune & Stratton, 1969.

CHESS, S., & ROSENBERG, M. Clinical differentiation among children with initial language complaints. *Journal of Autism and Childhood Schizophrenia,* 1974, *2,* 99-109.

CHILDREN'S DEFENSE FUND. *Your rights under the Education for All Handicapped Children Act P.L. 94-142.* Washington, D.C.: Children's Defense Fund, 1976.

CHRISTOPHERSEN, E. R., ARNOLD, C. M., HILL, D. W., & QUILITCH, R. H. The home point system: Token reinforcement procedures for application by parents of children with behavior problems. *Journal of Applied Behavior Analysis,* 1972, *4,* 485-98.

CICIRELLI, V. G., EVANS, J. W., & SCHILLER, J. S. *The impact of Head Start: An evaluation of the effects on children's cognitive and affective development* (2 vols.). Athens, Ohio: Ohio University-Westinghouse Learning Corp., 1969.

CLASTER, D. S. Comparison of risk perception between delinquents and nondelinquents. *Journal of Criminal Law, Criminology, and Police Science,* 1967, *58,* 80–86.

CLEARY, T. A., HUMPHREYS, L. G., KENDRICK, S. A., & WESMAN, A. Educational uses of tests with disadvantaged students. *American Psychologist,* 1975, *30,* 15–41.

CLEMENT, P. W. Elimination of sleepwalking in a seven-year-old boy. *Journal of Consulting and Clinical Psychology,* 1970, *34,* 220–26.

CLEMENTS, S. D., & PETERS, J. E. Minimal brain dysfunctions in school-age children. *Archives of General Psychiatry,* 1962, *6,* 185–97.

CLOSER LOOK. Due process in a nutshell. National Information Center for the Handicapped: A Project of the U.S. Dept. of HEW, Fall 1977.

CLOWARD, R. A., & OHLIN, L. E. *Delinquency and opportunity.* New York: Free Press, 1960.

COLLINS, R. C. Toward a future strategy for child development. *Children Today,* 1975, *36,* 11–13.

CONNELL, P. H. Medical treatment. In J. K. Wing (Ed.), *Early childhood autism: Clinical, educational, and social aspects.* London: Pergamon Press, 1966.

CONNOR, F. P. *Education of homebound or hospitalized children.* New York: Columbia University Bureau of Publications, 1964.

CONNOR, F. P., HOOVER, R., HORTON, K., SANDS, H., STERNFELD, L., & WOLINSKY, G. F. Physical and sensory handicaps. In N. Hobbs (Ed.), *Issues in the classification of children* (Vol. 1). San Francisco: Jossey-Bass, 1975.

CONNORS, C. K. A teacher rating scale for use in drug studies with children. *American Journal of Psychiatry,* 1969, *126,* 152–56.

CONNORS, C. K. Pharmacotherapy of psychopathology in children. In H. C. Quay & J. S. Werry (Eds.), *Psychopathological disorders of childhood.* New York: Wiley, 1972. (a)

CONNORS, C. K. Psychological effects of stimulant drugs in children with minimal brain dysfunction. *Pediatrics,* 1972, *49,* 702. (b)

CONNORS, C. K. A placebo—crossover study of caffeine treatment of hyperkinetic children. *International Journal of Mental Health,* 1975, *4,* 132–43.

COOK, M. Therapeutic preschool. In J. Hellmuth (Ed.), *Educational therapy* (Vol. 1). Seattle, Wash.: Special Child Publications, 1966.

COOPER, E. G. Recovery from stuttering in a junior and senior high school population. *Journal of Speech and Hearing Research,* 1972, *15,* 632–38.

COTT, A. Orthomolecular approach to the treatment of learning disabilities. *Schizophrenia,* 1971, *3,* 95–102.

COVERT, C. *Mental retardation: A handbook for the primary physician.* Report of the American Medical Association Conference on Mental Retardation. Chicago, April 9–11, 1964.

COWEN, E. L., UNDERBERG, R. P., VERILLO, R. T., & BENHAM, F. G. *Adjustment to visual disability in adolescence.* New York: American Foundation for the Blind, 1961.

COX, C. M. *The early mental traits of three hundred geniuses. Genetic studies of genius* (Vol. II). Stanford, Calif.: Stanford University Press, 1926.

CRAIG, P. A. Counting handicapped children: A federal imperative. *Journal of Educational Finance,* 1976, *1,* 318–39.

CRAIG, Y. The care of our dying child: A parent offers some personal observations based on recollection. In L. Burton (Ed.), *Care of the child facing death.* London: Routledge & Kegan Paul, 1974.

CRAMER, J. B. Psychiatric examination of the child. In A. M. Freedman, H. I. Kaplan, & B. J. Sadock (Eds.), *Comprehensive textbook of psychiatry* (Vol. II). Baltimore: Williams & Wilkins, 1975.

CRATTY, B. J., & SAMS, T. A. *The body-image of blind children.* New York: American Foundation for the Blind, 1968.

CREAK, M., CAMERON, K., COWIE, V., INI, S., MACKEITH, R., MITCHELL, G., O'GORMAN, G., ORFORD, F., ROGERS, W., SHAPIRO, A., STONE, F., STROH, G., & YDKIN, S. Schizophrenic syndrome in childhood. *British Medical Journal,* 1961, *2.*

CRINELLA, F. M. Identification of brain dysfunction syndromes in children through profile analysis: Patterns associated with so-called "minimal brain dysfunction." *Journal of Abnormal Psychology,* 1973, *82,* 33–45.

CRITCHLEY, E. M. R. Reading retardation, dyslexia, and delinquency. *British Journal of Psychiatry,* 1968, *115,* 1537–47.

CRONBACH, L. J. Psychological issues pertinent to recent American curriculum reforms. In G. Nielsen (Ed.), *Child and education, proceedings of the XIV International Congress of Applied Psychology.* Copenhagen: Munksgaard, 1962.

CRUCHON, G. *The transformations of childhood.* Dayton, Ohio: Pflaum Press, 1969.

CRUICKSHANK, W. M. Least-restrictive placement: Administrative wishful thinking. *Journal of Learning Disabilities,* 1977, *4,* 193–94.

CUMMING, J., & CUMMING, E. *Ego and milieu.* New York: Atherton Press, 1962.

CURRIER, L. S. Some poems. *Journal of Pediatric Psychology,* 1977, *2,* 81.

CUTTS, N. E., & MOSELY, N. *Teaching the bright and gifted.* Englewood Cliffs, N.J.: Prentice-Hall, 1957.

CYTRYN, L., & LOURIE, R. S. Mental retardation. In A. M. Freedman, H. I. Kaplan, & B. J. Sadock (Eds.), *Comprehensive textbook of psychiatry* (Vol. I) (2nd ed.). Baltimore: Williams & Wilkins, 1975.

DAHLLOF, U. S. *Ability grouping, content validity, and curriculum process analysis.* New York: Teachers College Press, Columbia University, 1971.

DARLEY, F. L. *Diagnosis and appraisal of communication disorders.* Englewood Cliffs, N.J.: Prentice-Hall, 1964.

DAUGHERTY, L. G., & RUDD, A. L. Compensatory education in an urban center. In P. A. Witty (Ed.), *The educationally retarded and disadvantaged NSSE yearbook.* Chicago: University of Chicago Press, 1967.

DAVIDS, A. Childhood psychosis: The problem of differential diagnosis. *Journal of Autism and Childhood Schizophrenia,* 1975, *5,* 129–38.

DEMAUSE, L. (Ed.). *The history of childhood.* New York: Psychohistory Press, 1974.

DEMYER, M. K. Research in infantile autism: A strategy and its results. *Biological Psychiatry,* 1975, *10,* 433–52.

DEMYER, M. K., CHURCHILL, D. W., PONTIUS, W., & GILKEY, K. M. A comparison of five diagnostic systems for childhood schizophrenia and infantile autism. *Journal of Autism and Childhood Schizophrenia,* 1971, *1,* 175–89.

DENHOFF, E., & TARNOPOL, L. Medical responsibilities in learning disorders. In L. Tarnopol (Ed.), *Learning disorders in children: Diagnosis, medication, education.* Boston: Little, Brown & Co., 1971, 65–118.

DENNIS, W. (Ed.). *Historical readings in developmental psychology.* New York: Appleton-Century-Crofts, 1972.

DENNISON, W. M. *Surgery in infancy and childhood.* London: Churchill Livingstone, 1974.

DES LAURIERS, A., & CARLSON, C. *Your child is asleep: Early infantile autism.* Homewood, Ill.: Dorsey Press, 1969.

DESPERT, J. L. *Schizophrenia in children.* New York: Robert Brunner, Inc., 1968.

DESPERT, J. L. *The emotionally disturbed child: An inquiry into family patterns.* New York: Anchor Books, 1970.

DEUTSCH, M. Facilitating development in the pre-school child: social and psychological perspectives. *Merrill-Palmer Quarterly,* 1964, *10,* 249–64.

DEUTSCH, M. The role of social class in language development and cognition. *American Journal of Orthopsychiatry,* 1965, *25,* 75–88.

DEUTSCH, M., & BROWN, B. R. Social influences in Negro-white intelligence differences. *Journal of Social Issues,* 1964, *20,* 24–35.

DIANA ET AL. v. STATE BOARD OF EDUCATION, United States District Court, Northern District of California, C–70 37 RFP, 1969.

DILLER, L. Psychological aspects of physically handicapped children. In B. B. Wolman (Ed.), *Manual of child psychopathology.* New York: McGraw-Hill, 1972.

DOLLARD, J., DOOB, L. W., MILLER, N. E., MOWRER, O. H., & SEARS, R. R. *Frustration and aggression.* New Haven: Yale University Press, 1939.

DOMBRO, R. H. Child life programs in ninety-two pediatric departments of general hospitals in the United States and Canada. In A. Haller (Ed.), *The hospitalized child and his family.* Baltimore: Johns Hopkins University Press, 1967.

DOMINO, E. F. Pharmacological analysis of the pathobiology of schizophrenia. In S. Sankar (Ed.), *Schizophrenia: Current concepts and research.* Hicksville, N.Y.: PJD Publications Ltd., 1969.

DONOFRIO, A. F. Child psychotherapy—help or hindrance? *Mental Hygiene,* 1970, 54.

DONOFRIO, A. F. Parent education vs. child psychotherapy. *Psychology in the Schools,* 1976, *13,* 176–80.

DOUBROS, S. G., & DANIELS, G. J. An experimental approach to the reduction of overactive behavior. *Behaviour Research and Therapy,* 1966, *4,* 251–58.

DOUGLAS, J. W. B. *The home and the school.* London: Mackgibbon & Kee, 1964.

DOUGLAS, J. W. B., & BLOMFIELD, J. M. *Children under five.* London: Allen & Unwin, 1958.

DOWN, J. L. Observations on ethnic classifications. *London Hospital Reports,* 1866, *3,* 229–62.

DRABMAN, R. S., SPITALNIK, R., & O'LEARY, K. D. Teaching self-control to disruptive children. *Journal of Abnormal Psychology,* 1973, *82,* 10–16.

DREVDAHL, J. E., & CATTELL, R. B. Personality and creativity in artists and writers. *Journal of Clinical Psychology,* 1958, *14,* 107–11.

DRUDGE, M. K., & PHILIPS, B. J. Shaping behavior in voice therapy. *Journal of Speech and Hearing Disorders,* 1976, *41,* 398–411.

DUFFY, J. K. Hearing problems of school age children. In I. S. Fusfeld (Ed.), *A handbook of readings in education of the deaf and postschool implications.* Springfield, Ill.: Charles C. Thomas, 1967.

DURR, W. K. *The gifted student.* New York: Oxford University Press, 1964.

EASSON, W. M. *The dying child: The management of the child or adolescent who is dying.* Springfield, Ill.: Charles C. Thomas, 1970.

EDELMAN, M. W., ALLEN, M., BROWN, C., & ROSEWATER, A. *Children out of school in America.* Cambridge, Mass.: Children's Defense Fund, 1974.

EDGINGTON, D. *The physically handicapped child in your classroom.* Springfield, Ill.: Charles C. Thomas, 1976.

EDUCATIONAL RESEARCH SERVICE, INC. *Gifted students: Identification techniques and program organization.* Arlington, Va.: Educational Research Service, Inc., 1975.

EISENBERG, L. The fathers of autistic children. *American Journal of Orthopsychiatry,* 1957, *27,* 715–24.

EISENBERG, L. The pediatric management of school phobia. *Journal of Pediatrics,* 1959, *55,* 758–66.

EISENBERG, L. Psychopharmacology in childhood: A critique. In E. Miller (Ed.), *Foundations of child psychiatry.* New York: Pergamon Press, 1968.

EISENBERG, L. The clinical use of stimulant drugs in children. *Pediatrics,* 1972, *49,* 709–15.

EISENBERG, L., & KANNER, L. Early infantile autism: 1943–1955. *American Journal of Orthopsychiatry,* 1956, *36,* 556–66.

EITZEN, D. S. The effects of behavior modification on attitudes of delinquents. *Behaviour Research and Therapy,* 1975, *13,* 295–300.

ELMER, E. *Children in jeopardy: A study of abused minors and their families.* Pittsburgh: University of Pittsburgh Press, 1967.

EMERY, R. E., & MARHALIN, D. An applied behavior analysis of delinquency: The irrelevancy of relevant behavior. *American Psychologist,* 1977, *32,* 860–73.

EMRICK, J. A., SORENSEN, P. H., & STERNS, M. S. *Interim evaluation of the national follow through program, 1969–1971.* Menlo Park, Calif.: Stanford Research Institute, 1973.

EPSTEIN, N. Priorities for change: Some preliminary proposals from the White House Conference on Children. *Children,* 1971, *18,* 2–7.

ERIKSON, E. H. *Identity and the life cycle: Selected papers.* New York: International University Press, 1959.

ERIKSON, E. H. *Childhood and society* (2nd ed.). New York: Norton, 1963.

ERIKSON, E. H. *Identity: Youth and crisis.* New York: Norton, 1968.

ESCALONA, S. Some considerations regarding psychotherapy with psychotic children. In M. Haworth (Ed.), *Child psychotherapy.* New York: Basic Books, 1964.

ESQUIROL, J. E. D. [*Mental Maladies*] (E. K. Hunt, trans.). Philadelphia: Lea & Blanchard, 1845. (Originally published as *Maladies mentales,* 1838.)

ESTES, W. K. *Learning theory and mental development.* New York: Academic Press, 1970.

EWING, I. R., & EWING, A. W. G. The ascertainment of deafness in infancy and early childhood. *Journal of Laryngology and Otology,* 1944, *59,* 309–38.

EYSENCK, H. J. *Crime and personality.* London: Routledge & Kegan-Paul, 1964.

EYSENCK, H. J. *Fact and fiction in psychology.* Baltimore: Penguin, 1965.

EYSENCK, H. J. Genetic factors in personality development. In A. R. Kaplan (Ed.), *Human behavior genetics.* Springfield: Charles C. Thomas, 1975.

EYSENCK, H. J. The learning theory model of neurosis—a new approach. *Behaviour Research and Therapy,* 1976, *14,* 251–68.

FARBER, B. Effects of a severely mentally retarded child on the family. In E. P. Trapp & P. Himelstein (Eds.), *Readings on the exceptional child.* New York: Appleton-Century-Crofts, 1962.

FARRELL, G. *The story of blindness.* Cambridge: Harvard University Press, 1956.

FASSLER, J. Performance of cerebral palsied children under conditions of reduced auditory input. *Exceptional Children,* 1970, *37,* 201–9.

FEINGOLD, B. F. Hyperkinesis and learning disabilities linked to artificial food flavors and colors. *American Journal of Nursing,* 1975, *75,* 797–803.

FEINMESSER, M., & BAUBERGER-TELL, L. Evaluation of methods of detecting hearing impairment in infancy and early childhood. Paper presented at the Conference on Newborn Hearing Screening (Bureau of Maternal & Child Health), San Francisco, 1971.

FELDMAN, F., CANTOR, D., SOLL, S., & BACHRACH, W. Psychiatric study of a consecutive series of 34 patients with ulcerative colitis. *British Medical Journal,* 1967, *3,* 14–17.

FELDUSEN, J. F., THURSTON, J. R., & BENNING, J. J. A longitudinal study of delinquency and other aspects of children's behaviour. *International Journal of Criminology and Penology,* 1973, *1,* 341–51.

FENICHEL, O. *The psychoanalytic theory of neurosis.* New York: Norton, 1945.

FERSTER, D. B. Positive reinforcement and behavioral deficits of autistic children. *Child Development,* 1961, *32,* 437–56.

FILLER, J. W., ROBINSON, C. R., SMITH, R. A., VINCENT-SMITH, L. J., BRICKER, D. D., & BRICKER, W. A. Mental retardation. In N. Hobbs (Ed.), *Issues in the classification of children* (Vol. I). San Francisco: Jossey-Bass, 1975.

FINCH, S. M. Psychophysiological disorders of children. In A. M. Freedman & H. I. Kaplan (Eds.), *The child: His psychological and cultural development* (Vol. 2). New York: Atheneum, 1971.

FINDLEY, W. G., & BRYAN, M. M. *Ability grouping: 1970 status, impact, and alternatives.* Athens, Ga.: Center for Educational Improvement, University of Georgia, 1971.

FISH, B. Drug therapy in child psychiatry: Pharmacological aspects. *Comprehensive Psychiatry,* 1960, *1,* 212–27.

FISH, B. Pharmacotherapy for autistic and schizophrenic children. In E. Ritvo (Ed.), *Autism: Diagnosis, current research and management.* New York: Spectrum Publications, 1976.

FISH, B., SHAPIRO, T., HALPERN, F., & WILE, R. The prediction of schizophrenia in infancy: III. A ten-year follow-up report of neurological and psychological development. *American Journal of Psychiatry*, 1965, *121*, 768–75.

FISH, B., WILE, R., SHAPIRO, T., & HALPERN, F. The prediction of schizophrenia in infancy: II. A ten-year follow-up report of predictions made at one month of age. In P. H. Hoch & J. Zubin (Eds.), *Psychopathology of Schizophrenia*. New York: Grune & Stratton, 1966.

FLEMING, J. W. *Care and management of exceptional children*. New York: Appleton-Century-Crofts, 1973.

FLETCHER ET AL. v. ILLINOIS, 52 Ill. 395 (1869).

FONDA, G. Definition and classification of blindness with respect to ability to use residual vision. *Blindness: 1960 AAWB annual*. Washington, D.C.: American Association of Workers for the Blind, 1960.

FONTANA, A. F. Familial etiology of schizophrenia. *Psychological Bulletin*, 1966, *66*, 214–27.

FONTANA, V. J. *Somewhere a child is crying*. New York: Macmillan, 1973.

FORCE, D. G. Social status of physically handicapped children. *Exceptional Children*, 1956, *23*, 104–7.

FRAIBERG, S. Intervention in infancy. *Journal of the American Academy of Child Psychiatry*, 1971, *10*, 381–405.

FRAIBERG, S. Separation crisis in two blind children. *Psychoanalytic Study of the Child*, 1972, *26*, 355–71.

FRAIBERG, S., SMITH, M., & ADELSON, E. An educational program for blind infants. *Journal of Special Education*, 1969, *3*, 121–39.

FRANK, G. H. The role of the family in the development of psychopathology. *Psychological Bulletin*, 1965, *64*, 191–205.

FRASER, G. R., & FRIEDMAN, A. I. *The causes of blindness in childhood: A study of 776 children with severe visual handicaps*. Baltimore: The Johns Hopkins Press, 1968.

FRENCH, J. L. (Ed.) *Educating the gifted*. New York: Holt, Rinehart and Winston, 1964.

FREUD, A. *The psychoanalytic treatment of children*. London: Imago, 1946.

FREUD, A. The role of bodily illness in the mental life of children. *Psychoanalytic Study of the Child*, 1952, *7*, 69–81.

FREUD, A. *Normality and pathology in childhood*. New York: International Universities Press, 1965.

FREUD, A. The concept of the rejecting mother. In E. J. Anthony & T. Benedek (Eds.), *Parenthood: Its psychology and psychopathology*. Boston: Little, Brown, 1970.

FREUD, S. Three essays on sexuality. In J. Stracey (Ed.), *Standard edition of the complete psychological works [of S. Freud]* (Vol. 3). London: Hogarth Press, 1953. (First German Language Edition, 1905.)

FRIEDMAN, E. Early infantile autism. *Journal of Child Clinical Psychology*, 1974, *3*, 4–10.

FROMMER, E. A. Treatment of childhood depression with antidepressant drugs. *British Medical Journal*, 1967, *1*, 729–32.

FROMM-REICHMANN, F. Notes on the development of treatment of schizophrenics by psychoanalytic psychotherapy. *Psychiatry*, 1948, *11*, 263–73.

FROSTIG, M., & HORNE, D. *The Frostig program for the development of visual perception: Teacher's guide*. Chicago: Follett, 1964.

FROSTIG, M., LEFEVER, D. W., & WHITTLESEY, J. R. B. *The Maryanne Frostig developmental tests of visual perception*. Palo Alto, Calif.: Consulting Psychologists Press, 1964.

FROSTIG, M., & MASLOW, P. *Learning problems in the classroom: Prevention and remediation*. New York: Grune & Stratton, 1973.

FULKER, W. H., & FULKER, M. *Techniques with tangibles: A manual for teaching the blind*. Springfield, Ill.: Charles C. Thomas, 1968.

FURTH, H. G. Research with the deaf: Implications for language and cognition. *Psychological Bulletin*, 1964, *62*, 145–64.

FURTH, H. G. *Thinking without language: Psychological implications of deafness*. New York: The Free Press, 1966.

FURTH, H. G. Linguistic deficiency and thinking: Research with deaf subjects, 1964–1969. *Psychological Bulletin*, 1971, *76*, 58–72.

GALLAGHER, J. J. *Research summary on gifted child education*. State of Illinois, Office of Superintendent of Public Instruction, 1966.

GALLAGHER, J. J. *Teaching the gifted child* (2nd ed.). Boston: Allyn & Bacon, 1975.

GALLAGHER, J. J. & WIEGERINK, R. Educational strategies for the autistic child. *Journal of Autism and Childhood Schizophrenia*, 1976, *6*, 15–26.

GAMPEL, D. H., GOTTLIEB, J., & HARRISON, R. H. Comparison of classroom behavior of special-class EMR, integrated EMR, low IQ, and nonretarded children. *American Journal of Mental Deficiency*, 1974, *79*, 16–21.

GARDINER, P. The "at risk" concept with reference to visual disorders. In P. Gardiner, R. MacKeith, & V. Smith (Eds.), *Aspects of developmental and paediatric ophthalmology*. London: Spastics International Medical Publications with W. Heinemann Medical Books, 1969.

GARDNER, G. E., & SPERRY, B. M. School problems—learning disabilities and school phobia. In G. Kaplan & S. Arieti (Eds.), *American handbook of psychiatry* (Vol. 2, 2nd ed.). New York: Basic Books, 1974.

GARDNER, W. I. *Behavior modification in mental retardation: The education and rehabilitation of the mentally retarded adolescent and adult*. Chicago: Aldine-Atherton, 1971.

GARDNER, W. I. *Children with learning and behavior problems*. Boston: Allyn & Bacon, 1976.

GARFINKEL, B. D., WEBSTER, C. D., & SLOMAN, L. Methylphenidate and caffeine in the treatment of children with minimal brain dysfunction. *American Journal of Psychiatry*, 1975, *132*, 723–28.

GARRARD, S. D., & RICHMOND, J. B. Mental retardation: Nature and manifestations. In M. F. Reiser & S. Arieti (Eds.), *American handbook of psychiatry* (Vol. 4, 2nd ed.). New York: Basic Books, 1975.

GEARHART, B. R., & WEISHAHN, M. W. *The handicapped child in the regular classroom*. St. Louis: C. V. Mosby Co., 1976.

GELLERT, E. Reducing the emotional stresses of hospitalization for children. *American Journal of Occupational Therapy*, 1958, *12*, 125–29, 155.

GEPPERT, T. V. Management of nocturnal enuresis by conditioned response. *Journal of the American Medical Association*, 1953, *152*, 381–83.

GERARD, M. W. Enuresis: A study in etiology. *American Journal of Orthopsychiatry*, 1939, *9*, 45–58.

GESELL, A. Cinemanalysis: A method of behavior study. *The Journal of Genetic Psychology*, 1935, *47*, 3–16.

GESELL, A., & AMATRUDA, C. S. *Developmental diagnosis: Normal and abnormal child development* (2nd ed.). New York: Harper & Row, 1947.

GESELL, A., & ILG, F. L. *Infant and child in the culture of today*. New York: Harper & Row, 1943.

GESELL, A., ILG, F. L., & BULLIS, G. E. *Vision: Its development in infant and child*. New York: Hoeber, 1949.

GETMAN, G. N. The visuomotor complex in the acquisition of learning skills. In J. Hellmuth (Ed.), *Learning disorders* (Vol. I). Seattle: Special Child Publications, 1965.

GETZELS, J. W., & JACKSON, P. W. *Creativity and intelligence: Explorations with gifted students*. New York: Wiley, 1962.

GIL, D. G. *Violence against children*. Cambridge: Harvard University Press, 1970.

GILES, D. K., & WOLF, M. M. Toilet training institutionalized, severe retardates: An application of operant behavior modification techniques. *American Journal of Mental Deficiency*, 1966, *70*, 766–80.

GINOTT, H. G. *Group psychotherapy with children*. New York: McGraw-Hill, 1961.

GIRARDEAU, F. L., & SPRADLIN, J. E. Token rewards on a cottage program. *Mental Retardation*, 1964, *2*, 345–51.

GITTELMAN, M., & BIRCH, H. G. Childhood schizophrenia: Intellect, neurologic status, perinatal risk, prognosis, and family pathology. *Archives of General Psychiatry*, 1967, *17*, 16–25.

GITTELMAN-KLEIN, R., KLEIN, D. F., ABIKOFF, H., KATZ, S., GLOISTEN, A. C., & KATES, W. Relative efficacy of methylphenidate and behavior modification in hyperactive children: An interim report. *Journal of Abnormal Child Psychology*, 1976, *4*, 361–79.

GLASSER, W. *Schools without failure*. New York: Harper & Row, 1969.

GLICKLICH, L. An historical account of enuresis. *Journal of Pediatrics*, 1951, 859–76.

GLUECK, S., & GLUECK, E. *Unraveling juvenile delinquency*. New York: Commonwealth Fund, 1950.

GLUECK, S., & GLUECK, E. *Family environment and delinquency*. Boston: Houghton Mifflin, 1962.

GLUECK, S., & GLUECK, E. *Delinquents and nondelinquents in perspective*. Cambridge, Mass.: Harvard University Press, 1968.

GOGGINS, E. L., LANSKY, S. B., & HASSANEIN, K. Psychological reactions of children with malignancies. *Journal of the American Academy of Child Psychiatry*, 1976, *15*, 314–25.

GOLD, M. J. *Education of the intellectually gifted*. Columbus, Ohio: Charles E. Merrill Books, 1965.

GOLD, S. Further investigation of a possible epileptogenic factor in the serum of psychotic children. *Australian and New Zealand Journal of Psychiatry*, 1967, *1*, 153–56.

GOLDFARB, W. *Childhood schizophrenia*. Cambridge: Harvard University Press, 1961.

GOLDFARB, W. Childhood psychosis. In P. H. Mussen (Ed.), *Manual of child psychology*. New York: Wiley, 1970.

GOLDFARB, W. Therapeutic management of schizophrenic children. In J. G. Howell (Ed.), *Modern perspectives in international child psychiatry*. New York: Brunner/Mazel, 1971.

GOLDSTEIN, J., FREUD, A., & SOLNIT, A. J. *Beyond the best interests of the child*. New York: Free Press, 1973.

GOLDSTEIN, K. *Aftereffects of brain-injuries in war*. New York: Grune & Stratton, 1942.

GOOD, H. G., & TELLER, J. D. *A history of western education*. New York: Macmillan, 1969.

GOODMAN, H., GOTTLIEB, J., & HARRISON, R. H. Social acceptance of EMR's integrated into a nongraded elementary school. *American Journal of Mental Deficiency*, 1972, *76*, 412–17.

GOODMAN, J. D., & SOURS, J. A. *The child mental status examination*. New York: Basic Books, 1967.

GORHAM, K. A., DES JARDINS, C., PAGE, R., PETTIS, E., & SCHEIBER, B. Effect on parents. In N. Hobbs (Ed.), *Issues in the classification of children* (Vol. 2). San Francisco: Jossey-Bass, 1975.

GOTTESMAN, I. I., & SHIELDS, J. *Schizophrenia and genetics*. New York: Academic Press, 1972.

GOTTLIEB, J., & BUDOFF, M. Social acceptability of retarded children in nongraded schools differing in architecture. *American Journal of Mental Deficiency*, 1973, *78*, 141–43.

GRAHAM, P. Management in child psychiatry: Recent trends. *British Journal of Psychiatry*, 1976, *129*, 97–108.

GRALIKER, B. V., FISHLER, K., & KOCH, J. Teenage reaction to a mentally retarded sibling. *American Journal of Mental Deficiency*, 1962, *66*, 838–43.

GRALIKER, B. V., KOCH, R., & HENDERSON, R. A. A study of factors influencing placement of retarded children in a state residential institution. *American Journal of Mental Deficiency*, 1965, *69*, 553–59.

GREENFIELD, J. *A child called Noah*. New York: Holt, Rinehart and Winston, 1972.

GRINKER, R. R. *Psychiatric diagnosis, therapy, and research on the psychotic deaf*. Washington, D.C.: U.S. Department of Health, Education, and Welfare, Social and Rehabilitation Service, 1971.

GROSSER, C., & MCGOWAN, B. *Case advocacy practice*. Paper presented at the meeting of the National Conference on Social Welfare, San Francisco, 1975.

GROSSMAN, F. K. *Brothers and sisters of retarded children: An exploratory study*. Syracuse, N.Y.: Syracuse University Press, 1972.

GROUP FOR THE ADVANCEMENT OF PSYCHIATRY. *Psychopathological disorders of childhood: Theoretical considerations and a proposed classification*. New York: Author, 1966.

GROUP FOR THE ADVANCEMENT OF PSYCHIATRY: COMMITTEE ON PUBLIC EDUCATION. *The joys and sorrows of parenthood*. New York: Charles Scribner's Sons, 1973.

GUILFORD, J. P. The structure of the intellect. *Psychological Bulletin*, 1956, *53*, 267–93.

GUILFORD, J. P. Traits of creativity. In H. A. Anderson (Ed.), *Creativity and its cultivation*. New York: Harper & Row, 1959, 142–61.

GUITAR, B. Pretreatment factors associated with the outcome of stuttering therapy. *Journal of Speech and Hearing Research*, 1976, *19*, 590–600.

GURALNICK, M. J. The value of integrating handicapped and non-handicapped preschool children. *American Journal of Orthopsychiatry*, 1976, *46*, 236–45.

GUSKIN, S. L., & SPICKER, H. H. Educational research in mental retardation. In N. R. Ellis (Ed.), *International review of research in mental retardation* (Vol. 3). New York: Academic Press, 1968.

HAGAN, J. W., & HUNTSMAN, N. J. Selective attention in mental retardation. *Developmental Psychology*, 1971, *5*, 151–60.

HALL, S. M., & TALKINGTON, L. W. Trends in programming for deaf mentally retarded in public residential facilities. *Mental Retardation*, 1972, *10*, 50–52.

HALLAHAN, D. P., & CRUICKSHANK, W. M. *Psychoeducational foundations of learning disabilities*. Englewood Cliffs, N.J.: Prentice-Hall, 1973.

HALLAHAN, D. P., & KAUFFMAN, J. M. *Introduction to learning disabilities: A psychobehavioral approach*. Englewood Cliffs, N.J.: Prentice-Hall, 1976.

HALVERSTADT, D. B. Enuresis. *Journal of Pediatric Psychology*, 1976, *4*, 13–14.

HANSON, D. R., & GOTTESMAN, I. I. The genetics, if any, of infantile autism and childhood schizophrenia. *Journal of Autism and Childhood Schizophrenia*, 1976, *6*, 209–34.

HAPEMAN, L. Reservations about the effect of P.L. 94–142 on the education of visually handicapped children. *Education of Visually Handicapped*, 1977, *9*, 33–36.

HARE, B. A., HAMMILL, D. D., & CRANDELL, J. M. Auditory discrimination ability of visually limited children. *New Outlook for the Blind*, 1970, *64*, 287–92.

HARPER, L. V. The scope of offspring effects: From caregiver to culture. *Psychological Bulletin*, 1975, *82*, 784–801.

HARRISON, S. I. Individual psychotherapy. In A. M. Freedman & H. I. Kaplan (Eds.), *Comprehensive textbook of psychiatry*. Baltimore: Williams & Wilkins, 1975.

HARTLAGE, L. C. Differences in listening comprehension of the blind and the sighted. *International Journal of Education for the Blind*, 1963, *13*, 1–6.

HAWKINS, R. P., PETERSON, R. F., SCHWEID, E., & BIJOU, S. W. Behavior therapy in the home: Amelioration of problem parent-child relations with the parents in a therapeutic role. *Journal of Experimental Child Psychology*, 1966, *4*, 99–107.

HAYES, S. P. *Contributions to a psychology of blindness*. New York: American Foundation for the Blind, 1941.

HEBER, R. F. A manual on terminology and classification in mental retardation. *American Journal of Mental Deficiency*, 1959. (Monograph Supplement)

HEBER, R. F. A manual on terminology and classification in mental retardation (2nd ed.). *American Journal of Mental Deficiency*, 1961. (Monograph Supplement)

HEBER, R. F., & GARBER, H. *An experiment in the prevention of cultural-familial mental retardation*. Madison, Wis.: Rehabilitation & Research Training Center, University of Wisconsin, 1971. (Mimeograph)

HEBER, R. F., & GARBER, H. *Rehabilitation of families at risk for mental retardation*. Madison, Wis.: Rehabilitation & Research Training Center, University of Wisconsin, 1974. (Mimeograph)

HEBER, R. F., GARBER, H., & FALENDER, C. *The Milwaukee Project:*

An experiment in the prevention of cultural-familial retardation.
Madison, Wis.: Rehabilitation & Research Training Center,
University of Wisconsin, 1973. (Mimeograph)

HEFFRON, W. A., BOMMELAERE, K., & MASTERS, R. Group discussions with parents of leukemic children. *Pediatrics*, 1973, *52*, 831–40.

HENDERSON, W. A review of current medical aspects of enuresis. *Journal of Pediatric Psychology*, 1976, *4*, 15–17.

HERBERT, E. W., & BAER, D. M. Training parents as behavior modifiers: Self-recording of contingent attention. *Journal of Applied Behavior Analysis*, 1972, *5*, 139–50.

HERSOV, L. A. Persistent nonattendance at school. *Journal of Child Psychology and Psychiatry*, 1960, *1*, 130–36.

HERTZLER, J. H., & MIRZA, M. *Handbook of pediatric surgery.* Chicago: Yearbook Medical Publishers, 1974.

HETHERINGTON, E. M., & MARTIN, B. Family interaction and psychopathology in children. In H. C. Quay & J. S. Werry, *Psychopathological disorders of childhood.* New York: Wiley, 1972.

HEWETT, F. Teaching reading to an autistic boy through operant conditioning. *The Reading Teacher*, 1964, *17*, 613–18.

HEWITT, L. E., & JENKINS, R. L. *Fundamental patterns of maladjustment: The dynamics of their origin.* Springfield, Ill.: State of Illinois, 1946.

HILDRETH, G. H. *Introduction to the gifted.* New York: McGraw-Hill, 1966.

HIMMELWEIT, H. T. A factorial study of "children's behavior problems." In H. J. Eysenck, *The structure of human personality.* London: Methuen, 1953.

HINGTGEN, J. N., & BRYSON, C. Q. Recent developments in the study of early childhood psychoses: Infantile autism, childhood schizophrenia and related disorders. *Schizophrenia Bulletin*, 1972, *5*, 8–53.

HINGTGEN, J. N., COULTER, S. K., & CHURCHILL, D. W. Intensive reinforcement of imitative behavior in mute autistic children. *Archives of General Psychiatry*, 1967, *17*, 36–43.

HINGTGEN, J. N., SANDERS, B. J., & DeMYER, M. K. Shaping cooperative responses in early childhood schizophrenics. In L. P. Ullmann & L. Krasner (Eds.), *Case studies in behavior modification.* New York: Holt, Rinehart and Winston, 1965.

HIRSCH, M. J. Survey of learning disorders. In D. B. Carter (Ed.), *Interdisciplinary approaches to learning disorders.* Philadelphia: Chilton Book Co., 1970.

HIRSCHI, T. *Causes of delinquency.* Berkeley, Calif.: University of California Press, 1969.

HIRSHOREN, A., SCHULTZ, E. W., MANTON, A. B., & HENDERSON, R. A. *A survey of public school special education programs for emotionally disturbed children.* Urbana, Ill.: University of Illinois, 1970. (Monograph)

HOBBS, N. Helping disturbed children: Psychological and ecological strategies. *American Psychologist*, 1966, *21*, 1105–15.

HOBBS, N. *The futures of children: Categories, labels, and their consequences.* San Francisco: Jossey-Bass, 1975.

HOBBS, T. R., & HOLT, M. M. The effects of token reinforcement on the behavior of delinquents in cottage settings. *Journal of Applied Behavior Analysis*, 1976, *9*, 189–98.

HOFFMAN, S. P., ENGELHARDT, D. M., MARGOLIS, R. A., POLIZOS, P., WAIZER, J., & ROSENFELD, R. Response to methylphenidate in low socioeconomic hyperactive children. *Archives of General Psychiatry*, 1974, *30*, 354–59.

HOLLINGWORTH, L. *Children above 180 IQ.* New York: World Book, 1942.

HOLT, K. S. Home care of severely retarded children. *Pediatrics*, 1958, *22*, 744–75.

HOWARTH, R. The psychiatric care of children with life-threatening illnesses. In L. Burton (Ed.), *Care of the child facing death.* London: Routledge & Kegan Paul, 1974.

HUGHES, J. G. The pediatric history and physical examination. In J. G. Hughes (Ed.), *Synopsis of pediatrics.* St. Louis: Mosby, 1975.

HUNT, J. McV. The psychological basis for using pre-school enrichment as an antidote for cultural deprivation. *Merrill-Palmer Quarterly*, 1964, *10*, 209–48.

HYATT, R., & ROLNICK, N. (Eds.). *Teaching the mentally handicapped child.* New York: Behavioral Publications, 1974.

HYMAN, I., PETRUZZI, R., & SCHLOSSMAN, T. Problems of defining and measuring child advocacy attitudes. *The Clinical Psychologist*, 1976, *29*, 25–27.

ILLICK, J. E. Child-rearing in seventeenth century England and America. In L. deMause (Ed.), *The history of childhood.* New York: Psychohistory Press, 1974.

INOUYE, E. Similarity and dissimilarity of schizophrenia in twins. *Proceedings of the Third International Congress of Psychiatry*, 1961, *1*, 524–30.

IN RE GAULT, 387 U.S. 1 (1967).

INTERNATIONAL LEAGUE OF SOCIETIES FOR THE MENTALLY RETARDED. *Newsletter*, Secrétariat: 12, rue Forestière, Bruxelles 5, Belgium, 1969, *7*.

ISHIHARA, T., & YOSHII, N. Multivariate analytic study of EEG and mental activity in juvenile delinquents. *Electroencephalography and Clinical Neurophysiology*, 1971, *33*, 71–80.

ITARD, J.-M.-G. *The wild boy of Aveyron.* New York: Appleton-Century-Crofts, 1962.

JACOB, T. Family interaction in disturbed and normal families: A methodological and substantive review. *Psychological Bulletin*, 1975, *82*, 33–65.

JACOBS, J. C. Teacher attitudes toward gifted children. *Gifted Child Quarterly*, 1972, *16*, 23–26.

JANSKY, J., & DE HIRSCH, K. *Preventing reading failure.* New York: Harper & Row, 1972.

JASTAK, J. F., & JASTAK, S. R. *The wide range achievement test* (Rev. ed.). Wilmington, Del.: Guidance Association of Delaware, 1965.

JEHU, D., MORGAN, R. T. T., TURNER, R. K., & JONES, A. A controlled trial of the treatment of nocturnal enuresis in residential homes for children. *Behavior Research and Therapy*, 1977, *15*, 1–16.

JENCKS, C., et al. *Inequality.* New York: Basic Books, 1972.

JOINT COMMISSION ON THE MENTAL HEALTH OF CHILDREN. *Crisis in child mental health: Challenge of the 1970s.* New York: Harper & Row, 1970.

JOINT COMMISSION ON THE MENTAL HEALTH OF CHILDREN. *The mental health of children: Services, research, and manpower.* New York: Harper & Row, 1973.

JOHNSON, A. Sanctions for superego lacunae of adolescents. In K. R. Eissler (Ed.), *Searchlights on delinquency.* New York: International Universities Press, 1949.

JOHNSON, D. J., & MYKLEBUST, H. R. *Learning disabilities: Educational principles and practices.* New York: Grune & Stratton, 1967.

JOHNSON, G. O. The mentally handicapped—a paradox. *Exceptional Children*, 1962, *29*, 62–69.

JOHNSON, S. M., & LOBITCH, G. K. Parental manipulation of child behavior in home observations. *Journal of Applied Behavior Analysis*, 1974, *7*, 23–32.

JONES, H. G. The behavioral treatment of enuresis nocturna. In H. J. Eysenck (Ed.), *Behavior therapy and the neuroses.* Oxford: Pergamon, 1960.

JONES, J. W. *Blind children: Degree of vision, mode of reading.* Wash., D.C.: U.S. Office of Education, 1961.

JONES, M. C. The elimination of children's fears. *Journal of Experimental Psychology*, 1924, *7*, 382–90.

JONES, M. H., BARRETT, M. L., OLONOSS, C., & ANDERSON, E. Two experiments in training handicapped children. *Clinics in Developmental Medicine*, 1969, *33*, 108–22.

JONES, R. L. &, SISK, D. A. *Early perceptions of orthopedic disability.* Paper presented at the meeting of the American Psychological Association, Washington, D.C., 1967.

KAHN, A., KAMERMAN, S., & MCGOWAN, B. *Child advocacy: Report of a national baseline study.* New York: Columbia University School of Social Work, 1972.

KAHN, J., & NURSTEN, J. P. School refusal: A comprehensive view of school phobia and other failures of school attendance. *American Journal of Orthopsychiatry*, 1962, *32*, 707–18.

KALLMANN, F. The genetic theory of schizophrenia: An analysis of 691 schizophrenic twin index families. *American Journal of Psychiatry*, 1946, *103*, 309-22.

KALNINS, I. V. The dying child: A new perspective. *Journal of Pediatric Psychology*, 1977, *2*, 39-41.

KAMERMAN, S., KAHN, A., & MCGOWAN, B. Research and advocacy. *Children Today*, March-April 1972, 35-36.

KANFER, F. H., & SASLOW, G. Behavioral analysis: An alternative to diagnostic classification. *Archives of General Psychiatry*, 1965, *12*, 529-38.

KANNER, L. Autistic disturbances of affective contact. *Nervous Child*, 1943, *2*, 217-50. (Reprinted in L. Kanner, *Childhood psychosis: Initial studies and new insights.* New York: Wiley, 1973.)

KANNER, L. Problems of nosology and psychodynamics in early infantile autism. *American Journal of Orthopsychiatry*, 1949, *19*, 416-26. (Reprinted in L. Kanner, *Childhood psychosis: Initial studies and new insights.* New York: Wiley, 1973.)

KANNER, L. Infantile autism and the schizophrenias. *Behavioral Science*, 1965, *10*, 412-20. (Reprinted in L. Kanner, *Childhood psychosis: Initial studies and new insights.* New York: Wiley, 1973.)

KANNER, L. The children haven't read those books: Reflections on differential diagnosis. *Acta Paedopsychiatrica*, 1969, *36*, 2-11.

KANNER, L. Follow-up study of eleven autistic children originally reported in 1943. *Journal of Autism and Childhood Schizophrenia*, 1971, *1*, 119-45.

KANNER, L. Linwood Children's Center: Evaluations and follow-up of 34 psychotic children. In L. Kanner, *Childhood psychosis: Initial studies and new insights.* New York: Wiley, 1973.

KAPLAN, B. J. Malnutrition and mental deficiency. *Psychological Bulletin*, 1972, *78*, 321-34.

KAPLAN, H. I. Classification of child psychiatric disorders. In A. M. Freedman, & H. I. Kaplan (Eds.), *The child: His psychological and cultural development* (Vol. 2). New York: Atheneum, 1971.

KARNES, M. B., & ZEHRBACH, R. Parental attitudes and education in the culture of poverty. *Journal of Research and Development in Education*, 1975, *8*, 44-53.

KAVALE, K., & HIRSHOREN, A. A teacher education and the behaviourally disordered child. *The Exceptional Child* (University of Queensland, Australia), 1977, *24*, 133-41.

KENNEDY, W. A. School phobia: Rapid treatment of fifty cases. *Journal of Abnormal Psychology*, 1965, *70*, 285-89.

KENNEDY, W. A. A behavioristic, community-oriented approach to school phobia and other disorders. In H. C. Rickard (Ed.), *Behavioral intervention in human problems.* New York: Pergamon, 1971.

KENNY, T. J. The hospitalized child. *Pediatric Clinics of North America*, 1975, *22*, 583-93.

KEPHART, N. C. *The slow learner in the classroom.* Columbus, Ohio: Charles E. Merrill, 1960.

KEPHART, N. C. *Learning disability: An educational adventure.* West Lafayette, Ind.: Kappa Delta Pi Press, 1968.

KERR, N., MEYERSON, L., & MICHAEL, J. A procedure for shaping vocalizations in a mute child. In L. P. Ullman & L. Krasner (Eds.), *Case studies in behavior modification.* New York: Holt, Rinehart and Winston, 1965.

KESSLER, J. W. Neurosis in childhood. In B. Wolman (Ed.), *Manual of child psychopathology.* New York: McGraw-Hill, 1972.

KHAN, A. U., HERNDON, C. H., & AHMADIAN, S. Y. Social and emotional adaptations of children with transplanted kidneys and chronic hemodialysis. *American Journal of Psychiatry*, 1971, *127*, 1194-98.

KIFER, R. E., LEWIS, M. A., GREEN, D. R., & PHILLIPS, E. L. Training predelinquent youths and their parents to negotiate conflict situations. *Journal of Applied Behavior Analysis*, 1974, *7*, 357-64.

KIRBY, F. D., & TOBER, H. C. Modification of preschool isolate behavior: A case study. *Journal of Applied Behavior Analysis*, 1970, *3*, 309-14.

KIRK, S. A. *Educating exceptional children.* Boston: Houghton Mifflin, 1972.

KIRK, S. A., & KIRK, W. D. *Psycholinguistic learning disabilities: Diagnosis and remediation.* Urbana, Ill.: University of Illinois Press, 1971.

KIRK, S. A., MCCARTHY, J. J., & KIRK, W. D. *The Illinois test of psycholinguistic abilities* (Rev. ed.). Urbana, Ill.: University of Illinois Press, 1968.

KIRKPATRICK, J., HOFFMAN, I., & FUTTERMAN, E. H. Dilemma of trust: Relationship between medical care givers and parents of fatally ill children. *Pediatrics*, 1974, *54*, 169-75.

KLEIN, G. S. Blindness and isolation. *Psychoanalytic Study of the Child*, 1962, *17*, 82-93.

KLEIN, M. *The psychoanalysis of children.* London: Hogarth, 1932.

KLEIN, P. S., FORBES, G. B., & NADER, P. R. Effects of starvation in infancy (pyloric stenosis) on subsequent learning abilities. *Journal of Pediatrics*, 1975, *87*, 8-15.

KLIMAN, G. *Psychological emergencies of childhood.* New York: Grune & Stratton, 1968.

KNITZER, J. E. Child advocacy: A perspective. *American Journal of Orthopsychiatry*, 1976, *46*, 200-216.

KNOBLOCH, H., & PASAMANICK, B. (Eds.). *Gesell and Amatruda's developmental diagnosis* (3rd ed.). New York: Harper & Row, 1974.

KNUDSON, A. G., & NATTERSON, J. M. Participation of parents in the hospital care of their children. *Pediatrics*, 1960, *26*, 482-90.

KOLVIN, I., OUNSTED, C., HUMPHREY, M., MCNAY, A., RICHARDSON, L. M., GARSIDE, R. F., KIDD, J. S., & ROTH, M. Six studies in the childhood psychoses. *British Journal of Psychiatry*, 1971, *118*, 381-419.

KOOCHER, G. P., & BROSKOWSKI, A. Issues in the evaluation of mental health services for children. *Professional Psychology*, 1977, *8*, 583-92.

KOPPITZ, E. M. *Psychological evaluation of children's human figure drawings.* New York: Grune & Stratton, 1968.

KOUGH, J. Administrative provisions for the gifted. In B. Shertzer (Ed.), *Working with superior students.* Chicago: Science Research Associates, 1960.

KRAGER, J. M., & SAFER, D. J. Type and prevalence of medication used in the treatment of hyperactive children. *New England Journal of Medicine*, 1974, *291*, 1118-20.

KRIPPNER, S., SILVERMAN, R., CAVALLO, M., & HEALY, M. A study of "hyperkinetic" children receiving stimulant drugs. *Academic Therapy*, 1973, *8*, 261-69.

LACHAR, D. The families of psychotic children (#1024). *Journal Supplement Abstract Service, Catalog of Selected Documents in Psychology*, 1975, *5*, 286.

LANGFORD, W. S. The child in the pediatric hospital: Adaptation to illness and hospitalization. *American Journal of Orthopsychiatry*, 1961, *31*, 667-84.

LAPOUSE, R., & MONK, M. A. An epidemiologic study of behavior characteristics in children. *American Journal of Public Health*, 1958, *48*, 1134-44.

LAPOUSE, R., & MONK, M. A. Behavior deviations in a representative sample of children. Variation by sex, age, race, social class and family size. *American Journal of Orthopsychiatry*, 1964, *34*, 436-46.

LARRY P. ET AL. v. *WILSON RILES ET AL.*, United States District Court, Northern District of California, No. C-71 2270 RFP, Order and Memorandum, June 20, 1972.

LAYCOCK, F., & CAYLOR, J. S. Physique of gifted children and their less gifted siblings. *Child Development*, 1964, *35*, 63-74.

LAZARUS, A. A. The elimination of children's phobias by deconditioning. In H. J. Eysenck (Ed.), *Behavior therapy and the neuroses.* London: Pergamon, 1960.

LAZARUS, A. A., & ABRAMOVITZ, A. The use of "emotive imagery" in the treatment of children's phobias. *Journal of Mental Science*, 1962, *108*, 191-95.

LEFF, R. Behavior modification and the psychoses of childhood. *Psychological Bulletin*, 1968, *69*, 396-409.

LEITENBERG, H., & CALLAHAN, E. J. Reinforced practice in the reduction of different kinds of fear in adults and children. *Behavior Research and Therapy*, 1973, *11*, 19–30.

LELAND, H., & SMITH, D. E. *Play therapy with mentally subnormal children.* New York: Grune & Stratton, 1965.

LELAND, H., & SMITH, D. E. Psychotherapeutic considerations with mentally retarded and developmentally disabled children. In I. Katz (Ed.), *Mental health services for the mentally retarded.* Springfield, Ill.: Charles C. Thomas, 1972.

LENNEBERG, E. H. *Biological foundations of language.* New York: Wiley, 1967.

LENNEBERG, E. H. What is meant by a biological approach to language? *American Annals of the Deaf,* 1970, *115,* 67–72.

LENNEBERG, E. H., REBELSKY, F. G., & NICHOLS, I. A. The vocalizations of infants born to deaf and to hearing parents. *Human Development,* 1965, *8,* 23–37.

LEVENTHAL, T., & SILLS, M. Self-image in school phobia. *American Journal of Orthopsychiatry,* 1964, *34,* 685–95.

LEVY, D. M. *Maternal overprotection.* New York: Norton, 1966.

LEWIS, E. D. Types of mental deficiency and their social significance. *Journal of Mental Science,* 1933, *79,* 298–304.

LIBERMAN, R. P., FERRIS, C., SALGADO, P., & SALGADO, J. J. Replication of the Achievement Place model in California. *Journal of Applied Behavior Analysis,* 1975, *8,* 287–300.

LICHTENSTEIN, P. E. Genius as productive neurosis. *Psychological Record,* 1971, *21,* 151–64.

LIDZ, T., FLECK, S., & CORNELISON, A. R. *Schizophrenia and the family.* New York: International University Press, 1965.

LILLIE, D. The parent in early childhood education. *Journal of Research and Development in Education,* 1975, *8,* 7–13.

LIPPMAN, L., & GOLDBERG, I. *Right to education: Anatomy of the Pennsylvania case and its implications for exceptional children.* New York: Teachers College Press, 1973.

LISS, E. Motivation in learning. *The Psychoanalytic Study of the Child,* 1955, *10,* 100–16.

LOTTER, V. Epidemiology of autistic conditions in young children, II: Some characteristics of the parents and children. *Social Psychiatry,* 1967, *1,* 163–73.

LOURIE, N. V. Operational advocacy: Objectives and obstacles. In I. N. Berlin (Ed.), *Advocacy for child mental health.* New York: Brunner/Mazel, 1975. (a)

LOURIE, N. V. The many faces of advocacy. In I. N. Berlin (Ed.), *Advocacy for child mental health.* New York: Brunner/Mazel, 1975. (b)

LOURIE, N. V., & BERLIN, I. N. Child advocacy: Political and legislative implications. In I. N. Berlin (Ed.), *Advocacy for child mental health.* New York: Brunner/Mazel, 1975.

LOURIE, R. S., & RIEGER, R. E. Psychiatric and psychological examination of children. In G. Kaplan & S. Arieti (Eds.), *American handbook of psychiatry (Vol. II): Child and adolescent psychiatry, sociocultural and community psychiatry.* New York: Basic Books, 1974.

LOVAAS, O. I. A program for the establishment of speech in psychotic children. In J. K. Wing (Ed.), *Early childhood autism: Clinical, educational and social aspects.* London: Pergamon Press, 1966.

LOVAAS, O. I., KOEGEL, R., SIMMONS, J. Q., & STEVENS-LONG, J. Some generalizations and follow-up measures on autistic children in behavior therapy. *Journal of Applied Behavior Analysis,* 1973, *6,* 131–65.

LOVAAS, O. I., SCHAEFFER, B., & SIMMONS, J. Q. Building social behavior in autistic children by use of electric shock. *Journal of Experimental Research in Personality,* 1965, *1,* 99–109.

LOVE, H. D. *Parental attitudes toward exceptional children.* Springfield: Charles C. Thomas, 1970.

LOVIBOND, S. H. *Conditioning and enuresis.* London: Pergamon, 1964.

LOWENFELD, B. (Ed.). *The visually handicapped child in school.* New York: John Day, 1973.

LUBAN-PLOZZA, B., & COMAZZI, A. The family as a factor in psychosomatic disturbances. *Psychotherapy and Psychosomatics,* 1973, *22,* 372–77.

LYON, H. Education of the gifted and talented. *Exceptional Children,* 1976–77, *43,* 166–68.

MACKEITH, R. The eye and vision in the newborn infant. In P. Gardiner, R. MacKeith & V. Smith (Eds.), *Aspects of developmental and paediatric ophthalmology.* London: Spastics International Medical Publications with W. Heinemann Medical Books, 1969.

MACKINNON, D. W. The nature and nurture of creative talent. *American Psychologist,* 1962, *17,* 484–95.

MACMILLAN, D. L. The problem of motivation in the education of the mentally retarded. *Exceptional Children,* 1971, *37,* 579–86.

MACMILLAN, D. L. *Mental retardation in school and society.* Boston: Little, Brown, & Co., 1977.

MACMILLAN, D. L., & KEOGH, B. K. Normal and retarded children's expectancy for failure. *Developmental Psychology,* 1971, *4,* 343–48.

MADSEN, C. H., BECKER, W. C., & THOMAS, D. R. Rules, praise, and ignoring: Elements of elementary classroom control. *Journal of Applied Behavior Analysis,* 1968, *1,* 139–50.

MAENCHEN, A. On the technique of child analysis in relation to stages of development. *Psychoanalytic Study of the Child,* 1970, *25,* 175–208.

MAHLER, M. On child psychosis and schizophrenia: Autistic and symbiotic infantile psychoses. In R. S. Eissler et al. (Eds.), *Psychoanalytic study of the child.* New York: International Universities Press, 1952, 286–305.

MARGOLIES, P. J. Behavioral approaches to the treatment of early infantile autism: A review. *Psychological Bulletin,* 1977, *84,* 249–64.

MARLAND, S. P., JR. *Education of the gifted and talented: Report to the Congress of the United States by the Commissioner of Education.* Washington, D.C.: U.S. Government Printing Office, 1972.

MARR, J. N., MILLER, E. R., & STRAUB, R. R. Operant conditioning of attention with a psychotic girl. *Behaviour Research and Therapy,* 1966, *4,* 85–87.

MARTIN, E. W. Breakthrough for the handicapped: Legislative history. *Exceptional Children,* 1968, *34,* 493–503.

MARTIN, E. W. The Deputy Commissioner of the Bureau of Education for the Handicapped talks about educational rights. *Teacher,* 1977, *94,* 44–46.

MARTINDALE, C. Degeneration, disinhibition, and genius. *Journal of the History of the Behavioral Sciences,* 1971, *7,* 177–82.

MATHENY, A. P., & VERNICK, J. Parents of the mentally retarded child: Emotionally overwhelmed or informationally deprived? In S. Chess & A. Thomas (Eds.), *Annual progress in child psychiatry and child development.* New York: Brunner/Mazel, 1970.

MATTSSON, A. Long-term physical illness in childhood: A challenge to psychosocial adaptation. *Pediatrics,* 1972, *50,* 801–11.

MAYER, C. L. The effects of early special class placement on the self-concepts of mentally handicapped children. *Exceptional Children,* 1966, *33,* 77–81.

MCCALL, R. B., HOGARTY, P. S., & HURLBURT, N. Transitions in infant sensorimotor development and the prediction of childhood IQ. *American Psychologist,* 1972, *27,* 328–34.

MCCARTNEY, J. L. A review of recent reseach in delinquency and deviance. *Journal of Operational Psychiatry,* 1974, *5,* 52–68.

MCCLURE, W. J. Current problems and trends in the education of the deaf. *The Deaf American,* 1966, *18,* 8–14.

MCCORMICK, M. Primary education for the disadvantaged: What the literature reveals. La Jolla, Calif.: Western Behavioral Sciences Instit., 1975.

MCDERMOTT, J., & FINCH, S. Ulcerative colitis in children: Reassessment of a dilemma. *Journal of the American Academy of Child Psychiatry,* 1967, *6,* 512–25.

MCGOWAN, B. *Case advocacy: A study of the intervention process in child advocacy.* Unpublished doctoral dissertation, Columbia University, 1973.

MEADOW, K. P. The development of deaf children. In E. M. Hetherington (Ed.), *Review of child development research* (Vol. 5). Chicago: University of Chicago Press, 1975.

MEDNICK, M. T., MEDNICK, S. A., & MEDNICK, E. V. Incubation of creative performance and specific associative priming. *Journal of Abnormal and Social Psychology*, 1964, 69, 84–88.

MEDNICK, S. A. The associative basis of the creative process. *Psychological Review*, 1962, 69, 220–32.

MEDNICK, S. A. Breakdown in individuals at high risk for schizophrenia. *Mental Hygiene*, 1970, 54, 50–63.

MEIER, J. H. *Developmental and learning disabilities.* Baltimore: University Park Press, 1976.

MELTON, D. *When children need help.* New York: Thomas Y. Crowell, 1972.

MENDELSOHN, G. A., & GRISWOLD, B. B. Assessed creative potential, vocabulary level, and sex as predictors of the use of incidental cues in verbal problem solving. *Journal of Abnormal and Social Psychology*, 1964, 68, 431–36.

MERCER, J. R. Psychological assessment and the rights of children. In N. Hobbs (Ed.), *Issues in the classification of children* (Vol. I). San Francisco: Jossey-Bass, 1975.

MERCER, J. R., & RICHARDSON, J. G. "Mental retardation" as a social problem. In N. Hobbs (Ed.), *Issues in the classification of children* (Vol. 2). San Francisco: Jossey-Bass, 1975.

MERRILL, E. J. Physical abuse of children: An agency study. In V. De Francis (Ed.), *Protecting the battered child.* Denver: American Humane Association, 1962.

MERZENICH, M. M., SCHINDLER, R. A., SOOY, F. A. (Eds.). *Proceedings of the First International Conference on Electrical Stimulation of the Acoustic Nerve as a Treatment for Profound Sensorineural Deafness in Man,* 1974.

MEYER, A. The anatomical facts and clinical varieties of traumatic insanity. *American Journal of Insanity*, 1904, 60, 373–441.

MILISEN, R. The incidence of speech disorders. In L. E. Travis, (Ed.), *Handbook of speech pathology and audiology.* Englewood Cliffs, N.J.: Prentice-Hall, 1971, 619–34.

MILLER, E. A. Cerebral palsied children and their parents. *Exceptional Children*, 1958, 24, 298–302.

MILLER, L. C., BARRETT, C. L., & HAMPE, E. Phobias of childhood in a prescientific era. In A. Davids (Ed.), *Child personality and psychopathology: Current topics* (Vol. I). New York: Wiley, 1974.

MILLER, L. C., BARRETT, C. L., HAMPE, E., & NOBLE, H. Comparison of reciprocal inhibition, psychotherapy and waiting list control for phobic children. *Journal of Abnormal Psychology*, 1972, 79, 265–79.

MILLER, N. E., SEARS, R. R., MOWRER, O. H., DOOB, L. W., & DOLLARD, J. The frustration-aggression hypothesis. *Psychological Review*, 1941, 48, 337–42.

MILLS v. BOARD OF EDUCATION OF THE DISTRICT OF COLUMBIA, 348 F. Supp., 866 (D.D.C., 1972).

MINDEL, E. D., & VERNON, M. *They grow in silence: The deaf child and his family.* Silver Springs, Md.: National Assoc. for the Deaf, 1971.

MINSKOFF, E. H. Creating and evaluating remediation for the learning disabled. In E. L. Meyen, G. A. Vergason, & R. J. Whelan (Eds.), *Alternatives for teaching exceptional children.* Denver: Love Publishing Company, 1975.

MINUCHIN, S., BAKER, L., ROSMAN, B. L., LIEBMAN, R., MILMAN, L., & TODD, T. C. A conceptual model of psychosomatic illness in children. *Archives of General Psychiatry*, 1975, 32, 1031–38.

MOGAR, R. E., & ALDRICH, R. W. The use of psychedelic agents with autistic schizophrenic children. *Behavioral Neuropsychiatry*, 1969, 1, 44–52.

MONROE, J. D., & HOWE, C. E. The effects of integration and social class on the acceptance of retarded adolescents. *Education and Training of the Mentally Retarded*, 1971, 6, 20–24.

MONTGOMERY, G. W. Relationship of oral skills to manual communication in profoundly deaf children. *American Annals of the Deaf*, 1966, 111, 557–65.

MOORE, D. F. A review of education of the deaf. In L. Mann & D. A. Sabatino (Eds.), *The third review of special education.* New York: Grune & Stratton, 1976.

MOORE, W. T. The impact of surgery on boys. *Psychoanalytic Study of the Child*, 1975, 30, 529–48.

MORGAN, E. S. *The Puritan family.* New York: Harper & Row, 1966.

MORGENSTERN, M., & MICHAL-SMITH, H. *Psychology in the vocational rehabilitation of the mentally retarded.* Springfield, Ill.: Charles C. Thomas, 1973.

MORRISSEY, J. R. Children's adaptations to fatal illness. *Social Work*, 1963, 8, 81–88. (a)

MORRISSEY, J. R. A note on interviews with children facing imminent death. *Social Casework*, 1963, 44, 343–45. (b)

MORSE, J. The goal of life enhancement for a fatally ill child. *Children*, 1970, 17, 63–68.

MORSE, W. C. If schools are to meet their responsibilities to all children. *Childhood Education*, 1970, 46, 299–303.

MOUSTAKAS, C. Creativity and conformity in education. In R. Mooney & T. Razik (Eds.), *Explorations in creativity.* New York: Harper & Row, 1967.

MOWATT, M. H. Group therapy approach to emotional conflicts of the mentally retarded and their parents. In F. J. Menolascino (Ed.), *Psychiatric approaches to mental retardation.* New York: Basic Books, 1970.

MOWRER, O. H., & MOWRER, W. M. Enuresis: A method for its study and treatment. *American Journal of Orthopsychiatry*, 1938, 8, 436–59.

MURRAY, M. *Needs of parents of mentally retarded children.* New York: National Association for Retarded Children, 1969.

MUSGROVE, W. J., & ESTROFF, E. H. Scale to measure attitudes of intellectually gifted toward an enrichment program. *Exceptional Children*, 1976–77, 43, 375–77.

MYKLEBUST, H. R. Learning disorders: Psychoneurological disturbances in childhood. *Rehabilitation Literature*, 1964, 354–60.

MYKLEBUST, H. R. Childhood aphasia: An evolving concept. In L. E. Travis (Ed.), *Handbook of speech pathology and audiology.* Englewood Cliffs, N.J.: 1971. (a)

MYKLEBUST, H. R. Childhood aphasia: Identification, diagnosis, remediation. In L. E. Travis (Ed.), *Handbook of speech pathology and audiology.* Englewood Cliffs, N.J.: Prentice-Hall, 1971. (b)

NATIONAL ADVISORY COUNCIL ON NEUROLOGICAL DISEASES AND STROKES. *Human communication and its disorders—an overview.* Bethesda, Md.: National Institute of Neurological Diseases & Strokes, 1969.

NATIONAL SOCIETY FOR THE STUDY OF EDUCATION. N. B. Henry (Ed.), *Forty-ninth yearbook (Part II): The education of exceptional children.* Chicago: Author, 1950.

NATIONAL SOCIETY FOR THE STUDY OF EDUCATION. *Fifty-seventh yearbook (Part II): Education for the gifted.* Chicago: Author, 1958.

NEISWORTH, J. T., & Smith, R. M. An analysis and redefinition of "developmental disabilities." *Exceptional Children*, 1974, 40, 345–47.

NEWLAND, T. E. *The gifted in socioeducational perspective.* Englewood Cliffs, N.J.: Prentice-Hall, 1976.

NEWMAN, M. H. Hearing loss. In M. Strome (Ed.), *Differential diagnosis in pediatric otolaryngology.* Boston: Little, Brown, 1975.

NOLAN, C. Y. Blind children: Degree of vision, mode of reading, a 1963 replication. *New Outlook for the Blind*, 1965, 59, 233–38.

NOLAN, C. Y. A 1966 reappraisal of the relationship between visual acuity and mode of reading for blind children. *New Outlook for the Blind*, 1967, 61, 255–61.

NORRIS, M., SPAULDING, P., & BRODIE, F. *Blindness in children.* Chicago: University of Chicago Press, 1957.

NORTHERN, J. L., & DOWNS, M. P. *Hearing in children.* Baltimore: Williams & Wilkins, 1974.

O'CONNER, R. D. Modification of social withdrawal through symbolic modeling. *Journal of Applied Behavior Analysis*, 1969, 2, 15–22.

O'DELL, S. Training parents in behavior modification: A review. *Psychological Bulletin*, 1974, 81, 418–33.

OFFIR, C. W. A slavish reliance on drugs: Are we pushers for our own children? *Psychology Today,* 1974, *8,* 49.

OHIO COMMISSION ON CHILDREN AND YOUTH. *Crippled children.* Columbus, Ohio: Department of Education, 1951.

O'LEARY, K. D. The assessment of psychopathology in children. In H. C. Quay & J. S. Werry (Eds.), *Psychopathological disorders of childhood.* New York: Wiley, 1972.

O'LEARY, K. D., & O'LEARY, S. G. (Eds.). *Classroom management: The successful use of behavior modification.* New York: Pergamon Press, 1972.

OMWAKE, E. B., & SOLNIT, A. J. "It isn't fair": The treatment of a blind child. *Psychoanalytic Study of the Child,* 1961, *16,* 353–404.

OPPEL, W., HARPER, R., & ROWLAND, V. The age of attaining bladder control. *Journal of Pediatrics,* 1968, *42,* 614–26.

ORNITZ, E. M. Childhood autism: A review of the clinical and experimental literature. *California Medicine,* 1973, *118,* 21–47.

ORNITZ, E. M., GUTHRIE, D., & FARLEY, A. H. The early development of autistic children. *Journal of Autism and Childhood Schizophrenia,* 1977, *7,* 207–29.

ORNITZ, E. M., & RITVO, E. R. Neurophysiologic mechanisms underlying perceptual inconstancy in autistic and schizophrenic children. *Archives of General Psychiatry,* 1968, *19,* 22–27. (a)

ORNITZ, E. M., & RITVO, E. R. Perceptual inconstancy in early infantile autism. *Archives of General Psychiatry,* 1968, *18,* 76–98. (b)

ORNITZ, E. M., & RITVO, E. R. Medical assessment. In E. R. Ritvo (Ed.), *Autism: Diagnosis, current research and management.* New York: Spectrum Publications, 1976.

ORTON, S. *Reading, writing, and speech problems in children.* New York: Norton, 1937.

OSMOND, H. The background to the niacin treatment. In D. Hawkins & L. Pauling (Eds.), *Orthomolecular psychiatry.* San Francisco: W. H. Freeman, 1973.

OWINGS, R. S. *Nonoperative aspects of pediatric surgery.* St. Louis: Warren Green, Inc., 1973.

OYERS, H. J., & FRANKMANN, J. P. *The aural rehabilitation process: A conceptual framework analysis.* New York: Holt, Rinehart and Winston, 1975.

PATTERSON, C. H. *Relationship counseling and psychotherapy.* New York: Harper & Row, 1974.

PATTERSON, G. R. An application of conditioning techniques to the control of a hyperactive child. In L. Ullman & L. Krasner (Eds.), *Case studies in behavior modification.* New York: Holt, Rinehart and Winston, 1965.

PATTERSON, G. R., & BRODSKY, G. A behavior modification program for a child with multiple behavior problems. *Journal of Child Psychology and Psychiatry,* 1966, *7,* 277–95.

PATTERSON, G. R., & GULLION, M. E. *Living with children: New methods for parents and teachers.* Champaign, Ill.: Research Press, 1968.

PATZ, A., & HOOVER, R. E. *Protection of vision in children.* Springfield, Ill.: Charles C. Thomas, 1969.

PAULING, L. Orthomolecular psychiatry. *Science,* 1968, *160,* 265–71.

PAULING, L. Orthomolecular psychiatry. In D. Hawkins & L. Pauling (Eds.), *Orthomolecular psychiatry.* San Francisco: W. H. Freeman, 1973.

PELONE, A. J. *Helping the visually handicapped child in the regular class.* New York: Teachers College Press, 1957.

PENNSYLVANIA ASSOCIATION FOR RETARDED CHILDREN (PARC) v. THE COMMONWEALTH OF PENNSYLVANIA, 334 F. Supp., 1257 (1971).

PERKINS, W. H. *Speech pathology: An applied behavioral science.* St. Louis: C. V. Mosby, 1971.

PETERSON, D. R. Behavior problems of middle childhood. *Journal of Consulting Psychology,* 1961, *25,* 205–9.

PETRILLO, M., & SANGER, S. *Emotional care of hospitalized children: An environmental approach.* Philadelphia: Lippincott, 1972.

PHILLIPS, E. L. Achievement Place: Token reinforcement procedures in a home-style rehabilitation setting for "pre-delinquent" boys. *Journal of Applied Behavior Analysis,* 1968, *1,* 213–23.

PHILLIPS, E. L., PHILLIPS, E. A., FIXSEN, D. L., & WOLF, M. M. Achievement Place: Modification of the behavior of pre-delinquent boys within a token economy. *Journal of Applied Behavior Analysis,* 1971, *4,* 45–59.

PIAGET, J. *The psychology of intelligence.* London: Routledge & Kegan Paul, 1950.

PIAGET, J. *Play, dreams and imitation in childhood.* New York: Norton, 1951.

PIAGET, J. *The growth of logical thinking.* New York: Basic Books, 1958.

PIAGET, J. *Six psychological studies.* New York: Random House, 1967.

PITFIELD, M., & OPPENHEIM, A. N. Child rearing attitudes of mothers of psychotic children. *Journal of Child Psychology and Psychiatry,* 1964, *5,* 51–57.

PLESS, I. B., & DOUGLAS, J. W. B. Chronic illness in childhood: Part I. Epidemiological and clinical characteristics. *Pediatrics,* 1971, *47,* 405–14.

PLESS, I. B., & ROGHMANN, K. J. Chronic illness and its consequences: Observations based on three epidemiologic surveys. *The Journal of Pediatrics,* 1971, *79,* 351–59.

POLIER, J. W. In defense of children. *Child Welfare,* 1976, *55,* 75–84.

POLLACK, M., & WOERNER, M. G. Pre- and peri-natal complications and "childhood schizophrenia": A comparison of five controlled studies. *Journal of Child Psychology and Psychiatry,* 1966, *7,* 235–42.

POLLIN, W., ALLEN, M. G., HOFFER, A., STABENAU, J. R., & HRUBEC, Z. Psychopathology in 15,909 pairs of veteran twins: Evidence for genetic factors in the pathogenesis of schizophrenia and its relative absence in psychoneurosis. *American Journal of Psychiatry,* 1969, *126,* 597–611.

POLLIN, W., STABENAU, J., MOSHER, L., & TUPIN, J. Life history differences in identical twins discordant for schizophrenia. *American Journal of Orthopsychiatry,* 1966, *36,* 492.

POWELL, L. The effect of extra-stimulation and maternal involvement on the development of low-birth-weight infants and on maternal behavior. *Child Development,* 1974, *45,* 106–13.

POWELL, W. C. Educational intervention as a preventive measure. *Criminal Justice and Behavior,* 1975, *2,* 397–407.

POWER, D. J., & QUIGLEY, S. P. Deaf children's acquisition of the passive voice. *Journal of Speech and Hearing Research,* 1973, *16,* 5–11.

POWERS, M. H. Functional disorders of articulation—symptomatology and etiology. In L. E. Travis (Ed.), *Handbook of speech pathology and audiology.* Englewood Cliffs, N.J.: Prentice-Hall, 1971.

POZNANSKI, E. O. Children with excessive fears. *American Journal of Orthopsychiatry,* 1973, *43,* 428–38.

PROCTOR, C. A., & PROCTOR, B. Understanding hereditary nerve deafness. *Archives Otolaryngology,* 1967, *85,* 23–40.

PRUGH, D. G. Toward an understanding of psychosomatic concepts in relation to illness in children. In A. J. Solnit & S. A. Provence (Eds.), *Modern perspectives in child development.* New York: International University Press, 1963.

PRUGH, D. G., & JORDAN, K. The management of ulcerative colitis in children. In J. G. Howells (Ed.), *Modern perspectives in international child psychiatry.* New York: Brunner/Mazel, 1971.

PRUGH, D. G., STAUB, E., SANDS, H. H., KIRSCHBAUM, R. M., & LENIHAN, E. A. A study of the emotional reaction of children and families to hospitalization and illness. *American Journal of Orthopsychiatry,* 1953, *23,* 70–106.

QUAY, H. C. Patterns of aggression, withdrawal, and immaturity. In H. C. Quay & J. S. Werry (Eds.), *Psychopathological disorders of childhood.* New York: Wiley, 1972, 1–29.

QUAY, H. C., MORSE, W. C., & CUTLER, R. L. Personality patterns of pupils in classes for the emotionally disturbed. *Exceptional Children,* 1966, *32,* 297–301.

QUIGLEY, S. P., WILBUR, R. B., & MONTANELLI, D. S. Complement structures in the language of deaf students. *Journal of Speech and Hearing Research,* 1976, *19,* 448–57.

RABIN, A. I., & MCKINNEY, J. P. Intelligence tests and childhood psychopathology. In B. B. Wolman (Ed.), *Manual of child psychopathology.* New York: McGraw-Hill, 1972.

RACHMAN, S., & SELIGMAN, M. E. P. Unprepared phobias: Be prepared. *Behaviour Research and Therapy,* 1976, *14,* 333–38.

REGER, R., SCHROEDER, W., & USCHOLD, K. *Special education: Children with learning problems.* New York: Oxford University Press, 1968.

RENSHAW, D. C. *The hyperactive child.* Chicago: Nelson-Hall, 1974.

REPORT OF THE PRESIDENT'S PANEL ON MENTAL RETARDATION. L. W. Mayo (Chair). Washington, D.C.: U.S. Government Printing Office, 1962. (In *Journal of Rehabilitation,* 1962, *28,* 40–43.)

RESNICK, R. *Sun and shadow.* New York: Atheneum, 1975.

REYNOLDS, M. C. A framework for considering some issues in special education. *Exceptional Children,* 1962, *28,* 367–70.

REYNOLDS, M. C. New alternatives through a new cascade. Paper presented at the Sixth Annual Invitational Conference on Leadership in Special Education Programs, Nov. 23, 1976.

RICHMOND, J. B., & WAISMAN, H. A. Psychological aspects of management of children with malignant diseases. *American Journal of the Diseases of Children,* 1955, *89,* 42–47.

RIE, H. E., RIE, E. D., STEWART, S., & AMBUEL, J. P. Effects of Ritalin on underachieving children: A replication. *American Journal of Orthopsychiatry,* 1976, *46,* 313–22.

RIMLAND, B. *Infantile autism.* New York: Appleton-Century-Crofts, 1964.

RIMLAND, B. The differentiation of childhood psychoses: An analysis of checklists for 2,218 psychotic children. *Journal of Autism and Childhood Schizophrenia,* 1971, *1,* 161–74.

RIMLAND, B. High-dosage levels of certain vitamins in the treatment of children with severe mental disorders. In D. Hawkins & L. Pauling (Eds.), *Orthomolecular psychiatry.* San Francisco: W. H. Freeman, 1973.

RIMLAND, B. Infantile autism: Status and research. In A. Davids (Ed.), *Child personality and psychopathology: Current topics.* New York: Wiley, 1974.

RITVO, E. E., YUWILER, A., GELLER, E., ORNITZ, E. M., SAEGER, K., & PLOTKIN, S. Increased blood serotonin and platelets in early infantile autism. *Archives of General Psychiatry,* 1970, *23,* 566–72.

ROBINS, L. N. Follow-up studies of behavior disorders in children. In H. C. Quay & J. S. Werry (Eds.), *Psychopathological disorders of childhood.* New York: Wiley, 1972.

ROBINSON, F. B. *Introduction to stuttering.* Englewood Cliffs, N.J.: Prentice-Hall, 1964.

ROBINSON, H. R., & ROBINSON, N. M. *The mentally retarded child* (2nd ed.). New York: McGraw-Hill, 1976.

ROSANOFF, A. J., HANDY, L. M., PLESSET, I. R., & BRUSH, S. The etiology of so-called schizophrenic psychoses with special reference to their occurrence in twins. *American Journal of Psychiatry,* 1934, *91,* 247–86.

ROSE, S. D. *Treating children in groups: A behavioral approach.* San Francisco: Jossey-Bass, 1972.

ROSEN, B. M., BAHN, A. K., & KRAMER, M. Demographic and diagnostic characteristics of psychiatric clinic outpatients in the U.S.A. *American Journal of Orthopsychiatry,* 1964, *34,* 455–68.

ROSS, A. O. *The exceptional child in the family.* New York: Grune & Stratton, 1972.

ROSS, A. O. *Psychological disorders in children.* New York: McGraw-Hill, 1974.

ROSS, A. O. *Psychological aspects of learning disabilities and reading disorders.* New York: McGraw-Hill, 1976.

ROUTH, D. K., & ROBERTS, R. D. Minimal brain dysfunction in children: Failure to find evidence for a behavioral syndrome. *Psychological Reports,* 1972, *31,* 307–14.

RUDESTAM, K. E., & BEDROSIAN, R. An investigation of the effectiveness of desensitization and flooding with two types of phobias. *Behaviour Research and Therapy,* 1977, *15,* 23–30.

RUFF, G., LEVY, E., & THALER, V. Factors influencing the reaction of reduced sensory input. In P. Solomon (Ed.), *Sensory deprivation.* Cambridge, Mass.: Harvard University Press, 1961.

RUTTER, M. (Ed.). *Infantile autism: Concepts, characteristics and treatment.* London: Churchill-Livingstone, 1971.

RUTTER, M. The development of infantile autism. *Psychological Medicine,* 1974, *4,* 147–63.

RUTTER, M., GREENFELD, D., & LOCKYER, L. A five to fifteen year follow-up study of infantile psychosis, II: Social and behavioral outcome. *British Journal of Psychiatry,* 1967, *113,* 183–99.

RUTTER, M., TIZARD, J., & WHITMORE, K. *Education, health, and behavior.* London: Longmans, Green, & Co., 1970.

RYAN, S. (Ed.). *A report on longitudinal evaluations of preschool programs.* Washington, D.C.: Department of Health, Education, & Welfare, 1974.

SABAGH, G., & WINDLE, C. Recent trends in institutionalization rates of mental defectives in the United States. *American Journal of Mental Deficiency,* 1960, *64,* 618–24.

SAFER, D. J., & ALLEN, R. P. *Hyperactive children: Diagnosis and management.* Baltimore: University Park Press, 1976.

SAFER, D. J., ALLEN, R. P., & BARR, E. Depression of growth in hyperactive children on stimulant drugs. *New England Journal of Medicine,* 1972, *287,* 217–20.

SANDERS, D. A. *Aural rehabilitation.* Englewood Cliffs, N.J.: Prentice-Hall, 1971.

SANDERS, W. B. *Juvenile delinquency.* New York: Praeger, 1976.

SANDLER, A. Aspects of passivity and ego development in the blind infant. *Psychoanalytic Study of the Child,* 1963, *18,* 343–60.

SATZ, P., & FRIEL, J. Some predictive antecedents of specific reading disability: A preliminary two-year follow-up. *Journal of Learning Disabilities,* 1974, *7,* 437–44.

SATZ, P., FRIEL, J., & RUDEGAIR, F. Differential changes in the acquisition of developmental skills in children who later became dyslexic. In D. G. Stein, J. J. Rosen & N. Butters (Eds.), *Plasticity and recovery of function in the central nervous system.* New York: Academic Press, 1974.

SCARR-SALAPATEK, S., & WILLIAMS, M. L. The effects of early stimulation on low-birth-weight infants. *Child Development,* 1973, *44,* 94–101.

SCHAEFER, E. Parents as educators: Evidence from cross-sectional, longitudinal, and intervention research. In W. Hartrup (Ed.), *The young child.* Wash., D.C.: National Association for the Education of Young Children, 1972.

SCHAIN, R., & REYNARD, C. Observations of effects of a central stimulant drug (methylphenidate) in children with hyperactive behavior. *Pediatrics,* 1975, *55,* 709–16.

SCHIFFER, C.G., & HUNT, E. P. *Illness among children: Data from U.S. national health survey.* Washington, D.C.: U.S. Department of Health, Education, & Welfare, 1963.

SCHILD, S. The family of the retarded child. In R. Koch & J. C. Dobson, (Eds.), *The mentally retarded child and his family.* New York: Brunner/Mazel, 1971.

SCHLESINGER, H. S., & MEADOW, K. P. *Deafness and mental health: A developmental approach.* San Francisco: Langley Porter Neuropsychiatric Institute, 1971.

SCHMITT, P. J. Some notes on the education of hearing impaired children. Urbana, Ill.: University of Illinois, n. d. mimeo.

SCHNACKENBURG, R. S. Caffeine as a substitute for schedule II stimulants in hyperkinetic children. *American Journal of Psychiatry,* 1973, *130,* 796–98.

SCHOPLER, E. Toward reducing behavior problems in autistic children. *Journal of Autism and Childhood Schizophrenia,* 1976, *6,* 1–13.

SCHOWALTER, J. E. The child's reaction to his own terminal illness. In B. Schoenberg, A. C. Carr, D. Peretz & A. H. Kutscher (Eds.), *Loss and grief: Psychological management in medical practice.* New York: Columbia University Press, 1970, 51–69.

SCHULMAN, J. L., STEVENS, T. M., SURAN, B. G., KUPST, M. J., & NAUGHTON, M. J. Modification of activity level through biofeedback and operant conditioning. *Journal of Applied Behavior Analysis*, 1978, in press.

SEAGOE, M. V. *Terman and the gifted.* Los Altos, Calif.: William Kaufmann, 1975.

SEARS, R. R. Sources of life satisfactions of the Terman gifted men. *American Psychologist*, 1977, *32*, 119–28.

SEARS, R. R., MACCOBY, E. E., & LEVIN, H. *Patterns of child rearing.* New York: Harper & Row, 1957.

SEIDEL, H. M. Educational needs and programs for the hospitalized child. In A. Haller (Ed.), *The hospitalized child and his family.* Baltimore: Johns Hopkins University Press, 1967, 53–65.

SEIDEL, H. M., & ZIAI, M. Pediatric history and physical examination. In M. Ziai (Ed.), *Pediatrics.* Boston: Little, Brown, 1975.

SEITZ, V., APFEL, N. H., & EFRON, C. Longterm effects of early intervention—the New Haven project. Paper presented at The American Association for the Advancement of Science, Denver, Col., Feb. 23, 1977.

SELLER, M. J., & GOLD, S. Seizures in psychotic children. *Lancet,* 1964, 1325.

SELVINI-PALAZZOLI, M. The families of patients with anorexia nervosa. In E. J. Anthony & C. Koupernik (Eds.), *The child in his family.* New York: Wiley, 1970.

SHAW, C. R. *The psychiatric disorders of childhood.* New York: Appleton-Century-Crofts, 1966.

SHEEHAN, J. G. Projective studies of stuttering. *Journal of Speech and Hearing Disorders*, 1971, *23*, 18–25.

SHEEHAN, J. G., & MARTYN, M. Stuttering and its disappearance. *Journal of Speech and Hearing Research*, 1970, *13*, 279–89.

SHELDON, W. H. (with collaboration of S. S. Stevens & W. B. Tucker). *The varieties of human physique: An introduction to constitutional psychology.* New York: Harper & Row, 1940.

SHORT, J. F., & NYE, F. I. Extent of unrecorded juvenile delinquency: Tentative conclusions. *Journal of Criminal Law, Criminology, and Police Science*, 1958, *49*, 296–302.

SIDMAN, M. Normal sources of pathological behavior. *Science*, 1960, *132*, 61–68.

SIGLER, A. T. The leukemic child and his family: An emotional challenge. In M. Debuskey (Ed.), *The chronically ill child and his family.* Springfield, Ill.: Charles C. Thomas, 1970.

SILBERMAN, C. E. *Crisis in black and white.* New York: Random House, 1964.

SILVER, H. K. History and physical examination. In H. Kempe, H. K. Silver & D. O'Brien (Eds.), *Current pediatric diagnosis and treatment.* Los Altos, Calif.: Lange, 1974.

SILVER, L. B. Acceptable and controversial approaches to treating the child with learning disabilities. *Pediatrics*, 1975, *5*, 406–15.

SKEELS, H. M. Adult status of children with contrasting early life experiences. *Monographs of the Society for Research in Child Development*, 1966, *31*, (Serial No. 105).

SKEELS, H. M., & DYE, H. A study of the effects of differential stimulation on mentally retarded children. *Convention Proceedings of the American Association of Mental Deficiency*, 1939, *44*, 114–36.

SKEELS, H. M., & HARMS, I. Children with inferior social histories: Their mental development in adoptive homes. *Journal of Genetic Psychology*, 1948, *72*, 283–94.

SKINNER, B. F. *The behavior of organisms.* New York: Appleton-Century-Crofts, 1938.

SKODAK, M. Children in foster homes. *University of Iowa Studies in Child Welfare*, 1939, *16*, 1–156.

SKODAK, M., & SKEELS, H. M. A final follow-up of one hundred adopted children. *Journal of Genetic Psychology*, 1949, *75*, 85–125.

SLAVSON, S. R. *Analytic group psychotherapy with children, adolescents, and adults.* New York: Columbia University Press, 1950.

SLINGERLAND, B. H. *Pre-reading screening procedures to identify first-grade academic needs.* Cambridge, Mass.: Educators Publishing Service, Inc., 1969.

SLIVKIN, S. E., & BERNSTEIN, N. R. Group approaches to treating retarded adolescents. In F. J. Menolascino (Ed.), *Psychiatric approaches to mental retardation.* New York: Basic Books, 1970.

SMITH, D. W., & WILSON, A. A. *The child with Down's Syndrome.* Philadelphia: Saunders, 1973

SOLNIT, A. J., & STARK, M. H. Mourning and the birth of a defective child. *Psychoanalytic Study of the Child*, 1961, *16*, 523–37.

SOLOMON, R. L. Punishment. *American Psychologist*, 1964, *19*, 239–53.

SOLOMON, R. L., TURNER, L. H., & LESSAC, M. S. Some effects of delay of punishment on resistance to temptation in dogs. *Journal of Personality and Social Psychology*, 1968, *8*, 233–38.

SOMMERS, V. S. *The influence of parental attitudes and social environment on the personality development of the adolescent blind.* New York: American Foundation for the Blind, 1944.

SOWELL, T. New light on black IQ. *The New York Times Magazine*, March 27, 1977, 56–61.

SPEERS, R. W., & LANSING, C. *Group therapy and childhood psychosis.* Chapel Hill, N.C.: University of North Carolina Press, 1965.

SPINETTA, J. J., RIGLER, D., & KARON, M. Anxiety in the dying child. *Pediatrics*, 1973, *52*, 841–50.

SPINETTA, J. J. The dying child's awareness of death: A review. *Psychological Bulletin*, 1974, *81*, 256–60.

SPITZ, R. Hospitalism: An inquiry into the genesis of psychiatric conditions in early childhood. *Psychoanalytic Studies of the Child*, 1945, *1*, 53–74.

SPITZ, R. A. On the genesis of superego components. *Psychoanalytic Study of the Child*, 1958, *13*, 375–404.

SPRAGUE, R. L., & WERRY, J. S. Psychotropic drugs and handicapped children. In L. Mann & D. A. Sabatino, *The second review of special education.* Philadelphia: JSE Press, 1974.

STATE-FEDERAL INFORMATION CLEARINGHOUSE FOR EXCEPTIONAL CHILDREN. *Second dimensions: Special education administrators view the field.* Arlington, Va.: Council for Exceptional Children, 1973.

STATISTICAL ABSTRACTS OF THE U. S.—1975. Washington, D.C.: U.S. Government Printing Office, 1976.

STEELE, B. F., & POLLOCK, C. B. A psychiatric study of parents who abuse infants and small children. In R. E. Helfer & C. H. Kempe (Eds.), *The battered child.* Chicago: University of Chicago Press, 1974.

STEINER, G. Y. *The children's cause.* Washington, D.C.: The Brookings Institute, 1976.

STEINHAUER, P. D., MUSHIN, D. N., & RAE-GRANT, Q. Psychological aspects of chronic illness. *Pediatric Clinics of North America*, 1974, *21*, 825–40.

STENNIS, W. Child psychiatry in the school. In S. Copel (Ed.), *Behavior pathology of childhood and adolescence.* New York: Basic Books, 1973.

STERNLICHT, M. Psychotherapeutic procedures with the retarded. In N. R. Ellis (Ed.), *International review of research in mental retardation* (Vol. 2). New York: Academic Press, 1966.

STEVENS, T. M. *Activity level: A comparison between objective and subjective measures and a classroom management approach.* Unpublished doctoral dissertation. Chicago: Northwestern University, 1977.

STEVENS-LONG, J., & LOVAAS, O. I. Research and treatment with autistic children in a program of behavior therapy. In A. Davids (Ed.), *Child personality and psychopathology: Current topics.* New York: Wiley, 1974.

STEVENSON, E. A. *A study of the educational achievement of deaf children of deaf parents.* Berkeley: California School for the Deaf, 1964.

STEVENSON, J., & RICHMAN, N. The prevalence of language delay in a population of three-year-old children and its association with general retardation. *Developmental Medicine and Childhood Neurology*, 1976, *18*, 431–41.

STRAUGHAN, J. H. Treatment with child and mother in the playroom. *Behaviour Research and Therapy,* 1964, *2,* 37-41.

STRAUSS, A. A., & KEPHART, N. C. *Psychopathology and education of the brain-injured child* (Vol. II). New York: Grune & Stratton, 1955.

STRAUSS, A. A., & LEHTINEN, L. E. *Psychopathology and education of the brain-injured child* (Vol. I). New York: Grune & Stratton, 1947.

STUART, R. A. *Trick or treatment: How and when psychotherapy fails.* Champaign, Ill.: Research Press, 1970.

STUART, R. A., & LOTT, L. B. Behavioral contracting with delinquents: A cautionary note. *Journal of Behavior Therapy and Experimental Psychiatry,* 1972, *3,* 161-69.

STUBBLEFIELD, R. L. Psychiatric complications of chronic illness in children. In J. A. Downey & N. L. Low (Eds.), *The child with disabling illness.* Philadelphia: Saunders, 1974.

SULLIVAN, H. S. *The interpersonal theory of psychiatry.* New York: Norton, 1953.

SULZBACHER, S. I., & HOUSER, J. A tactic to eliminate disruptive behaviors in the classroom: Group contingent consequences. In R. Ulrich, T. Stachnik & J. Mabry (Eds.), *Control of human behavior* (Vol. 2). Glenview, Ill.: Scott, Foresman, 1970.

SUPPES, P. A survey of cognition in handicapped children. In S. Chess & A. Thomas (Eds.), *Annual progress in child psychiatry and child development.* New York: Brunner/Mazel, 1975, 95-129.

SURAN, B. G., & HATCHER, R. P. The treatment of hospitalized children with failure-to-thrive. *Pediatric Nursing,* 1975, *1,* 10-17.

SURAN, B. G., & LAVIGNE, J. V. Rights of children in pediatric settings: A survey of attitudes. *Pediatrics,* 1977, *60,* 715-20.

SUTHERLAND, E. H., & CRESSEY, D. R. *Criminology.* Philadelphia: J. B. Lippincott, 1974.

SWANSON, F. L. *Psychotherapists and children.* New York: Pitman, 1970.

TAFT, L. T., & GOLDFARB, W. Prenatal and perinatal factors in childhood schizophrenia. *Developmental Medicine and Child Neurology,* 1964, *6,* 32-43.

TANNER, J. M., & INHELDER, B. (Eds.). *Discussions on child development.* New York: International University Press, 1971.

TARNOPOL, L. Introduction to neurogenic learning disorders. In L. Tarnopol (Ed.), *Learning disorders in children: Diagnosis, medication, education.* Boston: Little, Brown, 1971.

TARVER, S. G., & HALLAHAN, D. P. Attention deficits in children with learning disabilities: A review. *Journal of Learning Disabilities,* 1974, *9,* 560-69.

TAVORMINA, J. B. Basic models of parent counselling: A critical review. *Psychological Bulletin,* 1974, *81,* 827-35.

TAYLOR, C. W., & HOLLAND, J. Predictors of creative performance. In C. W. Taylor (Ed.), *Creativity: Progress and potential.* New York: McGraw-Hill, 1964.

TAYLOR, J. L. Educational programs. In B. Lowenfeld (Ed.), *The visually handicapped child in school.* New York: John Day, 1973.

TAYLOR, P. D., & TURNER, R. K. A clinical trial of continuous, intermittent and overlearning "bell and pad" treatment for nocturnal enuresis. *Behaviour Research and Therapy,* 1975, *13,* 281-93.

TERMAN, L. M., *Mental and physical traits of a thousand gifted children: Genetic studies of genius* (Vol. I). Stanford, Calif.: Stanford University Press, 1925.

TERMAN, L. M., & ODEN. M. *The gifted child grows up: Genetic studies of genius* (Vol. IV). Stanford, Calif.: Stanford University Press, 1947.

TERMAN, L. M., & ODEN, M. *The gifted group at mid-life: Genetic studies of genius* (Vol. V). Stanford, Calif.: Stanford University Press, 1959.

TERRIS, M., LAPOUSE, R., & MONK, M. A. The relation of prematurity and previous fetal loss to childhood schizophrenia. *American Journal of Psychiatry,* 1964, *121,* 476-81.

THARP, R. G., & WETZEL, R. J. *Behavior modification in the natural environment.* New York: Academic Press, 1969.

THOMAS, A., CHESS, S., & BIRCH, H. G. *Temperament and behavior disorders in children.* New York: New York University Press, 1968.

THOMAS, S. B. Neglecting the gifted causes them to hide their talents. *Gifted Child Quarterly,* 1973, *17,* 193-98.

THOMPSON, T., PICKENS, R., & MEISCH, R. A. (Eds.). *Readings in behavioral pharmacology.* New York: Appleton-Century-Crofts, 1970.

THORNDIKE, R. L. The measurement of creativity. *Teachers College Record,* 1963, *64,* 422-24.

TISDALL, W. J., BLACKHURST, A. E., & MARKS, C. *Divergent thinking in blind children* (Project No. OE-32-27-0350-6003). Washington, D.C.: U.S. Office of Education, 1967.

TIZARD, J. The residential care of mentally handicapped children. *Proceedings of the London Conference on the Scientific Study of Mental Deficiency,* 1962, *2,* 659-66.

TIZARD, J. *Community services for the mentally handicapped.* London: Oxford University Press, 1964.

TIZARD, J., & O'CONNOR, N. The employability of high-grade mental defectives (I). *American Journal of Mental Deficiency,* 1950, *54,* 563-76. (a)

TIZARD, J., & O'CONNOR, N. The employability of high-grade mental defectives (II). *American Journal of Mental Deficiency,* 1950, *55,* 144-57. (b)

TODD, D. D., SCOTT, R. B., BOSTOW, D. E., & ALEXANDER, S. B. Modification of the excessive inappropriate classroom behavior of two elementary school students using home-based consequences and daily report card procedures. *Journal of Applied Behavior Analysis,* 1977, *9,* 106.

TORRANCE, E. P. Developing creative thinking through school experiences. In S. J. Parnes & H. F. Harding, *A source book for creative thinking.* New York: Charles Scribner's Sons, 1962, 31-47. (a)

TORRANCE, E. P. *Guiding creative talent.* Englewood Cliffs, N.J.: Prentice-Hall, 1962. (b)

TORRANCE, E. P. *Creativity.* National Education Association, 1963. (a)

TORRANCE, E. P. *Education and the creative potential.* Minneapolis: University of Minnesota Press, 1963. (b)

TRACE, M. W., CUVO, A. J., & CRISWELL, J. L. Teaching coin equivalence to the mentally retarded. *Journal of Applied Behavior Analysis,* 1977, *10,* 85-92.

TRAVIS, L. The unspeakable feelings of people with special reference to stuttering. In L. Travis (Ed.), *Handbook of speech pathology and audiology.* Englewood Cliffs, N.J.: Prentice-Hall, 1971, 1009-34.

TREFFERT, D. A. Epidemiology of infantile autism. *Archives of General Psychiatry,* 1970, *22,* 431-38.

TWARDOSZ, S., & SAJWAJ, T. Multiple effects of a procedure to increase sitting in a hyperactive retarded boy. *Journal of Applied Behavior Analysis,* 1972, *5,* 73-78.

UNESCO. *Special education statistics.* Paris, France: UNESCO, 1974.

UNITED NATIONS GENERAL ASSEMBLY. The U.N. declaration of the rights of the child. New York: UNICEF, 1959.

U.S. DEPARTMENT OF THE CENSUS. *Historical statistics of the United States—colonial times to 1970.* Washington, D.C.: U.S. Government Printing Office, 1975.

U.S. DEPARTMENT OF HEALTH, EDUCATION, AND WELFARE, OFFICE OF YOUTH DEVELOPMENT. *Juvenile court statistics, 1972.* Washington, D.C.: U.S. Government Printing Office, 1973.

VAN RIPER, C. *Speech correction: Principles and methods.* Englewood Cliffs, N.J.: Prentice-Hall, 1972.

VAN RIPER, C. *The treatment of stuttering.* Englewood Cliffs, N.J.: Prentice-Hall, 1973.

VELTKAMP, L. J. School phobia. *Journal of Family Counseling,* 1975, *3,* 47-51.

VENEZIA, P. S. Delinquency prediction: A critique and a suggestion. *Journal of Research in Crime and Delinquency,* 1971, *8,* 108-17.

VERNON, D., FOLEY, J. M., SIPOWICZ, R. R., & SCHULMAN, J. L. *The psychological responses of children to hospitalization and illness.* Springfield, Ill.: Charles C. Thomas, 1965.

VERNON, M. Relationship of language to the thinking process. *Archives of General Psychiatry,* 1967, *16,* 325–33.

VERNON, M. *Multiply handicapped deaf children: Medical educational, and psychological considerations* (Research Monograph). Wash., D.C.: Council for Exceptional Children, 1969. (a)

VERNON, M. Sociological and psychological factors associated with profound hearing loss. *Journal of Speech and Hearing Research,* 1969, *12,* 541–63. (b)

VERNON, M., & KOH, S. D. Early manual communication and deaf children's achievement. *American Annals of the Deaf,* 1970, *115,* 527–36.

VERNON, M., & KOH, S. D. Effects of oral preschool compared to early manual communication on education and communication in deaf children. *American Annals of the Deaf,* 1971, *116,* 569–74.

VERNON, M., & PRICKETT, H., Jr. Mainstreaming: Issues and a model plan. *Audiology and Hearing Education,* 1976, *2,* 5–6, 10–11.

WAECHTER, E. H. Children's awareness of fatal illness. *American Journal of Nursing,* 1971, *71,* 1168–72.

WAHLER, R. G., WINKEL, G. H., PETERSON, R. F., & MORRISON, D. C. Mothers as behavior therapists for their own children. *Behaviour Research and Therapy,* 1965, *3,* 113–24.

WALD, P. Making sense out of the rights of youth. *Human Rights,* 1974, *4,* 13–29.

WALD, R. D. Some observations from the treatment of parents and their psychotic son. In S. A. Szurek & I. N. Berlin (Eds.), *Clinical studies in childhood psychosis.* New York: Brunner/Mazel, 1973.

WALDRON, S. The significance of childhood neurosis for adult mental health: A follow-up study. *American Journal of Psychiatry,* 1976, *133,* 532–38.

WALKER, S. Drugging the American child: We're too cavalier about hyperactivity. *Psychology Today,* 1974, *8,* 43–48.

WALLACH, M. A. Creativity. In P. H. Mussen (Ed.), *Manual of child psychology.* New York: Wiley, 1970.

WALLACH, M. A., & KOGAN, N. *Modes of thinking in young children: A study of the creativity-intelligence distinction.* New York: Holt, Rinehart and Winston, 1965.

WALLAS, G. *The art of thought.* New York: Harcourt Brace Jovanovich, 1926.

WALLEN, J. E. W. *Education of mentally handicapped children.* New York: Harper & Row, 1955.

WARD, A. J. Early infantile autism: Diagnosis, etiology, and treatment. *Psychological Bulletin,* 1970, *73,* 350–62.

WATSON, J.B., & RAYNER, R. Conditioned emotional reactions. *Journal of Experimental Psychology,* 1920, *3,* 1–14.

WATSON, L. S., & BASSINGER, J. F. Parent training technology. *Mental Retardation,* 1974, *12,* 3–10.

WEAKLAND, J. H. The "double-bind" hypothesis of schizophrenia and three-party interaction. In D. Jackson (Ed.), *The etiology of schizophrenia.* New York: Basic Books, 1960.

WECHSLER, D. *The measurement and appraisal of adult intelligence* (4th ed.). Baltimore: Williams & Wilkins, 1958.

WECHSLER, D. *Wechsler Intelligence Scale for Children–Revised.* New York: The Psychological Corporation, 1974.

WEIKART, D. P. *Preschool intervention: A preliminary report of the Perry preschool project.* Ann Arbor, Mich.: Campus Publication, 1967.

WEISBERG, P. Operant procedures with the retarded: An overview of laboratory research. In N. R. Ellis (Ed.), *International review of research in mental retardation* (Vol. 5). New York: Academic Press, 1971.

WEISS, D. A. *Cluttering.* Englewood Cliffs, N.J.: Prentice-Hall, 1964.

WENDER, P. H. *The hyperactive child: A handbook for parents.* New York: Crown Publishers, 1973.

WERNER, E. E., & SMITH, R. S. *Kauai's children come of age.* Honolulu: University Press of Hawaii, 1977.

WERNER, H., & STRAUSS, A. A. Pathology of figure-background relation in the child. *Journal of Abnormal and Social Psychology,* 1941, *36,* 236–48.

WERRY, J. S. Childhood psychosis. In H. C. Quay & J. S. Werry (Eds.), *Psychopathological disorders of childhood.* New York: Wiley, 1972.

WERRY, J. S. Psychosomatic disorders (with a note on anesthesia,

surgery, and hospitalization). In H. C. Quay & J. S. Werry (Eds.), *Psychopathological disorders of childhood.* New York: Wiley, 1972.

WERRY, J. S., & QUAY, H. C. The prevalence of behavior symptoms in younger elementary school children. *American Journal of Orthopsychiatry,* 1971, *41,* 136–43.

WEST, D. J. *Who becomes delinquent?* London: Heinemann, 1973.

WEST, R., & ANSBERRY, M. *The rehabilitation of speech.* New York: Harper & Row, 1968.

WEST, R., KENNEDY, L., & CARR, A. *The rehabilitation of speech.* New York: Harper & Row, 1937.

WHITE, J. H. Current medical treatment of hyperkinesis. *Journal of Pediatric Psychology,* 1975, *3,* 5–6.

WHITE, L. Organic factors and psychophysiology in childhood schizophrenia. *Psychological Bulletin,* 1974, *81,* 238–55.

WHITE, P. T., DEMYER, W., & DEMYER, M. EEG abnormalities in early childhood schizophrenia. *American Journal of Psychiatry,* 1964, *120,* 950.

WHITING, J. W., & CHILD, I. L. *Child training and personality.* New Haven: Yale University Press, 1969. (Originally published, 1953.)

WIENS, A. M., ANDERSON, K. A., & MATARAZZO, R. G. Use of medication as an adjunct in the modification of behavior in the pediatric psychology setting. *Professional Psychology,* 1972, *3,* 157–62.

WILKINSON, A. W. (Ed.). *Recent advances in pediatric surgery.* London: Churchill Livingstone, 1975.

WILLIAMS, C. *Prevalence of educable mentally retarded, behaviorally disturbed, and learning disabled pupils in Georgia public schools.* Athens, Ga.: University of Georgia, 1977.

WILLIAMS, C. D. The elimination of tantrum behavior by extinction. *Journal of Abnormal and Social Psychology,* 1959, *59,* 269.

WILLIAMS, M., & SCARR, S. Effects of short-term intervention on performance of low-birth-weight, disadvantaged children. *Pediatrics,* 1971, 289–98.

WILSON, H. Juvenile delinquency, parental criminality and social handicap. *British Journal of Criminology,* 1975, *3,* 241–52.

WILSON, L. *This stranger, my son.* New York: G. P. Putnam's Sons, 1968.

WILSON, T. G., & FRANKS, C. M. (Eds.). *Annual review of behavior therapy* (Vol. 3). New York: Brunner/Mazel, 1975.

WINITZ, H. *Articulatory acquisition and behavior.* New York: Appleton-Century-Crofts, 1969.

WINITZ, H. Articulation disorders: From prescription to description. *Journal of Speech and Hearing Disorders,* 1977, *42,* 143–47.

WITKIN, H. A., OLTMAN, P. K., CHASE, J. B., & FRIEDMAN, F. Cognitive patterning in the blind. In J. Hellmuth (Ed.), *Cognitive studies* (Vol. 2): *Deficits in cognition.* New York: Brunner/Mazel, 1971.

WITTENBERG, C. Studies of child abuse and infant accidents. In J. Segal (Ed.), *The mental health of the child.* (Public Health Service Publication No. 2168). New York: Arno Press, 1973.

WOLF, J. *Temple Fay, M.D.: Progenitor of the Doman-Delacato treatment procedures.* Springfield, Ill.: Charles C. Thomas, 1968.

WOLF, L. C., & WHITEHEAD, P. C. The decision to institutionalize retarded children: Comparison of individually matched groups. *Mental Retardation,* 1975, *13,* 3–7.

WOLFF, S. Dimensions and clusters of symptoms in disturbed children. *British Journal of Psychiatry,* 1971, *118,* 421–27.

WOLFF, S., & CHESS, S. A. A behavioral study of schizophrenic children. *Acta Psychiatrica Scandinavica,* 1964, *40,* 438–66.

WOLPE, J. *The practice of behavior therapy.* New York: Pergamon, 1973.

WOOD, N. *Verbal learning: Dimensions in Early learning series.* San Rafael, Calif.: Dimensions Publishing Company, 1969.

WOODS, C. L., & WILLIAMS, D. E. Traits attributed to stuttering and normally fluent males. *Journal of Speech and Hearing Research,* 1976, *19,* 276–78.

WRIGHTSMAN, L. S., ROGERS, C. M., & PERCY, J. *Conceptualization and measurement of attitudes toward children's rights.* Paper presented at the meeting of the American Psychological Association, Chicago, 1975.

WRIGHTSTONE, J. W., JUSTMAN, J., & MOSKOWITZ, S. *Studies of children with physical handicaps: The child with cardiac limitation.* New York: Board of Education of the City of New York, 1953.

WYATT v. *STICKNEY,* 344 F. Supp., 387 (M.D. Ala. 1972).

YAMAMOTO, K. Role of creative thinking and intelligence in high school achievement. *Psychological Reports,* 1964, *14,* 783–89.

YATES, A. J. *Behavior therapy.* New York: Wiley, 1970.

YOUNG, G. C., & MORGAN, R. T. T. Conditioning treatment of enuresis: Auditory intensity. *Behaviour Research and Therapy,* 1973, *11,* 411–16.

YOUNG, L. *Wednesday's children.* New York: McGraw-Hill, 1971.

YOUNG, M. A. Onset, prevalence, and recovery from stuttering. *Journal of Speech and Hearing Disorders,* 1975, *40,* 49–58.

YUWILER, A., GELLER, E., & RITVO, E. R. Neurobiochemical research. In E. R. Ritvo (Ed.), *Autism: Diagnosis current research and management.* New York: Spectrum Publications, 1976, 85–106.

ZEILBERGER, J., SAMPSON, S. E., & SLOANE, H. N. Modification of a child's behavior in the home with the mother as a therapist. *Journal of Applied Behavior Analysis,* 1968, *1,* 47–54.

ZIGLER, E. Motivational aspects of mental retardation. In R. Koch & J. C. Dobson (Eds.), *The mentally retarded child and his family.* New York: Brunner/Mazel, 1971. (a)

ZIGLER, E. The retarded child as a whole person. In H. E. Adams & W. K. Boardman (Eds.), *Advances in experimental clinical psychology.* New York: Pergamon Press, 1971. (b)

ZINK, G. D. Hearing aids children wear: A longitudinal study of performance. *Volta Review,* 1972, *74,* 41–51.

ZIPIN, D. Healthy minds for hospital children. *American Teacher,* 1947, *31,* 14–15.

ZUK, G. H., MILLER, R. L., BARTRAM, J. B., & KLING, F. Maternal acceptance of retarded children: A questionnaire study of attitudes and religious background. *Child Development,* 1961, *32,* 525–40.

Picture Credits

2	Scott Foresman
4	Christopher W. Morrow/Stock, Boston, Inc.
10	Elizabeth Hamlin/Stock, Boston, Inc.
14	Historical Pictures Service, Inc.
22	© David Powers 1978/Jeroboam, Inc.
25	Gesell Institute
31	Jon Erikson—1976
36	Yves De Braine/Black Star
42	Standford News Service, Stanford University (left)
42	Courtesy of Dr. Bandura (right)
50	Scott Foresman
56	George Roos/Peter Arnold, Inc.
61	Cary Wolinsky/Stock, Boston, Inc.
64	Cary Wolinsky/Stock, Boston, Inc.
72	Miriam Reinhart/Photo Researchers, Inc.
78	Photo by Allan Grant
88	Scott Foresman
96	Jack Corn/Image, Inc.
101	Julie O'Neil/Stock, Boston, Inc.
104	The Lambs, Inc.
106	Charles Harbutt/Magnum
108	Courtesy of United Cerebral Palsy
117	Susan Faludi/Leo de Wys, Inc.
120	Francis Laping/DPI
123	Pre-College Programs, Gallaudet College
127	George Bellerose/Stock, Boston, Inc.
132	Leo de Wys, Inc.
136	Elizabeth Hamlin/Stock, Boston, Inc.
144	Charles Harbutt/Magnum
148	Chuck Fishman/Leo de Wys, Inc.
154	Everett C. Johnson/Leo de Wys, Inc.
158	Everett C. Johnson/Leo de Wys, Inc.
161	Charles Harbutt/Magnum
170	J. Berndt/Stock, Boston, Inc. (left)
170	Everett C. Johnson/Leo de Wys, Inc. (right)
172	Werner Muckenhirn/DPI
178	© 1978 Doring-Stern/Black Star
182	Steve Hansen/Stock, Boston, Inc. (left)
182	John Robaton/Leo de Wys, Inc. (right)
184	Lynn Karlin/Leo de Wys, Inc.
187	George Bellerose/Stock, Boston, Inc.
192	Elliott Erwitt/Magnum
194	George Bellerose/Stock, Boston, Inc.
202, 204, & 212	Scott Foresman
218	Dr. James L. German III
219, 228, 234, 238 & 244	Scott Foresman
259	Elizabeth Hamlin/Stock, Boston, Inc.
262	E. F. Bernstein/Peter Arnold, Inc.
274	Al Kaplan/DPI
278	© Eric Kroll/Taurus Photos
281	Charles Gatewood
281	Burk Uzzle/Magnum
285 & 289	Scott Foresman
295	Arthur Tress/Magnum
297 & 302	Scott Foresman
304	Julie O'Neil/Stock, Boston, Inc.
311	E. F. Bernstein/Peter Arnold, Inc. (both)
317	David Seymour/Magnum
331	Mike Mazzaschi/Stock, Boston, Inc.
333	Bob Natkin (all three)
338	Jack Corn/Image, Inc.
345	Burk Uzzle/Magnum
347	Courtesy of The House of the Good Shepherd
348	Jack Corn/Image, Inc.
355	Scott Foresman
358 & 361	Jack Corn/Image, Inc.
366	Scott Foresman
372 & 388	E. F. Bernstein/Peter Arnold, Inc. (both)
391	Photo by Allan Grant (both)
396	Scott Foresman
398	From *Blue Rose,* Lawrence Hill and Company
402	Courtesy of the Children's Memorial Hospital and American Academy of Pediatrics, Inc.
406	E. F. Bernstein/Peter Arnold, Inc.
409	© Mitchell Payne 1978/Jeroboam, Inc.
419	Photograph by Ken Heyman
430	Esther Bubley
434	Ellis Herwig/Stock, Boston, Inc.
451	© Miriam Reinhart 1975/Photo Researchers, Inc.
454	Chuck Fishman/Leo de Wys, Inc.
455	Scott Foresman
457	© Van Bucher 1971/Photo Researchers, Inc.
460	E. F. Bernstein/Peter Arnold, Inc.
467	Eve Arnold/Magnum
470	Nicholas Sapieha/Stock, Boston, Inc.
476	Scott Foresman
481	© 1976 Joel Gordon (top left)
481	Ellis Herwig/Stock, Boston, Inc. (top right)
481	E. F. Bernstein/Peter Arnold, Inc. (bottom right)
481	Pre-College Programs, Gallaudet College (bottom left)

Name Index

Subject Index